THE TRINITY

AUGUSTINIAN HERITAGE INSTITUTE

THE WORKS OF SAINT AUGUSTINE

A translation for the 21st Century

Part I — Books

Volume 5: The Trinity

The English translation of the works of Saint Augustine has been made
possible with contributions from the following:

Order of Saint Augustine

   Province of Saint Thomas of Villanova (East)
   Province of Our Mother of Good Counsel (Midwest)
   Province of Saint Augustine (California)
   Province of Saint Joseph (Canada)
   Vice Province of Our Mother of Good Counsel
   Province of Our Mother of Good Counsel (Ireland)
   Province of Saint John Stone (England and Scotland)
   Province of Our Mother of Good Counsel (Australia)
   The Augustinians of the Assumption (North America)
   The Sisters of Saint Thomas of Villanova

Order of Augustinian Recollects

   Province of Saint Augustine

Mr. and Mrs. James C. Crouse
Mr. and Mrs. Paul Henkels
Mr. and Mrs. Francis E. McGill, Jr.
Mr. and Mrs. Mariano J. Rotelle

THE WORKS OF SAINT AUGUSTINE
A translation for the 21st Century

The Trinity

(De Trinitate)

introduction, translation, and notes
Edmund Hill, O.P.

editor
John E. Rotelle, O.S.A.

New City Press
Hyde Park, New York

Published in the United States by New City Press
202 Cardinal Rd., Hyde Park, New York 12538
©1991 Augustinian Heritage Institute

Cover painting: Augustine discusses with the child Jesus the mystery of the Trinity
(B. Gozzoli, 1465, Church of Saint Augustine, San Gimignano, Italy).

Library of Congress Cataloging-in-Publication Data:

Augustine, Saint, Bishop of Hippo.
    The works of Saint Augustine.

    "Augustinian Heritage Institute"
    Includes bibliographical references and indexes.
    Contents: — pt. 1, Books, v. 5. The Trinity
introduction, translation, and notes / Edmund Hill. —
— pt. 3, Sermons. v. 1.1-19 Introduction / Michele Pellegrino
    1.   Theology — Early church, ca. 30-600.   I. Hill,
Edmund.   II. Rotelle, John E.   III. Augustinian
Heritage Institute.   IV. Title.
BR65.A5E53   1990   270.2   89-28878
ISBN 1-54548-055-4 (series)
ISBN 0-911782-96-6 (pt. 1, v. 5 : pbk.)
ISBN 978-0-911782-89-9 (hardcover)

Nihil Obstat: John E. Rotelle, O.S.A., S.T.L., Censor Deputatus
Imprimatur: + Thomas V. Daily, D.D., Bishop of Brooklyn
              Brooklyn, New York: December 26, 1990

1st printing: September 1991
8th printing: April 2007

Printed in the United States of America

COLLEGIS DISCIPVLISQVE MEIS

AFRIS

CARISSIMIS

S. AVGVSTINI

AFRI

VNIVERSALIS ECCLESIAE

DOCTORIS EXIMII

HOC OPVS MAXIMVM

IN TERRA AFRICANA

ANGLICE VERSVM

LAETO CORDE

DEDICAVI

CONTENTS

Foreword 17

Introduction 18

    1. The place of the *De Trinitate* in Augustine's work — 18
    2. Structure and Contents of the *De Trinitate* — 21
    3. The Tradition behind Saint Augustine: Scripture — 27
    4. The Tradition behind Saint Augustine: Ecclesiastical Writers — 37
    5. Augustine's Contribution to the Tradition —45

Translator's Note 60

The Trinity

Prefatory Letter From Augustine to Aurelius, Bishop of Carthage 63

Book I
The Absolute Equality of the Divine Persons

Chapter 1 65
    The author comes to terms with his readers and outlines his method.

Chapter 2 69
    The unity and equality of the Father, the Son, and the Holy Spirit are proved from
    scripture.

Chapter 3 74
    The rule of interpretation that the Son is equal to the Father in *the form of God*, less than
    the Father in *the form of a servant;* that he will hand over the kingdom to the Father, and
    himself be subject to the Father (1 Cor 15:24-28), when he brings all his faithful to the
    contemplation of the three divine persons, and so completes and lays aside his office of
    mediator.

Chapter 4 82
    More applications of the rule of interpretation that the Son is equal to the Father in the
    form of God, less than the Father in the form of man; the proposal of another complemen-
    tary rule whereby some apparently subordinationist texts are interpreted as saying that
    the Son in his equality with the Father is yet from the Father; and of yet a third rule
    whereby, because of the unity of person in Jesus Christ, things are said of him in one
    nature which are in fact proper to him in virtue of the other; so that we can say, on the
    one hand that the Son of God was crucified, and on the other that the Son of man will
    judge the living and the dead.

Book II
Missions: Old Testament Theophanies

Prologue 97

Chapter 1 98
    Of the principle of interpretation whereby some texts are referred neither to the Son's

equality with the Father, nor to his being less than the Father in the form of a servant, but simply to his being, in his co-eternal equality, from the Father; with discussion in support of this principle of some of the things that are said about the Holy Spirit.

Chapter 2 101
In which the author begins to discuss the significance of the missions, the sendings of the Son and of the Holy Spirit; first arguing that to talk of their being sent does not jeopardize their equality with the Father; then proposing a preliminary definition or description of mission as the visible manifestation in time of these two divine persons; finally pointing out the crucial difference between the permanent visible manifestation of the Son in the flesh, and the transient visible manifestation of the Spirit in the forms of a dove, a gust of wind, and tongues of fire. It must be borne in mind by the reader that this discussion of the missions is subordinated to the argument of the previous chapter, although only toward the end of Book IV will the author explicitly define the missions as revealing in time the eternal processions of the divine persons, thus formally including the language of mission under the rule he has elaborated in chapter 1, as language which shows that the Son is from the Father and the Holy Spirit is from the Father and the Son. The involvement of mission with visible manifestation raises a series of problems which have to be solved before that final definition can be achieved.

Chapter 3 106
In which the author broaches the problems raised by his preliminary definition of mission, in the last chapter, as the visible manifestation of the person sent; dividing them into three groups of questions: i) which, if any, of the divine persons in particular were manifested in each of the Old Testament theophanies—this he will deal with in the remainder of this book; ii) how the visible manifestations in those theophanies were managed, whether by the agency of angels or no—this will form the subject of Book III; and iii) whether we can properly talk of the sending of the Son and the Holy Spirit before their visible manifestations in the New Testament—this will be settled in Book IV. Before going on, in the next chapter, to discuss the first group of questions, he turns aside to demolish a basic assumption of much of the cruder "economic" theology, that the Son is the essentially visible member of the trinity, while the Father alone has immortality and dwells in light inaccessible, whom no man has seen or can see, and is alone the invisible, only God (1 Tm 6:15; 1:17).

Chapter 4 109
The author investigates the theophanies in which God appeared to Adam and to Abraham.

Chapter 5 113
The various theophanies of Exodus are investigated.

Chapter 6 117
The special manifestation of God vouchsafed to Moses on Mount Sinai is discussed; it is treated allegorically, or at least typologically, because of the difficulty the author feels of giving any other interpretation to the concept of God having a face and a back.

Chapter 7 120
The author sums up the results of his investigation of the first of the three questions posed in chapter 3 of this book, noting also the bearing on the question of the vision in Daniel of the Ancient of Days and the Son of man.

Book III
Missions: The Work of Angels

Prologue 127

Chapter 1 128
In which the author recapitulates; and then goes on to discuss the second of the three questions posed in chapter 3 of Book II, above; and in this chapter he sets the framework for his discussion of the activities of angels in the Old Testament theophanies by first considering the general order of God's providential government of the universe, with

special reference to first and secondary causes, and to the significant, or meaningfully symbolic character of God's action in the world.

Chapter 2 134
The problem of miracles wrought by demonic agencies is discussed, with particular reference to the magicians of Pharaoh; that this kind of thing in no way derogates from divine providence and the unique creative efficacy of God the first cause is shown by illustration from the case of Jacob's stock-breeding experiments with Laban's flocks.

Chapter 3 137
The significance of the prodigies worked through the ministry of angels is examined more closely, and compared with the significance of the prophetic utterances and actions of people in the Old Testament.

Chapter 4 140
That it was angels who were the secondary agents of the Old Testament theophanies is proved from scripture; chiefly from certain New Testament passages, but also from a brief reconsideration of certain episodes already discussed at length in Book II.

Introductory Essay on Book IV 147

Book IV
Missions: The Work of the Mediator

Prologue 152

Chapter 1 153
Man's need, and God's response to it; the harmonies of the incarnation and redemption, in which Christ mediates between God and man by observing, as it were, the basic harmonious proportion of 1 to 2; and how Christ in his death and resurrection is both the sacrament of our spiritual death and resurrection, and the model for our bodily death and resurrection.

Chapter 2 158
The numerical harmony of 1 to 2, as manifested in the work of redemption, is further elaborated in terms of the number 6, treated mainly as symbolical of time; and the chapter closes with elevated reflections on the mystery of unity in multiplicity, harmony finally restored in the person and work of the one Word of God made flesh.

Chapter 3 162
The work of the true mediator to life is contrasted with the work of the false mediator to death, the devil; it is shown how Christ conquered the devil in a just contest, and justly delivered man from the quasi-just rights which the devil possessed over him as a result of sin; finally, the false sacrifices which the devil still deludes his followers into trusting in are contrasted with the one true and perfect sacrifice of Christ, in which the knot of perfect unity is perfectly tied.

Chapter 4 167
The pretension of platonic or plotinian philosophers to be able to purify themselves by their own intellectual and moral powers for the perfect contemplation of God is contrasted with the Christian dispensation, whereby man has to be purified for the contemplation of eternal things by submitting to faith in temporal things, namely, in the incarnation of the Word and the life, death, and resurrection of Christ; the philosophers' denial of the resurrection on philosophical grounds is also refuted, and the trustworthiness of the revelation contained in the scriptures on such matters is asserted.

Chapter 5 171
The author comes back at last to the topic of the mission of the Son and the Holy Spirit; he affirms once more that their being sent does not imply that they are not equal to the Father, and defines their being sent into the world in time as the making known to the world that they proceed from the Father in eternity; he states in passing that the Holy

Spirit proceeds eternally from the Son as well as from the Father, and that even though the Father is manifested to the world by sensible phenomena, we cannot say that the Father was ever sent, because he does not proceed from either of the other persons; and he concludes by discussing how the manifestations in time of the persons was brought about, without reaching any definite conclusions on the subject.

Foreword to Books V, VI, and VII 186

Book V
Linguistic and Logical: Substance and Relationship

Prologue 189

Chapter 1 190
On the basis of the principle, common to both parties, that nothing is predicated of God by way of modification of the divine being, that is by way of accident, he argues against the inference which the Arians drew from the names "unbegotten" for the Father and "begotten" for the Son that the Father and the Son must be of different substance from one another. He asserts that although nothing is predicated of God by way of modification, it does not follow that everything is predicated of him by way of substance; for some things are predicated by way of relationship, that is internal relationship within the godhead.

Chapter 2 195
The use of substantive predications of God is examined in more detail, with a short foray included into the terminology of *ousia* and *hypostasis* "substance" and "person," which will be discussed much more thoroughly toward the end of Book VII.

Chapter 3 197
The use of relative predications about God is examined in more detail; in particular the peculiarities of the names for the Holy Spirit of which "gift" is considered the most proper. Besides names by which the divine persons are referred to each other, names by which they are also referred to creation are discussed, like "origin" (*principium*), and even in some contexts "Father."

Chapter 4 200
A problem is discussed which is raised by those names that refer God to creation.

Book VI
Linguistic and Logical: The Problem of Appropriation

Chapter 1 205
The text Christ the power of God and the wisdom of God faces us with the possibility that perhaps all substantive predications, like goodness, greatness, and eternity, which do not seem to differ in quality from power or wisdom, should be treated really as quasi-relative predications, in such a manner that the Son is to be considered as the power, wisdom, goodness, greatness, and eternity by which the Father is powerful, wise, good, great, and eternal. The author plays sympathetically with this idea and shows that at least it does not involve any inequality between the divine persons.

Chapter 2 210
The question of the divine simplicity, raised by the discussion of the last chapter, is further examined, and how it is to be reconciled with the divine trinity; a divine triplicity is excluded by it; but the individuality of the divine persons, how far for example one can talk about "the Father alone," remains a problem; a quotation from Hilary is commented on at length in the hope that it might throw some light on this problem.

Book VII

Linguistic and Logical: The Problem Solved

Chapter 1 217

The question posed in the previous book is taken up and dealt with thoroughly; the tentative answer there assumed is set aside as having impossible logical consequences, and the definitive solution is proposed.

Chapter 2 222

Having established that "wisdom" is a substance and not a relationship word, the author goes on to inquire why in scripture it is almost always appropriated to the Son; he suggests it is because it is the Son who reveals the Father to us, and because our wisdom is to imitate the incarnate Son as the eternal Word imitates, by being the image of, the Father.

Chapter 3 224

The author investigates the logical status of the terms "person" and "substance" (Greek *hypostasis*); he concludes that they are simply terms of convenience which we have to use in order to be able to answer the question "Three what?" about the divine triad; we use them rather in spite of than because of their natural logical properties.

Chapter 4 230

The average sensual man just referred to is exhorted to cling to faith until he comes to some kind of understanding; in order to do this he is exhorted to activate in himself the image of the divine trinity, which is thus once more brought to our notice; and it is argued that this image does not mean likeness to the Son only, the equal and eternal image of the Father, but to all three persons. The book concludes with a quotation which sums up the whole approach of the first seven books, which began from the "initium fidei"—Unless you believe, you will not understand.

Introductory Essay on Book VIII 237

Book VIII

Through the Looking-Glass

Prologue 241

Chapter 1 242

God is nothing else but truth, and if we can see truth, we can see God; but our inner eyes are too weak to be able to gaze on truth itself.

Chapter 2 243

God is the good itself, the unchanging good, the good of all goods, in terms of which we love whatever good things we do love. So if we can see this good in which we love anything else that is good, and in which we live and move and are, we can see God.

Chapter 3 245

If we must love God in order to see him, as has been suggested in the last chapter, it might seem as if we are caught in a vicious circle. For we cannot love what we do not know, and therefore we must see God first, in the sense of know him, before we can love him. If the vicious circle is broken by faith, in that we can love something we believe but do not yet see or know, then faith too has a problem for us. For faith or belief in things we do not know presupposes a kind of general knowledge or experience about the things we believe, so that we can at least know what we believe; but about God, and especially about the trinity, we have no such general knowledge or experience, and so we are left with the question of how we can know what we believe about God.

Chapter 4 248

The problem raised in the last chapter is approached through the analogy of how we are able to love the just man, exemplified by Paul. The answer is found to be that we can only do this because we see and love within ourselves, or rather in-and-above ourselves, the very form or idea of justice, and this even though we may not be just ourselves.

Chapter 5 251
Having examined the notions of truth and of the good, and offered a solution, in terms of the notion of the form of justice, to the problem of how we can love by believing what we do not know, the author goes on to examine the notion of love or charity itself; he sets out the mutual coherence or reciprocity of the twin commandments to love God and our neighbor; achieves an identification of charity with truth and the good and the form of justice; and finally sketches a trinity in love or charity, thus opening a way to our understanding of the divine trinity through these notions he has displayed in the course of this book; according to his closing words they provide the warp on which he will weave the fabric of the trinitarian image in man.

Foreword to Books IX - XIV 258

Book IX
Psychological: Mental Image, First Draft

Prologue 270

Chapter 1 271
Starting from the trinity, triad or trio with which he concluded Book VIII, namely lover, what is loved, and love; and confining himself to *mens* or mind as its subject, Augustine expands this trinity into the apter one of mind, its knowledge and its love of self, *mens, notitia sui, amor sui;* and he establishes that these three are one substance, consubstantial, coequal, coinherent, and yet also distinct, unconfused, and mutually related.

Chapter 2 276
The author further investigates the knowledge which the mind has of things, and concludes that it essentially consists in a judgment of truth or of value about things, which can properly be called a mental word, or *verbum mentis*, which is a mental image of the thing known in the light of eternal truth. This word is provisionally defined as *amata notitia,* loved knowledge.

Chapter 3 280
The author looks for a reason why love should not be called word, or image, nor said to be begotten or conceived, like knowledge; this being a question that exercises him greatly with respect to the Holy Spirit. The reader must decide for himself what he makes of the suggested answer.

Book X
Psychological: Mental Image, Second Draft

Chapter 1 286
The author takes up the idea he has just employed in showing why love cannot also be called offspring and image, namely that of "inquisitiveness" or the *appetitus inveniendi*, and giving it now the name of *amor studentium*, the sort of love studious people have, he asks the question how it can be reconciled with the axiom that you cannot love what you do not know; he establishes that this kind of love is not a love of the unknown, but a love of the known which stimulates inquiry, either a love of knowledge itself, or a love of some object of knowledge in general that prompts an investigation of it in detail, or a love of some universal truth or value, that prompts one to verify some particular application of it.

Chapter 2 290
The problem raised by the mind wanting to know itself is much more difficult, because as the author argues at length the mind cannot not know itself, being immediately present to itself. What then is the meaning of the famous Delphic injunction "Know thyself"? The validity of this injunction is taken as axiomatic, and it is interpreted as meaning that

the mind ought to think about itself; it can be said to have forgotten itself as a consequence of being distracted from itself by its concern for material things, whose images it has absorbed in memory and imagination, so that it confuses itself with such things. It is clearly suggested that this distraction and confusion is a result of the original fall from the right order of creation by sin, or turning away from God.

Chapter 3 293

A number of erroneous ways in which people have thought about the nature of mind, all in varying degrees materialistic, are reviewed; it is suggested that they are due to mind's tendency to confuse itself with its images of things perceived by the senses. The right way for mind to think about itself, it is then argued, is not for it to go looking for something else outside itself which it might consist of, but to distinguish itself from its images; the process should be one of the mind distinguishing what it supposes it might be, but is not sure about being (for example, fire, brain, harmony of elements, etc.) from what it knows it is; it knows that it is, that it lives, that it understands, that it wills, judges, remembers, and so on. It does not know, but only guesses that it is made of any material stuff. Therefore, so the author concludes, it is not made of any material stuff, but is a living, understanding, willing, being substance.

Chapter 4 298

Of the many mental acts of which mind is certain, the author selects memory, understanding, and will from which to construct his final draft of the image of the divine trinity in the mind.

Book XI
Psychological: Mental Image, Lesser Analogies

Prologue 303

Chapter 1 304

The author picks out a trinity in the act of seeing, or looking at an external object, its members being the appearance or look or visibility of the object in itself, the form or likeness of it impressed on the sense of sight, and the deliberate intention or act of will that fixes the sense of sight on the object. The distinction between these three elements, their relationships and the kind of unity they have, are discussed, and implicitly compared, not so much with the trinity of divine persons as with the trinity of the mental image.

Chapter 2 307

A more inward trinity in the psychic functioning of the "outer man" is picked out and discussed, namely that which declares itself when one thinks about some remembered object or event in an act of recollection; here the intention of the will joins together the attention of the mind, the "mind's eye" or *acies animi* as the author calls it, which corresponds to the sense of sight in the previous trinity considered, and the image stored in the memory, corresponding to the visible object in the sense trinity. Such acts of recollection or imagination are discussed in a distinctly moralizing context.

Chapter 3 311

The two trinities of the outer man so far outlined are further discussed, with particular reference to the proper distinctions between their members, and their mutual relationships; as regards the order or relationship between the first two members of each trinity, this is seen as being one of quasi-parent and quasi-offspring; and as regards the relationship of the third member to the first two, it is found that it cannot be conceived of either as quasi-parent or quasi-offspring. In conclusion it is made clear that there is a dynamic link, or a chain of movement between the acts involved in the outermost trinity of sense and those comprised in the more inward one of memory or imagination. We are already embarked on the movement of the psyche inward and upward.

Chapter 4 317

The discussion of the limits, or *modus*, set by memory on thought and the pull or thrust exercised by the will in operation, with which the last chapter ended, leads the author into a concluding reflection on the text of Wisdom 11:21, *You have disposed all things in measure and number and weight*; a preliminary glance at imaginative or fictitious thinking introduces this reflection.

Book XII
Man's Case History: The Image Broken Up; The Fall

Chapter 1 322
The inner man, or mind, is distinguished into two departments or functions, a higher one concerned with contemplating eternal truth and making judgments in accordance with it, and in this function mind is most essentially itself; and a lower one concerned with the management of temporal and material affairs, which is derived from the higher function rather as the woman was derived from the man in the creation narrative of Genesis 2.

Chapter 2 324
Turning to the story of the first man and woman which he has introduced as an allegory of the two functions of the mind, he rejects another allegorical interpretation of it which sees the basic human family of man woman and offspring as the image of the divine trinity. Not only does this theory not fit the dogmatic requirements of trinitarian doctrine, it cannot either be reconciled with 1 Cor 11:7, where Paul asserts that the man alone is the image of God.

Chapter 3 327
The text from Paul quoted in the last chapter to demolish the opinion that the image of the trinity is to be found in the human trio of man, woman, and child presents an even greater problem itself, in that it seems to exclude woman altogether from being the image of God, in contradiction both to Christian good sense and to the text of Genesis 1:27. The problem is solved by explaining the apostle symbolically in support of the author's symbolic exegesis of the Genesis story of the first couple to represent the functional structure of the human mind. This exegesis is pursued to show the fall narrative as realized in the disordered psyche of Everyman.

Chapter 4 334
The distinction already briefly proposed between wisdom and knowledge, *sapientia* and *scientia*, is examined in detail, the former being the appropriate quality of the higher function of mind and the latter of the lower. In the course of the discussion Plato's theory of reminiscence is noticed and refuted. The quest for a trinity in knowledge is postponed to the next book.

Book XIII
Man's Case History: The Image Repaired; Redemption

Chapter 1 342
Taking as his text for analysis the prologue of John's gospel, the author proceeds to elaborate the distinction made in the previous book between wisdom as the proper activity of the higher reason and knowledge as the function of the lower reason. To this sphere of knowledge of temporal things he ascribes in particular faith, which he declares will be the main topic of this book.

Chapter 2 346
Taking up the idea of a common will, with which he was comparing a common faith at the end of the last chapter, he discusses at length the universal will to happiness. This seems at first to be a digression from the topic of faith, with which he professes to be concerned in this book; but in fact it is relevant to this topic, as he will go on to argue that faith is necessary if this desire for happiness, common to all men, is not to be frustrated.

Chapter 3 350
The author argues that real and total happiness implies and requires immortality; that it is therefore not available in this present life; hence that it is pursued by the philosophers in vain, and that faith alone guarantees the real possibility of a happy immortality through participation in the Word made flesh.

Chapter 4 353
The temporal content of faith is examined, namely the incarnation of the Son of God and the life, death and resurrection of the Son incarnate; and the propriety or congruity of this divine economy of salvation is set forth as achieving our deliverance from the evil one by divine justice as well as divine power; whereby a principle is archetypically exemplified, of great consequence for social and political morality, that justice should precede power, and not vice versa.

Chapter 5 358
The justice of God manifested in the redeeming death of Christ is further explored, as also the manifold quality of his grace presented to us in the mystery of the incarnation.

Chapter 6 362
The author places what he has said about the redemption in the last two chapters into his scheme of "wisdom" and "knowledge"; recapitulates the course of the whole book; and concludes by sketching a mental trinity of faith, which belongs to the lower activity of the inner man, and is not yet the mental image of the divine trinity.

Book XIV

Man's Case History: The Image Perfected

Chapter 1 370
The author turns to the discussion of wisdom and its appropriate function of contemplation, in which the true image of God is to be found; but first he picks up a thread from the previous book and examines in more detail why in fact a trinity of faith as the appropriate function of knowledge may not be said to be the image of God.

Chapter 2 374
The author now begins to look for a trinity in the inner man which will also be the image of God, and recalls what he said in the tenth book about the mind remembering, understanding, and willing itself; it is taken as axiomatic, though an axiom which raises problems, that the mind in some sense always remembers, understands, and loves itself; and yet this trinity is only actualized when the mind thinks about itself; so the place of thought or *cogitatio* in the production of the mental trinity is investigated more thoroughly and it is found that without thought there can be no mental word, and therefore no fully actual trinity which will be the actual image of God; thus we again are made to understand that the image of God is only fully realized in certain mental acts, not in mere mental potentialities.

Chapter 3 378
Continuing with his examination of the trinity of the mind's remembering, understanding, and willing itself, and comparing it with the lesser trinities hitherto described, the author finds it to be truly the image of God, because unlike these other trinities it is "coeternal" with the mind itself and is not adventitious to the mind, that is to say, it does not come to it from outside; his presentation of the case involves him in an important explanation or defense of his use of the term "memory" in this context.

Chapter 4 383
The final and perfect image of God is to be found not merely in the mind's remembering, understanding, and loving itself, but in its remembering, understanding, and loving God; it is shown that this trinity is no more adventitious to the mind than that of its self-awareness; and what can be meant by remembering God, understanding him and loving him is discussed.

Chapter 5 388
The analysis of the image of God in the mind is concluded with some reflections on the refashioning or refurbishing of the image in a man, which is presented as a lifelong process that will in fact only be completed when God is seen at last face to face.

Book XV
The Absolute Inadequacy of the Perfected Image

Prologue 395

Chapter 1 396
The author recapitulates the conclusions he has so far reached, in a brief summary of the previous fourteen books.

Chapter 2 399
On the strength of Romans 1:20, *For his invisible things are descried by being understood through the things that have been made*, the author now tests the possibility of directly descrying the divine trinity by inference from our understanding of creation; and he rules the possibility out, because all the divine perfections which we can infer in the creator from reflection on creation are identical with the divine substance—and thus of course substantively with each other—and therefore common to all three persons of the triad.

Chapter 3 405
Having shown that a direct intellectual understanding of the trinity in terms of the text of Romans 1:20 is not possible, the author turns to consider the possibility of an indirect vision of the mystery, in terms of 1 Corinthians 13:12: *We see now through a mirror in an enigma, but then it will be face to face*. The mirror is interpreted to mean the image of God, which is the human mind, and most of the chapter is devoted to discussing the enigmatic nature of this image, chiefly with respect to the mental word; the chapter closes with a suggested reason why it should have been the Word, not the Father or the Holy Spirit, that became man.

Chapter 4 411
The image seen enigmatically in the mirror is now examined to bring out its inadequacy, or unlikeness to the original; and first of all, in this chapter, with reference to the first eternal procession in God, that of the Son from the Father

Chapter 5 418
The author goes on to point out the dissimilarity of the mental image with reference to the second eternal procession, that of the Holy Spirit from the Father and the Son; though in fact he seems rather to forget his precise intention, only reverting to it at the very end of this chapter; and with scarcely any reference to the image, or its third element of will or love, he discusses at length the propriety of the names we give to the Holy Spirit.

Chapter 6 426
The author concludes his examination of the dissimilarity of the image trinity to the divine Trinity with some general observations, not peculiar to either of the divine processions or any of the divine persons; then commends the image trinity, for all its inadequacy, as a means of access to communion with the divine; and finally reverts as a kind of afterthought to the problem of why the Holy Spirit is not said to be born, though he proceeds from the Father; and the only reason he can find for this is that the Holy Spirit also proceeds from the Son as well as from the Father.

Epilogue 434
The author first addresses his soul in a soliloquy, and then concludes the work with a prayer to God

Prayer 436

Index of Scripture 445

Index 453

FOREWORD

Saint Augustine took a very long time writing this book; so much so that when he still had not finished it after fifteen years, some admirers got impatient and published the unfinished work with indecent haste, without the author's permission, and to his intense annoyance.

The case has been quite the reverse with this translation. I translated Book I in 1965 or 1966, while still in England at Hawkesyard Priory in Staffordshire. Then indeed I laid the project aside for some years when I was sent out to Saint Nicholas Priory, Stellenbosch in South Africa. But I took it up again in 1968 and completed it at Saint Peter's Seminary, Hammanskraal, in the Transvaal, in 1971. I took the opportunity of a sabbatical year in Manchester (1972-1973) to revise the introduction and some notes.

Already in 1970, when I had finished Book IV, I had started looking for a publisher. But for reasons totally incomprehensible to anyone outside the mysterious secret world of publishing, this translation has had to wait some years before being offered to the public.

I am therefore all the more grateful to John E. Rotelle, O.S.A., of the Augustinian Heritage Institute, for finally publishing it in this splendid series. We are friends of some years' standing, only, I regret to say, by correspondence and an occasional trans-Atlantic, trans-hemispherical telephone conversation.

My warmest thanks also to Martin Moynihan, whom I first had the pleasure of meeting when he was Her Majesty's High Commissioner in the Kingdom of Lesotho, and who did what he could, on his retirement, to secure a publisher, and who has been unfailing all along in his moral support.

I am also deeply grateful to Boniface Ramsey, O.P., of the American Saint Joseph's Province of the Order of Preachers, for all his help. He first expressed an interest in the translation during a visit to Lesotho in 1981. He has, in fact, been the midwife responsible for eventually bringing it to birth—Father Rotelle, you could say, being the family doctor.

Finally, my thanks and appreciation to Mrs. Jane Worsnip and Mrs. Val Hughes for producing a final typescript.

Edmund Hill, O.P.

Saint Augustine Seminary
Roma, Lesotho
Feast of Saint Augustine,
28 August 1990

INTRODUCTION

1

The place of the *De Trinitate* in Augustine's work

1. The most well known of all Saint Augustine's writings are the *Confessions* and *The City of God*. They are always known by their English rather than their Latin titles; they have long been available in a number of English translations. This is not the case with the *De Trinitate*, which it still feels more natural to refer to by its Latin name, and which was never translated until the late nineteenth century, when it appeared in the Library of the Nicene and Post-Nicene Fathers.

2. Yet these three works do form, in some sense, a kind of trilogy, and of the three the *De Trinitate* is the work of greatest genius and originality. I am not suggesting that Augustine wrote them as a trilogy, only that all three give expression in different modes to one of his basic theological intuitions. This was his keen sense of the historical, or perhaps a better word for it would be the dramatic, dimension to the truths of the Christian religion. He is indeed at his best, as a theological writer, in the dramatic presentation of truth, and at his weakest in the abstract statement of it. This goes a long way to explain, and even to excuse, his often tedious prolixity; to give expression to profound truths in dramatic form calls for a great many words. It is the merest commonplace, to be sure, that Christianity is a historical religion, even that its historical component is a dramatic one. But Augustine seems to have perceived, though he never explicitly defined this perception, that it is of the essence of Christian truth to be dramatic, to be an encounter cast in dramatic form between God revealing and man believing.

3. And so in the *Confessions* we have the history of his own personal drama, a drama primarily of faith. In *The City of God* we have the dramatic history of the Church, also a drama of faith, contrasted in a very complex pattern with unbelief. The book could in fact be called "A Tale of Two Cities," because it tells of the relations between the city of God and what Augustine calls the earthly city. And as each city is constituted by an appropriate kind of love,[1] one could call the work a kind of love story, telling of the drama of love. It is love that makes faith or its refusal dramatic.

4. But in the *De Trinitate*, with a stroke of almost unconscious genius, we are presented with the dramatic history of *God*. If you had asked Augustine whether God has a history, let alone a dramatic one, he would certainly have

When there is reference to the Introduction, the section numbers will be used.

answered "no." One of his most constantly reiterated axioms is that God is wholly unchanging and unchangeable, *incommutabilis*, and the unchanging is not a proper subject of either history or drama. And yet, by concentrating on the historical and dramatic revelation of the mystery of the Trinity, and by seeking to illuminate it through an examination of the divine image in man, which involves him in a kind of sub-plot of man's fall and redemption, he contrives to give the divine mystery itself a veritable dramatic quality.

5. Perhaps then it is not surprising that the *De Trinitate* has been less popular or influential than the other two classics. Saint Augustine's intuition was scarcely shared by his contemporaries, and was wholly alien to the middle ages. For the medievals neither history nor drama ranked high in the hierarchy of learned disciplines, and certainly neither of them had any serious connection with theology. History was no more than chronicle, of value sometimes for edification, and even for entertainment. So the *Confessions* could always be appreciated at this superficial level as the chronicle of a soul, and *The City of God* as the dramatic adventures of the Church from Abel onward. But the dramatic scope of the *De Trinitate* was not even suspected, and so its essential significance was lost on the Latin theology of succeeding ages. The work was indeed much copied and diligently mined; its more metaphysical section provided the scholastics and all subsequent theologians in the West with their language for expounding the doctrine of the Trinity; its description of the trinitarian image in man was adopted as standard in scholastic textbooks, though it was seriously misunderstood by Peter Lombard, for example, whose misunderstanding has been perpetuated up to present times and the old "Penny Catechism." But the central point was missed entirely, and that is that Augustine is proposing the quest for, or the exploration of, the mystery of the Trinity as a complete program for the Christian spiritual life, a program of conversion and renewal and discovery of self in God and God in self. Thus it has come about that the doctrine of the Trinity has been effectively detached from the wider movements of Christian spirituality and devotion in the West, and the mystery has come to be regarded as a curious kind of intellectual luxury for theological highbrows, a subject on which not many priests are eager to preach sermons, nor congregations to listen to them.

6. Saint Thomas Aquinas shows us the most skillful mining technique. His discussion of the Trinity in the *Summa Theologiae*, Ia, qq. 27-43 is a development and improvement of Saint Augustine's theology in many respects; it is in the same linguistic tradition. But it is significant of their very different approaches that Thomas begins with the divine processions in the godhead and ends with the missions of the divine persons, whereas Augustine, by and large, begins with the missions and ends with the processions. This is the historical approach; the other prescinds from, and indeed is scarcely aware of, the history of revelation. Then later on in the *Summa*, Ia, q. 93, when Thomas is discussing man as created by God, he reproduces accurately enough, though without any great profundity of insight, what Augustine says about the trinitarian image in man. He understood what Augustine said, and corrected Peter Lombard's

misunderstanding of it. But I have the impression that he did not really appreciate *why* Augustine said what he did. The very structure of his work compelled him to divorce his treatment of the Trinity from his treatment of its image in man, and so he misses the whole point and value of Augustine's coordinating them in a single work. And if Saint Thomas misses a point, the unfortunate consequence is likely to be that the whole subsequent tradition of Catholic theology will miss it too; which is what has happened.

7. It is time, then, to see why and in what circumstances Augustine wrote the *De Trinitate*. In the covering letter which he wrote to Bishop Aurelius of Carthage on sending him the finished work, he says he began it when he was a young man, and now publishes it when he is old. In fact he seems to have begun it about 400 and finished it soon after 420.[2] As he complains in the letter, tiresome admirers had got hold of his manuscript before he had finished the work and published it without his consent. One gathers from the letter that this happened when he was about halfway through Book XII. When he discovered what had happened, he registered his annoyance and his protest by stopping work on the project altogether. What he found particularly vexing was that it should be published before he had revised it as he would wish, and also that it was the sort of close-knit work which ought to be read as a piece, and was not in his opinion suitable for serial publication. However, his friends, and in particular Aurelius himself, eventually prevailed on him to finish the work. Even so, he felt unable to revise it to his own satisfaction, in case its final edition should differ too radically from the incomplete pirated edition.

8. This odd history accounts for some of the roughness which is undoubtedly one of the work's defects. But it also indicates that it was not an undertaking which Augustine felt to have an urgent public importance. It is not really a polemical work, though at times he puts himself into a kind of conventional polemic stance, as though it were a recognized and expected literary form that works on the Trinity should be written against somebody; nor was it undertaken to meet any particular need or occasion. The *Confessions* is an *apologia pro vita sua*, because like Newman he found himself the victim of a smear campaign which was spoiling his pastoral effectiveness, as well as doubtless wounding his *amour propre*. *The City of God* was written at the request of his friend Marcellinus to meet a kind of smear campaign against Christianity, occasioned by the fall of Rome to Alaric's Goths in 410. But the *De Trinitate* seems to be, so to say, a gratuitous work, undertaken to express the interest that lay nearest the author's heart.

9. That interest was the quest for God. All his life Augustine was a powerful seeker. He always asked far more questions than he answered; he was never easily satisfied that he had found what he was looking for, never lazily took anything for granted—not even his faith. Not that he was a prey to the torments of doubt. But his hard-won faith was a very open-eyed commitment, looking for God and incidentally for himself—for God in himself and for himself in God. The quest was a thoroughly intellectual one, but not academically so. Augustine had a greedy mind, a voracious intellectual appetite, and what he fed

it on was the whole range of his experience, his whole sensual, emotional, rational, and energetic life. This is the field in which he is looking for God.

10. But Augustine was very aware of himself as a public person; not only as a bishop with official and public responsibilities to his flock, but as a famous individual Christian whose most personal thoughts and aspirations were of common interest. He was a man quite without reserve (in an age that was anyhow not much inclined to respect people's reserves), who had the great gift of generalizing from his most intensely personal experiences, and distilling lessons from them about the Christian life in general. And so he presents his quest for God the Trinity as both an all-absorbing personal preoccupation, and a kind of plan for the spiritual life of any Christian. We are all urged to join in the quest, not just by Augustine, but by the Spirit of God in the scriptures. Three times, at key points of his work, he quotes Psalm 105:3-4: *Let their hearts rejoice who seek the Lord; seek the Lord and be strengthened; seek his face always.* It is a summons addressed in the plural to all who fear the Lord. We are reminded of it at the beginning of the quest, I, 2, 5; at the crucial turn it takes halfway through, IX, 1, 1; and at the end, when he is about to sum up and declare the quest a magnificent, a most successful failure, XV, 2, 2.

11. If we are to join him in this taxing quest, it will be convenient to have some plans or maps of the route. And so in the next section of this Introduction I shall analyze the structure of the *De Trinitate*; in the third and fourth I shall survey the legacy of scripture and tradition which Augustine inherited; and in the fifth I shall return to the *De Trinitate* and try to see with greater clarity how it contributed to this tradition.

2
Structure and Contents of the *De Trinitate*

12. The *De Trinitate* divides fairly obviously into two parts, Books I—VII, in which the mystery is discussed in itself, and Books VIII—XV, in which the image of God in man, which Augustine regards as a trinitarian image, is investigated, with the aim of inspecting the divine mystery, so to speak, at closer quarters. This obvious division of the work into two parts has commonly been thought[3] to correspond to the author's own declaration of intention in his introductory chapter in Book I, where he says that he will first establish the truth of the Catholic faith in the Trinity by the authority of scripture, and then go on to give rational arguments in support of this faith, as required by the rationalist opponents against whom he declares he has taken up his pen.[4]

13. However, there are a number of serious objections that can be made against this view of the matter. First, Book VIII does not fit easily into this division; it does not really belong more naturally to the second half than it does to the first. It is, as we shall see, a kind of keystone joining the two halves together, and this means that we shall have to look there, as well as at Book I, for a clue to Augustine's design. Secondly the second half of the work is occupied quite as much as the first

with the interpretation of scripture, and indeed the very idea of man being in the image of God is taken from scripture; it is as much a datum of faith as the mystery of the Trinity itself. These two objections will be substantiated, I hope, when we come to those parts of the work in the course of this survey. Thirdly, this view arises, it seems to me, from a natural but very misleading acceptation of Augustine's distinction between faith and reason, as if it were made in the medieval scholastic sense. This results, among other "inconveniences," in crediting him quite unjustly (if crediting is the word) with the theological naiveté of aspiring to prove the truth of the trinitarian mystery by reason. This objection we must now develop in more detail.

14. For nearly all of us who have grown up in the Catholic tradition today, whether we have formally studied theology or simply been instructed in the Catholic faith, it is the scholastic distinction between faith and reason that we are at least implicitly familiar with. It is really a distinction between truths of faith, things which can only be known by believing in divine revelation, like the mysteries of the Trinity and the incarnation, and truths of reason, things which can be ascertained by the human mind without recourse to divine revelation. This distinction is not meant to exclude the exercise of the mind's rational function from the things of faith or revelation; on the contrary, it is the basis for establishing theology as—in scholastic language—a *science* in its own right, which basing itself on a revelation received by faith tries to understand and organize its grasp of the revelation by rational procedures. Other "sciences" ranging from the physical and mathematical through the social to the metaphysical and philosophical do not differ from theology strictly so called because they employ reason in appropriate procedures and it employs faith, but because they employ their procedures on data and on principles ascertained by reason in the first place.

15. This is a perfectly valid and useful distinction within limits, the limits perhaps of a particular cultural outlook. But it does not happen to be the distinction made by either Augustine or his contemporaries. For example, Augustine made no distinction between theology and philosophy such as is involved in the scholastic faith/reason distinction we have been considering. He distinguished in fact between the true philosophy, which is orthodox Christianity, and what he often called false *theologies*, such as the doctrines of the Platonists and other pagan philosophers. For him the quest for truth is at heart a single and not a multiple effort, and if it is not directed toward the discovery of the supreme truth which is God, then it is not really a quest for truth at all. And in this single quest for truth no amount of rational effort, no high quality of rational procedure will be of any avail unless it starts from faith. One of his favorite quotations from scripture is Isaiah 7:9, which reads in his version, derived from the Septuagint, *Unless you believe, you will not understand.* Thus faith and reason are not distinguished as two parallel or concurrent mental procedures, nor as two distinct and autonomous spheres of intellectual activity, but as two consecutive steps in the only valid field of intellectual activity there is, which is the quest for saving, divine truth.

16. This distinction in fact expresses a much more starkly uncompromising view of man's proper intellectual pursuits than the scholastic one. In the *De Doctrina Christiana* Augustine seems to allow no native worth to the secular sciences, no autonomous dignity. They may be cultivated by the serious Christian only insofar as they serve the study of sacred scripture, which is the main highway to be followed in the quest for divine truth.[5] But whatever its dangers, this is the distinction Augustine makes between faith and reason, and unless we are clear about it we shall be quite mistaken in our analysis of the *De Trinitate*. It means that throughout the work he never leaves the field of theology in the strict sense. From the beginning to the end, in his quest for God, he is trying to understand what he believes, and never for one moment does he prescind from what he calls the *initium fidei*, the starting point of faith. Nowhere in the work is he trying to approach the mystery from other premises than those provided by revelation and accepted by faith. Never is he so naive as to think he can "prove" the mystery without recourse to faith.

17. So his declaration of intention in Book I, to which I have already referred, is less a sketch of the plan of the work than a statement of method. To the extent that it does indicate a plan, that plan is worked out in the first half of the work, in Books I to VII. After his introductory chapter he sets out, in I, 4, 7, a dogmatic statement of the mystery. "This," he concludes, "is my faith inasmuch as it is the Catholic faith." In our quest for God we are not seeking blindly; we know what we are looking for. Then he proceeds, in Books I-IV, to examine the scriptural revelation of the mystery. This is what he means by "establishing the starting point of faith"; he is proving it from scripture, to use a familiar but rather unsatisfactory expression. But more than that, he is in fact showing how the mystery was revealed. In particular, Books II-IV are occupied with a long discussion of the divine missions, the sendings of the Son and the Holy Spirit. In Books II and III he establishes that they were not sent under the Old Testament dispensation, in Book IV he discusses how they were sent in the new. Thus in these books he sketches the whole drama of God's self-revelation to man. The drama is complete in the New Testament when in the fullness of time *God sent his Son, born of woman, born under the law, to redeem those who are under the law, that we might receive adoption as sons; and because we are sons, God sent the Spirit of his Son into our hearts, crying Abba, Father* (Gal 4:4-6). By these sendings of the Son and the Spirit in time the heart of the divine mystery was revealed, which is the eternal divine processions, the eternal generation of the Son from the Father, and the eternal procession of the Spirit from the Father and the Son.

18. In Books V-VII Augustine turns to giving rational arguments in support of this faith. His actual expression in his introductory chapter in Book I is simply *reddere rationem*, which might in fact be better rendered as "give a rational account." He is not arguing in favor of the mystery in the sense of attempting proofs of it from reason, but he is arguing, chiefly against the Arians who seem to have been most accomplished "natural theologians," that the Catholic faith is not at variance with acceptable logic and metaphysics. What in fact he is

embarking on in these books is a discussion of the language in which we talk about the Trinity; he is not so much talking about the Trinity as talking about how to talk about it. He discusses words like "substance," and "person," and in particular he makes what seems to be an original and most important contribution to the theological terminology of the Trinity by developing the notion of relationship.[6] This is a section of the work that Saint Thomas will mine most diligently in his treatise on the Trinity. It is thoroughly theological, but there is very little reference to scripture except toward the end of Book VII. Thus, while it is not an exercise in purely natural reason, such as the scholastic distinction envisaged in the domain of the secular sciences, because it proceeds from and develops the assumptions of faith, neither is it an exercise in "establishing the starting point of faith," such as Augustine's own distinction envisaged, because it is not occupied with a direct examination of divine revelation as presented with the absolute authority of scripture. The section can only be governed then by Augustine's own rubric of *reddere rationem*.

19. One must conclude therefore that the last eight books of the *De Trinitate* are not directly taken into account by Augustine's statement of intention at the beginning of Book I, unless one treats that statement more as a basic principle of method than as a sketch of a plan of contents. In any case, one must look at the introduction of Book VIII for further indications of how the last eight books fit into the structure of the whole work. He ends his short preface to this book by saying that he is going to go over the things he has already treated of *modo interiore*, in a more inward or profound manner. In other words, he implicitly confesses, he has so far only scratched the surface of the mystery—seven books of surface exploration! This makes sense, however, if we keep in mind that the work is not an academic treatise, but a personal quest; he is a prospector looking for gold. It is a reasonable procedure when you are looking for something to search thoroughly on the surface first, before you start digging more deeply. At the end of Book VIII he has staked his claim and fixed the point where he is going to sink his shaft. We have not yet found what we are looking for, he says, but we have found the place where to look.

20. I must admit that I find Book VIII about the most difficult book of the whole work. What I think Augustine is doing in it is trying to establish a direct ontological link between the divine mystery of God himself (which we are in no position at all to inspect *interiore modo*), and the more accessible mystery of the human self. He finds this link in the categories of truth and goodness. God is absolute truth and absolute goodness—with his more concrete and less pretentious ways of speaking Augustine says that God is *ipsa veritas* and *ipsum bonum*. But now, truth is that in terms of which we know and understand whatever we do know and understand, and goodness is that in terms of which we desire, approve, and love whatever we do desire, approve, and love. That is what I mean by calling them categories (which is my word, not Augustine's in this context). They are the specifications or measurements of our knowing and our loving. So in fact, whether we notice it or not—and we seldom do—*God*, who is truth, and *God*, who is goodness, is the category in terms of which we know anything, and

the category or value in terms of which we love anything. God being truth and goodness, we really have to say that he is the very mold or structure, the very cast of the human self, of what Augustine calls the *mens* or mind.

21. Having established this dual ontological link between the divine and the human, we have a kind of guarantee that if we inspect the human mystery *interiore modo*, which should not be impossible since it is directly accessible to us, we shall indirectly be penetrating more deeply also into the divine mystery. This is the place we must stake our claim in and dig, which we proceed to do in the next seven books. The first spadeful of topsoil is removed at the very end of Book VIII by marking out a little trinity in the category of goodness and the activity of love which it governs: the trinity or threesome of the lover, the beloved, and the love that binds them together.

22. Thus Book VIII stands rather on its own, marking the transition to the second half of the whole work. This second half, Books IX-XV, corresponds very neatly, on the whole, and in reverse order to the first half, Books I-VII. In Books IX-XI the author is busy constructing a trinitarian image in man in much the same sort of way as in Books V-VII he was constructing a suitable trinitarian language in which to talk about God. I call it a construction, because it is being tailored deliberately all the time to the divine model which we are given in faith, and for which we have constructed a more or less suitable language. The style is philosophical, there is little or no reference to scripture, and the earlier books, Books V-VII, provide the terms of reference for the image being constructed. The construction is in fact complete at the end of Book X, but Book XI is devoted to elucidating it by providing lesser analogies at more external psychological levels. Thus in Book X the image is finally seen to consist in the consubstantial, coequal, really distinct acts of the inner self or *mens* whereby it remembers itself, understands itself, and wills or loves itself. Book XI throws some light on the more opaque corners of this inner world by looking at analogies in the field of the outer self, that is, at the sense relationships of external vision, and more significantly of internal vision or imagination.

23. This is perhaps the point at which to make clear that Augustine does not discern an image of the Trinity in the three faculties of the soul, memory, understanding, and will. He scarcely speaks of faculties at all, and for that matter he scarcely speaks of the soul. He unambiguously excludes the lower reaches of the soul, the sense faculties and appetites which belong to man's animal nature, and confines his quest or construction of the true image to the specifically human *mens*, which I here call the inner self. This serious misunderstanding of Augustine's thought is the responsibility of Peter Lombard,[7] and is faithfully reproduced in what we can now happily call, I trust, the late Penny Catechism,[8] in spite of the fact that it was explicitly corrected by Thomas Aquinas in his *Summa*.[9] It is a serious misunderstanding, because it deprives the whole doctrine of the divine image in man of any effective application to the spiritual life of the Christian.

24. The importance of appreciating that the image is a matter of mental activities and not of mental faculties or powers can be seen when we come to

the section initiated in Book XII. Augustine now proceeds to examine the history—we could almost call it the case history—of the image in man; and history is a matter of activities, not of faculties. This is a history of man's fall and redemption. It is examined in terms of the fall story in Genesis 3, which is given a highly idiosyncratic interpretation. At the stage of his investigation of the inner self he distinguishes between two functions or levels of activity, the lower function of practical intelligence or action, and the higher function of contemplation. Readers will recognize an echo of the traditional distinction between the active and the contemplative life. It is only in the activities of the contemplative function that the divine trinitarian image is to be found. Now what Augustine does is to apply the story of the fall to the personal history of Everyman. Everyman lives out the tale of Adam, Eve, the serpent, and the apple in himself. The apple is the external world, the serpent is man's lower nature or "sensuality," Eve is the lower mental function of action (women are the practical sex, so one wonders why men have not left them to get on with running the world), and Adam is the higher mental function of contemplation. Book XII is occupied with transposing the fall story into this key of psychological case history, which we are meant to understand as a defacement of the divine image, or rather as a failure to activate its potentialities. Book XIII goes on further to consider the restoration of the image, which is effected by God's redeeming activity in Christ, the term of the divine mission of the Son which was discussed at length in Book IV, and by man's response in faith to that mission, which is in fact a process of continuous conversion.

25. The supreme act of contemplative wisdom which rounds off this conversion process—and which is only intermittently achieved in this life—transforms the divine image, which we left at the end of Book X as consisting of inner self remembering itself, understanding itself, and willing itself into what we can here call the super-image of the inner self remembering God, understanding God, and willing or loving God. This forms the theme of Book XIV.

26. These three books, in which the dramatic history of the image in the spiritual life of Everyman is analyzed in terms of scripture, correspond neatly to II—IV in the first part of the work, where the drama of the scriptural revelation of the mystery of the Trinity was studied. Finally, XV is a ruthless exposé of the inadequacy even of the genuine trinitarian image in man at its highest peak of intensity for representing the divine Trinity itself, and thus a confession that the author has failed—but how splendidly!—in his quest. So it balances, by a pleasing contrast, the contents of I, where he sets out on the quest by establishing the absolute equality of the Son to the Father.

27. So our analysis has revealed a significant chiastic structure to the *De Trinitate,* which is most aptly suited to its dramatic theme of a quest for God. Merely "waiting for Godot" would never have satisfied so impatient a man as Augustine. He had to go on looking for God, in the confident knowledge that God was looking for him, and that he would find himself in the quest, and find God in finding himself. The *De Trinitate* does not in fact end with XV—it can only end with the beatific vision of God in the world to come. But as that stage

still escapes our analysis we can summarize its structure in the following parabola:

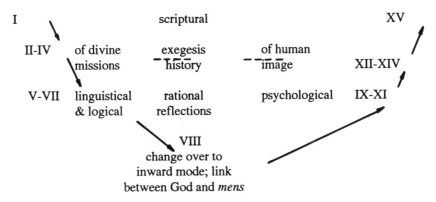

28. This symmetrical structure is of course an achievement of literary artifice, and to prevent its becoming inartistically mechanical, the author does in fact relieve it with certain asymmetries. Thus the division between I and II in the first half is not nearly as clear-cut as that between XIV and XV in the second, while on the other hand the division between IX-XI and XII-XIV is much more blurred than that between II-IV and V-VI. Indeed the six books IX-XIV could well be divided otherwise, with IX X XIV devoted to the construction of the image, interrupted by XI-XIII on its turbulent history.

29. To form a just conception of the work it is not enough, however, to grasp its structure. We shall also have to try to perceive something of the intellectual energy that powers the structure, to perceive the pattern of movement which Augustine's thought follows through this framework. But before we trace this movement of his thought from I to XV again, *interiore modo* and at the risk of some repetition, we must look at the history of the theological tradition he inherited, which naturally enough governed some of his concerns.

3
The Tradition behind Saint Augustine: Scripture

30. The tradition proper starts, of course, with the New Testament; we can say with certainty that the Trinity is a mystery which was only revealed in the New Testament, not in the Old. As we shall see, however, this is a certainty which we owe in large measure to Augustine himself. Since he deals with the New Testament evidence for the mystery more than adequately in Book I and elsewhere, there is no point in our summarizing it here. But in the New Testament revelation did not come wholly out of the blue; it was given in the context of the Old Testament tradition which was inherited and fulfilled by the New Testament. The vocabulary, the images in which the revelation was expressed

were provided by the Old Testament. Now Augustine's exegesis of the Old Testament is in this respect almost entirely negative; that is, it is devoted to proving against some of his forerunners that the mystery was not revealed in the Old Testament. So it may be of profit for us to begin our survey of the tradition he inherited by looking at the Old Testament background to the trinitarian language and imagery of the New Testament.

31. To provide us with a convenient New Testament starting point, we have a condensed statement of the revelation of the mystery in Galatians 4: *When the fullness of time came, God sent forth his Son, born of a woman, born under the law, that he might redeem those who are under the law, that we might receive the status of sons. And to show you are sons, God sent the Spirit of his Son into our hearts, crying Abba, Father* (Gal 4:4-6). Here we have the basic terms of the mystery, "God," "Father," "Son," "Spirit," "sending," to which we can attach other important words as we investigate these in turn.

32. Let us begin with the pair "Father and Son," and first just remind ourselves very briefly of the New Testament usage, whose Old Testament background we wish to elucidate. In the synoptics Jesus nearly always refers to God as "Father," hardly ever as "God"; but it is usually "my/your heavenly Father" in Matthew, "my/your Father" in Mark and Luke. There are in Matthew two passages, and in Mark and Luke one each, where he talks in a way familiar to us from John of "the Father and the Son."[10] In John "the Father" is usual, "my Father" common, and "your Father" quite exceptional. In Paul's letters the common expressions are "God and our Father" and "the God and Father of our Lord Jesus Christ." John's usage of "the Father" is the most unequivocally trinitarian, and also presumably the most developed and technical. As for "Son," there is the "Son of Man" formula, common in the gospels, but only used once elsewhere;[11] "the Son of God" and equivalents such as "his Son" and "my Son"; and finally John's "the Son" which corresponds to "the Father."

33. In the Old Testament we begin not so much with the idea of God being our father, as of his being "the God of the fathers."[12] It is Abraham, Isaac, and Jacob, rather than God, who are the first father figures in Israel's consciousness. In what relationship did the patriarchs themselves conceive that they stood to their God? Possibly, to judge by the most archaic names, such as Abraham and Abimelech, as sons; or even as younger brothers, as suggested by the name Achimelech. But the descendants of Abraham, Isaac and Jacob were at a remove from this intimate personal relationship; for them God was at first the God of their fathers.

34. Perhaps they were inhibited at first from thinking of themselves as sons of God, because this title usually signified what we can conveniently but too precisely call angels, divine beings remembered from the polytheistic past, and given the status in the bible of courtiers in the court of the Lord of hosts; they are sometimes also equated with the stars.[13] But then a remarkable thing happens in Israel's consciousness, and a most original use is made of this polytheistic or mythical inheritance; Israel is in some texts assimilated to the angelic and heavenly host. Thus the God of hosts is simultaneously and as it were identically

God of the angelic hosts and of the Israelite battle hosts. To our purpose here, Israel acquires the angelic status of "sons of God." Thus Psalm 82:6, *I said, You are gods, sons of the Most High*; and the interesting case of Deuteronomy 32:8, in which the Hebrew reads *When the Most High gave the nations their inheritance . . ., he fixed the bounds of the peoples according to the number of the sons of Israel*, while the Greek, representing a variant original—and we cannot say which is really the older—reads, . . . *according to the number of the sons of God* (that is, angels). This development culminates in three crucial texts: Exodus 4:22, *And you shall say to Pharaoh, Thus says the Lord, Israel is my firstborn son, and I say to you, let my son go that he may serve me*; and two prophetic allusions to this text, Hosea 11:1, *When Israel was a child I loved him, and out of Egypt I called my son*; and Jeremiah 31:9, *I am a father to Israel, and Ephraim is my firstborn.*[14]

35. Thus the nation comes to think of itself collectively as God's son, as well as continuing to think of itself as "the sons of the fathers, Abraham, Isaac, and Jacob." Once this idea takes root, it encourages the sacred writers to think of God as being like a father to individual persons, and of Israelites as being severally God's sons and daughters. God is *like* a father; not God *is* a father because that is a purely human relationship. He is also like a mother (and in texts that do not concern us, like a husband); he is like a parent in his constant care and provision for his people, whom he treats as his children.[15] Sometimes they are reminded what bad children they are, "faithless sons"[16] who have not treated God as a father should be treated;[17] sometimes they are called God's sons and daughters to distinguish them from the Gentiles, from among whom he has chosen them.[18] In some of the Wisdom literature the idea is extended, and we have Israelites being talked of as sons of the divine Wisdom, who thus becomes a divine mother figure, God's motherliness.[19]

36. Thus God mysteriously *is* the father of Israel collectively; Israel is his son in the same sort of way as the angels are. He is *like* a father to the children of Israel individually. Again, one has to stress "like," because their awareness of being sons of Abraham, of the fathers, the sacred ancestors, is still very strong. But eventually this "like" is forgotten or transcended, and we find texts in which God is "our father" quite simply, and in which he replaces the patriarchs in that role. He actually takes the place of Abraham, Isaac and Jacob. Thus in Isaiah 63:16, *For you are our father, though Abraham does not own us, and Israel*, (the patriarch Jacob) *does not acknowledge us; you, Lord, are our father, our redeemer is your ancient name; we the clay, you the potter, we are all the work of your hand*; and Malachi 2:10, *Have we not all one father? Did not one God create us? Why then do we break faith with one another, profaning the covenant of our fathers?*

37. There are two points to be made about this realization of God's fatherhood superseding, in a sense, that of the patriarchs: first, it arises most strongly out of a sense of anguish, of the need for God's fatherly care; and second, in spite of the appearances of the last two texts quoted, it has nothing to do with the doctrine of God being the creator. It is not a matter of God's common fatherhood

of all humankind, but of his special fatherhood of the sons of the patriarchs, whom he has specially created by bringing them out of Egypt. He has created them like a potter molding clay, by making them into a people, his chosen people. The writers of these texts were not thinking of the original creation of humankind in the common ancestor, Adam. In other words, this idea of God being father is linked with the consciousness of being chosen and redeemed by him, not with being his creatures.

38. This association of divine fatherhood with divine election is supremely shown in the last Old Testament development of the notion which we will consider. God, who said of the people as a whole "Israel is my firstborn," bestows a unique and privileged sonship on Israel's divinely chosen representative, the anointed king, the Messiah.[20] This idea of the king, in whom the Messiah *par excellence* was of course anticipated, being the son of God, is enriched by the picture given in Wisdom of the just man, whose portrait is drawn in a way reminiscent of Isaiah 53, being the son of God, and numbered among the sons of God.[21]

39. All this Old Testament development is summed up in the text of John 20:17: *Go to my brothers and say to them: I am ascending to my father and your father, to my God and your God.* "My father," the risen Christ says—and the parallel phrase "my God" shows that he is speaking as man—because he is the Messiah, the just man, the personification of Israel, God's firstborn; "your father," he says, because his brothers the disciples are true sons of Abraham, not just as Jews but as believers in the Messiah. If the disciples had not been familiar with this language of "my father and your father" and the correlative expressions "son of God" and "sons of God," they could surely never have either developed or grasped the strictly trinitarian language of "the Father and the Son."

40. Thus the revelation of the eternal and wholly divine father/son relationship is prepared for by the gradual unfolding of a temporal divine/human father/son relationship between God on the one side and Israel, Israelites and the Messiah on the other. This relationship is completely fulfilled in Jesus of Nazareth, who manifests himself to the disciples as the Messiah. What the trinitarian revelation does is to give an entirely new dimension to the messianic sonship of both Jesus the Messiah himself and of his disciples, whom he incorporates into himself as the *totus Christus*. But we can only come to a just appreciation of this bearing of the trinitarian mystery on *our* relationship with God, our sonship, if we have some awareness of what may be called its messianic antecedents.

41. To ascertain how the jump is made from the messianic language of "my father and your father," "son of God" and "sons of God," to the trinitarian language of "the Father" and "the Son," we must look at the history of the words "God" and "Lord." We can observe the whole span of the process in this chapter, John 20. First Jesus appears to Mary Magdalene and tells her to stop fondling him and to go and tell his brothers that *I am ascending to my Father and your Father, to my God and your God*—a purely messianic statement, were it not for

the hint, *Stop fondling me, for I have not yet ascended to "the Father"* (verse 17). Finally the chapter ends with Thomas being told to feel Christ's wounds and exclaiming *My Lord and my God,* a purely trinitarian expression. This text is indeed the nearest the New Testament gets, if I am not mistaken, to saying in so many words that Jesus Christ is God.

42. The point to note particularly is that before Thomas says "my God" he says "my Lord." It is this title of "Lord" which is the effectual key that actually achieves the transposition from messianic statements to trinitarian ones, from "my Father" to "the Father," from "the son of God" to "the Son." And it is able to do this because of its Old Testament history. This is a history, really, of implicit linguistic logic. The name "God," which for us is nearly always a proper name, and which we do not therefore use very much as a predicate by which to describe and classify a subject, was originally a common or generic noun, like "man" or "cat." In the Hebrew bible it is mostly used, in its plural form Elohim, as a proper name. But this use implies that the revelation of monotheism is already complete, and that there is only one being to whom this common name properly belongs; and there are evidences that this revelation was not fully acquired or clearly grasped until fairly late in Israel's history. The fact that the plural form is the usual one is itself rather significant—as though we were to recite in the creed "I believe in one Gods." However, long before this fairly late epoch—say from the time of Amos until the exile—Israel had been committed to the faithful service of only one god, the God of Israel. And from an early epoch, certainly from the time of Moses and possibly before, they had distinguished him from alien gods by the proper name YHWH, which in the story of Moses at the burning bush is related to the verb "to be" and explained as meaning "I am who I am," or "I am" *tout court.*[22] "YHWH is God," "YHWH" the proper name, "God" the predicate, came to be the typical Israelite slogan.[23] In Deuteronomy 6:4 this slogan receives its monotheistic form: *Hear, O Israel, YHWH our God YHWH one,* a succinct expression which can be construed in three ways: YHWH our God, YHWH is one; YHWH is our God, YHWH is one, YHWH is our God, YHWH alone. The only way, I would have thought, in which it cannot be construed is the way in which the Revised Standard Version takes it,[24] following Revised Version, Authorized Version, Vulgate and Septuagint: "the Lord our God is one Lord." For "YHWH" ("the Lord") is a proper name, and it is queer to treat it as a predicate—rather like saying "Elizabeth our queen is one Elizabeth."

43. Nevertheless I am sure the Revised Standard Version is quite right to stick to the tradition set by earlier versions. What makes sense of the tradition, however, is the substitution of the common noun "Lord," *Adonai* in Hebrew, for the proper name "YHWH"; a substitution which probably became customary from about the time of the exile, and was certainly well established by the end of the third century before Christ. The divine proper name was too sacred to be pronounced.

44. The deity thus comes to have, very commonly, a double-barreled name, consisting of two common nouns, "lord" and "god." They are combined in the

second creation narrative of Genesis 2: *The Lord God planted a garden in Eden,* etc. The difference between the two words, however, is to be noted. Once your monotheism is firmly established, the word "god" naturally acquires currency as a proper name, and is rarely used as a descriptive noun; we not only spell it, we think it with a capital G. We say about some insufferable office tyrant, "he thinks he's God," not "He thinks he's a god." "Lord," on the other hand, the substitute for God's *proper* name of YHWH, remains a descriptive noun in common use, applicable to various degrees of men and angels, as well as to God. It has a whole gamut of possible references, and can be the equivalent of "Sir" and "Mister," through "Lord," "M'lud," "sovereign lord the king," "messiah," to "the Lord God."

45. A key text for the New Testament use of the word, picked on by Jesus himself, is Psalm 110:1: *The Lord said to my Lord, Sit at my right hand; if David can call him Lord, then how can he be his son?* [25] The unique and special lordship which this text seems to ascribe to the Christ/Messiah is seen as implying a unique and special sonship. The way in which the revelation was "put across" to the disciples was possibly something like this: i) they called Jesus "Lord" as a title of human respect like "Sir," as they also called him "Master," "Teacher," "Rabbi"; ii) when they recognized him as the Messiah, he became "the Lord" in a special way, like our "sovereign lord the king," only more so; iii) but as they reflected on his deeds, what John calls his "signs," on his teaching and certain mysterious things he said about himself, above all on his resurrection, they came to see that he is "the Lord" in an even more unique and incomparable sense; he is the divine, not just the messianic Lord; he is the Lord, as that title stands for the ineffable name YHWH. So—"my Lord and my God."

46. John drives the lesson home by recording those strange "I am" sayings of Jesus: *before Abraham was, I am* (Jn 8:58); *when you have lifted up the Son of Man, then you shall know that I am* (Jn 8:28); *Who are you looking for? They answered, Jesus the Nazarene. He said to them, I am ... So when he said to them I am, they went backwards and fell to the ground* (Jn 18:5). In these passages John is no doubt deliberately pointing certain utterances of Jesus that were more obscure and less brutally shocking when he made them. It is hard to suppose that we have here his *ipsissima verba*. The purpose of these sayings in the evangelist's composition is to remind his readers of the full meaning of the title "Lord" which they gave to Jesus Christ.

47. So it happens that the double-barreled name of the Old Testament, the Lord God, gets distributed in the New Testament. "The Lord," when it is used as a name, or a title qualifying a proper name, is usually reserved for the Son—for the Son incarnate, of course, so it is a title now of divinity *and* humanity. "God," on the other hand, as a proper name, usually stands for the Father, even when it is not being explicitly linked with the name "Father"; as in the text from Galatians which we started with, *God sent his Son.* In Philippians 2:11 we have an illuminating juxtaposition of the two titles:. . . *and every tongue confess that Jesus Christ is Lord to the glory of God the Father.* Even more interesting is 1 Corinthians 8:6 . . . *but for us there is one God, the Father, of*

whom are all things and we for him; and one Lord, Jesus Christ, through whom are all things and we through him. Saint Paul really seems to be doing a trinitarian variation here on the text of Deuteronomy 6:4, *the Lord our God, the Lord one.*

48. But this man, who is thus recognized as Lord in this extraordinary sense, remains on record as having talked about God as "my Father." He has also talked mysteriously—much less often, no doubt, than one would infer from John, but in a manner striking enough to have been recorded in the synoptics—about the Father and the Son. John seizes on this expression to present us with the full revelation of the eternal, wholly divine father/son relationship within the life of the one true God.

49. We now turn to the consideration of associate "Son" words, in particular *Logos*, or "Word." It will be recalled that when we were examining the expression "son of God" in the Old Testament we discovered its origins to be at least partly mythological and polytheistic. Once it had meant divine beings, called the sons of gods, which is probably a semitic figure of speech meaning simply "gods." The biblical tradition downgraded these gods to angels, a rank in which they ceased to be a threat to the integrity of Israel's faith. But here in the New Testament, in a pagan world of the most uninhibited polytheistic pullulation of gods, we have a figure, called Christos, called Kyrios, called son of God, and explicitly upgraded—if I may so put it—to the divine level. There was surely a very great danger of the trinitarian revelation being interpreted by pagan converts in the primitive church as a modification of the stark Judaic monotheism in the direction of at least a philosophical polytheism. My guess is that it was to counter this danger that John introduced his concept of the *Logos* into his trinitarian theology, again very possibly developing some suggestion contained in the language used by Jesus himself. The anthropomorphism lurking in the terms "Father" and "Son" needed neutralizing by the introduction of impersonal terms. The chief of these is *Logos*, "Word"; other secondary ones are used in the New Testament, whose antecedents we need not examine, like "radiance," "character," and "image."[26]

50. I take it as established that the Old Testament source of *Logos* in John is the Wisdom literature, that is, those passages of it in which the divine Wisdom is personified as a feminine figure.[27] The best known is Proverbs 8 and 9. Others, perhaps even more important for the New Testament, are Wisdom 7—9, Sirach 24 and Baruch 3:9—4:4. Wisdom in these passages is personified as a feminine figure, one might almost say as Israel's *anima* in the Jungian sense, as Israel's better half; it is also identified with the Law. The personification and the attribute personified are ideal for John's purpose. This is what the Son is.[28] Unfortunately, the gender is wrong. The femininity of Wisdom is a valuable antidote in the Old Testament to what is otherwise an excessive projection of masculine characteristics onto the deity. There is really no reason why we should not call God mother as well as father—except perhaps that mother goddesses were far more dangerous rivals to the one true God than any mere Olympian male like Zeus. In fact, the divine Wisdom personified is the way in which the bible does call

God our mother. More to the point, it depicts this Wisdom as God's daughter. But for all the charm and rightness of this idea, this literary artifice of the Wisdom writers, it clearly would not do for John, who was expounding the gospel of Jesus Christ, a man not a woman, the Son not the Daughter of God.

51. The masculine *Logos* was a most convenient substitute for the feminine *Sophia*. As well as meaning the spoken word it also means in Greek the thought word, or simply reason, thought. Furthermore, it has close biblical affinities with *sophia*. I mentioned just now that in some passages, Baruch for example, Wisdom is identified with the Law. In others, for example Proverbs, she is represented as attending and assisting at the creation of the world. Now the world was created by the utterance of the divine words—*he spoke and they were made, he commanded and they were created* (Ps 148:5); and the heart of the Law is the decalogue, the ten *logoi*, ten words of God. Again, there are two psalm texts where the word of God is paired with his spirit, and they are both on the verge of being personified: Psalm 33:6, *By the word of the Lord the heavens were made, and all their host by the breath* (spirit) *of his mouth*; and even more apposite, Psalm 147:18, *He sends forth his word and melts them, he makes wind* (spirit) *blow, and the waters run.*

52. Finally, I think that long before John the latest of the Wisdom writers had already assimilated the ideas of *Logos* and *Sophia*. The last psalm text quoted speaks of the Lord sending his word. It is an idea you also get in the prophets; the word of the Lord comes to the prophet, or in the hand of the prophet, who is sent with the word of the Lord. "Word" and "sending" go together. Now the author of Wisdom says that he called upon God and the spirit of Wisdom came to him,[29] and later he says in a prayer, *Send her forth from the holy heavens, and from the throne of your glory send her, that she may be with me and toil* (Wis 9:10). Thus he uses *Logos* language about *Sophia*. Later he reverses the process. The most characteristic feature of Sophia language is the personification of Wisdom; but in one famous passage the author personifies the divine *Logos*: *For while gentle silence lay over all, and night had run the half of her swift course, down from the heavens, from the royal throne, leapt your all-powerful Word; into the heart of a doomed land the stern warrior leapt. Carrying your unambiguous command like a sharp sword, he stood and filled the universe with death; he touched the sky, yet trod the earth* (Wis 18:14). The reference, of course, is to the slaying of the firstborn in Egypt.

53. The New Testament, however, goes far further than the Old Testament in its use of these concepts and devices. In the Old Testament these personifications are no more than a literary device; what is signified remains a divine attribute or act. The New Testament says, in effect, that the personifications have come true. The personified *Logos* is a distinct subsistent reality, what later theology will call a person. But the language in which the New Testament expresses this revelation has been prepared by the Old Testament.

54. From "Word" to "Spirit" the transition is easy and natural. They are often paired, as we have seen in the two psalm texts above (Ps 33:6 and Ps 147:18). So it will be convenient to survey the history of the word "spirit" by a com-

parison with that of "word." I suggested above that John found in *Logos* a suitably impersonal term to correct aberrations that might spring from misunderstanding the highly personal terms "Father" and "Son." In comparison with these *Logos* is impersonal in that it does not signify a person, but only the activity or achievement of a person. But in comparison with *Pneuma Logos* is a personal term, since it refers to the sphere of personal activity, whereas the primary reference of *Pneuma* is to completely non-personal forces, such as wind and tempest. When the bible talks about God's word it is reminding us of God's being personal, of his "rational nature"; but when it talks about God's spirit it is reminding us that God is also non-personal and non-rational. There is more to God than can be contained in the category of "person." And so "spirit," applied both to God and human beings, is at once lower and higher than "word"; it is both subrational and suprarational; it heaves in the dark depths, and soars to the heights of light inaccessible.

55. Like God's word, the spirit of God is associated both with creation and with the giving of the Law; explicitly with creation,[30] implicitly with exodus and covenant under a number of symbols which later tradition interpreted of the Spirit, such as the pillar of cloud and fire, and the finger of God.[31] But this tradition, of which there is evidence in the Old Testament as well as in the New Testament, grows out of the Exodus narrative itself, and is not forced on it artificially. Again like God's Word, the Spirit of God is correlated with Wisdom in the sapiential books, perhaps even more emphatically so.[32] In fact, so similar sometimes in function are the word and the spirit as expressions of divine power or activity, that one is tempted to regard them as practically synonymous. One even finds this tendency to identification, or at least this difficulty of distinction between them, in the New Testament. Thus Christ and the Spirit seem almost to merge in this passage from 2 Cor 3:14: *Indeed to this very day that same veil is still there when the old covenant is being read, a veil never lifted, since Christ alone can remove it. Yes even today, whenever Moses is read, the veil is over their minds. It will not be removed until they turn to the Lord. Now this Lord is the Spirit, and where the Spirit of the Lord is, there is freedom. And we, with our unveiled faces reflecting like mirrors the brightness of the Lord, all grow brighter and brighter as we are turned into the image that we reflect; this is the work of the Lord who is Spirit.*

56. It is true that "spirit" is sometimes used, in a way that "word" never is, almost as a metaphysical term to describe the nature of the divine, "the stuff or matter of which God consists," in the words of G.L. Prestige.[33] This seems to be its meaning in the saying of Jesus to the Samaritan woman, *God is Spirit* (Jn 4:24) and we find a similar use of the word in Wisdom.[34] But I do not think this consideration will altogether solve the problem raised by Saint Paul's words just quoted.

57. Another difference between God's word and his spirit is the way in which we human beings are related to them. One could say that the relationship of men to God's word is more objective, it is something over against men, while our relationship to his spirit is more subjective, it is or can be something in us, in which we share. Men are the ministers of God's word, and proclaim it; but they

are seized or possessed by his spirit, it changes their spirit, it becomes a new principle of life in them. It is notoriously difficult to tell sometimes in Saint Paul whether "spirit" should be written with a capital S or a small s. This inwardness of the spirit is discernible in the most primitive Old Testament texts, where the spirit seizes men with its demonic power, as in the case of Samson or Saul,[35] and in the most developed, where it is seen as the interior principle of sanctification,[36] or as the equivalent of the divine presence.[37]

58. As the reader will no doubt have gathered, I find it hard to detect any great difference between the Old Testament and the New Testament in the range or reference of the word "spirit." The crucial difference is, of course, that in the Old Testament "spirit," whatever its reference, only signifies an attribute or activity of God, while in the New Testament it usually, though by no means always, signifies "the third person of the Trinity," just as "word" and "son" signify "the second person of the Trinity." But it is much more difficult to see how this development came about with the Holy Spirit than with the Son. The Son is conspicuously objectified for us by the incarnation, the Spirit, as we have noted, remains elusively experienced as subjective. It is obvious from the Acts and from the letters of the Apostles that they and their first converts enjoyed an overwhelmingly strong experience of the Spirit. It is also obvious that in the light of this experience they recognized the Spirit as a distinct, subsistent divine entity, and not merely as a divine attribute.[38] But it is not at all obvious why or how they came to this recognition. Nor, as we shall see, has the Church's theological reflection ever entirely succeeded in declaring what this recognition means. The Holy Spirit has always remained the most impersonal of the divine persons. Perhaps that is his (its?) chief significance for our faith.

59. It is possible that we have a slight clue to this problem in the notion of "sending," which is the last of the words presented for our investigation by our master text, Galatians 4:4-6, and is also of crucial importance for Augustine's *De Trinitate*. Perhaps this too is a word which has a kind of compulsive logic about it, as we saw to be the case with "Lord." Now we do not usually talk about people sending themselves; a person or thing sent is a subsistent entity distinct from the person or thing sending. As one of the most striking things about Jesus was that he claimed to be a man on a mission, claimed to have been sent by God, we spontaneously conclude that he is distinct from the one who sent him, and so we are driven to conclude that the Son is really distinct from the Father, because Jesus is the Son whom the Father sent.

60. There was nothing new about the idea of God sending various agents about his business, usually with a message or a revelation. In the Old Testament he is constantly sending prophets, and not infrequently angels, whose Greek name almost defines them as sendable beings. And it would be laboring the obvious to say that prophets and angels are distinct from the God who sends them. However, the Old Testament does sometimes rather stretch the inherent logic of the idea of "sending." There is nothing, perhaps, against this logic in God's sending plagues,[39] or serpents;[40] but for him to send out non-objective moods of his, like his fury or his terror,[41] is rather odd. What it means is that

these divine moods are being to some extent objectified, even on the way to being personified. It is the beginnings of the literary device of personifying abstract qualities or ideas.

61. The habit is widely developed, and in the later literature of the bible we have God sending his word, his spirit, and his wisdom, as we have already seen from a number of texts.[42] But these divine attributes remain attributes, for all that they are personified by a figure of speech. Thus it might be said that the compulsive logic in the idea of "sending" is not very powerful, seeing that it can be frustrated by a mere figure of speech. But the New Testament sees it pick up force again; there Jesus Christ is manifestly sent by God, sent by the Father, as the successor and fulfiller of all the prophets and angels who had been sent before him. But he is also identified with those attributes, word and wisdom of God, which were sent in the Old Testament in virtue of a figure of speech. So in him the attribute of *Logos/Sophia* becomes objectively distinct, with the distinctness of the Son from the Father.

62. Now the experience of the Spirit of God which the apostles and first converts had on and after Pentecost was of a—what? an en-thou-siasm?—that came upon them as something given or sent, something that Jesus had promised them they would receive.[43] If Jesus, being sent by the Father, is really distinct from the Father, then this something, this Spirit which Jesus promised, and which came from above as he had come from above, being sent as he had been sent, and given as he had been given[44]—then this Spirit too must be really distinct from both God (the Father) and the Son of God, and therefore really subsistent, and not just an attribute.

63. Correlated with the idea of "sending" or "mission" is the idea of "going forth" or "procession." One who is sent on a mission naturally proceeds or goes forth on his mission. So Wisdom came forth or proceeded from the mouth of the Most High,[45] so Jesus came forth from God and came into the world, so the Holy Spirit comes forth or proceeds from the Father. This term of "going forth" or "procession" is in later developments going to be given a reference, distinct from that of "mission," to eternal goings forth from the Father in the godhead, which precede the missions in time of the Son and the Spirit. Indeed Augustine's will be the main contribution to this development. In the New Testament, however, the words keep their natural association, whereby mission really precedes procession. But the later theological transposition of terms is harmonious and not forced, because it is the missions of the Son and the Spirit which reveal their distinction as persons in the godhead, and so manifest the eternal internal movements or acts in the divine being on which this distinction of persons is based.

4

The Tradition behind Saint Augustine: Ecclesiastical Writers

64. In examining the history of the terms used in scripture to declare what we call the mystery of the Trinity, we have been looking at the legacy left to the

Church by divine revelation, or to put it another way, the problem set before it. Now we go on to see what use the Church made of that legacy, and how Church thinkers and teachers set about trying to solve the problem. None of them, of course, ever solved the problem, because a divine mystery, and this particular mystery above all, is by definition insoluble as a problem. What happened was that each of them reset the problem in a slightly different form for their successors, and what we are interested in is how they had successively reset the problem for Augustine.

65. He, by his own confession, did not read Greek easily, or at least with any pleasure.[46] So it is with earlier Latin writers that we shall be chiefly concerned, that is with Tertullian in the early third century, Novatian some forty to fifty years later, Hilary and Victorinus Afer in the middle of the fourth century. It is extremely probable, indeed almost certain that Augustine had also read Irenaeus, from the end of the second century, in a Latin translation. I do not know whether any of the works of Justin Martyr, in the middle of the second century, had been translated into Latin. It is antecedently probable, since he lived and wrote at Rome. But in any case he is important for Irenaeus and Tertullian, who had certainly read him. So our survey will take us from Justin and Irenaeus in the second century, through Tertullian and Novatian in the third, on to Hilary and Victorinus in the fourth century. As for the great Greek fathers of the fourth century, it seems certain that Augustine had read the relevant writings of Gregory Nazianzen and Didymus the Blind, possibly also of Basil the Great and Epiphanius of Salamis.[47] In any case he had a general knowledge of the kind of problems, largely linguistic and metaphysical, that engaged their attention, and so we shall have to refer to them also. But for the most part we will confine ourselves to the Latin or Western tradition.

66. Before we begin, a word must be said in defense of this tradition, and to dissipate a prejudice against it which has been firmly established in theological circles by the great work of Dr G.L. Prestige already quoted, *God in Patristic Thought*. The author's contribution to theological learning is enormous, but we would be unwise to value his more sweeping generalizations as highly as his detailed scholarship and his particular inferences. In the first place, we really ought to demolish the distinction between the Latin and Greek traditions for this early period altogether—as he himself does when it suits his book, by claiming the Latin writer Tertullian for the Greek tradition, on the grounds that he read Greek with ease and familiarity, and had a more penetrating philosophical mind than other Latin writers.[48] The question-begging character of the argument will be apparent. What we have in fact at this early stage of theological history—and will continue to have—are various local traditions, African, Roman, Gallic in the West, Alexandrian, Antiochene, Cappadocian in the East. The only way in which language comes into it is that the Western traditions switched from Greek to Latin in the course of the third century. But we may take it that subsequent Latin writers were heirs to the whole of the Western tradition (or rather the whole of their local tradition at least), not just to those elements of it enshrined in the Latin language. Nor is it a very meaningful generalization that Greeks were of

a more philosophical mind, and their language a more subtle instrument for speculation. If the Latins have no one to compare as a polymath and a bold thinker with Origen, the Greeks can produce no one to equal Augustine for profundity and greatness of mind. And as for the quality of the two languages, the development of scholasticism shows what tricks Latin can be put to when philosophers and theologians are so minded. Nor was scholastic Latin merely a medieval phenomenon. The medievals inherited the makings of it from Boethius in the sixth century, and in the fourth we find Victorinus coining words like *filietas, intelligentialis, existentialitas* (do Existentialists recognize and acknowledge their debt, I wonder?), *essentitas, substantialitas*.[49] Whether Victorinus has a subtle metaphysical mind or not I cannot say, since I find him almost totally incomprehensible; but at any rate the Latin language was not stopping him from being subtle, even though his development of its latent possibilities did not help him to make himself clear.

67. Let us begin then with Justin and Irenaeus—in the West. Justin was, by his own reckoning, a philosopher, and the philosophy he professed was Christianity. He was concerned to present it persuasively to the unbelieving world, to the world of pagan and imperial philosophy in his *Apologies*, and to the Jewish world in his *Dialogue with Trypho*. In both works his central concern is to expound Christian belief in Christ, the Logos. The *Dialogue* is of the greater interest to us, as in it Justin is able to argue from the Old Testament, which he has in common with his adversary. He first proves to Trypho's satisfaction from the scriptures that Jesus is the Christ, thus following in the steps of the New Testament catechesis itself. Then Trypho says that while he can accept that Jesus is the Christ, he cannot yet concede that he is divine, and "pre-existed."[50] So Justin is committed to proving from the Old Testament the pre-existence of Christ, that is that the Word or Logos existed before the incarnation. He boldly undertakes to show "that there is, and is stated to be (in the scriptures) another God and Lord under the maker of all things," and "to provide evidence from the scriptures that in the beginning before all creatures God begot a certain 'logical' power out of himself, which is also called the glory of the Lord, and sometimes Son, sometimes Wisdom, sometimes Angel, sometimes God, sometimes Lord and Logos."[51]

68. He does this by reference to a great many texts, which we shall find are all discussed by Augustine, and by assuming that all the Old Testament theophanies, whether visible or audible manifestations of the divine, were appearances of the Son or Logos. In this he is developing a tradition of exegesis of which we have the beginnings perhaps in the New Testament itself (see Jn 12:41), and the first clear post-apostolic evidence in the epistle of Pseudo-Barnabas. It was destined to have a long history, and went quite unquestioned until Augustine criticized it ruthlessly. We find it again in Irenaeus. In his work *Adversus Haereses* he is writing against the Gnostics, not as a philosopher, but as a bishop. He is fighting on the opposite front to Justin, because while Trypho the Jew accepted the Old Testament but not the New Testament, the Gnostics accepted the New Testament, more or less, but definitely not the Old Testament. But in order to demonstrate that the God of the

Old Testament is the same as the God of the New Testament, it is very much to his purpose to show that "the Son of God is scattered (*inseminatus*) everywhere in the scriptures; sometimes talking to Abraham, sometimes to Noah, giving him the measurements (of the Ark), sometimes looking for Adam, sometimes bringing judgment on the men of Sodom; and again when he appeared and guided Jacob on his way, and talked to Moses from the bush."[52]

69. Irenaeus gives us a theological reason for this assumption that it was the Son or Word who figured in the Old Testament theophanies. It is that the Word is the means of communication between God the Father, God at his most ultimate, absolute and godly, and his creation. Irenaeus was no Gnostic, seeing how valiantly he labored to repel gnosticism from the Church, but he inhabited the same thought-world as the Gnostics. It was a world that almost axiomatically needed a link between the absolute being beyond being which is what nearly everyone meant by God, and the relative, corruptible sub-being of this visible world. The Gnostics postulated whole chains of emanating aeons; the Christians found the necessary link in Christ, or rather in the Logos incarnate in Christ. But his linking function did not just begin with the incarnation; it began with creation, and continued until the incarnation, when it reached its climax. Commenting on Exodus 3:7, *Seeing I have seen the affliction of my people in Egypt, and I have come down to deliver them,* Irenaeus writes: "The Word of God was accustomed from the beginning to go up and come down, for the salvation of those who were in evil straits."[53] His key statement is perhaps that "by the Word made visible and palpable (he is not here referring to the incarnation, but to Old Testament phenomena, especially those of the divine revelation at Sinai), the Father was being shown, even though all did not equally believe him. But all saw the Father in the Son; for the Father is the invisibility of the Son, and the Son is the visibility of the Father" (*invisibile etenim Filii Pater, visibile autem Patris Filius*).[54]

70. He later qualifies this statement, to forestall a crass misunderstanding which Augustine will belabor at great length, and which regarded the Son quite simply as the visible member of the Trinity; "it is not," says Irenaeus, "as some people say, that the Father of all things being invisible, there is another who could be seen by the prophets";[55] and he goes on to state the saving function of the Trinity in terms of this idea of visibility, or seeing the unseeable God: "Man of himself does not see God; but he is willingly seen by what men he will, when he will, as he will. For God is powerful in all things. He was seen then (in the Old Testament) through the Spirit of prophecy; he was seen (in the New Testament) through the Son adoptively (*adoptive*); he will be seen in the kingdom of heaven paternally (*paternaliter*). It is the Spirit who prepares man in the Son, it is the Son who leads to the Father, it is the Father who bestows incorruption unto eternal life, which comes to anyone from his seeing God."[56] Later on he says that "God's Word showed forth the glory of the Father in whatever way he willed, for the profit of those who see it, and expounded his plans," and he calls the Word "the interpreter of the Father."[57]

71. To sum up the contribution of Justin and Irenaeus, the pre-existence of

the Son, or Word, is clearly affirmed, and his distinction from the Father. This distinction is seen as lying in his function of being, with respect to the created world and to the world of men in particular, the operative principle in the divine order, that is being the creator, savior, revealer—above all perhaps the revealer of the Father. The problem this development set to the Church was above all the problem of the divine unity, or as it was usually termed, the divine monarchy. One reaction in defense of the monarchy of God went so far as to deny all real distinction between the three persons, regarding Father, Son and Spirit as no more than three names for the one God, or three modes of his manifestation to men. It was against this heresy of Modalism or Sabellianism that Tertullian wrote his *Adversus Praxeam* at the beginning of the third century, carrying on the work of Justin and Irenaeus, to whom he is greatly indebted.

72. To balance the principle of "monarchy," which of course he accepts, he brings in the principle of "economy." This term, employed by Paul in Ephesians 1:10, where the Greek *oikonomia* is usually translated "dispensation," means something like administration or plan. It is applied generally to God's providential administration of the world and his saving plan for humanity. The high point of the divine economy is the incarnation and the redemption achieved by Christ. What Justin and Irenaeus had said about the appearances and activities of the pre-existent Word in the Old Testament were preparatory instances of this divine economy. Now what Tertullian does is to explain the Trinity, that is the real distinctness of the Son and the Spirit from the Father, in terms of economy. All that monarchy means, he says, is unity of empire or rule, and its concentration in a single individual. But it does not rule out the monarch having a son, or administering (an economy word) his empire by whatever agents he likes, or sharing his monarchy with his son. "So if the divine monarchy or empire is administered by so many legions and armies of angels, and does not cease to be a monarchy for all that . . ., how is it that God should be thought to suffer division or dispersion in the Son and in the Holy Spirit, who share so intimately in the Father's substance, though he suffers none in all those angels, who are so alien to him in substance?"[58] Indeed he calls the Trinity "a mystery of economy" (*sacramentum oeconomiae*) "which arranges the oneness into threeness, setting forth three, Father, Son, and Holy Spirit."[59] And he goes on to say that his opponents "assume that the number and arrangement of a threesome (trinity) means the division of unity; whereas the unity, deriving the threesome out of itself, is not destroyed by it but administered."[60]

73. Tertullian is certainly not easy to understand. But I think it is clear from the context that the divine unity, like the monarchy which manifests it, is preserved and embodied in the person of the Father, who remains impregnably monarch, and one, while the mystery of the economy administers his unity into trinity by deriving the Son and the Spirit from his substance. Prestige considers that the idea of "economy" as used here by Tertullian does not mean quite the same thing as when the incarnation, for example, is called a divine economy, but that it has a secondary meaning of "arrangement of parts." He is trying to save Tertullian from putting the derivation of the Word and the Spirit from the

Father into the same category of act, that is to say an act in the order of creation, as the incarnation or any other saving act of God.[61] I do not think he really succeeds, as Tertullian's subsequent unfolding of his case makes clear. For example, with reference to the creation itself he writes, "It is then that the Word receives its shape and form, its sound and voice, when God says *Let there be light.* This is the complete nativity of the Word, when it proceeds from God" (presumably it was only conceived, but not yet born, while it was still only thought by God without being uttered).[62] Later still, developing and hardening Irenaeus' idea about the Son being what is visible of the Father, he says "and consequently we must understand the Father as invisible in the fullness of his majesty, but we must acknowledge the Son as visible in the measure of his derivation."[63] Finally, he treats the generation of the Son by the Father as being on a par with his being sent by the Father, and regards both as meaning a derivation of substance from the Father, which makes the Son less than the Father.[64]

74. Let us try to assess how Tertullian's contribution has reset the trinitarian problem. He has followed Justin and Irenaeus in asserting the real distinction of the Son and the Holy Spirit and the Father, and proved it by the same means, especially the manifestation of the Word in the Old Testament before the incarnation. He has defended the monarchy of God in the person of the Father. But his employment of the idea of economy to explain the relationship of Son and Spirit to the Father, and his association of this idea with the execution of God's providence as attested by scripture, and the whole drift of his argument, all means that the Son and Spirit have the function of lieutenants of the sole monarch, the Father. It also implies that God has become a trinity, the divine unity has been distributed into a trio, in the course of putting into effect the economies of creation and redemption. Tertullian is nowhere concerned to defend the equality of the divine persons. The last text quoted shows him quite happy with the idea of the Father being greater than the Son. It is true he vehemently maintains that the Son and the Spirit share in the Father's substance (a phrase which was going to give rise to the word *consubstantialis*, though Tertullian does not himself use it) and this makes them quite different from creatures. But his idea of the divine substance was such that it admitted of extension, and of gradation within it, differences of degree though not of kind.

75. So the effect of his use of economy, associated with the idea of the essential visibility of the Son and his frequent appearance in the Old Testament, is to subordinate the Son to the Father, that is to jeopardize his absolute equality with the Father. This was the tendency of most third century theology. Novatian in his *De Trinitate* does little more than put a kind of hard cutting edge on the tendencies that are beginning to show in Tertullian. For him, to argue the divinity of Christ, which he does with great vigor, actually involves arguing Christ's inequality to the Father. The assumption is that he can only be both divine and other than the Father if he is divine in a different and lesser degree. Novatian interprets the famous text of Philippians 2:6 as meaning that though Christ was divine, *in the form of God*, he never dreamed of claiming equality with God.[65]

Again, he states the visibility of the Son, as against the invisibility of the Father, even more unequivocally than Tertullian, and connects it with the Son's title of being the Image of the Father, the image according to which man was created.[66] Like Tertullian, he interprets the text *I and the Father are one* (Jn 10:30) as meaning that they are one by concord and love and unanimity.[67] Finally, he explicitly states, what I think Tertullian had not done, that the generation of the Son by the Father is an act of the Father's will, something he chose to do but need not have done.[68]

76. There were a number of latent confusions involved in all this; for example a curious confusion between the divine and the human sonship of Christ. It is as though the incarnation were projected backward into the generation of the Word— a natural enough mistake, no doubt, when we consider that the incarnation is our only evidence for the divine generation. But it was a dangerous mistake. Another was the failure really to distinguish between what we now call the eternal processions and the temporal missions of the divine persons. The most serious lack, though, was the want of a sufficiently rigorous and tough metaphysics of the divine nature. This moderate subordinationism of the third century, which strenuously asserted the divinity of Christ, and his distinction from the Father by an inequality signalized by his visibility, was inherently contradictory. The Arians in the next century were to solve the problem by boldly denying the genuine, proper divinity of the Son. But they were very acute practitioners of a metaphysical natural theology. And orthodoxy was going to be called on to make a stupendous effort of metaphysical reflection on God in order to meet the Arians.

77. If this is what an "economic" approach to the Trinity led to, then surely it was all a most unfortunate dead end. But this is not so; it had great virtues. Above all, it took the scriptural evidence seriously, and therefore it took the historical dimension seriously, and so kept the trinitarian mystery relevant to the historical human situation. The mystery of the Trinity is connected with the mystery of the incarnation; it is connected with the coming of the Spirit; and so it has everything to do with our redemption and sanctification. This was so obvious to the pre-Nicene theologians that they hardly labored the point. It was going to be obscured, however, by the "metaphysical" approach which Nicaea would canonize, and which would hold the field in trinitarian dogmatics until our own day. It was Augustine's great merit that he combined the virtues of both approaches; in his work neither swamps or wrecks the other; the economic approach is necessary to understand both the revelation and the relevance of the mystery; the metaphysical approach is necessary in order to safeguard the mystery itself in all its transcendence.

78. The definition of the Council of Nicaea in 325 did not solve the problem for the orthodox; it only forced them to realize that there was a problem to solve, by affirming that the Arian solution was unacceptable. It declared that the Son is in no sense a creature, and that therefore the generation of the Son is something quite different from creation; and that the Son is as fully and equally God as the Father, that he is consubstantial, *homo-ousios*, with the Father.

79. This left the orthodox with two questions to answer. First, what does

consubstantial really mean in this instance? Its primary meaning is "of the same substance or nature"; thus men are consubstantial with each other, having the same nature as each other. Is the Son consubstantial with the Father in this way? One school, rather unfairly dubbed semi-Arian by the history books, said "Yes," and they suggested that a better word than *homo-ousios* would be *homoi-ousios*, of like or similar substance. They were afraid that if you say *homo-ousios* you are in danger of fusing Father and Son into one numerically identical thing (as the Sabellian modalists did), and so denying any real distinction between them. However, if you limit yourself to saying they are of like substance, you in fact commit yourself to saying they are two Gods. In fact, *homo-ousios* in this instance has to be interpreted in the sense of being one numerically identical substance; Father and Son are numerically one and the same God. This was the line of Athanasius.

80. But this immediately poses us with the second question. If Father Son and Spirit are one numerically identical substance, in what sense are they really and distinctly three? Three what? In the third century from Tertullian on the habit had grown of calling them three persons, *prosopa* in Greek. But Basil of Ancyra, the leading theologian of the homoi-ousian party, and his Cappadocian namesake Basil the Great who was much influenced by him, were chary of this word, because they thought the Sabellians had used it, in its original sense of a theatrical mask (this too was the original meaning of the Latin *persona*), to mean that the three were only three modes, or facets, or faces of the one indistinguishable deity—thus making the God of the Christians a kind of three-faced Janus. So they answered the question "Three what?" by replying "Three *hypostaseis*." God is one *ousia*, three *hypostaseis*.

81. The trouble with this was that in Latin it could easily emerge as "God is one *substantia*, three *substantiae*"—which is clearly not very helpful. It is true that Victorinus, the ever ready coiner of terms, came to the rescue with the convenient expression "one *substantia*, three *subsistentiae*."[69] Like the two Basils, he shied away from the word *persona*: "one ought not to say, nor is it lawful to say, there is one substance, there are three persons."[70] Augustine will cut the Gordian knot by saying that it does not matter what word you choose, it is purely a matter of convention and convenience. And surely he is right; finding a word in this instance does not really tell us anything or solve anything. The question remains, *how* are the three persons, or subsistences, or hypostases, or substances, really distinguished from each other, while remaining numerically one and identically the same God, one divine substance. What are their distinguishing marks or properties? The fourth century wrestled with this question, and as far as I can see, without much success. Hilary, in his *De Trinitate*, contributes little or nothing to a solution. This is the only work of his predecessors that Augustine actually quotes by name, in Book VI of his own *De Trinitate*. But the quotation comes from the beginning of Book II of Hilary's work,[71] and I cannot resist the rather irreverent thought that Augustine read Hilary that far and then stopped. If this is true, he did not miss very much. In the passage quoted Hilary suggests distinguishing properties of the divine persons in terms of

certain attributes. Victorinus too will do the same. In a text already referred to he says that "the being (*esse*) which the Father is, the life which the Son is, the knowledge which the Holy Spirit is, are all one thing, one substance, and three subsistencies."[72] Elsewhere he says that the Father, in his absolute transcendence, is "*inoperans operatio*," the Son is "*operans operatio*." The Father as "*actio inactuosa*" is greater than the Son.[73] He insists, to be sure, on the equality of the divine persons, but one cannot help feeling that the Father is more equal than the other two!

82. But this attempt to distinguish the persons from one another in terms of divine attributes, or divine activities in the created order, is doomed to failure. For the attributes of God are not accidental qualities that adhere to him, nor are his actions things that he happens to do in time. As the Arians rightly insisted, in God all accidents become substance. God is his attributes, and his attributes are him, and the same goes for his actions. Therefore, if the Son and the Holy Spirit are truly God, they have (or rather are) all the attributes that belong to the Father, and they do (or rather are) all the acts which the Father does (is).

83. Two of the more philosophically experienced of the Greek Fathers of the fourth century, Gregory Nazianzen and Didymus the Blind, did propose what Augustine will develop in detail and with some originality as the definitive solution to this problem. What makes the divine persons really (and not just nominally) distinct from one another can only be their mutual relationships, which are expressed by their proper names, and which are relationships of origin. "For 'Father,' O wisest of men (the Arians), is not a name of substance or of activity, but of relationship (*schesis*), and of how the Father is related to the Son, or the Son to the Father."[74] So Gregory. Didymus will write in the same vein.[75] But on the question of how we are to distinguish the relationship of the Son to the Father (arising out of his generation by the Father) from that of the Holy Spirit to the Father (arising out of his procession from the Father), Didymus maintains a holy, and to be quite honest a rather irritating, agnosticism;[76] for what he thereby devoutly declines to examine is not the holy mystery itself, but our efforts to talk about it—and it is really obscurantist to be agnostic on principle about language.

84. It is on this point that Augustine will make one of his most original, and in this case fateful, contributions to trinitarian theology, and propose that the Holy Spirit can only be really distinguished from the Son if we say that he proceeds from the Father *and from the Son*, as from one source. In this too he had precursors, Ambrose[77] and Epiphanius of Salamis,[78] but it was he who watered the idea and made it grow.

5
Augustine's Contribution to the Tradition

85. We are now in a better position to appreciate the way in which the *De Trinitate* measures up to the task which had been set Augustine by the tradition. The first four books, in which according to his own terms he establishes the

starting point of faith from the scriptures, in fact take up the challenge of the
"economic" theology as it had developed from Justin to Tertullian and Novatian,
and give it a radical new look in order to eliminate all traces of the subordinationism which time had shown to be its great weakness.[79] This involves
Augustine in a wholesale reinterpretation of scripture. The next three books take
up the metaphysical and logical challenge of Arianism, as the author proceeds
to give a rational account of the faith he has established.

86. It will be worthwhile to quote extensively his statement of the faith which
he sets himself the task of establishing from the scriptures, because thanks to
Nicaea in 325 it is more sharply defined than any statement that might have been
made by the "economic" theologians of the second and third centuries. In Book
I, 7 he writes:

> The purpose of all the Catholic commentators[80] I have been able
> to read on the divine books of both testaments, who have written
> before me on the trinity which God is, has been to teach that
> according to the scriptures Father and Son and Holy Spirit in the
> inseparable equality of one substance present a divine unity; and
> therefore there are not three gods but one God; although indeed the
> Father has begotten the Son, and therefore he who is the Father is
> not the Son; and the Son is begotten by the Father, and therefore he
> who is the Son is not the Father; and the Holy Spirit is neither the
> Father nor the Son, but only the Spirit of the Father and of the Son,
> himself co-equal to the Father and the Son, and belonging to the
> threefold unity.

> It was not however this same three (their teaching continues) that
> was born of the virgin Mary, crucified and buried under Pontius
> Pilate, rose again on the third day and ascended into heaven, but the
> Son alone. Nor was it the same three that came down upon Jesus in
> the form of a dove at his baptism, or came down on the day of
> Pentecost after the Lord's ascension, with a roaring sound from
> heaven as though a violent gust were rushing down, and in divided
> tongues as of fire, but the Holy Spirit alone. Nor was it this same
> three that spoke from heaven *You are my Son*, either at his baptism
> by John or on the mountain when the three disciples were with him,
> nor when the resounding voice was heard, *I have both glorified it*
> (my name) *and will glorify it again*, but it was the Father's voice
> alone addressing the Son; although just as Father and Son and Holy
> Spirit are inseparable, so do they work inseparably. This is also my
> faith inasmuch as it is the Catholic faith.

87. This statement of faith, much more ample than the Nicene creed, seems
to me to be expressly intended to correct the subordinationist tendencies of the
"economic" theologians. There is the emphasis on the unqualified equality of
the divine persons, and there is the limitation of their revealed economy, their
manifestation as distinct persons, to the New Testament, because the custom of
seeing the Son distinctly manifested in the Old Testament had been largely

responsible for involving the "economic" theologians in subordinationism. In the first four books, therefore, Augustine will assiduously go over all the texts employed by these predecessors, and reinterpret them. In Book I he confines himself to the New Testament, and to establishing from it the equality of the Son—and the Holy Spirit—with the Father. The drift of his argument carries him against the current of Tertullian's, who was not worried about equality, and only concerned with establishing the real distinctness of the Son from the Father. No one in Augustine's time questioned this, but the Arians so asserted it that they denied even the divinity, let alone the equality of the Son. And so Augustine finds texts which were among Tertullian's favorites very problematical; notably John 14:28, *the Father is greater than I*, and 1 Corinthians 15:28, *When all things have been subjected to him, then the Son himself will also be subjected to the one who subjected all things to him, that God might be all in all.* He finds a solution in the principle which is echoed in the Athanasian creed (it could much more justly be called the Augustinian creed[81]), that the Son is equal to the Father in his divinity, less than the Father in his humanity. So he can interpret all seemingly subordinationist texts as referring to Christ's humanity.

88. This principle is not, however, universally applicable. In particular it will not work with texts that talk about the Son being sent. This is where Augustine comes up against the "economic" theology head on. The earlier writers assumed reasonably enough that sending, or mission, implies the superiority of the sender over the one he sends. Subordinates are sent by superiors. Furthermore, they did not distinguish between being sent and going forth or proceeding. When a man is sent, he naturally proceeds on his mission. As both the Son and the Holy Spirit are sent by God (the Father), so they proceed from the Father; and thus they are shown to be less than the Father by the very process which, in the view of the "economic" theologians, shows them to be divine, since they have been sent and have proceeded from the beginning, from creation onward, on the creative, redemptive and sanctifying work of God. Now Augustine could not break this chain of reasoning, which we saw to be almost explicitly set out by Novatian, by appealing to his principle that Christ is less than the Father in his humanity and equal in his divinity, because in the first place the Son was sent to become man, and not just after he had become man (the incarnation was the *term* of the divine mission), and in the second place the Holy Spirit was also sent, and he has no human nature in which he can be lawfully regarded as less than the Father.

89. Augustine here has to resort to simple assertion, but it is not, I consider, unreasonable assertion. He says that where the divine missions are concerned we do not have to take sending as necessarily implying inequality between sender and sent, but only as implying that the one sent is *from* the sender, as the Son is God from God. And of course it also implies that the one sent comes to be in the world to which he is sent in a new way—it implies a manifestation or revelation of the one sent among men. So the eternal Son, the Word, was manifested in the flesh, and the Holy Spirit was manifested at Pentecost, and previously at Christ's baptism, and began to be among men in a new way. Augustine also makes another crucial interpretative assertion; he firmly distin-

guishes between the mission and the procession of the divine persons, and contrary to the natural grain of the words, he makes procession *prior* to mission, treating procession as eternal and mission as temporal. Thus the temporal missions of the Son and the Spirit into the world reveal to men the eternal processions of these persons within the godhead, but do not constitute them. As he puts it toward the end of his long discussion of the missions in Book IV, 29:

> As being born[82] means for the Son being from the Father, so being sent means for the Son being known to be from the Father. And as being the gift of God means for the Holy Spirit proceeding from the Father, so being sent means for the Holy Spirit his being known to proceed from the Father.

90. Now the missions of the Son and the Holy Spirit are the climax of the divine economy of salvation. So Augustine modifies the "economic" theology by saying in effect that the economy (the missions) reveals the eternal mystery of God, whereas Tertullian had been constrained to say that the economy *constitutes* the mystery of God.

91. Before Augustine reaches this conclusion, though, he has to relieve the whole economic idea of the confusion in which the "economic" theologians had regrettably left it. We have it on the authority of Paul, in a text we have already made great use of, that it was only when the fullness of time had come, that is in the New Testament, that God sent his Son and sent his Holy Spirit.[83] But what about all those Old Testament theophanies which the "economic" theologians had assumed to be manifestations of the Son, because he is the visible, or at least the revealing member of the divine triad? Were they missions of the Son and sometimes of the Spirit? If so, does this not deprive the New Testament of all its definitive distinction, its proper newness? I think this is in fact the ultimate consequence of Justin's approach, and even to some extent of Irenaeus'. And if not, why not, seeing that sending appears to involve some kind of visible manifestation?

92. Augustine examines them all in detail in Book II. He affirms that in none of them—nor for that matter in the New Testament theophanies—is there any question of the invisible God being rendered visible (or audible) in his proper substance, but only of his being symbolically represented through some created medium. There are repeated sallies against the idea that the Son is essentially visible. And he also concludes that in most cases the text will not really allow one to assert that it is one of the divine persons and not another who is being so represented. But on this point he is not dogmatic; what he is dogmatic about is that whether it is the Father or the Son or the Holy Spirit, or just God without distinction, who is being represented in a theophany, he is being represented by some created effect, not being seen or heard in himself.

93. There was, he goes on to argue in Book III, mission of a sort involved in the production of these theophanies, but it was a mission of angels. Here he reverts to a rabbinic idea, which is also aired in the New Testament,[84] and which the "economic" theologians seem to have ignored or jettisoned. Then in Book IV he indulges in an elaborate piece of rhetorical sleight-of-hand; he goes into

a sustained digression, without a word of explanation, on the topic of the redemptive work of Christ, and his saving sacrifice. What, one asks, has this got to do with the Trinity? Suddenly, with a flourish, near the end of the book, he declares, "There you have what the Son of God was sent for."[85] There in fact you have the economy, the mystery of the divine plan of salvation, what Saint Paul calls *the economy of the fullness of the times* (Eph 1:10), and which he also says had been hidden from ages and generations, but was now made manifest to the saints.[86] Mission implies purpose; the Son and the Spirit were sent on a mission of redemption and sanctification. So until we find evidence of full divine redemption and sanctification, we cannot talk about divine mission; which means that we cannot talk about it until we come to the New Testament. And when we do come to the New Testament we find that the economy of redemption and sanctification, that is to say the mission of the Son and the Spirit, reveals to us the eternal mystery of the divine processions, and that redemption and sanctification are completed by our being admitted into a participation in that mystery, by being adopted into the sonship of the Son, and receiving the gift of the Holy Spirit. Thus Augustine, by his use of the idea of the mission of the divine persons, incorporates all that was most valuable in the work of the "economic" theologians, from Justin to Tertullian. It is a masterly achievement carried through by a painstaking reinterpretation of scripture.

94. Now he turns in Book V to the Arian metaphysicians of the fourth century, the chief of them being Eunomius, whom he probably knew through the polemical works of the Cappadocians, and deals with them in a similar manner. That is to say, he incorporates their metaphysics, while drawing its heretical sting. He found no difficulty in taking over their metaphysics, as he breathed the same neoplatonist atmosphere as they did. Philosophically the fourth century was much more sophisticated than its predecessors, in which the stock philosophy had been stoicism, which being mainly ethical in its concerns was weak in metaphysics. Tertullian, for instance, with his stoic background, could take it for granted that God is a body.[87] Perhaps this was just his, or the stoic, way of asserting that God is real and not an abstraction. If so, it is a very crude way of making the point. It is not surprising after this to find him talking about the Son as the visible one of the divine triad, or calling him a *portion* of the divine substance.

95. Neoplatonism with its idea of incorporeal, immaterial substance, to which the name "spirit" was usually appropriated, contributed to a much sounder and more acute manner of talking about God; though as a matter of fact it is more with the aristotelian than with the platonic element in fourth century metaphysics and natural theology that we shall find ourselves concerned. At least we must come to terms with Aristotle's ten categories, and realize that our metaphysics of the divine will be largely taken up with the right use of words; it will be a linguistic metaphysics. Aristotle, then, divided words which actually say something about things, that is excluding merely syntactical words like "and" and "because," into ten categories. The first is the category of substance, words which stand for what a thing is, like "man," "cat," "God"; then there are nine categories of what are called accidents (you could call them "concomitants"

as a slightly closer translation of his Greek term) which declare the different aspects of things, and by which we describe their qualities, quantities, actions, passions, times, places, etc. These accidents usually refer to changeable features of things. A substance goes through all sorts of changes while remaining the same substance, while remaining itself. I still remain me, a substance we call a man, though I am here one minute and there the next, though I am good and bad by turns, put on and lose weight, etc.

96. Now the Arians enunciated the supremely important principle that when we talk about God, although we use a lot of accident words, and say that God does things, that he is good and wise, etc., yet these words when applied to God do not state accidents about him, because he has not got any—nothing "happens" to him, and accidents mean happening; nothing is attached to him or taken away from him, he does not change, he is wholly simple, he just is, according to the text of Exodus 3:14, *I am who I am*. Given this principle—and it is a demonstrably sound one—they went on to argue that there cannot be any distinction in the divine substance as between distinct persons. God, they said, cannot be both unbegotten and begotten, because these words signify contradictory qualities which cannot both be identical with the divine substance. For whatever is predicated of the divine substance is the divine substance. If we say God is wise, this does not mean that God has an accidental quality called wisdom, but that God is his wisdom. So if God is called unbegotten, it means he is his unbegottenness; and if he is called begotten, it means he is his begottenness. He clearly cannot be both. *Ergo . . .*

97. Augustine argued that there is one modification to the rule of accident becoming substance when we talk about God. One of Aristotle's categories is that of relationship, which we usually signify by using the preposition "of." "Father" and "son" are obvious examples of relationship words. When applied to created substances they say accidents, because they imply change or becoming. Granted that we must rule out any such implication when we apply such words to God, since God has no accidents; yet it does not follow that when such words are used of God they say substance. What they state is relationship or reference. In fact we make a new distinction among words when we talk about God, and instead of distinguishing any longer between substance words and accident words, we distinguish between words which say something of the subject in itself or *absolutely*, without reference to another, and words which say something with such reference, or *relatively*. And it is only as terms of such mutual references or relationships that Father, Son and Holy Spirit are really distinct from one another. They cannot be distinguished, for example, in terms of such attributes as wisdom, understanding, eternity, divine will, divine action (as Victorinus and others thought they could), because all such things are predicated of God absolutely, in himself. In all these respects the divine persons are identical, one and the same substance. It is only as mutual subsistent relationships that they are distinct.

98. This is one of Augustine's most notable contributions to the debate, in which he followed, as we have seen, hints given by Gregory Nazianzen and

Didymus the Blind. You cannot distinguish the persons from each other in terms of function, as the "economic" theologians had done. Nor will it do to distinguish them in terms of divine attributes, as some of the anti-Arian fourth century theologians tried to do, because this introduces composition into the divine substance. Augustine's distinction of them in terms of relationship is the only consistent logical or linguistic key to the problem.

99. It is however important to realize that it is only a logical and verbal solution to a logical and verbal problem. The real heart of the mystery lies in the divine processions, the eternal generation of the Son and the eternal procession of the Holy Spirit. But one is directed to this mystery by getting straight the question of relationship words. While there is still confusion in this sphere of how we are to talk about the Trinity, we are in no position to carry on with the real quest for the real mystery.

100. Before Augustine comes to that, however, he has to face the fact that his logical linguistic solution raises further logical linguistic problems, and he deals with these in Books VI and VII. There is a special problem about the Holy Spirit which Augustine in fact never really succeeds in solving. The trouble is that this proper name "Holy Spirit" is not really a relationship or reference term in either of its parts. To be holy and to be spirit are divine attributes, attached by scriptural convention to the third person. The name does not seem to tell us anything about the constituent relationship of the Holy Spirit to the other two persons.[88] Augustine eventually opts for the name "Gift," which implies a relationship with the giver, as the key relationship name of the Holy Spirit. The trouble with this is that it also implies a relationship with the receiver of the gift, which takes us out of the purely divine sphere into the relationship of God with creatures. It is in fact a functional or "economic" name when all its implications are considered.

101. Another secondary problem he had to face was that of a word like "wisdom," which is used by scripture as a name for the Son. But it is not a relationship word; it states an attribute. One cannot deny wisdom to the Father or to the Holy Spirit. The same is true of "creator" used as a name for the Father, "redeemer" for the Son, "sanctifier" for the Spirit. Indeed it is supremely true for the name "God" used for the Father and "Lord" used for the Son. The solution is that we can use these names as improper names for the persons, provided we realize that they are improper and do not serve basically and properly to distinguish the persons. We apply them to the several persons by a linguistic process of "appropriation" ("distribution" or "application" might be less confusing terms). Or rather we interpret scripture as so using them, and thus telling us something about the persons in a non-technical way. This is a complexity of linguistic usage which has caused great trouble, and which led to subordinationism before it was carefully and minutely sorted out.

102. The last secondary problem raised is the status of the word *persona* for the Latins and *hypostasis* for the Greeks. These are clearly not relationship words, and yet we apply them to the three, and not to the one divine substance. But this is purely a matter of convenience or convention; we have to have an answer to the

question "Three what?" It does not matter very much what word we choose to answer this question with, provided we realize that whatever word we do choose it is a pure convention or label, and does not tell us anything real about the three. We should not, Augustine implies, waste our time by drawing out elaborate theological implications from these words, nor be particularly worried when we find that there are languages—such as the Bantu languages of Africa, for example—which do not provide obvious equivalents for the word "person."[89]

103. In the first seven books Augustine has been dealing with the problems set him by the tradition, and they have been mainly problems of words, the words of scripture and of logico-metaphysical speculation. In the course of his discussion he has, it is true, faced and clarified the reality of the divine missions, the reality of the revelation or presentation of the mystery to our faith. But he has not made contact with the divine mystery in itself, and as he is looking for God, this is what he wants to do above all else. That is why from Book VIII onward he decides to cover the same ground *interiore modo*. The inwardness of the divine mystery lies in the processions. However, the seeker has to face the hard fact that he has no direct access to the inwardness of God. God the absolute remains unapproachably "out there," to use an expression of John Robinson's *Honest to God*. This satisfies Augustine no more than it satisfies Robinson. But if man is made in God's image, as the bible assures us, then perhaps we can attain the inwardness of God indirectly, through entry into the inwardness of man, which ought to be accessible to us. Augustine prepares his ground by introducing the topic of the image toward the end of Book VII. Then he establishes the ontological link between God and the human self in Book VIII, in a manner we have already noticed.

104. I myself find it helpful to envisage the whole of the *De Trinitate* as an *Alice Through the Looking-Glass* exercise. We are looking-glass creatures living in a looking-glass world, which reflects the real realities of the divine world in a fragmentary manner, and back to front. In the first seven books Augustine has been discussing the language we use to talk about God "out there," God in his own divine world, and has also investigated God's incursion into our looking-glass world by the divine missions and by revelation. But now he withdraws wholly into the looking-glass world, in order to find God in his image, his reflection. Book VIII, you might say, marks the surface of the looking-glass, the point of contact between the two worlds, between God "out there" and God "in here" in his image. This being established we can go on to investigate the image with confidence. And we should not forget that what we are looking for above all else is a reflection in man, God's image, of the divine processions.

105. Book VIII, then, establishes contact in terms of the categories of truth and goodness, which mean in mental or psychological terms knowing and loving. So the first mental trinity he establishes in Book IX is *mens, notitia sui, amor sui* (mind, its knowledge of itself and its love of itself). This trio throws light on the divine trinity in terms of the proper trinitarian language Augustine has set up in the first seven books, which is his constant standard for assessing

the value of his image trinities. For mind, its self-knowledge, and self-love are all co-extensive, co-equal, consubstantial. Yet self-knowledge and self-love proceed from mind. Furthermore, all our knowledge is in terms of what we call ideas. We express, and indeed we think our ideas in words. So the very thought which is our knowledge can be called a word, a mental word, which precedes the spoken or uttered word. Clearly we are stressing the analogy with the *Logos*, the Word who was in the beginning with God, God's own idea of himself.

106. Again, we do spontaneously talk of conceiving ideas; we use a birth language for our thoughts. So the mind's self-knowledge, its word of itself, can naturally be regarded as its offspring, born of the mind. Finally, the mind's self-love proceeds from the mind and its self-knowledge—one does not love what one does not know. In the analogy, the Spirit proceeds from the Father and the Son. But this issue of self-love from mind and its self-knowledge is not naturally spoken of in birth language. It is not a generation or conception. It is rather an issue which joins together, as Augustine quaintly puts it, quasi-parent (mind) and quasi-offspring (mind's self-knowledge). We begin to have some inkling why the Holy Spirit also is not called Son, or said to be begotten.

107. There are however some obvious defects in this mental trinity as so far established. Knowledge and love signify acts, and acts that refer to an object; they are conjugated with the relative preposition "of," they are used *relatively*. But mind signifies just a thing, substance. It is said *absolutely*, without reference. We lack a relative term. This trinity of *mens, notitia sui*, and *amor sui* corresponds to God, Son, and Holy Spirit, not to Father, Son, and Holy Spirit.

108. In Book X Augustine proceeds to reduce this absolute term "mind" (God) to the relative term of "self-memory" (Father). And while he is about it, he modifies the other two to self-understanding and self-willing. So we come to the trinity enshrined in the Catechism, namely memory, understanding, and will—only, as we remarked in a previous section, it is a trio of mental acts, not faculties or powers; and acts of remembering self, understanding self, willing self. Augustine reduces "mind" to "memory," I suspect, because *memoria* is linguistically derived from *mens*, or at least from the same root. One can see the point by lapsing for a moment into Scotch, and observing that the proper act of mind is minding, in the sense of remembering. Here it is an act of minding or remembering oneself, which is a rather odd sort of remembering. Augustine says you can remember yourself in the same sort of way as you can forget yourself. You forget yourself by a kind of absence of mind, by not thinking. You remember yourself by a kind of presence of mind. Thus what he means in this context by self-memory, *memoria sui*, is the mind's sheer presence to itself, which is basically given in the very fact of its being mind; rather as you might say that the Father is the basically divine person, since he is just God, whereas the Son is God from God.

109. But as soon as mind activates its self-presence by remembering itself, this act of self-minding breeds the second act of understanding itself, thinking itself with the mental word of self-understanding, saying explicitly "Me"; and from these two conjoint, co-extensive, conmental acts of me minding me, and me saying me to myself, there issues the third co-extensive, conmental act, as

it were joining together quasi-parent, and quasi-offspring, of me liking me, me willing me, self-willing.

110. Thus by the end of Book X Augustine has completed his construction of the trinitarian image in man, which is so designed that it does throw light on the processions which constitute the trinity in God. I say "construct" advisedly, first because he is clearly being selective in his use of psychological activities, and is tailoring his selection to meet the requirements of the linguistic standards set in Books V-VII (which Books IX-XI are reflecting back to front, as it were); and secondly because he does not conceive the image of God in us as a static datum to be discovered and analyzed, but as a thing we are responsible for constructing. This explains why he does not stop at the end of Book X. We are looking for God. That is to say, God's image is looking for God. The only proper way for an image to find its exemplar is for it to realize its likeness. Our being in God's image is not just something given, like our having two ears; it is more a kind of program, which we have to execute. It is a kind of history, just as we have seen that the revelation of the divine Trinity is a history. Augustine gets on to the history of the image in Book XII. But he prepares for it in Book XI by examining certain submental trinities in human psychological activity, and he gives as his immediate and explicit reason the need to clarify certain obscurities in the trinitarian image he had elaborated in Book X. Is it perhaps after all no more than a merely verbal construction? In particular, is there any *real* distinction between remembering oneself and understanding oneself? He establishes to his satisfaction that there is, on the analogy of trinities he analyzes in the field of external visual perception and internal visual perception, that is the field of imagination or memory in the ordinary sense of the word. When I look at something, I have the threesome of the object, its impression in my sense of sight generated by the object, and my will or intention joining the two together. This of course is in no sense an image of the divine Trinity, because its three members are not consubstantial. But it illustrates the real distinction in the mental image between self-memory (= visual object), and self-understanding (= impression of object in the visual sense). The illustration is even more effective when we pass to the threesome in the inner sense of memory or imagination. Having seen Table Mountain, I have a memory of it; but I am not always adverting to it or actively remembering it. When I do this, then I have a trinity of the memory of it latent in my memory, the actual impress of this memory on what Augustine calls the *acies animi*, the mind's eye as you could call it, and again my will or intention keeping my mind's eye fixed on the object in my memory. When I am actually visualizing Table Mountain to myself, I cannot perceive the distinction between the latent memory and its impress on my mind's eye, because they coincide. But I infer there must be a real distinction, because I can stop visualizing Table Mountain when I turn my attention to something else, without thereby losing my memory of it altogether. In the same way the mind's self-memory, that is its sheer presence to itself, and its self-understanding, that is its conscious expression of itself in a word, can be seen to be really distinct, even when they coincide.

111. But as I have suggested, the chief though unexpressed function of Book XI is to introduce the image history of Book XII. For man's sense life plays a crucial part in this history, as we have seen earlier on. I have sufficiently summarized the history of the fall and restoration of the image, as outlined in Books XII-XIV, and need not repeat it here. I will just remind the reader that it ends in Book XIV with Augustine rephrasing his mental image of the Trinity as remembering, understanding, and willing God, rather than remembering, understanding, and willing self. The point, I think, is twofold. First, a true self-memory, self-understanding, and self-love or self-willing must emerge into a reference of these acts to God, because the self is in fact grounded in God, who in the famous Augustinian phrase is *interior intimo meo*, barely translatable as nearer to me than I am to myself. Secondly, it is by stopping at these acts at a self-directed level that Everyman in fact falls, and defaces the image. The true self is open to God; by closing itself to God the self-centered self loses its real self-possession, all its coherence, and tumbles down and outward, like Humpty Dumpty, scattering itself in pieces in the world of sensible material things. It practices a kind of parody of the divine missions, by the higher contemplative function of the mind sending the lower active function out into the world on lawless tasks of exploitation, in all the kinds of sin with which we are familiar.

112. The remedy for this state of affairs is the divine missions, and particularly the sending of the Son in the flesh. For as man fell and the image was fragmented by a downward and outward movement from the inner and upper citadel of the mind to the outer and lower reaches of the senses and their appetites, so he can only be raised up, and the image restored, by a reverse movement inward and upward; the restoration must start with the flesh. It must start with the humiliation, to the spiritual mind (the platonist in Augustine felt this far more keenly than we may do), of having to believe in the flesh of Christ, in the incarnation of the eternal Word, and his death on the cross. And it must go on to the restoration of the active function of the mind by the exercise of moral virtue, before it can reach the healing of the contemplative function, and the activation of the divine image in all its proper actuality of remembering, understanding, and loving God. The sequence is not, of course, purely temporal; but there is an element of the temporal in the process of restoring the image, a process of deepening the effect of conversion, of growing in faith and charity, in grace and the knowledge of Jesus Christ.

113. In his treatment of the image of God in man, I think Augustine was breaking wholly new ground, and owed little or nothing to the tradition. He does indeed criticize the traditional interpretation of Genesis 1:26, *Let us make man in our image and likeness*, which took it as meaning that the Father made man according to the image or model of the Son. One finds this exegesis from Irenaeus to Novatian. And of course, had Augustine accepted it, he could not have developed his argument at all. Tertullian does just hint at the idea which Augustine develops so elaborately, but it is no more than a passing illustration, to show how the Word could be generated by the Father.[90] If Augustine took a hint from Tertullian there, what he did with it was entirely the product of his own originality.

114. To conclude this introduction, we might ask ourselves where Augustine himself left the tradition of theological reflection on the Trinity for his successors. I have already stated my opinion that he did not, unfortunately, have any real successors. He succeeded in a masterly fashion in combining the "economic" and the "metaphysical" approaches to the mystery. But after his time the "metaphysical" approach became so entirely dominant that the point of his synthesis was lost. It is only one instance of the kind of marriage we are desiring to arrange today between the biblical exegete and the dogmatic theologian. I think the key word here—in the trinitarian field—is "mission." It gives us the historical dimension of the mystery. This is not of course the deepest dimension, but it serves to link us, historical beings, with that deepest dimension.

115. Augustine also finds another link by exploring the divine processions (which are the deepest dimension) in the historical image. Though his psychology and his exegesis of the Adam and Eve story are to modern eyes almost crudely archaic, they are nonetheless very powerful. He goes deep. He suggests, not just that the human self is a useful analogy through which to contemplate the divine exemplar, but that the divine exemplar of the threefold mutual relationships of origin is the ultimate authentic model for the true development of the human self, for the integration of the personality. He suggests that we will only find ourselves if we look for God (after all, Jesus made a similar suggestion somewhere in the gospel), and that only in finding ourselves will we find God. I think he has a lot in common with the *Honest to God* theologians, if there are such beasts. Perhaps there are not, but there are the millions of people in whom Robinson struck a responsive chord with his book. Augustine, or rather a development of some of his insights, might do far more to help them to a true and straight understanding and practice of Christianity than the "death of God" theologians. He can be, if people will only take the trouble to read him (and it does mean trouble), a true model, a patron saint for good actual theology today.

NOTES

1. *The City of God* XIV, 28.

2. For the dating of the *De Trinitate*'s composition see above all E. Hendrikx, "La Date de composition du *De Trinitate*," in *Bibliothèque Augustinienne*, Paris 1955, and A.-M. La Bonnardière, *Recherches de chronologie augustinienne*, Paris 1965. Mlle. La Bonnardière's learning is prodigious and her reasoning meticulous, but it does not always lead as compulsively to her conclusions as she would have us believe. She tends to push the writing of more and more of the work later and later. She marks the division in Book XII, the point at which the work was pirated, at chapter 14, and concludes that because the way in which these first fourteen chapters interpret Genesis 2 (which she quaintly calls "le livre second de la Genèse") bears many affinities to the treatment of the same topic in *The City of God*, XI-XIV, it was written about the same time, that is in 417 or 418. The conclusion does not seem to me to be a necessary one. But her researches certainly merit great respect.

I. Chevalier, in *Saint Augustin et la pensée grecque; les relations trinitaires* (Fribourg, 1940), also discusses the subject at length. But I find so many of his references to Augustine's letters absolutely baffling, and his opinion that with Letter 174 to Aurelius (translated below as an introduction to the work) Augustine sent his fellow bishop the first twelve books only of the work so gratuitously wrongheaded, that I cannot take his suggestions on chronology too seriously.

He is followed, in his opinions and his faulty references by E. TeSelle, *Augustine the Theologian* (London, 1970). This somewhat uncritical reliance on Chevalier mars an otherwise useful and well-considered book.

3. For example, by the editor of the Spanish translation, *Obras de San Agustin*, V (BAC., Madrid, 1956).

4. I, 4.

5. *Teaching Christianity*, II, 58 (PL 34, 62). But it should perhaps be borne in mind that this work was written as a guide for clergy in their professional studies.

6. The notion is used before Augustine by Gregory Nazianzen: in *Orationes* 29, XVI he says, "The name Father is not one of substance (*ousia*) or activity (*energia*), but relationship (*schesis*)," in *Orationes* 33, IX, he says the difference of the persons' mutual relationships has given rise to their names. Also Didymus the Blind, *De Trinitate* I, xi, says the divine hypostases are manifested in mutual relationship, *kat'allelon prosegoria*. It is almost certain that Augustine read both authors (see I. Chevalier, *op. cit.* above, note 2). But he used the notion so much more effectively than they, that he may be said to have introduced it into theological language.

7. *Sentences* I, dist. iii, c. 2.

8. Unhappily, we cannot call this Catechism late! A revised edition, 1971, authorized by the Bishops of England and Wales, still reproduces the same old mistake in questions 29 and 30.

9. Ia, 93, 7, ad 2.

10. See Mt 11:25; 24:36; Lk 10:21; Mk 13:32.

11. See Acts 7:56.

12. For example Gn 26:24; Ex 3:13.

13. See Gn 6:2; Ps 29:1; 89:6; Job 1:6; 38:7; Wis 5:5.

14. See also Wis 18:13.

15. See Ps 27:10; 103:13.

16. See Dt 32:20; Is 1:2.

17. See Mal 1:6; 3:17.

18. See Is 43:6; 45:11; Wis 9:7; 12:19; 16:10; 18:4.

19. See Prv 8:32; Sir 4:11; Bar 4:10, 14.

20. See 2 Sam 7:14; Ps 2:7; 89:26.27; see also Is 9:5.

21. See Wis 2:6, 18; 5:5.

22. See Ex 3:14.

23. See 1 Kgs 18:39.

24. The *Jerusalem Bible* also construes it this way, and thus presents us with its *reductio ad absurdum*, since it is committed to the use of the proper name "Yahweh." It softens the absurdity by the ingenious use of the article, but does not eliminate it: "Yahweh our God is the one Yahweh."

25. See Mt 22:44 and parallels.

26. See Heb 1:3; Col 1:15.

27. See *The Gospel according to John I-XII* by Raymond E. Brown (New York 1966) appendix II, page 519.

28. See 1 Cor 1:24.

29. See Wis 7:7.

30. See Gn 1:2.

31. For the finger of God (Ex 31:18) see Ps 8:4 and 32:6; also Lk 11:20 and Mt 12:28. The pillar of cloud and fire is a symbol of the divine presence, and this is represented by the Holy Spirit in Is 63:10.

32. See Wis 1:7; 7:25.

33. *God in Patristic Thought* (London, 1952), Introduction xix.

34. See Wis 1:6; 7:22.

35. See Jgs 14:6, 19; 1 Sam 10:10.

36. See Ps 51:13.

37. See Is 63:10; Ps 139:7.

38. See for example Gal 4:6; also Jn 14-16, *passim.*

39. See Ex 9:14; Am 4:10.

40. See Num 21:6.

41. See Ex 15:7; 23:27.

42. See Ps 147:18; 104:30; Is 9:7; 55:11; Wis 9:10; Sir 24:3.

43. See Lk 24:49; Jn 14:16, 26; 15:26; Acts 1:4, 8; Gal 4:6; Rom 5:5.

44. See Jn 3:13 and 1:32; 13:20 and 14:26; Jn 3:16 and Lk 11:13.

45. See Sir 24:3; Mk 1:38; Jn 8:42; 15:26.

46. *Confessions* I, 13, 20; 14, 23. See also Book III, prologue. Here, however, he talks about "our" difficulty with Greek books on this subject, and the plural is certainly meant to include his readers, and himself sympathetically. But the passage does not compel us to infer that he read no Greek authors on the subject of the Trinity.

47. See I. Chevalier, *Saint Augustin et la pensée grecque: les relations trinitaires* (Fribourg 1940, part ii, p. 98).

48. Op. cit. pp. 78, 97.

49. *Adv. Arium*: PL 8, 1060D, 1065A, 1078B, 1103C.

50. *Dial. c. Tryph* 48: PG 6, 580A.

51. *Ibid.* 56, 61: PG 6, 597B, 613C.

52. *Adv. Haer.* IV, 10, 1: PG 7, 1000A.

53. *Ibid.* IV, 12, 4: PG 7, 1006A.

54. *Ibid..* IV, 6, 6: PG 7, 989C.

55. *Ibid.* IV, 20, 5: PG 7, 1034C.

56. *Ibid.* IV, 20, 5: PG 7, 1035A, B.

57. *Ibid.* IV, 20, 11: PG 7, 1040A.

58. *Adv. Prax.* 3: PL 2, 158C.

59. *Ibid.* 2: PL 2, 157B.

60. *Ibid.* 3: PL 2, 158A.

61. *God in Patristic Thought*, pp. 99-106. See A. Grillmeier, *Christ in Christian Tradition* (London 1965) pp. 132ff.

62. *Adv. Prax.* 7: PL 2, 161B.

63. *Ibid..* 14: PL 2, 171A.

64. *Ibid.* 9: PL 2, 164B.

65. *De Trinitate* 22: PL 3, 958A.

66. *Ibid.* 18: PL 3, 946C, D, 28: PL 3, 970-971, 31: PL 3, 979B; cf 17 PL 3, 945B, C.

67. *Ibid*: PL 3, 966C; cf *Adv. Prax.* 22: PL, 183C.

68. *Ibid.* 31: PL 3, 978A.

69. *Adv. Arium* III, 9: PL 8, 1105B.

70. *Ibid.* I, 41: PL 8, 1072A.

71. II, 1: PL 10, 51A.

72. *Adv. Arium* III, 9: PL 8, 1105B.

73. *Ibid.* 1, 13: PL 8, 1047C.

74. *Orat.* 29, 16; see also *Orat.* 33, 9. See above, p.25 n. 7.

75. *De Trinitate* I, 11: PG 39, 293-294.

76. *Ibid.* I, 9: PG 39 (281-282); II, 1, 4: PG 39 (447-448, 481-482).

77. *De Spiritu Sancto* I, 11, 119: PL 16, 731.

78. *Ancoratus*, 6; *Panarion*, 76.

79. E. TeSelle, *Augustine the Theologian*, page 227, notes the same reference of these books to an archaic theology, and draws an inference about the current state of western theology that may or may not be justified. "It is a sign of the relatively undeveloped state of theology in the West," he writes, "that Augustine started out from the classic problem of earlier trinitarian thought, the view held by the Apologists and retained by the Arians, that the Word and Spirit are visible . . . . In his opening discussion of the theophanies (II, 8, 14) Augustine is in direct encounter with . . . Tertullian's *Adversus Praxeam*, for he explores much the same series of theophanies."

80. I doubt whether Augustine would count either Tertullian or Novatian among these, since they were both separated from the Catholic Church, and neither taught quite what he here sets out. His statement does not exactly bear out TeSelle's idea (see previous note) about "the relatively undeveloped state of theology in the West."

81. See J.N.D. Kelly, *The Athanasian Creed* (London 1964).

82. This is the Son's mode of proceeding from the Father.

83. See Gal 4:4.

84. See Gal 3:19; Heb 2:2.

85. Book IV, 19, 25.

86. See Col 1:26.

87. Quis negabit Deum corpus esse, etsi Deus spiritus est? Spiritus enim corpus sui generis: *Adv Prax* 7 (PL 2, 162C); cf *ibid* 9: PL 2, 164B.

88. Saint Thomas sees a kind of relationship connotation in "Spirit," in that its basic meaning is "breath," which implies reference to a breather (*Summa Theol.* Ia, q. 36, 1, ad 2). While Augustine nowhere uses this idea in the *De Trinitate*, he does do so in Letter 238 to the Arian count Pascentius. One infers he had published the *De Trinitate* by then. He writes: . . . et spiritus secundum id quod ad aliquid refertur spirantis alicujus est, et spirans utique spiritum spirans est.

89. See Raimundo Panikkar on this point, in *The Trinity and the Religious Experience of Man* (London/New York, 1973), page 41, where he says "During the Vatican Council some African Bishops confided to me their embarrassment at not being able to find in their own languages suitable words to convey the meaning of *nature* and *person*. In reply I could only express my admiration for such languages, and my hope that one day they would contribute notably toward the rejuvenation of the central body of dogma of Christianity."

90. *Adv. Prax* 5: PL 2, 160B, C.

Abbreviations in Notes:

CCL   editio W. J. Mountain, *De Trinitate*, T. L/La, *Corpus Christianorum*, Series Latina, 1968, Turnhout, Belgium.

M   editio monachorum Benedictionorum e Congregatione sancti Mavri, 1688, Paris.

PL   editio J. P. Migne, *Patrologia Latina*, t. 42, 1841, Paris (reprinted text of M above).

The translator is indebted to Brepols Publishers of Turnhout, Belgium, for use of the Latin text, critical edition, as published in *De Trinitate, Corpus Christianorum*, Series Latina, volume L and LA, 1968.

TRANSLATOR'S NOTE

I have made the translation from the text given in the *Corpus Christianorum, Series Latina, L* (Turnhout, 1968). Where it differs substantially from the Maurist edition reprinted by Migne, there will be a note to that effect; also where I occasionally prefer the Maurist reading.

As far as I can ascertain, the *De Trinitate* has been translated completely into English three times in the last century: Library of the Nicene Fathers in 1887; The Works of Aurelius Augustine (a series begun in 1872) in 1934; and in The Fathers of the Church (a USA series) in 1963. A great fault of all the series, to my mind, is the almost total dearth of introduction and notes. I frankly question the value of translating ancient texts simply to serve as reference books. A mere smattering of Latin will enable the students to go to the original for reference. But to read and study and profit by a writer like Augustine, the ordinary student needs a translation with full notes and introduction. That is what I try to provide in this volume.

A word about the chapter divisions of Augustine's text. The only division he made in his work was into books or volumes—of the length of a very long chapter in a modern book. It is a division that is slightly too long for the ordinary reader's concentration, and the books were very early divided up into chapters in the manuscripts. These chapters are indicated by the Roman numerals in the margins in the Latin text. To my way of thinking, however, they are not really at all helpful to the reader. They do not serve in the least to articulate the author's argument and line of thought, and so they are omitted in this translation. Even less useful for this purpose are the paragraph numbers (Arabic numerals in the margins) which were first inserted, I presume, for purposes of reference in the earlier printed editions. However, these have been retained for purposes of reference.

So I have taken the liberty of dividing the books into chapters on my own account, in a way that I hope will help the reader to follow the author's line of thought. With the same aim in mind I have given titles to the books, which are my own, not Augustine's, and have given a brief synopsis of each chapter. For this reason two rules or lines separate the chapter and the synopsis from the text.

Very occasionally I have put a section of Augustine's own text down into a footnote. The justification for this is that ancient writers, not having the practice of footnotes, sometimes incorporated asides or comments into the body of their text that modern practice would relegate to a note. To do this for them can be a help to the modern reader to keep his or her grasp on the sequence of thought. Where I have done it, I mark the note with an asterisk (*) instead of a 1), 2), etc. These notes are printed in the same point size as the text, unlike my own editorial notes and references at the end of each chapter which are printed in a smaller point size than the text.

THE TRINITY

(DE TRINITATE)

AUGUSTINE, to Pope[1] Aurelius, his good lord, his truly beloved revered and holy brother, and his fellow high priest, greetings in the Lord.

I was a young man when I began these books on the Trinity which the one true God is, and I am now an old man as I publish them. I stopped working on the project when I discovered they had been lifted from my possession, and prematurely at that since I had not completed them, nor revised and polished them as I had planned to do. It had been my intention to publish them all together and not one by one, because the inquiry proceeds in a closely-knit development from the first of them to the last. So when those people managed to get at some of them before I was ready, and thus made it impossible for me to carry out my plans, I did not resume the work of dictation that other preoccupations had interrupted; instead, I was seriously thinking of complaining about the matter in a special pamphlet, to make it as widely known as possible that those books had not been published by me but had been pirated before I considered them ready for publication.

However, at the urgent request of many of the brethren, and above all at your command, I have felt obliged to attend with the Lord's assistance to the completion of this laborious task. I have corrected the books as best I could, though hardly as I would or they might have varied too widely from the pirated copies that were already in people's hands. I now send them to your reverence by our dear son and fellow deacon,[2] and give permission for anyone to listen to them, read them, or have them copied. If I had been able to keep to my plans, the contents would indeed have been much the same, but their expression would have been much less knotty and much more lucid, as far as the difficulty of elucidating such deep matters and our own capacities would allow. Some people have the first four books, or rather five, without their prologues, and the twelfth without its considerable concluding section; but if they manage to learn about this edition, they will be able to correct their copies—if they want to and can afford it.[3] May I ask you to give instructions that this letter be placed at the head of these books, though of course separately? Pray for me.[4]

NOTES

1. The title pope was given widely to the bishops of the more important sees. The bishop of Carthage was the permanent president of the African synod.

2. Augustine, though a bishop, will usually address or refer to a presbyter as his fellow presbyter and a deacon as his fellow deacon, because his episcopal office was seen as including and sharing in their subordinate ministries.

3. These are presumably the pirates and their friends. Augustine cannot resist the sour comment, *si voluerint et valuerint*. Their action shows that they had little interest in the completeness and perfection of the author's work—and perhaps that they were more interested in getting copies on the cheap.

4. M: Farewell; pray for me.

BOOK I

THE ABSOLUTE EQUALITY OF THE DIVINE PERSONS

Chapter 1

The author comes to terms with his readers and outlines his method.

---

1. The reader of these reflections of mine on the Trinity should bear in mind that my pen is on the watch against the sophistries of those who scorn the starting-point of faith, and allow themselves to be deceived through an unseasonable and misguided love of reason. Some of them try to transfer what they have observed[1] about bodily things to incorporeal and spiritual things, which they would measure by the standard of what they experience through the senses of the body or learn by natural human intelligence, lively application, and technical skill. There are others whose concept of God, such as it is, ascribes to him the nature and moods of the human spirit, a mistake which ties their arguments about God to distorted and misleading rules of interpretation. Again, there is another type; people who indeed strive to climb above the created universe, so ineluctably subject to change, and raise their regard to the unchanging substance which is God. But so top-heavy are they with the load of their mortality, that what they do not know they wish to give the impression of knowing, and what they wish to know they cannot; and so they block their own road to genuine understanding by asserting too categorically their own presumptuous opinions, and then rather than change a misconceived opinion they have defended, they prefer to leave it uncorrected.

Indeed this disease is common to all three types I have mentioned—to those who conceive of God in bodily terms, those who do so in terms of created spirit such as soul, and those who think of him neither as body nor as created spirit, but still have false ideas about him, ideas which are all the further from the truth in that they have no place either in the world of body, or in that of derived and created spirit, or in the Creator himself. Thus whoever thinks that God is dazzling white, for example, or fiery red, is mistaken, yet these are realities of the bodily world. Or whoever thinks that God forgets things one moment and

65

remembers them the next, or anything like that, is certainly quite wrong, and yet these are realities of the mental world. But those who suppose that God is of such power that he actually begets himself, are if anything even more wrong, since not only is God not like that, but neither is anything in the world of body or spirit. There is absolutely no thing whatsoever that brings itself into existence.[2]

2. It was therefore to purify the human spirit of such falsehoods that holy scripture, adapting itself to babes, did not shun any words, proper to any kind of thing whatever, that might nourish our understanding and enable it to rise up to the sublimities of divine things. Thus it would use words taken from corporeal things to speak about God with, as when it says *Shelter me under the shadow*[3] *of your wings* (Ps 17:8); and from the sphere of created spirit it has transposed many words to signify what was not in fact like that, but had to be expressed like that; *I am a jealous God* (Ex 20:5) for example, and *I am sorry I made man* (Gn 6:7). But from things that simply do not exist it never has drawn any names to form into figures of speech or weave[4] into riddles. Hence those who are shut off from the truth by the third kind of error fade away into the meaningless even more disastrously than the others, since they imagine things about God that have no place either in him or in anything he has made.

The divine scriptures then are in the habit of making something like children's toys out of things that occur in creation, by which to entice our sickly gaze[5] and get us step by step to seek as best we can the things that are above and forsake the things that are below.[6] Things, however, that are peculiar to God and do not occur anywhere in creation are rarely mentioned by sacred scripture; an example would be what was said to Moses; *I am who I am*, and *He who is sent me to you* (Ex 3:14). Since in one way or another both body and spirit are said to be, scripture would not surely have said that, unless it were meant to be understood in some special way peculiar to God. Then there is the apostle's remark, *who alone has immortality* (1 Tm 6:16); since the soul too is called, and is, immortal in some way, he would not have said *who alone has*, unless it were the case that true immortality is unchangingness, which nothing created can have as it is peculiar to the creator. James too makes the point: *Every best bounty and every perfect gift is from above, coming down from the Father of lights, with whom there is no change nor moving shadow* (Jas 1:17), and so does David: *You will change them and they shall be changed, but you are the selfsame* (Ps 102:27).

3. So then it is difficult to contemplate and have full knowledge of God's substance, which without any change in itself makes things that change, and without any passage of time in itself creates things that exist in time.[7] That is why it is necessary for our minds to be purified before that inexpressible reality can be inexpressibly seen by them; and in order to make us fit and capable of grasping it, we are led along more endurable routes, nurtured on faith as long as we have not yet been endowed with that necessary purification. Thus the apostle indeed says that *all the treasures of wisdom and knowledge are hidden in Christ* (Col 2:3); yet to people who though reborn by his grace are still fleshly

and "all too human,"[8] like babies in Christ, he presents him not in the divine strength in which he is equal to the Father, but in the human weakness through which he was crucified. *Nor did I consider myself to know anything among you,* he says, *except Jesus Christ, and crucified at that;* then he adds, *and in weakness and fear and much trembling was I among you* (1 Cor 2:2). And a little later he says to them, *And I, brothers, could not speak to you as spiritual people, but only as fleshly; I gave you, like babies in Christ, milk to drink, not solid food, for you were not yet capable of it—indeed you are not capable of it even now* (1 Cor 3:1-2).

When some people are told this they get angry and think they are being insulted, and very often they prefer to believe that the ones they hear it from have nothing really to say, rather than consider themselves unable to grasp what they say. And sometimes we give them reasons—not indeed the ones they ask for when they inquire about God, since they are not capable of taking them, nor perhaps are we of mastering or presenting them—but reasons to show them how unfit they are, how little suited to receiving what they demand. But as they do not hear what they want, they presume that we are behaving craftily to conceal our lack of learning, or spitefully because we grudge them their learning, and so in ruffled indignation they take their departure.

4. That is why, with the help of the Lord our God, we shall undertake to the best of our ability to give them the reasons they clamor for, and to account for the one and only and true God being a trinity,[9] and for the rightness of saying, believing, understanding that the Father and the Son and the Holy Spirit are of one and the same substance or essence. In this way, instead of feeling that they have been fobbed off by my excuses, they may actually come to realize that that supreme goodness does exist which only the most purified minds can gaze upon, and also that they are themselves unable to gaze upon it and grasp it for the good reason that the human mind with its weak eyesight cannot concentrate on so overwhelming a light, unless it has been nursed back to full vigor on *the justice of faith* (Rom 4:13).[10]

But first we must establish by the authority of the holy scriptures whether the faith is in fact like that. Only then shall we go on, if God so wills and gives his help, to accommodate these talkative reason-mongers who have more conceit than capacity, which makes the disease they suffer from all the more dangerous. We shall do them such a service, perhaps, that they are able to discover reasons they can have no doubt about, and so in cases where they are unable to discover any they will sooner find fault with their own minds than with the truth itself or our arguments. In this way if there is a particle of the love or fear of God in them, they may return to the beginning and right order of faith, realizing at least what a wholesome regimen is provided for the faithful in holy Church, whereby the due observance of piety makes the ailing mind well for the perception of unchanging truth, and saves it from being plunged into opinions of a noisome falsehood by the random whims of temerity. Nor will I for my part, wherever I stick fast be loath to seek, nor wherever I go wrong be ashamed to learn.

5. Accordingly, dear reader, whenever you are as certain about something as I am go forward with me; whenever you stick equally fast seek with me; whenever you notice that you have gone wrong come back to me; or that I have, call me back to you. In this way let us set out along Charity Street together, making for him of whom it is said, *Seek his face always* (Ps 105:4).[11] This covenant, both prudent and pious, I would wish to enter into in the sight of the Lord our God with all who read what I write, and with respect to all my writings, especially such as these where we are seeking the unity of the three, of Father and Son and Holy Spirit. For nowhere else is a mistake more dangerous, or the search more laborious, or discovery more advantageous.

So whoever reads this and says, "This is not well said, because I do not understand it," is criticizing my statement, not the faith; and perhaps it could have been said more clearly—though no one has ever expressed himself well enough to be understood by everybody on everything. The person then who feels this grievance against my discourse should see if he can understand others who have busied themselves with such matters and such questions, when he fails to understand me. If so, let him lay my book aside (or throw it away if he prefers) and spend his time and effort on the ones he does understand.

However, he has no grounds to consider that I should have kept quiet, simply because I have not been able to express myself with such facility and clarity as those whom he can understand. Not everything, after all, that is written by anybody comes into the hands of everybody, and it is possible that some who are in fact capable of understanding even what I write may not come across those more intelligible writings, while they do at least happen upon these of mine. That is why it is useful to have several books by several authors, even on the same subjects, differing in style though not in faith, so that the matter itself may reach as many as possible, some in this way others in that. But if the person who complains that he has not understood this book has never been able to understand anyone else's painstaking and penetrating investigations of such subjects, he should set about improving himself with serious study, instead of trying to silence me with querulous abuse.

On the other hand, if anyone reads this work and says, "I understand what is being said, but it is not true," he is at liberty to affirm his own conviction as much as he likes and refute mine if he can. If he succeeds in doing so charitably and truthfully, and also takes the trouble to let me know (if I am still alive), then that will be the choicest plum that could fall to me from these labors of mine. If he cannot do me this service, I would be only too pleased that he should do it for anybody he can. All *I* am concerned with is *to meditate on the law of the Lord*, if not *day and night*, at least at whatever odd moments I can snatch (Ps 1:2), and to prevent forgetfulness from running away with my meditations by tying them down to paper; trusting in God's mercy that he will make me persevering in all truths I am sure of, and that *if in anything I am otherwise minded he will reveal this also to me himself* (Phil 3:15), either by hidden inspirations and reminders, or by his own manifest utterances,[12] or by discussions with the brethren. That is what I pray for, that is my deposit and my heart's desire, placed in the keeping of one who is a sufficiently reliable custodian of goods he himself has given and redeemer of promises he himself has made.

6. I do not doubt, of course, that some people who are rather slow in the uptake will think that in some passages in my books I meant what I did not mean, or that I did not mean what in fact I did. Nobody, I trust, will think it fair to blame me for the mistake of such people if they stray off the path into some falsehood in their effort to follow and their failure to keep up with me, while I am perforce picking my way through dark and difficult places. After all, no one would dream of blaming the sacred authors of God's own books for the immense variety there is of heretical errors, though all the heretics try to defend their false and misleading opinions from those very scriptures.[13]

Undoubtedly, though, it is required of me by the gentle authority of Christ's law, which is charity, that when people think I meant something false in my books which in fact I did not and this falsehood is disliked by one and welcomed by another, I should prefer to be censured by the censurer of falsehood than to receive its praiser's praises. The first, though he is wrong to blame me, since I did not in fact mean what he thinks I did, is right to blame the error; but the second is neither right in praising an opinion that truth condemns, nor right in praising me for something he thinks I meant that truth condemns. Without further ado, then, let us apply ourselves to the task we have undertaken.[14]

Chapter 2

The unity and equality of the Father, the Son, and the Holy Spirit are proved from scripture.

7. The purpose of all the Catholic commentators I have been able to read on the divine books of both testaments, who have written before me on the trinity which God is,[15] has been to teach that according to the scriptures Father and Son and Holy Spirit in the inseparable equality of one[16] substance present a divine unity; and therefore there are not three gods but one God; although indeed the Father has begotten the Son, and therefore he who is the Father is not the Son; and the Son is begotten by the Father, and therefore he who is the Son is not the Father; and the Holy Spirit is neither the Father nor the Son, but only the Spirit of the Father and of the Son, himself coequal to the Father and the Son, and belonging to the threefold unity.

It was not however this same three (their teaching continues) that was born of the virgin Mary, crucified and buried under Pontius Pilate, rose again on the third day and ascended into heaven, but the Son alone. Nor was it this same three that came down upon Jesus in the form of a dove at his baptism, or came down on the day of Pentecost after the Lord's ascension, with a roaring sound from heaven as though a violent gust were rushing down, and in divided tongues as of fire,[17] but the Holy Spirit alone. Nor was it this same three that spoke from heaven, *You are my Son,* either at his baptism by John (Mk 1:11), or on the mountain when the three disciples were with him (Mt 17:5), nor when the resounding voice was heard, *I have both glorified it* (my name) *and will glorify it again* (Jn 12:28), but it was the Father's voice alone addressing the Son; although just as Father and Son and Holy Spirit are inseparable, so do they work inseparably.[18] This is also my faith inasmuch as it is the Catholic faith.

8. Yet this statement of the faith worries some people, when they hear that the Father is God and the Son is God and the Holy Spirit is God, and yet this threesome is not three gods but one God. They wonder how they are to understand this, especially when it is said that the trinity works inseparably in everything that God works, and yet that an utterance of the Father was heard which is not the Son's utterance, and that on the other hand only the Son was born in the flesh and suffered and rose again and ascended;[19] and that only the Holy Spirit came in the form of a dove. They want to understand how that utterance which was only the Father's was caused by the three; and how that flesh in which only the Son was born of the virgin was created by the same three; and how that form of the dove in which only the Holy Spirit appeared was fashioned by the trinity itself. Otherwise the trinity does not work inseparably, but the Father does some things, the Son others and the Holy Spirit yet others; or if they do some things together and some without each other, then the trinity is no longer inseparable. Another puzzle is in what manner the Holy Spirit is in the three, being begotten neither by Father nor Son nor both of them, while being the Spirit both of the Father and the Son.[20]

People ask us these questions to the point of weariness, so we must set before them as far as we can what God has granted our weakness to understand, and on no account *take gnawing Envy as our traveling companion* (Wis 6:25). If we say that we do not usually think about these things, we are being untruthful; if we confess to our questioners that these matters live permanently in our thoughts because we are carried away by a love of tracking down the truth, then they can demand of us by right of charity that we should show them what conclusions we have been able to reach on the subject. *Not that I have already attained or am perfect*[21] (if not Paul the apostle, how much less may I, prostrate far below his feet, *count myself to have apprehended?*), but in my own poor measure *I forget what lies behind* and *stretch out to what lies ahead,* and *press on intently*[22] *to the palm of the supernal vocation* (Phil 3:12); and so I am desired to declare how much of the way I have covered and what point I have reached, from where in fine the rest of the course lies ahead of me, and free-born Charity compels me to be the slave of those who desire this of me. But it is proper, and God will surely grant it, that I should also do myself a little good by serving them with something to read; and that in being prompt to answer their questions I should also find the answers to my own. And so at the bidding of the Lord our God and with his aid I have undertaken, not so much to discuss with authority what I have already learned, as to learn by discussing it with modest piety.

9. Those who have affirmed that our Lord Jesus Christ is not God, or is not true God, or is not with the Father the one and only God, or is not truly immortal

because he is subject to change, have been confuted by the utterance of the clearest and most consistent divine testimonies, for example *In the beginning was the Word, and the Word was with God, and the Word was God* (Jn 1:1). It is clear that we are to take the Word of God for the only Son of God, of whom he goes on to say, *And the Word became flesh* (Jn 1:14), with reference to his incarnation birth which took place in time of the virgin. Now in this passage he clearly shows that he is not only God but also of the same substance as the Father, for after saying *and the Word was God*, he adds, *This was in the beginning with God; all things were made through him, and without him was made nothing* (Jn 1:2). By *all things* he means only what has been made, that is every creature. So it is crystal clear that he through whom all things were made was not made himself. And if he is not made he is not a creature, and if he is not a creature he is of the same substance as the Father. For every substance that is not God is a creature, and that is not a creature is God. And if the Son is not of the same substance as the Father he is a made substance; if he is a made substance then not all things were made through him. But[23] all things were made through him; therefore he is of one and the same substance as the Father. And thus he is not only God, but also true God;[24] as the same John says quite explicitly in his epistle: *We know that the Son of God has come and has given us understanding to know the true one[25] and to be in the true one, in his Son Jesus Christ. This is the true God and life everlasting* (1 Jn 5:20).

10. From this we can go on to infer that the apostle Paul's words, *who alone has immortality* (1 Tm 6:16),[26] do not refer to the Father alone but to the one and only God which the trinity is. For life everlasting can scarcely be mortal and subject to change, and thus the Son of God, being life everlasting, must also be meant with the Father by the words *who alone has immortality*. After all, it is by becoming partakers in his life everlasting that even we in our own little measure have been made immortal, though the life everlasting we have been made partakers of is one thing, and we who shall live forever by partaking of it are another.

Even if the whole passage ran, *whom in his own proper time* the Father *has manifested,[27] the blessed and only mighty one, King of kings and Lord of lords, who alone has immortality*—even then it ought not to be taken as excluding the Son. After all, in another place where the Son speaks with Wisdom's voice (for he is *the Wisdom of God*) (1 Cor 1:24) and says, *I compassed the circuit of heaven alone* (Sir 24:5), he has not excluded the Father; how much less need is there then to understand the words *who alone has immortality* of the Father only and exclude the Son, seeing that the passage in fact runs: *That you keep the commandment untarnished and irreproachable[28] until the coming of our Lord Jesus Christ, whom in his own proper times he has manifested who is the blessed and only mighty one, King of kings and Lord of lords, who alone has immortality and dwells in light inaccessible, whom no man has ever seen or can see, to whom is honor and glory for ever and ever* (1 Tm 6:14). In these words neither Father nor Son nor Holy Spirit is specifically named, but the blessed and only mighty one, King of kings and Lord of lords, which is the one and only true God, the three.

11. But perhaps this understanding of the phrase is spoilt by what follows, when he says, *whom no man has seen or can see*, though this too should be taken as applying to Christ in his divinity, which the Jews did not see, though they saw and crucified his flesh. Now divinity cannot be seen by human sight in any way whatever; it is seen by a power of sight which makes those who already see with it not human but superhuman. It is right therefore to take God the three as *the blessed and only mighty one, manifesting the coming of our Lord Jesus Christ in his own proper times.* For *who alone has immortality* is said in the same way as *who performs wonders alone* (Ps 72:18). I would like to know of whom they take it that is said. If of the Father only, then how can what the Son says be true, that *whatever the Father does, the same the Son also does likewise* (Jn 5:19)? Or which of his wonders is more wonderful than raising and giving life to the dead? Yet the same Son goes on to say, *As the Father raises the dead and gives them life, so also the Son gives life to whom he will* (Jn 5:21). How then can it be the Father who alone performs wonders, when these words do not allow us to understand either the Father only or the Son only as doing so, but simply the one true only God, that is Father and Son and Holy Spirit?

12. Take another saying of the same apostle: *For us there is one God the Father from whom are all things, and we in him, and one Lord Jesus Christ through whom are all things, and we through him* (1 Cor 8:6). Who can doubt that by *all things* he means all that is created, like John in *All things were made through him* (Jn 1:3)? So I ask whom does he mean in another place with the words, *Since from him and through him and in him are all things, to him be glory for ever and ever* (Rom 11:36).[29] If he means Father and Son and Holy Spirit, attributing a phrase apiece to each person—*from him*, from the Father; *through him*, through the Son; *in him*, in the Holy Spirit—then it is clear that Father and Son and Holy Spirit is what the one God is, since he concludes in the singular, *to him be glory for ever and ever.* As a matter of fact, he began the expression of this sentiment by saying, *Oh the depths of the riches of wisdom and knowledge*, not of the Father or of the Son or of the Holy Spirit, but *of God! How inscrutable are his judgments, and how unsearchable his ways! For who ever learned the mind of the Lord, or who was ever his counselor? Or who first gave,*[30] *and recompense shall be made him? Since from him and through him and in him are all things, to him be glory for ever and ever* (Rom 11:33-36).

But if they want all this to be understood of the Father alone, how in that case were all things made through the Father as it says here, and also all things through the Son as in 1 Corinthians, where he says *and one Lord Jesus Christ through whom are all things*, and as in John's gospel, *All things were made through him*? If some things were made through the Father, others through the Son, then it cannot be all things through the Father nor all through the Son. But if it is all things through the Father and all through the Son, then it is the same things through the Father as through the Son. So the Son is equal to the Father, and the work of Father and Son is inseparable. Because if it is even the Son merely that the Father made and the Son himself did not make, then not all things were made through the Son; but all things were made through the Son. Therefore he was not made himself, so that with the Father he might make all things that were made. In any case the apostle did not fail to use the very word "equal," and said as plainly as could be, *who being in the form of God did not think it robbery to be equal to God* (Phil 2:6),[31] here using "God" as a proper name for the Father, as he does in another text, *But the head of Christ is God* (1 Cor 11:3).

13. In the same way testimonies have been collected on the Holy Spirit and copiously employed by previous expositors of the subject to show that he too is God and not a creature.[32] And if he is not a creature then he is not only God—for even men have been called gods (Ps 82:6)—but also true God; therefore absolutely equal to the Father and the Son, and consubstantial and co-eternal in the oneness of the three. But the place which makes it most evident that the Holy Spirit is not a creature is the one where we are bidden not to serve the creature but the creator (Rom 1:25)—serve, not in the sense in which we are bidden to serve one another in charity, which is *douleuein* in Greek, but in the sense in which only God is served, *latreuein* in Greek, hence the name "idolaters" for those who offer to images the service owed to God. As regards this service it is said, *The Lord your God shall you adore, and him only shall you serve* (Dt 6:13). This is clearer in the Greek text, which has *latreuseis*. Accordingly if we are forbidden to serve the creature with such service as this, in that it is said *The Lord your God shall you adore, and him only shall you serve*—which is why the apostle abominates those who *have worshipped and served the creature instead of the creator* (Rom 1:25); then the Holy Spirit is certainly not a creature, since all the saints offer him such service, according to the apostle's words, *For we are the circumcision, serving the Spirit of God* (Phil 3:3), which in the Greek is *latreuontes*. Most of the Latin codices have this too: *qui spiritui dei servimus*, we who serve the Spirit of God; the Greek ones all have it, or nearly all. But in some Latin copies, instead of *spiritui dei servimus*, we find *spiritu deo servimus*, we who serve God in the Spirit.[33]

But now, can those who accept this wrong reading and decline to give in to weightier authority, can they find a variant reading in the codices for this text: *Do you not know that your bodies are the temple among you of the Holy Spirit, whom you have from God* (1 Cor 6:19)? Could anything be more insanely sacrilegious than to have the effrontery to call the members of Christ the temple of a creature who is inferior, in these people's opinion,[34] to Christ himself? For he says earlier on, *Your bodies are the members of Christ* (1 Cor 6:15). But if things that are the members of Christ are the temple of the Holy Spirit, then the Holy Spirit is not a creature, since we cannot but owe, to one whom we offer our bodies to as a temple, that service by which only God is to be served, which in Greek is called *latreia*. So he says in conclusion, *Glorify God therefore in your bodies* (1 Cor 6:20).

Chapter 3

The rule of interpretation that the Son is equal to the Father in the form of God, *less than the Father in* the form of a servant; *that he will hand over the kingdom to the Father, and himself be subject to the Father (1 Cor 15:24-28), when he brings all his faithful to the contemplation of the three divine persons, and so completes and lays aside his office of mediator.*

14. These and similar testimonies of the divine scriptures, used copiously by earlier writers, as I have said, to defeat such sophistries or errors of the heretics, present our faith with the unity and equality of the three. But because of the Word of God's incarnation, which for the sake of restoring us to health[35] took place that *the man Christ Jesus* might be *mediator of God and man* (1 Tm 2:5), many things are said in the holy books to suggest, or even state openly that the Father is greater than the Son. This has misled people who are careless about examining or keeping in view the whole range of the scriptures, and they have tried to transfer what is said of Christ Jesus as man to that substance of his which was everlasting before the incarnation and is everlasting still. They say that the Son is less than the Father because it is written in the Lord's own words, *The Father is greater than I* (Jn 14:28); the truth, however, shows that as far as that goes the Son is less even than himself. How could it be otherwise with him who *emptied himself, taking the form of a servant* (Phil 2:7)? For he did not so take the form of a servant that he lost the form of God in which he was equal to the Father. So if the form of a servant was taken on in such a way that the form of God was not lost—since it is the same only begotten Son of the Father who is both in the form of a servant and in the form of God, equal to the Father in the form of God, in the form of a servant the mediator of God and men the man Christ Jesus—who can fail to see that in the form of God he too is greater than himself and in the form of a servant he is less than himself? And so it is not without reason that scripture says both; that the Son is equal to the Father and that the Father is greater than the Son. The one is to be understood in virtue of the form of God, the other in virtue of the form of a servant, without any confusion.

And this rule for solving this question in all the sacred scriptures is laid down for us in this one passage of the apostle Paul's letter, where the distinction is clearly set out. He says: *Who being in the form of God thought it no robbery to be equal to God, yet he emptied himself taking the form of a servant, being made in the likeness[36] of men, in condition found as a man* (Phil 2:6). So the Son of God is God the Father's equal by nature, by condition his inferior. In the form of a servant which he took he is the Father's inferior; in the form of God in which he existed even before he took this other he is the Father's equal. In the form of God, the Word *through whom all things were made* (Jn 1:3); in the form of a servant, one *made of woman, made under the law, to redeem those who were under the law* (Gal 4:4). Accordingly, in the form of God he made man, in the form of a servant he was made man. For if the Father only without the Son had made man, it would not have been written *Let us make man to our image and likeness* (Gn 1:26).[37] In conclusion then, because the form of God took on the form of a servant, each is God and each is man, but each is God because of God taking on, and each is man because of man taken on. Neither of them was turned or changed into the other by that "take-over"; neither godhead changed into creature and ceasing to be godhead, nor creature changed into godhead and ceasing to be creature.

15. As for the apostle's words, *But when all things are made subject to him, then shall the Son himself also be made subject to the one who subjected all things to him* (1 Cor 15:28); either their meaning is such that one may not suppose the condition of Christ, received as a result of his being a human creature, is going to be changed afterward into divinity itself (or into deity, to put it more definitely[38]) which is not a creature, but is the unity of the three, incorporeal and unchanging, a nature consubstantial and co-eternal with itself; or at least, if anyone does argue for a view held by some,[39] that in the words *the Son himself shall also be made subject to the one who subjected all things to him* this subjection must be taken to mean a future change or conversion of creature into the very substance or essence of creator, that is, that what had been the substance of a creature, is to become the substance of the creator; at least he will surely grant this, something there can be no doubt about, that this had not yet happened when the Lord said *The Father is greater than I* (Jn 14:28). It was not merely before he had ascended into heaven that he said this, but even before he had suffered and risen from the dead. Now those who suppose that the human nature in him changes over into the substance of deity, and that the words *Then also shall the Son himself be made subject to the one who subjected all things to him* amount to saying, "Then also shall the son of man and the human nature taken by the Word of God be changed into the nature of the one who made all things subject to him"; these people consider that this will happen after the judgment day, *when he has handed over the kingdom to God and the Father* (1 Cor 15:24). And thus even according to this opinion the Father is still for the time being greater than the form of a servant which was taken from the virgin. And even if you assert that the man Christ Jesus has already[40] been changed into the substance of God, you surely cannot deny that the nature of man still remained when he said before his passion, *The Father is greater than I* (Jn 14:28). So there need be no hesitation from anyone in taking this to mean that what the Father is greater than is the form of a servant, whereas the Son is his equal in the form of God.

In the same passage the apostle has just remarked, *When it says that all things have been made subject to him, clearly he is excepted who subjected all things to him* (1 Cor 15:27);[41] and one ought not to think of the Father subjecting all things to the Son without allowing that the Son may also be thought of as having subjected all things to himself. The apostle makes this clear in Philippians: *But our residence is in heaven*, he says, *from where we are also awaiting as savior our Lord Jesus Christ, who will transfigure[42] the body of our lowliness to match the body of his glory, according to the working of that power of his by which he is able also to subject all things to himself* (Phil 3:20). For the Father's working and the Son's are inseparable. If it were not so, then it would not be true even that the Father has subjected all things to himself, but rather that the Son has subjected them to him by handing over the kingdom to him, and by cancelling all sovereignty and all authority and power. For that in fact is what is said of the Son: *When he has handed over the kingdom to God and the Father*, it goes, *when he has cancelled all sovereignty and all authority and power* (1 Cor 15:24). The one who cancels them is surely the one who subjects[43] them.

16. On the other hand we should not assume that Christ will so hand over the kingdom to God and the Father that he deprives himself of it—though even this belief can muster its collection of cranks. He is not excluded when it talks of the kingdom being handed over to God and the Father, since together with the Father he is one God. But these people, as casual about the divine scriptures as they are devoted to controversy, are caught by the word "until"; for the text continues, *He must reign until he has put all his enemies under his feet* (1 Cor 15:25), as though he will stop reigning when he has put them there. But they fail to see that it is exactly like the text, *His heart has been strengthened, he shall not be shaken until he looks down on his enemies* (Ps 112:8), where it is not suggested that he will be shaken the moment he does look down on them.

What then does it really mean, *When he hands over the kingdom to God and the Father* (1 Cor 15:24), as though at present God and the Father had not got a kingdom? The fact is that the *man Christ Jesus, mediator of God and men* (1 Tm 2:5), now reigning for all *the just* who *live by faith* (Hb 2:4),[44] is going to bring them to direct sight of God, to the *face to face* vision, as the apostle calls it (1 Cor 13:12),[45] that is what is meant by *When he hands the kingdom over to God and the Father*, as though to say "When he brings believers to a direct contemplation of God and the Father."[46] In his own words, *All things have been entrusted to me by my Father; and no one knows the Son except the Father, nor does anyone know the Father except the Son, and whomever the Son chooses to reveal him to* (Mt 11:27). It is *when he cancels all sovereignty and all authority and power* that the Son will reveal the Father, that is, when there is no more need for the regime of symbols administered by the angelic sovereignties and authorities and powers. It is in the name of these powers that we may suitably understand the word of the Song of Songs to be addressed to the bride: *We shall make you symbols of gold with variations of silver, as long as the king is in his bed-chamber* (Sg 1:10), that is, as long as Christ is in his place of withdrawal, for *our*[47] *life is hidden with Christ in God. When Christ your life*, he says, *is manifested, then shall you too be manifested with him in glory* (Col 3:3). Until that happens, *we see now through a glass in a puzzle*, that is in symbols, but *then it shall be face to face* (1 Cor 13:12).

17. This contemplation is promised us as the end of all activities and the eternal perfection of all joys. *For we are God's sons, and it has not yet been manifested what we shall be; we know that when he is manifested we shall be like him, for we shall see him as he is* (1 Jn 3:2). What we shall contemplate as we live for ever is what he told his servant Moses: *I am who I am. And so*[48] *you*

shall say to the children of Israel, He who is sent me to you (Ex 3:14). He himself said so, in fact: *This is eternal life, that they should know you, the one true God, and Jesus Christ whom you have sent* (Jn 17:3). This will happen when the Lord comes and lights up the *things hidden in the darkness* (1 Cor 4:5), when the darkness of this mortality and corruption passes away. That will be our morning, of which it says in the psalm, *In the morning I shall stand before you and contemplate* (Ps 5:5). It is of this contemplation that I understand the text, *When he hands over the kingdom to God and the Father* (1 Cor 15:24), that is, when *the man Christ Jesus, mediator of God and men* (1 Tm 2:5), now reigning for *the just* who *live by faith* (Hb 2:4), brings them to the contemplation of God and the Father. If I am being stupid in this, I hope anyone who has a better idea will correct me; I cannot think of one.

We will not seek anything else when we reach that contemplation of him, which is not yet ours as long as we are rejoicing only in hope.[49] *But hope which is seen is not hope; why should anyone also hope for what he can see? But if we hope for what we do not see, then we wait in patience* (Rom 8:24), *as long as the king is in his bed-chamber* (Sg 1:11). Then shall the psalm come true, *You will fill me with delight at your countenance* (Ps 16:11). Nothing further than that delight will be sought; there will be nothing further to seek. Philip understood this well enough to say, *Lord, show us the Father and it suffices us* (Jn 14:8). But he did not yet understand that he could just as well have said the same thing like this: "Lord, show us yourself and it suffices us." To make him understand, the Lord answered, *Have I been with you all this time and you do not know me? Philip, whoever has seen me has seen the Father too.* But he wanted him to live by faith before he could see that, and so he went on, *Do you not believe that I am in the Father and the Father is in me* (Jn 14:9-11)? For, *as long as we are in the body we are abroad from the Lord. For we walk by faith, not by sight* (2 Cor 5:6).

Contemplation in fact is the reward of faith, a reward for which hearts are cleansed through faith, as it is written, *cleansing their hearts through faith* (Acts 15:9). Proof that it is that contemplation for which hearts[50] are cleansed comes from the key text, *Blessed are the clean of heart, for they shall see God* (Mt 5:8). And that this is eternal life God makes clear in the psalms, *I will fill him with length of days, and I will show him my salvation* (Ps 91:16).[51] Whether we hear then "Show us the Son," or whether we hear "Show us the Father," it comes to the same thing, because neither can be shown without the other. They are indeed one, as he tells us, *I and the Father are one* (Jn 10:30). In a word, because of this inseparability, it makes no difference whether sometimes the Father alone or sometimes the Son alone is mentioned as the one who is to fill us with delight at his countenance.

18. Nor is the Spirit of each separable from this unity, the Father's Spirit, that is, and the Son's, the Holy Spirit which is given the proper name of *the Spirit of truth, which this world cannot receive* (Jn 14:17). For the fullness of our happiness, beyond which there is none else, is this: to enjoy God the three in whose image we were made. That is why it sometimes speaks of the Holy Spirit

as if he would suffice by himself for our bliss, and he does suffice by himself, for the good reason that he cannot be separated from the Father and the Son— just as the Father suffices by himself because he cannot be separated from the Son and the Holy Spirit, and the Son suffices by himself because he cannot be separated from the Father and the Holy Spirit. Is this not his point when he says, *If you love me keep my commandments, and I shall ask the Father, and he will give you another advocate to be with you for ever, the Spirit of truth which this world cannot receive* (Jn 14:15-17), the lovers of the world, that is? For *the unspiritual man does not perceive the things of the Spirit of God* (1 Cor 2:15).

It might, I suppose, be argued that his saying *I shall ask the Father and he will give you another advocate* really suggests that the Son by himself does not suffice. Here, on the other hand, is a passage where the Holy Spirit is spoken of as absolutely sufficing by himself: *When he, the Spirit of truth comes, he will teach you all truth* (Jn 16:13). Is the Son then to be excluded here, as though he did not teach all truth, or as though the Holy Spirit had to supplement what the Son was less able to teach? Let them say if they like, then, that the Holy Spirit whom they usually call inferior to the Son is greater than he. Or perhaps because it does not say "he alone," or "nobody but he will teach you all truth," they will allow us to believe that the Son also teaches with him? Then the apostle in that case excluded the Son from knowing the things that are of God when he said, *Thus also the things that are of God no one knows but the Spirit of God* (1 Cor 2:11). So now these perverse people are in a position to say that even the Son is only taught the things that are of God by the Holy Spirit, as an inferior by a superior; one to whom the Son himself attributed so much that he could say, *Because I have spoken these things to you sadness has filled your hearts. But I tell you the truth, it is expedient for you that I go; for if I do not go away, the advocate will not come to you* (Jn 16:6). But the point is, he did not say this because of any inequality between the Word of God and the Holy Spirit; it was as though he was telling them that the presence of the son of man among them would be a hindrance to the coming of him who was never an inferior, because he never *emptied himself, taking the form of a servant* (Phil 2:7), like the Son.

So it was necessary for the form of a servant to be removed from their sight, since as long as they could observe it they would think that Christ was this only which they had before their eyes. This explains his words, *If you loved me you should rejoice at my going to the Father, for the Father is greater than I* (Jn 14:28), that is, "This is why I must go to the Father, because while you see me like this you assume from what you see that I am inferior to the Father, and thus with all your attention on the creature and on the adopted condition, you fail to understand the equality I enjoy with the Father." It also explains that other text, *Do not touch me, for I have not yet ascended to the Father* (Jn 20:17).[52] Touching concludes as it were the process of getting acquainted. He did not want this heart, so eagerly reaching out to him, to stop at thinking that he was only what could be seen and touched. His ascension to the Father signified his being seen in his equality with the Father, that being the ultimate vision which suffices us.

Again, it is sometimes said of the Son by himself that he suffices us, and we are promised the vision of him as the whole reward of our love and desire. Thus he says, *Whoever has my commandments and keeps them he it is that loves me. And whoever loves me shall be loved by my Father, and I will love him and show myself to him* (Jn 14:21). Was he here excluding the Father because he did not say "I will show him the Father too"? The actual truth is that *I and the Father are one* (Jn 10:30), and therefore when the Father is shown, the Son who is in him is shown also, and when the Son is shown, the Father who is in him is shown too.

Thus just as it is understood, when he says *I will show myself to him*, that he also shows the Father; so when it says *When he hands over the kingdom to God and the Father* (1 Cor 15:24), it is to be understood that he does not deprive himself of it. When he brings the believers to the contemplation of God and the Father, he will assuredly bring them to the contemplation of himself, having said, *I will show myself to him* (Jn 14:21). And thus it follows naturally that when Jude said to him, *Lord, how is it that you will show yourself to us and not to this world, Jesus answered and said to him, If anyone loves me he will keep my word; and my Father will love him, and we shall come to him and make our abode with him* (Jn 14:22). There it is in black and white; it is not only himself he shows to one who loves him, since he comes and takes up his abode with him together with the Father.

19. Or perhaps while Father and Son take up their abode in their admirer, the Holy Spirit, you think, will be excluded from this abode? Then how about what he has just said above of the Holy Spirit: *whom this world cannot receive since it does not see him; you know him because he abides with you and is in you* (Jn 14:17)? So he is not excluded from this abode, since it is said of him that *he abides with you and is in you*—unless of course there is anyone absurd enough to suppose that when Father and Son arrive to take up their abode with their admirer the Holy Spirit will withdraw, and make room as it were for his betters. Even this crassly materialistic[53] opinion is met by the scriptures; a little earlier on he had said, *And I shall ask the Father, and he will give you another advocate to be with you for ever* (Jn 14:16). He will not therefore withdraw when the Father and the Son arrive, but will be with them in the same abode for ever; for as a matter of fact, neither does he come without them nor they without him. It is to make us aware of the trinity that some things are even said[54] about the persons singly by name; however, they must not be understood in the sense of excluding the other persons, because this same three is also one, and there is one substance and godhead of Father and Son and Holy Spirit.

20. Our Lord Jesus Christ, then, *will hand over the kingdom to God and the Father* (1 Cor 15:24)—and that phrase excludes neither the Holy Spirit nor himself—insofar as[55] he will bring believers to the direct contemplation of God, in which all good actions have their end, and there is everlasting rest and joy that shall not be taken away from us. He points this out himself when he says, *I shall see you again, and your heart shall rejoice, and your joy no one shall take away from you* (Jn 16:22). A sort of picture of what this joy will be like was sketched by Mary sitting at the Lord's feet, intent upon his words; at rest

from all activity and intent upon the truth, in such measure as this life allows of, but thereby nonetheless foreshadowing that joy which is going to last for ever. There was Martha her sister, busy doing what had to be done—activity which though good and useful is going to end one day and give place to rest. She, meanwhile, was already taking her rest in the word of the Lord. So when Martha complained that her sister was not helping her, the Lord replied *Mary has chosen the best part, which shall not be taken away from her* (Lk 10:38). He did not call what Martha was doing a bad part, but this which shall not be taken away he called the best part. For the part which is played in ministering to need will be taken away when need comes to an end, and in fact the reward of good works that are going to come to an end is a rest that will endure.[56]

In that contemplation, then, *God will be all in all* (1 Cor 15:28), because nothing further will be desired of him; to be illumined and rejoiced by him will be enough. And so the psalmist in whom *the Spirit makes intercession with inexpressible groanings* (Rom 8:26), *One thing*, says he, *have I asked, this will I desire, to dwell in the Lord's house all the days of my life, to contemplate the Lord* (Ps 27:4). For we shall contemplate God the Father and Son and Holy Spirit when *the mediator of God and men the man Christ Jesus* (1 Tm 2:5) has *handed over the kingdom to God and the Father* (1 Cor 15:24), and hence no longer *intercedes for us* as our mediator and priest,[57] son of God and son of man, but is himself subject as priest, in the *form of a servant* he has assumed for us (Phil 2:7), to the one *who has subjected all things to him*, and to whom he himself has subjected all things (1 Cor 15:28). So inasmuch as he is God he will jointly with the Father have us as subjects; inasmuch as he is priest he will jointly with us be subject to him. Accordingly, since the Son is both God and man, it is rather the man in the Son that differs in substance, than the Son in the Father;[58] just as the flesh of my soul differs more in substance from my soul, though in one and the same man, than another man's soul differs from mine.

21. When therefore *he has handed over the kingdom to God and the Father*, that is when he has brought those who believe and *live by faith* (Rom 8:34), for whom he now makes intercession as mediator, to that contemplation which we are sighing and yearning to attain, and when *weariness and weeping are at an end* (Is 35:10), he will then no longer intercede for us to God and the Father, once he has handed over the kingdom. He said as much in the words, *These things have I spoken to you in comparisons; the hour will come when I shall speak to you in comparisons no more, but shall tell you openly about the Father* (Jn 16:25), that is, there will be no more comparisons when there is direct vision face to face. That is what he means by *I shall tell you openly about the Father*, as though to say "I shall show you the Father openly." He uses the word "tell," presumably, because he is the Word. He goes on to say, *On that day you will ask in my name, and I do not say that I will beg the Father for you, for the Father himself loves you, because you love[59] me and have believed that I came forth from the Father and have come into this world; again, I am leaving the world and going to the Father* (Jn 16:26). *I came forth from the Father*, that is, surely, "It was not in the form in which I am equal to the Father that I was manifested,

but in another guise, namely as less than he in the creature I took on"; and *I have come into this world*, that is, "I have shown the form of a servant, which I emptied myself to take (Phil 2:7), even to the eyes of sinners who love this world"; and, *Again I am leaving this world*, "from the sight of those who love the world I am removing what they have seen"; and, *I am going to the Father*, "I am teaching my faithful ones that I can only be fully understood in my equality with the Father."

Those who believe this will be considered worthy of being brought from faith to sight, that is to the vision to which he brings us when he is said to *hand over the kingdom to God and the Father* (1 Cor 15:24). His faithful, after all, whom he bought with his blood, are called his kingdom (Rv 1:5), and he now makes intercession for them (Rom 8:34), but then he will attach them to himself there where he is equal to the Father, and will no longer beg the Father for them. *For the Father himself*, he says, *loves you* (Jn 16:27). It is as less than the Father that he begs for us, but as his equal he hearkens to us with the Father. So when he says *the Father loves you*, he is certainly not excluding himself, but would have us understand, according to the principle I have been rehearsing often enough, that one of the persons of the trinity is frequently mentioned in such a way that the others also are to be taken as being included. Thus here, what is said of the Father, that he *himself loves you*, is naturally to be understood of the Son and the Holy Spirit too.

Not that he does not love us now,[60] seeing that *he did not spare his own Son, but handed him over for us all* (Rom 8:32). It is not as we are, however, that God loves us, but as we are going to be. For it is as he loves us that he will keep us for ever, and that is as we shall be when he who now makes intercession for us (Rom 8:34) has handed over the kingdom to God and the Father (1 Cor 15:24), and will then no longer beg the Father for us, because the Father himself loves us. And how do we deserve this if not by faith, by which we believe before we have seen that which is promised us? It is through this faith that we come at last to sight, so that he may love us for actually being what he now loves us that we might be; and that we may no more be what he now hates us for being, and what he urges and helps us not to want to be for ever.

Chapter 4

*More applications of the rule of interpretation that the Son is equal to the Father in
the form of God, less than the Father in the form of man; the proposal of another
complementary rule whereby some apparently subordinationist texts are interpreted
as saying that the Son in his equality with the Father is yet from the Father; and of
yet a third rule whereby, because of the unity of person in Jesus Christ, things are
said of him in one nature which are in fact proper to him in virtue of the other; so
that we can say, on the one hand that the Son of God was crucified, and on the other
that the Son of man will judge the living and the dead.*

22. Provided then that we know this rule for understanding the scriptures
about God's Son and can thus distinguish the two resonances in them, one tuned
to the form of God in which he is,[61] and is equal to the Father, the other tuned
to the form of a servant which he took and[62] is less than the Father, we will not
be upset by statements in the holy books that appear to be in flat contradiction
with each other. In the form of God the Son is equal to the Father, and so is the
Holy Spirit, since neither of them is a creature, as we have already shown.[63] In
the form of a servant, however, he is less than the Father, because he himself
said *The Father is greater than I* (Jn 14:28); he is also less than himself, because
it is said of him that *he emptied himself* (Phil 2:7); and he is less than the Holy
Spirit, because he himself said, *Whoever utters a blasphemy against the Son of
man, it will be forgiven him; but whoever utters one against the Holy Spirit, it
will not be forgiven him* (Mt 12:32). He also worked his deeds of power through
him, as he said himself: *If I in the Spirit of God cast out demons, the kingdom
of God has come upon you for certain* (Lk 11:20). And he says in Isaiah, in a
lesson which he read in the synagogue and declared without the slightest hesitation to be fulfilled in himself, *The Spirit of the Lord is upon me; wherefore he
anointed me, to preach the gospel to the poor he has sent me, to proclaim release
to the captives* etc. (Is 61:1; Lk 4:18). It was precisely because the Spirit of the
Lord was upon him, he says, that he was sent to do these things.

In the form of God, *all things were made by him* (Jn 1:3); in the form of a
servant, he himself *was made of woman, made under the law* (Gal 4:4). In the
form of God, he *and the Father are one* (Jn 10:30); in the form of a servant, he
did not come to do his own will, but the will of him who sent him (Jn 6:38). In
the form of God, *as the Father has life in himself, so he gave the Son also to
have life in himself* (Jn 5:26); in the form of a servant, his *soul is sorrowful to
the point of death*, and *Father*, he said, *if it can be, let this cup pass by* (Mt
26:38).[64] In the form of God, *he is true God and life eternal* (1 Jn 5:20); in the
form of a servant, *he became obedient to the point of death, the death even of
the cross* (Phil 2:8). In the form of God, *everything that the Father has is* his (Jn
16:15), and *all yours is mine*, he says, *and mine yours* (Jn 17:10); in the form of
a servant, his *doctrine is not* his *own, but his who sent* him (Jn 7:16).

23. And likewise, *Of that hour and day no one knows, neither the angels in
heaven nor the Son, except the Father* (Mk 13:32).[65] What he does not know is

what he makes others not know, that is, what he did not know in such a way as to disclose there and then to the disciples. It is like what was said to Abraham, *Now I know that you fear God* (Gn 22:12), that is, "Now I have made you know," because in being tested by that trial he became known to himself. Well Christ was certainly going to tell his disciples that too about the day and the hour, when the right time came.[66] Indeed he spoke of that future time as though it were past when he said, *I call you no longer servants but friends. For the servant does not know the will of his master, but you I have called friends because I have made known to you everything that I have heard from my Father* (Jn 15:15). In fact he had not yet done so, but because he was certainly going to, he spoke as if he already had. For he went on to say, *I have many things to tell you, but you cannot take them now* (Jn 16:12); included among them, about the day and the hour. The apostle also uses the same manner of speaking: *I did not reckon myself to know anything among you,* he says, *but Christ Jesus, and that crucified* (1 Cor 2:2). For he had been speaking to people who were unable to grasp the deeper things of Christ's divinity. He also says to them shortly after, *I could not speak to you as spiritual but only as fleshly people* (1 Cor 3:1). So he did not know among them what they could not learn through him; and the only thing he said he did know was what they must learn through him. Finally, he did know among the perfect what he did not know among the little ones; you see, he says *We speak wisdom among the perfect* (1 Cor 2:6). It is by the same manner of speaking that one is said not to know something when one conceals it, as a corner that is concealed is called blind.[67] The scriptures employ no manner of speaking that is not in common human usage—they are, after all, speaking to human beings.

24. In the form of God, it says *Before all the hills he begot me* (Prv 8:25), that is, before all the immensities of creation, and also, *Before the daystar I begot you* (Ps 110:3), that is, before all time and things of time. But in the form of a servant it says *The Lord created me in the beginning of his ways* (Prv 8:22).[68] For he said *I am the truth* in the form of God, and *I am the way* (Jn 14:16) in the form of a servant; and it is because he,[69] *the firstborn from the dead* (Col 1:18, Rv 1:5), blazed a trail to the kingdom of God for his Church, whose head he is as regards even the body's immortality, it is for that reason that he was created in the beginning of God's ways in his work of creation. In the form of God, he is *the beginning which also speaks to us* (Jn 8:25),[70] *the beginning in which God made heaven and earth* (Gn 1:1); in the form of a servant, however, he is *the bridegroom coming forth from his chamber* (Ps 19:6).[71] In the form of God, *he is the firstborn of all creation, and he is before all, and all things hold together in him* (Col 1:15, 17); in the form of a servant, *he is the head of the body, the Church* (Col 1:18). In the form of God he is *the Lord of glory* (1 Cor 2:8; Ps 24:7); from this it is clear that it is he who glorifies his saints. For *whom he predestined, them he also called; and whom he called, them he also justified; whom he justified, them he also glorified* (Rom 8:30). Of him, after all, it is said that *he justifies the wicked* (Rom 4:5); of him it is said that *he is just and the justifier* (Rom 3:26). If then whom he justified them he also glorified, he who

justifies also glorifies, being, as I said, the Lord of glory. Yet in the form of a servant, he answered his disciples, carrying on about their own glorification, by saying, *To sit at my right hand or my left is not mine to grant you, but it is for those it has been prepared for by my Father* (Mt 20:23).

25. What has been prepared by the Father, however, has also been prepared by the Son, since he *and the Father are one* (Jn 10:30). We have already shown that with regard to this three the divine utterances have many ways of saying things about them individually which belong to them all, on account of the indivisible operation of their one and the same substance.[72] Thus he says of the Holy Spirit, *When I have gone I shall send him to you* (Jn 16:7). Not "we shall send" but as though only the Son would send him, and not the Father too; while elsewhere he says, *These things have I spoken to you while remaining among you; but the advocate, the Holy Spirit whom the Father will send in my name, he will make all things clear to you* (Jn 14:25). Here again it sounds as if the Son is not going to send him, but only the Father. As in this case then, so with those words of his, *but it is for those it has been prepared for by my Father* (Mt 20:23), he wished himself to be understood together with the Father as preparing thrones of glory for whom he would.

"But," someone objects, "when he was speaking there of the Holy Spirit, he said that he would send him without actually denying that the Father would do so too; and in the other text he said the Father would send him, without denying that he himself would also. Here, however, he says in so many words, *It is not mine to grant*, and then he goes on to say that it has been prepared by the Father." Yes, but this is the point we have been making all along; this is said in the form of a servant. So we should understand *It is not mine to grant you* as meaning "It is not in human power to grant this"; it is in virtue of being God and equal to the Father that he is to be understood as granting it. *It is not mine*, says he, *to grant*, that is, "I do not grant these things by human power," *but it is for those it has been prepared for by my Father*—"but now *you* must understand that if *all that the Father has is mine* (Jn 16:19), this surely is also mine, and I have prepared these things with the Father."

26. And then, you see, there is another text that I wonder about; in what sense does he mean, *If anyone does not listen to my words, it is not I that will judge him* (Jn 12:47)? Perhaps *it is not I that will judge him* in this text has the same sense as *It is not mine to give* in that. Yet how does it continue in this one? *For I did not come*, says he, *to judge the world but to save the world*; then he adds, *whoever spurns me and does not accept my words has one to judge him*. Here we would immediately take it that the Father was meant, did he not go on to say, *The word I have spoken, that is what will judge him on the last day* (Jn 12:47). So does it mean that the Son will not judge, as he said *It is not I that will judge him*, and that the Father will not either, but the word will which the Son has spoken? Well, but listen again to what follows: *Because I*, he says, *have not spoken as from myself, but the Father who sent me, he has given me commandment what to say and how to speak, and I know that his commandment means eternal life. All that I speak, I speak just as the Father told me* (Jn 12:49-50). If

then the Son does not judge, but the word the Son has spoken does, and if the reason why the word the Son has spoken judges is that the Son has not spoken as from himself, but the Father who sent him has given him commandment what to say and how to speak; then it is of course the Father that judges, whose word it is that the Son has spoken, whose Word indeed is the Son himself. The Father's commandment is not something different from the Father's word; it is the same thing that he called "commandment" one minute and "word" the next.

So then, let us see whether what he really wanted us to understand by *I have not spoken as from myself* is not "I was not born as from myself."[73] For if he speaks the Father's word, he speaks himself because he is the Father's Word. He often says *the Father has given me* (Jn 5:36; 14:31), by which he wants it to be understood that the Father has begotten him. This is not a case of giving something to someone who already exists and has not got it; here, giving him something to have is begetting him to be. The Son of God, the only-begotten *through whom all things were made* (Jn 1:3), is not like a creature (not at least before his incarnation and his taking on of a creature) in that what he is differs from what he has; what he is is the very same as what he has. This is stated more clearly (if there is any one at all who is capable of grasping it) in that other place where he says, *Just as the Father has life in himself, so has he given the Son to have life in himself* (Jn 5:26). It was not someone already existing and not yet having life, whom he gave to have life in himself, since by the very fact that he is, he is life. So this is the meaning of *he gave the Son to have life in himself*—that he begot the Son to be unchangeable life, that is to say eternal life. Since therefore the Word of God is the Son of God, and the Son of God is *true God and eternal life*, as John says in his letter (1 Jn 5:20), here too we can but recognize the same equation when the Lord says *It is the word I have spoken that will judge him on the last day* (Jn 12:48); this word he calls both the Father's word and the Father's commandment, and the commandment he calls eternal life. *And I know*, says he, *that his commandment is eternal life* (Jn 12:50).

27. The question then is how we are to understand *It is not I who shall judge, but the word will judge that I have spoken* (Jn 12:47). It is clear from what follows that this is another way of saying "It is not I who shall judge, but the word of the Father will judge." But the Father's Word is in fact the Son of God. Must we not then understand him really to be saying, "It is not I who shall judge, but I shall judge"? And in what other way can that be true but this: "I shall not judge on human authority, that is because I am the Son of man, but I shall judge on the Word's authority, because I am the Son of God"?

If you insist that "It is not I who shall judge, but I shall judge" is simply a contradiction in terms, then what are we to say to that other remark, *My doctrine is not mine* (Jn 7:16)? He did not say "This doctrine is not mine," but *My doctrine is not mine*. What he called his own he said was not his own. How else can this be true except by his calling it his own in one respect and not his own in another? His own in the form of God, and not his own in the form of a servant.[74] By saying *not mine but his who sent me*, he directs our attention to the Word. The Father's doctrine is the Father's Word, who is his only Son.

Then again, what about *He who believes in me does not believe in me* (Jn 12:44)? In him and not in him—how? How is such a self-contradiction to be understood—*He who believes in me*, he says, *does not believe in me, but in him who sent me*—unless you take it like this: "He who believes in me does not believe in what he sees," or our hope would in that case be in something created, but he believes in him who took a created form in which to appear to human eyes, and thereby to purify our minds for contemplating him by faith in his equality with the Father? So when he directs the aim of our faith onto the Father and says *does not believe in me but in him who sent me*, he does not of course want to separate himself from the Father, from him that is who sent him. He wants us to believe in him in the same way as we do in the Father whose equal he is. He says as much quite explicitly elsewhere: *Believe in God, believe in me too* (Jn 14:1), which amounts to, "Just as you believe in God, so too in me, because I and the Father are one God."

Just as in this place therefore he appears to deflect man's faith from himself and direct it onto the Father, by saying *does not believe in me but in him who sent me*, though in fact he did not separate himself from him, so it is with *It is not mine to give, but it is for those it has been prepared for by my Father* (Mt 20:23). I think it must be clear now in what respect each is to be taken. So also with *I shall not judge* (Jn 12:47), when he is in fact *going to judge the living and the dead* (2 Tm 4:1), not however on his human authority, and for that reason he turns our attention to the godhead and points the minds of men upward,[75] since to raise them up was the reason why he himself had come down.

28. However, if it were not one and the same person who is Son of God in virtue of the form in which he is, and Son of man in virtue of the form of a servant which he took, the apostle Paul would not have said, *If they had known, they would never have crucified the Lord of glory* (1 Cor 2:8).[76] It was in the form of a servant that he was crucified, and yet it was the Lord of glory who was crucified. For that "take-over" was such as to make God a man and a man God. Yet the careful and serious and devout reader will understand what is said of him for the sake of which, and what in virtue of which. For example, we said above[77] that it is in virtue of his being God that he glorifies his followers—in virtue, obviously, of his being the Lord of glory; and yet the Lord of glory was crucified, because it is quite correct to talk even of God being crucified—owing to the weakness of flesh, though, not to the strength of godhead.[78] In the same way we talk of him judging in virtue of his being God, that is by his authority as a divine, not as a human being, and yet it is that man who is going to judge, just as in the other case it was the Lord of glory who was crucified. He says so quite unequivocally himself: *When the Son of man comes in his glory and all the angels with him, then shall all the nations be herded together before him*, and so on through the description of the judgment to come, right up to the final sentence (Mt 25:31). And the Jews (those only of course who persist in their ill will and are therefore to be punished at that assize), as it says elsewhere, *will look upon him whom they pierced* (Rv 1:7).[79]

Both good and bad, of course, are going to look upon the judge of the living and the dead, but the bad, we may be sure, will only be able to see him in the form by which he is the Son of man, though in the proud splendor, certainly, that will be his as judge, not in the mean guise he once presented as prisoner in the dock. The form of God, however, in which he is equal to the Father, this the wicked will undoubtedly not see. They are not clean of heart, and *Blessed are the clean of heart, because they shall see God* (Mt 5:8). This is to be a *face to face* seeing (1 Cor 13:12), and it is promised to the just as their supreme reward, and it will happen *when he hands over the kingdom to God and the Father* (1 Cor 15:24) (in which we are also to understand the seeing of his own divine form), when every creature is made subject to God, including even the creature in which the Son of God became the Son of man, for in this created form *the Son himself shall also be made subject to the one who subjected all things to him, that God may be all in all* (1 Cor 15:28). Suppose on the other hand that the Son of God is manifested even to the wicked in the form by which he is equal to the Father, when he is about to judge them; what then becomes of the very special promise he makes to the one who loves him: *I in turn will love him and will show myself to him* (Jn 14:21)? So it is the Son of man who is going to judge, not though by his human authority but by his authority as Son of God. And again it is the Son of God who is going to judge, though he will not be manifested in the form by which he is equal to the Father, but in that by which he is the Son of man.

29. Thus you can have it both ways: both "the Son of man will judge," and "the Son of man will not judge." The Son of man will judge, to verify the text, *When the Son of man comes, then shall all the nations be herded together before him* (Mt 25:32), and the Son of man will not judge, to verify *I shall not judge* (Jn 12:47), and *I do not seek my own glory, there is one to seek it and to judge* (Jn 8:50). For insofar as at the judgment it will not be the form of God but the form of man that is manifested, not even the Father will judge. From this point of view it says, *The Father does not judge anyone, but has given all judgment to the Son* (Jn 5:22). Does this mean giving in the same manner of speaking as we mentioned above on the text, *So he has given the Son to have life in himself* (Jn 5:26),[80] where it means "So he has begotten the Son"; or in the manner the apostle uses when he says, *Therefore he raised him up and gave him the name above every name* (Phil 2:9)?—Here it is said of the Son of man, in whom the Son of God was raised up from the dead. For though of course equal to the Father in the form of God, from the moment he emptied himself and took the form of a servant it is in that servant form that he does and suffers and receives the things which the apostle threads one after the other into the same fabric: *He humbled himself, being made obedient to death, the death indeed of the cross. Therefore God surely exalted him and gave him the name above every name, that at the name of Jesus every knee should bend, of beings in heaven, on earth, and in the nether world; and every tongue should acknowledge that the Lord Jesus*[81] *is in the glory of God the Father* (Phil 2:8-11).

Is "giving" then meant after this manner of speech or that one, when he says, *He has given all judgment to the Son* (Jn 5:22)? The answer is clear enough from the context; if it were meant in the same way as *He has given the Son to have life in himself,* it would surely not have said *The Father does not judge anyone.* For inasmuch as the Father has begotten the Son as his equal, he judges together with him. The expression then must mean that in the judgment it will not be the form of God but the form of man that will be manifested. Not indeed that he who has given all judgment to the Son will not judge himself, since the Son says of him *There is one to seek and judge* (Jn 8:50); but it says *The Father does not judge anyone, but has given all judgment to the Son,* as though to say, "No one shall see the Father in the judgment of the living and the dead, but all shall see the Son"; because he is also the Son of man, and so can even be seen by the wicked, when they too *shall see him whom they have pierced* (Rv 1:7).

30. I consider that this is no mere conjecture of mine, but demonstrably correct; to clinch it and prove that his reason for saying *The Father judges no one, but has given all judgment to the Son* (Jn 5:22) was that he will be manifested as judge in the form of the Son of man, which is not the Father's form but the Son's only; and not the Son's form either in which he is equal to the Father, but the one in which he is less than the Father; to prove that he will be so manifested in order to be plainly visible to good and bad alike, we now bring forward the plain and unambiguous verdict of our Lord himself. A little later on he says, *Amen I tell you that he who listens to my word and believes him who sent me, has eternal life and shall not come under judgment, but shall pass from death to life* (Jn 5:24). This eternal life is that sight which the bad have no part in. Then he continues, *Amen I tell you, the hour will come and now is when the dead will hear the voice of God's Son, and those who hear shall live* (Jn 5:25). And this applies exclusively to loyal believers, who so hear of his incarnation that they believe him to be the Son of God, that is, they so accept him as having become less than the Father for their sakes in the form of a servant, that they believe him to be equal to the Father in the form of God. Thus he goes on to make this very point: *For just as the Father has life in himself, so he gave the Son also to have life in himself* (Jn 5:26). Then he comes to the sight of his splendor in which he will come to judgment, a sight that will be shared by wicked and just alike: *and he also gave him authority,* he continues, *to do judgment, because he is the Son of man* (Jn 5:27).

Nothing, I submit, could be plainer. As the Son of God and equal to the Father, he simply is, together with the Father, the hidden source of this authority, he does not receive it. But he does receive it, in order that both good and bad may see him judging, as Son of man. Yes, even the bad will be given a sight of the Son of man: a sight of the form of God will be granted only to *the pure of heart, because they shall see God* (Mt 5:8)—only, that is, to the loyal and true, whose love wins them the promise that he will show himself to them (Jn 14:21). So observe how he continues: *Do not be surprised at this,* he says—but what is to stop us being surprised except precisely the point that surprises anyone who fails to understand, namely his saying that it is because he is the Son of man that the Father has given him authority to judge, whereas one would rather expect him to say it is because he is the Son of God? But because the wicked cannot see the Son of God in his equality with the Father in the form of God, and because it is necessary for just and wicked alike to see the judge of the living and the dead when they are judged in his presence; that is why he says, *Do not be surprised at this, that the hour will come in which all in the graves shall hear his voice, and they shall come forth, those who have done good to the resurrection of life, those who have done evil to the resurrection of judgment* (Jn 5:28).

This then is why he had to receive that authority as Son of man; it is in order that all, as they rise again, may see him in the form in which he can be seen by all—by some however to their undoing, by others to eternal life. And what else is eternal life but that sight which is not granted to the wicked? *That they may know you*, he says of it, *the one true God, and Jesus Christ whom you have sent* (Jn 17:3), and in what way to know Jesus Christ as well, if not in the same way as the one true God, who will show himself to them, not in the same way as he will show himself even to the condemned in the form of the Son of man?

31. His essential goodness, in the last resort, is attained in that sight or vision in which God is manifested to the pure of heart—*How good is the God of Israel to the upright of heart* (Ps 73:1)! When the wicked see their judge, he will not seem good to them because the sight of him will not rejoice their hearts; on the contrary, *then shall all the tribes of the earth bewail themselves* (Rv 1:7; Zec 12:12)—represented, of course by all the wicked and unbelievers. This too is the explanation of the answer he gave the young man who called him good master and asked his advice about achieving eternal life: *Why ask me about the good? No one is good except the one God* (Mt 19:17; Mk 10:17). Yet our Lord himself talks about man as good: *The good man*, he says, *from the good treasure of his heart brings out good things, and the bad man from the bad treasure of his heart brings out bad things* (Mt 12:35). But that young man was seeking eternal life, and eternal life consists in that contemplation by which God is seen not to one's undoing but to everlasting joy, and he did not realize whom he was speaking to, imagining him to be only a son of man. So, *Why ask me about the good?*, that is, "Why ask this form which you see about the good, and why call me good master on the strength of what you can see? This is the form of the Son of man, this form has been received, this form will appear in judgment to the wicked as well as to the good, and the sight of this form will not bode well for those who do ill. There is however a sight of that form of mine in which I *thought it no robbery to be equal to God*, though I *emptied* (Phil 2:6) myself to take this one."

That one God, therefore, Father Son and Holy Spirit, whose manifestation will mean nothing but a joy which will not be taken away from the just (Jn 16:22; Lk 10:42), a joy to come for which someone sighs and says, *One thing have I begged of the Lord, this will I seek: to dwell in the house of the Lord all the days of my life, to behold the delight of the Lord* (Ps 27:4); that one God, therefore, alone is good, in that no one sees him for worse and for lamentation, but only for better and for true rejoicing. "If you understand me in that form, then I am indeed good, but if only in this visible one, why ask me about the good? If you are going to be one of those who *will see him whom they have pierced* (Rv 1:7), that sight will be evil for them, because it will mean punishment for them."[82]

That this was our Lord's meaning when he said, *Why ask me about the good? No one is good except the one God* (Mt 19:7), is shown to be likely from the texts I have mentioned. For that sight of God in which we shall behold his unchanging substance, invisible to human eyes and promised only to the saints and described by the apostle Paul as *face to face* (1 Cor 13:12), of which the apostle John says, *We shall be like him, because we shall see him as he is* (1 Jn 3:2), and of which it is said, *One thing have I begged of the Lord, to behold the delight of the Lord* (Ps 27:4), and of which our Lord himself says, *And I will love him and show myself to him* (Jn 14:21), in order to be *blessed the pure of heart, because they shall see God* (Mt 5:8), and whatever else is said about this sight, which anyone who directs the eyes of love to seeking it may find scattered plentifully throughout the scriptures; this sight alone is our supreme good, and it is to gain this that we are bidden to do whatever we do rightly. That other sight, however, of the Son of man, which has been announced for the day when all the nations are to be herded together before him and they will say, *Lord, when did we see you hungry and thirsty* etc. (Mt 25:37), that sight will be neither good for the wicked, who will be dispatched into everlasting fire, nor supremely good for the just. For he still calls them on to the kingdom which has been prepared for them from the beginning of the world. As he will say to those, *Go into everlasting fire*, so he will say to these, *Come, blessed of my Father, possess the kingdom prepared for you* (Mt 25:41.34). And as they will go into eternal burning, so will the just into eternal life.

And what is eternal life but *to know you the one true God*, as he says, *and Jesus Christ whom you have sent* (Jn 17:3)? To know him in this case, however, in that glory which, he says to the Father, *I had with you before the world was* (Jn 17:5). That is *when he will hand over the kingdom to God and the Father* (1 Cor 15:24), and the *good servant* will *enter into the joy of his Lord* (Mt 25:21), and *God will hide* those he possesses *in the hidden place of his countenance from the disturbance of men* (Ps 31:20), of those men namely who will be disturbed when they hear the sentence passed; *an evil hearing* of which *the just man will not be afraid* (Ps 112:7), provided he is now *protected in the tabernacle*, that is, in the right faith of the Catholic Church, *from the contradiction of tongues* (Ps 31:20), that is from the sophistries of heretics.

There are doubtless other ways of understanding our Lord's words, *Why ask me about the good? No one is good but the one God* (Mt 19:17). Provided however they do not favor belief that the Son's substance, by which he is *the Word through whom all things were made* (Jn 1:3), is of a lesser goodness than the Father's, and are not otherwise at odds with sound doctrine, we may cheerfully use not merely one interpretation but as many as can be found.[83] For the more ways we open up of avoiding the traps of heretics, the more effectively can they be convinced of their errors.

But let us now adjourn what remains to be considered, and take it up afresh in the next volume.

NOTES

1. *Notaverunt*; M *noverunt*, what they know about . . .

2. These two first paragraphs are full of allusions to the wisdom literature, in particular to Wis 9:13-16, 14:21-30, Eccl 25:16, Sir 1:15; 6:9

3. *Sub umbraculo*; M *in tegmine*, under cover.

4. *Sirparet*; M *spissaret*, pack.

5. *Aspectus*; M *affectus*, inclinations.

6. See Col 13:1.

7. Augustine is already laying down one of his governing principles, aimed especially at the "economic" theologians, the absolute immutability of God. He carefully talks about "God's substance" instead of just "God," in order to include Son and Holy Spirit, as well as Father, in the scope of this principle.

8. Literally "soul-ly" (silly?); *animales, psychikoi*, in Paul's Greek.

9. The word "trinitas" is more merely numerical in meaning than the English "trinity," which has come almost to demand a capital T. But it means no more than "threeness," or more concretely "threesome" "a three." My inclination will be to avoid the capital T mostly, and sometimes to substitute more numbersome English words.

10. See 1 Tm 6:16.

11. This is the theme-setting text for the whole work. See *Introduction* 12.

12. That is, the scriptures.

13. History was to show that Augustine had good reason to enter this defense in advance. He will be blamed—or praised—for being the *fons et origo* of almost as many uncatholic opinions and doctrines as have been fathered on the scriptures. This is more evidently so in matters to do with grace, predestination, and original sin than with the Trinity, but even here, as we have seen in the *Introduction*, he was subject to misunderstanding and straight incomprehension.

14. I have sometimes been inclined to interpret the involved polemic which Augustine engages in throughout this prologue to his work as a kind of literary convention; as though theological works in general, and ones on the Trinity in particular, had to be written *Contra Aliquem*. It is true that he does not seem to have had any particular opponents in mind, and that one cannot identify any of the opinions he has listed very satisfactorily with known heresies, the Arians for example. Indeed the third false idea about God which he lists at the beginning, according to which God begets himself, looks very like a piece of nonsense with which Arian controversialists might have reproached the Catholics.

But Augustine labors the point so, with what at times looks like hypersensitivity, that I do not think the literary convention hypothesis will do. His strangely defensive attitude recurs in prologues to later books of this work. What he is on the defensive against is not so much particular heresies or errors, as a certain attitude of mind, and he is so touchy about it that it is one he must have had a lot of experience of. It could be perhaps described as an attitude of coarse brash rationalism, self-assured, always ready with a definite opinion on any subject under the sun, trampling on truth with hobnailed yes-or-no, black-and-white, syllogistic boots. One finds it among the faithful quite as frequently as among unbelievers.

Augustine was unusually sensitive to the delicacy of truth, and to the inadequacy of human language to express it, and therefore of human reason to grasp it, without an infinite number of qualifications and distinctions and approximations and provisos. The interrogative form of sentence is far more characteristic of him than the affirmative. So one must take his defensiveness seriously. It is a standing protest against intellectual roughness and impatience which demands cut-and-dried solutions to problems, and quickly. This kind of impatience will never get far in the kind of quest on which Augustine is here engaged.

15. It is worth noting that Augustine takes it for granted that to write on the Trinity was to interpret the scriptures. There was no question of dogmatic writers and bible commentators belonging to different species.

16. M add *ejusdemque,* one and the same substance.

17. M add *sedisse super unumquemque eorum,* settled on each of them; a gloss in one manuscript completing the text of Acts 2:3.

18. This is a basic axiom of trinitarian theology. It is a necessary consequence of the truth that the divine substance is identical with the divine attributes, that there is no composition in God (see *Introduction* 93). What is true of divine attributes, like wisdom and goodness, is also true of divine activities, such as creation, redemption, revelation, mission. God is his actions just as he is his qualities. It is because of this absolute identity of God's substance with his attributes and with his actions, that we cannot distinguish the divine persons either in terms of divine attributes or in terms of divine actions. Therefore they work inseparably, just as they are inseparably good. It was the failure of the "economic" theologians to appreciate this point that was their chief weakness. Their failure jeopardized the divine transcendence. On the other hand, an over-emphasis on this principle can jeopardize the real distinction between the divine persons, and even if this is preserved, it can blot out any significance of that distinction for the believer. This was a tendency of later Catholic theology. If the divine persons work inseparably in creation, does it not follow that they can only be known, loved, worshipped inseparably by their creatures? And if that is the case, what is the point of making the distinction at all? Augustine avoids this anti-economy imbalance by stressing that it was only the Son who was incarnate, only the Spirit who was given at Pentecost, only the Father who spoke from heaven. This leads to the problem he puts in the next paragraph, which he will not be ready to answer until somewhere in books V-VII. The answer is, very briefly, that to make the divine persons the terms of distinct real relationships in creatures does not jeopardize the divine transcendence, nor impair the divine simplicity of being, because these real relationships of creatures to God, or to one or other of the divine persons, do not do anything to God, or modify any of the persons in any way. The Son was no different after the incarnation from what he was before—there is no real "before and after" for the Son; but the man Christ Jesus was very different. So he, and the pentecostal fire, and the baptismal dove, and the voice from heaven (all created effects of one kind or another) can have real distinct reference to one divine person and not another, belong to the Son and not the Father, or to the Spirit and not the Son, or to the Father and not the Spirit, and yet be the created effect of the three working inseparably. And so, therefore, can other creatures; we too can have different relationships to each of the divine persons.

19. M add *in caelum,* into heaven.

20. This problem will occupy him throughout the book, and he will not find a wholly satisfactory solution. It is a question of discovering and finding adequate expression for the specific or proper relationship of the Holy Spirit to the other two persons, and for his procession from them.

21. The CCL text adds *jam* a second time, which accords with the Vulgate—"or am already perfect." I follow M in omitting it, as copyists are more likely to emend Augustine to fit the Vulgate than otherwise.

22. Augustine's text reads *secundum intentionem,* which is a literal but inaccurate rendering of the Greek *kata skopon.* Vulgate translates correctly *ad destinatum,* "to the goal."

23. Following M; CCL adds *si*: but if all things were made through him, then he is . . .

24. The distinction between being God and being true God is not very easy for us to grasp, conditioned so thoroughly as we are to there being only one God, and to treating the word "God" as a proper name. The testimony of Jn 1:1 to the divinity of the Word is so manifest to us, that we cannot really see why Augustine has to spend a whole paragraph proving the obvious. But in the first place, the ancient world, and this includes the sophisticated world of neoplatonism as well as the popular world of polytheism, thought of the divine as covering a whole range of being in which the word "God" could be used with varying degrees of properness. Thus the Arians and other less thorough subordinationists read the same text in Jn 1:1 as Augustine and the orthodox, and did not find it impossible to interpret it in their own sense.

In the second place, the Greek text is in fact rather more subtle than either the Latin or the English translation shows. Greek regularly uses the definite article with "God," as it does with proper names like Jesus or Peter; and when it leaves it out, it might be the intention to make the word indefinite. Thus a literal rendering of Jn 1:1 would go, "In beginning was the word, and the word was with the god, and god the word was." It is clear that "god" in this sentence must have two different references each time it is used. The first time its reference is to the Father, with whom the Word was, but who the Word is not. The second time, where it is used without the article, it is the predicate describing the Word. Here you cannot take it as referring to the Father, unless you want to subscribe to the Sabellian heresy—which is doubtless what the Arians accused the orthodox interpretation of doing. For the Arians only the Father is the true God, and the Word can be called God only in a secondary and less proper sense. Thus the last phrase of Jn 1:1 could be rendered "and the Word was divine" (some modern commentators propose this), or "and the Word was a god." So it is that Augustine has to argue for his interpretation of this verse, even though he thought its testimony manifest, and he argues not from this verse, but from the next, "All things were made through him."

25. M add *Deum*, the true God; following Vulgate, but not the Greek text.

26. Augustine's discussion of this passage is a more or less direct refutation of the interpretation given by Tertullian (*Adv. Prax.* 14: PL 2, 171A) and Novatian (*De Trin.* 18: PL 3, 946CD).

27. *Ostendit*; M *ostendet*, with Vugate and Greek, will manifest. Augustine's reading (repeated at the end of the paragraph) is very curious. The verb could be parsed in the present tense, but I presume Augustine understood it as a perfect, referring to the first, not the second, coming of Christ.

28. In the Latin the adjectives qualify "the commandment"; in the Greek they can equally qualify "you," and are usually so translated.

29. M add *Amen*, here and twice below.

30. M add *illi*, to him.

31. Since Augustine does not think the meaning of this text needs to be discussed, it had presumably escaped his notice or slipped his mind that Novatian takes it to prove the Son's inequality (*De Trin.* 22: PL 3, 958A).

32. For example, Ambrose *De Spir. Sanc. Libri III* (PL 16); Damasus *Epist II* (PL 13: 351B).

33. This reading represents a Greek variant where "God" is in apposition to "Spirit," and both are in the dative, so that it should really mean "we who serve God the Spirit" and give even greater weight to Augustine's case.

34. The Macedonians (that is, followers of Macedonius) whose error was condemned at the Council of Constantinople in 381.

35. *Salus*, which of course is the Latin also for "salvation." It is a pity that "health" is not the usual English for "salvation."

36. *In similitudine*; M *in similitudinem*, into the likeness.

37. A passing but significant allusion to the great theme of the image in the second half of this work.

38. *Deitas*, a theological neologism on the model of the Greek *theotes*, more precisely means "Godness," whereas *divinitas* often has a wider reference, and can mean "godlikeness." See *The City of God* VII, 1; also below Book IV, 29.

39. Something like this view, not so crudely put, can be found in Gregory of Nyssa's *Adversus Apollinarem* 53 (PG 45: 1253B). I cannot find anything like it, to which Augustine could be referring, in Latin authors.

40. That is, before the last day. Gregory of Nyssa, in the work referred to, finds it ridiculous to think of Christ being corporeally present in heaven.

41. Commenting on Ps 8:8.

42. Reading *transfigurabit* with M; CCL has *transfiguravit*, has transfigured, which is undoubtedly the more difficult reading. But anyone who knows Spanish will appreciate how easily a copyist writing to dictation could write a "v" for a "b." This interchange of the two consonants might well have been a feature of African Latin pronunciation in the fifth century.

43. Reading *subicit* with M: CC has *subjecit*, who has subjected.

44. Quoted in Rom 1:17 and Gal 3:11.

45. See 2 Cor 5:7.

46. We come now to one of Augustine's long and significant digressions. Up till now his comments on the passage 1 Cor 15:24-28 have been simply in defense of his principle that the Son is less than the Father in his humanity, or in the form of a servant, and against various mistaken interpretations of the passage. Now in his own positive explanation of the apostle's meaning he

seems to leave the theme of the equality of the divine persons and its corollaries, to embark on a long and involved rhapsody on the topic of our final destiny.

But this is not really taking him away from his subject. He is in fact anticipating the end of his work again. By doing so he is reminding us early on of the essentially dramatic nature of the mystery of the trinity, or at least of its revelation. The revelation will only be complete when the drama reaches its climax and conclusion, and we are introduced to the full and perfect vision of the Father, which will of course include the vision of the Son and the Holy Spirit.

Our being made in the image and likeness of God, and our having to realize or activate this image by being converted to God in Christ is a constitutive part of the drama. That is the point of his reference to the angelic regime of symbols a few lines further on. The word translated "symbols" is *similitudines,* "likenesses," and it is only through such likenesses that under the present dispensation we have access to God. The administration of this regime by angels in the Old Testament will be the chief subject of Book III. But even after the advent of Christ, though the angels fall somewhat into the background, we are still under this regime, and the chief symbol or likeness through which we can approach God is that of the divine image or likeness in man, which is most perfectly found in Christ himself.

Another cardinal principle of the whole work which this digression is emphasizing is that the final contemplation of God face to face will be the reward of faith. We can only come to understanding—and that final vision will be perfect understanding—by living in faith, which is the proper response to the present regime of symbols.

47. *Nostra;* M *vestra,* your.

48. *Itaque;* M omits.

49. A favorite tag of Augustine's in his sermons is *nondum in re, tantum in spe,* "not yet in fact, only in hope."

50. For both the bible and Augustine the heart is the seat of thought and understanding, not of emotion.

51. I think Augustine interprets *I will show him my salvation* as meaning "I will show him my Son."

52. The Father, following M. CCL has *patrem meum,* my Father, which is the Vulgate reading, but not the Greek, and has little support in the manuscripts.

53. Literally, "carnal cogitation"; "carnal" is Augustine's usual word for materialism, or literal-mindedness, which was apparently as common a failing then as now.

54. M adds *separatim,* said separately about . . .

55. *quoniam,;* M *quando,* when he brings . . .

56. Mary and Martha are traditionally seen by the Fathers and subsequent writers as types of the contemplative and of the active life. Equally traditionally, the contemplative life is seen as the "heavenly" life, that is the mode of life which bears the most direct relationship and resemblance to that life which is our final eschatological goal. Other biblical types of these two modes of life which the Fathers liked to elaborate are Rachel and Leah, Jacob's two wives, and John and Peter, as they figure in the last chapter of John.

But Augustine's treatment of this theme always has a distinctive quality about it which one does not find either in his contemporaries or in later spiritual writers. For him the contemplative life is properly the life to which we look forward as the consummation of our destiny in Christ. It is significant that in describing Mary here, he says she was "at rest from all activities . . . in such measure as this life allows of"; the life proper to our earthly existence is in fact the active life. John, Rachel, Mary, symbolize for us the joys of the life to come; but they are scarcely presented as models of how to live it here and now. Augustine is always concerned that we should long for that life of perfect contemplation with a great desire; that we should in some measure anticipate it and prepare for it by assiduous attention to the word of God, by prayer, by faith seeking understanding, in this life. But he is firmly of the opinion that charity, and attention to the needs of ourselves and of our brothers, compel us to devote most of our energies in this earthly life to activity. He never, so far as I am aware, speaks of the contemplative life as a mode of life on this earth to which some Christians are called. Rather it is the mode of life to which all Christians are called as their final destiny. I think perhaps Saint Thomas Aquinas is heir to this Augustinian view of things, when he answers the medieval question on the comparative worth of the contemplative life and the active life, by giving the palm not to the contemplative life pure and simple, but to the mixed life, of contemplation issuing in activity.

Augustine will take up the theme later on in Books XII and XIII as he explores the dynamism of the divine image in the Christian life. There, activity will be coordinated with faith and the discipline of moral effort; contemplation with wisdom and direct contact with God. The first is the way to the second, and the second is not fully attainable in this life.

57. See Rom 8:34; Heb 7:25; 8:6; 9:15; 12:24.

58. Following M, supported by several manuscripts. In the Latin it runs *alia substantia homo potius in filio quam filius in patre,* a somewhat awkwardly constructed sentence, but clear in meaning. CCL follows other manuscripts in reading *alia substantia deus, alia homo, homo potius in filio quam filius in patre.* This I find impossible to translate in such a way that it makes any real sense. How to account for the three words *deus alia homo* getting added to the text, if they were not in the original? I would conjecture that first a copyist wrote *homo* twice by dittography; then another hand, copying from or correcting him, inserted the words *deus alia,* which at least gives the stock phrase *alia substantia deus alia homo,* though it finishes the wreck of the sentence as a whole.

59. *Amatis*; M *amastis,* you have loved.

60. To catch the movement of his thought, it is necessary to see that he has been interpreting "The Father himself loves you" of the future, when Christ hands over the kingdom.

61. M omits *est et,* reading "in which he is equal to . . ."

62. M reads *in qua* for *et;* "which he took, in which he is less . . ."

63. See above section 9; section 13.

64. M adds *a me,* from me.

65. What follows represents a certain incoherence in the writer's sequence of thought. The text is quoted as a "form of a servant" saying. Yet Augustine is side-tracked by it into a favorite groove of his, and by suggesting that the Son really did know the day and the hour, he makes the saying patient of a "form of God" interpretation.

66. That would be when the day actually arrived.

67. The Latin saying is *fossa caeca,* a blind ditch—a ha-ha, perhaps.

68. This is the Septuagint reading (Heb "The Lord possessed me"). The text was a real problem for earlier commentators, like Tertullian and Origen, and a godsend for the Arians. For Augustine to interpret it as a "form of a servant" text is somewhat of a *tour de force,* and he is obliged to give an involved and not altogether convincing explanation; as Wisdom is speaking, who was universally identified with the divine Son, or Word, I do not think he really makes his case.

69. Following M; CCL inserts *est,* he is the firstborn . . . , thus obscuring the argument of the sentence. The CCL editor does not always allow sufficiently for the unintelligence of officious copyists.

70. This is the Latin rendering of a very obscure saying in the Greek text, which, whatever it means, almost certainly does not mean this.

71. Referred to the incarnation and virgin birth.

72. See Book I, 18.

73. Here Augustine interrupts his discussion of the right way to understand the text *It is not I who will judge,* which he takes up again in the next paragraph and eventually settles in terms of Christ's two natures or "forms," and inserts in the merest aside his second important principle of interpretation, the eternal procession of the Son from the Father. This principle will be of crucial importance in the next book.

74. In his sermon on this passage in *Homilies on the Gospel of John* 29, 3 he explains the paradox rather more neatly in terms of what we here call his second principle. As he also says here, Christ is himself, as the Word, the Father's doctrine, and therefore precisely as Word, without reference to his human nature, he is both his own and not his own. For Augustine says in that place, *Quid tam tuum quam tu? Et quid tam non tuum quam tu, si alicujus est quod es?* What is more yours than yourself? And what is more not yours than yourself, if what you are is someone else's? When our Lord said "He that would save his life will lose it, and he that loses his life for my sake will find it,"

he was speaking not only from the depths of his own human experience—no one has ever been less able to call his soul his own than the man Christ Jesus who was assumed into personal union with the eternal Word—but also, one might say, from the experience of his divine being, which simply consists in belonging to the Father. But see below, Book II, 2, 4.

75. In the Latin, *sursum erigit corda,* an allusion to the *sursum corda* of the Mass. But for Augustine, like all the ancients, the heart is the organ and symbol of deliberate thought rather than of feeling; this was situated in the *viscera.*

76. Here he introduces his third principle, the unity of person in Christ; he is going to need it badly as he follows up the theme of judgment.

77. See Book I, 24.

78. Here Augustine very accurately anticipates the definition of the Council of Ephesus, 431, which ratified the title of Mary as *theotokos,* mother of God—mother of him who is God, in virtue however of his being man.

79. See Rv 19:37; Zec 12:10.

80. See Book I, 26.

81. M adds *Christus.*

82. One particular value of Augustine's long discussion of the judgment, and of this answer to the rich young man in relation to it, is that it provides a cogent and salutary corrective to an excessive emphasis on the humanity of Christ. The tendency in theology to explore to the limit all the implications of the incarnation and the humanity of Christ is valuable and sound. But like all good things it can be and is sometimes overdone. One is left wondering at times, when reading or listening to those who would stress the properly christocentric quality of Christian theology—christocentric instead of theocentric—whether there is any point or meaning in saying that Jesus Christ is true God as well as true man. From a miscontrued christocentricity it is only a step to a purely anthropocentric view, which soon leaves one wondering whether there is any point or meaning in saying God: period. And one answer that comes back honestly enough is "No, God is dead."

It does make all the difference where one puts the center. A fully humane, even humanist, anthropology is one thing, and a good one; but a Christian may question whether it is true to the deepest heart of man to put him at the center of things, even of himself. Again, a fully balanced christology, doing full justice to the human nature of Christ, is one thing and a good one, and even a christocentric approach to the Christian life is excellent in a limited context. But it leaves one with the question, what was the center of this Christ center, of Christ's own life? If one is going to be honest with the gospel, one must surely answer, God, the Father. So ultimately Christian theology must be unashamedly theocentric.

Augustine's certainly was so. It is the ultimate human destiny, and fulfillment, and "hominization" to find God, that is to know God, that is to see God. If it is also, according to the New Testament gospel, our ultimate destiny and fulfillment to know and see Christ, this can only be because Christ is God the Son of God, equal to the Father. Christ as man, true man, complete and perfect man though he be, cannot satisfy us as our final destiny, because he is, or will be, also available to the knowledge and sight of the wicked, that is to say, of those people who have somehow or other willfully foresworn their true destiny.

It is surely only with a very naive and fundamentalist eschatology that one could be contented with a description of our final destiny in terms of sharing in the glory of the Son of man as such—an eschatology which sees the bliss of the redeemed as consisting in the splendors of a purely material heaven, and the woes of the damned in the pains of purely material outer darkness. If one is going to interpret the eschatological images of scripture at all, to demythologize them, as the classical Christian tradition always has done, then with Augustine and this tradition, one must divinize them: divinize Christ and divinize humanity.

83. Augustine's lack of dogmatism is one of the most pleasing features of his exegesis. But it must be confessed that his happy pluralism as regards the meaning of scripture will not always satisfy modern standards of criticism.

BOOK II

MISSIONS: OLD TESTAMENT THEOPHANIES

Prologue

---

1. People who seek God, and stretch their minds as far as human weakness is able toward an understanding of the trinity, must surely experience the strain of trying to fix their gaze on *light inaccessible* (1 Tm 6:16), and the difficulties presented by the holy scriptures in their multifarious diversity of form, which are designed, so it seems to me, to wear Adam[1] down and let Christ's glorious grace shine through.[2] So they should find it easy, once they do shake off all uncertainty on a point and reach a definite conclusion, to excuse those who make mistakes in the exploration of so deep a mystery. But there are two things which are very hard to tolerate in the mistakes people make: presumption, before the truth is clear, and defense of the false presumption when it has become so. No two vices could be more of a hindrance to discovering the truth or to handling the divine and holy books. If God then, as I hope and pray, will defend me from them and fortify me *with the shield of his good will* (Ps 5:13) and the grace of his mercy, I will not be idle in seeking out the substance of God, either through his scriptures or his creatures.[3] For both these are offered us for our observation and scrutiny in order that in them he may be sought, he may be loved, who inspired the one and created the other.

Nor will I be diffident about expressing my sentiments, since my eagerness to have them scrutinized by the fairminded outweighs my fear of their being chewed to pieces by the spiteful. The keen eyes of the dove are most acceptable to Charity's modest beauty, while the teeth of the snarling dog are either dodged by Humility's caution or broken on the solid hardness of Truth. In any case I would rather receive any sort of censure than mistaken or flattering praise. No censure can be feared by the lover of truth. It will come, after all, either from friend or from foe; if it is a foe being offensive, he can be endured; if it is a friend being wrong, he can be put right; if it is a friend being right, he can be heeded.

But as for praise—if it is mistaken it confirms you in your mistakes, and if it is flattering it seduces you into making them. *May the just man*, therefore, *rebuke me in mercy and correct me, but let not the oil of sinners grease my head* (Ps 141:5).

Chapter 1

Of the principle of interpretation whereby some texts are referred neither to the Son's equality with the Father, nor to his being less than the Father in the form of a servant, but simply to his being, in his co-eternal equality, from the Father; with discussion in support of this principle of some of the things that are said about the Holy Spirit.

---

2. To resume then, we find scattered through the scriptures, and marked out by learned Catholic expositors of them, a kind of canonical rule, which we hold onto most firmly, about how our Lord Jesus Christ is to be understood to be God's Son, both equal to the Father by the form of God in which he is, and less than the Father by the form of a servant which he took. In this form indeed he is seen to be not only less than the Father, but also less than the Holy Spirit, less, what is more, than himself—and not a self that he was but a self that he is. For when he took the form of a servant he did not lose the form of God, as we learn from the evidences of scripture examined in the preceding book.

There are, however, some statements in the divine utterances of such a kind that it is uncertain which rule should be applied to them; should it be the one by which we take the Son as less than the Father in the created nature he took on, or the one by which we take him as equal to the Father, while still deriving from him his being God from God, light from light? We do, after all, call the Son God from God, but the Father we simply call God, not from God. Thus it is clear that the Son has another from whom he is and whose Son he is, while the Father does not have a Son from whom he is, but only whose Father he is. Every son gets being what he is from his father, and is his father's son; while no father gets being what he is from his son, though he is his son's father.

3. There are then some statements of scripture about the Father and the Son which indicate their unity and equality of substance, like *I and the Father are one* (Jn 10:30), and *Since he was in the form of God he thought it no robbery to be equal to God* (Phil 2:6), and any other such. And there are others which mark the Son as the lesser because of the form of a servant, that is because of the created and changeable human substance he took, like *The Father is greater than I* (Jn 14:28), and *The Father does not judge anyone, but has given all judgment to the Son* (Jn 5:22), for as he goes on to explain shortly after, *He also gave him power to do judgment because he is the Son of man* (Jn 5:27). Lastly there are others which mark him neither as less nor as equal, but only intimate that he is from the Father, like *As the Father has life in himself, so he also gave the Son to have life in himself* (Jn 5:26), and *Neither can the Son do anything of*

himself except what he sees the Father doing (Jn 5:19). If we take the reason for his saying this to be that in the creaturely form he took the Son is less than the Father, it will follow that the Father must first have walked upon the water,[4] and with spittle and mud opened the eyes of another man born blind,[5] and done all the other things done by the Son when he appeared among men in the flesh, to enable the Son to do them too, who as he said could do nothing of himself except what he saw the Father doing. Surely nobody, even out of his wits, could have such an idea.

So the reason for these statements can only be that the life of the Son is unchanging like the Father's, and yet is from the Father; and that the work of Father and Son is indivisible, and yet the Son's working is from the Father just as he himself is from the Father; and the way in which the Son sees the Father is simply by being the Son. For him, being from the Father, that is being born of the Father, is not something different from seeing the Father; nor is seeing him working something different from his working equally; and the reason he does not work of himself is that he does not (so to put it) be of himself; and the reason he does what he sees the Father doing is that he is from the Father.[6] He does not do other things *likewise*, like a painter copying pictures he has seen painted by someone else; nor does he do *the same* things differently, like the body forming letters which the mind has thought; but *Whatever the Father does*, he says, *the same the Son also does likewise* (Jn 5:19). "The same," he said; and also, "likewise"; thus showing that the working of the Father and of the Son is equal and indivisible, and yet the Son's working comes from the Father. That is why the Son cannot do anything of himself except what he sees the Father doing.

This then is the rule which governs many scriptural texts, intended to show not that one person is less than the other, but only that one is from the other. Yet some people[7] have extracted from it the sense that the Son is less than the Father. And on the other hand those amongst our people who are not so learned or so well versed in these matters, and try to measure these texts by the form-of-a-servant rule, find it very upsetting when they fail to make proper sense of them.[8] To avoid this, we should apply this other rule, which tells us not that the Son is less than the Father, but that he is from the Father. This does not imply any dearth of equality, but only his birth in eternity.

4. So then, as I started to say, there are some things so put in the sacred books that it is uncertain which rule they are to be referred to; should it be to the Son's being less than the Father because of the creature he took, or to his being shown to be from the Father in his very equality with him? And if the uncertainty is such that it can never be resolved, then in my opinion there is no harm in taking the passage according to either rule. For example, *My teaching is not mine, but his who sent me* (Jn 7:16); it can be understood by the form-of-a-servant rule, which is how we treated it in the previous book; and also by the form-of-God rule, of his being equal to the Father and yet from the Father.[9] For just as in this form the Son is not one thing and his life another, but the Son simply is his life; so also the Son is not one thing and his teaching another, but the Son simply is

his teaching. Therefore, just as *He gave the Son life* (Jn 5:26) means nothing else than "He begot the Son who is his life"; so also, when it says "He gave the Son teaching," it can well mean "He begot the Son who is his teaching." And thus *My teaching is not mine but his who sent me* (Jn 7:16) may be reduced to "I am not from myself but from him who sent me."

5. Let us compare the case of the Holy Spirit, who is not of course said to have *emptied himself, taking the form of a servant* (Phil 2:7). But the Lord does say, *When he comes, the Spirit of truth, he will teach you all truth. For he will not speak from himself, but whatever he hears he will speak, and will tell you of the things that are to come. He will glorify me, because he will receive of mine and will tell it to you* (Jn 16:13). Now unless he had gone on immediately to say *All that the Father has is mine; that is why I said, he will receive of mine and will tell it to you* (Jn 16:14), we might perhaps have supposed that the Holy Spirit is born of Christ as he himself is of the Father. About himself he says *My teaching is not mine, but his who sent me* (Jn 7:16); and about the Holy Spirit, *He will not speak from himself, but whatever he hears he will speak*; and, *because he will receive of mine and will tell it to you* (Jn 16:13). But he gives his reason for saying, *He will receive of mine*; namely, *All that the Father has is mine; that is why I said he will receive of mine* (Jn 16:14). And so we are left to understand that the Holy Spirit has of the Father's just like the Son. How does he? In the way we mentioned above:[10] *When the advocate comes whom I will send you from the Father, the Spirit of truth who proceeds from the Father, he will bear testimony about me* (Jn 15:26). So it is as proceeding from the Father that he is said not to speak from himself. And just as the Son is not made less than the Father by his saying, *The Son cannot do anything of himself except what he sees the Father doing* (Jn 5:19) (this is not spoken in the form of a servant but in the form of God, as we have already shown, and so these words do not indicate that he is less than the Father but only that he is from him); so here it does not make the Holy Spirit less to say of him, *He will not speak from himself, but whatever he hears he will speak* (Jn 16:13). This is said in virtue of his proceeding from the Father. But why then, since both the Son is from the Father and the Holy Spirit proceeds from the Father, are they not both called sons, both begotten? Why is the one alone the only-begotten Son, and the Holy Spirit neither a son nor begotten—he would of course be a son if he were begotten? This is a question we must discuss elsewhere, if God grants and in the measure he grants.[11]

6. Meanwhile this is the moment for those people to wake up if they can, who have imagined that they are supported in proving the Father to be greater than the Son by the Son's saying, *Father, glorify me* (Jn 17:1.5). For here we have the Holy Spirit glorifying him; is he then too greater than the Son? But if the reason the Holy Spirit glorifies the Son is that he will receive of the Son's, and the reason he will receive of the Son's is that all that the Father has is the Son's, then it is clear that when the Holy Spirit glorifies the Son the Father also glorifies the Son. Thus we ascertain that all that the Father has is not only the Son's but also the Holy Spirit's, because the Holy Spirit is competent to glorify

the Son, who is glorified by the Father. In any case, if he who glorifies is greater than the one he glorifies, let them at least grant that those who glorify each other are equal. Now it is written that the Son also glorifies the Father; *I*, he says, *have glorified you on earth* (Jn 17:4). Clearly they must take care that the Holy Spirit does not turn out to be greater than both of them, as he glorifies the Son, who glorifies the Father,[12] and is not himself said to be glorified by either the Father or the Son.

Chapter 2

In which the author begins to discuss the significance of the missions, the sendings of the Son and of the Holy Spirit; first arguing that to talk of their being sent does not jeopardize their equality with the Father; then proposing a preliminary definition or description of mission as the visible manifestation in time of these two divine persons; finally pointing out the crucial difference between the permanent visible manifestation of the Son in the flesh, and the transient visible manifestation of the Spirit in the forms of a dove, a gust of wind, and tongues of fire. It must be borne in mind by the reader that this discussion of the missions is subordinated to the argument of the previous chapter, although only toward the end of Book IV will the author explicitly define the missions as revealing in time the eternal processions of the divine persons, thus formally including the language of mission under the rule he has elaborated in chapter 1, as language which shows that the Son is from the Father and the Holy Spirit is from the Father and the Son. The involvement of mission with visible manifestation raises a series of problems which have to be solved before that final definition can be achieved.

---

7. Refuted here, they turn to another axiom: "The one who sends is greater than the one sent." So the Father is greater than the Son, who is constantly presenting himself as sent by the Father; he is also greater than the Holy Spirit, of whom Jesus said, *whom the Father will send in my name* (Jn 14:26). And the Holy Spirit is less than either, since besides the Father sending him, as mentioned, the Son sends him too, saying as he does, *But if I go away I will send him to you* (Jn 16:7).

On this question the first thing I want to ask is where the Son was sent from and where to. *I went forth from the Father*, he says, *and came into this world* (Jn 16:28). So that is what being sent is, going forth from the Father and coming into this world. Then what about something else the same evangelist said of him: *He was in the world, and the world was made through him, and the world did not know him* (Jn 1:10)? Then he adds, *He came into his own* (Jn 1:11). Where he came to, of course, is where he was sent. But if he was sent into this world because he went forth from the Father and came into this world, and if he was already in this world, then where he was sent to is where he already was.

Take some words spoken by God in one of the prophets: *Heaven and earth do I fill* (Jer 23:24); if they are ascribed to the Son—and it is he, so a number of authors prefer to think,[13] who spoke to and through the prophets—then where he was sent to must have been where he already was. One who could say *Heaven and earth do I fill* must be everywhere. Or suppose if you like it was the Father speaking; is there anywhere he could be without his Word and his Wisdom, who *stretches mightily from end to end, and disposes all things properly* (Wis 8:1)? Nor for that matter could he be anywhere without his Spirit. If God is everywhere, his Spirit is everywhere too. So the Spirit also was sent to where he was already. There was a man who found nowhere he could go from the face of God, and who said, *If I climb up to heaven, you are there; if I climb down to hell, there you are* (Ps 139:8). Wishing thus to convey that God is present everywhere, he had begun by mentioning his Spirit; for he had just said, *Where shall I withdraw to from your Spirit, and where shall I flee from your face* (Ps 139:7)?

8. If then both Son and Holy Spirit are sent to where they already are, the question arises what can really be meant by this sending of the Son or of the Holy Spirit—the Father alone is nowhere said to have been sent. About the Son the apostle writes, *When the fullness of time had come God sent his Son, made of woman, made under law, to redeem those who were under law* (Gal 4:4). He sent his Son, made of a woman—by "woman" of course, as presumably every Catholic knows, he did not intend to suggest loss of virginity, but merely difference of sex according to the Hebrew idiom.[14] So then, by saying *God sent his Son, made of woman* he shows plainly enough that it was in being made of woman that the Son was sent. Thus inasmuch as he was born of God he already was in this world; in that he was born of Mary he was sent and came into this world.

Furthermore, he could not be sent by the Father without the Holy Spirit. On principle, when the Father sent him, that is made him of woman, he cannot be supposed to have done it without his Spirit. And in any case there is the clear testimony of the answer given to the virgin Mary when she asked the angel *How shall this happen? The Holy Spirit shall come upon you and the might of the Most High shall overshadow you* (Lk 1:34), and Matthew says *She was found to be with child of the Holy Spirit* (Mt 1:18). There is even a prophecy of Isaiah in which Christ himself is to be understood as saying about his future coming, *And now the Lord, and his Spirit, has sent me* (Is 48:16).

9. Someone may now perhaps constrain me to say that the Son was also sent by himself. For Mary's conceiving and childbearing is the work of the three, by whose creative act all things are created. How then, he wants to know, can the Father have sent him if he sent himself? I answer first by asking him to tell me, if he can, how the Father can have sanctified the Son if he sanctified himself. Both are affirmed by one and the same Lord: *Do you say of him*, he asks, *whom the Father sanctified and sent into the world, that he is blaspheming,[15] because I said I am God's Son* (Jn 10:36)? And elsewhere he says, *For them do I sanctify myself* (Jn 17:19). Again I ask him how the Father can have delivered him up if he delivered up himself. The apostle Paul says both: *Who did not spare his own Son*, he says, *but delivered him up for us all* (Rom 8:32); and elsewhere he says

of the savior, *who loved me and delivered himself up for me* (Gal 2:20). I trust our friend will answer me, if he has a just appreciation of these matters, that Father and Son have but one will and are indivisible in their working. Let him therefore understand the incarnation and the virgin birth in the same way, as indivisibly wrought by one and the same working of Father and Son, not leaving out, of course, the Holy Spirit, of whom it is said in so many words that *she was found to be with child of the Holy Spirit* (Mt 1:18).

What we are saying may perhaps be easier to sort out if we put the question this way, crude though it is: In what manner did God send his Son? Did he tell him to come, giving him an order he complied with by coming, or did he ask him to, or did he merely suggest it? Well, whichever way it was done, it was certainly done by word. But God's Word is his Son. So when the Father sent him by word, what happened was that he was sent by the Father and his Word. Hence it is by the Father and the Son that the Son was sent, because the Son is the Father's Word. Would anyone adopt so blasphemous an opinion as to suppose that it was by a word in time that the Father sent the eternal Son to appear in the course of time in the flesh? Though it is true that in the Word of God which was in the beginning with God and was God,[16] that is to say in the Wisdom of God, there was timelessly contained the time in which that Wisdom was to appear in the flesh. So while without any beginning of time *in the beginning was the Word and the Word was with God and the Word was God* (Jn 1:1), without any time there was in the Word the time at which the Word would become flesh and dwell among us (Jn 1:14). And when this *fullness of time came, God sent his Son made of woman* (Gal 4:4), that is made in time, in order that the Word might be shown to men incarnate; and the time at which this should happen was timelessly contained within the Word. The whole series of all times is timelessly contained in God's eternal Wisdom.[17]

Since then it was a work of the Father and the Son that the Son should appear in the flesh, the one who so appeared in the flesh is appropriately said to have been sent, and the one who did not to have done the sending. Thus events which are put on outwardly in the sight of our bodily eyes are aptly called *missa*[18] because they stem from the inner designs of our spiritual nature. Furthermore, that form of the man who was taken on is the person[19] or guise of the Son only, and not of the Father too. So it is that the invisible Father, together with the jointly invisible Son, is said to have sent this Son by making him visible. If the Son has been made visible in such a way that he ceased to be invisible with the Father, that is if the substance of the invisible Word, undergoing change and transition, had been turned into the visible creature, then we would have had to think of the Son simply as sent by the Father, and not also as sending with the Father. As it is, the form of a servant was so taken on that the form of God remained immutable, and thus it is plain that what was seen in the Son was the work of Father and Son who remain unseen; that is that the Son was sent to be visible by the invisible Father together with the invisible Son. Then why did he say, *And I did not come from myself* (Jn 8:42)? He said it according to the servant form; as also *I do not judge anyone* (Jn 8:15).

10. If the Son is said to have been sent in that he appeared outwardly in created bodily form while inwardly in uncreated spiritual form remaining always hidden from mortal eyes, then it is easy to understand how the Holy Spirit can also be said to have been sent. He was visibly displayed in a created guise which was made in time, either when he descended on our Lord himself *in bodily guise as a dove* (Mt 3:16), or when ten days after his ascension *there came suddenly from heaven on the day of Pentecost a sound as of a violent gust bearing down, and there appeared to them divided tongues as of fire, which also settled upon each one of them* (Acts 2:2). This action, visibly expressed and presented to mortal eyes, is called the sending of the Holy Spirit. Its object was not that his very substance might be seen, since he himself remains invisible and unchanging like the Father and the Son; but that outward sights might in this way stir the minds of men, and draw them on from the public manifestations of his coming in time to the still and hidden presence of his eternity sublime.

11. Nowhere though do we find it written that God the Father is greater than the Holy Spirit, or the Holy Spirit less than God the Father; and the reason is that a created form was not assumed by the Holy Spirit to appear under in the same way that the son of man was assumed by the Word of God as the form in which to present his person to the world. The son of man was not assumed simply in order to have the Word of God, like other saints and wise men only more so, *above his fellows* (Ps 45:8);[20] not in order to have a more ample share in the Word of God and so excel the rest in wisdom, but quite simply to be the Word of God. The Word in flesh is one thing, the Word being flesh another; which means the Word in a man is one thing, the Word being man another. "Flesh" of course stands for "man" in the phrase *the Word became flesh* (Jn 1:14), as in that other text, *All flesh*[21] *shall see the salvation of God* (Is 40:5; Lk 3:6); not soulless, mindless flesh, but "all flesh" in the sense of "all men and women."

Not thus, therefore, was a creature taken by the Holy Spirit to appear under, in the way that that flesh, that human form, was taken of the virgin Mary. The Spirit did not make the dove blessed, or the violent gust, or the fire; he did not join them to himself and his person to be held in an everlasting union. Nor on the other hand is the Spirit of a mutable and changing nature, so that instead of these manifestations being wrought out of created things, he should turn or change himself into this and that, as water turns into ice. But these phenomena appeared, as and when they were required to, *creation serving the creator* (Wis 16:24), and being changed and transmuted at the bidding of him who abides unchanging in himself, in order to signify and show him as it was proper for him to be signified and shown to mortal men.

It is true that that dove is called the Spirit, and that of that fire it is said *There appeared to them divided tongues as of fire, which also settled on each one of them, and they began to speak with tongues as the Spirit gave them utterance* (Acts 2:3). But this is to indicate that it is the Spirit who was manifested by that fire, as by that dove. Yet we cannot say of the Holy Spirit that he is God and dove, or God and fire, as we say of the Son that he is God and man. Nor even as we call the Son the lamb of God, with both John the Baptist saying *Behold the lamb of God* (Jn 1:29), and John the evangelist seeing the *lamb as it were slain*, in the Book of Revelation.[22] That prophetic vision was not exhibited to bodily eyes in bodily shapes, but was seen in spirit by means of psychic images of things. But whoever saw that dove or that fire saw them with their real eyes. Though admittedly the point could be argued about the fire, whether it was seen with the eyes or in spirit, because of the words used. It does not say "They saw divided tongues as of fire," but "There appeared to them divided tongues as of fire." We do not usually mean the same thing by "There appeared to me" as by "I saw." It is indeed normal to say both "There appeared to me" and "I saw" in the case of visions in spirit of bodily images; but in the case of things offered to our eyes in their definite bodily shape we usually say "I saw" and not "There appeared to me." So in the case of the fire of Pentecost there is room for doubt about how it was seen; whether inwardly in spirit, only seeming to be real, or really outwardly by the eyes of the head. The dove however is expressly said to have descended in bodily guise, and nobody ever doubted that it was seen with the eyes.

Nor again can we call the Spirit a dove or fire as we call the Son a rock, as it is written, *And the rock was Christ* (1 Cor 10:4). That rock already existed as a created thing, and it was by reason of some dramatic action that it symbolized Christ and was called by his name; like that stone which Jacob had for a pillow and which he turned into a symbol of Christ by anointing it;[23] like Isaac, who became Christ when he carried the wood for his own sacrifice.[24] All these already existed and were given significance by certain symbolic actions. They did not, like this dove and fire, come suddenly into existence just to signify these things. These two cases seem to me more like that flame which appeared to Moses in the bush,[25] or like the pillar of cloud and fire which the people followed in the desert,[26] or like the thunders and lightnings which occurred when the Law was given on the mountain.[27] All these physical phenomena only happened in order to signify something and then to pass away.

Chapter 3

In which the author broaches the problems raised by his preliminary definition of mission, in the last chapter, as the visible manifestation of the person sent; dividing them into three groups of questions: i) which, if any, of the divine persons in particular were manifested in each of the Old Testament theophanies—this he will deal with in the remainder of this book; ii) how the visible manifestations in those theophanies were managed, whether by the agency of angels or no—this will form the subject of Book III; and iii) whether we can properly talk of the sending of the Son and the Holy Spirit before their visible manifestations in the New Testament—this will be settled in Book IV. Before going on, in the next chapter, to discuss the first group of questions, he turns aside to demolish a basic assumption of much of the cruder "economic" theology, that the Son is the essentially visible member of the trinity, while the Father alone has immortality and dwells in light inaccessible, whom no man has seen or can see, and is alone the invisible, only God (1 Tm 6:15; 1:17).

12. The Holy Spirit too, therefore, is said to have been sent because of these bodily forms which sprang into being in time in order to signify him and show him in a manner suited to human senses. But he is not said to be less than the Father as the Son is on account of his servant form. That form was attached in inseparable union to his person, whereas these other physical manifestations appeared for a time in order to show what had to be shown and then afterward ceased to be.

Why, in that case, is the Father not said to have been sent in those other physical manifestations, the fire in the bush,[28] the pillar of cloud and fire,[29] the lightnings on the mountain,[30] and whatever else occurred when he spoke to the fathers, as we learn from the evidence of scripture? Why not, if he was being manifested by these modulations of creation, these bodily forms presented externally to the sight of men? Or if it was the Son who was being manifested by them, why is he only said to have been sent such a long time afterward, when he was made of a woman? The apostle says, *When the fullness of time had come, God sent his Son, made of woman* (Gal 4:4); yet he had been sent already long before, if he appeared to the fathers in those created forms. If on the other hand he cannot properly be said to have been sent until the Word became flesh, why is the Holy Spirit said to have been sent at all, since he has never been embodied in that sort of way? Finally, if those visible occurrences we are told of in the law and the prophets manifested neither Father nor Son, but the Holy Spirit, why is he too only said to have been sent now, having on this supposition already been sent in these various ways before?

13. The first thing to be done in sorting out this tangled question is to ascertain, with God's help, whether it was the Father or the Son or the Holy Spirit who appeared under these created forms to the fathers; or whether it was sometimes the Father, sometimes the Son, sometimes the Holy Spirit; or whether it was simply the one and only God, that is the trinity without any distinction of persons. Next, whatever firm or tentative conclusion emerges on this point, we

must ask whether the creatures by which God would manifest himself as he judged opportune to the sight of men were formed for this function alone; or whether angels already in existence were sent to speak in God's name and made themselves material *media* out of created material for use in their duties as each required; or even, according to the power bestowed on them by the creator, turned and changed their own bodies, which they dominate and are not dominated by,[31] into whatever shapes they chose as most aptly suited to their activities. Finally, we shall see what we have set out to ascertain, whether the Son and the Holy Spirit were also being sent of old, and if they were, how such sending differed from the one we read of in the gospel; or whether neither of them was sent until the Son was made of the virgin Mary[32] and the Holy Spirit appeared in the visible shape of a dove and tongues of fire.

14. Let us pass over those people who have entertained excessively materialistic ideas about the nature of God's Word and Wisdom, which *abiding in itself renews all things* (Wis 7:27), which we call the only Son of God; they think of him as being not merely changeable but visible as well. With more effrontery than piety they have brought much crudeness of mind to bear on divine things. Even the human soul, a spiritual substance, something made and made through none other than him *through whom all things were made and without whom was made nothing* (Jn 1:3), though changeable is not also visible. Yet these people have thought this about the very Word and Wisdom of God, through whom the soul was made; whereas this divine Wisdom is not only invisible, which the soul is too, but unchangeable which the soul is not. This unchangeableness of Wisdom is rehearsed by the text, *Abiding in herself she renews all things* (Wis 7:27).

And yet they even try to prop up their tumble-down delusions by scriptural evidence, and quote the apostle Paul's authority; what he says of the one and only God, by which the triad is to be understood, they take as referring to the Father alone, and not also to the Son and Holy Spirit. He says, *To the king of ages, the immortal, invisible, only God, be honor and glory for ever and ever* (1 Tm 1:17), and again, *The blessed and only mighty one, king of kings and lord of lords, who alone has immortality and dwells in light inaccessible, whom no man has seen or can see* (1 Tm 6:15). I think I have already sufficiently discussed the interpretation of these texts.[33]

15. But those who prefer to take them as applying only to the Father and not to the Son and Holy Spirit say that the Son is visible not merely in the flesh which he took of the virgin, but even before that in himself. For it is he, they say, who showed himself visibly to the fathers. In that case, suppose you answer them, just as the Son is visible in himself, so he must also be mortal in himself, to suit your view of the text, which you maintain applies only to the Father, *who alone has immortality* (1 Tm 6:16). Or if you agree that what made the Son mortal was the flesh he took, then you must allow that was also what made him visible. They answer that they do not say that was what made him mortal; that in their view he was previously mortal just as he was previously visible. They have to do this, of course, because if they say it is the flesh he became which

made the Son mortal, then it is no longer the Father without the Son who alone has immortality; his Word too, *through whom all things were made* (Jn 1:3), will have immortality. Nor could it be said that he lost his immortality by taking on mortal flesh, because no such thing can happen even to the human soul to make it die with the body, given what the Lord himself says, *Do not fear those who kill the body, but cannot kill the soul* (Mt 10:28).

Nor, of course, did the Holy Spirit take flesh; and if the Son were mortal because of the flesh he took, the case of the Holy Spirit would certainly pose them a big problem in their insistence that it is the Father alone, without the Son and without the Spirit, who has immortality. But the Holy Spirit did not take flesh; so if he does not have immortality, then it is not because of the flesh he took that the Son is mortal. If on the other hand the Spirit does have immortality, then it is not said of the Father alone that he has immortality.[34]

For these reasons they think they can argue that the Son was mortal in himself even before the incarnation, because mere changeableness may be called, not improperly, mortality. It is after all in terms of this that we talk of the soul dying—by which we do not mean that it ceases to be itself by turning into body or some other substance. Anything that retaining its own identity is now different from what it was, is thereby shown up as being mortal to the extent that it has ceased to be what it was. And so, they say, because the Son of God appeared to our fathers even before he was born of the virgin Mary, and not in one constant guise either, but in many different forms, it follows both that he is visible in himself, because his substance was apparent to mortal eyes even before he took flesh; and that he is mortal insofar as he is changeable. So too with the Holy Spirit, who appeared now as a dove, now as fire. Therefore, they continue, it is not the three but solely and properly the Father to whom the text applies: *To the immortal, invisible, and only God* (1 Tm 1:17); and, *Who alone has immortality, and dwells in light inaccessible, whom no human being has seen or can see* (1 Tm 6:16).

16. So we leave these people on one side, people who have not even been able to conceive that the substance of the soul is invisible, and therefore are miles away from forming even the remotest idea that the substance of the one and only God, that is of the Father and of the Son and of the Holy Spirit, remains not only invisible but also unchangeable, and therefore abides in true and genuine immortality. As for us, we say that God has never shown himself to bodily eyes, neither the Father nor the Son nor the Holy Spirit, except through some created bodily substance at the service of his power. Let us then go on to investigate, in the peace of the Catholic faith, with peaceable persistence, ready to be put right by well-founded brotherly correction, ready even to be chewed up by an enemy provided what he says is true; let us go on to investigate whether God appeared to our fathers without distinction of persons before the Christ came in the flesh, or whether just one of the persons of the triad appeared, or whether all three appeared, if one may so put it, in turn.

Chapter 4

The author investigates the theophanies in which God appeared to Adam and to Abraham.

17. Let us begin then with the incident described in Genesis of God talking to the man he had made from the clay. If we leave aside the story's symbolic meaning and take it literally as a trustworthy account of events, it seems that God then talked to man in the guise of a man. The book does not indeed say so in so many words, but the details of the passage imply it, especially the bit about Adam hearing the voice of God as he was taking a walk round paradise in the evening, and hiding himself in the middle of the wood in paradise, and then when God says *Adam, where are you?* answering *I heard your voice and hid myself from your face, because I am naked* (Gn 3:9). How we can give a literal meaning to such walking and talking by God I cannot see, unless he appeared in human form.[35] It cannot be maintained that only a voice effect was produced from the place God was said to be walking in, or that he who was walking there was invisible, because Adam also says he hid from God's face. Who was it, then? Was it the Father or the Son or the Holy Spirit, or just God the three without distinction, that was talking to man in the guise of man?

It is true that the scripture narrative nowhere passes noticeably from person to person; the one who speaks to the first man appears to be the same as the one who had said *Let there be light*, and *Let there be a firmament* (Gn 1:3.6), and the other things on each of those days of creation. And we usually take this to be God the Father, saying let there be whatever he wished to make. For he made all things through his Word, and we know by the right rule of faith that his Word is his only Son. So if it was the Father who talked to the first man, and who used to walk about paradise of an evening; and if it was his face the sinner hid from in the middle of the wood in paradise; why should we not take it to be the Father who appeared to Abraham and Moses, and indeed to anyone he liked in any way he liked, by means of some changeable and visible creature under his control, while in himself and in his own changeless substance he remained invisible?[36]

But of course it could be that scripture passes imperceptibility from person to person, and that while it describes how the Father said *Let there be light* (Gn 1:3), and all the other things he is mentioned as making through his Word, it goes on to show us the Son speaking to the first man, not saying so explicitly, but hinting at it for those who are sharp enough to understand.

18. So if anyone is of sufficient intellectual caliber to get to the bottom of this mystery and tell for certain, either that the Father too can appear visibly to human eyes by means of some created thing, or that only the Son and the Holy Spirit can do so, let him go on studying the matter, and even publish the results. But in my opinion, at least as regards the scriptural evidence in this episode of God's speaking to man, the matter remains obscure. For one thing, it is not at all obvious whether Adam normally did see God with his physical eyes, as long

as the question remains unsettled what sort of eyes those were which were opened for them when they tasted the forbidden fruit, because before they tasted it those eyes remained shut.

In fact, I was almost too rash in affirming a little while ago that if scripture presents paradise as a physical locality, then God cannot have walked about in it except in some bodily form. After all, you could say that only sounds were produced for the man to hear, without his seeing any form. Again, just because it says *Adam hid himself from God's face* (Gn 3:8), it does not follow necessarily that as a rule he used to see his face. Suppose he himself could not see but was frightened of being seen by him whose voice he had heard and whose presence he had sensed as he walked about? After all Cain too said to God *I hid from your face* (Gn 4:14). But that does not oblige us to admit that he normally saw God's face with his physical eyes in some sort of bodily form, though he did hear his voice talking to him and interrogating him about his crime.

Again, it is not easy to decide by what sort of speech God used to make himself heard in those times by men's physical ears, particularly when he spoke to the first men; however, we are not concerned with that point in this discussion. But if voices and sounds alone were produced to make God's presence known to the senses of those first men, then I cannot see why I should not take this to be a manifestation of the person of God the Father. After all, it is his person which was manifested by the voice at the transfiguration of Jesus on the mountain in the presence of the three disciples;[37] and by the voice at his baptism when the dove came down upon him;[38] and by the voice which answered him, when he cried out to the Father about his glorification, *I have glorified and will glorify again* (Jn 12:28). Not that the voice could be produced without the activity of Son and Holy Spirit (the triad works inseparably); but it was produced to manifest the person of the Father alone, just as the three produced that human being of the virgin Mary and yet it is the person of the Son alone—the invisible three producing what is the visible person of the Son alone.[39]

However there is nothing in this text to prevent us from taking those voices which Adam heard as not only being produced by the three, but also as manifesting the person of the same three. In the other cases, where the voice says *This is my beloved Son* (Mt 3:17; 17:5), we are obliged to take it as being only the Father's, since neither faith nor reason allow us to suppose that Jesus is the son of the Holy Spirit or of himself. And where the voice resounded *I have glorified and will glorify again* (Jn 12:28), we also recognize only the Father's person; for it is in answer to our Lord's words, *Father, glorify your Son* (Jn 12:28),[40] which could only have been addressed to God the Father and not to the Holy Spirit as well, because he is[41] not his Son. But here the text runs, *The Lord God said to Adam* (Gn 3:9), and no reason can be given from the context against understanding this of the trinity.

19. The same holds good for the passage *And the Lord said to Abraham, Come away from your country and your kindred and your father's house* (Gn 12:1). It is not clear whether Abraham only heard a voice in his ears, or whether something also appeared before his eyes. A little further on, however, it says

rather more plainly, *And the Lord appeared to Abraham and said to him, To your seed will I give this land* (Gn 12:7). But even here it is not stated in what guise the Lord appeared to him, or whether the Father or the Son or the Holy Spirit appeared to him. Our friends may of course think it must have been the Son, because the text does not say "God appeared to him," but "The Lord appeared to him"; and Lord would seem to be a name proper to the Son, on the evidence of the apostle: *For even if there are those called gods in heaven or on earth, as indeed there are many gods and many lords; yet for us there is but one God, the Father, from whom are all things and we in him; and one Lord, Jesus Christ, through whom are all things and we through him* (1 Cor 8:5).[42] But God the Father is also unmistakably called Lord in many places—for example, *The Lord said to me, My son are you, I today have begotten you* (Ps 2:7), and *Said the Lord to my Lord, Sit at my right hand* (Ps 110:1). Indeed, so is the Holy Spirit unmistakably called Lord—where the apostle says, *And the Spirit is Lord* (2 Cor 3:17);[43] and in case anyone should consider that he means the Son, and is calling him spirit because of his immaterial substance, he goes on to add, *Where the Lord's Spirit is, there freedom is too* (2 Cor 3:17). And no one can doubt that the Lord's Spirit is the Holy Spirit. So then, in the passage we are discussing there is nothing to show whether one person of the three appeared to Abraham, or whether it was God the three, of which one God it is said elsewhere, *You shall worship the Lord your God, and him alone shall you serve* (Dt 6:13).

On another occasion, under the oak of Mambre, Abraham saw three men, whom he invited in and entertained to a meal. Scripture however does not begin the description of the episode by saying "Three men appeared to him," but by saying *The Lord appeared to him* (Gn 18:1). Then it proceeds to describe how the Lord appeared to him by introducing the story of the three men, whom Abraham invited in and entertained in the plural, but went on to speak to as one, in the singular; and he is also given a promise about a son for Sarah as by one, whom scripture calls the Lord, just as it says at the beginning of the story, *The Lord appeared to Abraham.* So he invites them in and washes their feet, and sets them on their way again as men; but he talks to them as the Lord God, both on being promised a son and on being informed about the imminent destruction of Sodom.

20. This passage of scripture calls for much more than a quick passing glance. If only one man, you see, had appeared to Abraham, the people who maintain that the Son was visible in his own proper substance even before he was born of the virgin would surely have been very quick to claim that this was he. Only the Father, they say, is referred to by the words *To the invisible and only God* (1 Tm 1:17). Yet even in this case I could still ask them how they would account for his *being found in the condition of a man* (Phil 2:7)—having his feet washed, sitting down to human victuals—before he took flesh. How could all this happen while he was still in the form of God, *not thinking it robbery to be equal to God* (Phil 2:6)? Surely he had not already *emptied himself, taking the form of a servant, made in the likeness of men and found in the condition of a man* (Phil 2:7)? We know, after all, that he did this by being born of the virgin. So how

could he appear to Abraham as one man before he had done this? Or was that apparition not a true human form perhaps? I could still ask them all these awkward questions even if only one man had appeared to Abraham, and he was too readily believed to be the Son of God. But in fact three men appeared to him, and none of them is said to have been superior to the others in stature or age or authority. So why may we not take the episode as a visible intimation by means of visible creations of the equality of the triad, and of the single identity of substance in the three persons?

21. Nor can you legitimately answer that one of the three is implicitly shown to be superior and is to be taken to be the Lord the Son of God while the other two are his angels, because Abraham only addresses one man as Lord while he sees three. Holy scripture took care to meet any future objection or view of this sort by providing evidence in contradiction of it, when it went on shortly afterward to describe how two angels came to Lot, and how that just man, found worthy to be delivered from the burning of Sodom, also addressed in them the one Lord. This is how it continues: *The Lord departed after he stopped speaking to Abraham, and Abraham returned to his own place. But the two angels came to Sodom in the evening* (Gn 18:33).

Here we must keep carefully in mind what it is I have undertaken to demonstrate; it is that Abraham was talking to three, and called him Lord in the singular. But perhaps, you say, he recognized one of the three as the Lord, and the other two as his angels. Then what does the scripture mean when it goes on to say, *The Lord departed after he stopped talking to Abraham, and Abraham returned to his own place; but the two angels came to Sodom in the evening* (Gn 18:33)? Perhaps one of them, who had been recognized as the Lord, departed— is that it?—and sent on the two angels he had with him to destroy Sodom. Well, let us see what follows: *The two angels came to Sodom in the evening. And when Lot saw them, he rose to greet them, and worshiped with his face to the ground, and said, Come, my lords, turn in to the house of your servant* (Gn 19:1). Here it is plain that there were two angels, that he offered them, in the plural, hospitality, and that he called them lords out of respect, taking them perhaps for men.

22. There is the point, though, that Lot would not have worshiped with his face to the ground if he had not recognized them as angels of God. So why does he offer them board and lodging as though they were in need of such human treatment?

But whatever hidden meaning there may be in this point let us carry on with what we have undertaken. Two appear, they are both called angels, they are invited in the plural to stay, he talks to them as two in the plural until they all leave Sodom. Then the scripture continues: *And it came to pass after they had led them out they said, Saving save your life; do not look back nor halt in all this region; go to the mountain, and there you will be safe, in case perhaps you are caught. But Lot said to them, Pray, Lord, since your servant has found favor before you*, etc. (Gn 19:17). How do you explain his saying *Pray, Lord*, if the one who was the Lord and who had sent the angels on had already departed?

Why *Pray, Lord* in that case, and not "Pray, lords"? Or if he only meant to address one of them, why does scripture say, *But Lot said to them, Pray, Lord, since your servant has found favor before you*? This time also, then, may we not understand two persons to be signified by the plural number, and the one Lord God of one substance by the fact of treating the same two as one? But in that case, which two persons are we to understand here—the Father and the Son, or the Father and the Holy Spirit, or the Son and the Holy Spirit? Perhaps the last pair I mentioned fits the case best; for the two angels said that they had been sent, and we say the same about the Son and the Holy Spirit. But nowhere in the scriptures do we find the Father being sent.[44]

Chapter 5

The various theophanies of Exodus are investigated.

---

23. When Moses received his mission to the people of Israel to lead them out of Egypt, this is how the text describes the way the Lord appeared to him: *He was feeding the sheep of Jethro his father-in-law, the priest of Midian, and he drove the sheep into the desert and came to the mountain of God, Horeb. Now the angel of the Lord appeared to him in a flame of fire from the bush. And he saw that the fire was burning in the bush, yet the bush was not being burnt up. And Moses said, I will go and look at this great sight I have seen, that the bush is not being burnt up. So when the Lord saw him coming to look, the Lord called to him from the bush and said, I am the God of your father, the God of Abraham and the God of Isaac and the God of Jacob* (Ex 3:1). In this case too he is first called the angel of the Lord and is then called God. This does not mean surely that an angel is the God of Abraham and the God of Isaac and the God of Jacob. Therefore we can be justified in taking it to be the savior himself, of whom the apostle says, *Theirs are the fathers, and of them is the Christ according to the flesh, who is God over all things blessed for ever* (Rom 9:5). So he who is God over all things blessed for ever may not unreasonably be understood here in the God of Abraham and the God of Isaac and the God of Jacob.

But why was he first called the angel of the Lord when he appeared in a flame of fire from the bush? Is it because he was in fact one of the multitude of the angels, but by a special arrangement was playing the part of the Lord? Or had some created thing been requisitioned to appear visibly for the business of the moment, and to produce audible voices which would convey the presence of the Lord by creature control as needed, even to a man's physical senses? If it was one of the angels, how can anyone easily tell whether the task imposed on him was to represent the person of the Son, or of the Holy Spirit, or of God the Father, or simply of the trinity itself who is the one and only God, in saying, *I am the God of Abraham and the God of Isaac and the God of Jacob*? We cannot possibly say that the God of Abraham and the God of Isaac and the God of Jacob is the Son of God but is not the Father. Nor will anyone dare to deny that the God of Abraham and the God of Isaac and the God of Jacob is the Holy Spirit, or the very trinity which we believe and recognize to be the one God. Only he qualifies to be not the God of those fathers who is not God. So then, if it is not only the Father who is God, as all heretics allow, but the Son too, which they must confess willy-nilly when the apostle says of him, *who is God over all things blessed for ever* (Rom 9:5); and the Holy Spirit as well, with the apostle saying, *Glorify God in your bodies* (1 Cor 6:20), having just previously said, *Do you not know that the temple among you of the Holy Spirit whom you have from God is your own bodies* (1 Cor 6:19)? And if these three are one God, according to the faith of Catholic sanity, then it does not clearly emerge which person that angel was playing the part of, if it was one of the angels, nor whether it was any of the persons in particular or the person of the trinity itself.

If on the other hand a created thing was requisitioned for use in this particular affair, which was to be seen by human eyes and heard by human ears and to be called the angel of the Lord, and the Lord, and God; then we cannot discern God the Father here, but only the Son or the Holy Spirit.[45] I cannot indeed think of any place where the Holy Spirit is actually called an angel, but he can be reckoned to be one from his activity; it is written of him that *He will announce to you the things that are to come* (Jn 16:13), and of course "angel" is only a Greek word meaning in English "announcer" or "messenger." But we find the Lord Jesus Christ being quite unmistakably called *angel of great counsel* by the prophet (Is 9:6, Septuagint). In themselves, of course, both the Holy Spirit and the Son of God are each God and the Lord of angels.

24. Again, it is said of the departure of the children of Israel from Egypt: *But God went before them by day in a pillar of cloud and showed them the way, and by night in a pillar of fire; and the pillar of cloud did not fail by day, nor the pillar of fire by night before the people* (Ex 13:21). No one will doubt, surely, that in this case God did not appear to mortal eyes in his own substance, but by creature control, and a physical creature at that. But whether it was the Father, the Son, the Holy Spirit, or the triad which is one God who thus appeared is not clear. Nor, as far as I can see, is any distinction of this sort made where it says, *And the majesty of the Lord appeared in the cloud, and the Lord spoke to Moses saying, I have heard the complaining of the children of Israel* (Ex 16:10).

25. But now what about the clouds and voices and lightnings, and the trumpet and the smoke of Mount Sinai, of which it says, *Sinai mountain was smoking all over, because God had come down upon it in fire, and smoke was rising from it like the smoke from a furnace, and the whole people was utterly bewildered; and there were trumpet blasts going on and on very loudly. Moses would speak, and God would answer him with a voice* (Ex 19:18). And a little further on, after the law had been given in the ten commandments, it says, *And all the people could see the voices and the flares and the trumpet blasts and the mountain smoking* (Ex 20:18). And a little further on still, *The whole people was standing far off, but Moses went into the mist where God was; and the Lord said to Moses* etc. (Ex 20:21). What is there to be said here, except that surely no one is crazy

enough to say that smoke, fire, clouds, mist and so forth are the very substance of the Word and Wisdom of God which is Christ, or of the Holy Spirit? As for God the Father, not even the Arians ever dared to say such a thing. So all these occurrences consisted of created things serving the creator and impressing themselves on the senses of men as the divine arrangements required. Unless of course the materialistic mind decides that because it says *Moses went into the mist where God was*, the mist was seen by the people, whereas inside the mist Moses saw the Son of God with his physical eyes, the Son who is to be seen, so raving heretics would have us believe, in his own substance. Sure, Moses saw him with his physical eyes if physical eyes can see not only the Wisdom of God which is Christ, but even that of any man however wise; sure, it says about the elders of Israel that *they saw the place where the God of Israel had stood*,[46] and that *under his feet there was a kind of work like sapphire stone, and like the appearance of the vault of heaven* (Ex 24:10); and so we must believe, I suppose, that the Word and Wisdom of God stood in a small space of earth—that Wisdom *who reaches from end to end mightily and disposes all things sweetly* (Wis 8:1); and that the Word of God *through whom all things were made* (Jn 1:3) is so changeable that it contracts and expands. May the Lord clear away such thoughts from the minds of his faithful!

No, as we have said often enough, it was by creature control that all these visible and perceptible exhibitions were staged, in order to represent the invisible and intelligible[47] God—not only the Father, but the Son too and the Holy Spirit, *from whom and through whom and in whom are all things* (Rom 11:36) although *the invisible things of God may be intelligibly perceived from the world's creation through the things that are made, as also his eternal might and divinity* (Rom 1:20).

26. But as far as our present discussion is concerned, Mount Sinai is yet another case in which I do not see how we can tell, in all those awful manifestations which struck the senses of mortal men, whether it was specifically God the three, or the Father, or the Son, or the Holy Spirit who was speaking. However, if one may be permitted a modest and hesitant conjecture, without asserting anything rashly, if one of the persons of the three can be discerned in these manifestations, why should we not give the preference to the Holy Spirit, seeing that the law which was given on this occasion is stated to have been inscribed on the stone tablets by the finger of God,[48] and we know that the Holy Spirit is indicated by this name in the gospel.[49] Furthermore, fifty days are reckoned from the slaying of the lamb and the celebration of the passover to the day on which these events on Mount Sinai began,[50] just as fifty days are reckoned after the Lord's passion from his resurrection to the coming of the Holy Spirit promised by the Son of God. And when he came, as we read in the Acts of the Apostles, he appeared in divided tongues of fire *which also settled on each one of them* (Acts 2:1). This corresponds to Exodus, where *Sinai mountain was smoking all over, because God had come down upon it in fire* (Ex 19:18), and a little later, *the appearance of the majesty of the Lord was like fire burning on the top of the mountain in the presence of the children of Israel* (Ex 24:17).

On the other hand, these things may only mean that neither the Father's presence nor the Son's could be indicated here in this fashion without the Holy Spirit, by whom the law was to be written. In that case we certainly know that it was God who was manifested under the guise of these created things—not of course in his own substance which remains invisible and changeless; but as far as I can grasp it, we do not discern any one person of the three by any sign or mark that is proper to him.

27. There is another place which shakes many people, where it says, *And the Lord spoke to Moses face to face, as a man speaks to his friend* (Ex 33:11), and yet a little further on this same Moses says, *If I have found favor before you, show yourself to me openly, that I may see you; that I may be one who has found favor before you, and that I may know that this nation is your people* (Ex 33:13); and again a little later, *And Moses said to the Lord, Show me your majesty* (Ex 33:18). How then, please, are we to suppose that in all that had happened up till now God appeared in his own substance, which is why these wretched people believe the Son of God is not just visible by means of created things but in himself; and that Moses went into the mist, so it seems, in order that while the people's eyes were shown only fog and mist he himself might hear God's words within as he gazed upon his face; and that, as it says, *the Lord spoke to Moses face to face, as a man speaks to his friend* (Ex 33:11), and yet here he is, saying *If I have found favor in your sight,*[51] *show yourself to me openly* (Ex 33:13).

Surely the answer is that he knew what he had seen was only physical, and he was demanding a true spiritual vision of God. Certainly, the words that those voices had conveyed to him had been arranged to sound like friend talking to friend. But who ever saw God the Father with his physical eyes? And who ever saw with his physical eyes the Word that *was in the beginning, and the Word was with God, and the Word was God and through it all things were made* (Jn 1:1)? And who ever saw *the Spirit of wisdom* (Is 11:2; Wis 7:7) with his physical eyes? On the other hand, what does *Show yourself to me openly that I may see you* (Ex 33:13) mean, if not "Show me your substance"? If Moses had not said this, then somehow or other we would have had to tolerate the fools who think that God's substance had been set visibly before his eyes in all that had happened previously. But as this place demonstrates in the clearest possible way, this favor was not granted to him, however much he longed for it.[52] How can anyone then presume to say that by such visible forms as appeared to Moses it is not some creation serving God's purposes, but what God is in himself, that has appeared to any mortal eyes?

Chapter 6

The special manifestation of God vouchsafed to Moses on Mount Sinai is discussed; it is treated allegorically, or at least typologically, because of the difficulty the author feels of giving any other interpretation to the concept of God having a face and a back.

28. Coming now to what the Lord goes on to say to Moses: *You cannot see my face and live, for a man shall not see my face and live. And the Lord said Behold, there is a place beside me, and you shall stand upon the rock the moment my majesty passes, and I will set you at a look-out*[53] *in the rock, and I will cover you with my hand until I have passed, and I will take away my hand, and then you shall see my back; for my face shall not appear to you* (Ex 33:20). This is usually understood, not inappropriately, to prefigure the person of our Lord Jesus Christ, taking his "back" to mean his flesh, in which he was born of the virgin, died and rose again. This flesh or human nature of his can suitably be called his back, either because it is mortal and so comes after, at the back of his immortal divine nature, or because he took it almost at the end, the back end, of this age or aeon. His face then is that form of God in which he *did not think it robbery to be equal to God* the Father (Phil 2:6), and which of course no man can see and live. And one reason why no man can see it and live is perhaps that we shall see him, as the apostle says, *face to face* only after this life (1 Cor 13:12), in which *we are away from the Lord* (2 Cor 5:6); and in which *the corruptible body weighs down the soul* (Wis 9:15); this life which is referred to in the psalm texts, *Yet utter vanity is every man living* (Ps 39:6), and, *For in your presence shall no man living be justified* (Ps 143:2); this life in which according to John *it has not yet appeared what we shall be. We know,* he adds, *that when he appears we shall be like him, because we shall see him as he is* (1 Jn 3:2); and he means, of course, that this will happen after this life, when we have paid the debt of death and received the promised gift of resurrection.

Or another reason why man cannot see his face and live may be that even now in this life, to the extent that we perceive in a spiritual way the Wisdom of God *through which all things were made* (Jn 1:3), we die to fleshly, materialistic attachments; and reckoning this world to be dead to us we ourselves die to this world and say what the apostle said, *The world has been crucified to me and I to the world* (Gal 6:14). Of this sort of death he says elsewhere, *But if you are dead with Christ, why do you lay down laws as though you were still living on*[54] *this world* (Col 2:20)? In either case, therefore, there is good reason why no man can see the face, that is the open manifestation, of God's Wisdom and live.

This is the sight which everyone yearns to behold who aims to *love God with all his heart and with all his soul and with all his mind* (Mt 22:37); and as far as possible he also builds up his neighbor by encouragement and good example to behold it, since he *loves his neighbor as himself; the two commandments on which the whole law depends and the prophets* (Mt 22:39). They are illustrated in this very case of Moses; after his love of God, with which above all else he was on fire, had prompted him to say, *If I have found favor in your sight, show yourself to me openly, that I may be one who has found favor before you,* he immediately added for love of his neighbor too, *and that I may know that this nation is your people* (Ex 33:13). This then is the sight which ravishes every rational soul with desire for it, and of which the soul is the more ardent in its desire the purer it is; and it is the purer the more it rises again to the things of the spirit; and it rises the more to the things of the spirit, the more it dies to the material things of the flesh. But while *we are away from the Lord and walking by faith and not by sight* (2 Cor 5:6), we have to behold Christ's back, that is his flesh, by this same faith; standing that is upon the solid foundation of faith, which is represented by the rock, and gazing at his flesh from the security of the lookout on the rock, namely the Catholic church, of which it is said, *And upon this rock I will build my church* (Mt 16:18). All the surer is our love for the face of Christ which we long to see, the more clearly we recognize in his back[55] how much Christ first loved us.

29. But as regards this flesh of his, it is faith in its resurrection that saves and justifies. *If you believe in your hearts,* it says, *that God raised him from the dead, you will be saved* (Rom 10:9); and again, *Who delivered himself up for our transgressions and rose again for our justification* (Rom 4:25). So it is the resurrection of the Lord's body that gives value to our faith. Even his enemies believe that that body died on the cross of pain, but they do not believe that it rose again. We however believe it absolutely, observing it so to say from the firmness of the rock, from where *we await our adoption, the redemption of our bodies,* in the certainty of hope (Rom 8:23). For we look forward in hope to the realization in Christ's members, which is what we are, of what right-minded faith assures us has already been achieved in him as our head. So this is why he does not wish his back to be seen until he has passed—he wants us to believe in the resurrection of his flesh. Pasch (Easter) is a Hebrew word meaning passage or passing, and so John the evangelist can say, *Before the feast day of the Pasch, Jesus knowing that his hour had come for him to pass from this world to the Father . . .* (Jn 13:1).

30. However, there are people who though they believe this, do not believe it in the Catholic church, but in some schismatical or heretical body; they do not see the Lord's back from a place there is beside him. What after all does it mean, the Lord's saying *There is a place beside me, and you shall stand upon the rock* (Ex 33:21)? Can there really be any terrestrial place beside the Lord, unless we regard that as being beside the Lord which borders upon him in a spiritual way? Or rather, can there be any place which is not beside the Lord, who himself *reaches from end to end mightily, and disposes all things sweetly* (Wis 8:1); of whom it is said that *the sky is his throne and the earth his footstool* (Is 66:1); and who could say himself, *What is the house you would build me, and what is the place of my rest* (Is 66:1)? But evidently the place beside him where one may stand on the rock is to be understood as the Catholic church, from where the man who believes in his resurrection may safely look upon the pasch of the

Lord, that is the passing of the Lord, and upon his back, that is his body, to his own good.

And you shall stand, it says, *upon the rock the moment my majesty passes* (Ex 33:21). And in very truth, the moment the majesty of the Lord passed, in the glory of the Lord's resurrection and ascension to the Father, we were firmly established upon the rock. It was then that Peter himself was firmly established, so that he could boldly preach Christ whom he had timorously thrice denied before he was firmly established. He had already, indeed, been placed by the divine predestination in the lookout of the rock, but the hand of the Lord was still covering him to prevent him from seeing. For he was going to see his back, and he had not yet passed, from death of course to life; he had not yet been glorified by rising from the dead.

31. As for the way the Exodus narrative proceeds: *I will cover you with my hand until I pass; and I will take away my hand, and then you shall see my back* (Ex 33:22); many Israelites, represented by Moses, believed in the Lord after his resurrection, as it were seeing his back after he had removed his hand from their eyes. That their eyes had previously been covered the evangelist declares by quoting the prophecy of Isaiah: *Make fat the heart of this people and block their ears and weigh down their eyes* (Mt 13:15; Is 6:10). And it is not too far-fetched to understand the psalmist as saying in their name, *Day and night your hand weighed heavy upon me* (Ps 32:4). By day, perhaps, when he did many open miracles, and yet was not acknowledged by them; by night, when he suffered and died and they thought for certain he was eliminated, liquidated like any other man. But when he had passed so that his back could be seen, and Peter preached to them that *the Christ had to suffer* and rise again (Lk 24:26), *they were pricked to the heart* with sorrow and repentance (Acts 2:37), and being baptized they verified the first verse of the psalm, *Blessed are they whose iniquities are forgiven and whose sins are covered* (Ps 32:1). And so whereas he had previously said *Your hand weighed heavy upon me* (Ps 32:4), now it is as though the Lord passes and takes away his hand so that his back can be seen, and thus we hear the repentant tones of one confessing and receiving the forgiveness of sins through faith in the resurrection of Christ: *I turned*, he says, *in my misery when a thorn was stuck in.*[56] *I recognized my sin, I did not cover up my injustice. I said, I will publish my injustice to the Lord against myself; and you have forgiven the wickedness of my heart* (Ps 32:4).

But however all this may be, some such interpretation of the story about Moses is required;[57] for we must not allow ourselves to be so befogged by literal-minded materialism that we imagine the Lord's face to be invisible and his back visible. Both of course were visible in the form of a servant; in the form of God—away with the possibility of such thoughts! Away with the idea that the Word of God and the Wisdom of God has a face on one side and a back on the other, like the human body, or that it undergoes any local movement or periodic change in appearance whatever!

Chapter 7

The author sums up the results of his investigation of the first of the three questions posed in chapter 3 of this book, noting also the bearing on the question of the vision in Daniel of the Ancient of Days and the Son of man.

32. To sum up, then: perhaps it was the Lord Jesus Christ who was being manifested in these voices of Exodus and all those other physical manifestations; or perhaps it was sometimes Christ, as we have reason to believe in the case of the narrative we have just been discussing, and sometimes the Holy Spirit, as we were led to suggest earlier on. But in either case this does not mean that God the Father never appeared to the fathers in this sort of guise. In those days there were many such manifestations, and though neither Father, Son, nor Holy Spirit was either named or unmistakably indicated in them, they still contained enough likely hints and probabilities to make it impossible without rashness to say that God the Father never appeared to the patriarchs or prophets under visible forms. This opinion stems from those people who could not recognize the unity of the triad in the words *To the king of ages, immortal, invisible and only God* (1 Tm 1:7), and *Whom no man has seen or can see* (1 Tm 6:16). But right-minded faith understands these words of the supreme and supremely divine and changeless substance in which the one and only God is both Father and Son and Holy Spirit. All these visions, however, were produced through the changeable creation subject to the changeless God, and they did not manifest God as he is in himself, but in a symbolic manner as times and circumstances required.

33. I must say, though, I do not see how these people explain the appearance to Daniel of the Ancient of Days, from whom the Son of man (which the Son agreed to be for our sakes) explicitly received the kingdom; from the same one, surely, who says to him in the psalms, *My son are you, I today have begotten you; ask of me and I will give you the Gentiles for your inheritance* (Ps 2:7), and who *subjects all things under his feet* (Ps 8:8; Heb 2:8; 1 Cor 15:26). So if both the Father bestowing the kingdom and the Son receiving it appeared to Daniel in physical form, how can they maintain that the Father never appeared to the prophets, and so alone can be regarded as the invisible one *whom no man ever saw nor can see* (1 Tm 6:16)?

This is how Daniel tells the story: *I watched*, he says, *while thrones were set, and the Age-old of Days took his seat; and his robe was white like snow, and the hair of his head like clean wool; his throne a flame of fire, its wheels blazing fire, and a river of fire was winding its way in his presence. And a thousand were serving him, and ten thousand times ten thousand were waiting on him. And he established the court and the books were opened,* etc. And a little later on: *I watched*, he says, *in the vision of the night, and behold with the clouds of heaven there was as it were a Son of man coming, and he came up to the Old one of Days, and was presented to him. And there was given to him the principality and the honor and the kingdom, and all peoples, tribes and tongues shall serve him. His authority is an everlasting authority which shall not pass away, and his kingdom shall not perish* (Dn 7:9-14). Here, surely, you have the Father giving and the Son receiving an everlasting kingdom, and they are both present to the prophet's sight in visible guise. So it is not improper to believe that God the Father was also accustomed to appear in that sort of way to mortal men.

34. Unless of course someone chooses to say, "No, no, the Father is not visible, for he only appeared to the vision of someone dreaming; but the Son is visible, and the Holy Spirit, because Moses was wide awake when he saw all those things." As though Moses could have seen the Word and Wisdom of God with his physical eyes of flesh; as though even the human spirit can be seen which gives life to the flesh—or even that material spirit, for that matter, which we call wind, let alone that Spirit of God who transcends the minds of all men and angels in the inexpressible sublimity of the divine substance! Or perhaps someone will rush in headlong with the crazy assertion that the Son and the Holy Spirit are even visible to men when they are awake, but the Father only when they are dreaming? But how do they square that with the text which they apply only to the Father, *whom no man has seen or can see* (1 Tm 6:16)? Do men cease to be men when they go to sleep? Or is the Father able to form a bodily likeness to represent himself in the dreams of men asleep, but unable to form an actual bodily creature to represent himself to the eyes of men awake?

In any case his substance, by which he is what he is, cannot be shown in itself either to a sleeping man in a bodily likeness or to a waking man in an actual bodily appearance; and "his substance" means not only the Father's but also the Son's and the Holy Spirit's. Even confining ourselves to the waking apparitions which evidently compel these people to suppose that only the Son and Holy Spirit, not the Father, have ever appeared to men's external gaze; and leaving aside all the vast extent of the sacred pages, and the infinite variety of ways they can be understood, which should surely prevent anyone who is right in the head from asserting that the Father's person was never presented in bodily guise to men's waking eyes; even leaving all this aside, what do they make of the case of our father Abraham, in which he was certainly wide awake and busy giving hospitality, which scripture heads by saying, *The Lord appeared to Abraham* (Gn 18:1), and in which he saw not one man or two, but three; none of them described as being taller than the others, or more resplendent in dignity, or acting with greater authority.

35. Finally, to conclude: the first point we undertook to investigate in our threefold division of the field was whether it was the Father or the Son or the Holy Spirit who appeared to the fathers in those various created forms; or whether it was sometimes the Father, sometimes the Son, sometimes the Holy Spirit; or whether it was simply the one and only God, that is the trinity itself, without any distinction of persons, as it is called. An examination of what seems a sufficient number of scriptural passages, and a modest and careful consideration of the divine symbols or "sacraments"[58] they contain, all served to teach us, I think, one lesson; that we should not be dogmatic in deciding which person of

the three appeared in any bodily form or likeness to this or that patriarch or prophet, unless the whole context of the narrative provides us with probable indications. In any case, that nature, or substance, or essence, or whatever else you may call that which God is, whatever it may be, cannot be physically seen; but on the other hand we must believe that by creature control the Father, as well as the Son and the Holy Spirit, could offer the senses of mortal men a token representation of himself in bodily guise or likeness. That being settled then, as this second volume is already rather too long, let us defer to the following ones our discussion of the two remaining topics.

NOTES

1. M reads *animam*, the soul.

2. *Dilucescat*; M reads *dulcescat*, let his grace soothe it.

3. Through creatures, particularly in the last seven books, when he is investigating the divine image in man.

4. See Mk 6:48; Jn 6:19.

5. See Jn 9.

6. M expands: the reason whatever he sees the Father doing the same the Son does likewise, is that . . .

7. The Arians, chiefly, but also "economic" theologians like Tertullian and Novatian.

8. "Proper sense" in this context means orthodox sense.

9. See Book I, 27, and note 74.

10. Possibly referring to Book I, 18 and 19. But a different point was being made there.

11. The question will preoccupy him intermittently throughout the work; his discussion of the image, Book IX on, will be aimed *inter alia* at solving it. See also Book V, 15 and Book XV, 45.

12. Augustine actually dictated, or his stenographer wrote, *quem glorificat Pater*, whom the Father glorifies; so read all the manuscripts. Yet surely we are compelled to suppose that this was a slip of the tongue, or of the pen, and that what he intended to write was *qui glorificat Patrem*, which is what I have translated: i) he has just quoted a text to make the point that the Son is said to glorify the Father, and as the reader will have discovered by now, it is his habit to repeat texts he quotes in slightly different words; ii) the logic of his ironical argument in this sentence will collapse if we stick to the Latin as it stands, which will only yield the conclusion that the Holy Spirit is greater than the Son but equal to the Father.

I will grant that if you bring the previous sentence but one into the argument, then it could yield the conclusion, even with the Latin text as it stands, that while the Son and the Father are equal, because they glorify each other, the Holy Spirit is greater than them both, because he glorifies one of these equals. But my emendation not only makes the argument more limpid, but also makes its irony more piquant by standing the Trinity wholly upside down, in a kind of extreme counter-sub-ordinationism, and making the Father the least of the three, with the Holy Spirit the greatest and the Son in the middle.

13. This was almost the universal assumption from Justin right down to Augustine's own day. He himself had his doubts about it.

14. In ordinary Latin usage *mulier* forms a pair by contrast with *virgo*, somewhat like English "wife" and "maid."

15. M *blasphemas*, you are blaspheming.

16. See Jn 1:1.

17. Sir 1:3; see Eccl 3:1-8. It may be worthwhile trying to appreciate the significance of this little digressive meditation on the relationship of time to the eternal, that is the timeless, Word. It is, to be sure, one of his favorite themes, which one would expect him to digress on. He discusses it at length in Book XI of the *Confessions* (especially from chapter 13 on) in the context of a long meditation on the creation narrative of Genesis 1. And it is woven into his *ex professo* treatment of creation in his monumental and supremely difficult *The Literal Meaning of Genesis.*

But this fascination with the theme of time is more than mere indulgence in a hobby horse; it seems to me that it is a consequence of what I called in the Introduction Augustine's intuition of the historical/dramatic pattern of Christian truth. What he here calls the *ordo temporum*, the whole series of all times, is of the essence of both history and drama. As he casts his whole quest for God in the *De Trinitate* into the mold of this dramatic or historical pattern, the question of how to relate the eternal, absolute, and unchanging God to this *ordo temporum* becomes urgent. Part of the solution is to say that while God indeed in himself is beyond history or drama, his revelation of himself, culminating in the divine missions, is historical and dramatic, to be dramatically grasped. But that, I think, is only half Augustine's answer, and does not in itself provide us with a wholly satisfying intrinsic link between God and history. This is quite a real problem for contemporary theology; one sometimes wonders if some writers are not so stressing the historical dimension of Christianity that they are even historicizing God, making him subject to change and development.

This, surely, is hardly an acceptable solution. It is certainly not Augustine's. For him God remains frankly outside or beyond history, and even his historical revelation of himself is so mediated by created agents, that it in no way renders the invisible one visible, or the unchanging one changeable. God remains outside history, outside the drama of human destiny and salvation; but the history and the drama are really inside God. That is Augustine's solution, in which he is faithful to the genuine insight of the "economic" theologians, very briefly adumbrated in this digression we are discussing, more fully developed elsewhere.

One relevant passage is his book, *Miscellany of Eighty-three Questions*, question 46, where he discusses the reality of platonic ideas and locates them in the creative mind of God. It is the divine Wisdom or reasonableness that guarantees the reasonableness and intelligibility of creation; and Plato's forms or ideas were, of course, a metaphysical device to account for the intelligibility of a material and changing world. It was the most natural thing in the world for Augustine to integrate this metaphysics into Christian theology by locating these forms or ideas in the divine mind.

However, I think Augustine's real concern was not so much to render the material and changeable world intelligible, as to historicize or dramatize God, if I may so put it; that is to render God available to dramatic appreciation without in any way diminishing his transcendence. This he does with remarkable skill and ingenuity in his *The Literal Meaning of Genesis.*

He interprets the six-day creation narrative as an analogical account of the simultaneous creation of the whole universe, for which he finds authority in Sir 18:1, which says that *he created all things together*, and in Gn 2:4, which talks of *the day on which the Lord God made heaven and earth*. This act of creation is extra-temporal, but it is unwrapped and displayed to us as the work of six days, precisely as a kind of dramatization of the hierarchy of being in the universe. Above all, there is a kind of dramatization of the creative relationship between God and his creation, which marries creation to the trinitarian mystery, without of course presenting it as a necessity for God and not as an act of pure divine freedom.

In the beginning God made heaven and earth: that is, in the Son the Father made as yet formless spiritual being and formless material being; in the Son, because he is the exemplar origin, or original of all created being, as will be seen more clearly in a moment; as yet formless, because all created being is made out of nothing and has a radical tendency or *penchant* toward nothingness, unless sustained in being by the creator: the "as yet" does not signify a temporal period of formless being at the beginning of time, because creation is taking place extra-temporally; but only that this formlessness is a basic and primary element in all created being. Over this formless void and waste hovered the Spirit of God, that is the cherishing love of God. Then *God said: Let there be light, and there was light*: that is he uttered the form of hitherto formless spiritual being in his Word, and formless spiritual being, by turning to the Word, was formed—the creation of angelic intelligence. *And it was evening and morning, one day*: that is the one and only day of creation: evening, the angels knew themselves in themselves, having been formed by turning to the Word: morning, they referred their knowledge of themselves in themselves to the praise of the creator by turning to the Word again for further (in)formation.

And now the next five days of creation unroll as a kind of dialogue between God in the Word and the angels. Creation proceeds as the unfolding of the divine mind, and also as a kind of response to this unfolding on the part of the created mind. In every day there are five stages:

i) *God said, Let there be x*: this is the utterance of the creature in the Word; of course in the Word all the utterances of all creatures are but one word or utterance, but we need to have it unfolded onto a space/time screen. The utterance is made to the angels, who see the creature first in the Word, in its exemplar in the divine mind.

ii) *And it was so*: this signifies the divine idea as impressed on the angelic intelligence, that is, the consequent existence of the creature in its secondary exemplar, the angelic idea in the angelic mind.

iii) *And God made x:* this signifies the existence of the creature now in itself.

iv) *And it was evening*: this signifies the angelic contemplation of the creature in itself, which is rightly called evening, both as marking the completion of the work, and as indicating the twilight character of knowledge of a thing in itself, compared with knowledge of it in its divine exemplar, the Word.

v) *And it was morning, the nth day*: this signifies the reference of the creature by the angelic mind to the praise of the creator, and the return, so to speak, of the angelic attention to the Word in readiness for the next series. Perhaps it can also be seen as declaring the participation by the angelic intelligence in the creative complaisance of the Holy Spirit in creation, signified by the repeated refrain, *And God saw that it was good*.

Augustine to some extent summarizes these ideas in *The Literal Meaning of Genesis* II, 8, 19 and at greater length in Book IV, especially 22, 39—23, 40; but he works them out tentatively, with a string of interminable questions and counter-questions, throughout the first four books, which as I have remarked, make very hard reading.

I would be inclined to sum up his view, which I think has validity in spite of the fact that his interpretation of the sacred text is more eisegetical than exegetical, as follows. Creation displays in a new mode (a spatio-temporal one, and thus a less perfect one, of course) the dramatic reality that is the divine tri-personal life. Created being, while very definitely not divine being, and quite other than divine being, is nevertheless rooted in divine being, and stays rooted there; it has not just been chucked out into the void by God to whirl away on its own. A creature exists at three levels: eternally in the Word, or the divine idea of it; in the knowledge other created intelligences have of it; and in itself. And this latter existence depends totally on the first, and is affected by the second.

What is true of created being is true of that dimension of it which we call time, or history. Therefore, what is true of the original creation is true of all created being throughout its history. And finally, though here I am more than usually tentative in my suggestion, the creaturely relationship to God is not one indistinguishable relationship to God without distinction of persons; nor is the creative work of God indistinguishably of the three. Without mitigating the principle Augustine is so strong on, that the divine persons are inseparable in their working in creation; and that they are not indeed to be distinguished from each other in terms of divine attributes; I think he is saying in his account of creation, and I think he is right to say it, that being created puts the creature into a distinct relationship with each of the divine persons; and so does being recreated or redeemed, or sanctified. As regards creation, we could perhaps say that it relates the creature to God the Father as its final cause, to God the Son as its exemplar cause, and to God the Holy Spirit as its efficient or effective cause.

In this way I think Augustine has succeeded in dramatizing God, or rather seeing that God is essentially dramatic, without dethroning him from his transcendence.

18. I think Augustine is illustrating his point by a common usage of popular Latin, by which public shows were called *missa*, that is, literally, "things sent." But he may just be generalizing the previous sentence, and saying that it is suitable to call visible human acts and artifacts "sent" because they issue from the inner intentions of the mind.

19. To call the man Jesus the *persona* of the Son is an unusual use of the word. It must here have

its primitive meaning of a mask (theatrical) or visible guise; a meaning that modern psychology has taken over.

20. See Heb 1:9.

21. M adds *pariter*, together.

22. See Rv 5:6.

23. See Gn 28:18.

24. See Gn 22:6.

25. See Ex 3:2.

26. See Ex 13:21.

27. See Ex 19:16.

28. See Ex 3:2.

29. See Ex 13:21.

30. See Ex 19:16.

31. Augustine took it for granted, with most contemporary philosophers, that angels and demons had airy bodies.

32. A very odd phrase; it is an allusion to Gal 4:4.

33. Book I, 10, 11; see also *Introduction* 67-74.

34. M, reading *qui* for *quia*, gives the following: then the text *who alone has immortality* is not said of the Father alone.

35. He will qualify this very shortly in section 18. I think in fact he probably has his tongue in his cheek here.

36. To get the point of this question, it must be remembered that throughout this book, and the next, Augustine is criticizing the "economic" commonplace that only the Son appeared visibly in the Old Testament.

37. See Mk 9:7 and parallels.

38. See Lk 3:22 and parallels.

39. The reader should bear in mind that in this sentence Augustine is not using "person" in the strict limited sense of the "three persons of the trinity." This becomes absolutely clear in the next sentence, where he talks of "the person of the trinity."

40. He misquotes here, though such a reading, "Son" for "name" is found. But in his *Homilies on the Gospel of John* he reads "name."

41. M *erat*, was.

42. See *Introduction* 41-48, especially 48.

43. It is clear that Augustine takes "Spirit" as subject and "Lord" as predicate, though he considers the opposite possibility in the next sentence.

44. It might help to summarize his argument, and once more state the point of it. He is inclined to favor the view, though he refuses to be dogmatic about it, that the three angels represent, or manifest, but of course are not, the three divine persons, while the fact of their sometimes being addressed in the singular signifies their unity of substance. Thus he makes the point that all Old Testament theophanies are not necessarily manifestations of the Son, and that therefore it is quite unnecessary to have a theory about the Son being the intrinsically visible member of the trinity.

45. In the previous paragraph he supposed that one of the creatures called angels appeared, and in this case there is nothing to prevent such an angel representing any of the persons. But now he supposes some *ad hoc* physical manifestation which is only called an angel etc.; and only the Son or the Spirit can suitably be called angel, in the sense of messenger or announcer, because only they are ever said to have been sent. If the manifestation is not an angel in the substantive or ontological sense, then its being called an angel in the functional sense can only have meaning with reference to the divine person being represented, and this cannot be the Father, because he never has this function.

46. The Septuagint reading, a pious interpretation. Hebrew reads, *they saw the God of Israel.*

47. Meaning perceptible by the mind as opposed to the senses.

48. See Ex 31:18.

49. See Lk 11:20; Mt 12:28.

50. There is no biblical evidence for this reckoning; Ex 19:1 says *In the third month*. Augustine is really relying on a liturgical tradition of later Judaism, which came to regard Pentecost, the Feast of Weeks, as commemorating the giving of the law.

51. *In conspectu tuo*; M *ante te*, before you.

52. In *The Literal Meaning of Genesis* XII, 27, 55, Augustine reverses this opinion to the extent of saying that Moses was granted what he calls at the beginning of this paragraph "a true spiritual vision of God."

53. Reading *in specula* with M and several manuscripts. CCL has *in spelunca*, in a cave. The reading *specula* is supported by allusions Augustine makes to it below, at the end of this section 28, and at the end of section 30. The Septuagint has the phrase *eis open tes petras*, at a hole of the rock, which can mean either a cave or a peephole.

54. While Greek and Vulgate read *in mundo*, Augustine reads *de hoc mundo*, on this world, as one lives on capital or on rents.

55. That is, his flesh.

56. Reading *infigeretur*, with M. CCL has *confringeretur*, was broken, with only one manuscript to support this reading.

57. This sentence is my own gloss, to bring out the run of Augustine's thought. As this whole chapter is a piece of allegorical or mystical interpretation, it does not really contribute to his argument, and is in the nature of a long digression. But like all his long digressions, it is germane to the whole purpose of his work. He is describing our quest for God, or in terms of this chapter, our longing to see God's face. And the only way we can come to that vision is by first seeing his back, that is, by faith in the human, slain, and risen flesh of Christ. This is our only way into an understanding or vision of the mystery of the Trinity. The point will be developed formally, first in Book IV, where it enters into his final explanation or definition of the divine mission of the Son; and then again in Book XIII, where it enters into his development of the divine image in man as a dynamic program for the Christian life.

58. *Sacramenta* is the word Augustine uses here. He is very fond of it in a sense far wider than that to which it has since been restricted in Latin theology. It includes the sacraments of the Church, but over and above this it embraces all scriptural symbols, types, and figures. This wide use serves to provide a context for the sacraments strictly so called, and remind us that they are essentially *signs*.

Book III

MISSIONS: THE WORK OF ANGELS

Prologue

---

1. Believe me, dear reader, I would much rather spend my time usefully by reading than by dictating material to be read by others. If you are not prepared to take my word for it and require experimental proof, then try providing me with something to read which will give me an answer to my inquiries, or for that matter to the questions of other people which I am compelled to face, both by the part of bishop which I play in Christ's service, and by my ardent concern to defend our faith against the errors of materialistic and unspiritual people. In this way you will appreciate how readily I would restrain myself from this task, and with what joy I would give my pen a holiday.

The fact, surely, is that sufficient works on this subject have not been published in Latin, or at least they are not at all easy to find; and as for Greek, though I do not doubt, from the few works that have been translated for us, that everything we might properly wish to know could be found there, most of us are hardly well enough acquainted with that language to be able to read Greek books on the subject with any real understanding. So I cannot decently refuse the brethren when they insist on their rights over me as their slave and demand that I should above all serve their praiseworthy studies in Christ by my tongue and my pen, a pair of horses in my chariot of which Charity is the driver. I must also acknowledge, incidentally, that by writing I have myself learned much that I did not know. So this work of mine should not be dismissed as superfluous either by the indolent or the learned, since it is very necessary to many who are neither indolent nor learned, myself included.

Certainly I have found that what I have read by other writers on the subject has provided me most helpfully with a framework for my own reflections. In undertaking, however, to investigate and discuss what I consider can be investigated and discussed about the trinity, the one supreme and supremely good

God, I have only followed the same God's invitation[1] and relied on his assistance. In this way I hope to provide those who want it and can use it with something to read on the subject, if there is nothing else of the kind available; and if there is, well then, the more books of the kind there are, the more likely are they to find what they are looking for.

2. What I desire for all my works, of course, is not merely a kind reader but also a frank critic.[2] This is peculiarly my desire for this work, treating as it does of so tremendous a subject, in which one wishes as many discoverers of truth could be found as it certainly has contradictors. But the last thing I want is a reader who is my doting partisan, or a critic who is his own. The reader will not, I trust, be fonder of me than of Catholic faith, nor the critic of himself than of Catholic truth. To the first I say: "Do not show my works the same deference as the canonical scriptures. Whatever you find in scripture that you used not to believe, why, believe it instantly.[3] But whatever you find in my works that you did not hitherto regard as certain, then unless I have really convinced you that it is certain, continue to have your doubts about it." To the second I say: "Do not criticize what I write by the standard of your own prejudices or contrariness, but by the divine text or incontrovertible reason. If you find any truth in it, then it does not belong to me just by being there, but rather to both of us by being understood and loved by us both. If you catch me out in anything that is not true, then I must own it for making the mistake; but from now on by being more careful, we can both repudiate its ownership."

Chapter 1

In which the author recapitulates; and then goes on to discuss the second of the three questions posed in chapter 3 of Book II, above; and in this chapter he sets the framework for his discussion of the activities of angels in the Old Testament theophanies by first considering the general order of God's providential government of the universe, with special reference to first and secondary causes, and to the significant, or meaningfully symbolic character of God's action in the world.

---

3. Let us then begin this third book where we left off the second. To recapitulate: we had first of all reached the point where we needed to show that the Son is not less than the Father simply because he was sent and the Father did the sending; and that the Holy Spirit is not less than either of them simply because he is declared in the gospel to have been sent by each. Next, since the Son was sent where he already was, as he both came into the world and *he was in this world* (Jn 1:10); and so was the Holy Spirit sent where he already was, as *the Spirit of the Lord has filled the world, and that which holds all things together has knowledge of speech* (Wis 1:7); we had therefore to find out if what constituted the sending of the Lord was

his being born in the flesh, his issuing, so to speak, from the hidden invisibility of the Father's bosom and appearing to the eyes of men in the form of a servant; and likewise for the Holy Spirit his being seen as a dove in bodily guise and as fire in divided tongues. So what their being sent would mean is their coming forth from the hidden world of the spiritual into the public gaze of mortal men in some bodily shape; and as the Father never did this, he is only said to have sent, not also to have been sent.

But then we went on to ask why in fact the Father was not sometimes said to have been sent, if he was signified by those bodily manifestations which were shown to the eyes of men in the Old Testament. If on the other hand these manifestations signified the Son, then why was he only said to have been sent *when the fullness of time came* for him to be *born of woman* (Gal 4:4)—seeing that on this supposition he would also have been sent before, when he appeared physically in those various guises. If, however, you argue that he cannot properly be said to have been sent until the Word became flesh, then why is the Holy Spirit ever said to have been sent at all, seeing that he had no such incarnation? If, finally, those Old Testament manifestations indicated neither Father nor Son but Holy Spirit, why should his being sent be confined to the New Testament, seeing that he had been previously sent in these ways in the Old?

Next, after raising these questions we divided the subject matter into three parts, in order to deal with them all more systematically. One part we have already been through, two are left to be tackled now. What we have already discussed and settled is that in those old time bodily manifestations and apparitions it was not only the Father, or only the Son or only the Holy Spirit who appeared; but it was either indistinguishably the one Lord God whom we know to be the triad, or any person of the three whom the context might most probably indicate.

4. So now we must go on to the second part of the inquiry. This is whether forms were simply created *ad hoc*, for God to appear by their means to mortal eyes as he judged most suitable; or whether angels who already existed were sent to speak as representing God, and accordingly used physical creatures to give themselves some bodily guise for the performance of their service; or perhaps they changed their own bodies, which they dominate and are not dominated by,[4] into whatever looks and shapes they chose to suit their activities, according to the power bestowed upon them by their creator. When this part of the inquiry has been completed as far as the Lord permits, we will go on to the point we first set out to decide, and see whether the Son and Holy Spirit were also sent in the Old Testament; and if so, what difference there is between that sending and the one we read of in the gospel; or whether in fact neither was sent until the Son was born of the virgin Mary, and the Holy Spirit appeared in bodily guise, whether as a dove or as tongues of fire.

5. I must confess it is beyond my powers of penetration to settle one question I have just alluded to: do angels work through the constant and stable spiritual quality of their own bodies to take and fit to themselves some grosser matter from the lower elements, which they can change and turn rather like clothes into any physical manifestation they please, even into true ones, as our Lord turned true water into true wine?[5] Or do they transform their own proper bodies into whatever form

they wish as it suits their purposes? Whichever the case may be, the point is not directly relevant to our present inquiry. As a mere man, of course, I cannot possibly have any first hand-knowledge of these things by direct experience, like the angels who do them. Indeed, they even know better than I do how my body changes according to the feelings or moods of my will, which is something I have experienced in myself and observed in others. I could, I suppose, try to work out what I should believe on this point on the authority of scripture; fortunately however there is no need to, as it would involve me in elaborating a proof that would take up more space than the matter really warrants.

6. What we have to investigate now is simply whether it was angels who produced the physical appearances that men saw and the sounds they heard, whenever the perceptible creation, in the manner described by the book of Wisdom, changed at the creator's beck and call into whatever was needed at the time: *For creation*, it says there, *in obedience to you its maker, exerts itself to punish the wicked, and relaxes for the benefit of those who trust in you; thus it became at that time, by a total transformation, the agent of your all-nourishing grace, conforming to the wish of those who longed for you* (Wis 16:24). The power of God's will, after all, extended to producing through created spiritual agents sensible and perceptible effects in the material creation. Is there indeed any place where the Wisdom of almighty God does not achieve what she will, Wisdom *who deploys her strength from one end of the universe to the other, ordering all things for good* (Wis 8:1)?

7. The order of nature, to be sure, declares itself in various ways; in all of them it serves the divine command, but in those changes and permutations of bodies which happen with steady regularity it ceases to astonish; as for example the changes that take place at frequent or at least regular intervals in the sky and the sea and on the earth, when things are born and die, rise and set, or regularly change their appearance. Other events, however, though products of the same natural order, are less familiar because they occur at longer intervals. Many people of course are amazed at them, but secular scientists come to an understanding of them, and as they are often repeated over several generations and known to more and more educated people, so they have come to seem less marvelous. As examples of such phenomena take eclipses and comets and earthquakes and monstrous births and similar things. Not one of them occurs independently of God's will, though many people do not see this. And so it has always been feasible for superficial philosophers to explain such things by other causes, true ones perhaps, but proximate and secondary, while the cause that transcends all others, namely the will of God, they have been quite unable to discern; or else they have even suggested false causes and explanations, derived not from objective research into physical bodies and their movements, but from their own guesswork and mistaken presuppositions.

8. Let me try to make the matter clearer with an example. The human body has its proper mass of living tissue, its shape and appearance, its coordination of various parts, its due balance of health. This body is governed by the soul breathed into it; this soul is rational, and so although it is subject to change, it is capable of sharing in that wisdom which is changeless. In this way *its sharing is in the selfsame*, as the psalm says of all the saints, who go like living stones into the building of that eternal Jerusalem *in heaven which is our mother* (Gal 4:26; Heb 12:22). The

psalmist sings, *Jerusalem which is built as a city, whose sharing is in the selfsame* (Ps 122:3). "The selfsame" here is to be understood of that supreme and changeless good which is God, and his wisdom and his will. Another psalm sings these words of praise to him: *You change the heavens and they are changed, but you are the selfsame* (Ps 102:26).

Let us then suppose such a wise man; his rational soul already shares in the changeless and eternal truth, and he consults it about all his actions.[6] Only if he sees in it that something must be done does he do it; and so by submitting to this eternal truth and obeying it he acts rightly. Now suppose he has consulted the highest principles of divine justice, which he listens to in the depths of his heart, and at her command he wears out his body in some work of mercy, and suffers a breakdown of health. Then he consults the doctors, and one tells him that the cause of his illness is the body's abnormal dryness, while another says the cause is an excess of moist humors. One of them is right and the other wrong, but in any case they are both pronouncing on the proximate, that is to say, the physical cause of his illness. If the doctor then looks for the reason of this abnormal dryness of body, and finds that it is overwork deliberately undertaken, he has come to a higher cause of the illness, which proceeds from the soul to affect the body it governs. But not even this is the primary cause of the matter. Without any doubt the first or ultimate cause must be looked for in that changeless wisdom which the soul of the wise man serves in charity, and in obedience to whose wordless and inexpressible command he has willingly undertaken to overwork himself. So it is in the will of God that the primary and ultimate cause of the man's illness can be located.

But now suppose further that in going about his loving and thoughtful labors this wise man uses servants to help the good work, and that these are not serving God with the same willing generosity as he is, but are prompted by the desire to use the wages offered for satisfying their worldly lusts, or for avoiding worldly inconveniences; suppose he also uses beasts of burden as required to get the work finished, and these being irrational animals would not of course carry their burdens with any thought for the good work they are engaged in, but simply as they are prompted to it by their natural appetite for pleasure and their natural avoidance of pain. Finally, suppose he also uses all sorts of wholly inanimate objects that are required for his undertaking, like corn, wine, oil, clothes, money, books, and so forth. In being applied to the work all these bodies, animate or inanimate, are moved about, damaged, repaired, destroyed, reconstructed, subjected to all sorts of changes in time and space; and of all these visible and changing events can any other cause be found but the invisible and unchanging will of God? From the soul of the just man as from the throne of wisdom the divine will uses the bad souls and the irrational souls, the animate and the inanimate bodies involved; indeed first and foremost it is the just man's good and holy soul which it has recruited to its service for this pious and religious purpose.

9. We have been illustrating the point from one wise man, wise although still carrying a mortal body, still only *seeing in part* (1 Cor 13:12); we could extend the point to cover a whole community of such wise men, or to the state—even to the whole world—provided the government of its human affairs were in the hands of wise men. However, this happy situation does not yet exist, for we first need to be

trained to mortality[7] in this exile of ours, and to have our capacity developed for gentleness and patience in affliction. And so let us apply the point to that heavenly country "far, far beyond the stars" from which we are at the moment exiles.

There the will of God presides, as in his house or his temple, over the spirits who are joined together in the highest concord and friendship, fused indeed into one will by a kind of spiritual fire of charity; as it is written, *He makes spirits his angel-messengers, and a burning fire his ministers* (Ps 104:4). From that lofty throne, set apart in holiness, the divine will spreads itself through all things in marvelous patterns of created movement, first spiritual then corporeal; and it uses all things to carry out the unchanging judgment of the divine decree, whether they be corporeal or incorporeal things, whether they be non-rational or rational spirits, whether they be good by his grace, or bad by their own will.

But just as the grosser, inferior bodies are governed in due order by the more subtle and potent ones, so too all bodies are governed by the spirit of life; and the non-rational spirit of life is governed by the rational spirit of life; and the rational spirit of life that has run away and sinned is governed by the rational spirit of life that has remained faithful and just; and that is governed by God himself. And so the whole of creation is governed by its creator, *from whom and by whom and in whom* (Rom 11:36) it was founded and established. And thus God's will is the first and highest cause of all physical species and motions. For nothing happens visibly and in a manner perceptible to the senses which does not issue either as a command or as a permission from the inmost invisible and intelligible court of the supreme emperor, according to his unfathomable justice of rewards and punishments, favors and retributions, in what we may call this vast and all-embracing republic of the whole creation.

10. If then the apostle Paul, though still carrying the burden of *the body which is perishing and weighing down the soul* (Wis 9:15), though still only seeing *in part and in a riddle* (1 Cor 13:12), still *wishing to cast off and be with Christ* (Phil 1:23), still *groaning in himself*, awaiting the adoption, *the redemption of his body* (Rom 8:23); if for all that he could use meaningful signs to proclaim the Lord Jesus Christ, in one way by using his tongue, in another by writing letters, in another by celebrating the Lord's body and blood;* need we be surprised if God produces visible and sensible effects as he pleases in sky and earth, sea and air, to signify and show himself as he knows best, without the very substance of

---

* Note that we do not call Paul's tongue or his paper and ink the body and blood of Christ, nor the significant sounds made by his tongue, nor the meaningful signs written on the pages of his letters, but only that which is taken from the fruits of the earth, and consecrated by mystic prayers, and taken by us for our spiritual salvation in memory of what the Lord suffered for us. The hands of men give this its visible appearance, but it can only be consecrated into being such a great sacrament by the invisible working of the spirit of God. For all the physical movements involved in the whole action are worked by God acting in the first place on what is invisible in the ministers, namely on the souls of men or on the services of the occult spirits who are subject to him.[8]

his being ever appearing immediately manifest, since it is altogether changeless, and more inwardly and mysteriously sublime than all created spirits?[9]

11. It is by the power of God administering the whole spiritual and corporeal universe that on certain days every year the waters of the sea are summoned and poured out as rain on the face of the earth. But once upon a time this happened at the prayer of Elijah, after such a long and unbroken drought that men were dying of famine; at the moment the servant of God made his prayer the weather had shown no signs, such as a damp and cloudy face to the sky, of the rain that was soon to come; thus when the rainstorm followed so rapidly and in such quantity on the heels of his prayer, the power of God was made manifest to those who were given the benefit of that miracle.[10] So too the recurrent phenomena of thunder and lightning are the work of God. But on Mount Sinai they occurred in an unusual manner, and there was unmistakable evidence that the sounds heard were no mere atmospheric disturbances, but meaningful signals, and so the phenomena were miraculous signs of divine power.[11]

Again, who but God draws up the sap from the roots of the vine into the grape clusters and makes wine, *God who gives the increase*, though man *plants and waters* (1 Cor 3:7)? But when water was turned into wine at the Lord's bidding with unusual speed, even fools admitted that it was a revelation of divine power.[12] Who but God annually clothes the bushes with leaves and flowers? But when the rod of Aaron the priest budded,[13] divinity was in a certain fashion conversing with a hesitant and doubtful humanity. And certainly all vegetation and all animal bodies are produced and fashioned from the one common material element of earth, and who makes them if not the one who commanded the earth to bring them forth,[14] who also controls and activates what he created by the same word of command? But when he suddenly and directly turned the same basic element from the staff of Moses into the flesh of a serpent, it was a miracle—a rather unusual mutation, certainly, but in a subject that was basically mutable. The one who animated that serpent for a few moments is no other than the one who animates all living things as they are born.

And is not he who has given back their souls to corpses when the dead have risen[15] the same as the one who animates cells in mothers' wombs that those who are going to die might be born? But when these things happen in the continuous flow and flux of things, traveling the usual road from darkness into light, and from the light back into the darkness, they are called natural; when however, to teach men some lesson, they are pressed forward in some abnormal transformation, they are called *the wonderful works of God* (Acts 2:11).

Chapter 2

The problem of miracles wrought by demonic agencies is discussed, with particular reference to the magicians of Pharaoh; that this kind of thing in no way derogates from divine providence and the unique creative efficacy of God the first cause is shown by illustration from the case of Jacob's stock-breeding experiments with Laban's flocks.

12. Here I see a somewhat specious difficulty may arise; why, that is, these miracles can be performed even by witchcraft. For Pharaoh's wizards also produced serpents and other such things. Though what is much more surprising is that the wizards' power could produce serpents, but when it came to the tiniest flies it failed completely. For "scinifs," which were the third plague to strike the pride of Egypt, are the minutest sort of flies. When the wizards failed hopelessly in this instance, they said, *This is the finger of God* (Ex 8:15). By which we are given to understand that even the rebel angels and the airy powers who have been thrust down from the purity of their ethereal dwelling place on high into this lower darkness as the prison of their kind,[16] and who give witchcraft whatever efficacy it has, are quite impotent unless they are *given power from above* (Jn 19:11). This power is given them, either to deceive the deceitful, as it was given for example to the detriment of the Egyptians and even of their wizards, since these performers of prodigies, condemned in fact by the truth of God, won a great reputation for what was no more than encouraging the Egyptians in delusions of grandeur; or else it is given to make faithful souls realize that they should not set any great store on being able to do such things; or finally it may be given in order to exercise, test, and display the patience of the just, as in the case of Job. For it was surely thanks to a very considerable satanic capacity for miracles that he lost all his possessions, and his children, and his health.[17]

13. It must not be supposed, however, that the material which visible things are made of is at the beck and call of the rebel angels, to serve them as they please; rather it is at God's disposal, and he gives them this power as he judges best in his sublime, spiritual, and immutable wisdom. In the same sort of way criminals condemned to the mines have water, fire, and earth at their disposal to do what they want with—but only in the measure they are allowed by their jailers. Clearly those bad angels cannot be called creators, just because the wizards in their competition with the servant of God made frogs and serpents with their help.[18] It was not they who created them. All things that come to corporeal and visible birth have their hidden seeds lying dormant in the corporeal elements of this world. There are of course the seeds plants and animals produce which we can see with our eyes; but of these seeds there are other hidden seeds from which, at the creator's bidding, water produced the first fishes and birds, and earth the first plants and animals of their kind.[19] Nor was this basic seminal force exhausted in that first primordial breeding; often, the suitable combinations of circumstances are lacking for particular species to burst into being and carry on their career.[20]

Observe for example a tiny cutting; it is a kind of seed, since if it is properly planted out in the ground it produces a tree. But this cutting has a finer seed in the seed of its kind properly so-called, the grain of seed which is also visible to our eyes. But though our eyes cannot see any further seed of this grain of seed, we can reasonably infer its existence, because if there were no such seminal force in the elements themselves, there would not be so many forms of life spontaneously generated from earth where nothing was sown; nor would there be so many animals on land and in water which have come into existence without any mating of male and female, though they themselves, born asexually, grow up and produce offspring by copulation.[21] Bees, in any case, do not conceive the seeds of their offspring by copulation, but collect them by mouth from where they have, so to say, been broadcast over the ground.[22] Thus it is the creator of all these invisible seeds who is the creator of all things, since whatever comes into our ken by a process of birth receives the beginnings of its course from hidden seeds, and derives its due growth and final distinction of shape and parts from what you could call the original programming[23] of those seeds.

So then, just as we do not call parents the creators of human beings, nor farmers the creators of their crops, though it is through the external action they provide that the power of God operates inwardly to create these things; so we are not permitted to call bad, or even good, angels creators, just because with their finer senses and more volatile bodies they perceive these seeds of things that are hidden from our gaze, and scatter them secretly among suitable combinations of the elements, and so seize the opportunity to bring things to birth and accelerate their growth in novel ways. No, the good angels only do such things as God commands them, and the bad ones, though they do them unjustly, only do them as far as he justly permits them. The unjust wills of the wicked angels are all their own, thanks to their malice; but their power is something they receive, and justly, whether for their own punishment, or the punishment of bad men, or for the praise and glory of the good.

14. This is the very way in which the apostle[24] distinguishes between God creating and forming from within and created agents working from without, and he takes his example from agriculture: *I planted*, he says, *and Apollos watered, but it was God who made things grow* (1 Cor 3:6). So, as in our Christian life it is only God who can give the right shape to our spirits by justifying us, while men can preach the gospel outwardly, and bad men too *under false pretenses*, as well as good men *in all sincerity* (Phil 1:18); in the same way it is only God who inwardly effects the creation of all visible things, while he applies to the nature in which he creates them the external activities of good and bad angels, of people and of animals, according to his decree and the capacities and appetites he has distributed to them all—rather in the same way as he applies the external activities of agriculture to the earth. Therefore I can no more call the bad angels who were conjured by witchcraft creators of those frogs and serpents, than I can call bad men creators of the crops which I see springing up as a result of their labor.

15. Again, Jacob was in no sense the creator of the piebald colors of the flocks he managed, just because he put the peeled and particolored rods in the drinking troughs for the ewes to gaze at as they conceived.[25] Nor for that matter were the ewes creators of the piebald effects in their young, just because the vivid impressions of piebaldness they received from looking at the particolored rods remained

embedded in their souls, and so could not help having a sympathetic effect on their bodies which were animated by these souls thus affected, so that the impression was passed on to color the progeny in their sensitive and impressionable beginnings. That soul and body should thus psychosomatically react upon each other is due to those archetypal harmonies of reason[26] which live immutably in the very wisdom of God, something that is not localized within the limits of space. While this wisdom is unchanging in itself, it does not hold itself aloof from anything that is, even in a changing mode of existence, because there is nothing that was not created by it. That the ewes gave birth to lambs and not to rods is due to the unchangeable and invisible disposition of God's wisdom by which all things were created; and that the lambs conceived were colored as an effect of the particolored rods was due to the souls of their pregnant mothers being affected from the outside through their eyes, and having inside them their own proper "program" of embryo formation which they received from their creator, whose power was active at the inner roots of their being.

It would take a long time, though, to discuss how great the power of the soul is to influence and change bodily matter, and it is not necessary at this point. In any case the soul cannot be called the body's creator, inasmuch as every cause of a changeable and sensible substance, and every measure and number and weight of it, from which it is made so that it might also exist, as well as its nature, so that it might exist in such and such a way, comes into being from the intellectual and unchanging Life that is over all things and that reaches as far as the uttermost extremes of earthly existence.

But I thought that what Jacob did with the flocks should be recalled so that it might be understood that if neither the man who maneuvered those rods in that way can be called the creator of the colors in the lambs and kids, nor the souls themselves of their mothers, which, as much as nature allowed, sprinkled the phantasm of color conceived through the eyes of the body with seeds conceived by the flesh, then all the less can it be said that the wicked angels (through which the magicians of Pharaoh did those things at that time) were the creators of the frogs and serpents.

16. It is one thing, after all, to establish and administer creation from the inmost and supreme pivot of all causes, and the one who does that is God the sole creator; it is another matter to apply activity from outside, in virtue of power and capacities distributed by him, so that the thing being created turns out like this or like that. All these things around us have been seminally and primordially created in the very fabric, as it were, or texture of the elements; but they require the right occasion actually to emerge into being. For the world itself, like mothers heavy with young, is heavy with the causes of things that are coming to birth; but these things are only created in it by that supreme being in which nothing is born or dies, nothing begins or ceases to be. But to apply secondary causes to things from outside, which even if they are not natural are applied all the same according to nature, and so to make things which lie hidden and secreted in nature's bosom burst forth and be created openly, by unfolding their measures and numbers and weights— which have been secretly assigned to them by him who *has arranged all things in measure and number and weight* (Wis 11:20)—this is something which bad men can do no less than bad angels, as I showed above in the case of agriculture.

17. It might be thought that this account will not do for explaining the sudden production of animals which have the spirit of life in them and the sensitive instinct to seek what is natural to them and avoid what is not. But here it is to be observed how many people there are who know what is the best compost of vegetable or animal matter, what is the best way to treat or cover up or crush or compound the right organic juices and humors in order to generate certain kinds of animal. Now none of these people, surely, would be so crazy as to call himself a creator. If then it is possible for any wicked man to know what materials grubs and maggots and flies are generated from, is it surprising that bad angels, with their keener perception of the hidden seeds of things in the elements, should know what frogs and serpents are generated from, and by putting these seminal materials of theirs through the appropriate hidden processes and motions, should have them created, but not, repeat not, create them?

However, people are not commonly astonished by what people commonly do. So if the speed of the process astonishes you by which those frogs and serpents were produced so suddenly, consider how comparable effects are produced by men, in the measure of human capacity; consider that the same organic matter will generate maggots more quickly in summer than in winter, or in hot places than in cold places. But men find it hard to produce startling results in this field because they lack the necessary keenness of perception, and with their earthly slow-moving bodies, the necessary agility of movement. So you could formulate the rule that the easier any sort of angels, good or bad, find it to bring together out of the elements the proximate causes of things, the more astonishing are their results for speed in this field.

18. But only he who fashions things in their principles is the creator; and only he can do this who has by him from the first the measures, numbers, and weights of all things that are; and he is God the one creator, by whose incomprehensible supremacy it happens that these angels cannot do, because they are not allowed to, what they could do if they were allowed to. The only possible reason I can think of why, having made frogs and serpents, they were unable to make the tiniest gnats, is that there was present the higher control of God's prohibition, working through the Holy Spirit. The wizards themselves admitted it, when they said, *This is the finger of God* (Ex 8:15). However it is difficult for us to ascertain what these angels can do by nature, but cannot do by divine prohibition, and what their own natural limitations prevent them from doing. Indeed it is impossible to ascertain this except by the gift of God, which the apostle alludes to when he says, *To another is given the discernment of spirits* (1 Cor 12:10).

For example we know that man can walk, and that he cannot even do this if he is not allowed to, whereas he cannot fly even if he is allowed to. So these angels can do some things if they are allowed to by stronger angels under God's direction; and some things they cannot do, even if they are allowed to, because God himself prevents it by limiting the scope of their nature. On the other hand, he frequently does not allow his good angels to do things which he has put within the scope of their natural capacities.

Chapter 3

The significance of the prodigies worked through the ministry of angels is examined more closely, and compared with the significance of the prophetic utterances and actions of people in the Old Testament.

19. Apart then from things that occur at frequent intervals in the normal course of nature, like the rising and setting of heavenly bodies, the births and deaths of animals, the countless variety of seeds and growths, clouds and fogs, snow and rain, thunder and lightning, thunderbolts and hail, wind and fire, cold and heat, and so forth; and apart from things that only happen rarely in the same course of nature, such as eclipses and comets, monstrous births, earthquakes and the like; apart from all these things whose first and supreme cause can only be the will of God—that is why, when the psalmist mentions *fire, hail, snow and ice and the stormy winds,* he adds, *which carry out his word* (Ps 148:8), in case anyone should imagine that they exist purely by chance, or as a result only of physical causes, or even spiritual ones, but without any reference to God's will—apart then from all these things, as I was trying to say, there are other things that occur equally in the physical realm, but are presented to our senses to tell us something from God. These are properly called miracles and signs. The very person of God, however, is not always represented in the things told us by the Lord God. When his person is represented, it is sometimes manifested in an angel, sometimes in an appearance or likeness which is not identical with an angel, though engineered by an angel; in this latter case it is sometimes a pre-existing body that is used and adapted for the manifestation, sometimes it is just produced *ad hoc,* and dissolved again when the business is complete.

In a similar fashion, when men convey the message, they sometimes speak the words of God in their own persons, as when they begin with "The Lord said," or "Thus says the Lord," or some equivalent; sometimes without any such introduction they play God's part and represent God's own person, as for example when the psalmist says, *I will give you understanding, and set you in the way you must go* (Ps 32:8). The prophets are sometimes also given the task of representing God's person in what they do as well as what they say; for example the prophet who divided his cloak into twelve parts and gave ten of them to Solomon's servant as the future king of Israel.[27] Sometimes a physical object distinct from the prophet himself is used to signify the person of God, as was done by Jacob with the stone he had used for a pillow, when he woke from his dream.[28] Sometimes a durable object is used for this purpose, like the brazen serpent lifted up in the desert,[29] or like written words; sometimes objects that cease to be when their significant function is complete, like the bread which is made for this purpose and is consumed when the sacrament is received.

20. But since people know that all such things are done or made by men, they cannot regard them with amazement as marvels or miracles, though they may treat them with reverence as objects of religion. The things done by angels, on

the other hand, seem marvelous to us the more difficult and mysterious they are, though to the angels themselves, being their own actions, they are quite straight-forward.

An example of an angel speaking in the person of God to a man is *I am the God of Abraham and the God of Isaac and the God of Jacob*—the text had just said, *An angel of the Lord appeared to him* (Ex 3:6, 2). An example of a man speaking in the person of God[30] is, *Listen, my people, and I will speak; Israel and I will testify against you; I am God your God* (Ps 50:7). A rod was used to mean something and changed by angelic skill into a serpent.[31] Man lacks this kind of skill, and yet a man took a stone and used it to signify the same sort of thing.[32] The first case was something both to wonder at and to understand, the second only something to understand. Perhaps what is understood as the mean-ing of both signs is the same, though the quality of the two signs differs—rather as if you were to write the Lord's name both in ink and in letters of gold. The gold letters are more valuable and the letters of ink cheaper, but they both mean the same thing.

As a matter of fact, although the serpent made out of Moses' rod has the same meaning as the stone set up by Jacob, Jacob's stone has a better meaning than the serpents produced by Pharaoh's wizards. The anointed stone stands for Christ in the flesh, in which he was anointed *with the oil of gladness above his fellows* (Ps 45:8); and Moses' rod turned into a serpent stands for Christ who *became obedient to death on the cross* (Phil 2:8). He himself says in the gospel, *As Moses lifted up the serpent in the desert, so must the Son of man be lifted up, so that everyone who believes in him might not perish, but have eternal life* (Jn 3:14), just as those who looked on that serpent in the desert *did not perish from the bites of the fiery serpents* (Nm 21:9). For *our old man has been nailed to the cross with him in order to nullify the sinful body* (Rom 6:6). Serpent stands for death (which was caused by the serpent in paradise) in virtue of the figure of speech by which the cause is used to mean the thing caused. So the rod turned into a serpent means Christ turned into death, and the serpent turned back again into a rod means Christ transformed in the resurrection—the whole Christ with his body the Church at the end of time; this is the meaning of the serpent's tail, which Moses caught hold of to turn it back into a rod again.

The serpents of the wizards, however, stand for the dead of this world, who will not be able to rise again with Christ unless by believing in him they are, as it were, devoured by him and incorporated into his body.[33] So Jacob's stone, as I said, represents something better than the wizards' serpents. Yet the action of the wizards was something much more wonderful than Jacob's. This however does not affect the relative value of the meanings; it is rather like writing a man's name in letters of gold and God's name in ink.

21. Take now the pillars of cloud and fire. Granted that they represented the Lord or the Holy Spirit, what man can possibly come to know how angels produced them or used them to signify what they declared? No more do the "infants"[34] know about what is put on the altar and is consumed at the end of the eucharistic celebration;[35] they do not know where it comes from, or how it

is effected, or how it gets its religious function. If they never learned by their own or other people's experience, and if they never saw that sort of thing except when it is offered and distributed at the celebration of the mysteries, and if they were told on the weightiest authority whose body and blood it is, they would imagine that this was the form, and no other, in which the Lord appeared to his disciples, that it was this sort of body which was pierced by the lance, and this sort of liquid which flowed from it.

Now it is just as well for me to remember my own limitations, and to remind my brothers to remember theirs, in case we should wander into deeper waters than human weakness can safely bear. How do angels do these things, or rather how does God do them through his angels, even through bad angels when he chooses, by permitting, commanding, or compelling them from his supreme and hidden seat of empire? I certainly lack the acuteness of vision to tell by observation, or the confidence of reason to work it out by calculations, or the range of intellect to grasp it in such a way that I could answer all the questions which might be asked here, with the same assurance as if I were an angel myself, or a prophet or an apostle. *The reasonings of mortals are unsure, and our forecasts uncertain. For a perishable body weighs down the soul, and a tent of clay presses down the mind full of thoughts. It is hard enough for us to work out what is on earth, laborious to discover what stares us in the face. But who has ever investigated*[36] *what is in the heavens* (Wis 9:14-16)? But he goes on to say, *As for your mind, who could learn it unless you granted wisdom, and sent your Holy Spirit from on high* (Wis 9:17)? So while we cannot investigate what is in the heavens, in the sense of knowing how to classify angels' bodies according to their special properties, or how to discern the pattern of their physical behavior, nonetheless by the Spirit of God sent us from on high, and by his grace bestowed on our minds, I can boldly say with complete confidence that neither God the Father nor his Word nor his Spirit, all of which is one God in being and identity, is in any way changeable or variable, let alone visible, like thoughts and memories and wishes, like any incorporeal creature. But nothing that is visible is not also variable. So then the substance, or if you prefer it the being[37] of God, in which we understand after our limited and partial human manner Father and Son and Holy Spirit, is in no way changeable or variable, and therefore cannot be in itself visible.

Chapter 4

That it was angels who were the secondary agents of the Old Testament theophanies is proved from scripture; chiefly from certain New Testament passages, but also from a brief reconsideration of certain episodes already discussed at length in Book II.

22. Accordingly, whatever it was that the Old Testament fathers saw whenever God showed himself to them, unfolding his plan of salvation in a manner

suited to the times, it is clear that it was always achieved through created objects. It may escape us how he did these things with angels to assist him, but that they were done through angels is not something we put forward as just our own idea; do not imagine we are *claiming a wisdom more than we ought to claim;*[38] *rather we are claiming wisdom with sobriety, according to the measure of faith which God has assigned to us* (Rom 12:3), *and we believe, therefore we also speak* (2 Cor 4:13). No, in this matter we have the authority of God's scriptures, which our minds should not stray from, the solid foundation of divine utterances which we must not leave, to plunge down the steep slopes of our own guesswork into places where neither our senses can guide us nor the clear reason of truth can enlighten us.

It is plainly stated in the letter to the Hebrews, where the author is distinguishing between the New Testament dispensation and the Old Testament dispensation, according to the requirements of different ages and times, that not only those visible phenomena of the Old Testament but also its verbal utterances were the work of angels. *To which of the angels,* he writes, *did he ever say, Sit at my right hand until I make your enemies your footstool? Are they not all serving spirits, sent on service for the sake of those who are going to possess the inheritance of salvation* (Heb 1:13a)?* Next he goes on to show clearly that the word which is now delivered through the Son was then delivered through angels; he says, *For that reason we should attend more closely to the things we have heard, in case we drift away. If the word spoken through angels had valid force, and every transgression or disregard of it received a just retribution, how shall we escape if we neglect such a great salvation* (Heb 2:1)? If you ask "What salvation?" he shows he is now speaking about the New Testament, that is the word spoken through the Lord, not through angels; *it was declared at first,* he goes on, *by the Lord, and it was attested to us by those who heard him, while God also bore witness by signs and portents and various miracles, and gifts of the Holy Spirit distributed according to his will* (Heb 2:3).

23. You might ask perhaps, "Then why does it read The Lord said to Moses, and not rather An angel said to Moses?" Well, when the clerk of the court pronounces the decision of the judge, it is not entered in the records as "Clerk So-and-so said," but as "Judge So-and-so said." Even when we say "The prophet said" about some prophetical utterance, we want it to be understood as "The Lord said," and if we say "The Lord said," we are not cutting out the prophet, but only emphasizing who it was who was speaking through him. In fact, that whole passage of scripture about Moses at the burning bush makes it clear that it is the angel of the Lord speaking when it says "The Lord said," as I have already shown.[39] But there are people who want to take the angel as meaning the Son of God speaking directly in his own person, because the prophet calls

---

* This shows, incidentally, that all those things, as well as being done by angels, were done for us, for the people of God who are promised the inheritance of eternal life. Compare a text from Corinthians: *All these things happened to them by way of example, but they were written down to put us right, on whom the end of the ages has come* (1 Cor 10:11).

him angel (Is 9:6), to signify that he is the messenger of the Father's—and his own—will. It was to counter this opinion that I preferred to use the evidence of Hebrews, where it does not say "through an angel" but "through angels."

24. Stephen too, in the Acts of the Apostles, tells of these things in the same sort of language as the Old Testament used. *Brothers and fathers, listen,* he says. *The God of glory appeared to our father Abraham when he was in Mesopotamia* (Acts 7:2). In case anyone should assume that the God of glory appeared to the eyes of mortals as he is in himself, he says further on that an angel appeared to Moses. *At this word,* he says, *Moses fled and became an exile in the land of Midian, where he had two sons. And when forty years had passed there, an angel of the Lord appeared to him in the desert of Mount Sinai in a flame of fire in the bush. When Moses saw it he was amazed at the sight. As he came up to look, the voice of the Lord came: I am the God of your fathers, the God of Abraham and the God of Isaac and the God of Jacob. Moses trembled and did not dare to look. The Lord said to him, Take your shoes off your feet,* etc. (Acts 7:29). Here, quite plainly, the same God of Abraham and God of Isaac and God of Jacob as is written about in Genesis is called both angel and Lord.

25. Perhaps you will say that the Lord appeared to Moses by means of an angel, but to Abraham directly himself? Let us not put this matter to Stephen to solve; let us interrogate the book Stephen was quoting from. Just because it says there that *the Lord God said to Abraham* (Gn 12:1), and a little later *And the Lord God appeared to Abraham* (Gn 12:7), must we conclude that it was not done by means of angels? Even though it says in a similar passage, *God appeared to him at the oak of Mambre, when he was sitting at the door of his tent at midday,* and yet it goes on, *Lifting up his eyes he saw, and there were three men standing over him* (Gn 18:1)? We have already discussed these texts.[40] How then can these people who are reluctant to rise from words to meaning, and so readily rush from meaning into words, how can they explain God appearing in the form of three men, unless they admit, as the story goes on to say in so many words, that the men were angels? Just because it does not say "An angel spoke or appeared to him," will they have the face to maintain that what Moses heard and saw was done through an angel, but that what Abraham heard and saw was God in his own substance, simply because an angel was not mentioned?

What if an angel was mentioned sometimes in connection with Abraham? Here is the story of his being asked to sacrifice his son: *And it came to pass after these things that God tested Abraham and said to him, Abraham, Abraham. He answered, Here am I. He said to him, Take your beloved son whom you love, Isaac, and go into the high country and offer him there as a holocaust on one of the mountains which I will show you* (Gn 22:1). To be sure, God is mentioned here, not an angel. But a little later the scripture runs, *Abraham stretched out his hand and took the sword to kill his son. And the angel of the Lord called to him from heaven and said to him, Abraham, Abraham, And he said, Here am I. And he said to him, Do not lay your hand on the boy or do anything to him* (Gn 22:10).

What will they answer to this? That God ordered the death of Isaac, and an angel forbade it? That his father obeyed the angel's command to spare him in the teeth of God's command to kill him? A ridiculous and untenable opinion. Anyway, scripture expressly excludes it by adding, *Now I know that you fear God, and for my sake have not spared your beloved son* (Gn 22:12). Whose sake can "my sake" be but his who had commanded Abraham to kill him? So then Abraham's God is identical with the angel, isn't he, or rather God is represented by the angel. See how it goes on; certainly the angel has already been expressly mentioned in the passage quoted. But see what follows: *Abraham lifted up his eyes and looked, and there was a ram caught in a sabek tree by its horns. And Abraham went and took the ram and offered it as a holocaust instead of Isaac his son. And Abraham named that place The Lord has seen, so that there is a saying today, On the mountain the Lord was seen* (Gn 22:13).*

So here then the angel is clearly called the Lord, surely because the Lord was represented by the angel. In what follows the angel speaks exactly in the prophetic style, and thus makes it quite clear that it is God who speaks through the angel: *The angel of the Lord*, it says, *called Abraham a second time from heaven, and said, By myself I have sworn, says the Lord, because you have done this thing, and for my sake have not spared your beloved son*, etc. (Gn 22:15). This expression "says the Lord" is one the prophets were in the habit of using, to show that they were the Lord's mouthpieces. Or is it perhaps the Son of God saying "says the Lord," meaning the Father, and is he the angel of the Father? But cannot people of this opinion see what difficulties those three men make for them who appeared to Abraham, with the introductory remark, *The Lord appeared to him* (Gn 18:2)? Do they maintain they cannot be angels because they are called men? They should read Daniel, who says *And behold the man Gabriel* (Dn 9:21).

26. But let us no longer defer stopping their mouths with another text of the weightiest and clearest kind, where it is not an angel in the singular or men in the plural that are mentioned, but simply angels, and where it is not any old utterance but the law itself which is clearly revealed through them, the law which as all the faithful know was given to Moses by God to tame the people of Israel, given however through angels. Here is Stephen again: *Stiff-necked men*, he says, *and uncircumcised of heart and ears, you have always withstood the Holy Spirit, just like your fathers. Which of the prophets did your fathers not persecute? They killed those who foretold the coming of the Just One, and now you have*

---

* Just as what God said through the angel a little earlier, *Now I know that you fear God*, does not mean that God then came to realize it, but that he made Abraham realize what strength of mind he had, to the point of sacrificing his only son in obedience to God—it is the figure of speech by which the cause is used to mean the thing caused, as when the cold is called numb because it makes people numb; thus God is said to have known because he made Abraham know—he might not have realized the strength of his faith unless it had been put to such a test; so here, *Abraham called the name of the place The Lord has seen*, meaning The Lord has made himself to be seen. Thus the text continues, *So that there is a saying today, On the mountain the Lord was seen.*

betrayed and killed him, you who received the law as proclaimed by angels and never kept it (Acts 7:51). What could be clearer? Could you find a more cast-iron authority for our case than that? The law was given to that people as proclaimed by angels, but the coming of our Lord Jesus Christ was being prepared and foretold by means of it; and he, as God's Word, was present in a wonderful and inexpressible way in the angels through whose proclamation the law was given. So he says in the gospel, *If you believed Moses, you would believe me too, since he wrote about me* (Jn 5:46).

So the Lord used to speak in those bygone days through angels, and through angels the Son of God, who would come from the seed of Abraham to mediate between God and men, was preparing his coming, arranging to find people to receive him by confessing themselves guilty, convicted of transgression by the law they had not fulfilled. That is what the apostle says to the Galatians: *Why the law then? It was put forth because of transgression until the seed should come to whom the promise had been made, who was prepared through angels in the hand of a mediator* (Gal 3:19),[41] that is, prepared through angels in his own hand; for he was not born in virtue of the natural condition of things, but in virtue of his own sovereign authority. When Saint Paul says "mediator" he does not mean one of the angels but the Lord Jesus Christ as having graciously become man; this is clear from another text of his: *There is one God, and one mediator between God and men, the man Christ Jesus* (1 Tm 2:5).

This then is the meaning and point of the lamb slain at passover; the meaning and point of all those things in the law which prefigured Christ who was to come in the flesh and to suffer and rise again, the law which was given as proclaimed by angels. Acting in and through these angels, of course, were the Father and the Son and the Holy Spirit. Sometimes it was the Father who was represented by them, sometimes the Son, sometimes the Holy Spirit, sometimes just God without distinction of persons. Even if he appeared in visible or audible fashion, it was by means of his creation and not in his own proper substance. To see that substance, hearts have to be purified by all these things which are seen by eyes and heard by ears.[42]

27. But the discussion, I think, has now gone on sufficiently long to demonstrate what we set out to show in this book. It has been established by all rational probability as far as man—or rather as far as I—can work it out, and by firm authority as far as the divine words of scripture have declared it, that whenever God was said to appear to our ancestors before our savior's incarnation, the voices heard and the physical manifestation seen were the work of angels. They either spoke and did things themselves, representing God's person, just as we have shown that the prophets used to do, or they took created materials distinct from themselves and used them to present us with symbolic representations of God; and this too is a kind of communication which the prophets made use of, as many cases in scripture show.

But now, when the Lord was born of the virgin, and when the Holy Spirit came down in bodily form like a dove, or in visible fiery tongues and a sound from heaven on the day of Pentecost after the Lord's ascension, what appeared to the bodily senses of mortals was not the very substance of the Word of God in which he is equal to the Father and co-eternal, nor the very substance of the Spirit of the Father and the Son in which he is co-equal and co-eternal with them both, but something created which could be formed and come into being in those ways. So it remains for us to see what the difference is between those Old Testament demonstrations and these proper manifestations of the Son of God and the Holy Spirit, even though these too were achieved through the visible creation. It will be more convenient, however, to tackle this question in a new volume.

NOTES

1. An allusion, doubtless, to Ps 105:4; see *Introduction* 10, and Book I, 5, and note 11.

2. A most necessary attitude for any honest theologian, honest bishop, and honest Christian, an attitude that has perhaps been rather wanting in Catholic theological and official circles.

3. But not, of course, before you have cautiously and undogmatically discovered what it really is, like Augustine himself.

4. See above Book II, 13, note 31.

5. See Jn 2:9.

6. This theme of participation by the rational soul in the eternal truth and goodness which is God will be developed at length in Book VIII.

7. *Mortaliter exerceri*, a difficult phrase; I think he means we need to be trained to accept our mortal condition in the spirit of the cross.

8. This strange little excursus into eucharistic theology throws an interesting light on Augustine's ideas on the subject, and must modify to some extent the impression we get of them, say from his commentary on John 6 (*Homilies on the Gospel of John* 26, 13-20). Augustine is customarily thought of, largely on the strength of that passage, as holding a "symbolist" view of the sacrament as against the "realist" view expressed for example by Ambrose in his *De Mysteriis* 9. On the whole this is true, as Augustine always lays great stress on the *significance* of the sacraments, which he classifies as signs, sacred signs, rather than as just things. In this he is firmly taken up by Thomas Aquinas, and again by the leading spirits in theology today, who are reacting, perhaps over-reacting, against a somewhat uncritical and mechanical "realism" that has colored Catholic sacramental thought and piety for rather a long time.

But this passage of ours here shows that Augustine's "symbolism" was not unqualified. He does indeed introduce the eucharist quite unequivocally in a "signs" context here. But then he introduces this section, which is in reality a footnote, to explain that the eucharist is a quite unique sort of sign, in that it is to be identified with the thing signified (the body and blood of Christ) in a way that no other sign can be. Furthermore a real and unique spiritual, divine, causality needs to be brought into play to effect this unique sign. It is interesting to observe that he thinks angels might well be co-ministers of the eucharist. Are they thought of perhaps as playing the same kind of role as the mysterious angel in the *Supplices te rogamus* prayer of Eucharistic Prayer I (the Roman Canon)?

9. This one-sentence paragraph, with its eucharistic parenthesis, introduces an important turn to his argument. It is that God not only orders all things, but speaks to us in all things. But as we are so used to the natural course of events that we fail to get the message, he drives it home by miracles, of which the essential point is that they are signs, which tell us about, but are not, God and his will.

10. See 1 Kgs 18.

11. See Ex 19:20.

12. See Jn 2:9.

13. See Nm 17:8.

14. See Gn 1:24.

15. See 1 Kgs 17:17; 2 Kgs 4:8; 13:21; Ez 37, 1-10, etc.

16. I do not think he is thinking of the darkness of hell, or tartarus (2 Pt 2:4) but of the sublunar atmosphere (see Eph 2:2; 6:12).

17. See Job 1:13.

18. See Ex 7:11; 8:3.

19. See Gn 1:20.24.

20. Augustine develops a kind of theory of what he calls *rationes seminales* or *causales* in *The Literal Meaning of Genesis*, Books V and VI especially. It follows from his view of the simultaneous creation of all things. It is hardly of course a theory of evolution, but it has a certain affinity with it as a dynamic view of the universe's unfolding.

21. The "fact" of spontaneous generation was as much a commonplace in the ancient world as the "fact" of evolution in the modern. The moral is, never treat as fact what is in fact only hypothesis or inference.

22. Vergil, *Georgics* 4, 200-202.

23. Augustine's pre-computer phrase is *ab originalibus tanquam regulis*.

24. M adds *Paulus*.

25. See Gn 30:37.

26. *Congruentiae rationis*: M reads *congruae rationes*, harmonious ideas. It is a thoroughly Augustinian expression, but he usually locates the *rationes*, which he terms *causales* (above section 13, note 20), in the created elements. As he here locates even more archetypal patterns in the divine wisdom. CCL's text is preferable.

27. See 1 Kgs 11:30.

28. See Gn 28:18.

29. See Nm 21:9.

30. M reads *Domini*, the Lord.

31. See Ex 4:3.

32. See Gn 28:18.

33. As Aaron's serpent devoured those of the wizards, Ex 7:12.

34. The newly baptized were known as *infantes*; they were not instructed in the mystery of the eucharist until after they had taken part in their first Mass during the Easter vigil.

35. Augustine's untranslatable phrase is *pietatis celebratione*.

36. *Investigavit*; M has *investigabit*, will investigate. It is peculiarly hard in this instance to decide which was the original. The manuscripts are fairly equally divided, and the confusion of sound between b's and v's could lead to a mistake from dictation in either direction. The Vulgate has *investigabit*, like M, and copyists are more likely to have altered a reading to conform to the Vulgate than to vary from it. But the Greek word being translated is one of those by no means common words in which the aorist and the future third singular are identical in form. The Revised Standard Version translates it as aorist; Jerusalem Bible neatly avoids the difficulty by rendering "Who can discover . . . ," though this is more likely to represent a decision in favor of the future.

37. *Essentia*: this word is briefly discussed below in Book V, 3 and extensively in Book VII, where I regularly render it "being." See below book V, 3, note 4.

38. Than we ought to claim, *praeter quam oportet sapere*, is omitted by M; presumably an inadvertent error in transcription.

39. Book II, 23.

40. Book II, 19-22.

41. Paul actually talks of the law being administered through angels etc.; the participle here rendered "who was prepared" being in agreement with "law." But Augustine's text translates it with a neuter form, in agreement with "seed."

42. He will elaborate this idea in Book XIII. What the heart needs to be purified by is faith, and faith is a response to the visible, symbolic economy of salvation presented in scripture and culminating in the *flesh* of the incarnate Word.

INTRODUCTORY ESSAY ON BOOK IV

This book is one of the most difficult and also one of the most important of the whole *De Trinitate*, and calls for special commendation to the reader. It contains some of the roughest, as well as some of the most splendid writing in the whole work, and had Augustine been able to revise as he wished, I think this book would perhaps have been one of the most thoroughly rewritten. I have remarked on some of the roughnesses, both of style and argument, in the footnotes.

But besides these particular difficulties there is a general difficulty of how the book as a whole fits into the development of his theme. In chapter 3 of Book II he set himself a program for discussing the idea of mission. The first part of this program, to decide whether any of the divine persons, and if so which, appeared to men in the Old Testament theophanies, he completed in the rest of Book II; the second part, to decide whether angels were employed in producing these theophanies, occupied Book III; and the third, to decide whether one could talk of the divine persons being sent in the Old Testament, and if not, what was special and unique about their being sent in the New Testament, this is the task that is scheduled for Book IV. Now he does eventually settle down to it and work out his final and complete definition of the divine missions, but only in chapter 5, in the last quarter of the book. The first four chapters are taken up with two accounts, and strange ones at that, of the redemption, or to be more accurate, of Christ's mediation. No word of explanation is given for this, and the reader is left wondering what it has to do with the subject of the trinity. This is of course a common rhetorical device to keep the audience alert, a kind of suspense technique. But to carry it to such lengths as this does seem to be to defeat the very purpose of such a device.

However, that is what he does. He gives us the key to the movement of his thought at the beginning of chapter 5, where he says "There you have what the Son of God has been sent for; indeed, there you have what it is for the Son of God to have been sent." He has been engaged all along in describing in concrete, actual terms what it means for the Word to be sent. We do not usually talk about people being sent except with reference to the purpose they are sent for; so much so that the word "mission" is more often used in English to mean what someone is sent for than to mean the actual sending. People go on fact-finding missions; forces return to base, mission accomplished. So the Son of God's mission was to be the mediator between man and God; the accomplishment of this mission required him to be incarnate and to offer himself as an acceptable sacrifice on our behalf; he cannot meaningfully be said to have been sent until he began to accomplish this mission; he did not do this until the New Testament; and so we conclude that he was not sent until the New Testament.

147

Augustine nowhere explicitly spells out this line of thought; I think he leaves us to assume it with him, and if we do so, then Book IV becomes coherent. Having then demonstrated in this oblique way that the mission of the Son is confined to the New Testament, he takes up the argument in chapter 5 where he had left it at the end of Book II, chapter 2 above. He shows (i) that even if (as the "economic" theologians assumed) being sent means being less than the sender, this does not involve us necessarily in saying that the Son is less than the Father except in the human form or nature in which he was sent; (ii) that in fact, however, being sent does not in this case mean being less than the sender, but only being from the sender, as light from light; and so he comes to his final and most important definition of divine mission, that it is the making known to us of the eternal processions: "being sent, for the Son, means his being known by men to be from the Father"—and similarly with the Holy Spirit. This definition of mission does not contradict his long description of the Son's mission as mediating between God and man; for the object of the mediation was by reconciling us to God to give us mortals access to eternal life; *and this is eternal life, that they may know you and Jesus Christ whom you have sent*; so it is by knowing that the Son is from the Father that we have eternal life, that we benefit from the mediating mission of the Son.

His definition of mission then leads him on to declare that the Holy Spirit proceeds from the Son as well as from the Father; given his definition of mission, this is an unavoidable conclusion, seeing that scripture speaks quite expressly about the Holy Spirit being sent by the Son as well as by the Father. But Augustine is careful to show why this does not derogate in any way from the Father's absolute priority as *principium*, "monarch," or ultimate source of all deity.

The vital importance of this definition of mission is that it has introduced the discussion to the key topic of the divine processions. So far all that has been established is the equality of the divine persons and their inseparability. But this gives no more than a surface impression of the mystery; the heart of it lies in the eternal generation of the Son and procession of the Spirit, and the missions open up this inner core of the mystery for our contemplation. But the reader must be warned that we will not proceed to attempt such contemplation until Book IX. There is more preliminary work to be done first, the refutation of the logical and metaphysical arguments of the Arians.

Besides describing what the Son of God was sent for, and so giving us in the concrete what his mission was, the first four chapters devoted to the mediation of the incarnate Word also have, I think, a secondary but related purpose. They serve to show up the difference in kind between his mission and the sort of mission on which angels were sent, which had been the subject of Book III. This purpose helps to explain why in chapters 3 and 4 Augustine describes Christ's mediation by contrasting it with the pseudomediation of the devil, and why indeed he makes mediation his key term at all, rather than say redemption or salvation. It is not, after all, as if it were a notably prominent concept in the New Testament. But let us look at chapters 1 to 4 as they come, and try to analyze what they have to say.

In the first two chapters the mediation is presented as the restoration of harmony to a discordant world. It is worked out in terms of a number symbolism against the background of the plotinian problematic of the one and the many. It was a problem that had been bothering the ancient world for centuries. The Gnostics had offered a variety of mystico-religious solutions. It was essentially a problem of mediation, of linking the One, the primal and ultimate reality, with the multiplicity of the world as we experience it. How did the many proceed from the One in the first place, and how could they be reduced or led back to it or reconciled with it in the second place? As a Christian Augustine finds the answer in the incarnation of the Word; as a man with a deep sympathy for the plotinian metaphysics he presents the mediation of the incarnate Word as an application of the single to the double, the basic musical harmony of the octave. This is the theme of chapter 1, and it leads him to the profound statement of the death and resurrection of Christ being the sacrament of our spiritual death and resurrection and the model of our bodily death and resurrection. Chapter 2 is a kind of baroque elaboration of this theme in terms principally of the symbolism of the number 6, treated as symbolic of time, and it concludes with a paean in praise of the mystery of unity, re-established by the mediation of Christ. In a note on the end of this chapter (section 12, note 46) I express a certain surprise at his seeing this re-establishment of unity as taking place primarily in moral terms. But his reason, I think, is a polemical one; he is disagreeing with the philosophical paganism of his day which looked for a more or less exclusively ontological mediation and restoration of unity.

So we come to chapters 3 and 4 in which Christ's mediation is regarded as primarily a work of purification. It is contrasted with the false mediation of the devil; the devil, that is to say, is a true mediator of death, but also tries to delude men into regarding him as a mediator of life by means of magico-religious rites. The chapter shows how Christ uses the devil's mediation of death to beat him on his own ground and mediate life to us by means of the death which he permitted the devil to inflict on him, thereby justly stripping the devil of the power and authority—Augustine uses the word *jus*—which he held over us. Then the chapter concludes by contrasting the vanity, indeed the baleful effect of the devil's rites of so-called purification with the one truly efficacious and purifying sacrifice of Christ. In a quite masterly way he also presents this sacrifice as being in itself a celebration of the mystery of unity.

The use made of the devil in working out a theology of redemption can be rather disconcerting to the modern reader. But it made very good sense in Augustine's day. If the devil was far more real for him than he is for us, this was because he lived in an age when Christianity was still faced with a vigorous *religious* paganism, as distinct from the religionless post-Christian neo-paganism of modern times. Whenever Augustine brings the devil into his discussion, you may be fairly sure that he is engaged in a polemic against paganism. That is certainly the case in this chapter, and for background reading to it I recommend *The City of God*, Books VIII, IX, and X. It seems to me very likely that Augustine was engaged in writing them about the same time as he was composing this book. He probably frequently interrupted his work on the *De Trinitate* to get on with *The City of God*, which he considered to be pastorally more urgent. In those books of that work we can see in more detail what kind of mediation the semi-philosophical paganism that went in for magical or "theurgical" rites was after. Between the celestial gods, who might either be identified with the One, or at least be regarded as proximate emanations from it, and terrestrial man, were the aerial demons; they were ontologically in the middle, above man in nature, below the gods, and so they were cultivated, often it appears with immoral rites, to mediate for man the way back to the divine sphere. In Augustine's view, of course, they were simply evil spirits bent on leading men astray, and the gods themselves were either false fictions or evil demons, all of them agents of the devil. The falsity of their mediation is shown by their claiming the divine honors of sacrifice, in contrast with the good spirits or angels, who only mediated God's commands and revelations to men, and directed the sacrificial worship of men to the one true God to whom alone it was due.

In the fourth chapter he goes on to attack the purely philosophical paganism of a man like Plotinus and perhaps his disciple Porphyry—though Porphyry is criticized in *The City of God* for being too tolerant of the magical cultivation of demons by theurgy—who claimed to be able to achieve the necessary purification for contemplation of the One by their unaided intellectual powers. The very claim itself involves them in the defilement of pride, and is based on an intellectual contempt for the flesh and matter, particularly for the flesh of the Word incarnate and the preposterous Christian claim that purification was achieved by his death. Against them Augustine argues for the necessity of purification by faith, faith precisely in the temporal and physical reality of the incarnation and in the death and resurrection of Christ. Faith is the proper response to temporal realities (see section 24, note 74), and the beauty of the mediation practiced by the Word incarnate is that he offers the same person in time to be the object of our faith as is intended to be the object of our contemplation in eternity. One of the salutary things about faith is that it is a hard form of intellectual humility, which thus purifies us of pride and makes us morally fit for contemplation.

Thus all these four chapters, and especially the third and fourth, can be seen as presenting the mediation of the Word incarnate in terms of a controversy with religious and philosophical paganism. One might think at first that such a controversy is not very relevant to a work on the Trinity. And it is true that it is various Christian unorthodoxies that provide the main controversial framework for Augustine to work out his own doctrine on. But a controversy with paganism provides a convenient and indeed organic link between the first few books in which he is engaged in refuting the unorthodox conclusions of the earlier "economic" theologians and the next three books in which he will be crossing swords with the Arians. For the Arian arguments against orthodoxy, unlike the erroneous conclusions of the earlier writers, have more of a metaphysical or rational basis than a purely scriptural one. They too, in other words, had been to school with the neoplatonists—and the aristotelians. So it is artistically neat of Augustine to lead up to his argument with the Arians by introducing and refuting the pagans; and because philosophic paganism was not indeed directly *ad rem* to trinitarian theology, he employs them as a foil in elaborating his theology of Christ's mediation, which is in fact relevant, as we have seen, to the theme of the divine missions. The execution of his scheme may well be rather clumsy here and there, but there is no denying that its conception is extremely ingenious, once we have been able to discern what it is.

BOOK IV

MISSIONS: THE WORK OF THE MEDIATOR

Prologue

---

1. The knowledge of earthly and celestial things is highly prized by the human race. Its better specimens, to be sure, attach even greater value to knowledge of self; and the mind that knows its own weakness deserves more respect than the one that, with no thought at all for a little thing like that, sets out to explore, or even knows already, the course of the stars, while ignorant of the course it should follow itself to its own health and strength. But take a man who has been roused by the warmth of the Holy Spirit and has already woken up to God; and in loving him he has become cheap in his own estimation; and being eager yet unable to go in to him, he has taken a look at himself in God's light, and discovered himself, and realized that his own sickness cannot be compounded with God's cleanness. So he finds it a relief to weep and implore him over and over again to take pity and pull him altogether out of his pitiful condition, and he prays with all confidence once he has received the free gratuitous pledge of health through the one and only savior and enlightener granted us by God. Well, such a man, poor[1] and grieving in this way, is not *puffed up* by *knowledge* because he is *built up* by *charity* (1 Cor 8:1), since he has valued knowledge above knowledge; he has put knowledge of his own weakness above knowledge of *the walls of the world,*[2] the foundations of the earth and the pinnacles of the sky; and by *bringing in* this *knowledge* he has *brought in sorrow* (Eccl 1:18),[3] the sorrow of the exile stirred by longing for his true country and its founder, his blissful God.

As one of this sort of men, O Lord my God, I sigh among your poor ones in the family of your Christ,[4] and I beg from you a morsel of your bread with which to reply to people who do not *hunger and thirst for justice* (Mt 5:6), but are well fed and have more than enough. What has satisfied them is their own imaginings, not your truth. This they thrust away from them, and so bounce back and fall into their own emptiness. I am fully aware how many fancies the human heart can breed—what is my own heart, after all, but a human heart? But what I pray for to the *God of my heart* (Ps 73:26) is that no such fancies should spill over into these pages masquerading as solidly true, but that the only things to appear on them should be what has come to me wafted by the fresh air of his truth, far though *I have been cast from his eyes* (Ps 31:23). But I am struggling to return from this *far country* (Lk 15:13)[5] by the road he has made in the humanity of the divinity of his only Son; and changeable though I am, I breathe in his truth the more deeply, the more clearly I perceive there is nothing changeable about it; not changeable in time and space like bodies, nor changeable only in time and quasi-space, like the wandering fancies of our spirits,[6] nor only in time and not even in imagined space, like some of the reasonings of our minds. For God's essence, by which he is, has absolutely nothing changeable about its eternity or its truth or its will; there truth is eternal and love is eternal; there love is true and eternity true; there eternity is lovely and truth is lovely too.

Chapter 1

Man's need, and God's response to it; the harmonies of the incarnation and redemption, in which Christ mediates between God and man by observing, as it were, the basic harmonious proportion of 1 to 2; and how Christ in his death and resurrection is both the sacrament of our spiritual death and resurrection, and the model for our bodily death and resurrection.

---

2. But we were exiled from this unchanging joy, yet not so broken and cut off from it that we stopped seeking eternity, truth, and happiness even in this changeable time-bound situation of ours—for we do not want, after all, to die or to be deceived or to be afflicted. So God sent us sights suited to our wandering state,[7] to admonish us that what we seek is not here, and that we must turn back from the things around us to where our whole being springs from—if it did not, we would not even seek these things here.

First we had to be persuaded how much God loved us, in case out of sheer despair we lacked the courage to reach up to him. Also we had to be shown what sort of people we are that he loves, in case we should take pride in our own worth, and so bounce even further away from him and sink even more under our own strength. So he dealt with us in such a way that we could progress rather in his strength; he arranged it so that the power of charity would be brought to perfection in the weakness of humility. This is the meaning of the psalm where it says, *O God, you are setting apart a voluntary rain for your inheritance, and it has been weakened; but you have perfected it* (Ps 68:9). What he means by voluntary rain is nothing other than grace, which is not paid out as earned but given gratis; that is why it is called grace. He was not obliged to give it because we deserved it; he gave it voluntarily because he wished to. Knowing this, we will put no trust in ourselves, and that is what to be weakened means. He however perfects us—as he said to the apostle Paul, *My grace is enough for you; strength is made perfect in weakness* (2 Cor 12:9). So we needed to be persuaded how much God loves us, and what sort of people he loves; how much in case we despaired, what sort in case we grew proud.

This is how the apostle explains this absolutely crucial point: *God shows the quality of his love for us in that Christ died for us while we were still sinners. Much more being justified now in his blood shall we be saved from the wrath by him. For if while we were enemies we were reconciled to God by the death of his Son, much more being reconciled shall we be saved in his life* (Rom 5:8). Again, he says elsewhere, *What then shall we say to this? If God is for us, who is against us? He did not spare his own Son but delivered him up for us all; how then has he not given us all things with him* (Rom 8:31)? Now what is proclaimed to us as already having been achieved was also shown to the just men of old as still to be achieved, in order that they too might be made weak through being humbled by the same faith as we[8] and once weakened might be perfected.

3. So because there is but one Word of God, *through which all things were made* (Jn 1:1-6), which is unchanging truth, in which[9] all things are primordially and unchangingly together, not only things that are in the whole of this creation, but things that have been and will be; but there it is not a question of "have been" and "will be," there they simply are; and all things there are life and all are one, and indeed there is there but one "one" and one life. For *all things were made through him* in such a way that *whatever has been made* in this world *was in him life* (Jn 1:3-4); and this life was not made, because *in the beginning* the Word was not made, but *the Word was, and the Word was*[10] *with God, and the Word was God, and all things were made through him* (Jn 1:1-3); and all things would not have been made through him unless he had been before all things and had not been made himself. Among the things made through him is the body which is not life, but which would not have been made through him unless it were life in him before it was made. For *what was made in him was* already *life* (Jn 1:4), and not any sort of life either. After all, the soul is the body's life, but this too was made since it is changeable, and what was it made by if not by the Word of God? *All things were made through him and without him was made nothing* (Jn 1:3). So *what was made was* already *life in him*, and not any sort of life, but *the life was the light of men* (Jn 1:4), the light that is to say of rational minds, which distinguish men from animals and precisely make them men. So it does not mean physical light, which whether it shines from the sky or is lit by fire on earth, is the light of bodies, and not of human bodies only but of brutes too, and right on down to the tiniest little worms; all these see this sort of light. But that *light of men* is what *life was* (Jn 1:4), *nor was it removed far from any one of us, for in it we live and move and are* (Acts 17:27). But *the light shines in the darkness and the darkness did not comprehend it* (Jn 1:5). The darkness is the foolish minds of men, blinded by depraved desires and unbelief.

4. To cure these and make them well *the Word* through which all things were made *became flesh and dwelt among us* (Jn 1:14). Our enlightenment is to

participate in the Word, that is, in that *life which is the light of men* (Jn 1:4). Yet we were absolutely incapable of such participation and quite unfit for it, so unclean were we through sin, so we had to be cleansed. Furthermore, the only thing to cleanse the wicked and the proud is the blood of the just man and the humility of God; to contemplate God, which by nature we are not, we would have to be cleansed by him who became what by nature we are and what by sin we are not. By nature we are not God; by nature we are men; by sin we are not just. So God became a just man to intercede with God for sinful man. The sinner did not match the just, but man did match man. So he applied to us the similarity of his humanity to take away the dissimilarity of our iniquity, and becoming a partaker of our mortality he made us partakers of his divinity.[11] It was surely right that the death of the sinner issuing from the stern necessity of condemnation should be undone by the death of the just man issuing from the voluntary freedom of mercy, his single matching our double.

This match—or agreement or concord or consonance or whatever the right word is for the proportion of one to two—is of enormous importance in every construction or interlock[12]—that is the word I want—of creation. What I mean by this interlock, it has just occurred to me, is what the Greeks call *harmonia*.[13] This is not the place to show the far-reaching importance of the consonant proportion of the single to the double. It is found extensively in us,[14] and is so naturally ingrained in us (and who by, if not by him who created us?), that even the unskilled feel it whether singing themselves or listening to others. It is what makes concord between high-pitched and deep voices, and if anyone strays discordantly away from it, it is not our knowledge, which many lack, but our very sense of hearing that is painfully offended. To explain it would require a long lecture; but anyone who knows how can demonstrate it to our ears with a tuning string, or tonometer.

5. As for our present concern, what has to be explained as far as God permits is how the single of our Lord Jesus Christ matches our double, and in some fashion enters into a harmony of salvation with it. We, for a start, and no Christian has any doubts about this, were dead in both body and soul—in soul because of sin, in body because of sin's punishment; and thus in *body* too *because of sin* (Rom 8:10). Each thing of ours, that is, both soul and body, was in need of healing and resurrection, in order to renew for the better what had changed for the worse. Now the death of the soul is ungodliness[15] and the death of the body is perishability, which ends in the soul's departure from the body. Just as the soul dies when God leaves it, so does the body when the soul leaves it. It becomes lifeless in this process, as the soul becomes wisdomless in that. The soul is resuscitated by repentance, and in the still mortal body the renewal of life takes its start from faith by which one *believes in him who justifies the ungodly* (Rom 4:5), and it grows and is strengthened by good behavior *from day to day*, while *the inner man is renewed* (2 Cor 4:16) more and more. However, the longer this life lasts, the more does the body, as *the outer man, decay* (2 Cor 4:16) whether by age or sickness or a whole variety of troubles, until it comes to the last of them which everybody calls death. Its resurrection is deferred to

the end, when our justification will be inexpressibly perfected. For then *we will be like him because we will see him as he is* (1 Jn 3:2). But meanwhile, as long as *the body which decays is weighing down the soul* (Wis 9:15), and *human life on earth is one long trial* (Jb 7:1), *in God's sight is no man living justified* (Ps 143:2), in comparison with that justice in which *we shall be equal to the angels* (Lk 20:36), and *with that glory which shall be revealed in us* (Rom 8:18).

Need I produce many examples to show the difference between the soul's death and the body's, when they can easily be told apart by anyone in that one sentence of the Lord's in the gospel: *Leave the dead to bury their dead* (Mt 8:22; Lk 9:60)? It was a dead body, of course, that had to be buried, but its buriers he meant us to understand as dead in soul through godless unbelief;[16] the sort of dead who are roused up in the text, *Awake, you who sleep and rise from the dead, and Christ will enlighten you* (Eph 5:14). Again, the apostle reprobates a death of this kind when he says of one sort of widow, *If she spends her time in pleasure, she is dead while she lives* (1 Tm 5:6). So the godly soul which had been godless is said to have returned to life from death and to live, thanks to the *justice of faith* (Rom 4:13). Of the body, however, it is not only said that it is going to die, thanks to the soul's departure in the future, but in one place of scripture that it is already dead, thanks to the great weakness of flesh and blood; the apostle says, *The body indeed is dead thanks to sin, but the spirit is life thanks to justice* (Rom 8:10). This life arises out of faith, since *the just man lives out of faith* (Rom 1:17).[17] But how does he go on? *If the Spirit of him who raised up Jesus from the dead dwells in you, he who raised up Jesus from the dead will also bring to life your mortal bodies through his Spirit dwelling in you* (Rom 8:11).

6. To balance this double death of ours the savior paid in his single one, and to achieve each resurrection of ours he pre-enacted and presented his one and only one by way of sacrament and by way of model. For he was not a sinner or godless, and so he had no need to be renewed in the inner man as though he were dead in spirit, or by regaining wisdom to be called back to a life of justice. But being clothed with mortal flesh, in that alone he died and in that alone he rose again; and so in that alone he harmonized with each part of us by becoming in that flesh the sacrament[18] for the inner man and the model for the outer one.

As a sacrament of our inner man he uttered that cry, both in the psalm and on the cross,[19] which was intended to represent the death of our soul: *My God, my God, why have you forsaken me* (Ps 22:1; Mk 15:34)? To this cry there corresponds what the apostle says, *Knowing that our old man was crucified together with him, in order to cancel the body of sin, that we might no longer be the slaves of sin* (Rom 6:6). By the crucifixion of the inner man is to be understood the sorrows of repentance and a kind of salutary torment of self-discipline, a kind of death to erase the death of ungodliness in which God does not leave us. And thus it is by this sort of cross that the *body of sin* is *cancelled* (Rom 6:6), so that we should *no* longer *offer* our *members to sin as the weapons of wickedness* (Rom 6:13). For surely, if it is *our inner man* that is *renewed from day to day* (2 Cor 4:16), then it must be old before it is renewed.[20] It all takes place within, this process that the apostle refers to in the words, *Strip off the old man and put on the new* (Eph 4:22). Indeed, he goes on to explain: *Therefore putting aside falsehood, speak the truth* (Eph 4:24). And where is falsehood put aside if not inside, that the man *who speaks the truth in his heart might dwell on God's holy mountain* (Ps 15:2.1)?

That the Lord's bodily resurrection is a sacrament of our inner resurrection is shown by the place where he said to the woman after he had risen, *Do not touch me, for I have not yet ascended to my Father* (Jn 20:17). To this mystery corresponds what the apostle says, *If you have risen with Christ, seek the things that are above, where Christ is seated at God's right hand; set your thoughts on the things that are above* (Col 3:1). Not to touch Christ until he has ascended to the Father means not to have materialistic thoughts about Christ.

Again, the Lord's death in the flesh is the model for the death of our outer man, because such sufferings were the greatest possible encouragement to his servants *not to fear those who kill the body but cannot kill the soul* (Mt 10:28). Thus the apostle can say, *That I may make up what is wanting from Christ's afflictions in my flesh* (Col 1:24). Likewise the resurrection of the Lord's body is found to serve as the model for our outer man's resurrection, since he said to the disciples, *Handle and see that a spirit does not have bones and flesh as you see that I have* (Lk 24:39). And one of his disciples felt his wounds and exclaimed, *My Lord and my God* (Jn 20:28)! Their being shown the complete integrity of his flesh like this was a demonstration of what he had said elsewhere to encourage them, *Not a hair of your heads will perish* (Lk 21:18).

How, after all, could he first say, *Do not touch me, for I have not yet ascended to my Father* (Jn 20:17), and then let himself be touched by the disciples before he ascended to the Father, unless on the first occasion he was suggesting the sacrament of the inner man, and on the second exhibiting the model of the outer man—unless of course anyone wishes to be so absurd and averse to the truth that he dares to suggest he could be touched by men before he ascended, but by women only after he had ascended. It is because this model of our bodily resurrection to come has been pre-enacted in the Lord's case that the apostle says, *Christ the beginning, then those who belong to Christ* (1 Cor 15:23). He is dealing there with the resurrection of the body, of which he says elsewhere, *He will transfigure[21] the body of our lowliness to match the body of his glory* (Phil 3:21). So then, the one death of our savior was our salvation from our two deaths, and his one resurrection bestowed two resurrections on us, since in either instance, that is both in death and in resurrection, his body served as the sacrament of our inner man and as the model of our outer man, by a kind of curative accord or symmetry.[22]

Chapter 2

The numerical harmony of 1 to 2, as manifested in the work of redemption, is further elaborated in terms of the number 6, treated mainly as symbolical of time; and the chapter closes with elevated reflections on the mystery of unity in multiplicity, harmony finally restored in the person and work of the one Word of God made flesh.

7. This proportion of the single to the double arises from the number 3; for 1 and 2 make 3. But all this I have just mentioned comes to the number 6; 1 and 2 and 3 make 6. This number is called perfect because it is made up of its parts, of which it has three, a sixth, a third, and a half; nor has it any other part which is a simple fraction of it. Its sixth part then is 1, its third part 2, and its half part 3. But 1, 2, and 3 added together make the same number 6. Sacred scripture commends its perfection to us above all in declaring that God completed his works in six days, and that on the sixth day man was made to the image of God.[23] And in the sixth age of the human race the Son of God came and was made the Son of man in order to refashion us to the image of God. That is the age we are now in, whether we allot the ages 1, 000 years each,[24] or whether we search the divine writings for certain memorable and outstanding turning points—as it were knuckles—of time. In this way we find the first age lasting from Adam to Noah, the second from him to Abraham, and from then on we follow the divisions of the evangelist Matthew, from Abraham to David, from David to the deportation to Babylonia, and from there to the virgin's child-bearing.[25] These three ages added to the first two make five. So the sixth began with the birth of the Lord, and still continues to the unknown end of time.

We see this number 6 being in some sense symbolic of time in that other tripartite division, by which we reckon one age before the law, another under the law, and the third under grace. In this last we receive the sacrament of our renewal, which is such that at the end of time we shall be renewed all through by the resurrection of the flesh, and healed of every infirmity both of body and soul. So we can see a type of the Church in that woman who was cured by the Lord and straightened up after being bound by Satan and bent double;[26] it is of this kind of unseen enemies that the psalm complains, *They have bent my soul double* (Ps 57:7). This woman had endured her infirmity for 18 years, which is 3 times 6. Now the months of 18 years add up to the cube of 6, that is 6 times 6 times 6. Beside this episode in the same passage of the gospel is that fig tree which the third year running was accusing of a miserable sterility. But the plea was made for it to leave it that year, and if it bore fruit, well and good; if not it should be cut down.[27] Its 3 years signify the same tripartite division of time,[28] and the months of 3 years add up to the square of 6, that is 6 times 6.

8. Even a single year, if it is thought of as consisting of 12 whole months of 30 days each (that was the month observed by the ancients, following the lunar cycle) is well furnished with the number 6. What 6 is in the first order of numbers, which consists of units and goes up to 10, that 60 is in the second order

which consists of tens and goes up to 100. So the number of 60 days is a sixth part of the lunar year. Thus, multiply the 6 number of the second order by the 6 number of the first order, and you get 6 times 60, 360 days, which are the 12 whole months. But while it is the lunar cycle that shows men the months, it is the solar cycle that marks the year, and so there remain 5 1/4 days over for the sun to complete its course and round off the year. Four quarters make up the day which has to be intercalated every fourth year on what they call the bissex-tile,[29] lest the order of the seasons should be upset. Now if we consider even these 5 1/4 days, we find the number 6 plays a great part in them; first, because if we follow the custom of counting a part as the whole, they are no longer 5 days but rather 6, taking that quarter for a whole day; secondly, because those 5 days are the sixth part of a month, and the quarter day has 6 hours to it. The whole day, that is the day with its night, has 24 hours, a quarter of which turns out to be 6 hours. So the number 6 plays a great part in the cycle of the year.

9. And therefore it is eminently proper that in the building of the Lord's body, which he meant to signify when he said that he would raise up in three days the temple destroyed by the Jews, the number 6 should stand for a year. They said, *In 46 years the temple was built* (Jn 2:19-21), and 6 times 46 makes 276. This number of days makes 9 months and 6 days, which are reckoned as 10 months for pregnant women, not because all reach the sixth day after the ninth month, but because the Lord's body is found to have been brought to perfection and birth in that number of days, according to the tradition of the fathers preserved by ecclesiastical authority. He is believed to have been conceived on 25 March, and also to have suffered on that day.[30] Thus to the new tomb he was buried in, where no dead body was laid before or after, there corresponds the womb he was conceived in, where no mortal body was sown before or after. But tradition has it that he was born on 25 December;[31] count from that day to this, and you will get 276 days, which contain the number 6 46 times. This was the number of years it took to build the temple, because in that number of 6's the Lord's body was perfected, the body which he raised up in three days after it had been destroyed by undergoing death. For *He was speaking of the temple of his body* (Jn 2:21), as is clearly shown by the strong evidence of the gospel.

10. This three days, however, of which he says, *As Jonah was in the belly of the whale three days and three nights, so will the Son of man be in the heart of the earth three days and three nights* (Mt 12:40),[32] this three days was not in fact full and complete, as scripture bears witness.[33] But the first day is reckoned as a whole one from its last part, and the third as a whole one from its first part. The one in between however, that is the second day, really is a whole one with its 24 hours, 12 of the day and 12 of the night. He was crucified, first by the cries of the Jews at the third hour of the sixth day of the week; then he was hung on the cross at the sixth hour, and he gave up the spirit at the ninth hour; he was buried *when it had already grown late*, as the gospel puts it (Mk 15:42), which is to be understood as the end of the day. So wherever you begin from, and even if you can give another account which will explain its not being against John's gospel to say he was hung up on the cross at the third hour,[34] you will not be

able to include the whole of the first day. So it must be reckoned as a whole one from the last part, as the third day is from its first part. For the night as far as the dawn on which the Lord's resurrection was revealed belongs to the third day; God is suggesting to us by implication that the day now takes its beginning from night—in the sense that he *told light to shine out of darkness* (2 Cor 4:6), in order that by the grace of the new covenant and a share in the resurrection of Christ we might hear it said to us, *You were once darkness, but now light in the Lord* (Eph 5:8). Just as the first days of creation are calculated from light to night[35] because of the fall of man that was to come, so these new days are calculated from dark to light because of man's restoration. So from the hour of his death to the dawn of the resurrection there are 40 hours, counting in the ninth hour.[36] This number corresponds to the 40 days of his life on earth after his resurrection. This number 40 is of very frequent occurrence in the scriptures,[37] to suggest the mystery of perfection in a quadripartite world.[38] There is a certain perfection about 10, and multiplied by 4 it makes 40.

But from his burial in the evening to the dawn of the resurrection 36 hours elapsed, which is 6 squared. This can also be reduced to that proportion of single to double in which is to be found the most complete harmony of the "interlock." For 12 to 24 has the proportion of single to double, and together they make 36, a whole night with a whole day and another whole night; this too is not without the kind of symbolic significance I mentioned above.[39] Thus it is not unreasonable to compare the spirit with day and the body with night. Now as we have seen, the Lord's body, in his death and resurrection, has the function of a type for our spirit and a model for our body. So here too, the proportion of single to double shows through in the 36 hours, which you get by adding 12 and 24.

Anyone else, of course, is at liberty to search out reasons why these numbers occur in the scriptures; they may find ones less convincing than those that I have given, or equally probable, or even more probable than mine. But at least no one will be so foolish and inept as to contend that they are there in the scriptures to no purpose, and that there are no mystical reasons for recording them. As for the reasons I have given, I have gathered them from the authority of the ecclesiastical tradition received from our fathers, or from the evidence of the divine scriptures themselves, or by a process of reason from the very character of the numbers and comparisons involved. And I hope no one in his senses will take sides against reason, no one who is a Christian against the scriptures, and no man of peace against the Church.[40]

11. This sacrament, this sacrifice, this high priest, this God, before he was sent and came, *made of woman* (Gal 4:4) —all the sacred and mysterious things that were shown to our fathers by angelic miracles, or that they themselves performed,[41] were likenesses of him, so that all creation might in some fashion utter the one who was to come and be the savior of all who needed to be restored from death. By wickedness and ungodliness with a crashing discord we had bounced away, and flowed and faded away from the one supreme true God into the many, divided by the many, clinging to the many.[42] And so it was fitting that at the beck and bidding of a compassionate God the many should themselves

acclaim together the one who was to come, and that acclaimed by the many together the one should come, and that the many should testify together that the one had come, and that we being disburdened of the many should come to the one; and that being dead in soul through many sins and destined to die in the flesh because of sin, we should love the one who died in the flesh for us without sin, and that believing in him raised from the dead, and rising ourselves with him in spirit through faith, we should be made one in the one just one; and that we should not despair of ourselves rising in the flesh when we observed that we the many members had been preceded by the one head, in whom we have been purified by faith and will then be made completely whole by sight,[43] and that thus fully reconciled to God by him the mediator, we may be able to cling to the one, enjoy the one, and remain for ever one.

12. So it is that the Son of God, who is at once the Word of God and the mediator between God and men the Son of man, equal to the Father by oneness of divinity and our fellow by taking of humanity, so it is that he intercedes for us insofar as he is man, while not concealing that as God he is one with the Father, and among other things he speaks as follows: *I do not ask for these alone,* he says, *but for all those who are going to believe in me through their word, that they may all be one as you, Father, in me and I in you, that they too may be one in us, that the world may believe that you have sent me. And I have given them the glory that you have given me, that they may be one as we are one* (Jn 17:20).

He did not say "that I and they may be one," though as he is the Church's head and the Church is his body he could have said "that I and they may be" not one thing but "one person," since head and body make the one Christ. But he is declaring his divinity, consubstantial with the Father—as he says elsewhere, *I and the Father are one* (Jn 10:30)—in his own proper way, that is, in the consubstantial equality of the same substance, and he wants his disciples to be one in him, because they cannot be one in themselves, split as they are from each other by clashing wills[44] and desires, and the uncleanness of their sins; so they are cleansed by the mediator that they may be one in him, not only by virtue of the same nature whereby all of them from the ranks of mortal men are made equal to the angels,[45] but even more by virtue of one and the same wholly harmonious will reaching out in concert to the same ultimate happiness, and fused somehow into one spirit in the furnace of charity.[46] This is what he means when he says *That they may be one as we are one* (Jn 17:22)—that just as Father and Son are one not only by equality of substance but also by identity of will, so these men, for whom the Son is mediator with God, might be one not only by being of the same nature, but also by being bound in the fellowship of the same love. Finally, he shows that he is the mediator by whom we are reconciled to God, when he says, *I in them and you in me, that they may be perfected into one* (Jn 17:23).

Chapter 3

The work of the true mediator to life is contrasted with the work of the false mediator to death, the devil; it is shown how Christ conquered the devil in a just contest, and justly delivered man from the quasi-just rights which the devil possessed over him as a result of sin; finally, the false sacrifices which the devil still deludes his followers into trusting in are contrasted with the one true and perfect sacrifice of Christ, in which the knot of perfect unity is perfectly tied.

13. This is our true peace, this is our firm bond with our creator, once we have been cleansed and reconciled by the mediator of life, just as we had withdrawn far away from him, being defiled and estranged by the mediator of death. Just as the devil in his pride brought proud-thinking man down to death, so Christ in his humility brought obedient man back to life. The devil grew high and mighty, he fell, and pulled down man who consented to him; the Christ came humble and lowly, he rose, and raised up man who believed in him. The devil did not sink to what he had brought man down to, for while he indeed bore the death of the spirit in his godlessness, he did not undergo the death of the flesh, not having clothed himself with any flesh in the first place;[47] and so he seemed a great chief with his battalions of demons to help him exercise his dominion of deceit. Thus he puffs man up with false philosophy or entangles him in sacrilegiously sacred rites, using them also first to deceive and make fools of the prouder souls who are too curious about magical tricks and then to ruin them;[48] and thus he holds him in subjection by his swollen self-esteem and his determined preference for power over justice. Then he also promises him purification of soul by what they call *teletai*,[49] *transforming himself into an angel of light* (2 Cor 11:14) by all sorts of contrivances, *with deceptive signs and portents* (2 Thes 2:9).

14. After all, it is easy for the wickedest spirits to do many things with their airy bodies that astonish souls burdened with earthly bodies, even though they may have more laudable dispositions than they. These earthly bodies themselves, if controlled by the right skills, treatment, and training, can exhibit such prodigious antics in circus shows that people who have not seen them can scarcely credit them when they are told about them. So why should it be difficult for the devil and his angels with their airy bodies to do things with the physical elements that astonish mere flesh? Why should he find it hard to contrive weird apparitions and images with which to make fun of human perception, introducing them by subliminal suggestion, and so to deceive men waking or sleeping, or to excite the mentally disturbed? Now it can well happen that a man of decent life and morals watches the most depraved rascals walking on tight-ropes or doing many incredible acrobatic feats with their bodies, and does not in the least want to do the same sort of things himself, or think that the acrobats are better men than he is because of them. So too a faithful and godfearing soul may perhaps not only see but also in the weakness of the flesh be struck dumb with amazement at demonic prodigies, and yet for all that he will not be sorry he

cannot do such things himself, or think them a reason for judging the demons to be better than he is. When all is said and done, he belongs to the company of the saints, both angels and men, and they by the power of God to whom all things are subject have done much greater things which are in no way deceitful.

15. Therefore such blasphemous symbols and godless curiosities[50] and magical consecrations are no use at all for purifying the soul and reconciling it to God; for the false mediator does not draw one to higher things, but rather blocks the way to them by inspiring men with proud and hence malignant desires to be his associates. Such desires cannot strengthen wings of virtue to fly with; all they can do is load down the soul with weights of vice to sink with, and insure that the higher the soul considers itself to be borne up, the heavier its collapse will be.

Accordingly, we should do as the Magi did when they received a warning from God after the star had led them to the Lord to worship him in his lowliness; like them we ought to *return to our own country by another way* (Mt 2:12),[51] and not by the way we came. This other way has been taught us by the humble king, and the proud king, adversary to the humble king, cannot block it. For we too have been brought to worship the humble Christ by *the heavens declaring the glory of God,* when *their sound went forth into all the earth, and their words to the ends of the world* (Ps 19:1.5).

For us the road to death was through sin in Adam; *by one man sin entered the world and by sin death, and so it passed into all men insofar as all sinned* (Rom 5:12).[52] The devil was the mediator of this road, persuading to sin and hurling down into death; he too brought his own single death to bear in order to operate our double death. By godlessness he died in spirit, though he did not die of course in the flesh; but he both persuaded us to godlessness and insured that because of it we should deserve to come to the death of the flesh. Persuaded thus by a crooked argument we set our hearts on one thing, and the other followed on our heels, condemned as we were by a just sentence. That is why it is written, *God did not make death* (Wis 1:13); he himself was not the cause of death, yet he imposed a wholly just death on the sinner as retribution. In the same way a judge imposes a punishment on a guilty man, and yet the cause of the punishment is not the justice of the judge but the deserts of the crime. So then, into the place where the mediator of death transported us without accompanying us there himself, that is into the death of the flesh, there the Lord our God by the hidden and wholly mysterious decree of his high divine justice introduced the healing means of our amendment, which he did not himself deserve.

The truth is, men were more inclined to avoid the death of the flesh which they could not avoid, than the death of the spirit; that is, they shrank more from the punishment than from what deserved the punishment. Few, after all, care—or care very much—about not sinning; but they make a great fuss about not dying, though it is in fact unobtainable. So then, in order that *as by one man came death so by one man there might come the resurrection of the dead* (1 Cor 15:21), the mediator of life came to show us how little we should really fear death, which in our human condition cannot now be avoided anyway, and how we should rather fear ungodliness which can be warded off by faith. And to do this he came to meet us at the end to which we had come, but not by the way we had come. We came to death by sin, he came by justice; and so while our death is the punishment of sin, his death became a sacrifice for sin.

16. So then—spirit is of more value than body; the death of the spirit is being forsaken by God, and the death of the body is being forsaken by the spirit; the death of the body is a punishment, in that because the spirit willfully forsook God, it has to forsake the body against its will, in that while the spirit forsook God because it wanted to, it has to forsake the body even though it does not want to,[53] nor does it forsake the body when it wants to—unless of course a man does violence to himself and commits suicide. This being the case, the spirit of the mediator demonstrated how he did not come to the death of the flesh as any punishment for sin by precisely not forsaking it against his will, but because he wanted to and at the time he wanted to and in the way he wanted to. In virtue of his being compounded into one being with the Word of God,[54] he said, *I have authority to lay down my life and I have authority to take it up again. No one takes it away from me, but I lay it down and I take it up again* (Jn 10:18). And indeed, as the gospel says, those who were present were quite amazed when *He gave up his spirit* (Jn 19:30; Mk 15:39), immediately after that cry he uttered in representation of our sin. Those who were hung up on gibbets used to endure the torments of a long slow death. That is why the robbers had their legs broken, to make sure they died forthwith and could be taken down from their gibbets before the sabbath. We are also told that Pilate was astonished when he was asked for the body of the Lord for burial.[55]

17. So that deceiver, man's mediator to death, falsely presenting himself as mediator to life under color of purification by sacred rites and sacrifices of blasphemy with which he hoodwinks the proud; that deceiver could have no share in our death and no resurrection from his own. And so while he could indeed apply his single death to our double one, he certainly could not apply that single resurrection which would provide the sacrament for our renovation and the model for the general awakening that is going to happen at the end. Accordingly, the true mediator of life, who being *alive in the spirit* (1 Pt 3:18) revived his own dead flesh, has cast that dead spirit and mediator of death out of the spirits of those who believe in him, so now that one no longer reigns inside them, but only attacks them from the outside without being able to overthrow them. The true one also allowed himself to be tempted by him, in order to be a mediator for overcoming his temptations by way of example as well as by way of assistance. For when the devil was driven off after attempting to insinuate himself by every entry into the inner citadel of Christ, after the one dead in spirit had completed every seductive temptation in the desert after the baptism, and had failed to force an entry into the living spirit,[56] being avid for human death in any shape or form he turned his attention to procuring the only death which he was able and permitted to, the death of that mortal element which the living mediator had received from us. And precisely there, where he was able really

to do something, was he well and truly routed; and by his receiving the exterior authority to strike down the Lord's flesh, the interior authority by which he held us captive was itself struck down.

For it came about that the chains of many sins in many deaths were broken by the one death of one man which no sin had preceded. For our sakes the Lord paid this one death which he did not owe in order that the death we do owe might do us no harm. He was not stripped of the flesh by right of any alien authority; he alone *stripped himself* (Col 2:15) of it.[57] As he was able not to die if he did not wish to, it follows since he did die that it was because he wished to; and thus *He made an example of the principalities and powers, confidently triumphing over them in himself* (Col 2:15). By his death he offered for us the one truest possible sacrifice, and thereby purged, abolished, and destroyed whatever there was of guilt, for which the principalities and powers had a right to hold us bound to payment of the penalty; and by his resurrection he called to new life us who were predestined, justified us who were called, glorified us who were justified.[58]

So by a death of the flesh the devil lost man, who had yielded to his seduction, and whom he had thus as it were acquired full property rights over, and being himself liable to no corruption of flesh and blood had held in thrall in his weakness and poverty and the frailness of this mortal body, like one seemingly rich and powerful, and all the prouder for that, lording it over a wretched ragged slave. He thrust down into death without following him there the sinner who fell; but he also drove to his death with a savage follow-through the redeemer who came down of his own accord.[59] Thus the Son of God did not disdain to become our friend in the companionship of death, * while the enemy considered himself to be better and bigger than we by not joining us there. For this reason the devil thought himself superior even to the Lord, seeing that the Lord gave way to him in his sufferings, because it is of him that the psalm text is to be understood, *You have made him a little less than the angels* (Ps 8:6). Yet in being slain in his innocence by the wicked one, who was acting against us as it were with just rights, he won the case against him with the justest of all rights, and thus *led captive the captivity* (Eph 4:8, Ps 68:19) that was instituted for sin, and delivered us from the captivity we justly endured for sin, and by his just blood unjustly shed *cancelled the I.O.U.* (Col 2:14) of death, and justified and redeemed sinners.

18. The devil, though, still uses this sort of argument to hoodwink his followers; he falsely presents himself to them as a mediator offering purification by his sacred rites, but in fact giving them only addiction and ruin; and then he easily persuades the proud to despise and scoff at the death of Christ, and to regard him, the devil, as all the more holy and divine for being immune from any such thing. However, very few such followers have remained with him, now that the nations acknowledge the price paid for them, and drink it with devout humility, and putting all their trust in it forsake their enemy and flock to their

---

* Our redeemer said himself, *Greater love has no one than to lay down his life for his friends* (Jn 15:13).

redeemer. The devil cannot understand how his snares and his rages are used by the sublime wisdom of God, which *reaches strongly from* the upper *end,* which is the origin of spiritual creation, *to* the lower *end,* which is the death of the body, *and disposes all things sweetly; for she reaches everywhere in her purity and no defilement touches her* (Wis 8:1; 7:24). But though the devil is immune to the death of the flesh, and therefore bears himself with overweening pride, another kind of death is being prepared for him in the everlasting fire of Tartarus, where spirits can be tormented who have airy bodies as well as those with earthy ones.

And proud men, who treat the great price which Christ bought us with as worthless because he died, both pay with other men the debt of this death to the sad condition which derives from the first sin, and will also be cast down into that death with the devil. They value him above Christ because he threw them down into this death without falling into it himself, thanks to his vastly different nature; whereas Christ came down to it for their sakes thanks to his enormous pity. Yet they do not hesitate to consider themselves better than the demons, and never cease reviling and execrating them with every sort of curse, knowing all the while that they too are immune from suffering the kind of death for which they despise Christ. They are not prepared to consider how it can be that the Word of God abides totally unchanged in himself and yet by taking on a lower nature can suffer what is proper to that nature, which an impure demon cannot suffer because he does not have an earthy body. Thus while they are themselves better than demons, they are clothed in flesh and so they can die in a way that demons who are not clothed in it certainly cannot.

And while they trust presumptuously in the deaths of their sacrificial victims, which they do not realize they are offering to proud and deceitful spirits—or perhaps they do realize it, and imagine they can get some advantage from courting the friendship of treacherous and jealous beings who have no other intention or business than to block our return to life.[60]

19. They will not understand that not even these proud spirits could enjoy the honors of sacrifice, unless true sacrifice were owed to the one true God in whose stead these spirits want to be worshipped. Nor will they understand that true sacrifice can only be correctly offered by a holy and just priest, and only if what is offered is received from those for whom it is offered, and only if it is without fault so that it can be offered for the purification of men with many faults. This is certainly what everyone desires who wants sacrifice offered for him to God.

What priest then could there be as just and holy as the only Son of God, who was not one who needed to purge his own sins by sacrifice,[61] whether original sin or ones added in the course of human life? And what could be so suitably taken from men to be offered for them as human flesh? And what could be so apt for this immolation as mortal flesh? And what could be so pure for purging the faults of mortal men as flesh born in and from a virgin's womb without any infection of earthly lust? And what could be so acceptably offered and received as the body of our priest which has been made into the flesh of our sacrifice? Now there are four things to be considered in every sacrifice: whom it is offered to, whom it is offered by, what it is that is offered, and whom it is offered for. And this one true mediator, in reconciling us to God by his sacrifice of peace, would remain one with him to whom he offered it, and make one in himself those for whom he offered it, and be himself who offered it one and the same as what he offered.

Chapter 4

The pretension of platonic or plotinian philosophers to be able to purify themselves by their own intellectual and moral powers for the perfect contemplation of God is contrasted with the Christian dispensation, whereby man has to be purified for the contemplation of eternal things by submitting to faith in temporal things, namely, in the incarnation of the Word and the life, death, and resurrection of Christ; the philosophers' denial of the resurrection on philosophical grounds is also refuted, and the trustworthiness of the revelation contained in the scriptures on such matters is asserted.

20. However, there are some people who think that they can purify themselves for contemplating God and cleaving to him by their own power and strength of character, which means in fact that they are thoroughly defiled by pride. No vice is more vehemently opposed by divine law, no vice gives a greater right of control to that proudest of all spirits, the devil, who mediates our way to the depths and bars our way to the heights, unless we avoid his hidden ambushes and go another way;[62] or unless his open assaults by means of a "falling people," which is what Amalek means,[63] disputing the passage to the promised land, are overcome by the Lord's cross, which was prefigured by the outstretched arms of Moses.[64] Their reason for assuring themselves of do-it-yourself purification is that some of them have been able to direct the keen gaze of their intellects beyond everything created and to attain, in however small a measure,[65] the light of unchanging truth; and they ridicule those many Christians who have been unable to do this and who *live* meanwhile *out of faith* (Rom 1:17) alone.[66] But what good does it do a man who is so proud that he is ashamed to climb aboard the wood, what good does it do him to gaze from afar on the home country across the sea? And what harm does it do a humble man if he cannot see it from such a distance, but is coming to it nonetheless on the wood the other disdains to be carried by?[67]

21. These people also find fault with us for believing the resurrection of the flesh, and would like men to believe them about such matters instead; as though, if you please, their ability to understand the sublime and unchanging substance of God by the things that are made (Rom 1:20) gives them a right to be consulted about the changes of mutable things or the interwoven series of the ages. But just because they can show very truly by the most persuasive arguments and convincing proofs that all temporal things happen according to eternal ideas,[68]

does it follow that they have been able to inspect these ideas themselves, and deduce from them how many kinds of animals there are, what are the seminal origins of each, what the measure of their growth, what the cycles of their conceptions, births, life spans, and deaths, how they are moved to seek what suits their natures and shun what harms them? Surely they have not sought the truth about these matters via that unchanging wisdom,[69] but by studying the natural history of times and places, and by believing what others have discovered and recorded. Small wonder, then, that they have not been able in any way to investigate the unfolding of the ages that stretch out ahead of us, or the turning point of the outward course which carries the human race down like a river, and the return from there to the end that is due to each one.[70] Not even historians have been able to write about these things that lie far in the future, and have not been experienced or described by anyone. Nor have these philosophers contemplated such things, even though they are superior to others in their understanding of the supreme eternal ideas. Otherwise they would not have to inquire into the same kind of past events as the historians have been able to investigate, but would rather know them beforehand while they are still in the future.[71]

22. Men who have been able to do this are called soothsayers by them, prophets by us, though the name of prophet is not altogether foreign to their literature.[72] But it makes all the difference how the future is foretold. It may be conjecturally forecast on the strength of past experience; doctors, for example, have committed many things to writing which they have observed from experience, in order to be able to make further prognoses; farmers too, and even sailors, can make many forecasts, and if such things happen over long intervals of time they are regarded as divinations. Or it may be that things which are going to come about have already started happening, and are seen approaching from afar by sharp-sighted individuals who promptly foretell them. When the airy powers do this, they are thought to be divining, but it is only like someone standing on a hilltop and seeing someone coming from a long way off, and telling the people in the plain nearby before he arrives. Or it may be that holy angels are shown these things by God through his Word and his Wisdom, where both past and future events are equally present and as it were stationary,[73] and they foretell them to some men, who then pass them on to other men. Or it may be that the minds of certain men are raised so high in the Holy Spirit that they see for themselves and not through angels the present causes of future things in that topmost citadel of all things. Now the airy powers also overhear these things, whether angels or men proclaim them, but they only hear as much as is judged expedient by him to whom all things are subject. Many things too are foretold with a certain intuition or movement of spirit by people who are unaware of it, as Caiaphas was unaware of what he was really saying, *but being high priest he prophesied* (Jn 11:51).

23. So then we should not consult the philosophers about the future succession of the ages or the resurrection of the dead, not even those who have understood to the best of their ability the eternity of the creator *in whom we live*

and move and are (Acts 17:28), *because knowing God by the things that are made they have not glorified him as God, or given thanks, but calling themselves wise they have become fools* (Rom 1:20). They were not capable, of course, of fixing the keen gaze of their intellects so constantly on the eternity of that spiritual and unchanging nature that they could see in the wisdom of the creator and ruler of the universe the rolled up scrolls of the centuries, which *there* already are and always are, but *here* only will be and so are not yet; or that they could see there the change for the better not only of the minds but also of the bodies of men, each to its own proper perfection. Not only were they quite incapable of seeing these things there, they were not either considered worthy of having them declared to them by holy angels, whether outwardly through the bodily senses, or by interior revelations impressed on their spirits. This, though, is how these things were shown to our fathers, who were marked with true piety. They foretold them and gained credence for their predictions either by the signs they performed there and then, or by the things they foretold for the near future coming true; and so they deservedly won an authority which could be trusted even about things they foretold of the far distant future right up to the end of the world. Now the proud and deceitful airy powers may well be found to have uttered through their soothsayers things they overheard from the holy angels and prophets about the company and city of the saints, and about the true mediator; but if so, they did it in order to suborn if they could even God's faithful by means of these alien truths to their own proper falsehoods. God however used them without their knowing it to insure that the truth would be heard on all sides, as a help for the faithful and a testimony to the godless.

24. To sum up then: we were incapable of grasping eternal things, and weighed down by the accumulated dirt of our sins, which we had collected by our love of temporal things, and which had become almost a natural growth on our mortal stock; so we needed purifying. But we could only be purified for adaptation to eternal things by temporal means like those we were already bound to in a servile adaptation. Health is at the opposite pole from sickness, but the cure should be halfway between the two, and unless it has some affinity with the sickness, it will not lead to health. Useless temporal things just delude the sick and disappoint them; useful ones help them to get well and lead them, once they have got well, to eternal things. Now just as the rational mind is meant, once purified, to contemplate eternal things, so it is meant while still needing purification to give faith to temporal things.[74] One of those men who were accounted wise among the Greeks himself said, *As eternity is to that which has originated, so truth is to faith.*[75] And it is indeed a true statement. What we call temporal he described as that which has originated. We too belong to this category, and not only our bodies but also our changeable spirits; a thing cannot properly be called eternal if it undergoes change in any way. So insofar as we are changeable, to that extent do we fall short of eternity.

But eternal life is promised us by the truth, from whose transparent clarity our faith is as far removed as mortality is from eternity. So now we accord faith to the things done in time for our sakes,[76] and are purified by it;[77] in order that when we come to sight and truth succeeds to faith, eternity might likewise succeed to mortality. Our faith will then become truth, when we come to what we are promised as believers; but what we are promised is eternal life, and the truth said—not the truth our faith will become in the future, but the truth which is always truth because it is eternity—the truth said, *This is eternal life, that they should know you the one true God, and Jesus Christ whom you have sent* (Jn 17:3); therefore when our faith becomes truth by seeing, our mortality will be transformed into a fixed and firm eternity.

Now until this happens and in order that it may happen, and to prevent the faith which we accord with all trust in this mortal life to things "that have originated" from clashing with the truth of contemplating eternal things which we hope for in eternal life, truth itself, co-eternal with the Father, *originated from the earth* (Ps 85:12)[78] when the Son of God came in order to become Son of man and to capture our faith and draw it to himself, and by means of it to lead us on to his truth; for he took on our mortality in such a way that he did not lose his own eternity. For *what eternity is to that which has originated, that truth is to faith.*[79] So it was proper for us to be purified in such a way that he who remained eternal should become for us "originated"; it would not do for there to be one person for us in faith, another in truth. Nor, on the other hand, could we pass from being among the things that originated to eternal things, unless the eternal allied himself to us in our originated condition, and so provided us with a bridge to his eternity.

As it is, our faith has now in some sense followed him in whom we have believed to where he has ascended, after having "originated," died, been raised to life, and taken up. Of these four stages we already knew the first two in ourselves; we know that men originate and die. As for the second two, being raised to life and taken up, we can justly hope that they are going to happen to us because we have believed that they happened to him. So because what has originated in him has passed over into eternity, so too will what has originated in us pass over when faith arrives at truth. To those who already believe he speaks as follows, in order that they may abide in the word of faith, and thence come to truth, and thus be set free from death and be conducted through to eternity: *If you abide in my word you are*[80] *really my disciples.* Then as though they asked "To what purpose?" he continues, *And you will know the truth.* Again as though they said "And what use is truth to mortals?" he concludes, *And the truth will set you free* (Jn 8:31). What from, if not from death, from perishability, from liability to change? Truth, surely, abides immortal, imperishable, unchanging. And true immortality, true imperishability, true unchangingness, that is eternity.

Chapter 5

The author comes back at last to the topic of the mission of the Son and the Holy Spirit; he affirms once more that their being sent does not imply that they are not equal to the Father, and defines their being sent into the world in time as the making known to the world that they proceed from the Father in eternity; he states in passing that the Holy Spirit proceeds eternally from the Son as well as from the Father, and that even though the Father is manifested to the world by sensible phenomena, we cannot say that the Father was ever sent, because he does not proceed from either of the other persons; and he concludes by discussing how the manifestations in time of the persons was brought about, without reaching any definite conclusions on the subject.

25. There you have what the Son of God has been sent for; indeed there you have what it is for the Son of God to have been sent. Everything that has taken place in time in "originated" matters which have been produced from the eternal and reduced back to the eternal, and has been designed to elicit the faith we must be purified by in order to contemplate the truth, has either been testimony to this mission or has been the actual mission of the Son of God. Some testimonies foretold that he was going to come, some testified that he had come. It was only fitting that when he through whom every creature was made became a creature himself, all creation should bear witness to him. Unless the one were proclaimed by the sending of the many, the one would not be held onto by the sending away or repudiation of the many.[81] And unless he were provided with such testimonies as would seem great to little ones, no one would believe that he who was sent as a little one to little ones was the great one who would make them great. Incomparably greater things were made by the Son of God than the signs and portents which broke out to bear him witness, namely *heaven and earth and all the things that are in them* (Ps 146:6)—*all things*, after all, *were made by him* (Jn 1:3). Yet in order for little men to believe that these great things were made by him, they had to be impressed and awestruck by these little things as though they were great.

26. *When therefore the fullness of time had come, God sent his Son made of woman, made under the law* (Gal 4:4), little to the extent that he was made, and therefore sent in that he was made. If then the greater sends the less,[82] we too confess that the one who was made was the lesser, lesser insofar as he was made, and made insofar as he was sent. *He sent his Son, made of woman* (Gal 4:4); but because *all things were made through* this Son (Jn 1:3), we also confess that he whom we call less when he had been sent was equal to the one who sent him not only before he was sent and so made, but before all things were.

How then before *the fullness of time* (Gal 4:4), which was the right time for him to be sent, how could he be seen by the fathers before he was sent, when various angelic demonstrations were shown them, especially considering that he could not even be seen, as he is in his equality with the Father, even after he had been sent? Why, otherwise, should he say to Philip, who of course saw him in the flesh just as those who crucified him did, *Am I with you all this time and you do not know me? Philip, whoever has seen me has seen the Father* (Jn 14:9).[83] Does this not mean that he both could and could not be seen? He could be seen as made and sent; he could not be seen as the one *through whom all things were made* (Jn 1:3). Or what about his saying, *He that has my commandments and keeps them is the one who loves me; and whoever loves me will be loved by my Father, and I shall love him and shall manifest myself to him* (Jn 14:21)? But there he was, manifest before their eyes; surely then it can only mean that he was offering the flesh which the Word had been made[84] in the fullness of time[85] as the object to receive our faith; but that the Word itself, *through whom all things had been made* (Jn 1:3), was being kept for the contemplation in eternity of minds now purified through faith.

27. If however the reason why the Son is said to have been sent by the Father is simply that the one is the Father and the other the Son, then there is nothing at all to stop us believing that the Son is equal to the Father and consubstantial and co-eternal, and yet that the Son is sent by the Father. Not because one is greater and the other less, but because one is the Father and the other the Son; one is the begetter, the other begotten; the first is the one from whom the sent one is; the other is the one who is from the sender. For the Son is from the Father, not the Father from the Son. In the light of this we can now perceive that the Son is not just said to have been sent because the Word became flesh, but that he was sent in order for the Word to become flesh, and by his bodily presence to do all that was written.[86] That is, we should understand that it was not just the man who the Word became that was sent, but that the Word was sent to become man. For he was not sent in virtue of some disparity of power or substance or anything in him that was not equal to the Father, but in virtue of the Son being from the Father, not the Father being from the Son.

The Son of course is the Father's Word, which is also called his Wisdom.[87] Is there anything strange, then, in his being sent, not because he is unequal to the Father, but because he is *a certain pure outflow of the glory of almighty God* (Wis 7:25)? But in this case what flows out and what it flows out from are of one and the same substance. It is not like water flowing out from a hole in the ground or in the rock, but like light flowing from light. It also says that Wisdom *is the brightness of eternal light* (Wis 7:26), and that means surely that it is the light of eternal light. The brightness of light is just light. And therefore it is co-eternal with the light from which it comes as light. The writer chose to say brightness of light instead of light of light, in case the light flowing out should be assumed to be dimmer than the light it flows out from. When we hear that this is the brightness of that, we are readier to believe that that is shining via this, rather than that this is shining less. There was no need to beware of that light which begot this one being thought to be less—no heretic has ever dared to say such a thing and it is impossible to believe that one ever will. So scripture concentrated on opposing the thought that this light which flows out might be dimmer than that light it flows out from, and it eliminated this notion by calling it the brightness of that eternal light, and in this way showed it to be equal. If this one is less, then it is the dimness, not the brightness of the other. If it is greater then it does not flow out from it—it could scarcely overpower the light it is begotten from. So because it flows from the other it is not greater, and because it is its brightness and not its dimness it is not less; therefore it is equal.

And do not be worried by its being called *a certain pure outflow of the glory of almighty God* (Wis 7:25), as though this means it is not almighty itself, but only an outflow of the almighty. It soon goes on to say of it, *While it is one, it can do all things* (Wis 7:27). And who is almighty if not one who can do all things? So it is sent by him from whom it flows. Thus a man who loved and desired this Wisdom could pray, *Send her out from your holy heavens, and send her from the throne of your greatness to be with me and labor with me* (Wis 9:10)—that is "to teach me to labor in case I should labor."[88] Her labors are virtues. But her being sent to be with man is one thing; that she was once sent to be man is another. *For she inserts herself into holy souls and makes them friends of God and prophets* (Wis 7:27), just as she also fills the holy angels and operates through them whatever belongs to the functions they perform. But when the fullness of time came she was sent, not to fill angels nor even to be an angel—except in the sense that she declared the counsel of the Father which was also her own[89]—nor to be with men or in men, since she had already been like this in the patriarchs and prophets; no, it was in order that the Word might become flesh, that is, become man. In this sacrament that was prophesied for the future lay the salvation of those wise and holy men also who were born of women before he was born of the virgin; and in this sacrament now proclaimed as achieved lies the salvation of all who believe, hope, and love. For this is *the great sacrament of piety, which was manifested in flesh, justified in spirit, was seen by angels, proclaimed among the nations, believed in the world, taken up in glory* (1 Tm 3:16).

28. So the Word of God is sent by him whose Word he is; sent by him he is born of. The begetter sends, what is begotten is sent. And he is precisely sent to anyone when he is known and perceived by him, as far as he can be perceived and known according to the capacity of a rational soul either making progress toward God or already made perfect in God. So the Son of God is not said to be sent in the very fact that he is born of the Father, but either in the fact that the Word made flesh showed himself to this world; about this fact he says, *I went forth from the Father and came into this world* (Jn 16:28). Or else he is sent in the fact that he is perceived in time by someone's mind, as it says, *Send her to be with me and labor with me* (Wis 9:10).[90] That he is born means that he is from eternity to eternity[91]—he is *the brightness of eternal light* (Wis 7:26). But that he is sent means that he is known by somebody in time.

But when the Son of God was manifested in the flesh, he was *sent into this world* (Jn 16:28), *made of woman in the fullness of time* (Gal 4:4). *For because in God's wisdom the world could not know God by wisdom (since the light shines in the darkness and the darkness did not comprehend it)* (Jn 1:5), *it was God's pleasure, to save those who believe by the folly of preaching* (1 Cor 1:21), *that the Word should become flesh and dwell among us* (Jn 1:14). When however he is perceived by the mind in the course of someone's spiritual progress in time, he is indeed said to be sent, but not into this world, for he does not then show himself perceptibly, that is he is not available to the physical senses. Of us too it can be said that when we grasp some eternal truth with the mind as far as we are capable of it, we are not in this world; and the spirits of all just men, even while still living in the flesh, are not in this world insofar as they have a sense of divine things.

But when the Father is known by someone in time he is not said to have been sent. For he has not got anyone else to be from or to proceed from. Wisdom says, *I went forth from the mouth of the Most High* (Sir 24:5), and of the Holy Spirit he says, *He proceeds from the Father* (Jn 15:26), but the Father is from no one.

29. Just as the Father, then, begot and the Son was begotten, so the Father sent and the Son was sent. But just as the begetter and the begotten are one, so are the sender and the sent, because the Father and the Son are one;[92] so too the Holy Spirit is one with them, because *these three are one* (1 Jn 5:7).[93] And just as being born means for the Son his being from the Father, so his being sent means his being known to be from him. And just as for the Holy Spirit his being the gift of God[94] means his proceeding from the Father, so his being sent means his being known to proceed from him.[95] Nor, by the way, can we say that the Holy Spirit does not proceed from the Son as well; it is not without point that the same Spirit is called the Spirit of the Father and of the Son.[96] And I cannot see what else he intended to signify when he breathed and said *Receive the Holy Spirit* (Jn 20:22). Not that the physical breath that came from his body and was physically felt was the substance of the Holy Spirit; but it was a convenient symbolic demonstration that the Holy Spirit proceeds from the Son as well as from the Father.[97] Surely you would have to be out of your mind to say that it was one Spirit which he gave by breathing and another which he sent after his ascension. No, the Spirit of God is one, the Spirit of the Father and of the Son, the Holy Spirit *who works all ways in all men* (1 Cor 12:6). That he was given twice was certainly a dispensation that meant something, and we will discuss it in due course as far as the Lord permits.[98]

By saying then, *Whom I will send you from the Father* (Jn 15:26), the Lord showed that the Spirit is both the Father's and the Son's. Elsewhere too, when he said, *whom the Father will send,* he added, *in my name* (Jn 14:26). He did not however say, "whom the Father will send from me" as he had said *whom I will send from the Father* (Jn 15:26), and thereby he indicated that the source of all godhead, or if you prefer it, of all deity,[99] is the Father. So the Spirit who proceeds from the Father and the Son is traced back, on both counts, to him of whom the Son is born.

As for what the evangelist says, *The Spirit was not yet given because Jesus was not yet glorified* (Jn 7:39), how are we to understand it, except as saying that there was going to be a kind of giving or sending of the Holy Spirit after Christ's glorification such as there had never been before? It is not that there had been none before, but none of this kind. If the Holy Spirit had not been given at all before, what were the prophets filled with when they spoke? No, scripture plainly says and demonstrates in many places that they spoke by the Holy Spirit;

it was said of John the Baptist, *He will be filled with the Holy Spirit right from his mother's womb* (Lk 1:15); and we find his father Zachary filled with the Holy Spirit to utter those words about him;[100] and Mary filled with the Holy Spirit to proclaim that praise of the Lord she was carrying in her womb;[101] and Simeon and Anna filled with the Holy Spirit to recognize the greatness of the infant Christ.[102] What then can it mean to say that *the Spirit had not yet been given because Jesus had not yet been glorified* (Jn 7:39), except that that giving or bestowal or sending of the Holy Spirit was going to have some special quality about it that there had never been before? Nowhere else do we read that men had spoken in languages they did not know as the Holy Spirit came upon them, in the way that occurred at Pentecost. For then his coming needed to be demonstrated by perceptible signs, to show that the whole world and all nations with their variety of languages were going to believe in Christ by the gift of the Holy Spirit, in order to fulfill the psalmist's prophetic song, *There are no languages or dialects whose voices are not heard; their sound has gone out to all the earth, and their words to the end of the world* (Ps 19:3).

30. So a man was coupled and even in a certain sense compounded, with the Word of God as one person,[103] when the Son of God was sent *into this world* (Jn 16:28; 3:17) *at the fullness of time, made of woman* (Gal 4:4), in order to be also the Son of man for the sake of the sons of men. Angelic beings could represent this person beforehand in order to foretell him; they could not take him over and just be him. But when it comes to the visible manifestation of the Holy Spirit, whether through the appearance of a dove or through tongues of fire, in which his substance, co-eternal with the Father and the Son and equally unchangeable, was manifested by a subject and compliant creation in temporal movements and forms; here I dare not say that no such things had happened before, since these visible manifestations were not coupled with him into one person, like the flesh which the Word became.[104] I will say however with absolute confidence that Father and Son and Holy Spirit, God the creator, of one and the same substance, the almighty three, act inseparably. But they cannot be manifested inseparably by creatures which are so unlike them, especially material ones; just as our words which consist of material sounds can only name Father and Son and Holy Spirit with their own proper intervals of time, which the syllables of each word take up, spaced off from each other by a definite separation. In their own proper substance by which they are, the three are one, Father and Son and Holy Spirit, without any temporal movement, without any intervals of time or space, one and the same over all creation, one and the same all together from eternity to eternity, like eternity itself which is never without verity and charity.[105] But in my words Father and Son and Holy Spirit are separated and cannot be said together, and if you write them down each name has its own separate space. Here is an example: when I name my memory, understanding, and will, each name refers to a single thing, and yet each of these single names is the product of all three; there is not one of these three names which my memory and understanding and will have not produced together.[106] So too the trinity together produced both the Father's voice and the Son's flesh

and the Holy Spirit's dove, though each of these single things has reference to a single person. Well, at least the example helps us to see how this three, inseparable in itself, is manifested separately through visible creatures, and how the three are inseparably at work in each of the things which are mentioned as having the proper function of manifesting the Father or the Son or the Holy Spirit.

31. If then you ask me how either the voices or the perceptible forms or likenesses were produced that occurred before the incarnation of the Word in order to prefigure that coming event, I answer that God worked them through angels, as I think I have sufficiently shown on the evidence of the holy scriptures.[107] If you go on to ask me how the incarnation itself was done, I say that the very Word of God was made flesh, that is, was made man, without however being turned or changed into that which he was made; that he was of course so made that you would have there not only the Word of God and the flesh of man but also the rational soul of man as well;[108] and that this whole can be called God because it is God and man because it is man. If this is difficult to understand, then you must purify your mind with faith, by abstaining more and more from sin, and by doing good, and by praying with the sighs of holy desire that God will help you to make progress in understanding and loving.

If finally you ask how the voice of the Father and the physical appearances which manifested the Holy Spirit were produced after the incarnation of the Word, I do not doubt that they were done by created means. It is difficult to discover though—and it would be most unwise to make any definite assertion— whether it only involved corporeal and perceptible creatures, or whether it meant bringing in a rational or intellectual* spirit, with the office merely of producing the symbolic effect as God judged opportune, and not of course with the object of becoming one person;[109] for surely no one wishes to say that whatever creature it is that produced the Father's voice is the Father, or that whatever creature it is that manifested the Holy Spirit in the form of a dove or in fiery tongues is the Holy Spirit, in the same way as the man who was made of the virgin is the Son of God. Or perhaps we should look for yet another explanation, but I personally do not see how these things could have happened without employing a rational or intellectual creature. However, this is not yet the occasion for me to explain why I hold this view, as far as the Lord may give me the power to do so.[110] For we first have to discuss and refute the arguments which the heretics bring, not from scripture but from their own reasonings, which absolutely compel them, so they think, to interpret the evidences of scripture about Father and Son and Holy Spirit in the way they want.[111]

32. For the moment, however, it has been sufficiently demonstrated, so I think, that the Son is not less than the Father just because he was sent by the Father, nor is the Holy Spirit less simply because both the Father and the Son sent him. We should understand that these sendings are not mentioned in scripture because of any inequality or disparity or dissimilarity of substance

---

* This is a word favored by some to render what the Greeks call *noeros*.

between the divine persons, but because of the created visible manifestation of the Son and the Holy Spirit; or better still, in order to bring home to us that the Father is the source and origin of all deity.[112] For even if the Father had chosen to appear visibly through the creation he controls, it would be quite absurd to talk about him being sent by the Son he begot or the Holy Spirit who proceeds from him.

So let us conclude this volume. In those that follow we shall see with the Lord's help what sort of subtle crafty arguments the heretics bring forward and how they can be demolished.

NOTES

1. *Egentem*: M reads *agentem*, acting and grieving . . .

2. Lucretius, *De Rerum Natura* 2, 73.

3. Augustine regularly connects the beatitude on those who mourn with the Holy Spirit's gift of knowledge.

4. See Ps 84:10.

5. A reference to the prodigal son.

6. "Spirits" is here a semi-technical term, meaning a kind of vaporous substance which fills the nervous system.

7. These are the various Old Testament manifestations which were discussed in Books II and III.

8. For Augustine, it is an essential characteristic of faith that it is humiliating to the natural pride of the intellect. The point will be elaborated in chapter 4 below.

9. *Ubi*: M reads *ibi*, in it. This would certainly save the sentence from being an anacolouthon, but it does not seem likely to be what Augustine wrote. This is the first of many rough pieces of writing in this book. And it is a significant one; in fact he finishes this sentence at the end of chapter 2 (11), where he rhapsodizes on the reintegration of the many in the one. The whole gist of his argument in the course of these two chapters is to present redemption, or the mediation of Christ—mediation seems to be his key concept in this book—as a work of restoring a fallen and fragmented mankind to a divine unity, of which the model is the unity of the three divine persons. This is the point of this opening phrase of this paragraph, "because there is but one Word of God." To make Augustine finish the sentence here, by changing *ubi* to *ibi*, would in fact be to cut him off in mid-argument—something the reader may often be tempted to do, but it does not help him to understand what the author is really trying to say.

10. M omits "and the Word was," with several manuscripts—a simple case of haplography.

11. See 2 Pt 1:4.

12. Augustine actually invents the word *coaptatio* here, so I feel constrained to invent a word too. See *The City of God* XXII, 24, 4 (PL 41, 791), where he uses the word, again as a translation of the Greek *harmonia*, of the construction of the human body.

13. The primary meaning of the Greek word is not musical, as with the English "harmony"; its primary meaning is a joint, fastener, or clamp—a carpenter's or shipwright's word.

14. In the whole construction of our nature, though he uses a musical illustration.

15. *Impietas*. Here and subsequently in this whole context I translate this word by "ungodliness" or "godlessness," *impius* by "ungodly" or "godless," *pius* and *pietas* by "godly" and "godliness" respectively. These are for various reasons unsatisfactory English words, but in this context one

wants something special for these Latin words. They do signify a special positive or negative attitude to our relationship with God; they mean acknowledging or refusing to acknowledge our creaturely or filial relationship. The English words chosen do convey this by their material form, though not so well in their overtones. I ask the reader simply to try to forget these overtones, and treat them as mere equivalents for the technical Latin terms.

16. *Infidelitatem impietatis*; M *infidelitatis impietatem*, unbelieving godlessness.

17. See Hb 2:4; Gal 3:11; Heb 10:38.

18. This is an unusually interesting use of the word sacrament, which Augustine develops in the rest of this chapter. His ordinary use of the word is of course much wider than that which it has come to receive in traditional theology and catechetics on the sacraments. For him, any material thing or historical event in scripture which can be read as symbolic of some deeper reality or future saving event is a sacrament—any "sacred sign." Very frequently Christ is the deeper reality or future event signified by such "sacred signs."

But here Christ himself, or rather his bodily death and resurrection, is the sacrament or sacred sign, and what his death and resurrection signify, and achieve, are hidden realities of our salvation. This brings Christ and his death and resurrection into close connection with the sacraments of the Church, which for Augustine both signify and achieve the Christian's inner saving relationship with Christ, by also signifying and making present his death and resurrection. We have here, in fact, a pretty explicit forestalling of Fr. Schillebeeckx' important theological idea of *Christ the Sacrament of the Encounter with God* (Sheed & Ward, 1963). Schillebeeckx alludes to this whole passage, with a short quotation that in fact seems to be a paraphrase, in his more monumental work, *De Sacramentele Heilseconomie* (Antwerp, 1952) on page 97.

Two points are worth making about Augustine's development of the idea: (i) Christ's death and resurrection do not only have the value of sacrament; they also have the value of model (*exemplum*). And he does not primarily mean a moral example or model; he means they are models of the Christian's physical death and resurrection too. If Christ were only a sacrament, then he would pass away when the present regime of signs and symbols, which is proper to the incomplete and imperfect condition of faith, has passed away, and faith has yielded to sight, and signs and symbols have faded before the presence of the realities they signify. But Christ is central to these ultimate realities. In his human nature, now glorified and indestructible, he is the means of access for us in our whole nature, body and soul, to those realities. For all his Platonism, Augustine never lost sight of the permanent, real, true value of the corporeal creation, and in particular of the human body, as something existing in its own right for its own sake, and not just as a symbol of something incorporeal and spiritual.

(ii) In his working out of the significance of Christ's death as sacrament there seems to be a certain oscillation or inconsistency in his thought. It represents the death of our inner man, both as our godforsakenness as a result of sin, our spiritual death in sin, *and* as our spiritual death to sin, our crucifying the old man and dying to self, the spiritual death of mortification which is the prelude to our spiritual resurrection and the regeneration of the new man. Indeed, it is the same reality as spiritual resurrection, seen from a different angle.

Perhaps I am wrong to call this an inconsistency; it is rather an added dimension to his thought. But it involves him in a certain equivocation which obscures his expression of his thought.

19. Christ is thought of not just as quoting the psalm written by someone else, but as having spoken the psalm, in the person of the psalmist, in the first place.

20. He is justifying his identification of "the old man" of Rom 6:6 with the "inner man" of 2 Cor 4:16.

21. Reading *transfigurabit* with several manuscripts. Both CCL and M have *transfiguravit*, has transfigured. But the whole sense of the passage shows that Augustine's text of the epistle correctly rendered Paul's future. The transcriptional error of writing *-avit* for *-abit* and vice versa is so common and so easy, that cases like this should be judged simply on the merits of the sense. To prefer in a case like this the more difficult reading even when it makes nonsense of the author's argument is itself nonsense.

22. It is possible that in elaborating this harmony theory of our redemption, or our cure, as he calls it here, Augustine had at the back of his mind the stories of how Elijah and Elisha each raised

a child from the dead—by placing their own bodies over those of the dead children in "a kind of curative accord or symmetry," *medicinali quadam convenientia*; see 1 Kgs 17:21, and 2 Kgs 4:34.

23. See Gn 1:26.

24. Evidently the calculations Augustine followed to determine the date of creation differed from those of Archbishop Ussher, who worked it out to 4004 B.C.

25. See Mt 1:17.

26. See Lk 13:11-16. That Augustine sees this woman as a type of the Church means that he regards the Church as co-eval with the world.

27. See Lk 13:6-9.

28. As the woman's 18 years. Augustine's number symbolism may leave the reader skeptical; but there can be little doubt that Luke thought these numbers significant. In the same chapter he mentions the 18 men on whom the tower fell, and the 3 measures of flour which the woman mixes with leaven.

29. In the Roman calendar the VI Kal. Mar. (Feb. 24) was repeated in a leap year; hence the name *bissextile*.

30. John Donne, in his poem *Upon the Annunciation and Passion Falling upon One Day* (1608), seems to be unaware of this tradition, and talks about the Church letting Good Friday fall on March 25, as a kind of occasional mystic lesson to us.

31. The earliest reference to December 25 being celebrated as the feast of Christ's nativity is found in the Philocalian calendar, compiled in 336 (Martimort, *L'Eglise en Prière*, Tournai, 1961, page 728). According to the scholars, the feast was probably instituted at Rome at the same time as the Vatican basilica was built by Constantine. The date, the winter solstice, marked the pagan feast of *Sol invictus*, and while the Roman Church would have seen in the institution of the feast of Christ's nativity a kind of counterblast to this pagan festival, it seems that Constantine might have had more syncretistic ideas about it.

About the origins of the feast of the Annunciation on March 25 the same learned work gives much less satisfactory information. The first mention it records of the feast is in the Martyrology of Jerome, dated shortly after 431, which declares under this date, *Dominus noster Jesus Christus crucifixu est et conceptus, et mundus factus est* (*op. cit.* pages 778, 754): and we are told that the Roman Church did not adopt the feast until the seventh century (page 775). Perhaps liturgical scholars do not cast their nets wide enough, but our passage here shows that the feast was firmly established at least in Africa before the fifth century.

32. I have here taken a considerable liberty with the text which I must explain. In the actual text this quotation, preceded by the words *quo ait*, follows immediately on the last sentence of the previous paragraph, which would then run: . . . "by the strong evidence of the gospel, in which he says, As Jonah" etc. But this makes no sense at all, since the text does nothing to prove that he was speaking of the temple of his body, and the strong evidence of the gospel is that this statement is contained in Jn 2:21.

Now the CCL edition which I am translating encloses the whole passage from *quo ait* to the end of the quotation in curly brackets, to indicate that it is a passage which was not in the original text Augustine dictated, but was added by him when he revised the text. The evidence for this supposition is that the passage is omitted by one whole family of manuscripts, and included by another.

I accept the supposition, but suggest that either Augustine's stenographer or an early copyist inserted the addition in the wrong place. The addition really ran, I suggest, *de quo ait* etc., and was added by the author to explain why we talk about a *triduum*, or three days in this whole connection. The *de* dropped out, and a clever but unintelligent stenographer or copyist added the passage where it made grammatical sense, but rational nonsense. One quality one must allow Augustine is intelligence.

33. In the passion narratives.

34. The difficulty about reconciling the gospel narratives of the passion in this respect is as follows: Mk 15:25 says It was the third hour and they crucified him; ibid: 33 *At the sixth hour there was darkness over the whole earth till the ninth hour*; ibid: 34-37 *At the ninth hour Jesus cried out . . . and shortly afterward breathed his last.* Mt and Lk agree. But in Jn 19:14 Jesus is still before Pilate at the sixth hour, and is crucified shortly afterward.

35. The first days of creation are in fact calculated from evening to morning, as days are still calculated by Jews for religious purposes, and as they were by Jews in Augustine's day, as I am sure he must have known. So his assertion here is extremely puzzling.

It is clear, in the first place, that he calculated the 24 hour day as beginning at midnight, just as we do still. Otherwise the night as far as the dawn of the resurrection would not have belonged to the third day. On this calculation, the day begins and ends with darkness; but the end of it is not in question; the point he is making is that the new day, of Christian reckoning, proceeds from darkness to light.

He could be saying that the 24-hour day, by Jewish reckoning, since it begins at sunset (6:00 p.m., let us say) proceeds from light to darkness, ending up again, of course, with light.

But I don't think that is quite what he is saying. The evidence from his work *On Genesis: A Refutation of the Manicheans* I, 10, 16 and *Unfinished Literal Commentary on Genesis* VII, 28, where he discusses the days of creation explicitly, shows that with a curious obtuseness he interpreted Genesis 1 as saying that the 24-hour day ran from morning to morning. To quote from the first work, *loc. cit.*: "Here the Manichees misrepresent the case, thinking that it says 'There was evening and there was morning one day' as though the day began from the evening. They do not understand that the work by which light was made, and a division was put between light and darkness, and light was called day and darkness night, that this whole work belongs to the day; and after this work, the day being now ended, it was evening. But because the night belongs to its day, it did not say that one day had passed until with the night now finished it was morning. So from then on the following days are reckoned from morning to morning. For now that it is morning, and one day has passed, the work begins from this morning, and after the work it is evening again, then morning, and so another day passes."

Perhaps, after all, he did not know that the Jews still reckoned the day from evening to evening; or if he did, he simply assumed that they like the Manichees were misrepresenting scripture.

36. That is to say, counting in the hour which ended at 3:00 p.m. on the Friday; from 2:00 p.m. on Friday to 6:00 a.m. on Sunday is the stretch of time he means, and the 36 hours from his burial to his resurrection which Augustine goes on to mention, he thinks of as running from 6:00 p.m. on Friday to 6:00 a.m. on Sunday. To count in the ninth hour in his first calculation was simply to count in the way the Romans were accustomed to do, by which they regarded the day before yesterday as being three days ago.

37. For example, the 40 years wandering in the desert, the 40 days spent by Moses on Mount Sinai, the 40-day journey of Elijah to Mount Horeb, the 40 days of our Lord's temptation.

38. That is, a world coordinated by the four points of the compass, the "four corners" of the earth. 4 is a common cosmic symbol, built into the cubic dimensions of the holy of holies, the four living creatures who support God's throne in Ezekiel's vision and in the Apocalypse—and according to the most ancient tradition into the four gospels.

39. Book IV, 4-6. In this last application of the proportion, the two nights and a day in which our Lord's body lay in the tomb represent the proportion of his body (one night) to our body and spirit (one night and one day) as model for the one and type or sacrament for the other.

40. It must be confessed that Augustine's number symbolism, which he indulged in with tireless ingenuity, no longer carries any conviction, though the extraordinary virtuosity of his interpretation of the 46 years it took to build the temple almost persuades me to be a disciple.

It is hard to say how far he meant his symbolic calculations to be taken seriously. To a large extent it was an intellectual pastime of the age, a kind of ancient equivalent to the modern crossword puzzle, and so we will nearly always find Augustine half apologizing for his performance, as here, by saying that perhaps someone else might do it better. On the other hand he is almost truculently insistent that we must accept the validity of the game.

And I think that to some extent he is right. Even though we do not subscribe to any kind of Pythagorean mystique of numbers, the fact is, as I suggested in an earlier note (section 7, note 28), the scriptures do themselves employ numbers symbolically, and we have no right to suppose that this use is limited to the elementary deployment of the number 7 in the Apocalypse, just because this is about the only case of a symbolic number we can recognize. Augustine today might well find the correct solution to the *Times* crossword equally unconvincing, and if we were to point out that within the conventions of crossword clues the solutions are correct, he would have every right to reply that within the conventions of ancient number symbolism, his solutions to biblical crossnumber puzzles, though he does not claim that they are the only correct ones, have a similar right to respect. And he would have a point.

41. As for example Jacob anointing the stone at Bethel, or Abraham ready to sacrifice Isaac at God's command.

42. The philosophical background to the language of this passage is the neoplatonism of Plotinus (let us call it plotinism and be done with it) rather than the plain palaeoplatonism of Plato. But while vitally stimulated by Plotinus, Augustine was even less his mere disciple than Aquinas was to be Aristotle's. Briefly, Plotinus saw the many proceeding from the One by a necessary emanation, and the first stage of this emanation is Mind or Nous (equivalent to the Johannine Logos for Augustine), where multiplicity first appears as the ideas contained in it; and the last stage is matter, which is evil itself, as the ultimate manifold or many in total antithesis to the One, which is good itself. See Copleston, *History of Philosophy*, Vol. I (London, 1946, pages 464-469). Augustine, on the other hand, introduces freedom into these processes all along the line. The many proceed from the One by a free act of creation; in the creative Logos, which is itself one with the One, the many are harmoniously unified; the disharmony of the many with the one (evil) is introduced by a free act of the rational creation; and harmony is restored by yet another free act of the divine One. In the next two chapters Augustine will be attacking many of the religious and philosophical ideas of Porphyry, Plotinus' faithful disciple, though he does not mention his name. See note 1 at the beginning of this book.

43. See Acts 15:9; 2 Cor 5:7.

44. *Voluntates*; M *voluptates*, pleasures.

45. Men will be given (by grace) an equality of nature with the angels when they receive the gift of immortality. I cannot help feeling that Augustine is suffering from a paucity of categories here, which limits him to a choice between ontological or substantial unity of nature, and moral unity of will. His interpretation of this passage simply in terms of the moral unity of charity, though valuable, does less than justice, I feel, both to the passage itself and to the whole drive of his own thought.

46. See Book III, 9.

47. The devil has a body (in Augustine's view), but it is an airy, not an earthy one like flesh, and so is not subject to corruption.

48. This last clause is syntactically incoherent with the rest of the sentence in the Latin.

49. A technical term for mystic rites, particularly for the rites of initiation into the mysteries of Isis, for example, or Mithras, which were still very much in vogue. In *The City of God* X, 9, 2 he describes the *teletai* as "theurgic (magical) consecrations."

50. *Curiositates*; Augustine's scornful word for the *arcana* or mysteries.

51. The interesting thing about this reference to the Magi is that it allows for our being introduced to Christ by a way that is at least analogous to "magical" experiences, etc.

52. "Insofar as" renders *in quo*, which Augustine normally interprets (incorrectly) as "in whom" (that is, in Adam). But such an interpretation hardly fits the grammar here. See Book XIII, 22, note 49.

53. This repetition of the explanatory clause in only slightly altered terms is evidence enough that Augustine did not have the chance to revise as he would have liked. Perhaps in fact he here corrected himself while dictating, rephrasing the clause more to his liking, and the stenographer included both texts by mistake.

54. The word *commixtus*, compounded, would be ruled out by Chalcedon. But Augustine certainly was no monophysite.

55. See Mk 15:44.

56. See Lk 4:1-13.

57. He, or his version, treats the first word of this verse, *apekdusamenos*, as reflexive, not as active with principalities and powers as object, like Vulgate and all modern versions. I think he is probably right.

58. See Rom 8:30.

59. As the previous sentence was hard to translate because it was so loosely written, so this one is impossible to translate because it is so beautifully composed: *Quo enim cadentem non secutus impulit peccatorem, illuc descendentem persecutus compulit redemptorem.*

60. This is Augustine's hostile interpretation of the more sophisticated pagan religiosity of his day, an equivalent of modern theosophy. It was sometimes called "theurgy," which literally means "working the gods." He describes it in detail in *The City of God* VIII, quoting Apuleius and Hermes Trismegistus.

61. See Heb 7:27.

62. Like the Magi; see section 15, note 51.

63. *Populum deficientem*: it could mean a "deserting people"; it is hard to figure out what bogus etymology lies behind it—possibly *am*, people, and *halak*, be hapless.

64. See Ex 17:8-16.

65. This is not said contemptuously, but because no man can achieve this in this life in any but a small measure.

66. "Faith alone" here does not of course have the same meaning as Luther's *sola fide*.

67. The wood, of course, is the cross, assimilated to Noah's ark. The text that governs and legitimates this typology is Wis 10:4, which declares that after water had destroyed the earth, "Wisdom healed it again, steering the just man (Noah) *per contemptible lignum*" (so the Vulgate), on a contemptible piece of wood. It is the use of the word *lignum* for both the ark in this passage, and frequently in the New Testament for the cross, that makes the link.

68. *Aeternae rationes*; see above Book II, 9 note 17; Book III, 13 note 20. These *aeternae rationes* are the platonic ideas or forms, located by Plotinus in the first emanation Mind or Nous, and by Augustine in the Logos or Word of God. See also, in this book, section 3. The *aeternae rationes* are not to be identified with the *seminales rationes*, which he was talking about in Book III, 13, note 20, and which are, as it were, products of the eternal ideas planted as "seeds" in the creation, or the eternal program for things, conceived in the Logos, written into the structure of the created universe.

69. That is, the Word, in which the eternal ideas are situated.

70. With this rather labored metaphor, derived from Eccl 1:7, he is signifying death (the turning point), heaven and hell; or perhaps the turning point represents rather the *parousia* and the general judgment.

71. His argument, stated baldly, is that philosophical knowledge of eternal realities does not give one access to knowledge of contingent things and events in the past, much less then to knowledge of contingent events, like the resurrection, that lie in the future. If *per impossible* one could look right into the eternal ideas in the Word, then one would know everything even before it happened.

This thought brings him on to the discussion in the next paragraph of claims to be able to foretell the future, or practice divination, and he sorts them out into various categories; forecasts based on experience, and the people who make these, are arranged in an amusing scale of social acceptability, with doctors at the top and "even sailors" at the bottom; sheer long sight, or excellent intelligence services, such as the "airy powers" enjoy; divine revelations made to angels or men, which the airy powers are quite capable of picking up by eavesdropping, and publishing through such agencies of theirs as the Delphic oracle, the Sybilline books, or Virgil's fourth Eclogue.

72. *Vates* was the classical word. It is not used at all in the Latin version of the scriptures, which adopted the Greek word *propheta* as the invariable Christian Latin term; either because *vates* had excessively strong pagan connotations, or because *propheta* was already being used by post-classical writers, like Apuleius, for example, to whom Augustine is probably referring here by the words "their literature."

73. I must humbly confess that "are equally present and as it were stationary" stands for the single monosyllable *stant*; and all unnecessary if *stare* was already beginning to be an equivalent for *esse*, as it would come to be in the Romance languages.

74. The author takes up the subject of faith again, and develops it more fully, especially what one might call the psychology of it, in Book XIII. Meanwhile it might help to say something about

the Augustinian perspective on faith, which differs in many respects from that which has become standard in the Church since his time. We are accustomed to regard faith as the appropriate intellectual response to truths which transcend the natural grasp of reason, thus of divine mysteries. For Augustine it is all rather different.

The proper intellectual response to divine mysteries, to what he calls eternal things, is contemplation—a timeless awareness of timeless truth. The unfortunate fact is that we are incapable of this response to any significant degree; but it is meaningless to substitute a faith response to these same eternal mysteries or truths, because faith does not touch them. Faith, which has affinities with platonic "opinion," is the proper response to temporal realities, which do not offer a proper object of timeless contemplation, because they are themselves not timeless.

How then are we to latch onto these eternal divine mysteries in the contemplation of which lies our ultimate salvation? The answer is that we cannot, of our own accord and by our own efforts; this is his objection to the philosophers he has just been arguing with. But the divine mysteries have by a pure act of grace reached down to us and entered into our temporal world of faith and opinion, the world of matter, time, and change. So what we can now do is respond in faith to what God has done, and become, in time. This purifies our minds and makes them capable of contemplating the divine mysteries themselves. How does faith purify our minds? Not by some quality inherent in the act of believing in itself, but in virtue of the temporal object to which we attach our faith—namely Christ. Because this object is identical with eternal truth, it acts as a vehicle to carry our minds up to contemplation.

The process is no more than begun in this life; contemplation belongs properly to a mode of existence in which we are totally liberated from the changing and the temporal. But in this life our faith can, as Augustine will say shortly, follow the risen Christ to heaven, and so introduce us to some foretaste of contemplation, and glimmerings of understanding.

To fit Augustine's perspective into another and perhaps more familiar frame of reference, one might put it this way. We distinguish between believing someone and believing that what they tell us is the case. We only believe in the second way of using the word—believing evidence given—because we first believe in the first way—trust the person giving the evidence. Now for Augustine faith certainly latches onto God in the first way. It is because he believes or trusts God that he believes the evidence of the scriptures, or what God says there. But what God says there, what Augustine believes on faith to be the case because he trusts God, is a lot of temporal, historical things and events, above all Christ, his death and resurrection. Even if God does tell us some eternal truths about himself, Augustine would say, he has to do it in temporal terms, by means of material symbols and sacraments, otherwise we would not be able to hear him. Time is our language, even for talking—baby-talking, really—about eternity. So we can, in a secondary sense, talk about believing by faith divine mysteries that surpass human reason, like the mystery of the Trinity. But what we are really believing in the strict sense, in Augustine's perspective, is the whole series of temporal, material and "sacramental" realities which confront us with the mystery; the mystery itself is properly an object of timeless contemplation, and the whole drive of our faith—and the whole effort of this work—is to achieve even some small measure of that contemplation, knowing full well that this will only be finally achieved when what is mortal has put on immortality.

75. Plato, *Timaeus* 29c. I think Augustine was probably using Cicero's translation. What is actually said in the Greek is, "As being is to becoming, so is truth to faith (belief)."

76. That is, principally to the incarnation and the life, death, and resurrection of the Word incarnate.

77. See Acts 15:9, a key text for Augustine's conception of faith and its function.

78. *Sprang from the earth*, had this translation not had to be accommodated to its peculiar context.

79. *Timaeus*, 29c.

80. *Estis*: M reads *eritis*, will be.

81. *Nisi enim multis missis praedicaretur unus, non multis dimissis teneretur unus*: a very obscure sentence. The Spanish BAC translation renders the apodosis ". . . many would not have been set free, one remaining bound," thus interpreting the second *unus* of the devil. In view of the way Augustine has throughout been identifying the "One" with the Word, I find this quite unaccept-

able. Taking as I do the second *unus* to have the same reference as the first *unus*, I have to translate *teneretur* as I do. *Multis dimissis*, however, could also mean, and probably does carry the overtone of meaning, "many sins having been forgiven." But I prefer to interpret it as primarily signifying our liberation from enslavement to "the many."

82. Augustine is here returning to the argument which he initiated back in Book II, 7 and 8 and conceding for the moment, for the sake of argument, the opinion of the "economic" theologians that the notion of sending implies that the one sent is less than the sender. But he only concedes it for the sake of argument, and to show that even on this premise one can still argue that the Son is only less than the Father in his human nature. At the beginning of the next paragraph he will state his own view that being sent does not in fact imply being less than the sender, but only being from the sender. He has to hold this view because, as he is going to say, the Word was not sent after he had become man, but precisely in order to become man. While the incarnation is in fact identical with the mission of the Son as realized, the mission is at least logically prior to the incarnation.

83. The argument is certainly very elliptical. He discusses the text a little more fully above in Book I, chapter 3, and from there we might spell out his argument as follows: Philip's saying *Show us the Father* could just as well have been put, had he known what he was talking about, "Show us yourself," given the Son's equality with the Father. And such a request would have made sense. But before it could be granted, Philip must first be purified by faith. So Jesus goes on to say to him, *Do you not believe that I am in the Father and the Father in me?*

84. See Jn 1:14.

85. See Gal 4:4.

86. That is, to fulfill the scriptures.

87. And Wisdom is feminine. This is going to involve me in some changes of gender, which I ask the reader to excuse.

88. It is a better pun in Latin than in English, but one does use the word "labor" to mean have difficulty as in labored jokes, or cars laboring as they go uphill.

89. See Is 9:6, where in the Septuagint "angel of good counsel" is one of the Messiah's titles.

90. This is what the scholastics would call invisible mission.

91. M omits the preposition in, giving the sense: What is born from eternity is eternal.

92. See Jn 10:30.

93. The famous Johannine comma, an interpolation into the text which probably occurred not long before Augustine's time.

94. Finding proper names for the Holy Spirit that will distinguish him from the other persons is a classic difficulty of trinitarian theology. Augustine opts for this title of "Gift," and will revert to the subject several times in the course of the work. What is required is a relational term, like "Father" and "Son."

95. These two sentences are the culmination of the whole discussion of the divine missions from Book II onward. They justify the space devoted to the topic, for they state that it is the missions which reveal the inner core of the trinitarian mystery.

96. See Mt 10:20; Gal 4:6.

97. Augustine will develop this doctrine of the double procession of the Holy Spirit more fully below in Book V, 15. This expression I have just used, "double procession," while convenient is not really accurate, and as the next few pages will show, Augustine is careful to state that the Spirit proceeds from the Father and the Son as from one principle or source, and that the Son receives from the Father his being, with the Father, that from which the Spirit proceeds. He is really compelled to formulate the doctrine, given his notion of mission, which we have just noted. For scripture plainly talks of the Son sending the Spirit, and if as we have seen the sendings in time manifest the eternal processions, then the sending of the Spirit by the Son must manifest the eternal procession of the Spirit from the Son.

98. He will discuss the point, briefly enough, below in Book XV, 46.

99. See above Book I, 15, note 38.

100. See Lk 1:67.

101. See Lk 1:46.

102. See Lk 2:25.

103. See above section 16, note 54.

104. He appears to be contradicting what he just said in the previous paragraph about the unprecedented character of Pentecost. But in fact, all he is allowing here is that the visible symbols employed in the New Testament may have been used before; what they symbolize, as described above, remains new.

105. See the end of the prologue to this book.

106. This is the first mention of the terms in which he is going to work out his theory of the image; they will be taken up again in Book X.

107. In Book III above.

108. This is a caution against the heresy of Apollinaris, who maintained that the Word took the place of a human soul in Christ.

109. With the Father and the Holy Spirit; it is hard to see how this possibility could even suggest itself. I think the thought is that the intellectual spirit brought in as agent might be thought of as analogous to the human soul of Christ, the animating principle of the voice, dove, etc., which, like Christ's soul in his body, could be hypostatically united to the divine person.

110. Another sentence which shows the roughness of an unrevised text. I have not yet been able to locate anywhere later on in the *De Trinitate* where he takes up this particular point.

111. He means the Arians, to whom he will turn his attention in the next three books.

112. *Propter principii commendationem.* That is, to keep before our eyes what the earlier "economic" theologians called the *monarchia*. I think *principium* is Augustine's word for this.

It is one of the Greek objections to the *Filioque* in the Latin creed, the doctrine of the Holy Spirit's proceeding from the Son as well as the Father, that it derogates from the Father's *monarchia*. It is clear that Augustine at least was aware of the need to safeguard this attribute, and that he so envisaged the double procession of the Holy Spirit that this *monarchia* was not impugned.

The following three books form a distinct unit, and should be read as such. Indeed, their division into three books is somewhat artificial, a contrivance to achieve the symmetrical form of the whole work, which I outlined in the introduction. In particular, the division between Books VI and VII has little substantive significance, since they are both concerned with all the ramifications of the problem raised by the text of 1 Corinthians 1:24, *Christ the power of God and the wisdom of God*. It is important that the reader should realize that in Book VI the author is only toying with a provisional solution to the problem, which he discards in Book VII where he propounds his definitive solution.

The argument through these books is with the Arians, not in terms of scripture, or what Augustine calls faith, but in terms of reason. If we can make a distinction between metaphysics and linguistic logic—though the distinction certainly becomes rather blurred when we are discussing how to talk about God—then the whole tenor of these three books is logical rather than metaphysical. This becomes most clear when Augustine is discussing the use of the terms "person" and "hypostasis" in Book VII. Here he deliberately eschews the attempt to give any metaphysical content to the terms, and perhaps this is what most notably marks off his trinitarian theology from that of his Greek contemporaries. In general, it is well to bear in mind that in these books he is not so much talking about God the Trinity, as talking about how to talk about God the Trinity.

The general line of his argument is simple enough, but in his characteristic fashion he complicates it with all sorts of variations and arabesques. His constant concern against the Arians is to safeguard the absolute equality of the Son and the Holy Spirit with the Father, while still maintaining their real distinction from each other. In Book V he sets out his basic principle. He agrees with the Arians that because of God's absolute simplicity and immutability, there can be no accidents in God, in the sense of Aristotle's nine categories of accidents; that is to say, that although we use accident words about God, like "good" and "great" etc., and say that God does things, such words in fact signify not divine quality or quantity or activity as happening to or adhering to the divine substance, but the divine substance itself, so that we have to qualify the statement "God is good" by adding that indeed God is his own goodness. Thus we can say, and the Arians very firmly did say, that all accident words, when predicated of God, turn into substance words.

Augustine makes one exception: relationship words like "Father" and "Son." Not that these words when predicated of God signify accidents that adhere to or modify the divine substance in any way, but that they signify mutual, and

186

therefore mutually exclusive, relationships within God, and not the divine substance. And so he will conclude that as regards all predications of substance, and of accident words that become substance words when predicated of God, like "good" and "great," the three divine persons are absolutely equal, and are indeed one. And yet the Father is not the Son, because he is the Father of the Son, and the Son is not the Father because he is the Son of the Father. This scheme applies too, though with certain linguistic difficulties and inadequacies, to the Holy Spirit.

But this satisfactory distinction between substance words and relationship words is called in question by St Paul's expression *Christ the power of God and the wisdom of God*. What the apostle is doing here, and what scripture frequently does with other words, is to use substance words, namely "power" and "wisdom," which have the same kind of status as "goodness" and "greatness," as relationship words, or at least in a relationship manner; the expression "wisdom of God" seems to have the same structure as "Son of the Father" or "Word of the Father."

Perhaps all the words we use to talk about God with are really relationship words, except wholly unassailable substance words like "God" itself or "substance"; and perhaps these irreducible substance words cannot be used of any of the divine persons individually, but only of all of them together. This seems to be the provisional solution Augustine works with in Book VI, his only concern being to show that even with such a way of looking at the matter, the Son is equal to the Father.

He demolishes this solution, however, in Book VII by showing that logically on this kind of supposition, if you reduce words like "wisdom" and "goodness" to relationship status, you are compelled in fact to reduce "God" to relationship status too; worse still "substance" or "being" will become relationship words, which is the height of absurdity. So he is brought back to his original distinction, but with an added qualification. Substance words like "God" or "good" or "wisdom" or "goodness" are *properly* predicated of the divine substance, or equally and identically of the divine persons without signifying their mutual relationships. Because the divine persons are not distinct from the divine substance, but only from each other, such names may be properly predicated of the persons individually, sometimes with an indication of the relationship sometimes not. Thus one can say "the Son is God (or good or wisdom or great) and the Father is God (or good etc.)"; and one can also say "the Son is God from God, light from light," as in the Nicene creed; and thus also if you like, "wisdom from wisdom."

But besides this *proper* use of substance words, there is also a perfectly legitimate *improper* use of them, as in the Pauline text which raised the whole problem; by which they are appropriated, to use the later scholastic term, which is not Augustine's own, to one of the persons. Thus in this text, *Christ the wisdom of God*, "wisdom" is appropriated to the Son and "God" to the Father; but this does not mean either that the Father is not wisdom, or that the Son is not God. Augustine suggests one or two reasons for this improper use of terms, which the reader will ascertain from the author; the main point is that scripture does so use terms improperly, and we have to be sure what inferences we may and what we may not draw from this usage.

The last point he touches on is a usage that is not scriptural but ecclesiastical, namely the use of the word "person," and by the Greeks of the word "*hypostasis*," of which the literal translation is "substance." We cannot possibly say that these are relationship words; yet we say "three persons" or "three *hypostaseis*," whereas with all the other substance words that are appropriated to this or that person we never say "three Gods," or "three wisdoms," but "one God" and "one wisdom." We do this, Augustine says bluntly, because we have to say "three something" in answer to the question "three what"? Greek theologians, so we are given to understand by Prestige,[1] tried to note a distinction of metaphysical content between *ousia* and *hypostasis* in order to justify their saying "one *ousia*, three *hypostaseis*." Augustine makes no such attempt—and I for my part think he is wise. For him the distinction between "substance" and "person" in the Latin terminology is purely and simply one of arbitrary linguistic convention. The words tell us nothing at all substantive about God, they merely help us to talk about him with less incoherence than would otherwise be the case.

NOTES

1. *God in Patristic Thought*, pages 157-178, 235ff.

BOOK V

LINGUISTIC AND LOGICAL: SUBSTANCE AND RELATIONSHIP

Prologue

---

1. From now on I will be attempting to say things that cannot altogether be said as they are thought by a man—or at least as they are thought by me. In any case, when we think about God the trinity we are aware that our thoughts are quite inadequate to their object, and incapable of grasping him as he is; even by men of the calibre of the apostle Paul he can only be seen, as it says, *like a puzzling reflection in a mirror* (1 Cor 13:12). Now since we ought to think about the Lord our God always, and can never think about him as he deserves; since at all times we should be praising him and blessing him, and yet no words of ours are capable of expressing him, I begin by asking him to help me understand and explain what I have in mind and to pardon any blunders I may make. For I am as keenly aware of my weakness as of my willingness. And I also ask my readers to forgive me, wherever they notice that I am trying and failing to say something which they understand better, or which they are prevented from understanding because I express myself so badly; just as I will forgive them when they are too slow on the uptake to understand what I am saying.

2. We will find it easier to excuse one another if we know, or at least firmly believe and maintain, that whatever we say about that unchanging and invisible nature, that supreme and all-sufficient life, cannot be measured by the standard of things visible, changeable, mortal and deficient. Indeed we find ourselves unequal, except with much difficulty, to achieving a scientific comprehension of what is accessible to our bodily senses or of what we ourselves are in the inner man. Yet for all that there is no effrontery in burning to know, out of faithful piety, the divine and inexpressible truth that is above us, provided the mind is fired by the grace of our creator and savior, and not inflated by arrogant confidence in its own powers. In any case, what intellectual capacity has a man

189

got to grasp God with, if his own intellect with which he wishes to grasp him still eludes his grasp? If he does comprehend his own intellect, he should bear firmly in mind that it is the best thing in his nature, and then ask himself whether he can see in it lines, shapes, bright colors, space, size, distinction of parts, extension of bulk, movement from place to place, or anything of that sort. We certainly find none of these things in what we find to be the best thing in our nature, that is in our intellect, in which we hold however much wisdom we have the capacity for. So what we do not find in our better part we should not look for in that which is far and away better than our better part. Thus we should understand God, if we can and as far as we can, to be good without quality, great without quantity, creative without need or necessity, presiding[1] without position, holding all things together without possession, wholly everywhere without place, everlasting without time, without any change in himself making changeable things, and undergoing nothing.[2] Whoever thinks of God like that may not yet be able to discover altogether what he is, but is at least piously on his guard against thinking about him anything that he is not.[3]

Chapter 1

On the basis of the principle, common to both parties, that nothing is predicated of God by way of modification of the divine being, that is by way of accident, he argues against the inference which the Arians drew from the names "unbegotten" for the Father and "begotten" for the Son that the Father and the Son must be of different substance from one another. He asserts that although nothing is predicated of God by way of modification, it does not follow that everything is predicated of him by way of substance; for some things are predicated by way of relationship, that is internal relationship within the godhead.

---

3. There is at least no doubt that God is substance, or perhaps a better word would be being; at any rate what the Greeks call *ousia*. Just as we get the word "wisdom" from "wise," and "knowledge" from "know," so we have the word "being" from "be."[4] And who can more be than he that said to his servant,[5] *I am who I am*, and, *Tell the sons of Israel, He who is sent me to you* (Ex 3:14)? Now other things that we call beings or substances admit of modifications,[6] by which they are modified and changed to a great or small extent. But God cannot be modified in any way, and therefore the substance or being which is God is alone unchangeable, and therefore it pertains to it most truly and supremely to be, from which comes the name "being." Anything that changes does not keep its being, and anything that can change even though it does not, is able to not be what it was; and thus only that which not only does not but also absolutely cannot change deserves without qualification to be said really and truly to be.

4. It is about these things which cannot be expressed as they are thought and cannot be thought as they are that we must now begin to reply to the critics of

our faith. Now among the many objections which the Arians are in the habit of leveling against the Catholic faith, the most cunning and ingenious device they think they can bring to bear is the following argument: "Whatever is said or understood about God is said substance-wise, not modification-wise. Therefore the Father is unbegotten substance-wise, and the Son is begotten substance-wise. But being unbegotten is different from being begotten; therefore the Father's substance is different from the Son's."

We answer: If everything that is said about God is said substance-wise, then *I and the Father are one* (Jn 10:30) was said substance-wise. So the substance of the Father and of the Son is one. Or if this is not said substance-wise, then there are some things that are not said about God substance-wise, and therefore we are not obliged to understand unbegotten and begotten substance-wise. Again, it is said of the Son, *He thought it no robbery to be equal to God* (Phil 2:6). What-wise equal? If he is not called equal substance-wise, then they are admitting that something is not said about God substance-wise; so they should admit that unbegotten and begotten need not be said substance-wise. But if they will not admit it, because they insist on everything being said about God substance-wise, then the Son is equal to the Father substance-wise.

5. We usually give the name "modification" to something that can be lost by some change of the thing it modifies. Even though some modifications are called inseparable, *achorista* in Greek, like the color black in a crow's feather, it does lose it, not indeed as long as it is a feather, but because it is not always a feather. The stuff it is made of is changeable, and so the moment it ceases to be that animal or that feather, and that whole body turns and changes into earth[7] it loses of course that color. As a matter of fact, even a modification that is called separable is not lost by separation but by change—like the blackness of people's hair which can turn white while still remaining hair. It is called a separable modification, but if we stop to think for a moment it will be evident that it is not a question of something being separated and departing from the head, or of blackness leaving and going somewhere else when whiteness takes its place but of that quality of color turning and changing there in the same place.

So there is no modification in God because there is nothing in him that can be changed or lost. You may also like to call anything that diminishes and grows a modification even though it cannot be lost, like the life of the soul—for the soul lives as long as it is soul, and since it is always soul it always lives; but it lives more when it is wise and less when it is unwise. So even here you have a change, not indeed one by which life is lost as wisdom is lost by the unwise, but one by which it diminishes. Well, there is nothing like that either with God, because he remains absolutely unchangeable.

6. Nothing therefore is said of him modification-wise because nothing modifies him, but this does not mean that everything said of him is said substance-wise. It is true that with created and changeable things anything that is not said substance-wise can only be said modification-wise. Everything that can be lost or diminished is a modification of such things, such as sizes and qualities, and whatever is said with reference to something else[8] like friendships,

proximities, subordinations, likenesses, equalities, and anything of that sort; as also positions, possessions, places, times, doings, and undergoings.[9]

With God, though, nothing is said modification-wise, because there is nothing changeable with him. And yet not everything that is said of him is said substance-wise. Some things are said with reference to something else, like Father with reference to Son and Son with reference to Father; and this is not said modification-wise, because the one is always Father and the other always Son—not "always" in the sense that he is Son from the moment he is born or[10] that the Father does not cease to be Father from the moment the Son does not cease to be Son, but in the sense that the Son is always born and never began to be Son. If he had some time begun or some time ceased to be Son, it would be predicated modification-wise. If on the other hand what is called Father were called so with reference to itself and not to the Son, and what is called Son were called so with reference to itself and not to the Father, the one would be called Father and the other Son substance-wise. But since the Father is only called so because he has a Son, and the Son is only called so because he has a Father, these things are not said substance-wise, as neither is said with reference to itself but only with reference to the other. Nor are they said modification-wise, because what is signified by calling them Father and Son belongs to them eternally and unchangeably. Therefore, although being Father is different from being Son, there is no difference of substance, because they are not called these things substance-wise but relationship-wise; and yet this relationship is not a modification, because it is not changeable.

7. They may argue back against this line of reasoning by saying that while indeed "Father" is said with reference to "Son" and "Son" with reference to "Father," "unbegotten" and "begotten" are said with reference to themselves and not to each other. To call him unbegotten is not the same as calling him Father, because there would be nothing to stop you calling him unbegotten even if he had not begotten a son; and if someone does beget a son it does not follow that he is unbegotten, since men who are begotten by other men beget yet others themselves. So they say, "Father is said with reference to Son and Son with reference to Father; but unbegotten is said with reference to itself and begotten is said with reference to itself. And so if whatever is said with reference to itself is said substance-wise; and if being unbegotten is different from being begotten, then there is here a difference of substance."

If that is what they say, then I grant that they are saying something about "unbegotten" that will have to be looked at more closely, because being father does not necessarily follow on being unbegotten nor being unbegotten follow on being father; and therefore it might be thought that unbegotten is said with reference to self and not to another. But they are marvelously blind if they fail to notice that begotten can only be said with reference to another. Being son is a consequence of being begotten, and being begotten is implied by being son. Just as "son" is referred to "father," so is "begotten" referred to "begetter," and as father is to son, so is begetter to begotten. So two distinct notions are conveyed by "begetter" and "unbegotten." Both indeed are said of God the Father, but the first is said with reference to the begotten, that is to the Son, and they do not deny this; while as for "unbegotten," they maintain that this is said with reference to self. So they say: "If the Father is called anything with reference to himself that the Son cannot be called with reference to himself; and if anything said with reference to self is said substance-wise, and 'unbegotten' which cannot be said of the Son is said with reference to self; then 'unbegotten' is said substance-wise, and because the Son cannot be called this, he is not of the same substance."

The answer to this subtlety is to oblige them to tell us what makes the Son equal to the Father;[11] is it what is said of him with reference to himself, or what is said of him with reference to the Father? Well, it cannot be what he is called with reference to the Father, because with reference to the Father he is called Son; and in this respect the other is not Son but Father, for father and son do not have the same sort of reference to each other as friends or neighbors. Friend of course has reference to friend, and if they love each other equally, there is the same friendship in each; and neighbor has reference to neighbor, and because they neighbor equally on each other (A is as near to B as B is to A), there is the same neighborness in each. But because son does not have reference to son but to father, it cannot be what he is called with reference to the Father that makes the Son equal to the Father. It remains that what makes him equal must be what he is called with reference to himself. But whatever he is called with reference to himself he is called substance-wise. So it follows that he is equal substance-wise. Therefore the substance of each of them is the same. And when the Father is called unbegotten, it is not being stated what he is, but what he is not. And when a relationship is denied it is not denied substance-wise, because the relationship itself is not affirmed substance-wise.

8. This point must be illustrated by examples. But first we must just establish that when we say "begotten" we mean the same as when we say "son." Being son is a consequence of being begotten, and being begotten is implied by being son. To call something unbegotten, then, is to show that it is not son. But while one can talk correctly about begotten and unbegotten, and while "son" is a perfectly good English word, our normal habits of speech will scarcely allow us to talk about "unson." But it makes no difference to the meaning if one says "not son," just as if you say "not begotten" instead of "unbegotten" you are not saying anything different. There are similar limitations with the relationship words "friend" and "neighbor." One can use the negative adjectives "unfriendly" and unneighborly" to correspond with "friendly" and "neighborly," but scarcely the negative nouns "unfriend" and "unneighbor."[12] It is as well to realize that what matters in considering actual things is not what our language usage will or will not allow, but what meanings emerge from the things themselves.

So let us stop saying unbegotten, although we can say it in English, and instead let us say not begotten, which has the same value. Are we saying anything else than not son? Now this negative particle does not have the effect that something said without it relationship-wise is said substance-wise with it;

its effect is simply to deny what without it is affirmed, as in all other predications. Thus when we say "It is a man," we indicate substance. If you say "It is not a man," you do not state another kind of predication, you merely deny this one. As I affirm substance-wise "It is a man," so I deny substance-wise when I say "It is not a man." And when you ask how big he is and I affirm "He is four foot"—that is, four feet tall[13]—someone who says "He is not four foot" is denying quantity-wise. "He is white" I affirm quality-wise; "He is not white" I deny quality-wise. "He is near" I affirm relationship-wise; "He is not near" I deny relationship-wise. I affirm position-wise when I say "He is lying down"; I deny position-wise when I say "He is not lying down." I affirm possession-wise when I say "He is armed" ; I deny possession-wise when I say "He is not armed"—and it would be exactly the same if I said "He is unarmed." I affirm time-wise when I say "He was born yesterday"; I deny time-wise when I say "He was not born yesterday." When I say "He is in Rome," I affirm place-wise; I deny place-wise when I say "He is not in Rome" I affirm action-wise when I say "He is beating"; but if I say "He is not beating" I deny action-wise to show that he is not acting like this. And when I say "He is being beaten" I affirm with the predication that is called passion; and I deny in the same way when I say "He is not being beaten." In a word, there is no kind of predication we may care to affirm with, which we are not obliged equally to employ if we wish to insert the negative particle.

This being so, if I affirmed substance-wise by saying "son," I would deny substance-wise by saying "not son." But because in fact I affirm relationship-wise when I say "son," since I refer it to father, I deny relationship-wise when I say "He is not a son," since I am referring the negation to parent, in wishing to declare that he has not got a parent. But if what is meant by saying "son" can be said just as well by saying "begotten" as I remarked above, then one can say "not son" just as well by saying "not begotten." Now we deny relationship-wise when we say "not son"; therefore we deny relationship-wise when we say "not begotten." And what does unbegotten mean but not begotten? So we do not leave the predication of relationship when we say unbegotten. Just as begotten is not said with reference to self but means being from a begetter, so unbegotten is not said with reference to self but simply means not being from a begetter. Each meaning belongs to the predication that is called relationship. And what is stated relationship-wise does not designate substance. So although begotten differs from unbegotten, it does not indicate a different substance, because just as son refers to father, and not son to not father, so begotten must refer to begetter, and not begotten to not begetter.[14]

Chapter 2

The use of substantive predications of God is examined in more detail, with a short foray included into the terminology of ousia *and* hypostasis, *"substance" and "person," which will be discussed much more thoroughly toward the end of Book VII.*

9. The chief point then that we must maintain is that whatever that supreme and divine majesty is called with reference to itself is said substance-wise; whatever it is called with reference to another is said not substance- but relationship-wise; and that such is the force of the expression "of the same substance" in Father and Son and Holy Spirit, that whatever is said with reference to self about each of them is to be taken as adding up in all three to a singular and not to a plural. Thus the Father is God and the Son is God and the Holy Spirit is God, and no one denies that this is said substance-wise; and yet we say that this supreme triad is not three Gods but one God. Likewise the Father is great, the Son is great, the Holy Spirit too is great; yet there are not three great ones but one great one. It is not, after all, about the Father alone that scripture says *You alone are the great God* (Ps 86:10), as they perversely consider, but about Father, Son and Holy Spirit. Again, the Father is good, the Son is good, the Holy Spirit too is good; yet there are not three good ones but one good one, of whom it is said *No one is good but the one God* (Mk 10:18; Lk 18:19). When the Lord Jesus was accosted just as a man by the young man who said *Good master*, he did not want to be taken for just a man, and so he significantly said, not "No one is good but the Father alone," but *No one is good but the one God* (Mk 10:18; Lk 18:19). The name "Father" signifies only the Father in himself[15] but the name "God" includes him and the Son and the Holy Spirit, because the one God is a trinity.

As for position, possession, times, and places, they are not stated properly about God but by way of metaphor and simile. Thus he is said to be *seated on the cherubim* (Ps 80:2), which is said with reference to position; and *the deep is his clothing like a garment* (Ps 104:6) which refers to possession; and *Your years will not fail* (Ps 102:28) which refers to time; and *If I climb up to heaven you are there* (Ps 139:8) which refers to place. As far, though, as making or doing is concerned, perhaps this can be said with complete truth only about God; he alone makes and is not made, nor does he suffer or undergo anything so far as his substance by which he is God is concerned. So then, the Father is almighty, the Son is almighty, the Holy Spirit is almighty; yet there are not three almighties but one almighty; *from whom are all things, through whom are all things, in whom are all things: to him be glory* (Rom 11:36).

So whatever God is called with reference to self is both said three times over[16] about each of the persons, Father, Son and Holy Spirit, and at the same time is said in the singular and not the plural about the trinity. As it is not one thing for God to be and another for him to be great, but being is for Him the same thing as being great, for that reason we do not say three greatnesses any more than we say three beings, but one being and one greatness. By "being" I mean here what is called *ousia* in Greek, which we more usually call substance.

10. The Greeks also have another word, *hypostasis*, but they make a distinction that is rather obscure to me between *ousia* and *hypostasis*, so that most of our people[17] who treat of these matters in Greek are accustomed to say *mia ousia, treis hypostaseis*, which in English is literally one being, three substances.[18] But because we have grown accustomed in our usage to meaning the same thing by "being" as by "substance," we do not dare say one being, three substances. Rather, one being or substance, three persons[19] is what many Latin authors, whose authority carries weight, have said when treating of these matters, being able to find no more suitable way of expressing in words what they understood without words. In very truth, because the Father is not the Son and the Son is not the Father, and the Holy Spirit who is also called *the gift of God* (Acts 8:20; Jn 4:10) is neither the Father nor the Son, they are certainly three. That is why it is said in the plural *I and the Father are one* (Jn 10:30). He did not say "is one," which the Sabellians say, but "are one." Yet when you ask "Three what?" human speech labors under a great dearth of words. So we say three persons, not in order to say that precisely, but in order not to be reduced to silence.

11. To return to the point I was discussing: just as we do not say three beings, neither do we say three greatnesses or three great ones. In things that are great by partaking of greatness, things where being is one thing and being great another, like a great house and a great mountain and a great heart, in such things greatness is one thing and that which is great with this greatness is another—thus greatness is certainly not the same thing as a great house. True greatness is that by which not only is a great house great or any great mountain great, but by which anything at all is great that is called great, so that greatness is one thing and things that are called great by it another. This greatness of course is primally great and much more excellently so than the things that are great by partaking of it. God however is not great with a greatness which he is not himself, as though God were to participate in it to be great; otherwise this greatness would be greater than God. But there is nothing greater than God. So he is great with a greatness by which he is himself this same greatness. And that is why we do not say three greatnesses any more than we say three beings; for God it is the same thing to be as to be great. For the same reason we do not say three great ones but one great one, because God is not great by participating in greatness, but he is great with his great self because he is his own greatness. The same must be said about goodness and eternity and omnipotence and about absolutely all the predications that can be stated of God, because it is all said with reference to himself, and not metaphorically either or in simile but properly—if anything, that is, can be said properly about him by a human tongue.

Chapter 3

The use of relative predications about God is examined in more detail; in particular the peculiarities of the names for the Holy Spirit of which "gift" is considered the most proper. Besides names by which the divine persons are referred to each other, names by which they are also referred to creation are discussed, like "origin" (principium), and even in some contexts "Father."

12. But as for the things each of the three in this triad is called that are proper or peculiar to himself, such things are never said with reference to self but only with reference to each other or to creation,[20] and therefore it is clear that they are said by way of relationship and not by way of substance. The triad, the one God, is called great, good, eternal, omnipotent, and he can also be called his own godhead, his own greatness, his own goodness, his own eternity, his own omnipotence; but the triad cannot in the same way be called Father, except perhaps metaphorically with reference to creation because of the adoption of sons.[21] The text *Hear, O Israel: the Lord your God is one Lord* (Dt 6:4) is not to be understood as excluding the Son or excluding the Holy Spirit, and this one Lord we rightly call our Father as well because he regenerates us by his grace.

In no way at all, however, can the trinity be called Son. As for Holy Spirit, in terms of the text *God is spirit* (Jn 4:24),[22] the triad can as a whole be called this, because both Father and Son are also spirit. So because Father and Son and Holy Spirit are one God, and because God of course is holy and *God is spirit*, the triad can be called both holy and spirit. And yet that Holy Spirit whom we understand as being not the triad but in the triad, insofar as he is properly or peculiarly called the Holy Spirit, is so called relationship-wise, being referred to both Father and Son, since the Holy Spirit is the Spirit of the Father and of the Son.[23]

This relationship, to be sure, is not apparent in this particular name, but it is apparent when he is called *the gift of God* (Acts 8:20; Jn 4:10). He is the gift of the Father and of the Son, because on the one hand he *proceeds from the Father* (Jn 15:26), as the Lord says; and on the other the apostle's words, *Whoever does not have the Spirit of Christ is not one of his* (Rom 8:9), are spoken of the Holy Spirit. So when we say "the gift of the giver" and "the giver of the gift," we say each with reference to the other. So the Holy Spirit is a kind of inexpressible communion or fellowship of Father and Son,[24] and perhaps he is given this name just because the same name can be applied to the Father and the Son. He is properly called what they are called in common, seeing that both Father and Son are holy and both Father and Son are spirit. So to signify the communion of them both by a name which applies to them both, the gift of both is called the Holy Spirit. And this three is one only God, good, great, eternal, omnipotent; his own unity, godhead, greatness, goodness, eternity, omnipotence.

13. Nor should the reader be worried by our saying that Holy Spirit (not the triad itself but the one member of the triad) is said relationship-wise, on the grounds that there does not seem to be a corresponding name to which this one

is referred. As we say servant of the master, so we say master of the servant, and likewise son of the father and father of the son, because these are all said relationship-wise; and it is true that we cannot say the same in this case. We say the Holy Spirit of the Father, but we do not reverse it and say the Father of the Holy Spirit, or then we should take the Holy Spirit to be his son. Again, we say the Holy Spirit of the Son, but we do not say the Son of the Holy Spirit, or we should take the Holy Spirit to be his father. But this happens in many relationships, where we cannot find two corresponding words to be referred to each other. Could anything more obviously be said relationship-wise than "pledge"? It is referred to that which it is a pledge of, and a pledge is always a pledge of something. So then when we say pledge of the Father and of the Son[25] can we turn it round and say Father of the pledge or Son of the pledge? When however we say gift of the Father and of the Son, it is true that we cannot say Father of the gift or Son of the gift, but to get a correspondence here we say gift of the giver and giver of the gift. Here in fact we can find an ordinary word, but in the other two cases we cannot.

14. Coming now to the Father, he is called Father relationship-wise, and he is also called origin relationship-wise, and perhaps other things too. But he is called Father with reference to the Son, origin with reference to all things that are from him. Again, the Son is so called relationship-wise; he is also called Word and image relationship-wise, and with all these names he is referred to the Father, while the Father himself is called none of these things. The Son, however, is also called origin; when he was asked *Who are you?* He replied, *The origin, because[26]I am also speaking to you* (Jn 8:25).[27] But surely not the origin of the Father? No, he wanted to indicate that he is the creator when he said he was the origin, just as the Father is the origin of creation because all things are from him. For creator is said with reference to creation as master is with reference to servant. And so when we call both the Father origin and the Son origin, we are not saying two origins of creation, because Father and Son are together one origin with reference to creation, just as they are one creator, one God.

Furthermore, if anything that abides in itself and produces or achieves something is the origin of the thing it produces or achieves, we cannot deny the Holy Spirit the right to be called origin either, because we do not exclude him from the title of creator. It is written of him that he achieves, and of course he abides in himself as he achieves; he does not turn or change into any of the things that he achieves. Observe what he achieves: *To each one*, it says, *is given a manifestation of the Spirit for advantage. To one is given through the Spirit a word of wisdom; to another a word of knowledge according to the same Spirit; to another faith in the same Spirit; to another the gift of healing in the one Spirit; to another workings of mighty deeds, to another prophecy, to another discrimination of spirits, to another varieties of tongues. But all these things are achieved by one and the same Spirit distributing them severally to each just as he wills* (1 Cor 12:7-11)—as God of course. Who but God can achieve such great things? *It is the same God who achieves all things in all of us* (1 Cor 12:6).

If, after all, we are asked specifically about the Holy Spirit, we reply with perfect truth that he is God, and with the Father and the Son he is together one God. So God is called one origin with reference to creation, not two or three origins.

15. But to return to the mutual relationships within the trinity: if the producer is the origin with reference to what it produces, then the Father is origin with reference to the Son, because he produced or begot him. But whether the Father is origin with respect to the Holy Spirit because it is said that *He proceeds from the Father* (Jn 15:26), that is quite a question. If it is so, then he will be origin not only for what he begets or makes, but also for what he gives. And here perhaps some light begins to dawn as far as it is possible on a problem that often worries many people, namely why the Holy Spirit too is not a son, seeing that he too comes forth from the Father, as it says in the gospel.[28] He comes forth, you see, not as being born but as being given, and so he is not called son, because he was not born like the only begotten Son, nor made and born adoptively by grace[29] like us. What was born of the Father is referred to the Father alone when he is called Son, and therefore he is the Father's Son and not ours too. But what has been given is referred both to him who gave and to those it was given to; and so the Holy Spirit is not only called the Spirit of the Father and the Son who gave him, but also our Spirit who received him. It is like salvation, which is called the salvation of the Lord who gives salvation, and also our salvation because we receive it.

So the Spirit is both God's who gave it and ours who received it. I do not mean that spirit of ours by which we are, which is also called *the spirit of man which is in him* (1 Cor 2:11); this Holy Spirit is ours in a different way, the way in which we say *Give us our bread* (Mt 6:11; Lk 11:3). Though as a matter of fact we also received that spirit which is called the spirit of man; *What have you, it says, that you did not receive* (1 Cor 4:7)? But what we received in order to be is one thing, what we received in order to be holy is another. So then, it is said of John that he would come *in the Spirit and power of Elijah* (Lk 1:17); it is called the Spirit of Elijah, but it means the Holy Spirit which Elijah received. The same is to be understood of Moses when the Lord said to him, *I will take some of your Spirit and give it to them* (Nm 11:17), that is, "I will give them a share in the Holy Spirit which I have already given to you."

If therefore what is given also has him it is given by as its origin, because it did not receive its proceeding from him from anywhere else,[30] we must confess that the Father and the Son are the origin of the Holy Spirit; not two origins, but just as Father and Son are one God, and with reference to creation one creator and one lord, so with reference to the Holy Spirit they are one origin; but with reference to creation Father, and Son, and Holy Spirit are one origin, just as they are one creator and one lord.

16. Now an even deeper[31] question arises: the Son by being born not only gets his being the Son but quite simply his being; does the Holy Spirit in the same way not only get his being gift by being given, but also quite simply his being? In that case we go on to ask whether he was even before he was given, but was not yet gift, or whether perhaps even before he was given he was gift

because God was going to give him. But if he only proceeds when he is given, he would surely not proceed before there was anyone for him to be given to. How could he already be that divine substance, if he only is by being given, just as the Son gets his being that substance by being born, and does not just get being Son, which is said relationship-wise? Or is the answer that the Holy Spirit always proceeds and proceeds from eternity, not from a point of time; but because he so proceeds as to be giveable, he was already gift even before there was anyone to give him to? There is a difference between calling something a gift, and calling it a donation; it can be a gift even before it is given, but it cannot be called in any way a donation unless it has been given.[32]

Chapter 4

A problem is discussed which is raised by those names that refer God to creation.

---

17. We should not be disturbed at the Holy Spirit, although he is coeternal with the Father and the Son, being said to be something from a point of time, like this name we have just used of "donation." The Spirit, to make myself clear, is everlastingly gift, but donation only from a point of time. But what about "lord"? If a man is not called a lord except from the moment he begins to have a slave, then this relationship title too belongs to God from a point of time, since the creation he is lord of is not from everlasting. But then how will we be able to maintain that relationship terms are not modifications with God, since nothing happens to him in time because he is not changeable, as we established at the beginning of this discussion?

Look, this is the problem: He cannot be everlastingly lord, or we would be compelled to say that creation is everlasting, because he would only be everlastingly lord if creation were everlastingly serving him. As there cannot be a slave who has not got a lord, so there cannot be a lord who has not got a slave.[33] Someone may now stand up and say that indeed God alone is eternal, and time is not eternal because of variability and changeableness, and yet that time did not begin to be in time (there was not any time for time to begin in before time began); and therefore it did not happen to God in time to be lord, because he was lord of time which did not begin to be in time. But what will he say about man, who certainly was made in time, and whose lord God was not before he, man, existed? Certainly it happened to God in time to be at least the lord of man; and to put the issue beyond all doubt, it happens to God in time to be my lord or your lord, seeing that we came to be pretty recently. Well, perhaps even this might be doubtful, given that there is a knotty question about the soul.[34] But then what about his being the Lord of the people of Israel? Even granting that the nature of the soul, which that people had, already existed—how, we will not inquire—yet that people did not yet exist, and we can point clearly to the moment when it began to be. Anyway to settle the matter, it happens to him in time to be the lord of this tree or of this crop of corn which has only recently begun to be. Even if the material it is made of was already there before, it is one thing to be lord of the material, another to be lord of the formed nature. Even man is at one time lord or owner of the wood and at another lord or owner of the chest; although the chest is made from the wood, he was not owner of the chest while he was just owner of the wood.

How then are we going to be able to maintain that nothing is said of God by way of modification? Well, we say that nothing happens to his nature to change it, and so these are not relationship modifications which happen with some change in the things they are predicated of. Thus it is true a man is called friend by way of relationship, and he does not begin to be a friend until he begins to be friendly; so there is some change in his will involved in his being called friend. But when a coin is called the price of something it is so called relationship-wise, and yet in this case no change occurs in it when it begins to be a price; and the same is true of pledge and similar things.[35] So if a coin can be talked of in relationship terms so often without any change in its form or nature as coin occurring whenever it starts or stops being talked of like that, how much more readily should we accept a similar position about the unchangeable substance of God? Thus when he is called something with reference to creation, while indeed he begins to be called it in time, we should understand that this does not involve anything happening to God's own substance, but only to the created thing to which the relationship predicated of him refers. *Lord*, says the psalm, *you have become our refuge* (Ps 90:1). God is called our refuge by way of relationship; the name has reference to us. And he becomes our refuge when we take refuge in him. Does this mean that something happens then in his nature, which was not there before we took refuge in him? No, the change takes place in us; we were worse before we took refuge in him, and we become better by taking refuge in him. But in him, no change at all. So too, he begins to be our Father when we are born again by his grace, because *He gave us the right to become sons of God* (Jn 1:12). So our substance changes for the better when we are made his sons; at the same time he begins to be our Father, but without any change in his substance. So it is clear that anything that can begin to be said about God in time which was not said about him before is said by way of relationship, and yet not by way of a modification of God, as though something has modified him. It is however said by way of a modification of that with reference to which God begins to be called it. That a just man begins to be called the friend of God means that he changes. But it is unthinkable that God should love someone temporally, as though with a new love that was not in him before, seeing that with him things past do not pass, and things future have already happened. So he loved all his saints *before the foundation of the world* (Jn 17:24; Eph 1:4), as he predestined them; but when they are converted and find him, then they are said to begin to be loved by him, in order to state the thing in a way that can be grasped by human feeling. So too when he is said to be angry with the wicked and pleased with the good, they change, not he; just as light is harsh to weak eyes, pleasant to strong; but it is the eyes, not the light, that change.

SAINT AUGUSTINE – THE TRINITY

NOTES

1. Reading *praesidentem* with M; CCL has *praesentem*, present. But though M's reading only has weak manuscript support, it has to be preferred as associating better with the category of *situs* or position, which concerns the body's physical posture. The omission of two letters is a very easy mistake for a copyist or stenographer to make.

2. Here Augustine runs through Aristotle's nine categories of accidental predication, and anticipates what he is going on to affirm, with the Arians, that all such apparent predications are predicated of God without signifying that he has accidents, or that they happen to him or modify him in any way. With the exception that we will see in due course, they are all predicated of him substance-wise. The categories are quality, quantity, relationship (that, I think, is what he is referring to when he says "creative without need or necessity"), position, *habitus* (which I translate possession, but which usually refers to clothing, for reasons best known to Aristotle), place, time, action, and passion.

3. It is a commonplace of classical theology, rather overdone by the pseudo-Denys under the influence of neoplatonism, that we are rather able to know what God is not than what he is. The *via negativa* has preference over the *via positiva*, apophatic over cataphatic theology.

4. *Sapientia* from *sapere, scientia* from *scire, essentia* from *esse*. The etymology looks much better in Latin. "Being" is not altogether satisfactory for *essentia*, because it also has sometimes to do for *esse*, the English gerund for the Latin infinitive. But it is better than "essence."

5. M adds *Moses*.

6. My translation from now on of the technical *accidentia*.

7. One of the four elements of ancient physical science.

8. A cumbersome rendering of *ad aliquid*, the succinct Latin term for the category of relationship.

9. See section 2, note 2 of this book.

10. *Aut*; M has *ut*, so that the Father.

11. A most extraordinary question to ask the Arians, whose whole aim was to deny that the Son is equal to the Father; it might perhaps be addressed to the semi-Arians or homoiousians, who thought of Father and Son as two equal, but different substances, like two men or two horses.

12. The Latin instances are rather different; he remarks that while you can say *inimicus* to correspond with *amicus*, you cannot say *invicinus* to correspond with *vicinus*.

13. His word is *quadripedalis*, which he explains as meaning *quattuor pedum*, I presume in case he should be understood to mean four-footed, which is what the word looks as if it ought to mean.

M adds here, *secundum quantitatem aio*, I affirm quantity-wise.

14. The distinction Augustine has elaborated in this chapter between substantive and relative predication in our talk about God, which underlies the whole of this and the next two books, and indeed the investigation of the divine image in man which occupies the second half of the work from Book IX onward, is going to prove perhaps his most influential contribution to Latin theology— rather unfortunately in one way, because this is not his cardinal insight into the trinitarian mystery.

But in fairness to Augustine himself we should remember that in this matter he seems to be a pioneer; this is only the first, and by no means the last word in trinitarian logic. So it is scarcely surprising that there should be a number of loose ends, which the reader skilled in predicamental logic will readily be aware of. The tying up of these loose ends was going to absorb a very considerable amount of theological energy in the West. First Boethius would wrestle with it in his *De Trinitate*, a work that only logicians are capable of reading, and that possibly introduced more smoke than light into the subject. He was followed by the early scholastics in the twelfth century, among them Gilbert de la Porré who argued himself, doubtless by a too rigid reading of Augustine, into the position that the relationships which constitute the divine persons are "externally affixed" to the divine substance, and not identical with it—a view which he duly recanted. Finally we have Saint Thomas, who may be said to have spoken the last word on the subject in the *Summa Theologiae*, 1a pars, q.28. He too leaves some obscurities, but I think we may say that what Saint Thomas cannot tidy up nobody else is likely to be able to, and that this theological subject (of trinitarian logic, not of the trinitarian mystery as a whole) has now been exhausted.

15. *Per se*, not *ad se*; what is said of the Father in himself is said of him with reference to another.

16. *Ter*, M reads *singulariter*, singly.

17. That is, the Catholics.

18. The words are etymologically identical, *sub-* and *hypo-* meaning under, *-stance* and *-stasis* coming from verbs meaning "stand."

19. M adds *quemamodum*, as many Latin . . ., which involves a different division of the sentences. I have myself changed CCL's division.

20. He rather confuses the issue by mentioning relationship words by which God is referred to creation, because they do not serve to distinguish the divine persons from each other, and therefore as far as trinitarian logic is concerned they are substantive and not relative predications. But of course, he is feeling his way and has to discover this fact by an examination of the language. Such confusions are part and parcel of Augustine's *via inventionis*, which is so different from Aquinas' *via doctrinae*.

21. See Gal 4:5. I am inclined to take issue with Augustine on this point. It is of course true that the trinity the one God can be called Father metaphorically by men. But the important question is whether we ought to consider ourselves as addressing the trinity when we say Our Father, or whether we should regard the prayer as addressed personally to God the Father. Augustine implies, and Thomas Aquinas explicitly follows him in this (*Summa Theologiae*. 1a, q. 33, a.3), that we are and ought to be addressing God the trinity as our Father. Their reason is the principle that all divine works *ad extra*, like creation and regeneration, are worked by the three persons inseparably. So as our sonship of God is a consequence of both our creation and our regeneration, it relates us to the three persons inseparably as to our Father.

But this seems to me to be an undue, and ultimately disastrous inference from a sound principle. The principle is necessary to safeguard the unity and equality of the persons. The inference, when carried to its logical conclusions, robs the distinction of persons in the trinity of all relevance to us. It totally severs the mystery of the trinity from the economy of salvation, and finally eliminates the genuine values for which the "economic" theologians stood. If we cannot enter into real and distinct several relationships with each of the divine persons, then they might as well not be distinct as far as we are concerned. And has not this in fact come to be the case with average Christian piety?

But the inference does not follow necessarily from the principle. The world is created and men are redeemed or regenerated inseparably by the three, but this does not mean that all distinction between the three is blurred in their inseparable activity; even less does it mean that the created and the redeemed cannot be really related by distinct relationships to each of the divine persons. And it seems to me that we have the support both of scripture and of the Church's liturgical practice for saying that the final effect of redemption or regeneration is to introduce us in the most perfect possible manner into a share in the distinct divine relationships of the three persons. In the liturgy we pray to the Father through the Son in the fellowship of the Holy Spirit. In scripture we are told that we have been made sons of the Father by a brotherly sharing in the sonship of the Son, as recipients of the gifts of the Holy Spirit.

No, here Augustine is not true to his own deepest insights. But see Book I, 7, note 18.

22. Also 3:26 in the Old Latin text.

23. Any word, practically, can be regarded as predicating relationship if it is construed with the genitive, the preposition "of."

24. This conclusion is scarcely an inference from the name "gift," but rather from his being the gift, and the Spirit, of each. One must be careful not to construe the idea as meaning that he is the gift of the Father to the Son.

25. See 2 Cor 1:22; 5:5; Eph 1:14.

26. *Quia*: M reads *quod*, who am also . . .

27. See above Book I, 24, note 70.

28. See Jn 15:26.

29. M adds *Dei*, God's grace.

30. This clause could also be rendered, rather less probably, "because the recipient did not receive what proceeds from him from anywhere else."

31. *Interius*; M reads *ulterius*, a further question.

32. The distinction is a little less artificial in Latin, between *donum*, gift, and *donatum*, meaning that which has been given. That is the sense in which we must here understand the English word "donation."

33. The current English use of "lord" as a title of rank obscures, but does not invalidate, this original force of the word.

34. This is the question whether the human soul pre-existed its embodiment in the human being, and was created at the beginning of creation, at the same time as time, and thus not in time.

Origen was the first to propose such an idea. In his ultra-platonic and spiritualist view, the soul's involvement with the body is a result of, and the punishment of, sin. He interprets the story of the creation of Adam and Eve, and their sojourn in paradise, of the soul in its original state, and the account of their expulsion from paradise clothed with skins as the clothing of fallen souls in mortal bodies (*Peri Archon* 1, 6; 2, 9: PG 11, 165.225). This opinion, along with many other tenets of Origen, was condemned as heterodox in the year 543.

Augustine discusses the question in his *Literal Meaning of Genesis* VII, 24 (32)—28 (40). He expressly repudiates the idea that material embodiment or incarnation is a punishment for the soul, but his peculiar theory of creation as a simultaneous act unfolded for us in the narrative of the six days makes it hard for him to conceive of the soul being created in the *seminales rationes* on the so-called sixth day like the body (see Book II, 9, note 17). So he inclines to the view that the soul was created at the beginning, with the rest of the spiritual creation, before the material creation. His thought too is governed by platonic concepts.

Aquinas, with the aristotelian frame of his thought, maintains that the soul is created with the body (*Summa Theologiae* 1a, q. 90, a. 4).

35. It is the difference between what the scholastics call real relationships which state some actual reality of the thing they are predicated of, and relationships of reason which are conceptual constructs of the mind organizing its knowledge of things.

BOOK VI

LINGUISTIC AND LOGICAL:
THE PROBLEM OF APPROPRIATION

Chapter 1

The text Christ the power of God and the wisdom of God *faces us with the possibility that perhaps all substantive predications, like goodness, greatness, and eternity, which do not seem to differ in quality from power or wisdom, should be treated really as quasi-relative predications, in such a manner that the Son is to be considered as the power, wisdom, goodness, greatness, and eternity by which the Father is powerful, wise, good, great, and eternal. The author plays sympathetically with this idea and shows that at least it does not involve any inequality between the divine persons.*

---

1. Some people find it difficult to accept the equality of Father and Son and Holy Spirit because of the text, *Christ the power of God and the wisdom of God* (1 Cor 1:24). Equality seems to be lacking here, since the Father is not himself, according to this text, power and wisdom, but the begetter of power and wisdom. And indeed the question how God can be called the Father of power and wisdom calls for and commonly receives very careful attention; there it is, in the apostle's words, *Christ the power of God and the wisdom of God* (1 Cor 1:24). On the other hand, some of our people have used this text to argue against the Arians with, or at least against the early ones who first set themselves up against the Catholic faith. Arius himself is said to have declared: "If he is Son, he was born; if he was born, there was a time when he was not." He did not understand that for God even being born is everlasting, so that the Son can be coeternal with the Father, just as the brightness which a fire begets and radiates is coeval with it, and would be coeternal if fire was eternal. So the later Arians rejected this statement, and admitted that the Son of God did not begin in time. But in the arguments which our people used to have with those who said "There was a time when he was not," they used to put forward this line of reasoning: "If the Son of God is the power and wisdom of God, and God was never without power or wisdom, then the Son is coeternal with God the Father. Now the apostle does

say, *Christ the power of God and the wisdom of God* (1 Cor 1:24), and it is crazy to say that there was a time when God did not have power or wisdom. Therefore there was no time when the Son was not."

2. This argument, however, forces us to say that God the Father is only wise by having the wisdom which he begot, and not by the Father being in himself very wisdom. And if that is the case, we have to consider whether the Son can be called wisdom from wisdom as he is also called God from God, light from light; it is hard to see how he could be, if God the Father is not very wisdom but only the begetter of wisdom. If we hold this view, then why should he not also be the begetter of his own greatness and goodness, his eternity and omnipotence, instead of being himself his own greatness and his own goodness and his own eternity and his own omnipotence? Thus he will be great with the greatness he has begotten, and good with the goodness, eternal with the eternity, omnipotent with the omnipotence which is born of him, just as he is not his own wisdom, but wise with the wisdom which is born of him.

We need not be afraid, of course, that we will be forced to say there are many Sons of God (apart from creatures who are sons by adoption) coeternal with the Father, if he is the begetter of his own greatness and goodness and eternity and omnipotence. There is an easy answer to this charge: listing many names does not make him the Father of many coeternal Sons, any more than the text *Christ the power of God and the wisdom of God* (1 Cor 1:24) makes him the Father of two Sons. The power of course is identical with the wisdom and the wisdom with the power. So it will be the same, surely, with the other things mentioned, and the greatness will also be identical with the power, and so will the other things we have named above and any other things that can be named.

3. But now if the Father is only called in himself what he is called with reference to the Son, that is his Father or begetter or origin* and if whatever else he is called, he is called it with the Son, or rather in the Son, so that he is called great with the greatness he has begotten, just with the justice he has begotten, good with the goodness he has begotten, powerful with the power he has begotten, wise with the wisdom he has begotten—and so the Father is not called greatness itself but begetter of greatness; while the Son too is indeed called Son in himself, which he is not called with the Father but only with reference to the Father, but is not in the same way called great in himself, but only with the Father whose greatness he is, and wise with the Father whose wisdom he is, just as he in turn is wise with the Son because he is wise with the wisdom he has begotten—then it follows that whatever they are called with reference to themselves, neither is called without the other; that is, whatever they are called to indicate their substance they are both called together.[1]

If this is so, then we must say further that the Father is not God without the Son, nor the Son God without the Father, but they are both God together; and the text *In the beginning*[2] *was the Word* (Jn 1:1) must be understood as "in the

---

* On the supposition that one who begets is thereby origin to that which he begets of himself.

Father was the Word." Or if "in the beginning" just means "before everything else," then there is a difficulty with the following words, *and the Word was with God* (Jn 1:1). The Word, of course, is to be taken as only the Son and not Father and Son together as if they were both one Word. Word is like image; Father and Son are not both image together, but the Son alone is the image of the Father, as he is also his Son; they are not both Son together. So as for these words that follow, *and the Word was with God* (Jn 1:1), it is asking too much if we must understand them as meaning that the Word, which is the Son alone, was with God, which is not the Father alone, but Father and Son who are both God together.

And yet perhaps this is not so strange, seeing that the same sort of thing can be said with two things that differ widely from each other. What could be more different than mind and body? Yet you could say "the mind was with the man," that is in the man, though the mind is not body, while man is both mind and body together. So we could understand what follows, *and the Word was God* (Jn 1:1), as meaning that the Word which is not the Father was God together with the Father. Are we therefore saying that the Father is the begetter of greatness, that is, the begetter of his power or begetter of his wisdom, while the Son is greatness, power, and wisdom, but that both together are the great, omnipotent, and wise God? Then what about "God from God, light from light"? They are not both together God from God, but only the Son is from God, namely from the Father; nor are they both together light from light, but only the Son is from light, from the Father. Perhaps, though, the creed says, "God from God, light from light" in order to suggest and inculcate in a nutshell that the Son is coeternal with the Father, and so with anything else that could be said in the same way. It could be spelled out into "this which the Son is not without the Father from this which the Father is not without the Son; that is, this light which is not light without the Father, from this light, the Father, which is not light without the Son." And so when it says "God," which the Son is not without the Father, and "from God," which the Father is not without the Son, it can be perfectly understood that the begetter did not precede what he begot. If this is the case, then the only sort of thing that cannot be said about them in the form of "that from that" is what they are not both together. So you cannot say "Word from Word," because they are not both Word together, but only the Son is; nor "image from image," because they are not both image together; nor "Son from Son," because they are not both Son together. It is in this sense that it says *I and the Father are one* (Jn 10:30); "are one" means "What he is, that I am too by way of being, not by way of relationship."

4. I do not know whether you can find "they are one" said in scripture of things that differ from each other in nature. And if there are several things of the same nature and of different minds, then they are not one precisely insofar as they are of different minds. If men were one simply by all being men, he would not have said *That they may be one as we are one* (Jn 17:22), when he was commending his disciples to the Father. But Paul and Apollos being both men and of the same mind, it could say, *He that plants and he that waters are*

one (1 Cor 3:8). So when "one" is predicated without its being stated "one what," and several things are just called one, it signifies sameness of nature and being without any variance or disagreement. But when a specification is added to state "one what," then it can signify one made out of several things, even though they differ in nature. Thus soul and body are certainly not one (could two things be more different?), unless you add or understand one what, namely one man or one animal. Thus the apostle says, *Whoever cleaves to a harlot is one body* (1 Cor 6:16). He did not say simply "they are one" (or "is one"), but he added "body" to signify one body composed of the joining together of two diverse things, male and female. Then he says, *Whoever cleaves to the Lord is one spirit* (1 Cor 6:17). He did not say, "Whoever cleaves to the Lord is one" (or "they are one") merely, but added "spirit." For the Spirit of God and the spirit of man differ by nature, and yet one spirit is made out of two different ones by cleaving, in the sense that the Spirit of God is indeed blessed and perfect without man's spirit, but the spirit of man is only blessed by being with God. Nor do I think it is without significance, seeing how much and how often the Lord spoke in the gospel according to John about unity, whether his with the Father or ours with each other, that he nowhere said "That we and they may be one," but *That they may be one as we are one* (Jn 17:22).[3] Father and Son are of course one with the unity of substance, and it is one God and one great one and one wise one, as we have seen.

5. So in what way can the Father be greater? If he is greater, he is greater with greatness. But since his greatness is the Son, and he of course is not greater than the one who begot him, the Father cannot be greater than the greatness he is great with. So he is equal. But for him being is not one thing and being great another; so what can he be equal with but that by which he is? Or if the Father is greater by eternity, then the Son is not equal to him in anything. How could he be equal? If you say in greatness, it is not an equal greatness which is less eternal or less anything else. Perhaps he is equal in power but not equal in wisdom? But how is power equal which is less wise? Or is he equal in wisdom and not equal in power? But how can wisdom be equal which is less powerful? It remains that if he is not equal in any one thing, then he is not equal.[4] But scripture cries out, *He did not think it robbery to be equal to God* (Phil 2:6). So any adversary of truth who in any way acknowledges the apostle's authority is obliged to admit that the Son is equal to God at least in one thing. He can take his choice about which; from this it will be proved to him that he is equal in all things that are said of his substance.

6. It is generally accepted to be the case with the human virtues which are to be found in the human spirit that although they each mean something different from the others, they can in no way be separated from each other, and so men who are equal for example in courage are also equal in sagacity and justice and moderation.[5] For if you say that they are equal in courage, but one man excels in sagacity, it follows that the other's courage is less sagacious, and thus they are not even equal in courage, since the former's courage is more sagacious; and you will find the same with the other virtues if you run through them all—it

is not of course a question of fortitude of body, but of fortitude or courage of spirit. How much more then will this not be the case in that unchanging and eternal substance which is incomparably more simple than the human spirit? For the human spirit it is not of course the same thing to be, and to be courageous or sagacious or just or moderate; it can be a human spirit and have none of these virtues. But for God it is the same thing to be as to be powerful or just or wise or anything else that can be said about his simple multiplicity or multiple simplicity to signify his substance. So whether you take "God from God" to mean that this name belongs individually to each person (not in the sense that they are both together two Gods, of course, but one God), * to avoid being landed in the absurdity of saying he is the Son of both of them when he is called Son of God, which would be the case if "God" could only be said of both persons together; or whether anything that is said of God to indicate his substance is in fact said of both persons together, indeed of all three together; whichever is the case—and it will have to be discussed more thoroughly in due course[6]—this at least is clear enough as far as we are concerned at present, that the Son is in no way equal to the Father, if he is found in any way that has to do with signifying his substance to be unequal.[7] We have already proved this. But the apostle called him equal. So the Son is equal to the Father in every respect, and is of one and the same substance.

7. Therefore the Holy Spirit too takes his place in the same unity and equality of substance. For whether he is the unity of both the others or their holiness or their charity, whether he is their unity because their charity, and their charity because their holiness, it is clear that he is not one of the two, since he is that by which the two are joined each to the other, by which the begotten is loved by the one who begets him and in turn loves the begetter. Thus *They keep unity of the Spirit in the bond of peace* (Eph 4:3),[8] not in virtue of participation but of their own very being, not by gift of some superior but by their own gift. We are bidden to imitate this mutuality by grace, both with reference to God and to each other, in the two precepts on which *the whole law and the prophets depend* (Mt 22:40). In this way those three are one, only, great, wise, holy, and blessed God. But we find our blessedness *from him and through him and in him* (Rom 11:36), because it is by his gift that we are one with each other; with him we are one spirit (1 Cor 6:17), because our *soul is glued on behind him* (Ps 63:8). And *for us it is good to cling to God, because he destroys everyone who goes awhoring away from him* (Ps 73:27, 28).

So the Holy Spirit is something common to Father and Son, whatever it is, or is their very commonness or communion, consubstantial and coeternal. Call this friendship, if it helps, but a better word for it is charity. And this too is substance because God is substance, and *God is charity* (1 Jn 4:8, 16), as it is

---

* For the two cohere with one another in a way that the apostle shows can happen even with widely differing substances; for the Lord by himself is spirit, and a man's spirit by itself is of course spirit, and yet *if he cleaves to the Lord he is one spirit* (1 Cor 6:17). How much more in that other case, where there is an absolutely inseparable and eternal mutuality!

written. But just as it is substance together with the Father and the Son, so is it great together and good together and holy together with them and whatever else is said with reference to self,[9] because with God it is not a different thing to be, and to be great or good etc., as we have shown above. If, after all, charity in this divine sphere is less than wisdom, it follows that wisdom is loved less than wisdom is; so it must be equal, in order that wisdom may be loved as much as wisdom is. But wisdom is equal to the Father, as we have proved; so the Holy Spirit is equal too, and if equal, equal in every respect, on account of the total simplicity which belongs to that substance. And therefore there are not more than three; one loving him who is from him, and one loving him from whom he is, and love itself. If this is not anything, how is it that *God is love* (1 Jn 4:8, 16)? If it is not substance, how is it that God is substance?

Chapter 2

The question of the divine simplicity, raised by the discussion of the last chapter, is further examined, and how it is to be reconciled with the divine trinity; a divine triplicity is excluded by it; but the individuality of the divine persons, how far for example one can talk about "the Father alone," remains a problem; a quotation from Hilary is commented on at length in the hope that it might throw some light on this problem.

---

8. If now you go on to ask in what way that substance is both simple and multiple, we must first observe how any created thing is multiple and in no way truly simple. First of all, take any body; it consists, of course, of parts, in such a way that one of its parts will be greater, another smaller, and the whole will be greater than even the greatest part. Even heaven and earth are parts of the whole mass of the cosmos, and earth alone or heaven alone consists of countless parts, and each in the third of its parts is smaller than in the rest, and in the half is smaller than in the whole, and the whole body of the cosmos which is usually said to consist of two parts, namely heaven and earth, is of course greater than heaven alone or earth alone. And in any body its size is one thing, its color another, its shape yet another. It can diminish in size and remain the same color or the same shape; it can change color and remain the same shape and the same size; its shape can alter while it remains the same size and the same color; and in a word, all the other things that can be said together about a body can all change together, or several can change without the others. This shows that the nature of body is multiple, and in no way simple.

When we come to a spiritual creature such as the soul, it is certainly found to be simple in comparison with the body; but apart from such a comparison it is multiple, not simple. The reason it is simpler than the body is that it has no mass spread out in space, but in any body it is whole in the whole and whole also in any part of the body. Thus when something happens even in some tiny little part of the body that the soul is aware of, the whole soul is aware of it because it does not escape the whole soul even though it does not happen in the whole body. And yet even in the soul it is one thing to be ingenious, another to be unskillful, another to be sharp, another to have a good memory; greed is one thing, fear another, joy another, sadness another; some of these things can be in the soul without others, some more, some less; countless qualities can be found in the soul in countless ways. So it is clear that its nature is not simple but multiple. Nothing simple is changeable; everything created is changeable.

God however is indeed called in multiple ways great, good, wise, blessed, true, and anything else that seems not to be unworthy of him; but his greatness is identical with his wisdom (he is not great in mass but in might), and his goodness is identical with his wisdom and greatness, and his truth is identical with them all; and with him being blessed is not one thing, and being great or wise or true or good, or just simply being, another.

9. Nor because he is three must we think of him as triple, or three by multiplication; otherwise the Father alone or the Son alone would be less than the Father and the Son together—though admittedly it is not easy to see how you can talk of the Father alone or the Son alone, since the Father is always and inseparably with the Son and the Son with the Father; not that both are Father or both Son, but that they are always in each other and neither is alone. However, we say that the trinity is God alone, though he is always with the holy spirits and souls; but we say he is God alone because these others are not God with him. In the same way we talk about the Father being the Father alone, not because he can be separated from the Son, but because they are not both the Father.

Since therefore the Father alone or the Son alone or the Holy Spirit alone is as great as Father and Son and Holy Spirit together, in no way can they be called triple, or three by multiplication. Now bodies of course grow by being joined together. Although it is true that whoever cleaves to his wife is one body,[10] nonetheless it becomes a bigger body than the man's alone or the wife's alone. In spiritual things however, when the lesser cleaves to the greater, as the creature to the creator, it becomes bigger than it was, but the other does not. For in things that are great without mass, to be bigger is to be better. And the spirit of any creature becomes better by cleaving to the creator than it would be if it did not cleave, and so it is bigger because it is better. So *whoever cleaves to the Lord is one spirit* (1 Cor 6:17), and yet the Lord does not thereby become bigger, although he who cleaves to him does. In God, therefore, when the equal Son cleaves to the equal Father, or the equal Holy Spirit to the Father and the Son, God is not made bigger than each of them singly, because there is no possibility of his perfection growing. Whether you take Father or Son or Holy Spirit, each is perfect, and God the Father and the Son and the Holy Spirit is perfect, and so they are a three, a triad or a trinity rather than triple or three by multiplication.[11]

10. Now that we have shown how it is possible to talk about "the Father alone," in the sense that none but he is the Father, we must go on to examine the opinion that *the only true God* (Jn 17:3)[12] is not the Father alone, but Father

and Son and Holy Spirit. After all, if anyone asks whether the Father alone, that is, on his own, is God, you can scarcely reply that he is not; unless perhaps you say that the Father is indeed God, but is not the only God, because Father, Son, and Holy Spirit are the only God. But what are we to make of the Lord's own evidence? He was speaking to the Father and he had named the Father he was speaking to, when he said *This is eternal life, that they should know you the one true God* (Jn 17:3).[13] The Arians like to take this as meaning that the Son is not true God. But let us forget them for the moment, and see whether we are obliged to understand his saying to the Father *that they should know you the one true God* as intended to suggest that the Father alone is also true God, in case we should suppose that only the three together, Father Son and Holy Spirit, are God. On the strength of this evidence of the Lord then, do we now say that the Father is the one true God, and the Son is the one true God, and the Holy Spirit is the one true God, and Father Son and Holy Spirit together, that is the trinity together, are not three true Gods but one true God? Or because he added *and the one you sent, Jesus Christ* (Jn 17:3), do we have to supply here the words "one true God," and read the whole sentence as "that they should know you and the one you sent, Jesus Christ, the one true God"?

Then why did he not mention the Holy Spirit? Was it perhaps because it follows that where one is mentioned cleaving to the other in such total peace that by this peace they are both one, this peace itself is to be understood, even though it is not mentioned? The apostle also seems to leave out the Holy Spirit in that other text, and yet he has to be understood: I mean the text, *All things are yours, and you are Christ's and Christ is God's* (1 Cor 3:22), and again, *The head of the woman is the man; the head of the man is Christ; the head of Christ is God* (1 Cor 11:3). But here again, if only the three all together can be called God, how is God the head of Christ—that is, on this supposition, the trinity the head of Christ—when Christ is included in the trinity to make it three? Or is it that what the Father and the Son are together is head of what the Son is alone? The Father and the Son together are God, but only the Son is Christ, especially as it is the Word already made flesh who is speaking[14] in the lowliness by which the Father is greater, as he says himself, *For the Father is greater than I* (Jn 14:28). So it might be that his being God, which he has in common with the Father, is head of the man mediator which he alone is. If we are right in saying that the mind is the chief part of man, that is to say the head of the human substance, though man is man with the mind; why should we not much more properly say that the Word which is God together with the Father is the head of Christ, although the man can only be understood as Christ together with the Word which became flesh? But as I have already remarked, we must consider this problem more thoroughly later on.[15] Meanwhile we have demonstrated as briefly as we could the equality of the triad and its one identical substance. So whatever may be the solution of this question, which we have put off for more searching examination, there is nothing now to prevent us from acknowledging the supreme equality of Father, Son, and Holy Spirit.

11. Someone who wished to put in a nutshell the special properties of each

of the persons in the trinity wrote: "*Eternity in the Father, form in the image, use in the gift.*"[16] He was a man of no small authority in the interpretation of the scriptures and the defense of the faith—it was Hilary who wrote this in his book on the subject. So I have examined as best I could the hidden meaning of these words, that is of "Father" and "image" and "gift," "eternity" and "form" and "use"; and I am afraid I do not follow him in his employment of the word "eternity," unless he only means that the Father does not have a father from whom he is, while the Son has it from the Father both to be and to be coeternal with him. For if an image perfectly matches that of which it is the image, it is coequated with that, not that with its image. As regards the image, I suppose he mentioned form on account of the beauty involved in such harmony, in that primordial equality and primordial likeness, where there is no discord and no inequality and no kind of unlikeness, but identical correspondence with that of which it is the image; where there is supreme and primordial life, such that it is not one thing to live and another to be, but being and living are the same; and where there is supreme and primordial understanding such that it is not one thing to understand and another to live, but understanding is identical with living, identical with all things, being as it were one perfect Word to which nothing is lacking, which is like the art of the almighty and wise God, full of all the living and unchanging ideas, which are all one in it, as it is one from the one with whom it is one. In this art God knows all things that he has made through it, and so when times come and go, nothing comes and goes for God's knowledge. For all these created things around us are not known by God because they have been made; it is rather, surely, that even changeable things have been made because they are unchangeably known by him.

Then that inexpressible embrace, so to say, of the Father and the image is not without enjoyment, without charity, without happiness. So this love, delight, felicity, or blessedness (if any human word can be found that is good enough to express it) he calls very briefly "use," and it is the Holy Spirit in the triad, not begotten, but the sweetness of begetter and begotten pervading all creatures according to their capacity with its vast generosity and fruitfulness, that they might all keep their right order and rest in their right places.

12. Thus all these things around us that the divine art has made reveal in themselves a certain unity and form and order. Any one of them you like is both some one thing, like the various kinds of bodies and temperaments of souls; and it is fashioned in some form, like the shapes and qualities of bodies and the sciences or skills of souls; and it seeks or maintains some order, like the weights or proper places of bodies, and the loves or pleasures of souls. So then, as we direct our gaze at the creator by *understanding the things that are made* (Rom 1:20), we should understand him as triad, whose traces appear in creation in a way that is fitting. In that supreme triad is the source of all things, and the most perfect beauty, and wholly blissful delight. Those three seem both to be bounded or determined by[17] each other, and yet in themselves to be unbounded or infinite. But in bodily things down here one is not as much as three are together, and two things are something more than one thing; while in the supreme triad one is as

much as three are together, and two are not more than one, and in themselves they are infinite. So they are each in each and all in each, and each in all and all in all, and all are one. Whoever sees this even *in part*, or *in a puzzling manner in a mirror* (1 Cor 13:12), should rejoice at knowing God, and should *honor and thank him as God* (Rom 1:21); whoever does not see it should proceed in godliness toward seeing it, not in blindness toward making objections to it. For God is one, and yet he is three. On the one hand the persons are not to be taken as muddled together in the text *From whom are all things, through whom are all things, for whom are all things*; and on the other, not to many Gods, but *to him be glory for ever and ever. Amen* (Rom 11:36).[18]

NOTES

1. A divine person is only called *in se* or *per se*, that is with a name that is proper to himself, what he is called *ad alterum*, that is with reference to another, like Father or Son. Anything that he is called *ad se*, with reference to himself, that is by way of predicating substance, he is called *cum altero*, with the other, because such names are common to all divine persons. So far this is standard trinitarian logic. But Augustine is here playing with a further inference from it, which he will finally repudiate in Book VII, that such common names cannot be predicated of the divine persons individually, but only all together.

2. *In principio:* that is, "In the origin," as I have been rendering this word *principium* above, where it has been treated as sometimes being a proper name for the Father.

3. He does not elaborate the significance of this formulation over against the alternative. What I think he implies is that though there is indeed an analogy between human unity and divine, divine unity is yet different in kind, admitting no possibility of inequality.

4. M adds *in omnibus*, he is equal in nothing.

5. The four cardinal virtues. As the author remarks, it was a commonplace among the moralists of antiquity that these virtues were interdependent, so that one could not be possessed if the others were lacking, and the perfection of one depended on the perfection of the others. Aquinas takes up and clarifies the point in his *Summa Theologiae* 1a 2ae, and in fact comments explicitly on this passage from Augustine's *De Trinitate* in q.65 a.1 and q.66 a.2. He meets the objection from common sense and experience against this theory that a man can be at the same time very brave and very immoderate or licentious, or wise and just in his dealings, but a coward, by saying that these are instances rather of natural inclination or temperament than of conscious deliberate virtue, which is essentially a freely chosen attitude (*habitus*). He cites the case, well illustrated by the merry monarch, of the genial type of man who is naturally disposed to be generous, but not naturally disposed to be chaste.

The theory, or perhaps insight would be a fairer word, holds good whether you take Aristotle's view of the cardinal virtues that each was concerned with a specific field of human activity, courage with being brave in the face of danger, justice with giving other people their rights, for example; or whether you regard them, like Augustine here and the other Fathers, who followed Cicero and the Stoics in this matter, as four key qualities that should govern all human behavior in all fields. In both views, the key to the insight is the fundamental premise or assumption that all virtue is essentially the expression of the control of *reason* over human behavior.

6. In Book VII, where he decides definitively in favor of the first alternative.

7. This long and excessively involved sentence is one which I like to think Augustine would have revised had he been able. It helps being able to take the parenthesis within a parenthesis out of the text altogether and put it in a footnote. But in addition to that step, which calls for no explana-

tion, I have had, in order to make sense of the sentence, to take a considerable liberty with CCL's usually excellent punctuation (M's punctuation here goes wild with despair) and to construe rather boldly. The clause in my version immediately after the first parenthesis in the text, beginning "to avoid . . ." and ending at the semicolon "both persons together," follows in the Latin immediately on the clause which I relegate to the footnote, and is included by CCL in the same parenthesis, so that it becomes a consequence (governed by *ne*) of the inseparability of the divine persons, which is nonsense. What I have done, in terms of the Latin, is close CCL's brackets after *aeterna connexio* (eternal mutuality), and construe the negative final clause *ne absurde dici videatur* (to avoid being landed in the absurdity of saying) as being governed by the first of Augustine's alternatives *sive ita dicatur* (whether you take). There is nothing syntactically impossible about this, and it does not involve emending the Latin text in any way; it is just that the subordinate clause is separated from its governing clause by a parenthesis and a parenthesis within a parenthesis, which puts rather a strain on the reader's memory.

8. A very bold application of the text.

9. That is, whatever is said *ad se*, as signifying substance, as distinct from relative names, said *ad alterum*, which are not common to the divine persons, but proper to each of them severally.

10. See Gn 2:24; Eph 5:31.

11. It is worth observing that to allow "trinity" and disallow "triplicity" is an act of linguistic convention that is not necessarily valid for all languages. I suppose the German *Dreifaltigkeit* could in fact represent both words.

12. "Only" here represents the same Latin word, *solus*, as "alone" in the phrase "the Father alone."

13. Here Augustine changes "only" to "one." Greek and Vulgate read "only."

14. Either he forgets he is quoting Paul, or he still has Jn 17 in mind, or possibly but less likely he is referring to the next quotation.

15. In Book VII. It is essentially the same problem which he raised and deferred in the previous chapter (above section 6 note 6).

16. Hilary, *De Trinitate* 2, 1 (PL10, 51A). It is not at all clear to me why he quotes and discusses Hilary at this point. It has no very obvious connection with what precedes or follows, and contributes nothing to his argument. This is perhaps in keeping with the rather shapeless and nondescript character of the whole of this Book VI. My guess is that Augustine had some notes on the passage, and decided to incorporate them somewhere. For a suggestion on the general bearing of Hilary's treatment on Augustine's task, see above, *Introduction* 81. It would at least explain why Augustine quotes him in the metaphysical or logical, rather than the scriptural part of the whole first part of his work.

The Latin wording of Hilary's text is as follows: *Aeternitas in Patre, species in imagine, usus in munere.* An alternative reading of the first phrase, followed by the translation in the library of the Nicene Fathers, is *Infinitas in aeterno*, which is perhaps more likely to be the original, but is not what Augustine read. The difficult words to translate are *species* and *usus*, both being such vague words with an enormous range of meaning. On reflection, I am quite content with "form" for *species*; but I only retain "use" for *usus*, as a piece of crass literalism, because Augustine is in fact going to explain what Hilary means by the word very effectively. From its primary meaning of "use," *usus* goes on to mean "habituation," or what one has got used to, or being used to something; hence familiarity, intimacy, intercourse between persons; hence it can be a euphemism for sexual intercourse; and finally it can mean and often does, "enjoyment," since use and enjoyment of things often go together, and tend at least legally to be synonymous.

In terms of a frankly erotic analogy Augustine interprets Hilary as meaning a combination of intimacy and enjoyment by *usus*. I did consider translating it myself as "intimacy", but there was a risk that this might practically involve Augustine in the bathos of interpreting intimacy as intimacy. So I went by my rule for quotations, which I find works well in most cases, that it is much better to translate them overliterally than to paraphrase them. Were I translating Hilary's work, I would certainly employ "intimacy" or a similar word for *usus* here, but then I would probably alter the whole structure of these three phrases. I cannot do that when they are in a quotation, cut out from their original context. So I am under a greater obligation, in fairness to both quoting and quoted author, to be even excessively literal in my translation.

17. *A se invicem*; M reads *ad se invicem*, with reference to each other.

18. "For whom" etc.; reading with CCL *in quem*, representing Greek *eis auton*. M reads *in quo*, in whom etc., following the Vulgate *in ipso*.

In previous quotations of the text Augustine has followed the Vulgate reading.

BOOK VII

LINGUISTIC AND LOGICAL: THE PROBLEM SOLVED

Chapter 1

The question posed in the previous book is taken up and dealt with thoroughly; the tentative answer there assumed is set aside as having impossible logical consequences, and the definitive solution is proposed.

---

1. It is now time to examine more thoroughly, as far as God enables us to, the question we postponed in the previous book, that is, whether we can predicate of each person in the trinity by himself, and not just together with the other two, such names as God and great and wise and true and omnipotent and just and anything else that can be said of God with reference to self as distinct from by way of relationship; or whether these names can only be predicated when the trinity or triad is meant. What gives rise to this question is the text *Christ the power of God and the wisdom of God* (1 Cor 1:24); does it mean that God is the Father of his wisdom and power in such a way that he is wise with this wisdom he has begotten and powerful with this power he has begotten, and that because he is always powerful and wise he has always begotten power and wisdom? And I said that if this is the case, why should he not also be the Father of his greatness by which he is great, and of the goodness he is good with and the justice he is just with, and all the other things said of him? But perhaps all these things signified by several words can be understood as contained in the same wisdom and power, so that greatness is the same as power and goodness the same as wisdom, and indeed wisdom the same as power, as we have argued above. Let us remember in that case that when I name one of these things it can be understood as amounting to my mentioning them all.

So the question is whether the Father taken singly is wise and is indeed his own wisdom, or whether he is wise in the same way as he is uttering.[1] He is uttering with the Word which he has begotten—not a word that is spoken and makes a sound and then ceases, but the Word which *was with God, and the Word was God, and all things were made through him* (Jn 1:1, 3); the Word equal to himself with which he always and changelessly utters himself. Clearly he is not himself Word, any more than he is Son or image. Now as uttering—apart from those temporal utterances of God which take place in creation, are heard, and then cease[2]—as uttering them with that coeternal Word, he is not to be understood singly but together with that Word, without which, of course, he would not be uttering.[3] So the question is, is he wise in the same way as he is uttering, so that wisdom is the same as Word, and being Word is the same as being wisdom, the same as being power; so that power and wisdom and Word are all the same, and all said by way of relationship, like Son and image; so that the Father is not powerful or wise taken singly, but only taken together with that power and wisdom which he has begotten, just as he is not uttering taken singly but only with the Word, and taken together with the Word which he has begotten; and so he will be great with and taken together with[4] the greatness he has begotten?

But now it is not one thing that makes him great and another that makes him God; what makes him great is what makes him God, because for him it is not one thing to be great and another to be God; so it will follow, presumably, that the Father is not God taken singly, but only with and taken together with the godhead he has begotten; and so the Son will be the godhead of the Father just as he is the wisdom and power of the Father, and just as he is the Word and image of the Father. And furthermore, because it is not one thing for him to be and another for him to be God, it follows that the Son will also be the being of the Father, just as he is his Word and his image. This means that apart from being Father, the Father is nothing but what the Son is for him. It is clear, of course, that he is only called Father because he has a Son, since he is called Father not with reference to himself but with reference to the Son. But now we are forced to say in addition that it is only because he has begotten his own being or "is-ness" that he is what he is with reference to himself. Just as he is only great with the greatness he has begotten, so he only is with the "is-ness" or being he has begotten, because for him it is not one thing to be and another to be great. Are we not then forced to say that he is the Father of his own being just as he is the Father of his own greatness, just as he is the Father of his own power and wisdom? For without doubt his greatness is the same as his power, and his being is the same as his greatness.

2. This problem has arisen from the text *Christ the power of God and the wisdom of God* (1 Cor 1:24). So our desire to express the inexpressible seems to have forced us into the position where *(i)* we either have to say that Christ is not the power of God and the wisdom of God, and thus shamelessly and irreligiously contradict the apostle; or *(ii)* we admit that Christ is indeed the power of God and the wisdom of God, but that his Father is not the Father of his own power and wisdom,[5] which would be no less irreligious, because in this case he will not be Christ's Father either, seeing that the power of God and the wisdom of God are Christ; or *(iii)* that the Father is not powerful with his power or wise with his wisdom,[6] and who would have the nerve to say that?; or *(iv)* that to be for the Father and to be wise must be understood as two different

things, so that he is not wise simply by being,[7] and is thus in the same case as the soul which is sometimes unwise sometimes wise, being a changeable nature, and not supremely and perfectly simple; or *(v)* that the Father is not anything with reference to himself, and that not only his being Father but also his simply being is said with reference to the Son.[8] How then can the Son be of the same being as the Father, seeing that his Father is not even being with reference to himself, but even his "is" or his "to be" is only a reference to the Son?

No, but surely this makes them even more of one and the same being; it means that Father and Son are one and the same being, seeing that the Father's very "is" has reference not to himself but to the Son, and that he has begotten this being, and by this being is whatever he is. So neither of them is with reference to himself, and each is said with reference to the other. Or perhaps only the Father is called not only Father but anything at all with reference to the Son, while the Son is called things with reference to himself? In that case, what is he called with reference to himself? Being? But on our present supposition the Son is the Father's being, just as he is the Father's power and wisdom, just as he is the Father's Word and the Father's image. Or if the Son is called being with reference to himself, while the Father is not being but the begetter of being, that is, he does not be with reference to himself, but with this being which he has begotten, just as he is great with this greatness he has begotten, then it follows that the Son is called greatness with reference to himself, so too power and wisdom and Word and image. And what could be more ridiculous than calling something image with reference to itself?[9] But perhaps being image and Word are not the same as being power and wisdom; perhaps the former are predicated by way of relationship, the latter with reference to self and not to another. In that case the Father is now no longer wise with the wisdom which he has begotten, because it is not possible for him to be called wise with reference to wisdom, and wisdom not to be predicated with reference to him. For the terms of any predication of relationship must have reference to each other.[10]

So we are left with the position that the Son is called being by way of relationship, with reference to the Father. And this leads us to the most unexpected conclusion that being is not being, or at least that when you say being you point not to being but to relationship; just as when you say master, you point not to a being but to a relationship, which refers to slave; but when you say man, or anything similar that has reference to self and not to another, then you point to a being. So when a man is called master, the man is the being, but he is called master by way of relationship, for man is predicated of him with reference to himself, master with reference to slave. But in the case we are considering, if being is predicated by way of relationship, then being is not being.

What it comes to is this: every being that is called something by way of relationship is also something besides the relationship; thus a master is also a man, and a slave is a man, and a draught-animal[11] is a horse, and a security is a sum of money. Man and horse and sum of money are said with reference to self, and signify substances or beings; while master and slave and draught-animal and security are said with reference to something else, to signify certain relationships. But if it were not, for example, a man, that is some substance, there would be nothing there that could be called master by way of relationship; and if a horse were not some kind of being, there would be nothing which could be called by way of relationship a draught-animal; so too if a sum of money were not a kind of substance, it could not also be called by way of relationship a security for something. So if the Father is not also something with reference to himself, there is absolutely nothing there to be talked of with reference to something else.

It is not the same case either as that of color, which always has reference to something colored, so that color is never predicated of itself, but always of that which it is the color of. And as for that which it is the color of, even if it is referred to color by being called colored, it is still called body with reference to itself. But this is no sort of comparison with the Father not being called anything with reference to the Son, while the Son is called things both with reference to himself and with reference to the Father;[12] with reference to himself when he is called great greatness and powerful power, with reference to the Father when he is called the greatness and power of the great and powerful Father, by which the Father is great and powerful. This is not the case, then; each, Father and Son, is substance, and each is one substance.

Just as it is absurd to say that whiteness is not white, so it is absurd to say that wisdom is not wise;[13] and as whiteness is called white with reference to itself, so is wisdom called wise with reference to itself. But a body's whiteness is not its being, for body signifies its being, and whiteness its quality by which it is called a white body, since it is not the same for it to be and to be white. Its shape is one thing and its color another, and neither is in itself but in some mass, and this mass is neither shape nor color, but shaped and colored. Wisdom however is both wise and wise with itself. A soul becomes wise by participating in wisdom, but if it then becomes unwise, wisdom remains in itself; it does not change when the soul changes over to folly. It is not the same with one who becomes wise with wisdom as it is with whiteness in a body which becomes white with it. When the body changes to another color, whiteness will not remain but simply cease to be.

But if the Father too[14] who begot wisdom becomes wise with it, and if for him to be is not the same as to be wise, then the Son will be a quality of his, not his offspring, and there will no longer be absolute simplicity in God. This however is unthinkable, since in fact we have there absolutely simple being. With God to be is the same as to be wise. If then in this case to be is the same as to be wise, it follows that the Father is not wise with the wisdom he has begotten; otherwise he did not beget it, but it begot him. When we say that for him to be is the same as to be wise, what else are we saying but that he is by that which he is wise by? So it follows that the cause of his being wise is the cause of his being at all. Therefore, if the cause of his being wise is the wisdom he has begotten, this will also be the cause of his being at all. And it can only be this by begetting him or making him. But no one has ever dreamt of saying that wisdom is the begetter or maker of the Father. Could you have a crazier notion? So the Father is himself wisdom, and the Son is called the wisdom of the Father in the same way as he is called the light of the Father, that is, that as we talk of light from light, and both are one light, so we must understand wisdom from wisdom, and both one wisdom. And therefore also one being, because there to be is the same as to be wise. What being wise is for wisdom, and being powerful for power, and being eternal for eternity, being just for justice, being great for greatness, that simply being is for being. And because in that ultimate simplicity to be is not different from to be wise, there wisdom is the same as being.

3. So the Father and the Son are together one being and one greatness and one truth and one wisdom. But the Father and the Son are not both together one Word, because they are not both together one Son. Just as Son is referred to Father and is not said with reference to self, so too Word is referred to him whose Word it is when it is called Word.[15] He is Son in the same way as he is Word and Word in the same way as Son. So because Father and Son are not of course together one Son, it follows that Father and Son are not both[16] together one Word. And therefore the Son is not Word in the same way as he is wisdom, because he is not called Word with reference to himself, but only in relationship to him whose Word he is, just as he is Son in relationship to the Father; but he is wisdom in the same way as he is being. And therefore one wisdom because one being. But because wisdom is also Word, though not Word in the same way as wisdom (for Word is to be understood relationship-wise, wisdom being-wise), let us take it as being the same, when it is called Word, as if it were called "born wisdom,"[17] and as such it can also be Son and image. When we use these two words "born wisdom," the first of them, "born," can be understood as signifying Word and image and Son, and none of these names indicates being, because they state a relationship; but the second word, "wisdom," having only a self-reference (it is wise with itself), indicates being, and its being[18] is the same as its being wise.

So Father and Son are together one wisdom because they are one being, and one by one they are wisdom from wisdom as they are being from being. And therefore it does not follow that because the Father is not the Son nor the Son the Father, or one is unbegotten, the other begotten, that therefore they are not one being; for these names only declare their relationships. But both together are one wisdom and one being, there where to be is the same as to be wise; they are not however both together Word or Son, because it is not the same here to be as to be Word or Son, since as we have quite sufficiently shown, these are terms of relationship.

Chapter 2

Having established that "wisdom" is a substance and not a relationship word, the author goes on to inquire why in scripture it is almost always appropriated to the Son; he suggests it is because it is the Son who reveals the Father to us, and because our wisdom is to imitate the incarnate Son as the eternal Word imitates, by being the image of, the Father.

4. The question then arises, why do the scriptures almost nowhere[19] say anything about wisdom except to show it as either begotten or made[20] by God? Begotten, that is to say, when it means the wisdom *through* whom *all things were made* (Jn 1:3); created or made as it is in men, when they turn to the wisdom which is not created or made but begotten, and are enlightened; then something is brought about in them which is called their wisdom. Or else wisdom is talked of as made when the scriptures are foretelling or just telling that *the Word was made flesh and dwelt among us* (Jn 1:14); in this sense Christ is made wisdom, because he was made man. Is it perhaps to commend to us for our imitation the wisdom by whose imitation we are formed, that wisdom in those books never speaks or has anything said about her but what presents her as born of God or made by him, although the Father too is wisdom itself? For the Father utters her to be his Word, not like a word spoken aloud from the mouth, or even thought of before it is pronounced—such a word is completed in a space of time, but this other Word is eternal; and she by enlightening us utters to us whatever needs to be uttered to men about herself and about the Father. Thus the reason it says *No one knows the Son but the Father, and no one knows the Father but the Son and whoever the Son chooses to reveal him to* (Mt 11:27) is that it is through the Son that the Father makes his revelation, that is through his Word.[21] If the temporal and passing word that we utter declares both itself and the thing we are speaking of, how much more is this the case with the Word through whom all things were made? This declares the Father as he is, because it is itself just like that, being exactly what the Father is insofar as it is wisdom and being. Insofar as it is Word it is not what the Father is, because the Father is not Word, and it is called Word by way of relationship, like Son, which of course the Father is not either.

Thus *Christ is the power and wisdom of God* (1 Cor 1:24), because he is power and wisdom from the Father who is power and wisdom, just as he is light from the Father who is light, and the fountain of life with God the Father who is of course the fountain of life. *For with you,* says the psalm, *is the fountain of life, and in your light we shall see light* (Ps 36:10), because *just as the Father has life in himself, so he has given the Son to have life in himself* (Jn 5:26); and, *that was the true light which enlightens every man as he comes into this world* (Jn 1:9), and this light is the Word which *was with God, and the Word was God* (Jn 1:1). But *God is light and there is no darkness in him* (1 Jn 1:5); not physical but spiritual light, and not even spiritual light in the sense that it was made by illumination, in the way the apostles were told, *You are the light of the world* (Mt 5:14); but *the light which enlightens every man* (Jn 1:9), that supreme, that very wisdom, God, which we are now talking about. So wisdom the Son is from wisdom the Father as light from light and God from God, so that the Father alone is light and the Son alone is light, and the Father alone is God and the Son alone is God; so the Father alone is wisdom and the Son alone is wisdom. And just as both together are one light and one God, so both are one wisdom. But the Son *was made for us by God wisdom and justice and sanctification* (1 Cor 1:30), because we turn to him in time, that is at a particular moment of time,[22] in order to abide with him for ever. And at a certain moment of time he too, *the Word, was made flesh and dwelt among us* (Jn 1:14).

5. This then is the reason perhaps why it is the Son who is being introduced to us whenever mention is made of wisdom or description given of her in scripture, whether she herself is speaking or being spoken about. Let us copy the example of this divine image, the Son, and not draw away from God.[23] For we too are the image of God, though not the equal one like him; we are made by the Father through the Son, not born of the Father like that image; we are image because we are illuminated with light; that one is so because it is the light that illuminates,[24] and therefore it provides a model for us without having a model itself. For it does not imitate another going before it to the Father, since it is never by the least hair's breadth separated from him, since it is the same thing as he is from whom it gets its being. But we by pressing on imitate him who abides motionless; we follow him who stands still, and by walking in him we move toward him, because for us he became a road or way in time by his humility, while being for us an eternal abode by his divinity.

To the pure intellectual spirits who did not fall by pride he offers a model *in the form of God* and as *equal to God* (Phil 2:6) and as God. But in order to offer a model of return to man who had fallen away and was unable to see God on account of the impurity of sin and the punishment of mortality, *he emptied himself* (Phil 2:6), not by changing his divinity but by taking on our changeability, and *taking the form of a servant* (Phil 2:6), *he came into this world* (1 Tm 1:15) for us, though he was already *in this world* because *the world was made through him* (Jn 1:10). Thus he could be a model for those who can see him as God above, a model for those who can admire him as man below; a model for the healthy to abide by, a model for the sick to get better by; a model for those who are going to die not to be afraid, a model for the dead to rise again, *in all things holding the first place himself* (Col 1:18). Man ought to follow no one but God in his search for bliss, and yet he was unable to perceive God; so by following God made man he would at one and the same time follow one he could perceive and the one he ought to follow. Let us love him and cling to him with the charity that *has been poured into our hearts through the Holy Spirit who has been given to us* (Rom 5:5). Thus to conclude, it is not surprising that scripture should be speaking about the Son when it speaks about wisdom, on account of the model which the image who is equal to the Father provides us with that we may be refashioned to the image of God; for we follow the Son by living wisely. Though we must not forget that the Father too is wisdom, just as he is light and God.[25]

6. As for the Holy Spirit, whether he is supreme charity conjoining Father and Son to each other and subjoining us to them, and it would seem a suitable name since it is written *God is love* (1 Jn 4:8, 16), he too must surely be wisdom, since he is light, because *God is light* (1 Jn 1:5); or whether the being of the Holy Spirit should be properly and distinctly indicated by some other name, it is still quite certain that he is light because he is God, and because he is light he is certainly wisdom. And that the Holy Spirit is God scripture cries aloud in the person of the apostle, who says , *Do you not know that you are God's temple*— and he adds straightaway, *and the Spirit of God dwells in you* (1 Cor 3:16)? But it is God who dwells in his temple.[26] The Spirit of God does not live in the temple of God as a minister; he makes this quite clear in another text: *Do you not know that the temple of the Holy Spirit in you is your bodies? You have him from God, and so you are not your own. For you have been bought with a great price. So glorify God in your body* (1 Cor 6:19).

But now what is wisdom but spiritual and unchanging light? The sun in the sky too is light, but physical light; the spiritual creation is also light, but not unchanging. So the Father is light, the Son is light, the Holy Spirit is light; but together they are not three lights but one light.[27] And so the Father is wisdom, the Son is wisdom, the Holy Spirit is wisdom; and together they are not three wisdoms but one wisdom; and because in their case to be is the same as to be wise, Father and Son and Holy Spirit are one being. Nor with them is to be anything else than to be God. So Father and Son and Holy Spirit are one God.

Chapter 3

The author investigates the logical status of the terms "person" and "substance" (Greek hypostasis*); he concludes that they are simply terms of convenience which we have to use in order to be able to answer the question "Three what?" about the divine triad; we use them rather in spite of than because of their natural logical properties.*

---

7. And so, for the sake of talking about inexpressible matters, that we may somehow express what we are completely unable to express, our Greek colleagues talk about one being, three substances, while we Latins talk of one being or substance, three persons, because as I have mentioned before,[28] in our language, that is Latin, "being" and "substance" do not usually mean anything different. And provided one can understand what is said at least in a puzzle,[29] it has been agreed to say it like that, simply in order to be able to say something when asked "Three what?" That there are three is declared by the true faith, when it says that the Father is not the Son, and the Holy Spirit which is the gift of God is neither the Father nor the Son. So when the question is asked "Three what?"[30] we apply ourselves to finding some name of species or genus which will comprise these three, and no such name occurs to our minds, because the

total transcendence of the godhead quite surpasses the capacity of ordinary speech. God can be thought about more truly than he can be talked about, and he is more truly than he can be thought about.

When we say that Jacob is not the same as Abraham, and that Isaac is neither Abraham nor Jacob, we admit that they are three. When we are asked "Three what?" we reply "Three men," using a species name to call them by in the plural; we would use a genus name if we said "Three animals"—for man, as defined by the ancients, is a rational mortal animal;[31] or as our scriptures are in the habit of saying, we could say "Three souls," since it is customary to name the whole from its better part, that is, to name both body and soul, which is the whole man, from soul. Thus it is written that with Jacob there went down to Egypt seventy-five souls,[32] meaning that number of men and women.

Again, when we say that your horse is not the same as mine, and a third horse belonging to somebody else is neither mine nor yours, we admit that they are three, and when someone asks "Three what?" we reply "Three horses" using a species name, "Three animals" using a genus name. Yet again, when we say an ox is not a horse, and a dog is neither a horse nor an ox, we say three things; and when we are asked "Three what?" we can no longer use a species name and say three horses or three oxen or three dogs, because they do not belong to the same species; but we use the genus name and say three animals; or even turn to a higher genus and say three substances or three creatures or three natures.

Any things that can be named in the plural with one specific name can also be named generically, but we cannot also give one specific name to any things that share one generic name. Three horses, a specific name, we also call three animals; but a horse and an ox and a dog we only call three animals or substances, which are generic names, and anything else that can be said about these three generically; we cannot however call them three horses or three oxen or three dogs, which are specific names. We predicate of them with one name, though in the plural, whatever they have in common that is signified by such a name. Thus Abraham and Isaac and Jacob have in common what is meant by man, and so they are called three men; a horse and an ox and a dog have in common what is meant by animal, and so they are called three animals. In the same way, if we have three bay trees, we can also call them three trees; but a bay tree and a myrtle and an olive tree we can only call three trees or three substances or natures. Similarly three stones are also three bodies; but a stone and a piece of wood and a lump of iron can only be called three bodies, or by some even higher generic name.

So Father and Son and Holy Spirit being three, we ask three what, meaning what do they have in common? They do not have in common what is meant by Father, so that they are three fathers to each other, as friends who are so called with reference to each other can be called three friends, which they are toward each other. But that is not the case here, because here only the Father is father, nor is he father of two but only of his only Son. Nor are they three Sons, since the Father is not son nor is the Holy Spirit. Nor are they three Holy Spirits, because neither the Father nor the Son is holy spirit in that name's proper signification, by which it also signifies gift of God. So three what, then? If three persons, then what is meant by person is common to all three. So this is either their specific or their generic name, if we consider normal habits of speech. But where there is no diversity of nature, several things that can be named together generically can also be named together specifically. It is a difference of nature that prevents us from calling a bay tree, a myrtle and an olive tree, or a horse, an ox, and a dog by one specific name, three bay trees for example in the first case, or three oxen in the second; we are confined to generic names, three animals in this case, three trees in that. Here however there is no diversity of being, and so these three ought to have a specific name, and yet none can be found. For person is a generic name; so much so that even a man can be called person, even though there is such a great difference between man and God.

8. But anyway, take this generic name; if we call them three persons because what is meant by person is common to them—otherwise they could certainly not be called this, just as they are not called three sons because what is meant by son is not common to them—why can we not also call them three Gods? Clearly it is because the Father is a person and the Son is a person and the Holy Spirit is a person that we can say three persons. But the Father is God and the Son is God and the Holy Spirit is God, so why not three Gods?[33] If on the other hand these three are together one God because of their inexpressible mutuality, why are they not one person for the same reason? Thus we should not be able to call them three persons, although we call each one of them person, any more than we can call them three Gods, although we call each one of them God, whether Father or Son or Holy Spirit. Is it just because scripture does not say three Gods? But neither do we find scripture talking anywhere about three persons. Perhaps because scripture calls these three neither one person nor three persons—we read of *the person of the Lord* (2 Cor 2:10),[34] but not of the Lord called person—we are allowed to talk about three persons as the needs of discussion and argument require; not because scripture says it, but because it does not gainsay it. Whereas if we were to say three Gods scripture would gainsay us, saying *Hear, O Israel, the Lord your God is one God* (Dt 6:4).[35]

But if this is the only reason, why are we not allowed to say three beings, which scripture likewise neither says nor gainsays? If being is a specific name common to the three, why are they not called three beings just as Abraham, Isaac, and Jacob are three men, because man is the specific name common to all men? Or if being is not a specific name but a generic one, seeing that man and beast and tree and star and angel are called beings, why should these three not be called three beings as three horses are called three animals, or three bay trees three trees, or three stones three bodies? Or if it is because of the unity of the triad that we do not say three beings but one being, why is this same unity not a good reason for our not saying three substances or three persons, but one substance or one person? For just as the name being is common to them, so that each of them can be called being, so is the name substance or person common to them. What, of course, we have been saying about persons in our way of talking must be understood about substances in the Greek way of talking. They say three substances, one being, just as we say three persons, one being or substance.

9. What are we left with then? Perhaps we just have to admit that these various usages were developed by the sheer necessity of saying something, when the fullest possible argument was called for against the traps or the errors of the heretics. Human inadequacy was trying by speech to bring to the notice of men what it held about the Lord God its creator, according to its capacity, in the inner sanctum of the mind, whether this was held by devout faith or by the least amount of understanding. It was afraid of saying three beings, in case it should be taken as meaning any diversity in that supreme and ultimate equality. On the other hand it could not say that there are not three somethings, because Sabellius fell into heresy by saying precisely that. For it is known with complete certainty from the scriptures and is thus to be devoutly believed, and the mind's eye can also achieve a faint but undoubted glimpse of the truth, that the Father is and the Son is and the Holy Spirit is, and that the Son is not the same as the Father is, nor is the Holy Spirit the same as the Father or the Son. So human inadequacy searched for a word to express three what, and it said substances or persons. By these names it did not wish to give any idea of diversity, but it wished to avoid any idea of singleness; so that as well as understanding unity in God, whereby there is said to be one being, we might also understand trinity, whereby there are also said to be three substances or persons.[36]

Of course, if it is the same for God to be as to subsist, then it ought not to be said that there are three substances any more than it is said that there are three beings. It is because it is the same for God to be as to be wise that we do not say three wisdoms any more than we say three beings. So too, because it is the same for him to be God as to be, it is as impious to talk about three beings as about three Gods. But if it is one thing for God to be, another for him to subsist, as it is one thing for him to be, another for him to be Father or be Lord, then substance will no longer be substance because it will be relationship.* For just as the name being is derived from to be, so we get substance from to subsist. But it is ridiculous that substance should be predicated by way of relationship; every single thing that is, after all, subsists with reference to itself. How much more God, if indeed it is proper to talk about God subsisting?

10. The word is rightly used for ordinary things which provide subjects for those things that are said to be in a subject, like color or shape in a body. Thus body subsists, and is therefore substance; but those things are in the subsisting, in the subject or underlying body, and so they are not substances, but in substance. Therefore if that color or shape ceases to be, it does not stop the body being body, because it is not the same for it to be as to retain this or that shape or color. So things that are changeable and not simple are properly called substance.[38] But if God subsists in such a way that he can properly be called

---

* That he is, is said of God with reference to himself; that he is Father is said with reference to Son, and that he is Lord is said with reference to the creation that serves him; so on this supposition, he subsists by way of relationship, just as he begets by way of relationship and lords it by way of relationship.[37]

substance, then something is in him as in its underlying subject, and he is not simple—he for whom it is the same thing to be as to be whatever else is said of him with reference to himself, such as great, omnipotent, good, and anything of that sort that is not unsuitably said of God. But it is impious to say that God subsists to and underlies his goodness, and that goodness is not his substance, or rather his being, nor is God his goodness, but it is in him as in an underlying subject. So it is clear that God is improperly called substance, in order to signify being by a more usual word. He is called being truly and properly in such a way that perhaps only God ought to be called being. He alone truly is, because he is unchanging, and he gave this as his name to his servant Moses when he said *I am who I am*, and, *You will say to them, He who is sent me to you* (Ex 3:14). But in any case, whether he is called being, which he is called properly, or substance which he is called improperly, either word is predicated with reference to self, not by way of relationship with reference to something else. So for God to be is the same as to subsist, and therefore if the trinity is one being, it is also one substance.

11. Perhaps then it is more correct to say three persons than three substances. But we must inquire further into this, in case it looks[39] like special pleading for our own usage against that of the Greeks.* Now exactly the same arguments hold in the case of persons; it is not one thing for God to be and another for him to be person, but altogether the same. If he is said to be with reference to himself, and called person by way of relationship, then we could call Father and Son and Holy Spirit three persons in the same way as we talk about three friends or three neighbors or three relatives with reference to each other, not each with reference to himself. So each of them is the friend or neighbor or relative of the other two, because these names signify relationships. What have we got then? Is it agreed that we can call the Father the person of the Son and of the Holy Spirit, or the Son the person of the Father and of the Holy Spirit, or the Holy Spirit the person of the Father and of the Son? But that is not how we are in the habit of using person in any context; nor in the case of the trinity do we mean anything else when we say the person of the Father but the substance of the Father. Thus as the substance of the Father is just the Father, not insofar as he is Father, but insofar as he just is; so too the person of the Father is nothing but just the Father. He is called person with reference to himself, not with reference to the Son or Holy Spirit; just as he is called God with reference to himself, and great and good and just and anything else of that sort. And just as it is the same for him to be as to be God, to be great, to be good, so it is the same for him to be as to be person.

So the only reason, it seems, why we do not call these three together one person, as we call them one being and one God, but say three persons while we never say three Gods or three beings, is that we want to keep at least one word for signifying what we mean by trinity, so that we are not simply reduced to

---

* As a matter of fact, if they like, they could also say three persons, *tria prosopa*, just as they say three substances, *treis hypostaseis*. But they prefer this latter expression, because I imagine it fits the usage of their language better.

silence when we are asked three what, after we have confessed that there are three. For if, as some people consider, being is a genus word, substance or person a species word—I will pass over what I have already said, that you would have to say in this case three beings if you say three substances or persons, just as you have to say three animals where you say three horses, though horse is the species, animal the genus. You do not put the species in the plural and the genus in the singular and say three horses one animal, but you call them three horses with the specific name and three animals with the generic one. But if you say that the name substance or person does not signify species but something singular and individual, so that substance or person is not predicated like man which is common to all men, but more like this man, say Abraham or Isaac, or Jacob, or anyone else who could be pointed to with your finger, you will still be caught by the same argument; just as Abraham, Isaac and Jacob are called three individuals, so are they called three men or three souls. So if we try to explain these words in terms of genus and species and individual, why are the Father and the Son and the Holy Spirit not called three beings just as they are called three substances or persons? But as I said, I will pass over this.[40]

What I am saying is that if being is a genus word, it does not follow that one being contains several species, just as one animal does not contain several species simply because animal is a genus word. So the Father and the Son and the Holy Spirit are not three species of one being. If however being is a species word like man, and those three which we call substances or persons have the same species in common, as Abraham, Isaac, and Jacob have in common the species which is called man; and if while man can be subdivided into Abraham, Isaac, and Jacob, it does not mean that one man can be subdivided into several single men—obviously he cannot, because one man is already a single man; then how can one being be subdivided into three substances or persons? For if being, like man, is a species, then one being is like one man.

But perhaps it is like our saying that three men of the same sex, the same physique and the same character[41] are one nature—they are three men but one nature; so here perhaps we say three substances, one being, or three persons, one substance or being. There is at least this similarity here, that the ancients who spoke Latin before they had these terms, that is being or substance[42]—it is not all that long since they came into use—used to talk about nature instead. So now we are not talking anymore in terms of genus and species, but rather in terms of what you could call the same common material. For example, if three statues were made of the same gold we would say three statues, one gold; and here we would not be using statue as a specific and gold as a generic term, nor even gold as a specific term and statue as an individual one. For no species extends beyond the individuals of it to include something outside. When I define what man is, a specific name, every single man, all the individuals of the species are contained within that definition, nor does anything belong to the definition which man is not. But when I define gold it is not only statues, if they are made of gold, but also rings and anything else made of gold that will come under the definition. Even if nothing is made out of it, it is still called gold, and statues will still be statues even if they are not made of gold.[43] Again, no species extends beyond the definition of its genus. When I define animal, since horse is a species of this genus, every horse will be an animal. But not every statue is gold. So although with three golden statues we rightly say three statues, one gold, we do not say it in such a way that we understand gold to be the genus and statues the species.

Well now, it is not in this way either that we talk about the trinity as being three persons or substances, one being and one God, as though they were three things consisting of one material, even if whatever that material might be it were wholly used up in these three; for there is nothing else, of course, of this being besides this triad. And yet we do talk of three persons of the same being, or three persons one being; but we do not talk about three persons out of the same being, as though what being is were one thing and what person is another, as we can talk about three statues out of the same gold. In this case being gold is one thing, being statues another. And when three men are said to be one nature, or three men of the same nature, they can also be called three men out of the same nature, since other men can also emerge out of the same nature. But in the case of the being of the trinity, it is quite impossible for any other person at all to emerge out of the same being. Finally, with these ordinary things, one man is not as much as three men together, and two men are something more than one man; and in equal statues, there is more gold in three together than in each one of them, and less gold in one than in two. But that is not how it is in God; Father and Son[44] together are not more being than Father alone or Son alone, but those three substances or persons together, if that is what they must be called, are equal to each one singly, which *the sensual*[45] *man does not perceive* (1 Cor 2:14). He can only think of masses and spaces, little or great, with images of bodies flitting around in his mind like ghosts.[46]

Chapter 4

The average sensual man just referred to is exhorted to cling to faith until he comes to some kind of understanding; in order to do this he is exhorted to activate in himself the image of the divine trinity, which is thus once more brought to our notice; and it is argued that this image does not mean likeness to the Son only, the equal and eternal image of the Father, but to all three persons. The book concludes with a quotation which sums up the whole approach of the first seven books, which began from the initium fidei—*Unless you believe, you will not understand.*

---

12. Until a man is purified of this sort of uncleanness, he must just believe in the Father and the Son and the Holy Spirit, one only God, great, omnipotent, good, just, merciful, creator of all things visible and invisible, and whatever else humanity is capable of saying of him that is true and worthy of him. And when he hears the Father called the only God,[47] he must not exclude the Son or the

Holy Spirit from that title, for he is of course the only God together with whomever he is the one God with; so too when we hear the Son called the only God, we must accept it without in any way excluding the Father or the Holy Spirit. And this man must also say one being, in order to avoid thinking that one is greater or better than another, or in any way different; yet not in such a way that he takes the Father to be himself Son and Holy Spirit and whatever else they are each called with reference to each other, like Word which only the Son is called, or gift which only the Holy Spirit is called. This is why we can talk about them in the plural, as for example the gospel does where it is written, *I and the Father are one* (Jn 10:30). He said both "one" and "are"; "one" in terms of being, because he is the same God; "are" in terms of their relationship, because one is Father, the other Son.

Sometimes the unity of being is even passed over in silence, and only the relationships are mentioned in the plural; thus, *We will come to him*, I and the Father, *and will dwell with him* (Jn 14:23). "We will come and dwell" is in the plural, because the subject is "I and the Father," that is, the Son and the Father, which signify mutual relationships. Sometimes even the relationships are no more than implicit in the text, as in Genesis: *Let us make man to our image and likeness* (Gn 1:26). "Let us make" and "our" are in the plural, and must be understood in terms of relationships. For he did not mean that gods should do the making, or do it to the image and likeness of gods, but that the Father and the Son and the Holy Spirit should do it; do it therefore to the image of Father and Son and Holy Spirit, so that man might subsist as the image of God; and God is the three.

But that image of God was not made in any sense equal, being created by him, not born of him; so to make this point he is image in such a way as to be "to the image"; that is, he is not equated in perfect parity with God, but approaches him in a certain similarity. One does not approach God by moving across intervals of place, but by likeness or similarity, and one moves away from him by dissimilarity or unlikeness. Some people see the following distinction here: they like to take only the Son as being image, and man as being not image but "to the image." However, the apostle refutes them by saying, *The man ought not to cover his head, as he is the image and glory of God* (1 Cor 11:7). He did not say "he is to the image," but just "he is the image." Another thing, when this image is said in the other text to be "to the image," this is not said as though it meant "to the Son," who is the image equal to the Father; otherwise it would not have said *to our image* (Gn 1:26). How could it be our image when the Son is the image of the Father alone? But as I said, man is said to be "to the image" because of the disparity of his likeness to God, and "to our image" to show that man is the image of the trinity; not equal to the trinity as the Son is equal to the Father, but approaching it as has been said by a certain likeness, as one can talk of a certain proximity between things distant from each other, not proximity of place but of a sort of imitation. To this kind of approximation we are exhorted when it says, *Be refashioned in the newness of your mind* (Rom 12:2), and elsewhere he says, *Be therefore imitators of God as most dear sons* (Eph 5:1), for it is with reference to the new man that it says, *Who is being renewed for the recognition of God according to the image of him who created him* (Col 3:10).

However, it is now generally agreed to use the plural with other names besides those signifying relationships, as required by the necessities of argument, in order to have a name to answer the question "Three what?" with, and so to say three substances or persons. But when we use such words we must remember not to think in terms of mass and space, nor to take it that one is even a little bit less than another, in whatever way one thing can be less than another, not even by the distance of even the slightest dissimilarity or of place.[48] There must be neither confusion or mixing up of the persons, nor such distinction of them as may imply any disparity. If this cannot be grasped by understanding, let it be held by faith, until he shines in our minds[49] who said through the prophet, *Unless you believe, you will not understand* (Is 7:9).[50]

NOTES

1. The comparison is more effective in the Latin, in which "wise" as well as "uttering" has the form of a participle; *sapiens*, compared with *dicens*; as though in English one were to compare "knowing" or "understanding" with "uttering." But the translation of *sapiens* by "wise" is really mandatory.

2. See Mt 3:17; 17:5; Jn 12:28.

3. What is said here is not easy to harmonize, as far as the trinitarian logic is concerned, with what was said above Book VI, 3, note 1. For there we saw that a divine person is only called *cum altero*, together with another, what he is called *ad se*, that is by a substantive predication; but whatever he is called by a relative predication, *ad alterum*, like Father, he is called *in se* or *per se*, alone and not together with another. Now here he takes as his model the predication *dicens*, which is clearly a relative predication, because it refers to *Verbum* exactly as *gignens* refers to *genitum*, and says that the Father is not called *dicens* or "uttering" alone, but only with the Word; "with" not only in the sense of an ablative of respect (in this sense he is equally "Father with the Son"), but in the sense of "together with."

But there are several reasons for us to absolve Augustine from contradicting himself; in the first place and in general he is to some extent deliberately confusing the categories of substantive and relative predication in order to test the validity of the distinction between them. But in the second place and in particular, we can say that the point made about trinitarian logic in Book VI, 3, and explained there in section 4, holds good; whatever name a divine person is called *ad alterum* is proper to him, not common to the triad, and so he is called it alone, and not together with the other persons. And so the Father is called *dicens* with reference to the *Verbum*, and so the Father alone is called *dicens*, and it is not a name common to the Son and Holy Spirit as well. In this place, however, Augustine is rather examining the relationship involved in such names; he is not saying that the Father is called *dicens* together with the Word in the sense that the Word is also called *dicens*, but that *dicens* necessarily and always involves or implies Word, and that you cannot say the one without bringing in the other. And he is asking whether *sapiens*, which we usually (and correctly) regard as a substantive predication, is not in fact *ad alterum*—namely *ad sapientiam*—in exactly the same way as *dicens* is *ad verbum*—is not in fact a relative predication. He is going to suppose that it is, and then reduce this supposition to absurdity. In the previous book he was careful not to make the supposition so clear-cut, and also not to press it to absurdity, in the interests of his dramatic technique of intellectual suspense.

4. Ablative of respect (with), and *cum* with the ablative (taken together with). The *reductio ad absurdum* argument involves two false premises that will later in fact be repudiated—or perhaps

they should be called two equivocations. The first equivocates with the ablative, and assumes that whatever a person is called a name with, as wise with wisdom (ablative of respect), he is called the name together with the person designated by that noun (ablative of association?). It is this equivocation that is effectively confusing substantive and relative predication.

The second premise involves a false distinction, and assumes that whatever name a person is called together with, or in common with another person, he cannot be called that name singly, or by himself; that either the Father is called God by himself, or he is called God together with the Son. But this will turn out to be a false alternative, and Augustine will conclude that each divine person is called God, etc., singly and by himself and alone, and is also called God together with and in common with the other persons. By then the first false premise or equivocation will have been sorted out, and it will be clear that calling the Father God together with the Son does not presuppose calling him God with the godhead which the Son is for him.

5. In order to avoid concluding that he is the Father of his own "is-ness" or being.

6. In order to avoid concluding that he is with the "is-ness" or being he has begotten.

7. Thus breaking the inference from how wisdom is predicated to how being is predicated.

8. The conclusion that all the other alternatives were designed to avoid, and which repeats what was said at the end of the previous paragraph. Needless to say, none of these is Augustine's final solution.

9. "Image" is by its very meaning an *ad alterum* word.

10. This is the first glimpse of the final solution; the Father is not wise with the wisdom which he has begotten, but with the wisdom which he is.

11. *Jumentum*, meaning a beast precisely as referred to its burden, or what it draws, by its *jugum* or yoke.

12. It is no sort of comparison, because color is only a quality, not a substance; you do not predicate "being" of it but only "being in" or "inbeing" with respect to its subject; and this is clearly not the case with God.

13. One is tempted to retort that it is also a very odd use of language to talk about whiteness being white. But perhaps this platonic way of speaking is coming into its own again with such slogans as "Omo washes whiter than white."

14. Like the soul, now, no longer like color.

15. He might have said that Word is referred to *dicens* or him who utters it.

16. *Ambo*; M has *amborum*, are not one Word of both.

17. See Sir 24:3.

18. This second "being" renders *esse*, the first *essentia*.

19. *Nusquam*; M reads *nunquam*, never.

20. A reference probably to Prv 8:22, which reads in the Greek and the Latin versions from it "The Lord created me at the beginning of his ways," a very embarrassing text for the Fathers embattled with the Arians. Hebrew has "possessed me."

21. An important theme with Irenaeus. See *Introduction* 69–70.

22. It is the phrase "in time" in the causal clause that explains the "was made" in the main clause. What needs explaining is how the uncreated wisdom could be made. The reason or cause is man being in time, because temporality and createdness go together.

23. Augustine is at pains in this Book VII, the last of the first half of the work, to introduce the image theme which will dominate the second half. He does it twice, as a coda to the two main topics of this book; here following on the long discussion of the previous chapter on the logical status of "wisdom" and words like it; and again in chapter 4 after the long discussion on the logical status of "person" and "substance." Thus he gives a simple balance to this Book VII that was rather lacking in the previous book.

It is to be noted that from the first the idea of image is linked with the idea of imitation. The link between the two ideas, illustrated by their etymological relationship, was a commonplace for the Latin writers in the Church of all ages. But it means, what is sometimes perhaps overlooked, that the doctrine of the image is a practical doctrine. Man's being in the image of God is not just a theological fact to be observed and interpreted as throwing light on the nature of the Trinity; it is also an imperative, a program to be carried out in order to discover the mystery of the Trinity by achieving its likeness in oneself. Augustine reminds us at the beginning that this will be one of his chief interests in exploring the image of God in the human *mens* or mind.

24. Note the connection between image and light. The primary form of image for Augustine was not, as it is for us, the statue or picture, but the reflection in water or in a glass.

25. This paragraph briefly echoes the view of the incarnation developed at length in Book IV. See in particular sections 4 and 24.

26. See Ps 11:4, Hb 2:20.

27. In Augustine's view the word "light" is not applied to God, or to the spiritual creation metaphorically, but properly. This is clear every time he discusses the verse *God said, "Let there be light" and there was light* (Gn 1:3). For him light is a transcendental idea, like "being"; there is uncreated light, which is God, and there is created light, which is the participation by creatures in the uncreated light, and is spiritual or physical (his word is *corporalis*) according to the nature of the creature participating.

28. Book V, 10.

29. See 1 Cor 13:12.

30. Augustine here gives a choice of gender, *quid tria vel quid tres*, which is not necessary in English, though perhaps it could be rendered "three what or three who."

31. Quoted from Quintilian; Aristotle omitted "mortal," because he did not include angels or gods in the genus "animal."

32. See Gn 46:27; Ex 1:5 (both Septuagint); Acts 7:14.

33. Latin lacks the added refinement of the indefinite article, so the comparison between person and God is more effective in that language. You could say that it is because we cannot decently say the Father is a God etc., that we cannot say three Gods.

34. Which actually talks of the *persona Christi*.

35. The text actually runs *the Lord your God is one Lord*, or *the Lord your God, the Lord is one*. See *Introduction* 42-43.

36. Thomas Aquinas takes issue, very discreetly, with Augustine on the opinion stated in this paragraph. In the *Summa Theologiae*, 1a, q.29 he defines and analyzes the word *persona* at length in four articles; he concludes the fourth by saying that "the name person was adapted to stand for relationship owing to the suitability of its meaning; that is to say, it is able to stand for relationship not just because of usage, as the first opinion (Augustine's in fact) would have it, but because of what it really means."

He agrees with Augustine, of course, that *persona* is not itself a relationship word. But he accepts the definition of Boethius that "person means individual substance of a rational nature," and thereby avoids the tangle of species and genus which Augustine has been weaving for us up to this point. Person means the distinct individual within a species or nature. Now whatever distinguishes individuals from each other in human nature, or angelic nature for that matter, we have already established, with Augustine, that the only thing that distinguishes the three from each other in divine nature is relationship. Thus "person," while not directly signifying relationship, is able to "stand for relationship" in God because it signifies what is really and subsistently distinct in God in virtue solely of distinct relationships. What it signifies directly, in virtue of its proper meaning, is hypostasis, or the subsistent; and thereby it signifies indirectly the relationship by which one divine hypostasis or subsistent is distinguished from another.

Augustine is just going on to examine the case of subsistence or hypostasis, and to find it hard to say why, except purely for reasons of usage, we should not say that God is one hypostasis or *substantia*, just as we say he is one being, or *essentia*, or in ordinary Latin usage *substantia*. And then he is going on to consider the point that person might mean individual, and to find no solution along that line, because as his illustration of three statues made out of one material will show, he takes the Aristotelian position that what individuates one individual from another in any one nature or species is matter, and this clearly has no place in the divine nature or God.

Aquinas clearly has a point when he says that if these words are just taken arbitrarily and by the convention of usage, in spite of their proper signification, to stand for the three, in order to meet the objections and traps of the heretics, this will rather provide the heretics with more ammunition than confound their arguments. And Augustine too has a very important point when he insists at such length on the almost total inadequacy of these words to say what we want them to say. Thus we have to allow, in a way which Aquinas could scarcely do, that there are contexts in which we can legitimately talk about God as "a person," just as much as we can also talk about him (them) as "three persons."

37. He rather confuses the issue by bringing in "lord" as a relationship word like "Father." In spite of "lord" being a relationship word, he would neither want to say there are three lords, nor to say that the name is applicable only to one person. He dealt with one aspect of names like "lord" in Book V, 17.

38. Because they "stand under" their accidents or their predicates. Thus *substantia* is equated with *suppositum* (what is placed under) or *subjectum* (what is laid under), as the Greek equivalent *hypostasis* is equated with *hypokeimenon*.

39. *Videatur*; M has *videar*, in case I should seem to be doing some special pleading.

40. A very notable and gallant piece of "passing over," important, because in it he offers one criticism of the view that "person" can be put in the plural with God because it signifies not species or genus, but individual; see above section 9, note 36.

41. That is, three men who are absolutely equal, to make the trinitarian comparison as exact as possible.

42. *Substantia* and *essentia* were first used by Quintilian at the end of the first century AD. The ancients mean the classical writers, chiefly Cicero and Lucretius.

43. I have taken a slight liberty with this sentence, which runs in the Latin: *Etsi nihil inde fiat, aurum dicitur quia etiamsi non sint aureae, non ideo non erunt statuae*. I confess that *quia* baffles me; it seems a perfect *non sequitur*.

44. M adds *et Spiritus Sanctus*, and Holy Spirit.

45. Latin *animalis*, a literal translation of Paul's *psychikos*.

46. Another slight liberty with the text. The concluding clause is an ablative absolute, running: *volitantibus in animo ejus phantasmatis tamquam imaginibus corporum.*

Phantasmatis is a less correct form for *phantasmatibus*, but this is not an uncommon occurrence with Augustine. But even so, and treating it without a qualm as ablative and not genitive, at first sight it looks as if he is saying "with fancies flitting around in his mind like images of bodies"; and that simply does not fit the sense of the whole passage, or what we know from elsewhere of Augustine's view of the sensual man. His trouble is that he cannot rise above the imagination; he takes the bodily images that stock it absolutely literally, instead of interpreting them intelligently or spiritually. Augustine does not think of him as being particularly ghostridden.

So I treat *tamquam* as governing the noun that precedes it. This is very unusual in prose, but not impossible in poetry, and let us allow Augustine to use a poetic idiom for once.

47. Aquinas discusses the use of the word *solus*, only or alone, with respect both to God and to the divine persons in *Summa Theologiae* 1a q.31, a.3-4, and both shares and clarifies the reserve that Augustine clearly feels about it. He concludes a.4 by saying that this way of speaking is not to be extended, but is to be "piously explained" wherever it is found in authentic scripture.

48. Reading *ubi* with CCL, and interpreting it as meaning the category of *ubi* or place. M reads *ibi*, there, which involves construing the sentence in a different, and, it must be confessed, a much simpler way. Here the difficulty of the reading *ubi*, which can however be made sense of, is in favor of its authenticity.

The text of the main clause (roughly from "we must remember" in my version) runs in the two editions as follows:

CCL: . . . *nullae moles aut intervalla cogitentur, nulla distantia quantulaecumque dissimilitudinis* aut ubi *intellegatur aliud alio vel paulo minus quocumque modo minus esse aliud alio potest . . .*

M: . . . *nullae moles aut intervalla cogitentur, nulla distantia quantulaecumque dissimilitudinis,* ut ibi *intelligatur aliud alio vel paulo minus, quocumque modo minus esse aliud alio potest. . .*

Thus to be quite accurate, where CCL reads *aut ubi* M reads *ut ibi*.

49. See 2 Pt 1:19.

50. This is perhaps Augustine's favorite quotation, or in fact misquotation, from scripture. He misquotes not from carelessness, but because his text is a mistranslation.

I touched on the special position or function of Book VIII with regard to the whole *De Trinitate* in the Introduction 20-23 and again 103-105. Here I want to enlarge on what I said there, and also by discussing some of its difficulties and key points to try and get at the basic assumptions and movement of the author's mind, which are often only implicit in what he wrote.

First of all another word on the title I have given the book, "Through the Looking-Glass." I will not labor the justification for using the symbol which I gave in section 104 of the Introduction, except to say that Lewis Carroll's fantasy seems peculiarly appropriate to a work cast in a platonic mold, or at least written in platonic language, such as the *The Trinity* in general and this Book VIII in particular, with its assumption of a real, eternal world of ideas—or of God for the Christian platonist—and a seeming, less than real world of time, the world inhabited by man, which more or less remotely reflects the real world from which it derives and in which it imperfectly participates. Augustine's whole use of the idea of the image encourages one to use the looking-glass symbol, and in the first chapter of this book he expresses his sense of the two worlds in a passing use of another image, which we could call that of the aquarium (Book VIII, 2-3). In terms of this image, we could entitle this book "Breaking the Surface."

It might be urged that this would be a better title in one respect, in that it would suggest correctly the direction in which the seeker for God is moving, that is from his own murky world into the clarity of the divine world; whereas the title "Through the Looking-Glass" suggests movement in precisely the opposite direction. But as I suggested in the Introduction, Augustine is in a sense moving in the opposite direction; and in any case his movements are more complex than a simple one-way system will allow for; his preferred direction of movement is as much inward as upward. But whichever direction one moves in, the chief significance of both images is that the point of contact between the two worlds is also a barrier between them. There is a fundamental problem of communication.

It is this problem to which Augustine turns his attention in chapters 3 and 4 of this book. It is an indication of his keen sense of structure that in the central section of the central book of the *De Trinitate* he discusses what is the key structural problem of the work, the key problem for the man engaged in the quest for God. If it is so important, one might wonder how he has managed to write seven books without discussing it. The answer is that he has assumed an *ad hoc* solution to the problem, and indeed written that solution into his program for the first seven books. The *ad hoc* solution to the communications problem between man and God is faith. For God, it is assumed, there is no problem; he can communicate as and when he pleases by revelation, and if man responds to this revelation in faith, the barrier is broken. Hence Augustine's insistence at the beginning of Book I on starting from faith in order to arrive at understanding; and he concludes his prologue to this Book VIII by reiterating this standing rule of all his teaching.

But then in these central chapters of the book he submits this standing rule, this *ad hoc* solution to the ultimate communications problem, to the most radical criticism. The ultimate solution of the communications problem, the aim of the mind in search of God, is to know as we are known; faith is proposed as an *ad hoc* and temporary substitute for the knowledge of God or for the face to face vision of him, inadequate of course, but enough to start us off with and get us through life on our way to God. But then the question arises, is faith even a possible substitute for knowledge? If we look at what we ordinarily mean by faith, or believing something, say that Jesus Christ was a man born of a virgin who was crucified under Pontius Pilate and rose on the third day from the dead, we find that it presupposes knowledge; not knowledge of course of the particular thing or event we believe, but knowledge of what believing it means. We have some knowledge, not necessarily very profound or extensive, but still some knowledge of what men are, and virgins, and crosses and days, and we know what it means to talk about being born and dying, life and death. In other words we have certain categories of knowledge, what Augustine here calls species and genera, which make it possible for us to define the object of our belief, and in a word to know what we mean and to talk sense when we state our belief. Without this kind of presupposed knowledge belief is simply meaningless, and psychologically impossible. If I were to see a Chinese newspaper, I would be unable to believe a single word of it, not because I mistrust communists, but because I would not know what it meant; I would be equally incapable of actively disbelieving it.

Now it is certain that I have no categories of knowledge, in the sense just illustrated, into which I can fit God. As Aquinas says in a nutshell, *Deus non est in genere*,[1] God is not classifiable by genus and species, and Augustine himself elaborated on this theme at the beginning of Book V. And yet if I have no knowledge about God whatsoever, it will be quite simply impossible for me to have any faith or belief about him either. Is it perhaps a kind of general awareness of this shocking logical truth that has caused God's death to spread so infectiously in recent years? Neither Aquinas nor Augustine, however, was prepared to accept the impossibility of faith in God so easily. The former found the solution in saying that we can have a certain knowledge of God as of a cause in its effect.[2] Augustine takes a more subjective line, and says in substance that we have direct knowledge, and not in terms either of genus and species, of certain values, truth, the good, justice, and hence an indirect knowledge of God as the guarantor of these values, or the source from which they derive.

That knowledge of these values does not give us direct knowledge of God is clear, in spite of the way in which in the first two chapters Augustine eagerly identifies truth and the good with God (justice is a subordinate value, introduced mainly for purposes of illustration); otherwise he would not be constrained to raise the whole question the way he does in chapter 3. Not that he withdraws the identification, but that in fact it is one that is made in faith, and is not self-evident to pre-faith knowledge. Anyway, it is an affirmation that God is truth, or God is the good, not that truth is God, or the good is God. But the knowledge of these values does give us sufficient indirect knowledge of God to provide a meaning for the word "God," and so for us to make faith affirmations about God. And a further examination of such values will enable us to deepen our apprehension of the meaning of the affirmations we make in faith. Truth and goodness will thus be the categories in terms of which we will continue to pursue our search for God the trinity, or as Augustine himself puts it in his closing sentence, the warp on which we can weave the further understanding of our trinitarian faith.

Thus what in fact he does in Book VIII is to reverse the movement of thought which had governed the first seven books. Up till now it has been a movement from faith to consequent understanding; from now on, without in any sense repudiating his rule that we must believe first if we would understand, and must not stop believing simply because we do not understand, the movement is going to be from a kind of antecedent knowledge to faith.

Truth and goodness—even though we call it the good—sound rather abstract. But Augustine succeeds in concretizing or existentializing the warp on which his thought is going to move from now on by introducing love, not just as the mind's response to the value of the good, but as a value in its own right. Indeed, awareness of love as a value, and love of love, is almost sufficient in itself to overcome the whole communications problem. Love is perhaps the all-embracing notion which covers the whole double movement of faith to understanding, and antecedent knowledge to faith. In the first place, Augustine introduces his communications problem as a love problem: in order eventually to see God we must love him first; but how can we love what we do not know, and so on. In the second place, when he first brings in faith as the obvious solution to this conundrum, he talks about "loving by believing." In the third place, he suggests in his last chapter that loving is in itself a kind of knowing; at least that seems to be the implication of the stirring exhortation in section 12. Thus we can restate the double movement of the whole work as first a movement from loving by believing to understanding in loving, and second a movement "in a more inward fashion" from knowing by loving to loving by believing now immeasurably deepened and matured.

The introduction of love as a value in its own right definitively sets the stage for the books that are to come, because as it is not just a superior or abstract value to which the mind adheres, like truth and goodness, but an act which the mind performs, it means that we can bring the warp of our subsequent investigations right down into the mind itself. That is why Augustine is careful to discover a trinity, not in truth or the good, but in love. This opens the way to his discovering one in the mind which is the subject of love.

The thing that makes it hardest to appreciate or even to understand the drift of what Augustine is saying in this book is, to my mind at least, the platonic style of his discourse. I think it is more than a little a matter of language; you could talk like that in Latin, treating notions like truth, the good, justice, and love as if they were independently existing substances, but you cannot really talk like that in English. On the other hand, you can talk in English about such things being real, objective values, but perhaps you could not say that in Latin. Certainly one cannot imagine Augustine talking about *veritas, ipsum bonum, justitia* or *caritas/dilectio* as *valores*, even if the word had existed in the Latin of his time, which seems unlikely. So when he wished to state their wholly objective character, as elements or standards in the real world perceived by the mind, and not mere constructs imposed by the mind on its experience of the world, he had little alternative but to talk of them, in platonic terms, as real forms. That he regarded them as objective absolutes there is no doubt at all, and this is what enabled him to see them as means of knowing God. That he in fact identified them with God is part of his Christian rather than his platonic style of thought. And so perhaps, after all, is much of what at first sight we regard as his platonism; if the Bible could hypostatize and personify wisdom in the way it does, Augustine could see no reason why he should not do the same for love, or truth, or the form of justice. But it makes hard reading for people whose thought is controlled by a very different linguistic tradition.

NOTES

1. *Summa Theologiae* Ia, q. 3, a. 5.
2. *Summa Theologiae* Ia, q. 12, a. 12.

Book VIII

Through the Looking-Glass

Prologue

---

1. We have remarked elsewhere that any names that are predicated with reference to each other like Father and Son and the gift of each, the Holy Spirit, are said properly in that triad or trinity, that is, they belong distinctly to the several persons; the trinity is not Father, the trinity is not Son, nor is the trinity Gift. But whatever they are each and severally called with reference to self the trinity is also called, not three such in the plural but one such; thus the Father is God, the Son is God, the Holy Spirit is God; and the Father is good, the Son is good, the Holy Spirit is good; and the Father is almighty, the Son is almighty, the Holy Spirit is almighty; yet there are not three Gods, or three good ones, or three almighty ones, but one God, good and almighty, the trinity itself;[1] and the same goes for anything else that they are each called not with reference to one another but to self. For they are called such things with respect to being, because in this case to be is the same as to be great, to be good, to be wise, and to be anything else that each person or the trinity itself is called with reference to self. And the reason there are said to be three persons or three substances is not to signify any diversity of being, but to have at least one word to answer with when asked three what or three who. And finally we observed that so total is the equality in this triad that not only is the Father not greater than the Son as far as divinity is concerned, but also Father and Son together are not greater than the Holy Spirit, nor any single person of the three less than the trinity itself.

All this has been said, and if it has been repeated rather often in various ways, this only means that we become all the more familiar with it. But we must put some limits to repetition, and beseech God as devoutly and earnestly as we can to open our understandings and temper our fondness for controversy, so that our minds may be able to perceive the essence or being of truth without any mass, without any changeableness.[2] Now therefore, as far as the wonderfully merciful

241

creator may assist us, let us turn our attention to the things we are going to discuss[3] in a more inward manner than the things that have been discussed above, though in fact they are the same things; but let us all the while still keep to the rule that just because a thing is not yet clear to our understanding, we must not therefore dismiss it from the firm assent of our faith.[4]

Chapter 1

God is nothing else but truth, and if we can see truth, we can see God; but our inner eyes are too weak to be able to gaze on truth itself.

2. We are saying then that in this trinity two or three persons are not any greater than one of them alone, and a flesh-bound habit of thought cannot grasp this for the simple reason that, while it perceives as far as its powers extend true things that have been created, it cannot gaze upon the truth itself which they were created by. If it were able to, then this physical light around us would in no way at all be clearer or more obvious than what we have just said. Now in the substance of truth, since the only way it is is truly, nothing is greater unless it is more truly. And where things are intelligible[5] and unchangeable one is not truer than another, because each is equally unchangeably eternal; and what makes a thing great in this sphere is simply the fact that it truly is. So where greatness is simply truth itself, anything that has more greatness must have more truth; and anything that does not have more truth does not have more greatness. Then of course whatever has more truth is truer, just as whatever has more greatness is greater; so in this sphere greater is the same as truer. But now the Father and the Son together do not be more truly than the Father alone or the Son alone. So both together are not something greater than each one of them singly. And since the Holy Spirit equally truly is, Father and Son together are not something greater than he is, because neither are they something truer. Again, Father and Holy Spirit together do not excel the Son in truth since they do not be more truly; so neither do they excel him in greatness. And thus Son and Holy Spirit together are something as great as the Father alone, because they as truly are. So too the trinity itself is as great as any one person in it; what is not truer is not greater where greatness is truth itself, because in the essence or being of truth to be true is the same as to be, and to be is the same as to be great; so to be great is the same as to be true. Here then what is equally true must be equally great.

3. But with bodies it can happen, for instance, that this gold is as equally true as that, and yet this is greater than that, because here greatness is not the same as truth and it is one thing for it to be gold, another to be great. So too with the nature of the human spirit[6] it is not called a true spirit by the same kind of token as it is called a great spirit. A man who is not great-spirited or magnanimous still has a true spirit. In both cases the reason is that the essence or being of body

and of spirit is not the being or essence of truth; but the trinity is, which is the one, only, great God, true, truthful, truth. If we try to think of him as far as he allows and enables us to, we must not think of any special contact or intertwining as it were of three bodies, any fusion of joints in the manner in which the fables picture the three-bodied Geryon.[7] Any such thing that occurs to the mind so as to make the three bigger than any one of them, or one less than two, must be rejected without hesitation. Indeed any and every bodily conception is to be so rejected.

As for spiritual conceptions, anything that is changeable about them must not be thought to be God. For it is no small part of knowledge, when we emerge from these depths to breathe in that sublime atmosphere,[8] if before we can know what God is, we are at least able to know what he is not.[9] He is certainly not the earth, nor the heavens, nor like earth and heavens, nor any such thing as we see in the heavens, nor any such thing as we do not see in the heavens and yet may perhaps be there all the same. Nor if you increase the light of the sun in your imagination as much as you can, whether to make it greater or brighter a thousand times even or to infinity, not even that is God. Nor is he as you may think of angels, pure spirits "inspiriting"[10] the heavenly bodies and changing and turning them as they judge best in their service of God; not even if all *thousand times a thousand* (Dn 7:10; Rv 5:11) of them were lumped together to make one, is God anything like that; not even if you think of these same spirits as being without bodies, which is extremely difficult for flesh-bound thoughts to conceive of.[11]

Come, see if you can, O *soul weighed down with the body that decays* (Wis 9:15) and burdened with many and variable earthy thoughts, come see it if you can—God is truth. For it is written *that God is light* (1 Jn 1:5) not such as these eyes see, but such as the mind sees when it hears[12] "He is truth." Do not ask what truth is; immediately a fog of bodily images and a cloud of fancies will get in your way and disturb the bright fair weather that burst on you the first instant when I said "truth." Come, hold it in that first moment in which so to speak you caught a flash from the corner of your eye when the word "truth" was spoken, stay there if you can. But you cannot; you slide back into these familiar and earthy things. And what weight is it, I ask, that drags you back but the birdlime of greed for the dirty junk you have picked up on your wayward wanderings?[13]

Chapter 2

God is the good itself, the unchanging good, the good of all goods, in terms of which we love whatever good things we do love. So if we can see this good in which we love anything else that is good, and in which we live and move and are, we can see God.

---

4. Once more come, see if you can. You certainly only love what is good, and the earth is good with its lofty mountains and its folded hills and its level

plains, and a farm is good when its situation is pleasant and its land fertile, and a house is good with its harmonious symmetry of architecture so spacious and bright, and animals are good with their animated bodies, and the air is good when mild and salubrious, and food is good when tasty and health-giving, and health is good being without pains or weariness, and a man's face is good when it has fine proportions and a cheerful expression and a fresh complexion, and the heart of a friend is good with its sweet accord and loving trust, and a just man is good, and riches are good because they are easily put to use, and the sky is good with its sun and moon and stars, and angels are good with their holy obedience, and speech is good as it pleasantly instructs and suitably moves[14] the hearer, and a song is good with its melodious notes and its noble sentiments. Why go on and on? This is good and that is good. Take away this and that and see good itself if you can. In this way you will see God, not good with some other good, but the good of every good. For surely among all these good things I have listed and whatever others can be observed or thought of, we would not say that one is better than another when we make a true judgment unless we had impressed on us some notion of good itself by which we both approve of a thing, and also prefer one thing to another. That is how we should love God, not this or that good but good itself, and we should seek the good of the soul, not the good it can hover over in judgment but the good it can cleave to in love, and what is this but God? Not good mind or good angel or good heavens, but good good.

Perhaps it will be easier to perceive what I want to say if we put it like this. When I hear it said, for example, "a good soul,"[15] just as there are two words used, so do I understand two things from these words, one by which it is a soul, another by which it is good. And of course in order to be a soul it did not do anything itself; it was not already there to do anything[16] in order to be. But in order to be a good soul I see that it must deliberately choose to do something. Not of course that simply being a soul is not something good—how else could it be said, and very truly said, to be better than the body? But the reason it is not yet called a good soul is that it still remains for it to act by deliberate choice in order to acquire excellence. If it neglects to do this it is justly blamed and rightly said to be not a good soul; for it diverges from one that does so act, and as this one is praiseworthy, so it follows that the one who does not act is blameworthy. But when it does act with this intention and become a good soul, it cannot in fact achieve this unless it turns to something which it is not itself. And where is it to turn to in order to become a good soul but to the good, when this is what it loves and reaches for and obtains? And if again it turns away from it and becomes not good by the very fact of turning away from good, it will have nowhere to turn to again if it wishes to reform, unless that good which it has turned away from remains in itself.

5. And thus it is that there would be no changeable good things unless there were an unchangeable good. So when you hear a good this and a good that which can at other times also be called not good, if without these things, that are good by participation in the good, you can perceive good itself by participating in

which these other things are good—and you understand it together with them when you hear a good this or that—if then you can put them aside and perceive good itself, you will perceive God. And if you cling to him in love, you will straightaway enter into bliss. But when other things are only loved because they are good, you should be ashamed of so clinging to them that you fail to love the good itself which makes them good.[17]

Then there is also the point that the soul just because it is soul, even though not yet good in that way of turning to the unchangeable good, but just the soul, as I said, is indeed esteemed so highly by us when we understand it rightly that we prefer it to anything material, even light; and yet we do not value it in itself but in the art by which it was made. For the reason we value it once made is that we see the reason why it was worth making. This reason, this art is truth, and the simple good;[18] for it is nothing else but the good itself, and thus it is also the highest good. The only good, after all, that can diminish or increase is one that gets its being good from another good.

So the good the soul turns to in order to be good is the good from which it gets its being soul at all. This is when the will accords with nature to perfect the soul in good, when the will turns in love toward that good by which the soul is what it does not forfeit being, even if the will turns away again. By turning away from the highest good the soul forfeits being a good soul; but it does not forfeit being soul, and even this is still a good that is better than the body. So the will can forfeit what the will can obtain; the soul was already there to will to turn toward that from which it was, but it was not already there to will to be before it was. This then is our good, in which we see why anything ought to be or to have been that we understand ought to be or to have been; and in which we see that nothing can have been unless it ought to have been, even though we do not understand why it ought to have been.[19] This good then *is not situated far from anyone of us; for in it we live and move and are* (Acts 17:27).

Chapter 3

If we must love God in order to see him, as has been suggested in the last chapter, it might seem as if we are caught in a vicious circle. For we cannot love what we do not know, and therefore we must see God first, in the sense of know him, before we can love him. If the vicious circle is broken by faith, in that we can love something we believe but do not yet see or know, then faith too has a problem for us. For faith or belief in things we do not know presupposes a kind of general knowledge or experience about the things we believe, so that we can at least know what we believe; but about God, and especially about the trinity, we have no such general knowledge or experience, and so we are left with the question of how we can know what we believe about God.

---

6. But[20] we also have to stand by and cling to this good in love, in order to enjoy the presence of him from whom we are, whose absence would mean that

we could not even be. For since *we are still walking by faith and not by sight* (2 Cor 5:7) we do not yet see God, as the same apostle says, *face to face* (1 Cor 13:12). Yet unless we love him even now, we shall never see him. But who can love what he does not know? Something can be known and not loved; what I am asking is whether something can be loved which is unknown, because if it cannot then no one loves God before he knows him. And what does knowing God mean but beholding him and firmly grasping him with the mind? For he is not a body to be examined with the eyes in your head.

But then to behold and grasp God as he can be beheld and grasped is only permitted to the pure in heart—blessed are the pure in heart, because they shall see God (Mt 5:8); so before we are capable of doing this we must first love by faith, or it will be impossible for our hearts to be purified and become fit and worthy to see him.[21] Where after all are those three things to be found which the whole gear of all the inspired books is set up to build in the human spirit,[22] where are faith, hope, and charity to be found if not in the spirit that believes what it cannot yet see, and hopes in and loves what it believes? So something[23] can be loved which is unknown, provided it is believed. But naturally the spirit which believes what it does not see must be on its guard against fabricating something that does not exist, and thus hoping in and loving something false. If this happens, then it will not be charity from a pure heart and a good conscience and an unfabricated faith (1 Tm 1:5), as the same apostle puts it.

7. But now, when we believe some material or physical facts we read or hear about but have not seen, we cannot help our imaginations fabricating something with the shape and outline of bodies as it may occur to our thoughts, and this will either not be true, or if it is true, which can only happen extremely rarely, this is not what it profits us to hold on faith. Our faith is directed to something else of use and importance which is represented by this picture in our imagination. Anyone, surely, who has read or heard what the apostle Paul wrote or what was written about him, will fabricate a face for the apostle in his imagination, and for everybody else whose name is mentioned in these texts. And every one of the vast number of people to whom these writings are known will think of their physical features and lineaments in a different way, and it will be quite impossible to tell whose thoughts are nearest the mark in this respect. Nor is our faith bothered with what physical features those men had, but only with the fact that they lived like that by the grace of God and did the things which those scriptures bear witness to. This is what it is useful and desirable to believe and there is no need to despair of its possibility.[24] Even the physical face of the Lord is pictured with infinite variety by countless imaginations,[25] though whatever it was like he certainly only had one. Nor as regards the faith we have in the Lord Jesus Christ is it in the least relevant to salvation what our imaginations picture him like, which is probably quite different from the reality. What does matter is that we think of him specifically as a man; for we have embedded in us as it were a standard notion of the nature of man, by which whenever we see some such thing we immediately recognize it as a man, or at least as the shape of a man.

It is in terms of this sort of notion that our thoughts are framed when we believe that God became man for us as an example of humility and to demonstrate God's love for us. This indeed it is useful for us to believe and to hold firm and unshaken in our hearts, that the humility thanks to which God was born of a woman, and led through such abuse at the hands of mortal men to his death, is a medicine to heal the tumor of our pride and a high sacrament to break the chains of sin.[26] So too with his miraculous powers and his resurrection; we know what omnipotence is and so we believe these things of the omnipotent God, and we think about them in terms of the species and genera of things which are either connatural to us or gathered from our experience of this sort of facts, and in this way our faith is not fabricated. Nor do we know what the virgin Mary looked like, from whom he was marvelously born although she was untouched by man and remained intact even in childbirth; nor have we seen Lazarus and what kind of figure he had, nor Bethany nor the tomb and the stone which he ordered to be removed when he raised him to life; nor the new tomb cut in the rock which he rose from himself, nor the Mount of Olives from where he ascended into heaven. Nor do we have the slightest idea, we who have not seen these things, whether they are like what we think of them as being; indeed we assume that in all probability they are not. After all, when our eyes are confronted with the features of a man or a place or any physical object which turns out to be exactly the same as we pictured it to ourselves when we were thinking about it before we had ever seen it, we treat it as no little miracle, so rarely, almost never in fact, does it happen.

And yet we firmly believe those things because we think of them in terms of general and specific notions that we are quite certain of. Thus we believe that the Lord Jesus Christ was born of a virgin who was called Mary. What a virgin is, and what being born is, and what a proper name is we do not believe, we just know. But whether Mary's face was like what occurs to our imaginations when we talk of or remember these things we neither know nor believe. And so without prejudice to faith it is permissible to say "Perhaps she had a face like this, perhaps she did not." But nobody can say "Perhaps Christ was born of a virgin" without prejudice to his Christian faith.

8. So then, since we desire to understand as far as it is given us the eternity and equality and unity of the trinity, and since we must believe before we can understand,[27] we must take care our faith is not fabricated. This is the trinity we are to enjoy in order to live in bliss; but if we have false beliefs about it our hope is vain and our charity is not chaste. How then are we to love by believing this trinity which we do not know? In terms perhaps of the kind of general and specific notions which enable us to love the apostle Paul? In his case, even if his features were not as we imagine them when we think of him, and of this we are totally ignorant, at least we know what a man is. To go no further, it is what we are ourselves and clearly what he was too, so that with his soul joined to his body he lived a mortal life. So we believe about him what we experience in ourselves, in terms of the species and genus in which every human nature is equally included.

What then do we know, either generically or specifically, about that transcendent trinity, as though there were many such trinities and we had experience of some of them, and thus could believe according to a standard of likeness impressed on us or in terms of specific and generic notions that that trinity is of the same sort, and hence could love the thing we believe and do not yet know from its likeness to what we do know? But this of course is simply not so. Or is it like our loving in the Lord Jesus Christ that he rose from the dead, although we have never seen anyone rise from there? Can we love the trinity by believing like that, even though we do not see it and have never seen anything like it? But we know what it is to live and what it is to die because we live ourselves and have sometimes seen and had experience of people dying or dead. And what else is rising but reviving, that is coming back from death to life? In the same way perhaps, when we say and believe that there is a trinity, we know what a trinity is because we know what three are. But then this is not what we love. We can always have that when we want, simply by flashing three fingers, to say nothing else. Perhaps then what we love is not what any trinity is but the trinity that God is. So what we love in the trinity is what God is. But we have never seen or known another God, because God is one, he alone is God whom we love by believing, even though we have not yet seen him. What we are asking, though, is from what likeness or comparison of things known to us we are able to believe, so that we may love the as yet unknown God.

Chapter 4

The problem raised in the last chapter is approached through the analogy of how we are able to love the just man, exemplified by Paul. The answer is found to be that we can only do this because we see and love within ourselves, or rather in-and-above ourselves, the very form or idea of justice, and this even though we may not be just ourselves.

---

9. So come back a step or two with me, and let us consider why we love the apostle. Is it after all because of the species "man" which is so well known to us, and because we believe him to have been a man? Surely not; otherwise there would be no one in this case for us to love, since that man is now no more; his soul has been separated from his body. But what we love in him we believe to be living even now—we love his just mind.[28] And by what generic or specific standard could we do this, were it not that we know what mind is and also what just is? Not implausibly we say that we know what mind is for the simple reason that we ourselves also have a mind. At least we have never seen one with our eyes, or gathered a generic or specific notion of what it is from the likeness of several we have seen. But it is rather, as I said, that we have one ourselves. What after all is so intimately known and so aware of its own existence as that by which things enter into our awareness, namely the mind? So too it is by com-

parison with ourselves that we recognize the body movements which tell us that other people besides ourselves are alive; we too in living make the same body movements as we notice those other bodies making. It is not after all as though, when a living body moves, our eyes had an aperture opened for them through which they could see its mind, a thing that cannot be seen by eyes. But we are aware of something being in that mass like what there is in us to move our mass in the same way, and this is life and soul. Nor is this as it were an inference proper to human sagacity or reason. Animals too are aware not only of themselves but also of each other and of us too as being alive. They do not see our souls, but they perceive it immediately and readily, by a kind of natural affinity, from our body movements. So we know anyone else's mind[29] from our own, and from our own we believe any mind we do not know. Indeed we are not only aware of mind but we are even able to know what mind is from a consideration of our own; for we have a mind.

But how do we know what "just" is? I said, you remember, that the only reason we love the apostle is because he is a just mind. Therefore we know both what "just" is and what mind is. But we know what mind is, as has been said, from ourselves; there is a mind in us. How though do we know what "just" is if we are not just ourselves? And if nobody knows what "just" is unless he is just himself, then nobody loves the just man except a just man. A man cannot love someone he believes to be just for the reason that he believes him to be just, if he does not know what "just" is, according to the rule we have demonstrated above that nobody loves what he believes and does not see except by some standard of generic or specific notions. And thus if only a just man loves the just man, how can someone ever wish to be just who is not so yet? Nobody wishes to be something he does not love. But in order for someone who is not yet just to be so, he must of course wish to be just; and in order to wish it he must love the just man. But he cannot love the just man if he does not know what "just" is. So even the man who is not so yet knows what "just" is.

But what does he know it from? Has he ever seen it with his eyes, or some just body perhaps, like a white or a black or a square or a round one? Who would ever say such a thing? All he has ever seen with his eyes is bodies, and it is only the mind in man that is just, and when a man is called just he is called it from his mind not his body. For justice is a sort of beauty of mind by which many men are beautiful even though they have ugly misshapen bodies. But just as mind cannot be seen with the eyes, so neither can its beauty. So how does a man who is not yet just know what "just" is, and in order to be so himself love the just man? Are there perhaps some signs evident in the movements of the body which make it clear that this or that man is just? If so, how does someone who is entirely ignorant of what "just" is know what those signs are of a just mind? He must know therefore what "just" is.

But where have we learnt what "just" is even when we are not yet just? If we have learnt it outside ourselves then we have learnt it in some body. But this is not a body reality. So it is in ourselves that we have learnt what "just" is. When I seek to express what it is I do not find the answer anywhere but with myself;

and if I ask someone else what "just" is, he searches in himself to find the answer. And anyone who has ever been able to answer the question truly has found the answer in himself. When I want to express Carthage I search about in myself in order to express it and in myself I find the image of Carthage. But I got this through the body, that is through the senses of the body, because I have been present there in body and seen and perceived it and kept it in my memory, so that I could find a word about the city to say when I wanted to say the city. Its image in my memory is its word,[30] not this sound of two syllables made when "Carthage" is named, nor even the name thought of silently in a space of time, but that which I am aware of when I utter these two syllables with my voice or even before I utter them. So too when I wish to express Alexandria which I have never seen I have its image ready to hand within me. I have heard about it from lots of people, and believed it to be a great city as people have been able to describe it to me, and so I have fabricated its image as best I could in my mind, and this is its word for me when I wish to express it even before I utter these five syllables which are its name and known to practically everyone. But if I could produce this image from my mind and show it to the eyes of men who know Alexandria, they would all say at once "That isn't it"; or if by any chance they said "That's it," I would be very astonished indeed; yet looking at it in my mind, that is at its image, like a picture of it, I still would not know that this was really Alexandria but I would believe it from those who held in their minds the picture of what they had seen.

But this is not how I search for what "just" is, nor how I find it, nor how I look at it when I express it, nor how I am agreed with by someone who hears me, nor how I agree with someone when I hear him, as though I had seen such a thing with my eyes or learnt it by any of my senses or heard about it from others who had so learnt it. For when I say, and say with full knowledge, "That mind is just which knowingly and deliberately, in life and in conduct, gives each man what is his own,"[31] I am not recalling something absent like Carthage, or fabricating it as best I can like Alexandria, whether it is like my fabrication or not like it; but I am perceiving something that is present to me, and it is present to me even if I am not what I perceive, and many will agree with me when they hear me. And anyone who hears me and knowingly agrees with me also perceives the same thing in himself, even if he is not what he perceives. When a just man says it he perceives and says what he himself is. And where would he too perceive it if not in himself? But this of course is not surprising; where after all would he perceive himself if not in himself?

What is wonderfully surprising is that a mind should see in itself what it has seen nowhere else, and see something true, and see something true that is a just mind, and be itself mind, and not be the just mind which it sees in itself. Is there then another just mind in the mind that is not yet just? If not, then what is it seeing there when it sees and says what a just mind is, and does not see it anywhere but in itself, though it is not itself a just mind? Or is perhaps what it sees the inner truth[32] present to the mind which is capable of beholding it? Not all are so capable, and of those who are, not all are what they behold, that is to say they are not just minds in the same way as they can see and say what a just mind is. And how will they ever be able to be so but by cleaving to that same form which they behold, in order to be formed by it and become just minds, now no longer merely perceiving and saying that the mind is just which "knowingly and deliberately in life and in conduct gives each man what is his own," but themselves now living justly and conducting themselves justly by giving each man what is his own, in order to *owe no man anything but to love one another* (Rom 13:8)? And how is one to cleave to that form except by loving it? Why then do we love another man whom we believe to be just, and not love this form in which we see what a just mind is, so that we too may become just? Or is it perhaps the case that unless we also loved this form we would in no wise love him whom we love and appreciate by this form, but that as long as we are not just we love it less than is necessary for us to be able to become just ourselves?

So then a man who is believed to be just is loved and appreciated according to that form and truth which the one who is loving perceives and understands in himself; but this form and truth cannot be loved and appreciated according to the standard of anything else. We simply cannot find anything else besides this, which is such that from this something else that we know we can love by believing this form and truth, while it is still unknown to us. If in fact you ever observe any such thing else, it is this form and truth, and so is not any such thing else, because this form and truth alone is such as this form and truth is.

Whoever therefore loves men should love them either because they are just or in order that they might be just. This is how he ought to love himself, either because he is just or in order to be just; in this way he can love *his neighbor as himself* (Mk 12:33) without any danger. Anyone who loves himself any other way loves himself unjustly, because he loves himself in order to be unjust, in order therefore to be bad, and thus in fact he no longer really loves himself; for *the man who loves iniquity hates his own soul* (Ps 11:5).

Chapter 5

Having examined the notions of truth and of the good, and offered a solution, in terms of the notion of the form of justice, to the problem of how we can love by believing what we do not know, the author goes on to examine the notion of love or charity itself; he sets out the mutual coherence or reciprocity of the twin commandments to love God and our neighbor; achieves an identification of charity with truth and the good and the form of justice; and finally sketches a trinity in love or charity, thus opening a way to our understanding of the divine trinity through these notions he has displayed in the course of this book; according to his closing words they provide the warp on which he will weave the fabric of the trinitarian image in man.

10. Thus it is that in this question we are occupied with about the trinity and about knowing God, the only thing we really have to see is what true love is; well in fact, simply what love is. Only if it is true love does it deserve to be

called love, otherwise it is covetousness; and thus covetous people are said improperly to love, and those who love are said improperly to covet. True love then is that we should live justly by cleaving to the truth, and so for the love of men by which we wish them to live justly we should despise all mortal things.[33] In this way we will be ready and able even to die for the good of our brethren, as the Lord Jesus Christ taught us by his example. And while there are *two commandments* from which *the whole law and the prophets depend* (Mt 22:40), love of God and love of neighbor, scripture not unsuitably often puts just one for both of them. Sometimes just love of God, like *We know that all things work together for good for those who love God* (Rom 8:28); and again, *Whoever loves God is known by him* (1 Cor 8:3); and, *Since the love of God has been poured out in our hearts through the Holy Spirit who has been given to us* (Rom 5:5); and many other instances, because if a man loves God it follows that he does what God has commanded and loves God to the extent that he does this; it follows in fact that he loves his neighbor too, because God has commanded this. And sometimes scripture only mentions love of neighbor, like *Bear one another's burdens, and thus you will fulfill the law of Christ* (Gal 6:2); and, *The whole law is fulfilled in one word, in that which is written: You shall love your neighbor as yourself* (Gal 5:14); and in the gospel, *All the good things*[34] *you want men to do to you, do these yourselves to them; for this is the law and the prophets* (Mt 7:12). And we find many other cases in the sacred writings where only love of neighbor seems to be required of us for perfection and the love of God seems to be passed over in silence, though the law and the prophets depend on both commandments. But this is because if a man loves his neighbor, it follows that above all he loves love itself. But *God is love and whoever abides in love abides in God* (1 Jn 4:16). So it follows that above all he loves God.

11. Therefore those who seek God through these powers which rule the world or parts of the world are in fact being swept away from him and cast up a long way off, not in terms of distance but of divergence of values; they are trying to go by an outer route and forsaking their own inwardness, where God is present more inwardly still. So even supposing they could hear or in any manner raise their thoughts to some holy power of heaven, it would be rather his mighty deeds they would be after, which amaze human weakness; they would not think of imitating his piety, by which the divine rest is attained. They would rather proudly be able to do what an angel can than devotedly be what an angel is. For no really holy being takes pleasure in his own power, but rather in the power of him from whom he receives the power to do whatever he appropriately can do; and he knows it is far more effective to be bound to the almighty by a devout and dutiful will than by his own will[35] to be able to do things that overawe those who cannot do them. And so though the Lord Jesus Christ himself did such things, he wished to open the eyes of men who were amazed and spellbound by such unusual temporal deeds to larger perspectives, and convert them to eternal and more inward realities; so he said, *Come to me, you*[36] *who toil and are heavy burdened, and I will refresh you; take my yoke upon you*—and he did not add "Learn of me, because I raise those who have been four days[37] dead," but he

said *Learn of me because I am meek and lowly of heart* (Mt 11:28). A down-to-earth lowliness is stronger and safer than a wind-swept *hauteur*. And therefore he goes on to say, *and you will find rest for your souls* (Mt 11:29). For *love is not inflated* (1 Cor 13:4), and *God is love* (1 Jn 4:8), and *those who are faithful in love will repose with him* (Wis 3:9), called away from the din outside to the joys of silence. There you are, *God is love*. Why should we go running round the heights of the heavens and the depths of the earth looking for him who is with us if only we should wish to be with him?[38]

12. Let no one say "I don't know what to love." Let him love his brother, and love[39] that love; after all, he knows the love he loves with better than the brother he loves. There now, he can already have God better known to him than his brother, certainly better known because more present, better known because more inward to him, better known because more sure. Embrace love which is God, and embrace God with love. This is the love which unites all the good angels and all the servants of God in a bond of holiness, conjoins us and them together, and subjoins us to itself. And the more we are cured of the tumor of pride, the fuller we are of love. And if a man is full of love, what is he full of but God?

"Yes I can see charity, and to the best of my ability grasp it with my mind, and I believe the scripture when it says that *God is charity and whoever abides in charity abides in God* (1 Jn 4:16). But when I see it, I don't see any trinity in it." Oh but you do see a trinity if you see charity. I will just remind you of a few things, and so help you if I can to see that you see it; only let charity herself be present so that we may be moved by her to something good. For when we love charity, we love her loving something, precisely because she does love something. What then does charity love that makes it possible for charity herself also to be loved? She is not charity if she loves nothing; but if she loves herself, she must love something in order to love herself as charity.[40] Just as a word indicates something and also indicates itself, but does not indicate itself as a word unless it indicates itself indicating something; so too charity certainly loves itself, but unless it loves itself loving something it does not love itself as charity. So what does charity love but what we love with charity? And this, to move beyond our neighbor, is our brother.[41]

But let us observe how much the apostle John commends brotherly charity: *Whoever loves his brother*, he says, *abides in the light, and there is no scandal in him* (1 Jn 2:10). It is clear that he sets the perfection of justice in the love of one's brother; for a man in whom there is no scandal is clearly perfect. And yet he seems to pass the love of God over in silence. He would never do this unless he wished God to be understood in brotherly love. He says it quite openly a little further on in the same letter: *Beloved, let us love each other because love is from God, and everyone who loves is born of God and knows God. Whoever does not love does not know God, because God is love* (1 Jn 4:7). This passage shows clearly and sufficiently how this brotherly love—it is of course brotherly love that we love each other with[42]—is proclaimed on the highest authority not only to be from God but also simply to be God. When therefore we love our brother out of love, we love our brother out of God; and it is impossible that we should not love especially the love that we love our brother with. Thus we infer that those two commandments cannot exist without each other: because God is love the man who loves love certainly loves God; and the man who loves his brother must love love. And that is the reason for what he goes on to say a little later: *Whoever does not love the brother whom he sees cannot love God whom he does not see* (1 Jn 4:20); for the cause of his not seeing God is that he does not love his brother.[43] Whoever, you see, does not love his brother is not in love, and whoever is not in love is not in God, because *God is love* (1 Jn 4:8). Accordingly whoever is not in God is not in light, because *God is light and there is no darkness in him* (1 Jn 1:5). Is it surprising then that a man who is not in light should not see light, that is not see God, because he is in darkness? Now he sees his brother with ordinary human vision which God cannot be seen by. But if he were to love with spiritual charity the one he sees with human vision, he would see God who is charity with the inner vision which he can be seen by. How therefore can the man who does not love the brother he sees love God, whom he does not see for the reason that God is the love which he lacks by not loving his brother? So now we need not let that question worry us about how much love we should expend on our brother, how much on God. On our brother as much as on ourselves;[44] and we love ourselves all the more, the more we love God. So with one and the same charity we love God and neighbor; but God on God's account, ourselves and neighbor also on God's account.

13. After all, why is it, I would like to know, that we catch fire when we hear and read: *Behold now is the acceptable time, behold now is the day of salvation. Giving no offense in anything that our ministry may not be criticized, but in all things commending ourselves as the ministers of God, in much patience, in troubles, in need, in difficulties, in blows, in prisons, in riots, in labors; in vigils, in fasts, in chastity, in knowledge, in long-suffering, in goodness, in the Holy Spirit, in charity unfeigned, in the word of truth, in the power of God; with the weapons of justice in the right hand and the left, with glory and obscurity, with ill repute and good repute, as seducers and yet truthful, as ones who are ignorant and yet known, as dying and behold we are alive, as coerced and not done to death, as sad but always rejoicing, as poor but enriching many, as having nothing and possessing all things* (2 Cor 6:2-10)? What is it that fires us with love for the apostle Paul when we read this, if not that we believe he himself lived like that? But that God's ministers should live like that we do not believe on hearing it from someone else, we observe it within ourselves, or rather above ourselves in truth itself. So it is from what we see that we love the man we believe to have lived like that; and unless above all we loved this form which we perceive always enduring, never changing, we would not love him merely because we hold on faith that his life when he lived in the flesh was harmoniously adjusted to this form.

Yet I do not know how it is, but we are stirred all the more largely to love of that form by the faith with which we believe that someone lived like that, and by the hope that does not allow us to despair of ourselves living like that, men though we are, seeing that other men have lived like that; so that we desire this all the more ardently and pray for it all the more confidently. Thus on the one hand love of that form we believe they lived up to makes us love their life, and on the other belief in their life stirs us to a more blazing charity toward that form; with the result that the more brightly burns our love for God, the more surely and serenely we see him, because it is in God that we observe that unchanging form of justice which we judge that a man should live up to. Faith therefore is a great help for knowing and loving God, not as though he were altogether unknown or altogether not loved without it, but for knowing him all the more clearly and loving him all the more firmly.

14. What then, after all that, is this love or charity which the divine scriptures praise and proclaim so much, but love of the good?[45] Now love means someone loving and something loved with love. There you are with three, the lover, what is being loved, and love. And what is love but a kind of life coupling or trying to couple together two things, namely lover and what is being loved? This is true even of the most external and fleshly kinds of love. But in order to quaff something purer and more limpid, let us trample on the flesh and rise to the spirit.[46] What does spirit love in a friend but spirit? So here again there are three, lover and what is being loved, and love.

It still remains to rise from here and investigate these things on a higher plane as far as it is granted man to do. But here let us rest our effort for a little, not supposing that it has already found us what we are looking for, but as if finding a place where something has to be looked for. It has not yet been found, but we have found where to look for it. Thus we have said enough to provide ourselves as it were with the frame of a kind of warp on which we can weave what remains to be said.

NOTES

1. This is one of the more striking "echoes" of the *Quicunque vult*, or the so-called Athanasian creed, to be found in the *De Trinitate*. The reader will doubtless have noticed others, and will continue to do so as he reads on. It has of course been universally accepted at least since the beginning of the eighteenth century that Athanasius was not the author. The creed is in fact a Latin composition, and has never played any significant part in the tradition of the Greek Church, where it was unknown until the twelfth century.

It is also universally agreed that the creed is a thoroughly Augustinian document. The question discussed by modern scholars is whether it derives from Augustine's doctrine, above all from his *De Trinitate*, or whether it was a formula that he knew and made use of. The question really seems to have been definitively settled by J.N.D. Kelly in his lectures *The Athanasian Creed* (London, 1964). He argues convincingly that the author, or better the compiler, of the creed was Caesarius of Arles, bishop of that see from 502 to 542 A.D. Its earliest name was "the faith of Athanasius" or sometimes "the Catholic faith," and the theory is that the bishop compiled it as a statement of the orthodox trinitarian faith, of which Athanasius had become the traditional patron, for the instruction of his clergy and their charges. His reason for thinking such a statement necessary, over and above the official creeds already in liturgical use, would have been the domination of his part of Gaul by the Arian Visigoths and Burgundians. He was a devoted disciple of Augustine.

2. *Mutabilitate*: M reads *mobilitate*, mobility.

3. Reading *tractabimus* with M: CCL reads *tractavimus*, in which case we either have "let us turn our attention to the things we have discussed in a more inward manner than the above," which scarcely makes sense; or a clumsy anacoluthon, "let us turn our attention to the things which in a more inward manner than we have discussed above." The crucial declaration of intention is that we are now going to go over the same ground of trinitarian theology all over again *modo interiore*. This governs all the subsequent books.

4. See the first chapter of Book I, especially where this rule is laid down.

5. That is spiritual as opposed to material things, which are intelligible as opposed to sensible. Material things as such are not intelligible except insofar as they participate in intelligible forms. Thus the platonic point of view.

6. *Animus*: the word occurs frequently in this book; next time I render by "soul" and later still by "mind." Basically it is the human *anima* or principle of life precisely as rational or spiritual and not merely "anima-l."

7. A mythical king of Erythia, slain by Hercules. see Vergil's *Aeneid* 6, 289; 7, 662; 8, 202.

8. This image of man living as it were in subaqueous depths, and emerging into the upper air to breathe the divine atmosphere, conveys the same idea as I try to give by talking about "through the looking-glass" in the title I have given this book.

9. See Book V, 2, note 3.

10. *Inspirantes* here analogous to *animae animantes*.

11. Augustine himself seemed to have found this very difficult, or perhaps he simply went along with the more common view of his time that spiritual beings, angels and demons, have "airy" bodies. But whatever his own view, here at least he gives the three classical opinions about superior beings:

i) that they are, as it were, the souls, or rather the spirits of the heavenly bodies;

ii) that they have proper airy bodies of their own;

iii) that they are purely spiritual substances, or "separated intelligences," in the aristotelian expression.

12. *Audit*: M reads *audis*, you hear.

13. This image of man as a dirty tinker sadly attached to the squalor of his life, a son of Cain in fact, will recur frequently from Book IX onward when Augustine is investigating the image of the trinity in man, and the moral difficulties of its realization.

14. *Movens*: M reads *monens*, advising.

15. *Animus*: see note 6 above.

16. *Non iam erat qui ageret*: M has . . . *quod ageret*, there was not yet anything it could do.

17. This last sentence implicitly explains why we fail to carry out the program proposed in the previous two, and find instant bliss. While created things ought to be introducing us, by the platonic analyses outlined, to God the truth and the good, in fact they crowd so closely on our weakened intellects and twisted appetites that they obscure our vision and distract our affections.

18. It is interesting and possibly significant that in this context he regularly talks about truth, the abstract noun, and identifies God with it, but never about goodness, the abstract noun, only identifying God with "the good," *ipsum bonum*.

19. A roundabout reference to the problem of evil, seen as totally absorbed in the goodness of God.

20. The implicit sequence of thought is: "It is not enough to live and move and be in this good; we also etc."

21. The argument hangs on an allusion to Acts 15:9, *purifying their hearts by faith.*

22. *Animus*: see note 6 above.

23. *Amatur quod ignoratur*: M has *qui ignoratur*, someone . . . who . . .

24. Literally: This is useful to believe and not to be despaired of and to be sought after. He might in fact mean that we should not despair of living likewise, and should seek to do so, encouraged by our faith that these men did.

25. Not yet stereotyped and sterilized by vile holy pictures and cheap commercialized religious art.

26. See Book IV especially chapter 1, and chapter 4.

27. See Is 7:9 (Septuagint) *Unless you believe you will not understand.*

28. *Animus:* see note 6 above.

29. Not in the usual sense of this English phrase of knowing what they are thinking, but of knowing that they have a mind, and also knowing, as he goes on to say, what any mind is.

30. He is pressing the meaning of "word," *verbum,* into the mold of the Greek *logos,* meaning in this case "idea," for theological purposes which he will be working out in the subsequent books.

31. This seems to be Augustine's personal variation on the theme of the traditional definition of justice, made perhaps because he is not defining justice, but "just."

32. Here the form of justice is concretely identified with the truth discussed in chapter 1, just as the good itself was identified with that truth at the end of chapter 2, section 5.

33. A singularly unromantic definition of love. But it must be realized that he is not defining the passion of *amor* but the act or virtue of intelligent spirit which he calls *dilectio.* In English we have to make do with the same word. Note too how he puts the traditional *contemptio mundi* in its proper context.

34. *Omnia . . . bona, haec;* M has *Omnia . . . ita,* All that you want men to do to you, so do yourselves to them.

35. M has *potestate et voluntate,* power and will.

36. M adds *omnes,* all you.

37. Reading with M *quia quatriduanos:* CCL reads *quia triduanos,* because . . . three days . . . Both readings are supported by only one manuscript, and that the same one, CCL following a correction in it. All the rest read simply *quatriduanos.* Perhaps the original secretary wrote *quiatriduanos,* an easy slip. The allusion is clearly to Jn 11:39.

38. This whole paragraph seems to be a curiously inconsequential digression. It echoes Book IV chapter 3. Perhaps it serves here to introduce the idea of humility, which is an essential prerequisite of charity, which cannot find any room for itself in a spirit inflated by pride.

39. *Diligat:* M has *diliget* and he will love. But the argument here requires that this love too be made an imperative, and not a consequence of the preceding imperative.

40. Reading here and in the following sentence *caritatem* with M. CCL in both has *caritate,* with charity. But this does not really fit his argument, nor the analogy he makes with a word indicating itself as a word.

41. Here the argument, involved enough already, gets completely sidetracked, and we do not return to there being a trinity in love until right at the end of the book several paragraphs further on, where his conclusion appears to owe nothing to the argument he is beginning to sketch here. The truth is that in his characteristically "baroque" style he is engaged on several themes at once; he wants to tie in to what he has to say about the trinitarian character of charity what he has already said about the two commandments, and the form of justice, and the good, and truth. What his treatment loses thereby in the elegance of clarity it gains in richness and depth.

42. The point of this brief aside is obscure; perhaps to distinguish brotherly love from carnal affection?

43. Augustine quite alters the bearing of John's statement by taking it as meaning "Whoever does not love his brother cannot in consequence see God, and therefore he cannot love God"; and this he goes on to prove.

44. M begins the sentence: *incomparabiliter plus quam nobis deo; fratri autem . . .* Incomparably more on God than on ourselves; on our brother . . . But this is to give the trite answer to the question which we have just been told not to worry about.

45. He is defining *dilectio (caritas),* the kind of love he has been exclusively talking about till now, as a kind of *amor,* an altogether wider term (see above, note 33). And in so doing he finally ties the notion of love, already almost identified with truth and the form of justice, to the notion of the good.

46. *Animus* again; see above, note 6.

In my analysis of the structure of the *De Trinitate* in the Introduction (12-29), I suggested that Books IX-XIV in the second half of the work correspond in reverse order to Books II-VII in the first half; and more particularly that Books IX-XI, which are mainly psychological, correspond to Books V-VII, which are mainly linguistic and logical, while Books XII-XIV correspond to Books II-IV, both sets being mainly historical and scriptural.[1] I still have the courage of the conviction there expressed, but discretion obliges me to qualify it. As it stands, it is a little too neat. Taking the looking-glass as our model of the work's structure,[2] in which the last seven books are to be seen as somehow reflecting the first seven back to front, we must say that the glass is not quite flawless, and that the image it reflects is rather distorted—and as the subject of the last seven books is the image of God in man, that is artistically speaking just as it should be. To speak plainly the six books we are here concerned with do not have the clear-cut structure of the six in the first half of the work, Books II-VII, to which they correspond. The author is employing a greater number of structural elements, which both serve to bind these six books together without any such clean *caesura* as can be observed between Books IV and V in the first half, and also make it possible to discern a variety of structures, according to which structural element you may choose to emphasize.

But before we attempt to discern these complexities of structure a little more closely, it will be necessary to see something of the model of the human *psyche* with which Augustine is working here, because this provides one of the crucial structural elements of this part of the work. And then it will be as well to see if we can crystalize some of the trinitarian doctrine that emerges from these books; for, as we pointed out in the Introduction,[3] his examination of the image of God in man is primarily intended to throw light on the mystery of the divine processions within the godhead. Thus we can divide this foreword into three parts:

Augustine's psychology;
the complexities of structure of these Books IX-XIV;
their doctrine about the divine processions.

Augustine's Psychology

Augustine really had little interest in, and nothing original to say about, the *nature* of the soul; what fascinated him was its functioning. In this respect at least his approach has more in common with that of moderns like Freud and Jung than with the theories and speculations of ancient philosophers. We can say that he took for granted the language and for that matter the concepts of Platonism in this field, that is, he took for granted that man consists of an immaterial soul and a material body, and even talked at times as if man were an immaterial soul simply inhabiting a material body—a dualist way of looking at the matter which has commonly been assumed for most of the Christian era to be a Christian way. It is not, of course, the Aristotelian or the Thomist way, which takes a more unitary view of man as physical body organized or given living form by the life principle or soul, which in this system is defined as "the form of the body."[4] It is my feeling that Augustine would have been quite content with this system had he known about it; but he was misled, by Cicero among others,[5] into thinking that Aristotle had a materialistic view about the nature of the human soul, saying that it consisted of a "fifth element" or quintessence, a substance which Aristotle really introduced over and above the four common elements of fire, air, water and earth to account for the apparently incorruptible nature of the heavens. And one thing Augustine was quite determined about was that the soul is not any kind of body whatsoever.

His disproof of all materialistic theories of the soul in Book X, as the reader will observe, proceeds entirely in terms of its functions or activities. The argument may be allowed to speak for itself, and there is no need to summarize it here. Augustine's starting point, though, his basic assumption in all his psychological explorations, is that the soul, or the mind as he calls it in that particular context, is primarily a center of self-awareness, of reflexive presence. It knows itself, and for the matter of that it loves itself, simply by being itself.

Working out from this center of self-awareness Augustine builds up a model of the *psyche* as a structure of functions. Above, and within itself it is able to know God; or to put it another way, it is open to and in contact with truth, in the light of which it makes whatever true judgments it does make about anything whatever.[6] Below, and outside itself it is open through the bodily senses to the physical universe. This structure of cognitive functions is of course coordinated with a structure of affects; perhaps coordinated is not quite the right word, because the affective structure has been disordered by sin, with the consequence that the whole psychic structure of man has been turned upside down and inside out.

To my mind the best way of picturing this structure of the *psyche*—disregarding its sinful disorder for the moment—is to see it like one of those cooling towers we are so familiar with at power stations nowadays. These are just hollow concrete tubes, open at the top and the bottom, where they are supported on struts. They narrow in the middle and flare out at the top and bottom, so that they may be considered to have a top half and a bottom half. So too with the *psyche* according to Augustine—only he prefers to talk about an inner and an outer man, Pauline terms which he happily identifies at the beginning of Book XI with the platonic ones of intellectual and sensitive. Each section or "man" is again subdivided, so that the outer man has as the outermost, or lowest, function that of sensation, and as his inner function, one in or one up from sensation, that of sense memory/imagination; the inner man for his part has as his lower or outer function that of rational judgment and decision about material and temporal things, which Augustine will call *scientia* or knowledge in a fairly strict sense, and as his innermost or uppermost function that of contemplating eternal and immaterial truth, which Augustine will call *sapientia* or wisdom.

Here a word or two may be in place about the three words Augustine uses for the subject of these psychic functions. The first and most characteristic of him is *mens*, which I have, with absolute consistency as far as I can recall, translated "mind." But it means more than "mind" commonly means in English; it is the subject of the higher psychic functions, volitional and affective as well as cognitive. One might be inclined to say that it is practically synonymous, or at least coterminous, with what he calls the inner man; only he seems most to use it when he is talking about the highest or the innermost functions of the inner man, so in that respect it would be a narrower term than "mind" in ordinary English usage. However, he is not over-precise in his usage, and at the beginning of Book XII, in which he first broaches the distinction between the two functions of the inner man, he uses the phrase *mens humana* to cover them both.

The second word he uses with great frequency, and a word that is far harder to translate, is *animus*. It is a far more inclusive word than *mens*, and yet it always carries the connotation of rationality about it. It stands for the human soul precisely as rational, and could never be used for the souls or life principles of animals. It has not been possible to find a consistent translation of it, but I have inclined wherever I could to translate it by "consciousness." His third term is *anima*, which I have nearly always translated by "soul"; but it is important to realize that it is not a specifically human term; it can be used of animals too. On the other hand, again he is not precise in his use of it, and does not confine it to being the subject of the lower sense functions of the outer man, though that would seem to be its proper usage, were you to attempt to use these terms strictly. We can say, then, that *mens* is confined to the upper half of our cooling tower image of the *psyche*, sometimes even to the uppermost section of the upper half; *animus* represents the whole cooling tower, with the emphasis on the upper half; *anima* represents the whole tower, with the emphasis on the lower half. The time has come, perhaps, to offer the reader a visual aid in the form of a diagram.

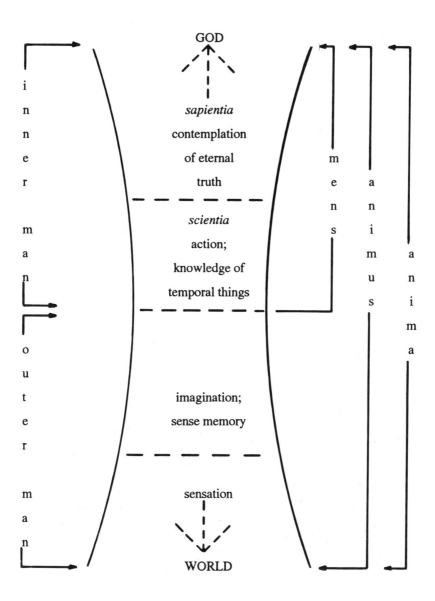

A diagram, however, is a static kind of thing, and the whole virtue of Augustine's structure of the *psyche* is that it is pregnant with dynamic possibilities; it is in constant movement, either in the right or the wrong direction.

This is why in Book XII he casts it into the dramatic form of a paradise story in microcosm. He has certain polemical and exegetical motives too, as the reader will discover, and it also suits his taste for baroque complexity of symbolism and embellishment. But his main purpose, it seems to me, is to introduce the historical dimension into his exploration of the human *psyche* as the image, or rather as the bearer of the image of God. And so, in brief, he identifies the sapiential function of the *mens* with Adam, the sciential or active function with Eve, and the sensuality of the outer man, which is the affective counterpart of the cognitive function of imagination and sense memory, with the serpent. In this way he graphically suggests the defacement of the divine image and the calamitous disorientation or indeed collapse of the human *psyche* caused by sin; sin being, of course, not a mere breach of some regulation or other, but the turning away from God through pride and self-love, through a preference for private possession over common participation—the political and social implications of his doctrine in this respect are really rather revolutionary and subversive. The consequence is a disruption of the divinely appointed order by which man is under the dominion of God and exercises dominion over the world; by rejecting the lordship of God, and seeking to be his own master, he finds himself in effect dominated or fascinated by the material world.

This parable is explicitly worked out in Book XII. Its obverse is suggested in Book XIII. In sin the highest or sapiential function of the human *psyche* falls down from its lofty contemplation of spiritual truth, by consenting to the lower sciential function's lust for material power, into the depths of carnal enslavement. In redemption the right order is restored by a movement in the opposite direction, initiated by the Word made *flesh*. It is only when the sciential function has consented to this divine condescension by *faith,* and begun to control the appetites of the outer man by *virtue,* that the highest sapiential function can begin to be released once more for the loving contemplation of the divine. Augustine does not in fact allegorize or parabolize this redemptive process for the *psyche* in terms of Christ and Mary. Perhaps he felt it would be taking too great a liberty with the historical objectiveness of the gospel narrative. But the possibility of such a counter-allegory is there in Augustine's account of redemption in Book XIII, and I think it may help us to appreciate the dramatic quality of his thought if we supply it. So we can now give a further complexion to our diagram, and with it conclude this sketch of Augustine's psychology.

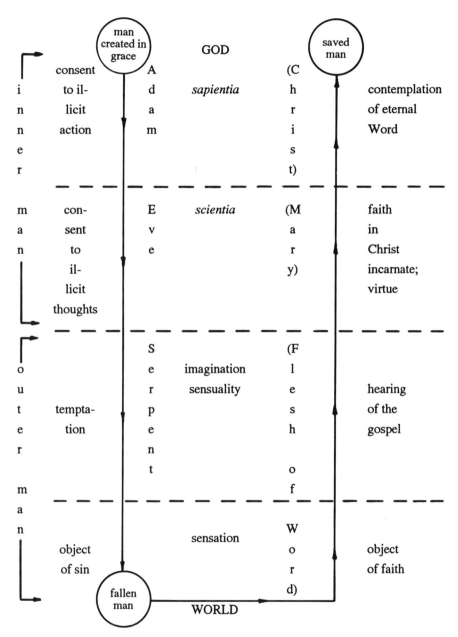

The Complex Structure of Books IX-XIV

It is in terms of this dramatic, historical, or dynamic dimension of Augustine's psychology, and in consequence of his exploration of God's image in man, that these books have the structure outlined in the Introduction. Books IX-XI are not concerned with the history of the image in Everyman; Books XII-XIV certainly are. In consequence the latter three books are much more scriptural than the former three. That is the view of the matter taken in the Introduction, which, as I have said, I have no desire to recant. Another point favoring the view is that the *scientia/sapientia* distinction is first introduced in Book XII and governs the two following books.

But there is no doubt that these books also have another structure, and it depends on the way the reader focuses on them which structure he will see as dominant. In terms of the actual subject matter of the whole work, I must confess that it is the second structure which I am about to sketch that seems to be the more basic. I remarked earlier on that there is no clear *caesura* between Books XI and XII. There is however a fairly definite one, though nothing so decisive as that between Books IV and V, between Books X and XI. In Books IX and X Augustine is constructing, as I remarked in the Introduction,[7] images of the divine trinity in the *mens*. At the end of Book X, but only at the end of it, he has produced his final and finished image of *memoria sui, intelligentia sui* and *voluntas sui*, self-memory, understanding and will. There he breaks off, and in order to elucidate certain obscurities in this mental trinity, he starts in Book XI to examine other psychological trinities, in the outer man and in the lower function of the inner man. This occupies him through to Book XIII. It is only in Book XIV that he returns to the mental trinity he had evolved in Book X, and develops it from a trinity of the remembering, understanding, and willing of self to a trinity of remembering, understanding, and willing God. Thus we still have a pattern of these six books divided into two sets of three, but this time one of the sets is broken. We get the following pattern:

Book IX   first sketch of mental trinity - image;
Book X   second sketch of mental trinity - image;
   Book XI   two "outer man" trinities - not image;
   Book XII   the structure of the inner man;
   Book XIII   trinity of sciential function - not image;
Book XIV   mental trinity of sapiential function - image.

However, we have to realize that there is no break between Books XIII and XIV to correspond to that between Books X and XI. Book XIV flows on very smoothly from Book XIII, tied to it very closely by the continued use of the *scientia/sapientia* distinction. It is more in terms of its content than of its structural elements that we are able to group Book XIV in this pattern with Books IX and X. We have then, in fact, the possibility of discerning a third structural pattern in these six books, which divides them not into two sets of three, but into two uneven sets of two and four. Seen in this way, Books IX and X provide the terms of reference for our exploration of the image, while Books XI to XIV explore the image in the light of these terms, and end in Book XIV by achieving the goal set in Book X. This pattern can either be set out rather flatly as follows:

Book IX
Book X
  Book XI
  Book XII
  Book XIII
  Book XIV;

or less neatly, but more effectively in showing the way the author's thought moves, and illustrating that these books have their own internal, if lopsided, chiastic structure, as follows:

Book IX $\Big)$
Book X

Book XI $\subset$ Book XII $\subset$ Book XIII $\subset$ Book XIV

I suspect the reader may be beginning to feel that all this pattern making is a waste of time. My excuse is that we cannot hope to appreciate what Augustine says unless we have some idea how his mind moves. Its movements are undoubtedly tortuous, but not irrational or inconsequential. And not either, in my opinion, inartistic. If I have succeeded in suggesting some of the intricacy of the figures to which his mind dances, then I do not think my pattern making has been entirely in vain.

Augustine's Doctrine about the Divine Processions

In the dogmatic sense, Augustine's doctrine about the divine processions has already been given; it is the *datum* of orthodoxy which he is investigating through the image in order to be able to understand or see it. Briefly, it is that the Son is eternally begotten by the Father in total equality of nature, or that he proceeds eternally by way of generation as the Word of the Father; and that the Holy Spirit eternally proceeds from the Father and the Son as from one principle or origin. All this is no more, really, than a rigorous conclusion from the revealed data of scripture—that at least would be Augustine's view, and he has a very good case to support it.

What we are now concerned with is seeing how, if at all, he succeeded in understanding this dogmatic faith in the light of the mental image of the divine trinity which he works out in these six books before us. Our task, in fact, will be to translate what he says about memory, understanding, and will, and about the lesser trinities with which he tries to elucidate this major one, into language appropriate to the Father, the Son, and the Holy Spirit.

I think the key term in Augustine's understanding of the trinitarian mystery is the term "Word." It is very probably the use of this name by John for God the Son that prompted Augustine to seek the divine image in man in his key mental activities. As there is a Word of God, so there is a word of man; and it is not just the vocal word uttered in speech. This itself represents a mental word—and not, as Augustine makes quite clear, simply the word in Latin or English or whatever language you think in, the word thought before being uttered. No, behind this word-in-a-language there is the word-beyond-language which is formed in the mind when it sees something to be true. Of course, we do not usually use the English term "word" in this kind of sense, but it is a natural meaning of the Greek *logos*, and Augustine did a little perfectly justifiable violence to the Latin *verbum* to produce his idea of the *verbum mentis* or mental word. It is this mental word then that lies behind and is expressed by any language word that I may speak or even just think to myself without speaking.

Now clearly this mental word, being what my mind forms when it sees something to be true, is intimately connected with understanding, one of the terms in Augustine's mental trinity. But it cannot simply be identified with understanding, in particular not with self-understanding. A man may, and usually does, understand lots of things, but when he is concentrating on one of them it is about that one alone that a mental word is formed in his mind. And when he turns his attention to something else, the first mental word is replaced by another. The way the mental word is formed is by turning the attention (by an act of *cogitatio* or thought) to the object of understanding latent in the *memoria* or memory. When this is done the mental word is produced, in an act of active understanding, as a mentally visible replica or image of the object of understanding latent in the memory. It can thus be regarded as an offspring (*proles*) conceived from the parent (*parens*) memory, but this conception or generation of the mental word from the memory is only done by an act of thought.

Now as regards self-remembering, self-understanding and self-willing, Augustine is insistent that there is never a time when the mind, in virtue of its nature as a center of self-awareness, does not remember, understand, and will itself, but it only produces a mental word of itself when it actually thinks about itself. At other times, he says, when it is not actually thinking about itself, its perpetual self-memory, self-understanding and self-willing belong to memory, which in this case may be defined as sheer self-presence. This self-presence is perpetually actual, but not perpetually active; or you could say it represents the mind's perpetually actual potential, which is only intermittently activated. This actual potential is memory in one sense. Yet it does not cease to be memory when it is activated by an active thought to generate a mental word of active self-understanding; it then becomes active memory, or an act of remembering, recollecting, or calling to mind, which is inseparable and yet distinct from the mental word or active understanding that it generates.

Applying this model now to the divine trinity and the procession of the Son from the Father by way of generation, can we describe the Father, represented by memory, as the eternal actual potential of the godhead? I am tempted to say yes, and to say that this is what Augustine, along of course with the whole tradition, means by calling the Father the *principium*, or origin or source, not only of creatures but of uncreated deity—*principium deitatis*. This helps us to see why it is that the Father only reveals himself, only can reveal himself, through the Word, as Irenaeus long ago understood. It is because the Father only activates this actual potential, and indeed only constitutes himself as Father, by uttering or generating his Word, an act represented in the model by the act of thought, identical with the act of recollection or calling to mind.

We must be careful, though, to change what has to be changed when we apply the model to the divine reality. There is of course no question of merely intermittent activation of the potential; the act is eternal. Furthermore there is no real distinction between potential and activation thereof in God. God is whatever he has, and he is whatever he does; so the potential he has is simply identical with the activation of it he does. But at least this way of talking helps us to understand the real inseparability and equality of the Father and the Son. If memory is only activated into an act of remembering by generating a mental word in an act of understanding, and if it is only through this mental word that we have access to the memory; then it is only by uttering his Word, that is generating his Son, that the Father realizes himself as Father, and it is only through his Word, co-equal to him, that we can have access to the Father. Eternal, active divine self-presence generates eternal active self-expression, and only in that self-expression is the self-presence so to say realized and also made open or available to our participation.

Augustine is less successful, as I think he himself would be inclined to admit, in his attempts to elucidate the procession of the Holy Spirit. His mental model for the third person of the trinity is love, beginning in his first sketch in Book IX with *amor*, correlative to the general word *notitia*, or knowledge in no very specific sense, as the second element in that first trinity of the *mens*. But *amor* is transformed in his second and final mental trinity into *voluntas*, even though his favorite and one might say sublimated names for the Holy Spirit in this regard are *caritas* and *dilectio*. It is hard to say why he put *voluntas* instead of *dilectio* as the third term of his mental trinity. Perhaps to his mind it conveyed much better than the English word "will" the act of willing, better than *dilectio* denotes the act of loving, and it is essential to his purposes that the mental trinity should be a trinity of mental acts. Perhaps also he felt that *caritas* and *dilectio* were too strong for the kind of affective act which he points to in the lesser psychological trinities that he traces.

In any case, the question he is constantly posing himself is why the Holy Spirit, who proceeds from the Father in absolute equality, just as the Son does, is not also called Son. It is an answer to this question that he hopes to find by examining the image of the mental trinity and its lesser declensions. His answer seems to be that it is this third element in these trinities that holds the other two together as parent to offspring, or quasi-parent to quasi-offspring. My mental word, generated as offspring from my mental memory by an act of thought or recollection, is kept in being by continuing to issue from my memory as long as I go on thinking about it, and I go on thinking about it as long as I want to. So it is my act of will that joins my mental word and my memory together, thus ensuring that there is a word of this particular memory, that there is therefore an actual activation of this memory. So in the divine trinity Augustine's favorite way of envisaging the Holy Spirit is as the love which is common to the Father and the Son, their mutual participation in love, their fellowship. That is why, he has already suggested as early as Book V,[8] his proper name consists of two terms that are each common to all three persons, who are all holy and all spirit.

This idea of the Holy Spirit being the bond or communion between the other two persons can be misunderstood. Augustine certainly does not mean that the Holy Spirit constitutes the relationship between Father and Son; that is only constituted by the Father's generation of the Son, and consists simply in the Father/Son relationship. What then does he really mean by this act of conjunction—his usual expression is that *tertia voluntas conjungit utrumque*—will as the third element joins the other two together? In some ways, in the psychological trinities, it merely seems to be a prerequisite of the memory/mental word relationship, which is set up by an act of thought, which is performed and maintained because it is willed. As such it is not a very useful model for the relationship or procession of the Holy Spirit, which is consequent on and not a prerequisite of the procession of the Son.

So, in the mental model, that act of will that *conjungit utrumque* must be taken to be an act of will consequent upon the formation of the mental word. There is no doubt this is how Augustine intends it to be taken, though he does not always make himself as clear about it as he might. It is the act of love consequent upon the act of knowledge, in accordance with his tirelessly repeated maxim that you cannot love what you do not know. It is the act of will, taking pleasure in the idea seen to be true in the mental word formed from memory, that joins the two together; and in this particular trinity this act of taking pleasure is really the third element, although it might well be a previous act of will, forming part of a previous trinity of mental acts, that prompted the mind to turn its attention to this particular object or idea, and so activated this particular trinity.

With the divine trinity, however, we do not face any possibility of successive trinities of mental acts—there is only one eternal trinity constituted by the two eternal processions. And so we can perhaps, in terms of our mental model, which has to be handled with great delicacy, describe the procession of the Holy Spirit as the eternal act of divine self-loving or self-willing—issuing eternally from the divine self-presence eternally activated in self-expression, and by so issuing or proceeding, "joining the two together" and being their communion, their fellowship, their gift.

It must be emphasized that Augustine's whole understanding of the procession of the Holy Spirit, and his explanations for why the Holy Spirit is not also said to be born and to be a Son, depend on his theological conviction that the Holy Spirit proceeds from the Father and the Son together. His understanding and his explanations of the matter may indeed be hesitant and confused; but his clear statement of what is called the double procession of the Holy Spirit seems to me to be one his most valuable contributions to trinitarian theology. If we do not say that the Holy Spirit proceeds both from the Father and from the Son (as from one principle, or origin, of course, a qualification Augustine is most careful to make), but only from the Father, then there really is no way to distinguish his procession from that of the Son, no way therefore to distinguish the Holy Spirit from the Son. In that case we either reduce the trinity to a duality and sacrifice orthodoxy to reason; or we maintain an orthodox trinity by a sheer act of faith which we have rendered intrinsically impervious to reason thanks to the theological stance adopted. This would mean sacrificing reason, and hence theology, to orthodoxy and faith, and this would mean depriving orthodoxy and faith of any significance or human relevance. And this would mean to stop being Augustine.

NOTES

1. See Introduction 21-23.

2. *Ibid.*, 104.

3. *Ibid.*, 104-109.

4. Aristotle, *De Anima*, 2. 11 (414a12): Aquinas, *Summa Theologiae*, la. q. 76, a.l.

5. For example in the *Tusculan Disputations* 1, 10, 22; 1, 17, 41.

6. For a full treatment of Augustine's so-called illuminationism see E. Gilson, *The Christian Philosophy of St Augustine* (New York, 1960); A. Gardeil, *La structure de l'âme et l'expérience mystique* (Paris, 1927); also A. Gardeil, "Le 'mens' d'apres S. Augustin et S. Thoma d'Aquin," *Revue des sciences philosphiques et théologiques* 13 (1924).

7. See Introduction 22-23.

8. See Book V, 12.

BOOK IX

PSYCHOLOGICAL: MENTAL IMAGE, FIRST DRAFT

Prologue

---

1. A trinity is certainly what we are looking for, and not any kind of trinity either but the one that God is, the true and supreme and only God. Wait for it then, whoever you are that are listening to this; we are still looking, and no one can fairly find fault with someone who is looking for such things as this, provided that in looking for something so difficult either to know or to express, he remains absolutely firm in faith. When a man actually affirms something, though, well then anyone who sees or teaches better can promptly and with justice find fault with him. *Look for God,*[1] it says, *and your souls shall live*; and in case anyone should be too quick to congratulate himself that he has got there, *look for his face*, it goes on, *always* (Ps 105:4). And the apostle says, *If anybody thinks he knows anything, he does not yet know as he ought to know. But anyone who loves God, this man is known by him* (1 Cor 8:2). Even in this case, you notice, he did not say "knows him," which would be a dangerous piece of presumption, but "is known by him." It is like another place where as soon as he had said *But now knowing God,* he corrected himself and said, *or rather being known by God* (Gal 4:9). Above all there is this text: *Brothers*, he says, *I do not consider that I myself have got there; one thing, though, forgetting what lies behind, stretching out to what lies ahead I press on intently*[2] *to the palm of our upward calling from God in Christ Jesus. As many of us therefore as are perfect, let us set our minds on this* (Phil 3:13). Perfection in this life, he is saying, is nothing but forgetting what lies behind and stretching out to what lies ahead intently. The safest intent, after all, until we finally get where we are intent on getting and where we are stretching out to, is that of the seeker. And the right intent is the one that sets out from faith. The certitude of faith at least initiates knowledge; but the certitude of knowledge will not be completed until after this life when we see *face to face* (1 Cor 13:12). Let this then be what we set our

minds on, to know that a disposition to look for the truth is safer than one to presuppose that we know what is in fact unknown. Let us therefore so look as men who are going to find, and so find as men who are going to go on looking. For *when a man has finished, then it is that he is beginning* (Sir 18:7).

About what is to be believed let us not have any faithless doubts, about what is to be understood let us not make any hasty affirmations; in the case of the former we must hold fast to authority, in the case of the latter we must search out the truth. As far then as this question of ours is concerned, let us believe that Father and Son and Holy Spirit are one God, maker and ruler of all creation; and that the Father is not the Son, and the Holy Spirit is neither the Father nor the Son, but that they are a trinity of persons related to each other, and a unity of equal being. But let us seek to understand this, begging the help of him whom we wish to understand; and as far as is granted us[3] let us seek to explain what we understand with such a solicitous care for piety,[4] that even if we say something about one which really belongs to another, at least we say nothing unworthy. For example, if we say something about the Father which does not properly belong to the Father, let it belong at least to the Son or the Holy Spirit or the trinity itself; and if we say something about the Son which does not fit the Son, let it at least fit the Father or the Holy Spirit or the trinity; finally if we say something about the Holy Spirit which does not really express[5] what is proper to the Holy Spirit, let it not at any rate be alien to the Father or the Son or the one God the trinity itself. For instance, we are now eager to see whether this transcendent charity is peculiarly the Holy Spirit. If it is not, then at least either the Father is charity, or the Son or the trinity itself is, since we cannot withstand the certitude of faith and the great weight of scriptural authority which says *God is charity* (1 Jn 4:8.16). What we have to avoid is the sacrilegious mistake of saying anything about the trinity which does not belong to the creator but rather to the creature, or which is fabricated by vain imaginings.

Chapter 1

Starting from the trinity, triad or trio with which he concluded Book VIII, namely lover, what is loved, and love; and confining himself to mens *or mind as its subject, Augustine expands this trinity into the apter one of mind, its knowledge and its love of self,* mens, notitia sui, amor sui; *and he establishes that these three are one substance, consubstantial, coequal, coinherent, and yet also distinct, unconfused, and mutually related.*

2. This being agreed, let us take another look at that trio which we seem to have found. We are not yet speaking of things above, of God the Father and the Son and the Holy Spirit, but about this disparate image, yet image nonetheless, which is man; it is likely to be easier, after all, and more familiar for our mind in its weakness to examine.

Here you are then—when I who am engaged on this search love something, there are three: I myself, what I love, and love itself. For I do not love love unless I love it loving something, because there is no love where nothing is being loved.[6] So then there are three, the lover, and what is being loved, and love. But supposing I only love myself, are there now not two merely, what I love and love? Lover and what is being loved are the same thing when he loves himself, just as loving and being loved are likewise the same thing when someone loves himself. You are only saying the same thing twice when you say "he loves himself" and "he is loved by himself." In this case loving and being loved are no more different things than lover and beloved are different people. Love, however, and what is being loved are still two things. For it is not the case that anyone who loves himself is love except when love loves itself.[7] It is one thing to love oneself and another to love one's love. For love is not loved unless it is already loving something, because where nothing is being loved there is no love. So there are two things when someone loves himself, namely love and what is being loved; for in this case lover and what is being loved are one thing. It seems then after all that there are not necessarily three things to be perceived wherever there is love.

Now let us remove from our consideration of this matter all the many other things of which man consists, and to find what we are looking for with as much clarity as is possible in these matters, let us only discuss the mind.[8] So when the mind loves itself it reveals two things, mind and love. But what does loving itself mean but wanting to be available to itself in order to enjoy itself? And since it wants itself as much as it is, will exactly matches mind here, and love is equal to lover. And if love is a kind of substance,[9] it is certainly not body but spirit, just as mind too is not body but spirit. Love and mind, however, are not two spirits but one spirit, not two beings but one being; and yet they are two somethings, lover and love, or if you like beloved and loved. And these are called two things relatively to one another. Lover has reference to love, and love to lover; for lover loves with some love, and love is of some lover. Mind and spirit, however, are not said relatively but state being. It is not because it is mind and spirit of some man that it is mind and spirit. Take away its being man, which is said with the addition of body, take away body therefore, and mind and spirit remain. But take away lover and there is no love; take away love and there is no lover. So then, insofar as they are referred to each other they are two; but insofar as they are stated with reference to self they are each spirit and they are both together one spirit, they are each mind and both together one mind. Where then is a trinity? Let us look into the matter as closely as we can, and call upon the everlasting light to enlighten our darkness (Ps 18:28), and let us see in ourselves as far as we are permitted the image of God.

3. Now the mind cannot love itself unless it also knows itself. How can it love what it does not know? Or if anyone says that in terms of general and specific notions the mind believes itself to be such as it has experienced others to be and so loves itself, he is talking very great nonsense. How can the mind know another mind if it does not know itself? You cannot say the mind knows

other minds and is ignorant of itself in the same sort of way as the bodily eye sees other eyes and does not see itself. We see bodies with our bodily eyes because the rays which shoot out from them touch whatever we observe;[10] but we cannot snap off these rays and bend them back into our own eyes except when we look in a mirror. This question is discussed with great subtlety, and will continue to be so until it is clearly demonstrated that sight works like that or does not work like that. But whatever kind of power it is by which we see with our eyes, we certainly cannot see this power with our eyes, whether it is rays or anything else. What we look for it with is our minds, and if it can be done we grasp even this matter with our minds. So the mind itself assembles notions both of bodily things through the senses of the body, and of non-bodily things through itself. Therefore it knows itself, because it is non-bodily. Anyhow, if it does not know itself, it does not love itself.[11]

4. Just as you have two somethings, mind and its love, when it loves itself, so you have two somethings, mind and its knowledge,[12] when it knows itself. The mind therefore and its love and knowledge are three somethings, and these three are one thing, and when they are complete they are equal. If the mind loves itself less than it is—for example if the mind of a man loves itself only as much as a man's body should be loved though it is itself something more than body—then it sins and its love is not complete. Again if it loves itself more than it is, for example if it loves itself as much as God is to be loved, though it is itself incomparably less than God, here too it sins by excess, and does not have a complete love of itself. It sins of course with even greater perversity and wickedness when it loves the body as much as God is to be loved.

Again, if knowledge is less than what is known and can be fully known, then it is not complete. If it is greater, that means that the nature which knows is greater than the nature which is known, as for example knowledge of a body is greater than the body which is known with that knowledge. For this knowledge is a kind of life in the reason of the knower, but body is not life. And any life is greater than any body not in mass but in force. But when mind knows itself it does not excel itself with its knowledge, since it is knowing and it is being known. So when it knows its whole self and nothing else together with itself, its knowledge exactly matches itself because its knowledge does not belong to another nature when it knows itself. And when it perceives its whole self and nothing else, it is neither less nor greater. So we have been right in saying that when these three are complete they are consequently equal.

5. At the same time we remind ourselves, if we are at all able to see it, that these things come to light in the soul—where they are, so to say, all rolled up and have to be unrolled in order to be perceived and enumerated—substantially or being-wise, if I may so put it, and not as in a subject, like color or shape in a body, or any other quality or quantity. Whatever is of this nature does not go beyond the subject in which it is; this color, or the shape of this body, cannot belong to another body too. But mind can also love something besides itself with the love it loves itself with. Again mind does not only know itself but many other things as well. Therefore love and knowledge are not in the mind as in a

subject, but they too are substantially, just as mind itself is; and even if they are posited relatively to each other, still each of them is its own substance. It is not like color and the colored thing being posited relatively to each other in such a way that color is in the colored subject without having any proper substance in itself, since the colored body is the substance while color itself is in substance. But it is more like two friends also being two men which are substance things, since they are not called men relatively to each other but they are called friends relatively to each other.[13]

6. The comparison holds further; lover or knower is substance, knowledge is substance and love is substance; yet lover and love, knower and knowledge are said with reference to each other, like friends. Mind and spirit, however, are not terms of reference, just as men are not terms of reference. Lover and love, though, or knower and knowledge, cannot be separated from each other as can two men who are friends. Yet even of friends you could say that they may seem to be separated in body, but they cannot be so in spirit insofar as they are friends. Still it can happen that friend begins to hate friend and thereby ceases to be friend, while the other does not know this and still loves him. But if the love which mind loves itself with ceases to be, then mind thereby ceases to be lover. Again if the knowledge mind knows itself with ceases to be, mind thereby ceases to know itself. Perhaps it is comparable to a head, which is of course the head of something headed. They are so called with reference to each other, though they are also both substances, since head is a body and so is the headed thing. And if there is no head,[14] neither will there be a headed thing. But these can be separated from each other by beheading, while in our case the pair cannot.

7. There may of course be some bodies that are quite impossible to cut up or divide;[15] but even so, if they did not consist of their parts they would not be bodies. So even in these the part is so called with reference to the whole, because every part is part of some whole and a whole is whole with all its parts. But as both part and whole are body, these are not only posited relatively to each other, they also are substantially. So perhaps the mind is a whole, and the love it loves itself with and the knowledge it knows itself with are quasi-parts of it, two parts of which the whole consists? Or are they three equal parts which make up one whole? But no part encompasses the whole it is a part of. When mind however knows its whole self, that is knows itself completely, its knowledge pervades the whole of it; and when it loves itself completely it loves its whole self and its love pervades the whole of it. Are we then to think of these three together, mind, love, knowledge, as being like one drink made out of wine and water and honey, in which each pervades the whole and yet they are three? After all, there is no part of the drink which does not have these three in it; they are not joined together as if they were water and oil but completely mixed up together, and they are all substances, and that liquid is some one substance made out of three. However, water, wine, and honey are not of one substance, even though one substance of a drink is made out of mixing them. As for our trio, though, I cannot see how they are not of the same being,[16] since mind is itself loving itself and itself knowing itself, and these three are such by our definition that mind is not being

loved or known by any other thing. So these three must be of one and the same being. And if they were confused together in a mixture they would no longer in any way be three, or be able to be referred to each other. This for the same reason as if you were to make three similar rings out of one and the same gold and link them together, they would be referred to each other as similar, since every similar is similar to something; and you would have a trinity of rings and one gold. But if they are mixed up together and each dispersed through the whole lump, then that trinity will collapse and simply cease to be; it will still be called one gold as it was called in those three rings, but now no longer three gold things as well.

8. But with these three, when mind knows and loves itself the trinity remains of mind, love, knowledge. Nor are they jumbled up together in any kind of mixture, though they are each one in itself and each whole in their total, whether each in the other two or the other two in each, in any case all in all. Thus mind is of course in itself, since it is called mind with reference to itself, though it is called knowing or known or knowable relative to its knowledge; also as loving and loved or lovable it is referred to the love it loves itself with. And while knowledge is referred to the mind knowing or known, it is also called knowing and known with reference to itself; the knowledge the mind knows itself with cannot be unknown to itself. And while love is referred to the mind loving, whose love it is, nonetheless it is also love with reference to itself, so that it is also in itself, because love too is loved, nor can it be loved with anything but love, that is with itself. Thus each of them is in itself.

But they are in each other too, because the mind loving is in love, and love is in the knowledge of the lover, and knowledge is in the mind knowing. They are each in the other two, because the mind which knows and loves itself is in its love and knowledge, and the love of the mind loving and knowing itself is in the mind and its knowledge, and the knowledge of the mind knowing and loving itself is in the mind and its love, because it loves itself knowing and knows itself loving. And hence also each pair is in the other single, because the mind which knows and loves itself is in love together with its knowledge and in knowledge together with its love; and love and knowledge are together in the mind which loves and knows itself. How they are all in all[17] of them we have already shown above; it is when the mind loves all itself and knows all itself and knows all its love and loves all its knowledge, when these three are complete with reference to themselves. In a wonderful way therefore these three are inseparable from each other, and yet each one of them is substance, and all together they are one substance or being, while they are also posited with reference to one another.[18]

Chapter 2

The author further investigates the knowledge which the mind has of things, and concludes that it essentially consists in a judgment of truth or of value about things, which can properly be called a mental word, or verbum mentis, *which is a mental image of the thing known in the light of eternal truth. This word is provisionally defined as* amata notitia, *loved knowledge.*

9. But when the human mind knows itself and loves itself, it does not know and love something unchangeable. And a man is acting in one way when he looks at what is going on in himself and speaks to declare his mind; but in quite another when he defines the human mind in terms of specific or generic knowledge. So when he speaks to me about his own particular mind, saying whether he understands this or that or does not understand it, and whether he wishes or does not wish this or that, I believe it. When however he says something true, specifically or generically, about the human mind, I acknowledge and agree with it. Clearly then what anybody can see in himself, which someone else he tells it to can believe but not see, is one thing; what he sees in truth itself, which someone else can also gaze upon, is another. And one of these changes with time, while the other stands fast in unchangeable eternity. Nor do we assemble a specific or generic knowledge of the human mind by seeing many minds with our bodily eyes, but we gaze upon the inviolable truth from which we define as perfectly as we can, not what kind of thing any particular man's mind is, but what kind of thing by everlasting ideas it ought to be.[19]

10. So too we absorb the images of bodily things through the senses of the body and transfer them somehow to the memory, and from them we fabricate images with which to think about things we have not seen, whether differently from what they actually are or by a chance in a million as they are; but whenever we correctly approve or disapprove of something represented by such images, we have the inescapable conviction that we make our judgment of approval or disapproval within ourselves by altogether different rules which abide unchangeably above our minds. Thus when I call to mind the ramparts of Carthage which I have seen, and also form a picture of those of Alexandria which I have not seen, and prefer some of these forms in my imagination to others, I make a rational preference. The judgment of truth is shining vigorously from above, and it is firmly supported by the wholly unbiased rules of its own proper law, and even if it is somewhat veiled by a kind of cloud of bodily images, still it is not entangled and confused by them.

11. But it does of course make some difference whether I am as it were shut off from the transparent sky under or in that fog, or whether as happens on high mountains I can enjoy the free atmosphere between the two, and look upon the fair light above and the swirling mists below. From where, after all, is the fire of brotherly love kindled in me when I hear about some man who has endured severe tortures in the fine constancy of his faith? And if this man is pointed out to me, I am dead set at once on getting in touch with him, on getting to know

him, on binding him to myself in friendship. So when I get the chance I approach him, speak to him, engage him in conversation, express my regard for him with whatever words I can, and in turn I hope he will develop and express a regard for me; and I try to achieve spiritual rapport with him by believing his inner disposition, because I am quite unable in so short a time to judge it on the basis of thorough observation. And so I love a faithful and brave man with a chaste and brotherly love. But now suppose that in our mutual conversation he confesses or carelessly betrays himself in some fashion as having unworthy beliefs about God and looking for some material benefit from him, and as having suffered what he did for some such mistaken notion, whether in the greedy hope of financial gain or the vain pursuit of human praise; immediately that love which carried me out to him is brought up short and as it were repulsed and withdrawn from an unworthy man; but it remains fixed on that form by which I loved him while I believed him to be like it. Except of course that I might still love him hoping that he may become like it, though I have discovered him not to be like it. Yet in the man himself nothing has changed; though it could change so that he became what I believed he already was. In my mind however there is a change from the estimation which I had of him to the one I now have of him; and at the bidding from above of unchanging justice the same love of mine is deflected from the intention of enjoying him to the intention of counseling him. But the form itself of unshaken and abiding truth, in which I would enjoy the man while I believed him to be good and in which I now counsel him to be good, continues unruffled as eternity to shed the same light of the purest incorruptible reason both on the vision of my mind and on that cloud of imagination which I perceive from above when I think of this man I had seen.

Or take another example; I turn over in my mind an arch[20] I have seen in Carthage embellished with a beautifully intricate pattern; here a particular thing, brought to the mind's notice through the eyes and transferred to the memory, produces an observation in the imagination. But with the mind I observe something else, in terms of which I take pleasure in this work of art, in terms of which I would put it right if it displeased me. Thus it is that we make judgments about these things according to that form of truth, and we perceive that by insight of the rational mind. These things however we touch with our bodily sense when they are present, or recall their images fixed in the memory when they are absent, or else we fabricate composite images, from elements similar to these, of what we would try to put into effect in a work of our own if we had the will or the ability. But our shaping the images of bodies in our consciousness[21] or our seeing bodies through the body is one thing; quite another is our grasping by simple intelligence the proportions,[22] the inexpressibly beautiful art of such shapes, existing above the apex of the mind.

12. Thus it is that in that eternal truth according to which all temporal things were made we observe with the eye of the mind the form according to which we are and according to which we do anything with true and right reason, either in ourselves or in bodies.[23] And by this form we conceive true knowledge of things, which we have with us as a kind of word that we beget by uttering inwardly, and

that does not depart from us when it is born. When we speak to others we put our voice or some bodily gesture at the disposal of the word that abides within, in order that by a kind of perceptible reminder the same sort of thing might happen in the mind of the listener as exists in and does not depart from the mind of the speaker. And so there is nothing that we do with our bodies in deeds or words to express approval or disapproval of the behavior of men, which we have not anticipated with a word uttered inside ourselves. Nobody voluntarily does anything that he has not previously uttered as a word in his heart.

13. This word is conceived in love of either the creature or the creator, that is of changeable nature or unchangeable truth; which means either in covetousness or in charity. Not that the creature is not to be loved, but if that love is related to the creator it will no longer be covetousness but charity. It is only covetousness when the creature is loved on its own account. In this case it does not help you in your use of it, but corrupts you in your enjoyment of it.[24] Now a creature can either be on a par with us or lower than us; the lower creature should be used to bring us to God, the creature on a par should be enjoyed, but in God. Just as you ought to enjoy yourself not in yourself but in him who made you, so too with the one whom you love as yourself. Let us then enjoy both ourselves and our brothers in the Lord, and from that level let us not dare to lower ourselves down even to our own, and so slacken off in a downward direction.

Now this word[25] is born when on thinking over it we like it either for sinning or for doing good. So love, like something in the middle, joins together our word and the mind it is begotten from, and binds itself in with them as a third element in a non-bodily embrace, without any confusion.

14. But the conceived word and the born word are the same thing when the will rests in the act itself of knowing, which happens in the love of spiritual things. For example, someone who perfectly loves justice is thereby already just even if no occasion exists for him to do justice externally in bodily activity. But in the love of temporal and material things the conception of a word is one thing and its birth another, as it is with the breeding of animals. In this case the word is conceived by wanting and born by getting, as it is not enough for greed to know and love money unless it also has it, or to know and love eating or copulating unless it also does them, or to know and love honors and political power unless they are also forthcoming. Yet as a matter of fact none of these things satisfies even when you get it; Whoever drinks of this water, it says, *will be thirsty again* (Jn 4:13); and thus it says in the psalms, *He conceived pain and brough forth iniquity* (Ps 7:14). Pain or labor is said to be conceived when things are conceived that it is unsatisfying simply to know and want, and so the soul is in a burning fever of need until it gets hold of them and so to say brings them forth;* *for when lust conceives it brings forth sin* (Jas 1:15). So the Lord cries

---

* So in Latin you can say rather elegantly that things which are *reperta* or *comperta*, words that sound as if they came from *partus*, are *parta*; or in English you could say that things which have been brought out or brought to light, in the sense of found out, have been brought forth.

out, *Come to me, all you that labor and are heavy burdened* (Mt 11:28);[26] and in another place, *Woe to those that are with child and giving suck in those days* (Mt 24:19). And thus when he would refer all good deeds or sins to this bringing forth of a word, he said *Out of your mouth you will be justified and out of your mouth you will be condemned* (Mt 12:37); by "mouth" he wished to signify not this visible one but the inner invisible one of the thoughts and the heart.

15. It is right then to ask whether all knowledge is a word, or only loved knowledge. We also know what we hate, but we can scarcely talk of things we dislike being either conceived or brought forth by the consciousness. Not everything that touches our mind in any way is conceived, so it may only be known without being called the kind of word we are now talking about.[27] In one sense we give the name of word to whatever occupies a space of time with its syllables, whether it is spoken aloud or merely thought; in another, everything that is known is called a word impressed on the consciousness, as long as it can be produced from the memory and described, even when we dislike it; but in the sense we are now using, that is called a word which we like when it is conceived by the mind.[28] It is in terms of this kind of word that we must take what the apostle says, *Nobody says "Jesus is Lord" except in the Holy Spirit* (1 Cor 12:3), though in terms of the other notion of word those people also say this of whom the Lord himself says, *Not everyone who says to me "Lord" will enter the kingdom of heaven* (Mt 7:21).

And yet even when we rightly dislike things we hate, and disapprove of them, we like and approve of our disapproval of them, and this is a word. Nor as a matter of fact is it the knowledge of vices that we dislike, but the vices themselves. It pleases me that I can know and define what immoderation is, and this is its word. In any art or craft the relevant faults are known, and knowledge of them is rightly applauded when the connoisseur distinguishes the quality[29] of some relevant excellence from the defect of it, on the analogy of affirming and denying, being and not being;[30] and yet for the practitioner to lack this excellence and lapse into this defect is a black mark against him. Now to define immoderation and utter its word belongs to the art of morals; but to be immoderate belongs to what that art condemns. Likewise to know and define what a solecism is belongs to the art of grammar; but to commit one is something that the same art reprehends. The kind of word then that we are now wishing to distinguish and propose is "knowledge with love." So when the mind knows and loves itself, its word is joined to it with love. And since it loves knowledge and knows love, the word is in the love and the love in the word and both in the lover and the utterer.

16. But all positive knowledge of quality[31] is like the thing which it knows. There is another knowledge of defect which we express when we find fault, and this finding fault with defect commends the corresponding quality, and is therefore approved of. So the consciousness has some kind of likeness to the positive quality known, either when it takes pleasure in it or when it is displeased with the lack of it. It follows that insofar as we know God we are like him, but never like him to the point of equality, since we never know him as much as he himself

is. When we learn about bodies through our bodily senses a kind of likeness of them occurs in our consciousness which is their image in the memory. The bodies themselves of course are certainly not in our consciousness when we think of them but their likenesses, and so when we make a judgment[32] on these instead of on those we make a mistake; that is what a mistake is, judging one thing for another. Yet for all that the image of the body in our consciousness is better than the reality of the body itself insofar as it is in a better nature, that is, in a living substance such as the consciousness. By the same token when we know God we are indeed made better ourselves than we were before we knew him, especially when we like this knowledge and appropriately love it and it becomes a word and a kind of likeness to God; yet it remains inferior to God because it is an inferior nature, our consciousness being a creature, but God the creator.

From this we can gather that when the mind knows and approves itself, this knowledge is its word in such a way that it matches it exactly and is equal to it and identical,[33] since it is neither knowledge of an inferior thing like body nor of a superior one like God. And while any knowledge has a likeness to the thing it knows, that is to the thing it is the knowledge of, this knowledge by which the knowing mind is known has a perfect and equal likeness. And the reason it is both image and word, is that it is expressed[34] from the mind when it is made equal to it by knowing it; and what is begotten is equal to the begetter.

Chapter 3

The author looks for a reason why love should not be called word, or image, nor said to be begotten or conceived, like knowledge; this being a question that exercises him greatly with respect to the Holy Spirit. The reader must decide for himself what he makes of the suggested answer.

---

17. What then about love? Will love not be image, nor word, nor begotten? Why does the mind beget its knowledge when it knows itself, and not beget its love when it loves itself? If the reason it is the cause of its notion of itself is that it is knowable, then equally it is the cause of its love of itself because it is lovable. So why it should not have begotten both it is difficult to say. The same question often bothers people about the supreme trinity, God the almighty creator *to whose image man was made* (Gn 9:6); the truth of God invites them by human speech to faith,[35] and they wonder why the Holy Spirit too may not be believed or understood to be begotten by the Father and so be called Son in his turn.

What we are now trying to do is to examine this question in the human mind; here our own nature can, so to say, answer our questions more familiarly; and so after practicing the mind's gaze on the lower image we may be able to shift it from the illuminated creature to the unchangeable illuminating light. This presupposes that truth itself has convinced us the Holy Spirit is charity, just as no Christian doubts that the Son is the Word of God. Let us return then to the created image, that is to say to the rational mind, and examine and question it more thoroughly about this matter. Here there exists in the time dimension a knowledge of some things that was not there before, and a love of some things that were not loved before. So this examination will reveal to us more distinctly what we are to say, since it is easier for speech which has to proceed in a time dimension to explain something which is comprehended in the time dimension.

18. First of all then let it be accepted that it can happen that something is knowable, that is can be known, and yet is not known. What cannot happen is that something is known that was not knowable. Evidently then we must hold that every single thing whatsoever that we know co-generates in us knowledge of itself; for knowledge issues from both, from the knower and the thing known. So when mind knows itself it is the sole parent of its knowledge, being itself the thing known and the knower. It was however knowable to itself even before it knew itself, but its knowledge of self was not in it while it did not know itself. Therefore as it gets to know itself it begets a knowledge of itself that totally matches itself, since it does not know itself less than it is, nor is its knowledge different in being from itself, not only because it is doing the knowing but also because what it is knowing is itself, as we have said before.

What then is to be said about love, to show why even when the mind loves itself it cannot also be regarded as having begotten its love of itself? It was of course lovable to itself even before it loved itself, since it was able to love itself; just as it was knowable to itself even before it knew itself, since it was able to know itself. After all, if it had not been knowable to itself it could never have got to know itself; so too if it had not been lovable to itself it could never have loved itself. So why may it not be said to have begotten its love by loving itself, just as it begot its knowledge by knowing itself? Perhaps all that this clearly shows is that this is the origin of love from which it proceeds. For obviously it proceeds from the mind which is lovable to itself before it loves itself, and thus is the origin of the love of self with which it loves itself.

But the reason it is not right to say that love is begotten by it like the knowledge of itself by which it knows itself, is that knowledge is a kind of finding out what is said to be brought forth or brought to light,[36] which is often preceded by an inquisitiveness[37] that is going to rest in that end. Inquisitiveness is an appetite for finding out, which amounts to the same thing as "bringing to light." But things that are brought to light are so to speak brought forth, which makes them similar to offspring. And where does all this happen but in knowledge? It is there that they are as it were squeezed out[38] and formed. Even if the things we have found out by inquiry already existed, still knowledge of them did not yet exist, and it is this that we reckon as the offspring coming to birth. Now this appetite shown in inquiring proceeds from the inquirer, and it is left somewhat hanging in the air and does not rest assuaged in the end it is stretching out to, until what is being looked for has been found and is coupled with the inquirer. This appetite, that is inquisitiveness, does not indeed appear to be the love with which what is known is loved (this is still busy getting known), yet it is something of the same kind. It can already be called will because everyone who inquires wants to find out, and if what is being inquired about belongs to knowledge,[39] then everyone who inquires wants to know. If he urgently and passionately wants to know he is said to be studious, a term which is commonly used about the pursuit and acquisition of various kinds of learning. So parturition by the mind is preceded by a kind of appetite which prompts us to inquire and find out about what we want to know, and as a result knowledge itself is brought forth as offspring; and hence the appetite itself by which knowledge is conceived and brought forth cannot appropriately itself be called brood or offspring. The same appetite with which one longs open-mouthed to know a thing becomes love of the thing known when it holds and embraces the acceptable offspring, that is knowledge, and joins it to its begetter. And so you have a certain image of the trinity, the mind itself and its knowledge, which is its offspring and its word about itself, and love as the third element, *and these three are one* (1 Jn 5:8)[40] and are one substance. Nor is the offspring less than the mind so long as the mind knows itself as much as it is, nor is love any less so long as it loves itself as much as it knows and as much as it is.

NOTES

1. Reading *deum*, with M and all the manuscripts but one. CCL reads *dominum*, the Lord, with that odd manuscript. It is hard to see why, since *dominum* is a Vulgate reading, and easier for a scribe inadvertently to correct to than from. Augustine is quoting from memory.

2. See Book I, 8, note 22.

3. *Tribuitur*: M reads *tribuit*, as far as he grants us.

4. M adds *cupientes*, which alters the whole run of the sentence after the semi-colon, making it a second participial clause, running "and desiring as far as he grants us to explain what we understand etc."

5. *Doceat*: M reads *deceat*, befit, following what is perhaps a correct, and certainly a shrewd, emendation by one copyist.

6. I think the point of this remark is to exclude the possibility of a mere duet, one that would not help him in his argument, namely, me loving love, and love being loved by me. He made the point before, Book VIII, 12. The duet he wishes to concentrate on is the one we are reduced to in the case of me loving myself.

7. *Cum amatur ipse amor*. This seems to me a clear case where the Latin passive must be interpreted as a reflexive, like the Greek middle.

8. *Mens*. See page 253.

9. Augustine's use of Aristotle's ten categories in Book V makes it clear that he does not really think love is a substance, and knows perfectly well that in our normal use of the word we mean by it an act, a quality, or a relationship. At the same time, as we discovered in Book VIII, being accustomed to a neoplatonist manner of speaking, he feels less incongruity in substantifying love than we do, and as a Christian neoplatonist, with John for his authority, he is quite sure that God is love substantively. So this is a first step in tailoring the image trinity of the mind to suit the divine trinity which it reflects. But in Book XV he is going to come clean and admit that this is precisely one of the ways in which the image falls short of its prototype, that the trio of mental acts which he

is going to evolve are not really substantial, and so do not constitute three persons or hypostases in one being or substance, but only three accidental attributes in one person or hypostasis. However, for the sake of his argument we must allow him to treat them *as if* they were substantive (see Book XV, 42).

10. A theory of vision propounded by Plato, *Timaeus* 45b-d; disputed by Aristotle, *De Sensu* 431b. Augustine clearly has no intention of being dogmatic about it.

11. The whole paragraph is, it must be said, a rather slack piece of argument. But it is as though the point he is making is too obvious to need argument, and however the mind comes to know itself, it must do so before it can love itself.

12. *Notitia*; Augustine's most general and untechnical word for knowledge. It is a pity one cannot find distinct English words for his *notitia, cognitio, and scientia*. But English makes its distinctions, for example, between "knowledge," "cognition," "notion," "science" on quite a different plane.

13. Another paragraph of slack and confused argument. For my attempt at pious interpretation of his substantifying of love and knowledge, see above, section 2, note 9. Here the whole concern is clearly to tailor the image to the substance/relationship language established in Books V-VII. For a more thorough use of the "color" and "friends" comparison, see Book VII, 2 and 10.

14. Reading *caput* with M, and one manuscript. CCL with the weight of the manuscripts behind it reads *corpus*, which involves recasting the whole pair of sentences to run, "They are so called with reference to each other, though they are also both substances, since head is a body and so is the headed thing, and if it is not a body, neither will it be a headed thing." And neither, one might add, will there be any point to the whole laborious comparison, which will be decapitated as neatly as the headed thing in the next sentence. The mistake arises, I suspect, from the faulty punctuation of most manuscripts. Augustine's last sentence here, as so often, is the conclusion to the main clause of his first sentence. But it is separated from it by a considerable concessive parenthesis; and with this parenthesis still in his mind a scribe could almost without thinking substitute *corpus* for *caput*.

15. The "atoms" or "indivisibles" postulated by the early Greek physicist Democritus, for whom Aristotle had a great admiration, as the basic stuff of all things.

16. *Essentiae*; M reads *substantiae*.

17. *Tota* in *totis*; this use of *totus*, whole, in the plural is not classical, and indeed poses a certain problem for the translator. It can only, of course, be translated "all," and yet it carries a nuance that *omnes* lacks; it eliminates, so to say, any idea of discreteness between the individuals lumped together as "all." I cannot help feeling, in fact, that it is an Augustinism which the author feels peculiarly apt for use when talking about the trinity. It reoccurs in the Athanasian creed, a thoroughly Augustinian document, in the phrase *totae tres personae*. See above Book VIII, 1, note 1.

18. Augustine has here been descrying in the image what is known in the archetypal trinity as the circumincession of the three divine persons, their mutual coinherence.

19. The twist given to the whole argument by the last sentence is disconcerting at first, but should not really surprise us, so utterly characteristic is it of Augustine's mind. It shows that he is not thinking of ontological judgments or definitions but moral ones. In the next paragraph he introduces aesthetic ones, and then in the following two paragraphs gives illustrations of each. For him the platonic idea seen in the eternal truth consists much more of an ideal of behavior or action, than of a definition of nature.

20. *Arcum*. It could also mean a bow, and his describing it as *pulcre . . . intortum* tempted me so to translate it—some civic heirloom in a Carthage museum perhaps? But as his previous reference to the city was architectural, I think arch is the more likely meaning.

21. *Animo*; here rather contrasted with *mens*.

22. *Rationes*; "ratios" would almost do as a translation here. Augustine's classical view of art hardly allows for cultural variations of its canons.

23. That is, either morally or aesthetically.

24. In his *Teaching Christianity* Augustine introduces and elaborates his distinction between *frui* and *uti*, enjoying and using. Enjoying he defines as "adhering with love to some thing for its own sake"; using as "referring what comes into your use to the acquisition of what you love" (*Teaching Christianity* 1, 4). Later in the same book he goes on to say that only those things should be enjoyed which are eternal and unchangeable, that is, divine things (1, 22, 20). This raises the

question of our proper attitude to created things. Briefly, his answer is that we must love ourselves and other men, *non propter se, sed propter aliud*, not for our own sake, but for God's sake. This is not properly speaking, according to his own definition, to enjoy ourselves and others, though it can also be called enjoying ourselves and others in God; it can be called using and loving, using because we thus refer ourselves and others to the supreme good, loving because we value ourselves in ourselves, but not however purely for ourselves. This, he is careful to point out, does not dishonor ourselves or others but simply treats human beings according to their deepest ontology as creatures, that is as beings with a built-in reference or orientation on their creator (1, 22, 21).

He then goes on to explore the extent of this right self- and other-love, and goes on to explain at length that it includes love of our own and other people's bodies—this against the various extreme forms of spiritualist moral dualism, Manichaeism for example, widespread in his day (23-27). As for all other material things, they ought not to be enjoyed or loved, but only used.

By any interpretation this is an austere morality, utterly unhedonistic; so much so that in the hands of persons of narrow intelligence and determined will it can—and often has—become frighteningly inhuman. But we have to remember that Augustine carefully defines what he means by enjoying and using. What he means by the former is something much more precise, deliberate, intellectual and spiritual than what we ordinarily mean by enjoying. So he is not in fact forbidding us to enjoy our food, our sleep, our work, our play, good weather, good company, good entertainment, and so forth. What he is telling us to do is to *use* the pleasure we take in such things by referring it, in one way or another, to the only wholly satisfying object of enjoyment, namely God; and to avoid making these things ends in themselves. The same is true for the idea of using; he is not telling us to take a purely exploitative utilitarian attitude to the created world, because he had never heard of Jeremy Bentham; he is merely warning us against idolizing the world.

But it cannot be denied that the whole ethos of puritanical philistinism which has so long haunted the European outlook is descended—as a bastard indeed, but still descended—from Augustine's distinction between *frui* and *uti*.

25. That is, the word conceived in love.

26. Augustine interprets this metaphorically, of the labor of childbirth.

27. *Ut tantum nota sint non tamen verba dicantur ista de quibus nunc agimus.* I take *ista* etc., as qualifying *verba*, because of what he goes on to say, not as the subject of this clause, which other things being equal would be the more natural thing to do. M inserts a *sicut* immediately before *ista*. This alters the whole structure of the sentence, but at least supports me as taking the *omnia* (which I translate by the singular "everything") of the main clause as subject of the subordinate clause. M would require the following translation: "Not everything that touches our mind in any way is conceived, so it may be known without being called a word, like the things we are now talking about."

28. That is, in fact, a judgment. We would not make any judgment unless we approved of it.

29. *Speciem.*

30. The axiom here at work is that all evil, moral or technical, that is all vices and faults are a kind of lack of being, they are that which is not.

31. *Speciem.*

32. *Approbamus, approbatio.* He cannot just mean preferring our imaginations to reality, because that does not in itself involve making a mistake. Nor can he just mean our mistaking our mental images for external reality, because that would not necessarily involve approval. Judgment is clearly involved, the kind made by people who, we say, see the world through rose-colored spectacles—or with jaundiced eyes for that matter.

33. *Identidem.* In classical Latin this word means "frequently," "again and again." But here it cannot possibly mean that, and it seems clear that Augustine uses it as a reduplicated or strengthened form of *idem.*

34. Here Augustine is echoing what he says *ex professo* about the distinction between "image," "likeness" and "equality" in his *Miscellany of Eighty-three Questions* 74. There he says that for one thing to be the image of another it is not enough for it to be like it—otherwise we could say that a father was the image of his son as well as the other way round, or that my face is the image of its reflection in the mirror, or that one egg is the image of another egg; none of which things we do say. For a likeness also to be an image, it must, he says, be in some way or other derived, *or expressed,*

from that of which it is the image; not necessarily materially so, but at least formally. He takes the word *imago* as deriving from the word *imitor*, to imitate, and he is not altogether wrong.

35. His meaning is that God invites us to faith through the human speech of the scriptures, which thus provide us with the ultimate canon of the language in which we express our faith. It is this language of scripture that does not allow us to say the Holy Spirit was begotten, and we want to know why.

36. See section 14, footnote. Now that elegant piece of Latin word play is being put to a constructive purpose that the reader may well feel it is not logically strong enough to bear. An argument relying on word play that can scarcely be translated into other languages is suspect of equivocation.

37. *Inquisitio*. Augustine is again stretching the proper Latin meaning of a word. His definition of it as *appetitus inveniendi* would have surprised all previous uses of it.

38. *Expressa*, the key word for allowing a likeness also to be "image."

39. That is, is not just something you are looking for, like a lost umbrella.

40. From the famous Johannine comma, a gloss that seems to have crept into certain Latin manuscripts toward the end of the fourth century; it is not found in any Greek manuscript of the New Testament before the ninth century, nor in the best manuscripts of the Vulgate. But this allusion of Augustine's suggests that it had already found its way into his text, and so it would seem to be an error on the part of the Nestle/Kilpatrick edition of the Greek New Testament, produced for the British and Foreign Bible Society in 1958, to list Augustine among the witnesses for the uninterpolated text. He is still included among these witnesses by the Aland/Black/Metger/Wikgren edition published under the same Society's auspices in 1966.

Unfortunately, his discourses on this first Letter of John do not go beyond 1 John 5:3. Perhaps there are other places in his works which show clearly that his text lacked the comma. If so, at least this apparently clear allusion to the comma would render his testimony on the point doubtful.

BOOK X

PSYCHOLOGICAL: MENTAL IMAGE, SECOND DRAFT

Chapter 1

The author takes up the idea he has just employed in showing why love cannot also be called offspring and image, namely that of "inquisitiveness" or the appetitus inveniendi, *and giving it now the name of* amor studentium, *the sort of love studious people have, he asks the question how it can be reconciled with the axiom that you cannot love what you do not know; he establishes that this kind of love is not a love of the unknown, but a love of the known which stimulates inquiry, either a love of knowledge itself, or a love of some object of knowledge in general that prompts an investigation of it in detail, or a love of some universal truth or value, that prompts one to verify some particular application of it.*[1]

---

1. We must go on now to remove some of the knots and polish some of the roughnesses out of our draft presentation of these matters. But first of all, remembering that absolutely no one can love a thing that is quite unknown, we must carefully examine what sort of love it is that the studious have, that is people who do not yet know but still desire to know some branch of learning. Even over matters where we do not usually talk about studiousness, love commonly results from hearing; thus the spirit[2] is roused by talk of someone's beauty to go and see and enjoy it, since it has a general knowledge of physical beauty, having seen many examples of it, and has something inside[3] by which to judge and approve of what it hungers for outside. When this happens love is not being aroused for something totally unknown, since the kind of thing it is is known in this way. And when we love a good man whose face we have not seen, we love him out of a knowledge of the virtues which we know in truth itself.

As for branches of learning, our interest in studying them is very often aroused by the authority of those who commend and popularize them; and yet unless we had at least some slight notion of any subject impressed on our consciousness,[4] it would be quite impossible for us to be kindled with enthusiasm for studying it. Would anyone take any trouble or care to learn rhetoric, for example, unless he knew beforehand that it was the science of speaking?

Sometimes too we are amazed at what we hear or experience about the results of these disciplines, and this makes us enthusiastic to acquire by study the means of being able to reach such results ourselves. Suppose someone who does not know about writing is told that it is a discipline by which you can make words in silence with your hand and send them to somebody else a long way away, and by which this person they are sent to can pick them up not with his ears but his eyes; surely when he longs to know how he can do that himself, his enthusiasm is stirred by that result which he has now got the message about. This is the kind of way the enthusiasm and studiousness of learners is enkindled. What you are absolutely ignorant of you simply cannot love in any sense whatever.

2. Thus suppose someone hears an unknown sign, like the sound of some word which he does not know the meaning of; he wants to know what it is, that is, what thing that sound was fixed on to remind us of; he hears someone say "metheglin"[5] for example, and not knowing what it is he asks. Now he must already know that it is a sign, that is, that it means something and is not just that mere vocal noise; otherwise he already knows this trisyllabic sound, and has its articulated form impressed on his consciousness through his sense of hearing. What more could he ask for in order to know it better, seeing that he knows all its letters and its stresses and quantities, were it not that he realized simultaneously that it was a sign, and was prompted by a desire to know what thing it was a sign of? The more therefore the thing is known without being fully known, the more does the intelligence desire to know what remains; if it only knew that there was a vocal sound like this and did not know that it was the sign of something, it would not look further for anything else, having already perceived as much as it could about a sensible object by sensation. But as it knows that this is not just a vocal sound but also a sign, it wants to know it completely; and no sign is completely known unless it is known what thing it is the sign of.

If a man then earnestly, enthusiastically, and persistently seeks to know this, can he be said to be without love? What does he love, in that case? It is quite certain that nothing can be loved unless it is known. On the other hand, he does not love those three syllables which he already has by heart—and if he does love in them the fact that he knows they mean something, that is not precisely what we are concerned with, because this is not what he wants to know. The object of our inquiry is what it is that he loves in that which he is studious to know. Clearly he does not know it yet, and so we are wondering why he loves it, since we know for certain that things cannot be loved unless they are known. So what does he love then? It must be that he knows and sees by insight in the very sense of things[6] how beautiful the discipline is that contains knowledge of all signs; and how useful the skill is by which a human society communicates perceptions between its members, since otherwise an assembly of human beings would be worse for its members than any kind of solitude, if they could not exchange their thoughts by speaking to each other. This then is the lovely and useful form which the soul discerns and knows and loves, and anyone who inquires about the meaning of any words he does not know is studiously trying to perfect it in himself as far as he can; for it is one thing to observe it in the light of truth, another to desire to have it at one's disposal.

What one observes in the light of truth is what a great and good thing it would be to understand and speak all the languages of all peoples, and so to hear nobody as a foreigner,[7] and to be heard by no one as such either. The loveliness of such knowledge is now perceived in thought, and the thing so known is loved. This in turn is contemplated, and so inflames the studiousness of learners that they get all excited about it and hunger for it in all the work they put into acquiring such a competence that they may embrace in actual use what they have prior knowledge of in reason; and the more hope anyone has of coming by such a competence the more ardent is his love for it. You put more passion into your study of a discipline if you do not despair of being able to master it. But if you have no hope at all of acquiring a thing, you are lukewarm in your love for it or you do not love it at all, even though you are quite aware how beautiful it is.

And so it is that since practically everybody despairs of knowing all languages, you tend to be most studious about knowing the language of your own people. You may of course feel that you are not up to mastering it to perfection; but surely no one is so totally indifferent to this kind of knowledge that when he hears an unknown word he does not want to know what it is, and does not ask if he can and find out. When he does ask he is of course being studious to find out, and he appears to love something unknown, which is not the case. There is that form in contact with his consciousness which he knows and considers, in which is manifested the loveliness of linking minds together by hearing and exchanging known vocal sounds; it stimulates a certain studiousness in the man, who is indeed asking about something he does not know, but at the same time observing and loving a form he knows to which that something belongs.

So when someone asks, for instance, what metheglin is (that was the example I suggested), and you reply, "What has that got to do with you?" he will no doubt answer, "I might hear someone use the word and not understand; or perhaps I might read it somewhere and not know what the writer meant." Would anyone, I ask you, round off the conversation by saying "Don't bother to understand what you hear; don't bother to know the meaning of what you read"? It is plain for almost any rational soul to see that there is a beauty about this skill that enables men to know each other's thoughts by uttering meaningful sounds; and because this beauty is known, and loved because known, this word that is unknown is studiously asked about. So when he hears and gets to know at last that metheglin is what the ancients called fermented liquors, but that the word has now died out of current use, he may reckon that he still needs to know it in order to read the classics. If however he regards these as superfluous, then he may not think it worth the trouble of committing this word to memory, seeing that it scarcely belongs after all to that form of learning which he knows and contemplates with the mind and loves.

3. And so we see that all the love of a studious spirit, that is of one who wishes to know what he does not know, is not love for the thing he does not know but for something he knows, on account of which he wants to know what he does

not know. Even if he is so curious that he is carried away by the mere love of knowing unknown things for no known reason, such a curious man is indeed to be distinguished from the studious man; and yet not even he loves the unknown. Indeed it would be truer to say that he hates the unknown, since he would like nothing to be unknown and everything known. In case anyone should throw the question back to us with an added complication, and say that it is as impossible to hate what you do not know as to love what you do not know, we will not deny the truth of this, but merely make the point that to say "He loves to know the unknown" is not the same as saying "He loves the unknown"; it can happen that a man loves to know the unknown, but that he should love the unknown is impossible. "To know" is not put groundlessly in that first sentence, because the man who loves to know the unknown loves not the unknown but the actual knowing. And unless he had known what this was, he would not be able to say with confidence either that he knew something or that he did not know something. It is not only the man who says, and says truly, "I know" that must know what knowing is; the man who also says "I don't know," and says it confidently and truly and knows he is saying the truth, this man too obviously knows what knowing is, because he distinguishes one who does not know from one who does when he looks honestly at himself and says "I don't know." He knows what he says is true; how could he know this if he did not know what knowing was?

4. So no studious man, no curious man whatever loves the unknown even when he exhibits a ravenous appetite for knowing what he is ignorant of. Either he already has a general kind of knowledge of what he loves and longs to know it in some particular or in all particulars which are still unknown to him and have perhaps been recommended to his attention; so he fabricates in his consciousness some imaginary form which will stir him to love such particulars.* Or else we see something in the form of everlasting reason, and then we believe and love some expression of it in the formation of some temporal thing when we hear the praises of those who have experienced this particular; here too we are not loving something unknown, as we have already sufficiently explained above. Or else we love something known and because of it look for something unknown, and it is not at all the love of this unknown thing that holds us but love of that known thing; for we know that it is relevant to it that we should know this unknown thing that we are looking for, as I have just illustrated in the case of the unknown word. Or else everybody loves knowing, which cannot be

---

* And what can he fabricate such a form out of but things he already knew? And if he discovers that the thing recommended to him is different from this form he has shaped in his consciousness and got to know so well in his thoughts, perhaps he will not love it; if he does love it, he will begin to love it from the moment he gets to know it. A little earlier there was something else he loved, which his consciousness was in the habit of fashioning and showing him. If however he finds that the thing which reports had spoken so well of is like that form he had imagined, so that he can truly say to it, "I have already loved you," even then he was not loving something unknown because he knew it in that likeness.

unknown to anyone desirous of knowing the unknown. These are the reasons why people who want to know something they do not know seem to love the unknown; and because of their keen appetite for inquiry they cannot be said to be without love. But if you look at the matter carefully I think I have truly made out the case for saying that in fact it is otherwise, and nothing at all is loved if it is unknown. However, the examples I have given are of people wanting to know something which they are not themselves; so we must see if some new issue does not arise when the mind desires to know itself.

Chapter 2

The problem raised by the mind wanting to know itself is much more difficult, because as the author argues at length the mind cannot not know itself, being immediately present to itself. What then is the meaning of the famous Delphic injunction "Know thyself"? The validity of this injunction is taken as axiomatic, and it is interpreted as meaning that the mind ought to think about itself; it can be said to have forgotten itself as a consequence of being distracted from itself by its concern for material things, whose images it has absorbed in memory and imagination, so that it confuses itself with such things. It is clearly suggested that this distraction and confusion is a result of the original fall from the right order of creation by sin, or turning away from God.

5. What is it then that the mind loves when it ardently seeks to know itself while still unknown to itself? Here you have the mind seeking to know itself and all afire with this studious concern. So it is loving. But what is it loving? If itself, how, since it does not yet know itself and no one can love what he does not know? Has some report told the praises of its beauty, in the way we often hear about absent people? Perhaps then it does not love itself, but loves something it has imagined about itself, very different perhaps from what it really is. Or it may be that what the mind imagines itself as being is really like itself, and so when it loves this image it is loving itself before it knows itself, because it is looking at what is like itself; in this case it knows other minds from which it forms an image of itself, and so it is already known to itself in general terms. Seeing that it knows other minds, then, why does it not know itself, since nothing could be more present to it than itself? Or if it is like the eyes of the body which know other eyes better than themselves, then it should stop looking for itself because it is never going to find itself; eyes will never see themselves except in mirrors, and it is not to be supposed that in the contemplation of non-bodily things a similar device can be provided, so that the mind can know itself as in a mirror.

Can it be that it sees in the canon of eternal truth how beautiful it is to know oneself, and that it loves this thing that it sees and is at pains to bring it about in itself, because although it does not know itself, it knows how good it would be to know itself? But this is passing strange, not yet to know oneself, and already to know how beautiful it is to know oneself. Perhaps then the mind sees some excellent end, that is its own security and happiness, through some obscure memory which has not deserted it on its travels to far countries[8] and it believes it can only reach this end by knowing itself. Thus while it loves this end it seeks knowledge of itself, and it is on account of the known thing it loves that it seeks the unknown. But why in this case could the memory of its happiness remain with it while the memory of itself could not, so that as well as knowing that which it wants to reach it might also know itself who wants to reach? Or is it that when it loves knowing itself it is not itself that it loves, which it does not yet know, but the very knowing; and it finds it a bitter pill to swallow that it should itself be missing from its knowledge, with which it wishes to comprehend all things? It knows what knowing is, and while it loves this that it knows it also longs to know itself.

But where in this case does it know its knowing, if it does not know itself? Well, it knows that it knows other things, but does not know itself; thus it also knows what knowing is. How comes it then that a mind which does not know itself knows itself knowing something else? It is not that it knows another mind knowing, but itself knowing. Therefore it knows itself. And then when it seeks to know itself, it already knows itself seeking. So it already knows itself. It follows then that it simply cannot not know itself, since by the very fact of knowing itself not knowing, it knows itself. If it did not know itself not knowing, it would not seek to know itself. For it knows itself seeking and not knowing, while it seeks to know itself.

6. What are we to say then? That the mind knows itself in part and does not know itself in part? But it is absurd to say that the whole of it does not know what it knows: I am not saying "It knows the whole," but "What it knows, the whole of it knows." And so when it knows some of itself, which only the whole of it can do, it knows its whole self. For it knows itself knowing something, and only the whole of it can know something; so it knows the whole of itself. Again, what is so known to the mind as that it is alive? It cannot both be mind and not be alive, particularly as it has in addition the fact that it is intelligent; even the souls of animals live, though they are not intelligent. So just as the whole mind is, in the same way the whole mind lives. But it knows that it lives; therefore it knows its whole self. Finally, when the mind seeks to know itself it already knows that it is mind; otherwise it would not know whether it was seeking itself, and might perhaps be seeking something else by mistake. It might happen after all that it was not itself mind, and so while it was seeking to know mind it would not be seeking itself. Therefore since the mind seeking what mind is knows that it is seeking itself, it follows that it knows itself to be mind. Accordingly, if it knows about itself that it is mind and that the whole of it is mind, it knows the whole of itself.

But all right then, let us suppose it does not know it is mind; all it knows when it is looking for itself is that it is looking for itself. In this way it is possible for it in ignorance to look for one thing in mistake for another; but if it is not going to look for one thing in mistake for another, then without a shadow of doubt it must know what it is looking for. But if it knows what it is looking for, and it is looking for itself, then of course it knows itself. In that case, why does it go on looking? If it knows itself in part and goes on looking for itself in part, then it is not looking for itself but for its part; for when we say "itself" we mean "the whole of itself." Accordingly, as it knows that the whole of itself has not yet been found by itself, it must know how much the whole is. And so it must be looking for what is still missing, in the way we are in the habit of looking for something to come back to our minds that has slipped out of them; something that has not wholly slipped out of them, since when it comes back to us it can be recognized as what we were looking for. But how can the mind come back to the mind, as though the mind were able not to be in the mind? What it comes to is that if it is not looking for its whole self because it has already found part of itself, at least the whole of it is looking for itself. In that case the whole of it is available to itself, and so there is nothing that still needs to be looked for, since anything that is being looked for is missing, and what is doing the looking is not. So as the whole mind is doing the looking for itself, none of it is missing. Or if it is not the whole of it that is doing the looking, but the part that has been found is looking for the part that has not yet been found, then the mind is not looking for itself, because no part of it is looking for itself. The part that has been found is not looking for itself; nor is the part that has not yet been found looking for itself, since it is being looked for by the part that has already been found. So it would follow that since neither the whole mind is looking for itself, nor any part of it looking for itself, the mind is quite simply not looking for itself.

7. Why then is the mind commanded to know itself?[9] I believe it means that it should think about itself and live according to its nature, that is it should want to be placed according to its nature, under him it should be subject to and over all that it should be in control of; under him it should be ruled by, over all that it ought to rule. In fact many of the things it does show that it has twisted its desires the wrong way round as though it had forgotten itself. Thus, for example, it sees certain inner beauties in that more excellent nature which is God; but instead of staying still and enjoying them as it ought to, it wants to claim them for itself, and rather than be like him by his gift it wants to be what he is by its own right. So it turns away from him and slithers and slides down into less and less which is imagined to be more and more; it can find satisfaction neither in itself nor in anything else as it gets further away from him who alone can satisfy it. So it is that in its destitution and distress it becomes excessively intent on its own actions and the disturbing pleasures it culls from them; being greedy to acquire knowledge of all sorts from things outside itself, which it loves as known in a general way and feels can easily be lost unless it takes great care to hold onto them, it loses its carefree sense of security, and thinks of itself all the less the more secure it is in its sense that it cannot lose itself[10]

So then it is one thing not to know oneself, another not to think about oneself—after all we do not say that a man learned in many subjects does not know the art of grammar just because he does not think about it when he is thinking about the art of medicine; so it is one thing not to know oneself, another not to think about oneself. Yet such is the force of love that when the mind has been thinking about things with love for a long time and has got stuck to them with the glue of care, it drags them along with itself even when it returns after a fashion to thinking about itself. Now these things are bodies which it has fallen in love with outside itself through the senses of the flesh and got involved with through a kind of long familiarity. But it cannot bring these bodies themselves back inside with it into the region, so to say, of its non-bodily nature; so it wraps up their images and clutches them to itself, images made in itself out of itself. For it gives something of its own substance to their formation; but it also keeps something apart by which it can freely make judgments on the specific bearing of such images; and this is more truly mind, that is rational intelligence which is kept free to judge with. For we observe that we share even with animals those other parts of the soul which are impressed with the likenesses of bodies.

Chapter 3

A number of erroneous ways in which people have thought about the nature of mind, all in varying degrees materialistic, are reviewed; it is suggested that they are due to mind's tendency to confuse itself with its images of things perceived by the senses. The right way for mind to think about itself, it is then argued, is not for it to go looking for something else outside itself which it might consist of, but to distinguish itself from its images; the process should be one of the mind distinguishing what it supposes it might be, but is not sure about being (for example, fire, brain, harmony of elements, etc.) from what it knows it is; it knows that it is, that it lives, that it understands, that it wills, judges, remembers, and so on. It does not know, but only guesses that it is made of any material stuff. Therefore, so the author concludes, it is not made of any material stuff, but is a living, understanding, willing, being substance.

8. But the mind is mistaken when it joins itself to these images with such extravagant love that it even comes to think it is itself something of the same sort. Thus it gets conformed to them in a certain fashion, not by being what they are but by thinking it is—not of course that it thinks itself to be an image but simply to be that of which it has the image by it. Naturally it is capable of the judgment which distinguishes the body it leaves outside itself from the image of it which it carried with it inside, except in cases where such images are reproduced as if they were being felt outside and not thought up inside, as commonly happens to people who are asleep, or raving, or in an ecstasy. So in short, when the mind thinks of itself like that, it thinks it is a body.

9. And because it is perfectly conscious of the control it exercises over the body, it has come about that some people started looking for some part of the body that had the highest value in the body, and imagined that this was mind, or quite simply the whole soul.[11] Thus some thought it is the blood, others the brain, others the heart—not in the sense in which scripture says I will confess

to you, Lord, with all my heart (Ps 9:2), and You shall love the Lord your God with all your heart (Dt 6:5); here the word is being used improperly or by transference from body to soul.[12] No, they mean quite simply that organ of the body which we can see when carcasses are gutted. Others believed that it is put together from minute indivisible corpuscles, which they called "atoms," coming together and coalescing. Some said its substance is air, some fire. Others said it is not a substance at all, because the only substance they could conceive was body and they found no evidence that mind is body. Instead they supposed that it is the very organization of the body, or the structure of primordial elements which so to say holds this flesh together. All these of course conceived it to be mortal, since whether it is body or some arrangement of body, it cannot continue immortally.

Others however found the substance of mind to be life and not in the least bodily, seeing that it is life that animates and vivifies every living body. These tried, as best as each of them could, to prove that mind is immortal, since life cannot lack life. Some of them said the soul is heaven knows what fifth kind of body[13] which they add to the four elements of the world that we all know about; but I do not think this is the place to discuss that at any length. For either they mean the same as we do by body, that is something whose part in a localized space is smaller than the whole, and hence are to be counted among those who have fancied that mind is something bodily; or if they call every substance, or at least every changeable substance, body, while knowing that not every changeable substance is contained three-dimensionally in localized space, then there is no point in fighting them over a matter of words.

10. Looking at all these opinions, anyone who sees that mind is in nature both substance and not body, that is that it does not occupy a smaller space with its smaller part and a bigger space with its bigger one, should also see at the same time that those who think it is body do not make their mistake because mind is not available to their knowledge, but because they add those things to it without which they cannot think about any nature; if they are told to think about something without imagining bodies, they suppose that it is simply nothing. Therefore the mind does not have to look for itself as if it were not available to itself. What after all is so present to knowledge as what is present to mind, and what is so present to mind as the mind itself?

Now let us trace the origin of the word *inventio* (finding);[14] surely it suggests that *invenire* (finding) is simply *venire in* (coming on) what you are looking for. The reason then why things that seem to come of their own accord into the mind are not usually said to be *inventa* (found), although they can certainly be said to be known, is that we were not approaching them in a search in order to *venire in* them, that is to *invenire* them. Now it is the mind that looks for things that are being looked for by the eyes or any other sense of the body (since it is the mind which directs the sense of the flesh); and it is the mind that finds what is being looked for when the sense comes upon it. So too, when the mind comes on other things that it has to know by itself and not through the intermediary of a bodily sense, it finds them either in a higher substance, that is in God, or in other parts of the soul, as when it makes a judgment about the images of bodies; it finds them within, impressed by bodies on the soul.

11. So now then, in considering how the mind is to look for itself and find itself, we are faced with a very odd question: where does it go to look for, and where does it come in order to come upon itself? What after all can be as much in the mind as mind? But it is also in the things that it thinks about with love, and it has got used to loving sensible, that is bodily things; so it is unable to be in itself without their images. Hence arises its shameful mistake, that it cannot make itself out among the images of the things it has perceived with the senses, and see itself alone; they are all stuck astonishingly fast together with the glue of love. And this is its[15] impurity, that while it attempts to think of itself alone, it supposes itself to be that without which it is unable to think of itself. So when it is bidden to know itself, it should not start looking for itself as though it had drawn off from itself, but should draw off what it has added to itself. For it is more inward, not only than these sensible things[16] which are obviously outside, but also than their images which are in a part of the soul that animals have too, though they lack intelligence which is proper to mind. While then mind is at the inner level, it comes out of itself in a kind of way when it puts out feelings of love toward these images which are like the traces of its many interests. These traces are as it were imprinted on the memory when these bodily things outside are perceived by the senses, so that even when these things themselves are absent their images are available to be thought about. Let the mind then recognize itself and not go looking for itself as if it were absent, but rather turn on to itself the interest of its will, which had it straying about through other things, and think about itself. In this way it will see that there never was a time when it did not love itself, when it did not know itself. What it did was to mix itself up with something else that it loved together with itself and to coalesce with it in some way or other; and as a result, by comprising divergent things as a unity in itself, it came to think that these things which really are divergent were one with itself.

12. Let the mind then not go looking for a look at itself as if it were absent, but rather take pains to tell itself apart as present. Let it not try to learn itself as if it did not know itself, but rather to discern itself from what it knows to be other.[17] How will it see to act on the command it hears, *Know thyself,*[18] if it does not know what "know" is or what "thyself" is? If however it knows both, then it knows itself. The mind you see is not told *Know thyself* in the same way as it might be told "Know the cherubim and seraphim"; of them, as absent beings, we believe what they are declared to be, that they are certain heavenly powers. Nor is it like being told "Know the will of that man," which is not available in any way to our sense perceptions, nor even to our intelligence unless certain bodily signs of it are given, and this in such a way that we must rather believe than be intellectually aware of what it is. Nor is it like a man being told "Look at your face," which he can only do in a mirror; even our own face is absent from our sight, because it is not in a place our sight can be directed at. But when the mind is told *Know thyself*, it knows itself the very moment it understands what "thyself" is, and for no other reason than that it is present to itself. If it does

not understand what is said, then naturally it does not do it. So it is being commanded to do something which it automatically does the moment it understands the command.

13. Let it therefore avoid joining anything else to its knowing of itself when it hears the command to know itself. It knows for certain the command is being given to itself, the self which is and lives and understands. But a carcass is too, and a beast lives too; neither carcass nor beast though understands. So the mind knows that it is and that it lives, in the way intelligence is and lives. And so when it thinks, for example, that it is air, it thinks it understands air, it knows it understands itself; and it does not know but only thinks it is air. Let it set aside what it thinks it is, and mark what it knows it is;[19] in this way it will be left with something that even people who have thought mind is this or that sort of body can have no doubt about. After all, not every mind supposes it is air; some have supposed it to be fire, others brain, others this body and others that, as I described it all above.[20] But all these minds have known that they understand, and are, and live; though of course they have related understanding to what they understand, being and living to themselves.[21] And none of them have doubted that no one understands who does not live, and no one lives who does not be. The consequence is that whatever understands also is and lives, not as a carcass is which does not live, nor as a soul[22] lives which does not understand, but in its own proper and more excellent way.

Again they know that they will, and they know likewise that no one can do this who does not be and does not live, and again they relate this will to something that they want with this will.[23] They also know that they remember, and at the same time they know that no one would remember unless he was and unless he lived. This memory too we relate to something that we remember with it. Two of these three, memory and understanding, contain the awareness and knowledge of many things; will is there for us to enjoy them or use them. We enjoy things we know when the will reposes in them because it is delighted by them for their own sakes; we use things when we refer them to something else we would like to enjoy. And what makes the life of men vicious and reprehensible is nothing but using things badly and enjoying them badly; but this is not the place to discuss that.[24]

14. But we are concerned now with the nature of mind; so let us put aside all consideration of things we know outwardly through the senses of the body, and concentrate our attention on what we have stated that all minds know for certain about themselves. Whether the power of living, remembering, understanding, willing, thinking, knowing, judging comes from air, or fire, or brain, or blood, or atoms, or heaven knows what fifth kind of body besides the four common elements; or whether the very structure or organization of our flesh can produce these things; people have hesitated about all this, and some have tried to establish one answer, others another. Nobody surely doubts, however, that he lives and remembers and understands and wills and thinks and knows and judges. At least, even if he doubts, he lives; if he doubts, he remembers why he is doubting; if he doubts, he understands he is doubting; if he doubts, he has a will to be

certain; if he doubts, he thinks; if he doubts, he knows he does not know; if he doubts, he judges he ought not to give a hasty assent. You may have your doubts about anything else, but you should have no doubts about these; if they were not certain, you would not be able to doubt anything.[25]

15. Those who think mind is a body or an arrangement or organization of body would like these things to be regarded as "being in a subject"; thus the substance would be air or fire or any other body they think mind is, while understanding would be in this body as a quality of it, so that this body would be the subject and understanding would be in the subject; that is to say, mind which they consider to be a body would be the subject, and understanding or any of those other things we have mentioned, as being what we are certain about, would be in the subject. Those who deny that mind is a body but say it is the structure or organization of the body will have a similar view. The difference between them is that the former say the mind itself is the substance which understanding is in as in a subject; while the latter say that mind itself is in a subject, namely the body whose structure or organization it is. It follows surely that they must suppose understanding to be in the same subject, namely the body.

16. But what none of them notice is that the mind knows itself even when it is looking for itself, as we have shown above. Now properly speaking a thing cannot in any way be said to be known while its substance is unknown. Therefore when mind knows itself it knows its substance, and when it is certain of itself it is certain of its substance. But it is certain of itself, as everything said above convincingly demonstrates. Nor is it in the least certain whether it is air or fire or any kind of body or anything appertaining to body. Therefore it is not any of these things.[26] The whole point of its being commanded to know itself comes to this: it should be certain that it is none of the things about which it is uncertain, and it should be certain that it is that alone which alone it is certain that it is. For instance, it thinks fire in the same sort of way as it thinks air or anything else that belongs to body; but it could not possibly happen that it should think what it is itself in the same way as it thinks what it is not. It thinks all these other things with the images of the imagination, whether fire or air or this or that body or part of a body or structure and organization of a body; nor of course is it ever said to be all these things but only one or other of them. But if it were one of these things it would think that thing differently from the others, not that is to say with a construct of the imagination as absent things are thought that have been contacted by one of the senses of the body, either actually themselves or something of the same kind; but with some inner, non-simulated but true presence (nothing after all is more present to it than itself), in the same way as it thinks its living and remembering and understanding and willing. It knows these things in itself, it does not form images of them as though it had touched them with the senses outside itself, as it touches any bodily things. If it refrains from affixing to itself any of these image-bound objects of its thoughts in such a way as to think it is that sort of thing, then whatever is left to it of itself, that alone is what it is.

Chapter 4

Of the many mental acts of which mind is certain, the author selects memory, understanding, and will from which to construct his final draft of the image of the divine trinity in the mind.

17. Now let us put aside for the moment the other things which the mind is certain about as regards itself, and just discuss these three, memory, understanding, and will. It is usual to examine these three things in children, to see what kind of promise they show. The more easily and firmly a boy remembers things and the more acutely he understands and the keener his application to study, the more admirable is considered his disposition. On the other hand, when one inquires about someone's learning, one does not ask how easily or tenaciously he remembers things or how sharply he understands, but what he remembers and what he understands. And because a person's character[27] is considered praiseworthy according to how good it is as well as how learned, one pays attention to what he wills as well as to what he remembers and understands. Not with what ardor he wills, but first of all what he wills, and only then how much. A character after all is only to be praised for loving passionately when what it loves deserves to be passionately loved.

So when one talks about these three things in a person, disposition, learning, practice,[28] one judges the first according to what he can do with his memory, his understanding, and his will; one estimates the second according to what he actually has in his memory and understanding, and where he has got to with his will to study; the third however is to be found in the use the will now makes of what the memory and understanding hold, whether it refers them to something else or whether it takes delight in them as ends in themselves. To use something is to put it at the will's disposal; to enjoy it is to use it with an actual, not merely anticipated joy.[29] Hence everyone who enjoys, uses; for he puts something at the disposal of the will for purposes of enjoyment. But not everyone who uses, enjoys, not if he wants what he puts at the disposal of the will for the sake of something else and not for its own.

18. These three then, memory, understanding, and will, are not three lives but one life, nor three minds but one mind. So it follows of course that they are not three substances but one substance. When memory is called life, and mind, and substance, it is called so with reference to itself; but when it is called memory it is called so with reference to another. I can say the same about understanding and will; both understanding and will are so called with reference to another. But each of them is life and mind and being with reference to itself. For this reason these three are one in that they are one life, one mind, one being; and whatever else they are called together with reference to self, they are called it in the singular, not in the plural. But they are three in that they have reference to each other. And if they were not equal, not only each to the other but also each to them all together, they would not of course contain each other. In fact

though they are not only each contained by each, they are all contained by each as well. After all, I remember that I have memory and understanding and will, and I understand that I understand and will and remember, and I will that I will and remember and understand, and I remember my whole memory and understanding and will all together. If there is any of my memory that I do not remember, then it is not in my memory. But nothing is more in the memory than memory itself. Therefore I remember the whole of it. Again, whatever I understand I know that I understand, and I know that I will whatever I will; and whatever I know I remember. So I remember my whole understanding and my whole will.

Likewise when I understand these three I understand the whole of them together. For the only understandable things I do not understand are the ones I am ignorant of. But what I am ignorant of I neither remember nor will. So it follows that any understandable thing which I do not understand, I do not remember or will either. Therefore whatever understandable thing I remember and will I also understand in consequence. My will also contains my whole understanding and my whole memory while I use the whole of what I understand and remember. Therefore since they are each and all and wholly contained by each, they are each and all equal to each and all, and each and all equal to all of them together, and these three are one, one life, one mind, one being.

19. Are we already then in a position to rise with all our powers of concentration to that supreme and most high being of which the human mind is the unequal image, but the image nonetheless? Or have we still to clarify the distinctions between these three in the soul by comparing them with our sensitive grasp of things outside, in which the awareness of bodily things is imprinted on us in a time sequence? We were in the process, you remember, of bringing the mind to light in its memory and understanding and will of itself, and discovering that since it was seen always to know itself and always to will itself, it must at the same time be seen always to remember itself and always to understand and love itself,[30] although it does not always think about itself distinctly from things that are not what it is. And thus it seems to be difficult to distinguish in it between its memory of itself and its understanding of itself. That these are not in fact two things, but one thing called by two names, is the impression you might get in this case where they are joined together very closely and one is not prior at all in time to the other; love too is not felt so obviously to be present when no neediness exhibits it, because what is being loved is always to hand. And so even those who are slower on the uptake will find some light shed on these matters if we discuss things that are added to our awareness in time, and what happens to it in a time sequence when it remembers something it did not remember before, and sees something it did not see before, and loves something it did not love before. But this discussion calls for another commencement, since this book is already long enough.

NOTES

1. To follow the line of his thought, the reader must always bear in mind that the kind of knowledge and love Augustine is interested in is the mind's knowledge and love of itself. So at the end of the last book, the idea of inquisitiveness which he introduced to help him in his difficulty was in fact inquisitiveness about self—and not just the person's curiosity about himself, which is not necessarily very problematic, but the mind's curiosity about itself. This is his real problem: how does it make sense to talk about the mind wanting to know itself? He will deal with it in his next chapter, to which this first chapter is merely a general introduction. If he cannot deal with it satisfactorily, then his tentative solution at the end of Book IX to the question why the Holy Spirit is not also said to be begotten and called Son will simply fall to the ground.

His treatment of this matter leads him to introduce the notion of *cogitatio* or "thought," just as in the previous book he introduced the notion of a "word"; and, indeed, just as the *verbum mentis* in the image is the analogue of the divine Word in God, so will *cogitatio* play a part in the image analogous to the generation or utterance of the divine Word. Then from his discussion of the mind thinking about itself, he goes on to draw out his final draft of the image as a triad of the mind's remembering, understanding, and willing itself.

It is interesting to note that he begins his exploration of the image in Book IX, and his deeper analysis of it in Book X, each time from the starting point of love. The point, I think, is that though love is more difficult to understand than knowledge, just as the Holy Spirit is more difficult to name and find suitable analogous concepts for than the Word, it is for all that more immediate to our experience; more immediate to experience, though less accessible to reflection. The practical theological implication of this for the Christian life is that although the Holy Spirit is a more shadowy person for us than the Word, who is made objectively accessible to us in the incarnation, still he is more immediate to our religious experience than the Word, that is to say than Christ; it is only in the Spirit that we can recognize Christ, and can say *Jesus is Lord* (1 Cor 12:3). This is the point that has been all too seriously neglected in the Church's theology, and hence in its piety and its practice of the Christian life.

2. *Animus.*

3. That is an idea or canon of beauty, seen in truth itself.

4. *Animus.*

5. In the Latin *temetum,* an obsolete word whose meaning is going to be explained in due course.

6. *In rationibus rerum.* These *rationes* are perceived by direct insight in truth itself.

7. Reading *nullumque ut alienigenam audire.* There is a bit of a crux here. CCL reads *nullamque ut alienigenam,* M reads *nullamque ut alienigena,* and two manuscripts support the reading I adopt.

To get the picture and the points of argument, here is the pertinent text of the whole sentence, with the disputed words in my reading: *Conspicit . . . quam bonum sit omnes. . . linguas intelligere ac loqui, nullumque ut alienigenam audire, et a nullo ita audiri.*

It is the last phrase that seems to me to determine the issue; it is clearly parallel to the preceding one in which the disputed words occur. This in my view settles the gender of *nullumque* as masculine, balancing the *a nullo* of the sister clause. This leaves the case of *alienigena/am* to be decided. What it is parallel to in the second phrase is *ita,* "like this" or "as such." What this last clause is clearly saying is that the man sees what a good thing it is not to sound like a foreigner when he is heard speaking by anybody else. He does not want to sound like a foreigner when others hear him speak, and so presumably, in parallel, he does not want others to sound foreign when he hears them speak. So I conclude that we should read *alienigenam* in the accusative, agreeing with *nullumque.* But clearly this last argument is nothing like as compelling as the former; the parallelism would still hold if one read *alienigena* in the nominative, and it would mean that it would be very nice neither to feel like a foreigner when you listen to anyone, nor sound like a foreigner when you speak to anyone. The English translation, in any case, leaves this particular point ambiguous.

Assuming then that *nullumque* is the original reading, it is easy to see how it could be turned almost inadvertently into *nullamque.* The previous clause mentions *omnes linguas,* all languages; it is a natural assumption that this one refers to "no language"; hence the gender is changed to agree with *lingua.*

How then to account for changing *alienigenam*, if that was the original reading, to *alienigena*, as M reads it with 5 manuscripts? I think the explanation would be a knowledgeable, if somewhat pedantic, scribe; . . . *nullamque ut alienigenam* looks very obvious and reasonable on the face of it, but it means treating the last word as an adjective, meaning "foreign." Originally, indeed, it was, and is sometimes so used by the earlier classical authors. But by far the commonest usage of it is as a masculine noun of the first declension. Our well-educated scribe, knowing this, would not like to find Augustine talking about "a foreigner language," and so would solve the problem by changing the word into the nominative, giving the meaning "to hear none as a foreigner." If, on the other hand, *alienigena* was the original, we merely have to postulate a half-educated instead of well-educated scribe. Both are equally plausible suppositions; so neither case is proven.

8. An allusion to the prodigal son, Lk 15:13.

9. An allusion to the famous words inscribed over the shrine at Delphi, *Gnôthi seauton*. But it seems to have been recalled by Augustine through a Ciceronian filter. In his *Tusculan Disputations*, 1.22, 52, Cicero expressly intellectualizes the precept: *Cum igitur "Nosce te" dicit, hoc dicit "Nosce animum tuum."*

10. In this paragraph Augustine for the first time explicitly introduces the theme of the fall, in a psychological key, into his construction of the image in man; but it will not be until Book XII that he takes it up *ex professo*. It is of course implied in the moral slant which he gives to his whole discussion of the image, which we saw coming out strongly in Book IX, chapter 2, when he was discussing how knowledge of self produces a mental word (see sections 10 and 13). Compare what he said above in Book IV, chapter 1, section 4 about the "dissimilarity" in which sin had involved us, the distortion of the image we were created in.

11. The opinions of the ancient philosophers which he proceeds to list were of course commonplaces in educated circles. But a very likely immediate source for him was doubtless Cicero's *Tusculan Disputations* which we have already referred to (above, n. 9). They are mostly the opinions of the pre-Socratic physicists.

12. *Animus.*

13. Cicero, *Tusc. Disp.* 1.12, 26, mistakenly ascribes this opinion to Aristotle, who certainly posited a fifth element or quintessence in addition to the terrestrial four of earth, water, fire, and air, but only to make it the material out of which the heavens are constructed. His reason is *(De Caelo* 1.2, 269) that each element has its proper or natural motion, earth and water downward, fire and air upward. But the heavens move neither up nor down, but round and round, which is the perfect motion. Therefore they must consist of some proper celestial element whose natural motion is circular.

Plato in the *Timaeus* (30-37b) gives a weird account of the creation of the cosmos (or rather puts it into the mouth of Timaeus) in which the world soul is described as being circular in its motions, to correspond to the perfect spherical shape of the cosmic body; and by derivation and analogy it could be inferred that all minds or souls have affinity with the circle or sphere. Hence doubtless Cicero's mistake arose from a conflation of Aristotle's astronomy with the Pythagorean mythology of the *Timaeus*.

14. By this exceedingly abrupt diversion Augustine is only preparing himself for the knock-out blow that will settle the point of the mind's immediate and unassailable self-presence.

15. Reading *ejus* with M. CCL reads *eis*, their impurity.

16. That is, things perceived by the senses, bodies.

17. Two sentences of untranslatable word play: *Non itaque velut absentem se quaerat cernere, sed praesentem se curet discernere. Nec se quasi non norit cognoscat, sed ab eo quod alterum novit dinoscat.*

18. Delphic oracle; see above, n. 9.

19. Another word play on *cernere: Secernat quod se putat, cernat quod scit.*

20. Section 9.

21. He is reminding us of the substance/relationship framework of the image, in preparation for his final draft of it.

22. *Anima*, meaning here an animal soul. It is tempting to emend to *animal*, but no manuscript supports this.

23. This sentence illustrates clearly that by *voluntas* he means the act of willing more than the faculty of will.

24. See Book IX, 13, note 24.

25. This is directed against the school of the Academics, who maintained that certain knowledge about anything is impossible. They derived, curiously enough, from the Academy of Plato, their founder being one Carneades. They could be described as Platonists who had lost their nerve; retaining the platonic distrust of the senses as reliable sources of knowledge, while having lost Plato's confidence in the unchanging reality of intellectually perceived truths and values.

When Augustine finally gave up Manichaeanism, he took up with the Academics (*Confessions* V, 10, 19) no doubt influenced by Cicero, whose lost work *Hortensius* had earlier inspired in him a keen interest in philosophy (*Confessions* III, 4, 7). Thus it is natural that in this place in the *De Trinitate*, where he is drawing fairly heavily on Cicero, his thoughts should turn to the Academics, and he should insert this criticism of their views. Toward the end of Book XIV he will be quoting *in extenso* from the *Hortensius,* and there voice again his criticism of the master for having joined the Academic school. The very first work Augustine wrote after his conversion, before even he was baptized, was called *Contra Academicos.* But his most famous anti-skeptical aphorism, sometimes called the Augustinian *Cogito,* on analogy with Descartes' *Cogito, ergo sum,* is *Si fallor, sum;* If I am mistaken, I am; and it occurs in *The City of God,* XI, 26. See Gilson's *The Christian Philosophy of Saint Augustine,* page 42-43.

26. What saves the argument from being mere specious dialectic is the fundamental premise of the mind's presence to itself, of which he is just about to spell out the implications.

27. *Animus.*

28. *Ingenium, doctrina, usus.* In these two paragraphs Augustine is manipulating certain commonplaces of classical ethics in order to explain his selection of the three mental acts of memory, understanding, and will. The first commonplace involved is Cicero's division of the cardinal virtue of prudence (I have hitherto translated this by "sagacity") into *memoria, intelligentia,* and *providentia.* It is for these three, presumably, that "it is usual to examine the dispositions of children." Augustine lists these three in a summary of Cicero's relevant passage from *De Inventione* 2, 53, 160 in his *Miscellany of Eighty-Three Questions* 31.

But here he does not require *providentia* or foresight, but will. And so he introduces the other commonplace trio, *ingenium, doctrina, usus,* from the same work of Cicero's, where they are declared to be the three things of which the art of rhetoric consists. The point is that *usus,* which as we have seen before he consistently pairs and contrasts with *fruitio,* is an act of will.

Within the actual context of the *De Trinitate,* however, it is not the term will that calls for explanation, but that of memory. According to the suggestion I made in the Introduction 106-109, he picks on this term because of its close association, etymologically and even psychologically according to Augustine's own system, with the term *mens* or mind.

29. . . . *Cum gaudio non adhuc spei sed jam rei;* this rhyming play on the words *spes* and *res* is a favorite trick of style with Augustine. It is a neat nutshell for his eschatology.

30. In this sentence he is explaining the transition from the first draft of the trinity image, consisting of *mens notitia amor,* to the second one consisting of *memoria intelligentia voluntas.* But he rather carelessly mixes his terms up, and so makes things rather more obscure than they need be. According to the first set of terms he had shown that the mind always knows itself and always loves itself, and he is saying that this implies, according to the second set, that it always remembers, always understands and always wills itself. But he in fact puts "wills" for "loves" in the first set, and "loves" for "wills" in the second.

BOOK XI

PSYCHOLOGICAL: MENTAL IMAGE, LESSER ANALOGIES

Prologue

---

1. No one will doubt that just as the inner man is endowed with understanding, so is the outer man with sensation. Let us try then if we can to pick out some trace of trinity in this outer man too. Not that he is also the image of God in the same way as the inner man; the apostle's verdict is quite clear which declares that it is the inner man *who is being renewed for the recognition[1] of God according to the image of him who created him* (Col 3:10); since elsewhere he says, *Even if our outer man is decaying, the inner man is being renewed from day to day* (2 Cor 4:16).

As best we can then let us look for some model of the trinity in this man who is decaying; even if it is not a more accurate model, it may perhaps be easier to distinguish. It is not without reason that this too is called man; but it would not be unless he bore some resemblance to the inner man. And by the very logic of our condition, according to which we have become mortal and carnal, it is easier and almost more familiar to deal with visible than with intelligible things, even though the former are outside and the latter inside us, the former sensed with the senses of the body and the latter understood with the mind, while we conscious selves[2] are not perceptible by the senses, not bodies that is, but only intelligible, because we are life. And yet, as I have said, we have grown so used to bodies, and our interest slips back and throws itself out into them in such a strangely persistent manner, that when it is withdrawn from the uncertainties of bodies to be fixed with a much more assured and stable knowledge on things of the spirit, it runs away again to those things and seeks to take its ease in the place where it caught its disease. Well, we have to adapt ourselves to this illness, and when we are trying to distinguish inner spiritual things as accurately and to propound them as simply as we can, we must take lessons in comparison from these outer bodily things.

So then, the outer man is endowed with sensation, and with it perceives bodies; and this sensation, as can be readily verified, is divided into five parts, seeing, hearing, smelling, tasting, touching. But it would be too much, and quite unnecessary, to ask all these five senses about what we are looking for. What one tells us will go for the others. So let us use for preference the evidence of the eyes; this is the most excellent of the body's senses, and for all its difference in kind has the greatest affinity to mental vision.

Chapter 1

The author picks out a trinity in the act of seeing, or looking at an external object, its members being the appearance or look or visibility of the object in itself, the form or likeness of it impressed on the sense of sight, and the deliberate intention or act of will that fixes the sense of sight on the object. The distinction between these three elements, their relationships and the kind of unity they have, are discussed, and implicitly compared, not so much with the trinity of divine persons as with the trinity of the mental image.

2. When we see some particular body, there are three things which we can very easily remark and distinguish from each other. First of all there is the thing we see, a stone or a flame or anything else the eyes can see, which of course could exist even before it was seen. Next there is the actual sight or vision, which did not exist before we sensed that object presented to the sense. Thirdly there is what holds the sense of the eyes on the thing being seen as long as it is being seen, namely the conscious intention. These three are not only manifestly distinct, but also of different natures.

The first of them, the visible body, is of quite another nature from the sense of the eyes which lights upon the body so as to produce sight, and also from the actual sight itself, which is clearly nothing but this sense informed by the thing which is capable of being seen; but still the body by which the sense of the eyes is informed when this same body is seen is in no way at all the same sort of substance as the form which it impresses on this sense, which we call sight. The body is separable in its nature from sight.[3] But the sense which was already there in the living being even before it saw what it could see when it lit upon something visible, or the sight which arises in the sense from the visible body when it is already joined to it and being seen—the sense therefore or the sight, that is to say the sense not formed from without or the sense[4] as formed from without, belongs to the nature of the living being, which is quite different from that body that we perceive by seeing; and this body does not form the sense into becoming sense but into becoming sight. If the sense did not exist in us even before the sensible thing were presented to it, we would be no different from blind men when we see nothing either because it is dark or because we have our eyes shut. But we do differ from them precisely in this, that even when we are not seeing we have something in us by which we can see, which we call the sense; they lack this in them, and it is because they lack it that they are called blind.

Again, the conscious intention which holds our sense on the thing we are seeing and joins the two together not only differs in nature from that visible thing, since it is consciousness while that is body, but it also differs from the sense itself and the sight, since this intention belongs only to the consciousness. The sense of the eyes, however, is called a sense of the body precisely because the eyes too are parts of the body; and although an unconscious or lifeless body does not sense anything, yet it is through a bodily instrument that the conscious soul mixed with the body senses, and it is this instrument that is called a sense. When someone goes blind through some affliction of the body this sense is cut off and extinguished, but the consciousness remains the same; and though its intention, now that the eyes have been lost, has no sense of the body which it can join in the act of seeing to a body outside, and keep its gaze fixed on it once seen, nonetheless it shows by its very exertions that it neither perishes nor even diminishes with the loss of the bodily sense; the desire to see remains intact, whether this happens to be possible or not. So these three, the body which is seen, and the actual sight, and the intention joining the two together, are clearly distinguished not only by what is proper to each but also by the difference of their natures.[5]

3. And while it is true that in their case the sense does not proceed from the body that is seen but from the body of the sentient living being to which the soul is adjusted in its own wonderful fashion, still sight is begotten of the body which is seen; that is, the sense itself is formed by it so that it is no longer just the sense, which can remain entire even in the dark provided the eyes are unharmed, but it is now the informed sense which we call actual sight. So sight is begotten of the visible thing but not from it alone; only if there is a seeing subject present. Sight then is the product of the visible object and the seeing subject, where the seeing subject of course provides the sense of the eyes and the intention of looking and holding the gaze; but the information of the sense, which is called sight, is imprinted on it only by the body which is seen, that is by some visible thing. Take this away, and the form which was in the sense while the thing being seen was present does not remain; but the sense itself remains, as it was there even before anything was sensed by it. Just as water retains the trace of a body as long as the body being imprinted is in the water; but take this away, and no trace will remain, though the water will still remain which was there even before it received the form of that body. Therefore we cannot say that the visible thing begets sense; but it does beget a form as a likeness of itself, which occurs in the sense when we sense anything by seeing it.

However, we cannot tell the form of the body we see apart from the form which it produces in the sense of the seer—not at least by the same sense, because the two coincide so exactly that there is no overlap to tell them apart by. It is by reason that we gather we could not possibly sense unless there were produced in our sense some likeness of the body observed. When a signet ring is imprinted in wax, it does not mean that there is no image of it just because it cannot be made out until the wax is removed. But when the wax is removed, what took place in it remains and can be seen, and so one is easily persuaded that the form impressed by the ring was in the wax even before it was removed from it. If the ring however is put to the surface of a liquid, no image of it appears when it is taken away. Still, that does not mean one cannot infer by reason that before the ring was taken away its form was in the liquid and there derived from the ring; and that this form is to be distinguished from the form which is in the ring, from which this one is derived that will cease to be when the ring is taken away, even though that one which produced this one will remain in the ring. In the same way it does not mean that the sense of the eyes does not have the image of the body it sees for as long as it sees it, just because the image does not remain when the body is taken away. However, it does mean that it is very difficult to persuade the slower of mind that an image of the visible thing is formed in our sense when we see it, and that this image is sight.

4. And yet if they have noticed a fact I am going to mention, they may not make such heavy weather of this investigation. It often happens that when we look at some lights for a little while and then close our eyes, certain luminous colors continue to revolve in our vision, changing their hues and gradually becoming less bright until they cease altogether. We can understand them as being the remnants of that form which was produced in the sense while we were looking at the luminous body, which gradually change colors and little by little fade away. What shows that this is a way our sense is affected by the impression received from the thing seen, is that the bars of the window panes[6] often appeared in those colors if our gaze happened to dwell on them. So that impression was there even while we were seeing; but it coincided so exactly with the form of the thing we were looking at that it simply could not be distinguished from it, and this is what our actual sight was.

Again, sometimes the flame of a candle can seem to be doubled somehow or other by the rays from the eyes spreading out,[7] and then we see double, with two actual sights, even though there is only one thing being seen. The rays issuing from each eye are affected singly and severally by the object as long as they are not allowed to converge or focus equally and together on the body being looked at, so as to produce one view out of them both. So if we shut one eye we no longer see a double flame but just one as it really is. Why it is that when we shut the left eye the right hand appearance stops being seen, and when we shut the right eye the one on the left dies out, would take too long to investigate and work out, and in any case is of no relevance to our present concern. All that matters for the question we have taken up is that unless some image exactly like the thing we are looking at were produced in our sense, the form of the flame would not be doubled according to the number of our eyes, when we adopt a certain mode of looking which makes it possible to separate the convergence of their rays. With one eye shut it is absolutely impossible to see a thing double with the other, however much you squint with it or screw it up or squeeze it.[8]

5. This being so, let us remember that although these three differ in nature they are compounded into a kind of unity, that is to say that form of the body

which is seen, and its image imprinted on the sense which is sight or formed sense, and the conscious will which applies the sense to the sensible thing and holds the sight on it. The first of these, that is the visible thing itself, does not pertain to the nature of the living being except when we look at our own body. The next pertains to it in that it happens in the body, and through the body in the soul; it happens in the sense, which is neither without body nor without soul. The third belongs only to the soul, because it is will. While then the substances of these three differ so widely, they nonetheless come together in so close a unity that the first two can scarcely be told apart even when reason intervenes as judge—that is, the form of the body which is seen and the image of it which is produced in the sense, namely sight. And the will exerts such force in coupling the two together that it applies the sense to be formed to the thing that is being looked at and holds it there once it is formed. And if it is violent enough to be called love or covetousness or lust, it will even deeply affect the rest of the living being's body, and where the body's material does not obstruct this by its intractability and hardness, it will even change it into a similar appearance and color. You can see the chameleon's little body transformed with the greatest facility into the colors which it sees. The grossness of other animals is not susceptible to such transformations, but their offspring frequently reveal the special caprices of their mothers, and what they have looked at with peculiar pleasure. The more tender are the first stages of the embryo, and the more formable if I may so put it, the more receptively and effectually do they reflect the intention of the mother's soul and the image produced in it by the body it has greedily gaped at. There are many instances that could be mentioned, but one is enough from the most trustworthy of all books; what Jacob did to ensure that the ewes and she-goats would bring forth particolored lambs and kids, by setting particolored rods before their eyes in the water troughs, so that they would gaze on them as they drank at the time they had just conceived (Gn 30:37).[9]

Chapter 2

A more inward trinity in the psychic functioning of the "outer man" is picked out and discussed, namely that which declares itself when one thinks about some remembered object or event in an act of recollection; here the intention of the will joins together the attention of the mind, the "mind's eye" or acies animi *as the author calls it, which corresponds to the sense of sight in the previous trinity considered, and the image stored in the memory, corresponding to the visible object in the sense trinity. Such acts of recollection or imagination are discussed in a distinctly moralizing context.*

6. But the rational soul lives a misshapen kind of life when it lives according to the trinity of the outer man; that is, when instead of bringing a praiseworthy will to bear on the things that form the senses from outside and referring them

to some useful end, it fastens on them with sordid greed. For even when the form of the body is taken away which was perceived by the bodily senses, there remains a likeness of it in the memory, to which the will can again turn the attention to be formed by it from within, just as the sense was formed from without by the sensible body presented to it. And so one gets another trinity, out of the memory and internal sight and the will which couples them together; and when these three are *coagitated* into a unity the result is called cogitation or thought, from the very act of *coagitation*.[10] Here there is no sensible body which is altogether separate from the nature of the living being; no sense of the body being formed to become sight; no will applying the sense to the sensible thing in order to have it formed by it and keeping it there once formed. But instead of the look of the body which was sensed outside, there now appears memory retaining that look which the soul drank in through the sense of the body; and instead of that external sight of the sense being formed from the sensible body, we now have a similar internal sight when the conscious attention is formed from what the memory retains, and absent bodies are thought about; and the same will that in the first case applied the sense for formation to the body presented to it outside and kept it joined to it once formed, now turns the conscious attention to the memory in an act of recollection for it to be formed from what the memory has retained, and there is produced in thought something like sight.

But it took some reasoning to distinguish between the visible look which formed the body's sense and the likeness of it which was produced in the formed sense to get sight—otherwise one would have thought they were one and the same thing, so completely did they coincide. In the same way this image you get when the consciousness thinks about the look of some body it has seen, does in fact consist both of the body's likeness held in the memory and that which is formed from it in the conscious attention as you actually recall something; and yet in appearance there is only one single image, and it takes a judgment of reason to discover two things there. We make it when we realize that what remains in the memory even while we are thinking of something else is one thing, and quite another is what is produced when we actually recall, that is go back to the memory and there find this same look or image. If it was not there we would say we had totally forgotten it beyond all possibility of recollection; and if on the other hand the attention were not formed from what was there in the memory in its act of recollection, there would be no seeing by thinking.[11] But the coincidence of the two images, namely the one held in the memory and the one off-printed from it to form the attention in the act of recall, makes them appear as one because they are so exactly alike. But when the attention that has recalled this thing turns away from it and stops gazing at what it was observing in the memory, not a trace of the form that was impressed on the attention will remain, and instead it will be formed from what it turns to next in thinking about something else. And yet the thing it dropped remains in the memory, where the attention turns to it when we recall it again, and when it turns to it it is formed by it again and becomes one with what is forming it.

7. The will, then, turns the attention here and there and back again to be formed, and once formed keeps it joined to the image in the memory. But if it concentrates its whole energy on the inner image, and withdraws the conscious attention altogether from the presence of bodies that surround the senses, and from the senses of the body themselves, and directs it utterly on the image that is perceived within, then the likeness of a bodily appearance printed off from the memory looms so large,[12] that it does not even allow the reason to tell whether a real body is being seen outside or something like it is being thought about inside. Sometimes people are so attracted or so terrified by their excessively vivid thoughts about visible things, that they actually give sudden vocal expression to the corresponding emotion as though they were really and truly caught up in such actions or experiences. I remember once hearing a man say that it was usual with him to see the form of a woman's body so vividly and as it were so solidly in his thoughts that he would as good as feel himself copulating with her and seed would even flow from his genitals. Such is the force the soul can exert on the body; such is the capacity to turn and change the garment according to his feelings which the wearer has who molds his garment to himself.[13] Our being deluded by images in dreams is the same kind of experience, but it makes all the difference whether on the one hand the senses of the body are lulled in sleep, or shaken from their inner moorings by madness, or otherwise alienated in divination or prophecy, so that the conscious attention comes captive upon the images that rise before it out of the memory, or from some other hidden power through various spiritual mixtures of a similarly spiritual substance;[14] or whether on the other hand, as sometimes happens to people who are awake and in their right minds, the will is so preoccupied with its thoughts that it turns its back on the senses, and so forms the conscious attention with various images of sensible things that it is as if the sensible things themselves were being sensed. And it is not only when the will stretches out to such things in desire that these vivid images are impressed on the attention, but also when the consciousness is drawn to observing things it shrinks from in order to avoid or beware of them. So it is by fear as well as by desire that the senses are directed to sensible things, to be formed by them. The more vehement the fear or the desire, the deeper is the impression made on the attention, either by the body you perceive with the senses in the place near you, or by the image of the body you are thinking about which is contained in the memory.

As a body in place, then, is to the senses of the body, so is the likeness of a body in the memory to the conscious attention; and as the sight of one looking at something is to that look of a body which forms the sense, so is the inner sight of one thinking about something to the image of a body fixed in the memory which forms the conscious attention; and what the intention of the will is to the coupling of a body seen to the sight, so that a kind of unity of three is produced even though they are of such different natures, that the same intention of the will is to the coupling of the image of a body in the memory to the sight of the one thinking about it, which is the form grasped by the conscious attention as it goes back to the memory; and here too a unity is produced out of three, which are not now differentiated by diversity of nature but are of one and the same substance, because all this is inside and it is all one consciousness.

8. Now just as the will cannot call the sense of the observer back to a bodily form or look that has vanished, so neither will there be anything for the will to bend the conscious attention back to in order to be formed by it in an act of recollection, if the image carried in the memory has been erased by being forgotten. However, the consciousness has the power of fabricating not merely things that have been forgotten but even things that have never been sensed or experienced; it can compose them out of things that have not dropped out of the memory, by increasing, diminishing, altering, and putting them together as it pleases. Thus it often pictures something as if it were like what it knows it is not like, or at least what it does not know that it is like. Here one has to be careful neither to lie and so deceive others nor to make an assumption and so deceive oneself. But if you avoid these two evils, there is no harm in such imaginative fancies, just as there is no harm in experiencing sensible things and retaining them in the memory, provided you do not desire them covetously if they are nice nor shirk them shamefully if they are nasty. But when the will forsakes better things and avidly wallows in these it becomes unclean, and in this way such things can be thought about disastrously when they are present and even more disastrously when they are absent.

This is how one lives a bad and misshapen life according to the trinity of the outer man; for even this second trinity which is busy imagining things inside is still imagining things of the outer world, and is generated for the sake of using sensible and bodily things. For no one could even use them well unless he kept the images of things he had sensed in the memory. And if the greater part of our will is not dwelling amid higher and more inward things, and if that part of it which is applied to bodies outside or to their images inside does not refer whatever it fixes on in them to the better and truer life, and does not rest in that end which it has its eye on when it judges that these outward actions are to be performed, what else are we doing but what the apostle forbids us to do when he says, *Do not be conformed to this age* (Rom 12:2)?

This trinity therefore is not the image of God. For it is produced in the soul through the senses of the body out of the lowest level of creation, which is the bodily one, and the soul itself is higher than this. And yet it is not altogether unlike God. Is there anything, after all, that does not bear a likeness to God after its own kind and fashion, seeing that God made all things very good for no other reason than that he himself is supremely good? Insofar then as anything that is is good, to that extent it bears some likeness, even though a very remote one, to the highest good, and if this is a natural likeness it is of course a right and well-ordered likeness; if it is faulty, then of course it is a sordid and perverted one. Even in their very sins, you see, souls are pursuing nothing but a kind of likeness to God with a proud and topsy-turvy and, if I may so put it, a slavish freedom. Thus our first parents could not have been persuaded to sin unless they had been told, *You will be like gods* (Gn 3:5). It is true that not everything in creation which is like God in some way or other is also to be called his image, but only that which he alone is higher than. That alone receives his direct imprint which has no other nature interposed between him and itself.

Chapter 3

The two trinities of the outer man so far outlined are further discussed, with particular reference to the proper distinctions between their members, and their mutual relationships; as regards the order or relationship between the first two members of each trinity, this is seen as being one of quasi-parent and quasi-offspring; and as regards the relationship of the third member to the first two, it is found that it cannot be conceived of either as quasi-parent or quasi-offspring. In conclusion it is made clear that there is a dynamic link, or a chain of movement between the acts involved in the outermost trinity of sense and those comprised in the more inward one of memory or imagination. We are already embarked on the movement of the psyche inward and upward.

9. So it is that sight, that is the form which is produced in the sense of the beholder, has its quasi-parent in the form of the body from which it is produced. But this is not a true parent, and so the former is not a true offspring; it is not wholly begotten by it since something else is presented to the visible body for sight to be formed out of it, namely the sense of the one who is seeing. For this reason to love the body seen means being alienated.[15] So the will which joins them both together as quasi-parent and quasi-offspring is more spiritual than either of them. The body which is seen is of course quite simply not spiritual; the sight that is produced in the sense has a certain mixture of the spiritual about it since it cannot occur without the soul, and yet it is not wholly spiritual because what is being formed is a sense of the body. So the will which joins the two together, as I said, is recognized as being more spiritual, and thus it begins to suggest the person of the Spirit in that other Trinity.[16] But it has more in common with the formed sense than with the body from which it is given form. Both the sense of the living being and the will belong to the soul, not to a stone or any kind of body that can be seen. It does not therefore proceed from that quasi-parent, or for that matter from this quasi-offspring, that is from the sight or form which is in the sense. The will was already there before sight occurred, and it applied the sense to the body to be formed from it by observing it. However, it was not yet pleased; how could it be with something not yet seen? Now being pleased means a will at rest. Therefore we can neither call the will the quasi-offspring of sight, because it was there before sight, not its quasi-parent, because sight is not formed and molded from the will but from the body that is seen.

10. Perhaps we can say that sight is the end and resting place of the will, at least in this one particular respect; for of course it does not mean that it is going to will nothing else, just because it sees something it wanted to. So I am not talking about the will of man as such, which has no other final end but happiness; but for the time being in this one particular instance the will to see has no end

but sight, whether it also refers this to some further end or not. If it does not refer sight to something else but has simply wanted it for the sake of seeing, then there is no problem about showing that the end of the will is sight; it is obvious. If it does refer it to something else, then it wants this something else and will no longer be a will to see, or if it is a will to see it is not at least a will to see this. For example, if someone wishes to see a scar in order to prove that here has been a wound; or if he wishes to see the window in order to see the passers-by through the window; all such wishes or willings as these have their own proper ends which are referred to the end of that wish or will by which we wish to live happily and to come to that life which is not to be referred to anything else but will be all-sufficient to the lover in itself. So the will to see has sight as its end, and the will to see this thing has the sight of this thing as its end. The will to see a scar aspires to its end which is a sight of the scar, and nothing further concerns it; for the will to prove there has been a wound is another will, though linked to the first, and its end is wound-proving. And the will to see the window has as its end the sight of the window; the will to see passers-by through the window is another will joined onto this one, and again its end is the sight of passers-by. Now all wills or wishes are straight, and all the ones linked with them too, if the one to which they are all referred is good; but if that is bent then they are all bent. And thus a sequence of straight wishes or wills is a ladder for those who would climb to happiness, to be negotiated by definite steps; but a skein of bent and twisted wishes or wills is a rope to bind anyone who acts so, and have him *cast into outer darkness* (Mt 8:12). Happy then are they who in their deeds and behavior sing the *song of steps*,[17] and *woe to those who trail sins like a long rope* (Is 5:18). But if the will is still referred to something else, its resting place which we call its end is rather like what we could call the resting place of the foot in walking, when it is set down in a place from which the other foot can be supported as it takes another step. If however something pleases the will in such a way that it rests in it with a certain delight, and yet is not the thing it is tending toward but is also referred to something else, it should be thought of not as the home country of a citizen but as refreshment, or even a night's lodging for a traveler.[18]

11. Now we come to that other trinity, which is indeed more inward than this one of the senses and sensible objects, and yet derives from it; here it is not a sense of the body being formed from a body, but the conscious attention being formed from the memory, when the look of a body we have sensed outside has lodged in the memory. So here we can say that this look in the memory is the quasi-parent of the one which is produced in the imagination of the thinking subject. There it was in the memory even before we started thinking about it, just as a body was in its place before we started sensing it so that sight resulted. But when we think about the look retained in the memory, this other look is "printed off" in the attention of our thoughts and formed in the act of remembering, and this is a quasi-offspring of the one held in the memory. Not even here, however, do we have true parent and true offspring. After all, the conscious attention which is formed from the memory when we recall something and think

about it, does not itself proceed from the look which we remember as something seen (we could of course not remember them[19] unless we had seen them); the conscious attention which is formed by remembering was there even before we saw the body we remember. How much more then before we committed it to memory. So although the form which is produced in the attention of the recalling subject is produced from the one which is in the memory, still the attention itself does not derive from it, but was there before it. It follows that if the one form is not true parent, the other is not true offspring. However, as quasi-parent and quasi-offspring they suggest points which may help us to see truer and more inward things with a surer and more practiced eye.

12. In the case of this second trinity it is already more difficult to tell whether the will which couples inner sight to memory is not either the parent or the offspring of one or other of them, and what makes it difficult is its likeness and equality in identity of nature and substance. It was easy in the outer case to tell the formed sense apart from the sensible body and the will apart from them both, because of the diversity of nature in all three with respect to each other, which we have examined enough above; but here it cannot be done so easily. It is true that this trinity we are now asking about has been carried into the consciousness from outside, but still it is all happening inside and there is nothing in it apart from the nature of the consciousness itself. So how can we set about demonstrating that the will is neither quasi-parent nor quasi-offspring of either the bodily likeness contained in the memory or the one that is printed off from it when we remember? After all, it so couples the two together in the act of thinking that it all seems to be one thing in the singular and cannot be sorted out except by reason. The first thing to see is that there can be no will to remember, unless either the whole or part of the thing we want to remember is held in the storerooms of memory. Where we have utterly and entirely forgotten something the will to remember cannot even arise, because if we want to recall anything it means that we have already recalled that it is or was in our memory. For instance, if I want to recall what I had for dinner yesterday, I have already recalled that I had dinner; or if not even that yet, I have certainly recalled something about that time, at least if nothing else that there was a yesterday and a part of it at which one usually has dinner, and also what it is to have dinner. If I had recalled none of this sort of thing whatever, then I could not possibly want to recall what I had for dinner yesterday.

So we can take it that the will to remember proceeds from things contained in the memory, together with things which are printed off from them through recollection in the act of observing, that is it proceeds from the coupling of something we have recalled to the sight which is produced from it in the attention of our thoughts when we have recalled it. The will itself which couples the two together now looks for yet another thing which is as it were nearby and within reach of recollection.[20] So there are as many trinities of this kind as there are recollections, because in every one of them you find these three: the thing stowed away in the memory even before it is thought about, and the thing that is produced in thought when it is looked at, and the will joining the two together and arising from both and itself as the third element completing one event or reality.

Or should we rather recognize one trinity in this kind of thing, and talk about whatever bodily looks are latent in the memory as one thing in general, and again about the sight of the consciousness recalling and thinking about such things as one thing in general, and to the coupling of these two add the coupling will as the third element, so that it all makes some one thing out of some three things? But the conscious attention cannot look at everything contained in the memory at one glance, and so trinities of thoughts follow one another in succession, and one gets this innumerably numerous trinity. It is not however an infinite one if it does not exceed the number of things stowed away in the memory. After all, from the moment a person begins to sense bodies with any of his bodily senses, they add up to a definite and determinate number, though an innumerable one, even if you add the things he has forgotten. It is not only infinite numbers that we call innumerable, but also finite ones that exceed our capacity to count.

13. But at least this shows us another way in which we can make it clearer that the thing stowed away in the memory is one thing, and the thing printed off from it in thought and recollection is another, although when they are coupled together they appear to be one and the same. We can only remember as many looks of bodies as we sensed, and as big as what we have sensed and like what we have sensed, because it is from bodily sensation that consciousness gulps them down in the memory. But the sights seen in our thoughts, while they do indeed derive from the things in the memory, can still be multiplied and varied to an innumerable and really infinite extent. I remember one sun because I have only seen one, as it actually is. But if I want to I can think of two or three, or as many as I like, and the attention of me thinking about many suns is formed from one and the same memory by which I remember one. I only remember it as big as I have seen it; if I remember it bigger or smaller that I have seen, then I am not remembering what I have seen, and so I am not in fact remembering. But because I am remembering, I remember it as big as I have seen it. However, I can think of it as bigger or smaller, just as I want. So I remember it as I have seen it, but I think of it moving as I wish or standing still where I wish, or coming from where I wish or going where I wish. It is easy for me to think of it square though I remember it round, and of any color at all, though I have never seen a green sun and therefore do not remember it. As with the sun, so with anything else. But these forms of things are all bodily and sensible, and so the consciousness is mistaken when it supposes that outside they are exactly as it thinks of them inside, either when they have already ceased to be outside and are still retained in the memory, or when what we remember is shaped in our thoughts otherwise than it is, not by faithful recollection but by variable cogitation.

14. Though as a matter of fact we very frequently believe people when they tell us true things which they have themselves perceived with their senses.[21] Such things we think about as they are told us and as we actually hear them, and so it does not seem in this case as if the attention is being bent back to the memory

to produce think sights; after all, we are not thinking about them because we are recalling them but because someone else is telling us them. So in this case we do not appear to realize that trinity which is produced when the look lying around in the memory and the sight of recollection are coupled together by the will as the third party. When I am told something, I do not think about what was lying around in my memory but about what I am actually hearing now. I do not mean of course the actual sounds uttered by the speaker, or the reader might suppose I have gone out again to that trinity which functions in sensible things and the senses; no, I mean that I think about those bodily appearances which the narrator signifies by the words he utters, and it is these I think about as I listen, and not as I remember. However, if we look at the matter a little more closely, not even in this case do we depart from the limits set by memory. I could not even begin to understand what he was telling me if I was hearing all the things he said and what they added up to for the first time, and did not have a general memory of each of them. Suppose someone tells me about a mountain that has been stripped of its woods and planted with olives, he is telling it to one who remembers what woods and olives and mountains look like. If I had forgotten all this I simply would be unable to think about his account of it. Thus it happens that everyone who thinks about bodily things, whether he makes them up himself or hears or reads someone else describing past events or forecasting future ones, has to have recourse to his memory and there bring to light the limits and measure of all the forms which he looks at in his thoughts. It is simply impossible for anyone to think about a color or a shape he has never seen, a sound he has never heard, a flavor he has never tasted, a smell he has never smelled, or a feel of a body he has never felt. But the reason why no one can think about anything bodily unless he has sensed it is that no one remembers anything bodily unless he has sensed it. So the limits of thinking are set by the memory just as the limits of sensing are set by bodies. The senses receive the look of a thing from the body we sense, the memory receives it from the senses, and the thinking attention from the memory.

15. Just as it is the will which fastens sense to body, so it is the will which fastens memory to sense and the thinking attention to memory. And what fastens them together and assembles them also unfastens and separates them, namely the will again. It is by movements of the body that it separates the senses of the body from the bodies to be sensed, either to avoid sensing or to stop sensing something; as when we shut our eyes or turn them away from something we do not want to see. In the same way we avert our ears from noises and our nostrils from smells. So too it is by shutting our mouths or spitting something out of them that we avoid flavors. As for touch, we draw back the body in order not to touch what we do not want to, or if we have already touched it we throw or push it away. Thus it is by moving the body that the will avoids coupling the senses of the body to sensible things. And it does it as far as it can. When it suffers difficulty in this respect because of our condition of servile mortality, the result is torment, and nothing is left to the will but endurance.

Memory is averted from sensation by the will when, intent on something else, it does not allow it to fix itself on what is present. This is easy to observe when, as often happens, we are with someone talking to us and appear not to have heard what they are saying, because we are thinking of something else. It is not true, though; we have heard, but we do not remember the sounds slipping that very instant through our ears, because the will has been disinclined to give the permission which is needed as a rule to fix them in the memory. So it would be truer to say "We don't remember" than "We didn't hear" when something like that happens. It also happens to people reading, extremely often at any rate to me, that I find I have read a page or a letter and have not the slightest idea what I have read, and have to repeat it. The will's interest has been intent on something else, and so the memory has not been applied to the sense of the body as that sense has been applied to the letters. So too, you go for a walk with your will intent on something else and you do not know what path you have taken. If you actually had not seen, you would either not have gone for the walk or you would have walked by feeling your way with great attention, especially if you were going along a way you did not know. But you walked quite easily, so of course you saw. However, while the sense of your eyes was connected with the places you were going through, your memory was not connected with your senses, and so you could not remember what you had seen even though it was extremely recent. Finally, the way the will averts the conscious attention from what is in the memory is simply by not thinking about it.

16. So it is that in this series which begins with the look of a body and ends with the look which is produced in the thinking gaze, four looks are brought to light, born as it were step by step one from the other; the second from the first, the third from the second, the fourth from the third. From the look of the body which is being seen arises the look which is produced in the sense of seeing, and from this the one which is produced in the memory, and from this the one that is produced in the attention on thinking. So the will couples quasi-parent with its offspring three times: first the look of the body with the one it begets in the sense of the body; next this with the one that is produced from it in the memory; and then a third time this with the one that is brought forth from it in the gaze of thought. But the middle or second couple, while nearer to the first, is not so similar to it as the third one is.[22] For there are in the series two sights, one of sensation, the other of thought. It is to make possible the sight of thought that there is produced from the sight of sensation something similar in the memory which the conscious attention can turn to in thought, just as the attention of the eyes turns to the body in actual observation. That is why I have wished to propose two trinities of this kind, one when the sensation of sight is formed from the external body, the other when the sight of thought is formed from the internal memory. But I did not wish to propose a middle trinity in between, because it is not usually called a sight when the form that is produced in the sense of the observer is committed to memory. In every instance, however, the will only appears as coupling quasi-parent with its offspring. And for this reason, wherever it proceeds from, it cannot itself be called either parent or offspring.

Chapter 4

The discussion of the limits, or modus, *set by memory on thought and the pull or thrust exercised by the will in operation, with which the last chapter ended, leads the author into a concluding reflection on the text of Wisdom 11:21,* You have disposed all things in measure and number and weight; *a preliminary glance at imaginative or fictitious thinking introduces this reflection.*

17. But then if we only remember what we have sensed, and only think what we have remembered, how is it that we often think false things though we do not of course remember falsely what we have sensed?[23] It must be that the will, which I have been at pains to present to the best of my ability as coupler and separator of this kind of thing, it must be that the will leads the thinking attention where it pleases through the stores of memory in order to be formed, and prompts it to take something from here out of the things we remember, something else from there, in order to think things we do not remember. All these assembled in one sight make something that is called false because it is not to be found outside in the nature of bodily things, or because it does not seem to have been derived from memory, since we do not remember ever having sensed such a thing. Has anyone ever seen a black swan? So no one remembers one. But is there anyone who cannot think of one? It is easy enough to suffuse that shape which we know from seeing it with the color black which we have seen no less in other bodies, and because we have sensed them both we remember them both. Nor do I remember a four-footed bird, because I have never seen one;[24] but it is very easy for me to look at such a fancy when to some winged shape I have seen I add two more feet of a sort that I have also seen. So when we think of two things in combination which we remember having sensed one by one, we appear to think of something which we do not remember, though we do it under the limitations set by memory, from which we take all the things that we put together in many and various ways as we will.

Again, we cannot think of bodies of a size we have never seen without the aid of memory. We can extend the masses of any bodies when we think of them to the maximum extent of space that our gaze is accustomed to range over through the magnitude of the universe. Reason can go further, but fancy does not follow,[25] inasmuch as reason declares an infinity of number, and this no thinking about bodily things can grasp with inner sight. The same reason teaches that even the smallest corpuscles can be divided to infinity; but when we reach the limits of minuteness or fineness that we remember having seen, we cannot now gaze on any slighter or minuter fancies, though reason does not stop proceeding to divide. So we do not think of any bodily things except what we remember or unless they are composed out of what we remember.

18. Because, however, the things that have been severally impressed on the memory can be thought about in numerous ways, it seems that measure belongs to memory while number belongs to sight. Though there may be an innumerable multiplicity of such sights, still each of them has its unpassable limits prescribed

for it in memory. So measure appears in memory and number in sights; just as there is a certain measure in visible bodies to which the sense of sight is adjusted in exceedingly numerous ways, and from one visible object the gaze of many observers is formed; indeed even one observer, thanks to the number of his two eyes, can often see things double, as we explained above. So in the things from which sights are printed off there is a certain measure, and in the sights themselves number. But the will which joins and arranges these pairs and couples them in a kind of unity, and only applies the appetite for seeing or thinking to the achievement of rest in the things from which sight are formed, the will is like *weight*. I must confess I like to taste the pleasure of observing these three, *measure, number, and weight*,[26] in all other matters as well.

But now to conclude, I have demonstrated as best I could and to whom I could that the will which couples together visible thing and sight as quasi-parent and quasi-offspring, whether in sensation or in thought, cannot itself be called either parent or offspring. So time is pressing us to begin looking for this same trinity[27] in the inner man; to turn inward from this animal and fleshly one called the outer man whom we have been talking about so long. There, inside, we hope we shall be able to find the image of God in a trinity, provided our efforts are assisted by him who according to the testimony of scripture and the very evidence of things themselves *has arranged all things in measure and number and weight* (Wis 11:20).

NOTES

1. *In agnitionem*: M reads *in agnitione*, in recognition. As far as one can be sure of the original reading, it seems that Augustine changed the text he used later on. At any rate when this text is quoted again in Books XIV and XV, he reads *in agnitione*. Where he really departs from both Greek and Vulgate is in adding *Dei*, and in this he is consistent.

2. *Nosque ipsi animi.* My translation does not perhaps bring out the full platonic force of the expression. It is not, as a matter of fact, altogether characteristic of Augustine. Elsewhere he is quite emphatic that the soul, *anima* or *animus*, is not the man, and therefore presumably not entitled to be called *ego*, or in the plural *nos*. In this very passage he has just talked about "we having become mortal," and this is clearly in respect of our bodies.

But as regards what it has to say about the cognitive functioning of the human being, this whole passage is entirely typical; that the author regards not merely our moral enslavement to the senses but our cognitive dependence on them as the result of the fall, not as a consequence of the kind of nature we have been created with; that this dependence is a kind of sickness—all this marks off the Augustinian view from the more genuinely humanistic aristotelianism of Thomas Aquinas.

This dependence does indeed, as he has put it, follow on "the logic of our condition," *ipso ordine conditionis nostrae*; but this order or logic is the crazy logic of disorder, which has turned us upside down and inside out.

Augustine does not go anywhere near so far as Origen and say that our very bodies and their senses are our punishment for sin (the garments of skin with which God clothed Adam and Eve when he turned them out of paradise); but he does not think that our intellectual powers depend by nature for their functioning on our senses, as Aristotle and Aquinas do. And what those two thinkers take as evidence of this dependence, he takes as evidence that the proper order of things has been upset by sin.

3. *A visu*: M reads *visum*, The body seen is separable in its nature.

4. M omits the words "not formed from without or the sense."

5. In the divine trinity and in its mental image the three constituents are of the same nature, and only distinguished by their properties, that is by the peculiar relationships which are proper to each. It is these properties that are obscure in the higher trinities and which he is hoping to illustrate in this lower one, where the manifest difference of natures will make the illustration easier. He is now going on to pinpoint the distinction between the three elements by their properties, that is to say their mutual relationships. According to the scheme, body, sight and intention in this lowest trinity are equivalent to self-memory, self-understanding, and self-willing in the mental image, which are equivalent to Father, Son, and Holy Spirit in the divine trinity. Now in the higher trinities the distinctions by proper relationships between the terms in each set are obscure: why is the Holy Spirit not also called Son, that is to say, how does his proper relationship to the Father differ from that of the Son; and in the image, to what extent is there a real distinction, founded on mutual relationship, between memory and understanding? So if he can show in this trinity of the outer man that the elements, which are manifestly different in nature, also have relational properties with respect to each other that are analogous to the as yet obscure relational properties in the higher trinities, he will have succeeded in his aim of casting light on those distinctions in the higher levels.

6. *Insertarum fenestrarum cancelli*. The exact meaning of *insertarum* is unclear. It seems to be a literary allusion to Virgil, *Aeneid* 3, 152. The dictionary's suggestion that it means "inserted in the wall" makes the poet guilty of the most meaningless padding. According to the editor of my pocket Virgil, the classical commentator Servius thought that *insertas* in the poet's line meant *non seratas*, that is, not bolted, meaning I imagine with the shutters back, an open window, being the only kind that could let the moonlight in, which Virgil's line is describing.

In the times of Aeneas, of course, there was no glass, and a window was no more than a hole in the wall, which could be closed by a wooden shutter. But I am assuming that by Augustine's time there was at least something equivalent to window panes, in the kind of house at any rate that the bishop of Hippo would have lived in. So I have myself taken *insertarum* to mean here "inserted windows" in the sense of "windows fitted in, with some translucent material inserted in them," as distinct from windows that were still just holes in walls.

7. See Book IX, 3, number 10.

8. What a homely vision these paragraphs conjure up of the bishop of Hippo sitting in his study and conducting simple optical experiments, no doubt getting his stenographer to join in!

9. See Book III, 15. One wonders what the many other instances he could have mentioned were, whether from Pliny and other ancient natural historians or instances he himself had been told about or had observed.

10. *Cogitatio*, from *cogito*, a frequentative form of *cogo*, itself a contraction of *coago*, to push together.

11. *Visio cogitantis*.

12. *Tanta offunditur similitudo*; the figure is of something like a pall of smoke spreading out and obliterating all visible objects. M reads *offenditur*, so great a likeness is stumbled on.

13. Another thoroughly platonic figure for the relationship of soul to body, that causes the writer to identify self with soul.

14. The "other hidden power" probably means angelic or demonic agencies; but the "various spiritual mixtures of a similarly spiritual substance" are impressions or images inserted into the imagination by the "hidden power," and are called "spiritual" in a different sense from the normal one. In his *Literal Meaning of Genesis* XII, 6, 15, Augustine distinguishes three kinds of sight or vision: that of the outer senses, *per oculos*; that of the memory or imagination which he is talking about here, and which he there describes as being *per spiritum*; and that of the mind, which sees intelligible ideas independently of bodily images.

Thus in this context "spirit" and "spiritual" have a more material or physical meaning than in their more normal use—not perhaps very different from "spirits" and "spirituous" applied to certain liquors. According to the commonplace ideas of ancient physiology the nerves contained "spirits" by which they transmitted sensations and impulses, and it is this kind of "spiritual mixture" and "spiritual substance" that Augustine has in mind in this passage.

15. In the *Revisions* he comments that this is only true if one so loves a body as to think one can find beatitude in the enjoyment of it, but not if one so loves its beauty as to turn it to the praise of the creator, and make it a part of one's finding beatitude in him (2, 15).

It is interesting to find the marxist term "alienation" in Augustine; is Marx's concept in any way Augustinian? Both seem to mean a forfeiture of captaincy of one's soul.

16. A purely verbal, and curiously feeble analogy. He has no need to offer it, as he has already established the will as the analogue in these lesser trinities to the Holy Spirit.

In his discussion of the relationship of the act of will to the two other elements involved in an act of sight he runs into certain difficulties, so far as his aim of throwing light on the divine procession of the Holy Spirit is concerned. He goes on to show easily enough how the will cannot be either quasi-parent or quasi-offspring of the formed sense of sight or the actual sight. This is helpful in illustrating how the Holy Spirit cannot be regarded as a second Son, or as a second parent to the Son. But it also proves a little too much, because the same argument shows that the will does not proceed either from the body seen or the sight of it which is the form of the body in the seeing eye. And of course Augustine is bound to maintain by faith, and desires to apprehend by understanding, that the Holy Spirit proceeds from the Father and the Son.

So in the next paragraph he goes on to refine a little more his idea of the precise act of will involved in the business of seeing. He asks if it is not the act of will which consists in resting in, or taking pleasure in the achieved object of the will, namely seeing what you want to see. Such an act could be said to proceed from both the object seen and the seeing of it—though he does not actually dot the "i"s and cross the "t"s of this conclusion, because he gets side-tracked into a discussion of how we will ends and means. But I think that is the conclusion he is feeling his way to. The trouble, as I see it, is that if you take will in this precise and limited sense, then the whole argument by which he showed that will cannot be regarded as quasi-offspring falls to the ground, because that was about will in a rather different sense. He does in fact seem to fall into a certain equivocation.

The only way we can save his dialectical honor in this case is by recognizing that he is not asserting arguments dogmatically, but proposing them, as always, in a tentative and exploratory manner. But see also note 20 below.

17. The title of the "gradual psalms," 120-134.

18. By his use here of this classical figure for the Christian life, he effectively qualifies the apparently harsh distinction he has made earlier between using and enjoying (Book IX, 13, note 24); no harm in enjoying the material world as traveler's refreshment.

19. *Eorum*; two manuscripts emend reasonably enough *ejus*, it; but it seems to be one of the cases of careless or rough composition which he would have corrected if he had been able to revise his text as he would have liked.

20. Augustine has here succeeded in completing a demonstration which we saw him only partially successful with in terms of the sensation trinity in section 9. There he proved easily enough that the act of will can be neither quasi-parent nor quasi-offspring; but in so doing he made it clear that the act of will does not in that trinity proceed in any way from the other two members of the trinity. With this more inward trinity, however, he succeeds in showing how the will act proceeds from the other two elements, and proceeds from them, what is more, as coupled together in one source from which the act of will proceeds. He does not, however, really show in this inner memory trinity how will cannot be called quasi-parent or quasi-offspring, except insofar as its function of coupling the other two elements together is incompatible with such a status.

So it seems to me that we should take his two analyses of these two trinities as amounting to two parts of one total demonstration; namely that the act of will, analogue of the Holy Spirit, does not stand in a generation relationship with either of the other two members of these trinities, analogues of the Father and the Son (this demonstrated from the sensation trinity); and yet that it does (with the memory trinity) proceed from them precisely as they are united in one act.

Again however it is clear that his demonstration by analogy is not perfect. For as he immediately goes on to remark, there are many such memory trinities constantly succeeding one another; and as his illustration from yesterday's dinner makes clear, the will to remember which forms part of trinity

C, say remembering what I had for dinner yesterday, does not proceed from the other two elements of trinity C, namely the look of yesterday's dinner stored in my memory and the look of it reproduced therefrom in my conscious attention, but from the two corresponding elements of trinity B, which is concerned, let us say, with remembering what a bad dinner I had today.

That is why, I think, he goes on to ask himself if he cannot treat all these successive trinities of successive recollections as one generic kind of trinity. But even if he does this, he realizes it will not save his analogy from the particular defect we have noticed.

21. This hanging concessive clause at the beginning of a new paragraph is little disconcerting. The general bearing of the whole paragraph is clear enough—a new variation on the working of his second trinity. It is the manner of its connection with what precedes it that is odd. I think the line of thought is that it is curious how our own memory can appear to deceive us (though it is really our thoughts that are guilty, not memory), while we rightly have every confidence in what other people tell us.

22. Reading *tertia* with M: CCL has *tertiae*, as it is to the third one.

23. When our memory "plays us false," it is really our thinking, our judgment, that is at fault, as he was maintaining above, sections 13, 14. See note 21.

24. In *Revisions* 2, 15 he has a scruple about this, saying he had forgotten what the Law has to say about four-footed "birds," *volatilia*, Lv 11:20. The reference is to winged insects.

25. Reading with M and most manuscripts *non sequitur, quippe cum* . . . CCL reads, it is hard to see why, *non sequitur. Sequitur quippe cum* . . . with two manuscripts; a dittography that makes nonsense of what he is saying in the whole passage.

26. This is indeed one of Augustine's favorite texts. He comments on it at some length in *The Literal Meaning of Genesis* IV, 3, 7-12. Besides the obvious meaning of the text, as saying in effect "You have arranged all things to have their appropriate measure, number, and weight," he also sees another by pressing the preposition "in" to its limits. If God arranged all things in these three, these three must have existed before all things; which is only possible if they are God. And so he interprets them as a trinitarian formulation; God (Father) is measure without measure, as that which prescribes *modus* or limits to everything; God (Son) is number without number, as that which provides everything with its *species* or look or beauty or proper nature; God (Holy Spirit) is weight without weight as that which draws everything to its proper rest and stability. Thus the text can be read as expressing succinctly the doctrine that all creation bears a trace or *vestigium* of the trinity, which seems to be the reason for his bringing it in here. The trinities we have been examining in the outer man are not the image of God; but they are, as found in the most noble of creatures, the highest kind of trinitarian *vestigium* in creation, and short of the image they are the best example of the divine measure, number and weight.

27. That is, of will coupling together a "parent" and an "offspring."

BOOK XII

MAN'S CASE HISTORY: THE IMAGE BROKEN UP; THE FALL

Chapter 1

The inner man, or mind, is distinguished into two departments or functions, a higher one concerned with contemplating eternal truth and making judgments in accordance with it, and in this function mind is most essentially itself; and a lower one concerned with the management of temporal and material affairs, which is derived from the higher function rather as the woman was derived from the man in the creation narrative of Genesis 2.

---

1. Well now, let us see where we are to locate what you might call the border between the outer and the inner man. Anything in our consciousness that we have in common with animals is rightly said to be still part of the outer man. It is not just the body alone that is to be reckoned as the outer man, but the body with its own kind of life attached, which quickens the body's structure and all the senses it is equipped with in order to sense things outside. And when the images of things sensed that are fixed in the memory are looked over again in recollection, it is still something belonging to the outer man that is being done. In all these things the only way that we differ from animals is that we are upright, not horizontal, in posture. This is a reminder to us from him who made us that in our better part, that is our consciousness, we should not be like the beasts we differ from in our upright posture. Not indeed that we should throw ourselves heart and soul onto what is most sublime in bodies; for to seek satisfaction for the will even in such noble bodies is to fell the consciousness into a prone position.[1] But just as our body is raised up by nature to what is highest in bodies, that is, to the heavens, so our consciousness being a spiritual substance should be raised up toward what is highest in spiritual things—not of course by the elevation of pride but by the dutiful piety of justice.

2. So animals too can both sense bodies outside with the senses of the body, and remember them as fixed in the memory, and seek in them whatever is advantageous and shun whatever is harmful. But to take note of such things, and

to retain not only what has been naturally caught in the memory but also what has been committed to it on purpose, and by recollection and thought to impress on it again things that were fast slipping into oblivion, so that just as thought is formed out of what the memory carries, what is in the memory is fixed firmly there by thought; to compose fabricated sights by taking all sorts of things recorded from here and there and as it were sewing them together; to observe how in this kind of thing what is like truth is to be distinguished from what is actually true—in bodies I mean, not in spiritual things; all this kind of conscious activity, while it is carried on with sensible things and with what the consciousness has imbibed from them through the senses of the body, is nonetheless not without its share in reason, and so is not common to man and beast.[2] But it pertains to the loftier reason to make judgments on these bodily things according to non-bodily and everlasting meanings;[3] and unless these were above the human mind they would certainly not be unchanging, and unless something of ours were subjoined to them we would not be able to make judgments according to them about bodily things. But we do make judgments on bodily things in virtue of the meaning of dimensions and figures[4] which the mind knows is permanent and unchanging.

3. However, while that part of us, which is occupied with the performance of bodily and temporal actions in such a way that it is not common to us and beasts, is indeed rational, still it has so to say been led off from that rational substance of our minds by which we cling from underneath to the intelligible and unchanging truth, and deputed to the task of dealing with and controlling these lower matters. Just as among all the beasts there was not found for the man an assistant like himself, and only something taken from himself and formed into a consort could fill the bill,[5] so too our mind, with which we consult the highest and innermost truth, has no assistant like it in the parts of the soul we have in common with the beasts, for making use of bodily things in a way to satisfy the nature of man. And therefore something rational of ours is assigned the duty of this work, not in the sense of being divorced from the mind in breach of unity, but as derived from it in a helpful partnership. And just as male and female are two in one flesh, so our understanding and activity, or counsel and execution, or reason and reasonable appetite, or whatever other more meaningful terms you may find,[6] are embraced in the one nature of mind. Thus as it was said of those *They shall be two in one flesh* (Gn 2:24), so it may equally be said of these "Two in one mind."

4. So when we discuss the nature of the human mind we are certainly discussing one thing, and we are not doubling it into the two aspects I have mentioned except in terms of functions. It follows that when we are looking for a trinity in it we are looking in the whole of it; we are not separating rational activity in temporal things from contemplation of eternal things in such a way that we now have to look for some third thing to complete the trinity. No, a trinity has to be discovered in the whole nature of the mind in such a way that if on the one hand temporal activity stops—it is only for this that an assistant is needed and that something of the mind is drawn off to administer these lower

affairs—this trinity is found in one quite simply undivided mind; and if on the other hand one makes this distribution of functions, only in that part which is concerned with the contemplation of eternal things can one find something that is not only a trinity but also the image of God; while in the part that is drawn off for temporal activity one may perhaps find a trinity, but certainly not the image of God.[7]

Chapter 2

Turning to the story of the first man and woman which he has introduced as an allegory of the two functions of the mind, he rejects another allegorical interpretation of it which sees the basic human family of man woman and offspring as the image of the divine trinity. Not only does this theory not fit the dogmatic requirements of trinitarian doctrine, it cannot either be reconciled with 1 Cor 11:7, where Paul asserts that the man alone is the image of God.

---

5. It will be clear that I do not find the opinion very convincing which supposes that the trinity of the image of God, as far as human nature is concerned, can be discovered in three persons; that is, that it may be composed of the union of male and female and their offspring, in which the man suggests the person of the Father, what proceeds from him by way of birth that of the Son, and thus the third person of the Holy Spirit, they say,[8] is represented by the woman, who proceeds from the man in such a way that she is not son or daughter, although it is by her conceiving that offspring is born; for the Lord said of the Holy Spirit that he *proceeds from the Father* (Jn 15:26), and yet he is not a son. The only thing about this mistaken opinion that carries any conviction is the point that, as the origin of woman according to the reliable authority of scripture shows clearly enough, not everything that comes into being from one person to make another can be called son, seeing that the person of the woman came into being out of the person of the man without all the same being called his daughter. The rest of the theory is so absurd, indeed so false, that it can easily be refuted. I pass over what an error it is to think of the Holy Spirit as the mother of the Son and the wife of the Father. This objection could possibly be met by replying that such ideas may be offensive in carnal affairs while you are thinking of the conception and birth of bodies, but that they can be thought about in all chasteness by the pure to whom all things are pure; while to the impure and unbelievers whose mind and conscience are defiled nothing is pure,[9] so much so that some of them are even offended at the thought of Christ being born of the virgin according to the flesh.[10] But at that supreme level of spirituality there is nothing that can be violated or corrupted, nothing born in time or formed out of formless matter. Furthermore it is to the likeness of things up there that all the different kinds of things in this lower creation were made, even though the likeness is a very remote one. So to talk about them in this kind of way ought not to upset

anyone of sober good sense, or he might find that by shrinking from a bogus horror he falls into a disastrous error. He must get accustomed to discovering the traces of spiritual things in bodies in such a way that when he turns upward from here and starts climbing with reason as his guide in order to reach the unchanging truth itself *through* which these *things were made* (Jn 1:3), he does not drag along with him to the top anything that he puts little value on at the bottom. There was, after all, a man who did not blush to choose wisdom as a wife for himself,[11] merely on the grounds that the word "wife" makes one think of the corruption of copulation in the begetting of offspring,[12] and for the matter of that wisdom is not female in sex just because it is called in Greek and Latin by a word of the feminine gender.

6. The reason then why we dislike this opinion is not that we are afraid of thinking about inviolate and unchanging charity as the wife of God the Father, who comes into being from him, though not as offspring, in order to bring to birth the Word *through whom all things were made* (Jn 1:3), but that the divine scripture shows quite clearly that it is false. God said *Let us make man to our image and likeness* (Gn 1:26), and a little later on it adds, *And God made man to the image of God* (Gn 1:27).[13] "Our," being plural in number, could not be right in this place if man were made to the image of one person, whether of the Father or the Son or the Holy Spirit; but because in fact he was made in the image of the trinity, it said *to our image*. And then in case we should suppose that we have to believe in three gods in the trinity, while this same trinity is in fact one God, it goes on to say, *And God made man to the image of God*, which amounts to saying "to his image."

7. Such turns of phrase are quite common in the scriptures, but quite a number of people, including ones who champion the Catholic faith, fail to notice them with sufficient care, and so they think "God made to the image of God" means "The Father made to the image of the Son."[14] What they are intending thereby is to vindicate the claim that the Son too is called God in the holy scriptures, as though there were no other perfectly plain and reliable texts in which the Son is not merely called God but also true God.[15] As for this text which they produce as evidence, while they set about solving one problem with it, they get themselves so tied up in another that they cannot extricate themselves. If the Father, you see, made man to the image of the Son in such a way that man is not the Father's image but only the Son's, then the Son is unlike the Father. But if devout faith teaches, as indeed it does, that the Son is like the Father to the point of being equal in being, then whatever is made to the likeness of the Son must also be made to the likeness of the Father. Finally, if the Father did not make man to his own image but to the Son's, why did he not say "Let us make man to your image and likeness" instead of saying "our"? The reason must be that it was the image of the trinity that was being made in man, and this is how man would be the image of the one true God, since the trinity itself is the one true God.

Now there are hundreds of such turns of phrase[16] in scripture, but it must suffice to quote the following. It says in the psalms *Salvation is the Lord's, and your blessing upon your people* (Ps 3:8), as though it were spoken to someone else and not to him about whom it said in the third person *Salvation is the Lord's.* Again, *By you*, it says, *I shall be snatched from temptation, and hoping*[17] *in my God I shall leap over the wall* (Ps 18:29), as though it were someone else to whom he had said *By you I shall be snatched from temptation.* Again, *Peoples shall fall beneath you in the heart of the king's enemies* (Ps 45:5), which amounts to saying "in the heart of your enemies"; he was of course addressing to the king, that is to the Lord Jesus Christ, the words *Peoples shall fall beneath you*, and it was the same king he meant when he added *in the heart of the king's enemies.*

Such turns of phrase are more rarely found in the New Testament writings, but still we have the apostle saying to the Romans, *About his Son, whom he acquired*[18] *from the seed of David according to the flesh, who was predestined Son of God in power according to the Spirit of sanctification as a result of the resurrection from the dead of Jesus Christ our Lord* (Rom 1:4), as though he were speaking about someone else above. But what in fact is the Son of God, predestined as a result of the resurrection from the dead of Jesus Christ, but the same Jesus Christ[19] who was predestined Son of God? So in this place, though we hear "Son of God in the power of Jesus Christ," or "Son of God according to the Spirit of sanctification of Jesus Christ," or "Son of God as a result of the resurrection from the dead of Jesus Christ,"[20] when he could have said more normally "in his power" or "according to the Spirit of his sanctification" or "as a result of his resurrection from the dead" or "from his dead,"[21] we are not for all that obliged to understand some other person but one and the same, namely the Son of God our Lord Jesus Christ. In exactly the same way, though we hear *God made man to the image of God* (Gn 1:27), when it could have said more normally "to his own image," still we are not obliged to understand another person in the trinity, but one and the same trinity itself which is one God, to whose image man was made.

8. This being established, what happens if we take this image of the trinity as realized not in one but in three human beings, father and mother and son? It would seem to follow that man was not in fact made to the image of God until a wife was made for him and until they had produced a son, because there was as yet no threesome or trinity. Is someone going to say, "The trinity was there all right, because in their germinal nature even if not in their proper form the woman was there in the side of her husband and the son was there in the loins of his father"? If that is the case, why did scripture go on, immediately after saying *God made man to the image of God*, to add, *He made him male and female, he made them and blessed them* (Gn 1:27)?* What I mean is, why does scripture make no mention of anything besides male and female in the nature

---

* The text could if you like be divided as follows: And *God made man*, then adding, *to the image of God he made him*, and finally the clause, *male and female he made them.* Some people, you see, have shrunk away from saying *He made him male and female* in case it should be understood as some monstrous formation, like those they call hermaphrodites. Yet even with my reading each could be understood in the singular number without falsehood, seeing that it later says, *Two in one flesh* (Gn 2:24).

of man made to God's image? To complete the image of the trinity it ought to have mentioned a son also, even though he was still in the loins of his father like the woman in his side. Or was the woman already made perhaps, scripture compressing in a short summary what it would later describe the manner of in greater detail, so that the son could not be mentioned because he was not yet born? As though the Spirit could not have included this too in the brief summary, though he would tell of the birth of a son in its proper place, just as he later told in the proper place of the woman being taken from the man's side, and yet did not omit to mention her here.[22]

9. We should not then understand man being made to the image of the supreme trinity, that is, to the image of God, as meaning that this image is to be understood in three human beings. Particularly so in view of what the apostle says about the man[23] being the image of God, for which reason he removes the covering from his head while he warns the woman to wear it: he says, *The man ought not to cover his head, since he is the image and glory of God. But the woman is the glory of the man* (1 Cor 11:7). Now what are we to say to this? If the woman in her own person completes the image of the trinity, why is the man still called the image when she has already been extracted from his side? Or if one human person of the three can be called the image of God in the same way as in the supreme trinity each person is God, why is the woman too not the image of God? That, you see, is why she is told to cover her head, which the man is forbidden to do because he is the image of God.

Chapter 3

The text from Paul quoted in the last chapter to demolish the opinion that the image of the trinity is to be found in the human trio of man, woman, and child presents an even greater problem itself, in that it seems to exclude woman altogether from being the image of God, in contradiction both to Christian good sense and to the text of Genesis 1:27. The problem is solved by explaining the apostle symbolically in support of the author's symbolic exegesis of the Genesis story of the first couple to represent the functional structure of the human mind. This exegesis is pursued to show the fall narrative as realized in the disordered psyche of Everyman.

10. But we must see how what the apostle says about the man and not the woman being the image of God avoids contradicting what is written in Genesis: *God made man to the image of God; he made him male and female; he made them and blessed them* (Gn 1:27). It says that what was made to the image of God is the human nature that is realized in each sex, and it does not exclude the female from the image of God that is meant. For after saying *God made man to the image of God*, it says *he made him male and female*—or at least with the other punctuation, *male and female he made them*. So how are we to take what we have heard from the apostle, that the man is the image of God, and so he is

forbidden to cover his head, but the woman is not and so she is told to do so?[24] In the same way, I believe, as what I said when I was dealing with the nature of the human mind,[25] namely that the woman with her husband is the image of God in such a way that the whole of that substance is one image,[26] but when she is assigned her function of being an assistant, which is her concern alone, she is not the image of God; whereas in what concerns the man alone he is the image of God as fully and completely as when the woman is joined to him in one whole.[27] We said about the nature of the human mind that if it is all contemplating truth it is the image of God; and when something is drawn off from it and assigned or directed in a certain way to the management of temporal affairs, it is still all the same the image of God as regards the part with which it consults the truth it has gazed on; but as regards the part which is directed to managing these lower affairs, it is not the image of God. Now the more it reaches out toward what is eternal, the more it is formed thereby to the image of God, and so it is not to be curbed or required to moderate or restrain its exertions in this direction, and therefore *the man ought not to cover his head* (1 Cor 11:7). But as regards that rational activity which is occupied with bodily and temporal things, too many advances into this lower territory are dangerous, and so it *ought to have authority over its head* (1 Cor 11:10); this is indicated by the covering, which symbolizes its need to be curbed. This hallowed and pious symbolism is pleasing to the angels.[28] For God does not see in time, nor does anything new happen in his sight or his knowledge when some temporal and transitory action is performed, in the way that such actions affect either the fleshly senses of animals and men, or even the celestial ones of angels.[29]

11. That the apostle Paul had worked out a symbolism of something more mysterious in the obvious distinction of sex between male and female can be gathered from the following: while he says elsewhere that the true widow is one who is left all alone without sons or grandchildren and yet that she ought to *hope in the Lord and persist in prayer night and day* (1 Tm 5:5), here he says that the woman after being *led astray and falling into deviationism will be saved through bearing children*, and he added, *If they remain in faith and love and sanctification with sobriety* (1 Tm 2:14).[30] As though it could count against a good widow if she did not have any children, or if those she had refused to remain in good behavior.[31] But what we call good works are like the children of our life, in the sense in which one asks what sort of life a man lives, that is, how he conducts his temporal affairs—the life which the Greeks call *bios* not *zoe*—and these good works most frequently consist of services of mercy.* So it is clear what the apostle intended to signify, and he did it symbolically and mystically because he was talking about the covering of the female head, and if this does not refer to some hidden sacramental or symbolic meaning, it will remain quite pointless.

12. After all, the authority of the apostle as well as plain reason assures us

---

* No works of mercy, however, will stand to the credit of pagans or Jews who do not believe in Christ, nor of heretics or schismatics either, among whom there is no faith and love and sober sanctification to be found.[32]

that man was not made to the image of God as regards the shape of his body, but as regards his rational mind. It is an idle and base kind of thinking which supposes that God is confined within the limits of a body with features and limbs.[33] And does not the blessed apostle say, *Be renewed in the spirit of your mind, and put on the new man, the one who was created according to God* (Eph 4:23); and even more clearly elsewhere, *Putting off the old man,* he says, *with his actions, put on the new who is being renewed for the recognition of God according to the image of him who created him* (Col 3:9)? If then we are being renewed in the spirit of our mind, and if it is this new man who is being renewed for the recognition of God according to the image of him who created him, there can be no doubt that man was not made to the image of him who created him as regards his body or any old part of his consciousness, but as regards the rational mind, which is capable of recognizing God.

Now it is with respect to this renewal that we are also made sons of God through Christian baptism, and when we put on the new man it is of course Christ that we put on through faith.[34] Is there anyone then who would exclude females from this association, seeing that together with us men they are fellow heirs of grace, and the same apostle says somewhere else, *You are all sons of God through faith in Christ Jesus. For all you who were baptized in Christ thereby put on Christ. There is no Jew nor Greek, there is no slave nor free, there is no male nor female; for you are all one in Christ Jesus* (Gal 3:26). Surely this does not mean, does it, that female believers have lost their bodily sex? But because they are being renewed to the image of God[35] where there is no sex, it is there where there is no sex that man[36] was made to the image of God, that is in the spirit of his mind. Why is it then that *the man*[37] *ought not to cover his head because he is the image and glory of God,* while the woman ought to because *she is the glory of the man* (1 Cor 11:7), as though the woman were not being renewed in the spirit of her mind,[38] which is *being renewed for the recognition of God according to the image of him who created him* (Col 3:10)? Well, it is only because she differs from the man in the sex of her body that her bodily covering could suitably be used to symbolize that part of the reason which is diverted to the management of temporal things, signifying that the mind of man does not remain the image of God except in the part which adheres to the eternal ideas to contemplate or consult them: and it is clear that females have this as well as males. So in their minds a common nature is to be acknowledged; but in their bodies the distribution of the one mind is symbolized.

13. As we climb up inward then through the parts of the soul by certain steps of reflection, we begin to come upon something that is not common to us and the beasts, and that is where reason begins, and where we can now recognize the inner man. But through that reason which has been delegated to administer temporal affairs he may slide too much into outer things by making unrestrained advances; and in this the active reason may have the consent of her head; that is to say the reason which presides as the masculine portion in the control tower of counsel may fail to curb her. In such a case the inner man grows old among his enemies,[39] demons and the devil their chief who are jealous of virtue, and

the sight of eternal things is withdrawn from the head himself as he eats the forbidden fruit with his consort, so that the light of his eyes is no longer with him.[40] Thus they are both stripped naked of the enlightenment of truth, and the eyes of conscience are opened to see what a shameful and indecent state they have left themselves in. So they sew together as it were the leaves of delightful fruits without the fruits themselves, which is to say, they sew together fine words without the fruit of good works, in order while living badly to cover up their baseness by speaking well.[41]

14. What happens is that the soul, loving its own power, slides away from the whole which is common to all into the part which is its own private property.[42] By following God's directions and being perfectly governed by his laws it could enjoy the whole universe of creation; but by the apostasy of pride which is called the beginning of sin[43] it strives to grab something more than the whole[44] and to govern it by its own laws; and because there is nothing more than the whole it is thrust back into anxiety over a part, and so by being greedy for more it gets less. That is why greed is called the root of all evils.[45] Thus all that it tries to do on its own against the laws that govern the universe it does by its own body, which is the only part it has a part-ownership in. And so it finds delight in bodily shapes and movements, and because it has not got them with it inside, it wraps itself in their images which it has fixed in the memory. In this way it defiles itself foully with a fanciful sort of fornication by referring all its business to one or other of the following ends: curiosity, searching for bodily and temporal experience through the senses; swollen conceit, affecting to be above other souls which are given over to their senses; or carnal pleasure, plunging itself in this muddy whirlpool.

15. What it comes to then is that if the soul consults its own interests or those of others with good will, it aims at obtaining those inner and higher things that are not possessed privately but in common by all who love them, possessed in a chaste embrace without any limitations or envy; even if it goes wrong through ignorance of temporal matters (for here too temporal action is involved) and does not keep to the limits it ought to in its action, this is only a human temptation. It is a great thing to lead this life, which we are traveling along like a road on our return journey, in such a way that *no temptation takes hold of* us *but what is human* (1 Cor 10:13). This is a sin apart from the body, and is not to be put down to fornication, and is therefore very easily forgiven. But when the soul, greedy for experience or for superiority or for the pleasure of physical contact, does something to obtain the things that are sensed through the body to the extent of setting its end and its proper good in them, then whatever it does it does basely and *commits fornication, sinning against its own body* (1 Cor 6:18).[46] It drags the deceptive semblances of bodily things inside, and plays about with them in idle meditation until it cannot even think of anything divine except as being such, and so in its private avarice it is loaded with error and in its private prodigality it is emptied of strength. Nor would it come down at a single jump to such a base and wretched fornication, but as it is written, *He who despises trifles will fall away little by little* (Sir 19:1).

16. For just as a snake does not walk with open strides but wriggles along by the tiny little movements of its scales, so the careless glide little by little along the slippery path of failure, and beginning from a distorted appetite for being like God they end up by becoming like beasts. So it is that stripped naked of their first robe[47] they earned the skin garments of mortality.[48] For man's true honor is God's image and likeness in him, but it can only be preserved when facing him[49] from whom its impression is received. And so the less love he has for what is his very own the more closely can he cling to God. But out of greed to experience his own power he tumbled down at a nod from himself into himself as though down to the middle level. And then, while he wants to be like God under nobody, he is thrust down as a punishment from his own half-way level to the bottom, to the things in which the beasts find their pleasure. And thus, since his honor consists in being like God and his disgrace in being like an animal, *man established in honor did not understand; he was matched with senseless cattle and became like them* (Ps 49:12).

And how could he travel this long way from the heights to the depths except through the half-way level of self? If you neglect to hold dear in charity the wisdom which always remains the same, and hanker after knowledge[50] through experience of changeable, temporal things, this knowledge puffs up instead of building up.[51] In this way the consciousness is overweighted with a sort of self-heaviness, and is therefore heaved out of happiness, and by that experience of its half-wayness it learns to its punishment what a difference there is between the good it has forsaken and the evil it has committed; nor can it go back up again, having squandered and lost its strength, except by the grace of its maker calling it to repentance and forgiving its sins. For *who will ever free* the hapless soul *from the body of this death except by the grace of God through Jesus Christ our Lord* (Rom 7:24)? We will discuss this grace in its proper place as far as[52] he himself permits.[53]

17. And now with the Lord's assistance let us carry on with the consideration we have embarked upon of that part of reason to which knowledge belongs, that is to say, the knowledge of changeable and temporal things that is needed for the conduct of the business of this life. Now with that evident couple of the two human beings who were first created the serpent did not eat from the forbidden tree but only incited to eat, and the woman did not eat alone but gave some to her husband and they ate together, although she alone spoke to the serpent and she alone was led astray by it. So too with this kind of hidden and secret couple that is distinguishably exhibited even in one man the carnal, or if I may so put it the sensual, motion of the soul which is channeled into the senses of the body, and which is common to us and the beasts, is shut off from the reasoning of wisdom. With bodily sensation, after all, bodily things are sensed; but eternal, unchangeable and spiritual things are understood with the reasoning of wisdom. But the appetite[54] is very close to the reasoning of knowledge, seeing that it is the function of this knowledge to reason about the bodily things that are perceived by bodily sensation. If it does this well, it does it in order to refer them to the highest good as their end; if badly, in order to enjoy them as goods of a

sort it can take its ease in with an illusory happiness. So this channel of the mind is busy reasoning in a lively fashion about temporal and bodily things in its task of activity, and along comes that carnal or animal sense with a tempting suggestion for self-enjoyment, that is, for enjoying something as one's very own private good and not as a public and common good which is what the unchangeable good is; this is like the serpent addressing the woman. To consent to this temptation is to eat of the forbidden tree. But if this consent is satisfied merely with the pleasure of thought, while the authority of the higher counsel restrains the members of the body *from offering themselves to sin as weapons of iniquity* (Rom 6:13), then I think it should be regarded as if the woman alone ate the forbidden food. If however in consenting to the bad use of things that are perceived by bodily sensation it is decided to commit some sin or other with the body as well should the possibility present itself, then it is to be understood as the woman giving the unlawful food to her husband to eat together with her. For the mind cannot decide to perpetrate a sin in very deed, and not merely wistfully in thought, unless that channel of the mind which has the supreme power to move the limbs to action or restrain them from action also yields to the bad action and enslaves itself to it.

18. To be sure, one cannot deny that it is a sin when the mind takes pleasure in just thinking about unlawful acts, not indeed deciding to do them but just holding them, so to say, and fondly turning them over in its hands, when they should have been thrown away the moment they touched the consciousness. Still, it is much less of a sin than it would be if it were decided to complete it with action. And so we have to ask pardon for such thoughts and beat our breasts and say *Forgive us our debts*; and we have to do what follows and include in our prayer, *as we forgive our debtors* (Mt 6:12). With those two first human beings, of course, each was a person acting his or her own part, and so if the woman alone had eaten the unlawful food she alone would have been punished with death. But the same sort of thing cannot be said with one human being; if he willfully feeds his thoughts on unlawful pleasures from which he should have turned away immediately, not deciding to do anything wrong but only holding it fondly in recollection, one cannot say that "the woman" in him is condemned without "the man." A ridiculous idea. This after all is one person, one human being, and the whole of him will be condemned unless these things that are generally felt to be sins of thought alone, without any will to act but with a will to please the consciousness with such things, are forgiven by the grace of the mediator.

19. So we have been looking for a kind of rational couple of contemplation and action in the mind of everyman, with functions distributed into two several channels and yet the mind's unity preserved in each; all this of course without prejudice to the historical truth of what divine authority tells us about the two first human beings, the man and woman from whom the human race has been propagated. The point of staging this discussion has simply been to help us understand why the apostle attributes the image of God to the man only and not to the woman as well, and to see that he did it because he wanted to use the

distinction of sex between two human beings to signify something that must be looked for in every single human being.

20. I have not forgotten that some of the outstanding defenders of the Catholic faith and interpreters of the divine utterances who have gone before us have felt that the good soul is in its totality a kind of paradise, and so in looking for these two in the individual man they have said that the man stands for the mind and the woman for the senses of the body.[55] And if you go through the whole story carefully everything in it seems to fit this distribution very neatly, in which the man represents mind and the woman bodily sensation, except for the bit where it says that among all the beasts and birds *there was not found for the man an assistant like himself* (Gn 2:20), and so then the woman was made for him from his side. That is why I did not think the woman should be made to stand for the senses of the body which we observe to be common to us and the beasts. I wanted her to stand for something the beasts do not have, and reckoned that the senses of the body should rather be represented by the serpent, who is *wiser*, so we read, *than all the beasts of the earth* (Gn 3:11). For among all the natural endowments that we observe to be shared in common by ourselves and irrational animals, the power of sensation excels by a certain liveliness[56]—I do not mean the sense referred to in the letter to the Hebrews where it says, *Solid food is for the perfect who have their senses trained by habit for separating good from evil* (Heb 5:14); these senses are rational in nature and belong to the understanding. No, I mean this fivefold power of sensation in the body by which beasts as well as we sense bodily appearances and movements.

21. But whether it is this, that or any other way you interpret what the apostle said about the man being the image and glory of God, the woman the glory of the man,[57] it is clear that when we live according to God our mind should be intent on his invisible things and thus progressively be formed from his eternity, truth and charity,[58] and yet that some of our rational attention, that is to say some of the same mind, has to be directed to the utilization of changeable and bodily things without which this life cannot be lived; this however not in order to be *conformed to this world* (Rom 12:2) by setting up such goods as the final goal and twisting our appetite for happiness onto them, but in order to do whatever we do do in the reasonable use of temporal things with an eye to the acquisition of eternal things, passing by the former on the way, setting our hearts on the latter to the end.

Chapter 4

The distinction already briefly proposed between wisdom and knowledge, sapientia *and* scientia, *is examined in detail, the former being the appropriate quality of the higher function of mind and the latter of the lower. In the course of the discussion Plato's theory of reminiscence is noticed and refuted. The quest for a trinity in knowledge is postponed to the next book.*

For knowledge too is good within its own proper limits if what puffs up or tends to puff up in it is overcome by the love of eternal things, which does not puff up but builds up, as we know.[59] Indeed without knowledge one cannot have the virtues which make for right living and by which this woeful life is so conducted that one may finally reach the truly happy life which is eternal.

22. However, action by which we make good use of temporal things differs from contemplation of eternal things, and this is ascribed to wisdom, the former to knowledge. For although wisdom itself can also be called knowledge, as when the apostle says, Now I know in part, but then I shall know even as I am known (1 Cor 13:12), and by this knowledge he clearly means the contemplation of God which is to be the supreme reward of the saints; still, when he says, To one is given through the Spirit the word of wisdom, to another the word of knowledge through the same Spirit (1 Cor 12:8), he is without any doubt distinguishing the two, although he does not here explain what the difference is or how they can be told apart. But after searching the multiple stores of the holy scriptures I find it written in the book of Job, in the holy man's own words, *Behold piety is wisdom, while to abstain from evil things is knowledge* (Jb 28:28). This distinction can be understood as meaning that wisdom belongs to contemplation, knowledge to action. He put "piety" here for "worship of God," which in Greek is *theosebeia*; and this is the word found in this sentence in the Greek codices. And what among eternal things is more excellent than God whose nature alone is unchangeable? And what is the worship of him but the love of him by which we now desire to see him, and believe and hope that we will see him? And however much progress we make, we see now *in a puzzling reflection in a mirror, but then it will be* "in clear"; for this is what the apostle Paul means by *face to face* (1 Cor 13:12); and also what John means: *Beloved, we are now sons of God, and that which we shall be has not yet appeared.*[60] *We know that when he appears we shall be like him, because we shall see him as he is* (1 Jn 3:2). As I see it, a word about these and suchlike things is a word of wisdom. To abstain from evil things, however, which Job called knowledge, is without doubt a matter of temporal things, because it is in terms of time that we are in the midst of evils, which we should abstain from in order to arrive at those eternal good things. Thus anything that we do sagaciously, courageously, moderately, and justly belongs to this knowledge or discipline with which our activity sets about avoiding evil and seeking good; and so does whatever historical knowledge[61] we gather for the sake of examples to be avoided or imitated and for the sake of the necessary information about anything at all that has been provided for our use.

23. So whenever there is a word about these I think it is a word of knowledge, to be distinguished from the word of wisdom which is concerned with things that neither were nor will be but just are, and which because of the eternity in which they are, are talked about as having been and being and going to be without any change of real tense. It is not that they were in such a way that they ceased to be, or that they will be in such a way that they are not yet, but that they always had the same being and always will have it. They do not abide fixed locally in space like bodies, but in non-bodily nature; thus as intelligible they are available to the inspection of the mind just as bodies are visible or touchable to the body's senses. And it is not only the intelligible and non-bodily ideas of sensible localized things that abide without themselves being localized, but also those of movements passing through time that stand unmeasurable in time— these too also intelligible, of course, not sensible. Few have the acuteness of mind to reach these ideas, and when someone does manage as far as possible to attain them he does not abide in them, because his very acuteness of mind gets blunted so to say and beaten back, and there is only a transitory thought about a non-transitory thing.

However, this transient thought is committed to memory through the disciplines the consciousness is trained in,[62] and so there is something that the thought which is forced to leave it can go back to. Though even if thought did not go back to the memory and there find what it had entrusted to it, it would be led back to it like a novice, as indeed it had been led there in the first place, and find it where it had found it in the first place, namely in incorporeal truth from which it could again as it were take a copy to fix in the memory.[63] The non-bodily and unchanging idea of a square body, for example, may abide for ever the same; but a man's thought does not abide in it in the same way, if that is to say he could ever attain to it without a spatial image.[64] Or if the sheer arithmetic[65] of a beautiful piece of music that passes through a temporal rhythm is comprehended without time, standing still in some high and secluded silence, it can at least only be thought for as long as that tune can be heard. Yet even though the mind's inspection of it was only transient, it could snatch something from it and deposit it in the memory as though swallowing it down into its stomach, and by recollection it will be able somehow to chew this in the cud and transfer what it has learnt into its stock of learning. And if this memory is erased by total oblivion, it will be possible under the guidance of science to recover what had completely lapsed and to discover it again exactly as it was before.

24. This is why that noble philosopher Plato tried to persuade us that the souls of men had lived here[66] even before they wore these bodies, and therefore learning things is more a remembering of things already known than a getting to know new things. He told the story of some boy asked goodness knows what questions about geometry and answering as if he were most learned in that science. He was of course interrogated step by step very skillfully, and so he saw what was to be seen and said what he saw. But if this were recollection of things previously known, not everybody or practically everybody would be able

to do the same if interrogated in that way; it is unlikely that everybody was a geometer in a previous life, seeing that they are such a rarity in the human race that it is a job even to find one. The conclusion we should rather draw is that the nature of the intellectual mind has been so established by the disposition of its creator that it is subjoined to intelligible things in the order of nature, and so it sees such truths in a kind of non-bodily light that is *sui generis*, just as our eyes of flesh see all these things that lie around us in this bodily light, a light they were created to be receptive of and to match. It is not because the eyes already knew the difference between black and white before they were created in this flesh, that they can tell the difference now without being taught it. In any case, why should it only be intelligible things that shrewd interrogation will get answers about from someone, answers belonging to some science he is ignorant of? Why can no one do this about any sensible things except those he has seen in the body, or heard about by word of mouth or in writing from people who have known? We cannot really believe those who say that Pythagoras of Samos recalled things of this sort that he had experienced when he had been here in another body;[67] and there are other tales of yet other people having experienced something of the sort in their minds. But these are false memories, such as we often experience in dreams when we seem to ourselves to remember seeing or doing things we have never seen or done at all; and the minds of those people were touched even while they were awake by the promptings of malignant and deceitful spirits whose concern it is to deceive men by sowing and strengthening false ideas about the successive states of souls.[68] One can gather that this is so, because if these things were true memories of what they had previously seen here in other incarnations, this sort of thing would happen to lots of people, indeed to almost everybody, seeing that the theory is that the living come from the dead as the dead from the living, like wakers from sleepers and sleepers from wakers, without interruption.

25. If then this is the correct distinction between wisdom and knowledge, that wisdom is concerned with the intellectual cognizance of eternal things and knowledge with the rational cognizance of temporal things, it is not hard to decide which should be preferred and which subordinated to the other. Perhaps of course some other distinction might be offered to tell the two apart by—for there can be no doubt that they do differ, seeing that we have the apostle's teaching, *To one is given through the Spirit the word of wisdom, to another the word of knowledge according to the same Spirit* (1 Cor 12:8). Yet even so there is a manifest difference between the two things we have just mentioned, namely the intellectual cognizance of eternal things and the rational cognizance of temporal things, and no one has any hesitation about preferring the former to the latter.

So then as we leave behind what belongs to the outer man, and desire to climb up inward from what we have in common with the beasts, before we come to the cognizance of intelligible things that are supreme and everlasting, we meet the rational cognizance of temporal things. Here too let us find some trinity if we can, just as we found one in the sensation of the body and another in the images that entered our soul or spirit through the senses, in such a way that for bodily things placed outside us which we attain with a bodily sense we have the likenesses of bodies inside impressed on the memory; and we have thought being formed from them with the will as the third element joining the two together, just as on the outside the attention of the eyes was formed, with the will again presenting it to the visible object to produce sight and joining the two together, and here too coming in itself as the third element. But this project must not be squeezed into the limits of this book; in the one that follows we can with God's help look for such a trinity at our convenience and analyze it when we have found it.

NOTES

1. He is probably referring to the sin of astrology.

2. He had in fact been analyzing all this kind of conscious activity in the second trinity of the outer man in Book XI. But there he was prescinding from the rationality of it. Here he is reminding himself and us that the analytic distinction of psychological levels does not mean an existential separation of them.

3. *Rationes.*

4. When we are doing geometry.

5. See Gn 2:20.

6. The scholastics called them *ratio superior* and *ratio inferior* (*Summa Theologiae* 1a, q.79, a.9). One can compare the distinction to that of Aristotle's between the speculative intellect and the practical intellect, though it is made on a rather different basis.

7. He will give his reasons for saying that the trinity in the lower function of the mind is not the image of God in Book XIV, 4-5. He illustrates this trinity mainly in the act of faith or the act of the virtues, and finds that these are not "co-eternal" or contemporal with the mind itself (Book XIV, 4-5); and also that the objects of faith and other such knowledge are adventitious to the mind, coming to it from outside (Book XIV, 11).

8. There is little evidence in written sources for this opinion. Victorinus Afer in the middle of the fourth century cautiously endorses calling the Holy Spirit "the mother" of Jesus, both as regards the eternal generation of the Son, and his birth in time (*Adv. Arium* 1, 58: PL8, 1084). Irenaeus in the second century quotes some Gnostics as interpreting the Genesis story of Adam and Eve in a sense vaguely similar to the one outlined here by Augustine. It might have filtered through from Gnostic to more orthodox circles, whom Augustine is here refuting. See Irenaeus, *Adv. Haereses*, 1, 30, 1: PG7, 695.

9. See Ti 1:15.

10. A reference, probably, to the Manichees.

11. See Wis 8:2.

12. Augustine takes for granted the widely accepted commonplace that the sexual act is in itself something dirty or impure—a now rightly discredited commonplace for which he is very often and quite unfairly saddled with a prime responsibility. But it was a commonplace assumption in the ancient world, implicit both in ritual practices and in the general platonic world view. Augustine indeed may be credited with taking some of the sting out of it by teaching that the corruption assumed to be inherent in the sexual act is not there by nature but as a consequence of sin, the sin of our first parents which he himself never regarded as a sexual sin. But this sin, by upsetting the moral order of nature, vitiated in particular that order at its most delicate point. Or one could say that for him the disorder consequent on the fall is most evident in the sexual act, in which the inherent concupis-

cence is not under the control of reason; and so it is the bearer or carrier of the inherited infection of original sin.

13. Augustine's text renders the Greek Septuagint and not the Hebrew of the masoretic text. The Septuagint misses out the words "to his own image" from this verse. But Augustine further complicates the matter by opting for a very idiosyncratic punctuation of the verse. He will be remarking on it himself in a footnote in the next page or two, but it might help the reader if we set the matter out here.

Without punctuation the Septuagint reads: And God made man to the image of God he made him male and female he made them (28) and blessed them God . . .

The most natural punctuation, and the one most consonant with the Hebrew, runs: And God made man, to the image of God he made him, male and female he made them. (28) And God blessed them.

Augustine chose to punctuate: And God made man to the image of God, he made him male and female, he made them and blessed them.

14. This is a much more widely held and reputable patristic view than the opinion that he is combating here in this chapter. Indeed one might say that before Augustine the common interpretation of the image text in Genesis 1 was that man as made "to the image" was modeled on the Son, who is the image par excellence. He has already commented on this view in Book VII, 12.

15. For example Jn 1:1; 1 Jn 5:20; for the distinction between God and true God, see above, Book I, 9, note 24.

16. As "God made to the image of God," where either a noun occurs instead of a pronoun, or a different pronoun from what one would expect.

17. Reading *sperans* with M and four manuscripts. CCL omits it; but as it is not in the Vulgate or the Septuagint it is hard to see where it could have got into the text from.

18. *Qui factus est ei*: the Greek is not burdened with an equivalent of *ei*, which makes the sense much easier. In the apparatus criticus of A. Merk's *Novum Testamentum Graece et Latine* (Rome, 1944) Augustine is cited in support of omitting *ei* from the Latin, and also of reading *gennomenou* instead of *genomenou* in the Greek. In view of our text, both citations seem dubious.

19. *Idem Jesus Christus*; M reads *ejusdem Jesu Christi*, untranslatable because nonsense.

20. All ways of construing which are more plausible in the Latin text than in the English—but only just.

21. Here he carries the grammatical possibilities of construing the text to the extreme of absurdity.

22. Augustine's interlocutor could have replied that the Spirit did here include the couple's offspring in the brief summary, as the text continues, *And God blessed them and said, Increase and multiply and fill the earth* (Gn 1:28).

The idea of a trinity of human persons representing the trinity of divine persons in God, as presented here, is rightly rejected by Augustine. But it is possible that he has merely set up something of an Aunt Sally of his own in order to knock it down. At any rate, I think he has missed a genuine suggestion of Paul's in this same chapter that interpersonal human relationships can to some extent be regarded as a reflection of the interpersonal divine relationships.

In 1 Cor 11:3 the apostle writes, *I want you to know that the head of every man is the Christ, and the head of woman is the man, and the head of the Christ is God.* The relationship signified by "head of" is not merely one of dominion or priority, but of origin, as is clear from what he later says, *The man is not from the woman, but the woman from the man* (verse 8). So here we have a chain of relationships or origin, God—Christ—man—woman; for God and Christ we can read Father and Son; and so we can set up a proportion: as the Son is to the Father, so is the woman to the man; as the Son is from the Father, so is the woman from the man. The man and the woman are of course Adam and Eve; in the case of that pair the woman is from the substance of the man in equality of nature just as the Son is from the substance of the Father in equality of nature.

This seems to me to be a fair interpretation of Paul. The analogy has its limitations, of course; the woman does not proceed from the man by way of generation; and in any case it is a dyadic rather than a triadic analogy. But then dyadic formulae, mentioning only the Father and the Son, are very common in the New Testament. If one wished to convert it into a triadic analogy, I think one would introduce as the analogue of the Spirit not the offspring of man and woman, but in typically Augustinian fashion the mutual love which joins them together and proceeds from them both.

23. *Vir*, of course, not *homo*.

24. See 1 Cor 11:4-10.

25. See above, section 4.

26. The whole of that substance is *two in one flesh*, representing "two in one mind" (above, section 3.)

27. Here I must try to save Augustine from being torn to pieces by his feminist critics. He is not anti-feminist; indeed his whole effort in this chapter is to maintain the equality of women as human beings with men, and their equal status as made to the image of God. That is why he insists on interpreting Paul here symbolically. The reader must therefore bear continually in mind that the author is not talking about man and woman in themselves or about their real personal relationships, but about man and woman as symbols of two aspects or functions of the human mind. What woman symbolizes as female is subordinate to what man symbolizes as male. It does not follow that what woman is as person is subordinate, let alone inferior to what man is as person, or that men do not engage as much, if not more, in the "feminine" function of mind as do women.

28. Augustine's explanation of the puzzling *because of the angels* (1 Cor 11:10). Why, one wonders, should symbolism (here *significatio*) be particularly pleasing to angels? Perhaps we have a clue in something he said in Book I, 16 (see note 46). There he says that the Son will fully and finally reveal the Father *when he cancels all sovereignty and all authority and power* (1 Cor 15:24), that is, when there is no more need for the régime of symbols administered by the angelic powers. (The word here translated "symbols" is *similitudines*.) This present world or *aeon* is symbolic through and through—an axiomatic notion for a platonist—and it is administered by angels, as God's agents. So it is to be assumed that they have a natural predilection for and skill in all the infinite possibilities of symbolic signification.

29. The point of this sentence seems to be that God does not need symbols, and so the observance of symbolic actions, like women covering their heads in church, is not necessary in order to please him, but only in order to instruct ourselves and delight the aesthetic sensibilities of the angels.

30. This quotation shows up Augustine's critical sense at its very lowest. First, he quotes it as if it were part of the text of 1 Corinthians 11, probably as coming after verse 10. This is made absolutely clear in the closing sentence of the paragraph. It is very hard to believe that it was found in his copy of the letter. 1 Timothy 2:13-15 is indeed a parallel passage, and might have been written in his margin at 1 Corinthians 11:10. Just possibly it might have crept into the text of one of his copies. And yet he must have known his New Testament so well that he really knew this passage did not belong in 1 Corinthians 11. And if it does not belong there, the whole peculiar argument of this paragraph collapses.

Secondly, his understanding of the concluding conditional clause as referring to the children remaining in faith etc. is a mistake only possible in the Latin text, because the Greek rendered by *filiorum generationem*, bearing children, is one word in the singular meaning childbearing. So the antecedent of the subject of the conditional sentence cannot possibly be children. He was quite capable of referring to the Greek text when he wanted to.

31. *Moribus*; M reads *operibus*, works.

32. I would like to think this sentence, which I have treated as an Augustinian footnote, was interpolated as a comment by some more bigoted copyist. But there is no manuscript evidence to this effect.

The argument of this extraordinarily slovenly paragraph depends on the mistaken assumptions commented on in note 30 above. Given those assumptions, Augustine still seems to offer us a circular argument. He wants to prove that Paul is talking about man and woman symbolically; he chooses a text where he supposes the apostle talks about widows literally, not symbolically; then he opposes to it another which seems to contradict it, and so must be taken symbolically and he explains this symbolism, in which children stand for good works. This suits his general theme very well, because it is his position that the performance of good works is the responsibility of the lower function of the mind, symbolized by woman. Then he seems to clinch his assertion that this passage about the children is to be taken symbolically on the grounds that in the context the apostle is talking about women covering their heads, which must be symbolic or it would be pointless. But this is what at the beginning of the paragraph he set out to prove. This is the kind of penalty he occasionally pays for an over-subtle mind and an over-fertile imagination.

33. This is the judgment of plain reason.

34. See Gal 3:26; Col 3:10.

35. See Col 3:10.

36. *Homo.*

37. *Vir.*

38. See Eph 4:23.

39. See Ps 6:7.

40. See Ps 38:10.

41. I suppose he has in mind the universal human habit of rationalization to cover up our faults, but in particular he probably has the philosophers in mind.

42. Augustine's view of the fall and sin is thoroughly socialist or even communist in its orientation. Any notion of the sacred rights of property would have been abhorrent to him. The desire for private possession is a kind of mark of Cain, the stigma of man alienated from God.

43. See Sir 10:13.

44. This is the absurd implication of being discontented with the whole, or of wanting to be equal to and independent of God.

45. See 1 Tm 6:10.

46. In *Revisions* I, 15, 3 he takes back this figurative interpretation, as the apostle clearly means it literally.

47. See Lk 15:22; the prodigal son parable is frequently connected with the fall story, the first robe of the parable being the innocence of paradise.

48. See Gn 3:21.

49. *Ad ipsum*, a pregnant expression; the honor, the image is reflected light, and the reflector must be turned toward the source.

50. *Scientia*, knowledge in a specialized sense contrasted with wisdom. The twin idea will be developed in the next chapter. Here there is clearly an allusion to the tree of knowledge of good and evil.

51. See 1 Cor 8:1.

52. *Quantum* with M; CCL reads *quando*, when.

53. This will be in Book XIII.

54. That is, the sensitive appetites precisely as sensual. I do not think he ever uses the word *appetitus* for will, but I may be mistaken.

55. For example, Ambrose, *De Noe et Arca* 92. This is certainly a more anti-feminist interpretation than Augustine's.

56. And so is suitably represented by the cunning of the serpent, while our other vital organic functions are represented by the other animals.

57. See 1 Cor 11:7.

58. See Book IV, prologue, above.

59. See 1 Cor 8:1.

60. Reading *nondum apparuit quod erimus*: M has . . . *quid erimus*, with the Vulgate and Greek. Augustine's text turns an indirect question into a relative clause. I have found no evidence that he ever used *quod* interrogatively, though perhaps the old Latin Bible sometimes did.

61. This includes natural history, a subject zealously pursued in aid of morals from Pliny the Elder to Saint Francis of Sales.

62. He clearly has in mind the mathematical sciences, geometry, music, and astronomy.

63. Here we find memory playing a new role, the retaining and making available for recollection of intellectual impressions received by the mind from intelligible and eternal ideas, and no longer merely the sensible impressions received from bodies through the senses. And here too, I think we have the Achilles' heel of Augustine's theory of knowledge, insofar as he had one. He seems, indeed,

as this paragraph unfolds, to be half aware of this himself. I would almost be inclined to say that he is teetering on the edge of conversion from the platonic to the aristotelian system in this matter.

The indispensable function of memory with regard to sense impressions is manifest; he has analyzed it at length in Book XI. The fact of memory retaining intellectual impressions and of the part it plays in acquiring and using intellectual disciplines like mathematics is also plain, which is why Augustine brings it in here.

But it is not so plain how he is to account for it in his own ideas about intellectual knowledge. In his view intelligible ideas or *rationes* are available to the mind by direct vision rather as material objects are available to the senses. But unlike material objects, these *rationes* abide unchanging, always present, always available. As he makes clear in this paragraph, there is no danger of their being lost; so there does not seem to be any real need to remember them—and yet we do so, and don't always find them easy to recapture when we have forgotten them. He would answer here, I imagine, that if our psychological order had not been upset by sin, these abiding *rationes* would indeed always be readily available and perceptible by the inner sight of the mind. But sin has weakened and partially blinded this mental sight; it is soon dazzled by strong intellectual light; and it is all misted up by a disordered predilection for material objects and their images. So once an intelligible idea has been seen, while it remains there unchanging, the mind cannot look at it unchangingly, nor can the mind find it in itself in the first place, or return to a sight of it without difficulty. It is easier for it to look at the intelligible idea or *ratio* through the dark glasses of its memory of it.

The next question, though, for him to face is *how* one remembers such *rationes*, ideas or truths. Presumably not by sensible images; and yet he is shortly to wonder whether the mind can either perceive, or presumably remember, the idea of a square body, the mathematical intelligible idea of squareness, without a spatial image; and the same with the "arithmetical" idea of a piece of music. He is in fact, so it seems to me, having good aristotelian doubts whether we do not derive our knowledge of the intelligible ideas of quantity and movement, non-bodily, non-temporal *rationes* which make bodies and time and movement intelligible, from bodies and movements themselves, rather than seeing them directly in a platonic world of forms and imposing them on the sensible world of matter and temporal change.

When it comes to the kind of intellectual memory, the memory of "wisdom" that he is primarily interested in, that is to memory of self and memory of God, it seems to me that he is genuinely successful in working out an analogous concept of memory as one of immediate presence of the object remembered, self or God, to the subject remembering, self. Here he is able to avoid even describing this kind of memory in imaginative terms of retaining sensible images. But he does not avoid this, and I do not think he can, when it comes to describing the memory of the *rationes* of the created eternal truth. Here he fails to analogize his concept of memory satisfactorily.

In this matter Augustine is not a full-blooded platonist, as his criticism of Plato's theory of reminiscence will show. It is his Christianity, really, that forces him to reject Plato here—a Christianity that is more hardheaded than Plato about the real truth value of the material temporal world, and much more precise, and personal, and theist than Plato about God. But Plato's theory of reminiscence is an integral part of a much more consistent theory of knowledge than Augustine's half-platonism can produce. It is to Augustine's credit that he was not enslaved to the platonic system, and that he was finding its conceptual apparatus inadequate for expressing his thought. But he never quite got round to replacing it with the more flexible because in fact less pretentious instrument of the aristotelian apparatus, which for a whole variety of reasons he was never fully introduced to.

64. This is what I regard as an example of his "aristotelian doubt."

65. *Numerositas*; "arithmetic" is the best I can do for this word, but the reader must try to give it a more poetic, less prosaic feel than it ordinarily has in English.

66. That is, here in previous incarnations in this world. It is true that in the *Meno* (81d-84), where the story about the boy and geometry is taken from, Socrates is only talking about transmigration or re-incarnation of souls. But from other texts (*Phaedo*, 72e, *Phaedrus* 249c-250), it is clear that the theory of reminiscence involves a pre-existence of the soul, unincarnate, in the pure world of form or ideas.

67. *Pre-socratic fragments, Empedocles, frag. 129* (Diels).

68. *De revolutionibus animarum.*

BOOK XIII

MAN'S CASE HISTORY: THE IMAGE REPAIRED; REDEMPTION

Chapter 1

Taking as his text for analysis the prologue of John's gospel, the author proceeds to elaborate the distinction made in the previous book between wisdom as the proper activity of the higher reason and knowledge as the function of the lower reason. To this sphere of knowledge of temporal things he ascribes in particular faith, which he declares will be the main topic of this book.

---

1. In the previous book, the twelfth of this work,[1] we had our hands full distinguishing between the function of the rational mind in temporal matters, in which our activity as well as our awareness is engaged, and the superior function of the same mind which is engaged in contemplating eternal things and terminates in awareness alone. Here I think it may help if I insert something from the holy scriptures which may make it easier to tell the two apart.

2. John the evangelist thus begins his gospel: *In the beginning was the Word, and the Word was with God and the Word was God; this was in the beginning with God. All things were made through him, and without him was made nothing. What was made in him was life, and the life was the light of men, and the light shines in the darkness, and the darkness did not comprehend it. There was a man sent from God whose name was John. This man came for a witness, to bear witness about the light that all might believe through him. He himself was not the light, but to bear witness about the light. The true light was that which enlightens every man coming into this world. He was in the world, and the world was made through him, and the world did not recognize him. He came to his own estates, and his own people did not receive him. But as many as did receive him, he gave them the right[2] to become sons of God, those who believe in his name, who are born not of blood, nor of the will of the flesh, nor of the will of the man,[3] but of God. And the Word became flesh and dwelt amongst us. And we have seen his glory, glory as of the only begotten from the Father, full of grace and truth* (Jn 1:1-14).

342

The first part of this passage from the gospel I have quoted contains what is unchangeable and everlasting, and it is the contemplation of this that makes us happy or blessed. In what follows eternal things are mentioned mixed up with temporal things. And thus some things here belong to the field of knowledge, others to wisdom, as our distinction went in the twelfth book. For, *In the beginning was the Word, and the Word was with God, and the Word was God; this was in the beginning with God. All things were made through him, and without him was made nothing. What was made in him was life, and the life was the light of men, and the light shines in the darkness, and the darkness did not comprehend it*—all this calls for the contemplative life, and is perceived by the intellectual mind. The more anyone makes progress in this matter, the wiser without any doubt he will become. But because of what he said, *The light shines in the darkness and the darkness did not comprehend it,* faith is needed by which to believe what cannot be seen. What he means by darkness of course is the hearts of mortal men turned away from this sort of light and unfit to look upon it; that is why he goes on to say, *There was a man sent from God whose name was John; this man came for a witness, to bear witness about the light, that all might believe through him.* This is already something that happened in time and belongs to the knowledge which is contained in awareness of history. When we think about the man John we do it with an image which has been impressed on our memory from our notion of human nature. And this is the way people think about him, whether they believe these things or not. In either case they know what a man is, having learnt his outer part, that is his body, with the eyes of the body; his inner part, that is his soul, they have knowledge of because they are men themselves and take part in human society;[4] so they are able to think about the meaning of *There was a man whose name was John,* as they also know about names from talking and listening. As for *sent from God,* though, those who accept it accept it by faith, and those who do not accept it by faith either hesitate and "don't know," or disbelieve and pooh-pooh it. Both sorts, however, provided they are not of the number of the extra foolish who say in their hearts: *There is no God* (Ps 14:1), on hearing these words have a thought both about what God is and what being sent by God is, and even if their thought does not match the reality, it at least matches their own capacity.

3. As for faith itself, which every man sees to be in his heart if he believes, or not to be there if he does not believe, we know it in another sort of way; not like bodies which we see with the eyes of the body, and think about even when absent through their images which we hold in the memory; nor like things which we have not seen and form somehow or other by thought out of things we have seen, and which we commit to memory so that we can go back to it when we like and see them there again by recollection, or rather whatever images of them we have fixed there; nor like a living man whose soul we infer from our own, even though we do not see it, and whom we have recognized as alive from seeing the movements of his body, so that we can also picture him as such by thinking about them. This is not how faith is seen in the heart it is in by him whose it is, but it is grasped with the knowledge of absolute certitude, and proclaimed by

knowledge of self.[5] So while we are indeed commanded to believe because we cannot see what we are commanded to believe, still faith itself when we have it is something that we see in ourselves, because faith in things absent is itself present, and faith in things outside is itself inside, and faith in things that are not seen is itself seen; and yet it occurs itself in the hearts of men in time, and if from being believers they become unbelievers it vanishes from them. Sometimes of course faith is accorded to things that are false; for example we sometimes say, "People put their faith in him and he deceived them." There is no blame in such faith as this, if it can really be called faith, vanishing from men's hearts when it is driven out of them by the discovery of the truth. And what we hope for is that faith in true things will eventually be transformed into the things themselves;[6] and it is hardly right to say "Faith has vanished" when things that used to be believed come to be seen. Yet it can no longer be called faith, can it, seeing that faith is defined in the Letter to the Hebrews as being *the conviction of things that are not seen* (Heb 11:1)?

4. What comes next, *This man came for a witness, to bear witness about the light, that all might believe through him,* is a temporal action, as we have said. For witness is borne in time even about something everlasting such as the intelligible light. To bear witness about this came John, who *was not the light, but to bear witness about the light.* For he continues, *The true light was that which enlightens every man coming into this world. He was in the world and the world was made by him, and the world did not recognize him. He came to his own estates, and his own people did not receive him.* Anyone who knows English[7] understands these words from things he knows. Some of these things have become known to us through the senses of the body, like man, like the world itself whose obvious bulk we observe, like the sounds of the words themselves; for hearing too is a sense of the body. Others have become known to us through the reasoning of consciousness, like *His own people did not receive him*; this is understood to mean "they did not believe in him," and what this is we know, not through any sense of the body, but through conscious reasoning. As for the meanings, as distinct from the sounds of the words, we have learnt them partly through the sense of the body, but partly through conscious reasoning. We have not heard those words just now[8] for the first time; having heard them before, we had them as known in the memory, and recognized them there, and not only the mere words but also what they meant. This monosyllabic noun "world," being a sound, is of course a bodily thing and has come to our knowledge through the body, that is through the ear; and so too has what it means come to our knowledge through the body, that is through the eyes of flesh. Insofar as the world is known, it is known to those who see it. But this two-syllable verb "believed" is a body indeed as regards its sound, and so slips in through the ear of flesh; but what it means is perceived by no sense of the body, but only by conscious reasoning. Unless we knew through the consciousness what "believed" is, we would not understand what those people did not do, of whom it is said *and his own people did not receive him.* So the sound of a word strikes the ears of the body outside and reaches the sense which is called hearing.

The look[9] of a man too is both known to us in ourselves and is outwardly presented to the senses of the body in others; to the eyes when we see it, to the ears when we hear it, to the touch when we hold and touch it. And it has its image in our memory, non-bodily indeed, but still like a body. Finally, the marvelous beauty of the world itself is available to our gaze outside, and also to the sense called touch when we come into contact with any part of it. It too has its image in our memory to which we have recourse when we think about it, even if we are enclosed in four walls or in the dark. But we have already talked enough in the eleventh book about these images of bodily things which are not bodily themselves but yet bear a resemblance to bodies and belong to the life of the outer man. Now, however, we are dealing with the inner man and that knowledge of his which is about temporal and changeable things. When anything is taken up in pursuit of this knowledge from things that belong to the outer man, it is taken up for the lesson it can provide to foster rational knowledge; and thus the rational use of things we have in common with non-rational animals belongs to the inner man, and cannot properly be said to be common to us and non-rational animals.

5. What we are now obliged by the prescribed course of our plan to discuss at somewhat greater length in this book is faith, which gives the name of the faithful to those who have it and of the unfaithful, or unbelievers, to those who do not, like those people who did not receive the Son of God when he came into his own estates. And although *faith comes* to us *by hearing* (Rom 10:17), it does not belong to that sense of the body that is called hearing, because it is not a sound; nor does it belong to the eyes of this flesh, because it is not a color or a bodily shape; nor to the sense called touch, because it has nothing material about it; nor in a word to any of the senses of the body, because it is a thing of the heart not the body; nor is it outside us but deep inside us; nor does any man ever see it in another, but everyone sees it in himself; and lastly people can pretend to have it and be thought to have it who in fact do not. So everyone sees his own faith in himself; he only believes and does not see it to be in someone else, and he believes all the more firmly, the more he is aware of its fruits, which it is of the nature of faith to produce by *working through love* (Gal 5:6).

So to all those about whom the evangelist goes on to say, *But as many as did receive him, he gave them the right to become sons of God, those who believe in his name; who are born not of blood, nor of the will of the flesh, nor of the will of the man, but of God*, this faith is common; not as some bodily shape is common, as far as seeing goes, to the eyes of all it is available to (the gaze of all who observe it is informed somehow or other by this one thing) but as the human face can be said to be common to all men. We say this, though everyone actually has his own. We certainly say very truly that faith has been impressed from one single teaching on the hearts of every single believer who believes the same thing; but what is believed is one thing, the faith it is believed with is another. What is believed is in things that we say are or have been or will be; faith is in the consciousness of the believer, evident only to him who has it, though it is also in others—not the numerically identical faith, but a faith like it. For it is not one in number but in kind; and yet because of its likeness and lack of diversity, we call it one rather than many. It is like when we see two men exactly alike; we say in astonishment that the two have one face. In fact, while it is not too difficult to talk about the many single souls of all single individuals whom we read about in the Acts of the Apostles as having one soul,[10] one would scarcely dare to say that there are as many faiths as there are faithful, when the apostle has said *one faith* (Eph 4:5). And yet he who says, *O woman, great is your faith* (Mt 15:28), and to someone else, *Little faith, why did you doubt?* (Mt 14:31), shows that each person has his own. But we talk about one and the same faith of believers in the same way as about one and the same will of people who will; they all want the same thing, but while his own will is evident to each, that of the other man is concealed from him though he wants the same thing, and even if he indicates his will by certain signs, it is believed rather than seen. But everyone who is aware of his own consciousness does not of course believe but clearly sees that this is his will.

Chapter 2

Taking up the idea of a common will, with which he was comparing a common faith at the end of the last chapter, he discusses at length the universal will to happiness. This seems at first to be a digression from the topic of faith, with which he professes to be concerned in this book; but in fact it is relevant to this topic, as he will go on to argue that faith is necessary if this desire for happiness, common to all men, is not to be frustrated.

---

6. There is indeed such a unanimity within the same living and reason-using nature, that while to be sure it is hidden from one man what another man wants, there are some wishes that all have which are known to every single individual. While each man is ignorant of what another man wants, in some matters he can know what all men want. There is the story of a comedian and his witty pleasantry when he promised in the theater that at his next show he would tell the audience what they all wanted. So on the appointed day a greater crowd than usual came along full of great expectations, and as the silence and suspense grew he said, so the story goes, "You all want to buy cheap and sell dear." In this saying of a frivolous comedian all found their own self-awareness expressed, and in their admiration for his telling them so unexpectedly a truth that was as plain to all of them as their own noses, they warmly applauded him. Now why should his promise to tell them what they all wanted have aroused such great expectations, if not because a man is normally in the dark about the wishes of other men? But was this man in the dark about this wish? Is anybody in the dark about it? And how can this be if not because there are some things which a man not inappropriately infers in other people from himself, since all suffer together from the same fault, or accord together in the same nature? But it is one thing

to see one's own wish, another to infer someone else's, however sure the inference. I am as certain in human affairs about the foundation of Rome as I am of Constantinople's, since I have seen Rome with my own eyes, while I know nothing about the other city except what I believe on other people's evidence.[11]

Now that comedian, by looking at himself or by his experience of others, believed that the wish to buy cheap and sell dear was common to all. But in fact this is a vice, so it is possible a man could acquire the corresponding quality of justice, or alternatively contract the infection of some opposite vice which would withstand and overpower this one. Thus I myself know a man who was offered a codex for sale, and when he realized that the seller was ignorant of its real value and was therefore asking for much too little, he gave him the just price which was far more than he expected. On the other hand, what about someone so enslaved by wickedness that he sells cheap what his parents have left him and buys dear what he needs to feed his lusts? Such profligacy, I imagine, is not inconceivable; such people can be found if you look for them; even without looking for them you might come across people of greater wickedness than the comedian's who make nonsense of the actor's proposition or utterance[12] by paying a great price for their debaucheries and selling their lands for a small one. Then we know of people who as a political investment[13] have bought corn dear and sold it cheap to their fellow citizens.

Another instance is given in what the ancient poet Ennius said, "All mortal men would praised be."[14] Presumably he inferred it in others from himself and from those he had experience of, and he appears to be declaring something that all men want. So if that comedian had said: "You all want to be praised; none of you wants to be disparaged," it would have been thought that he was expressing something common to the will of all men. And yet there are people who hate their vices, and do not want to be praised by others for what they dislike in themselves, and who are grateful for the good will of those who scold them when they are disparaged in order to be corrected. But if he had said "you all want to be happy; you do not want to be unhappy," he would have said something that no one at all could fail to recognize in his own will. Whatever else anyone may wish for secretly, he never forgoes this wish which is well known to all and in all.

7. But the strange thing is, seeing that all men have one common will to obtain and retain happiness, where does the enormous variety and indeed contrariety of wishes about happiness come from—not that anyone does not want it, but that not everyone knows it? If everybody knew it, it would not be reckoned by some to consist in conscious virtue,[15] by others in bodily pleasure, by others in both, by yet others in this, that and the other. Whatever has given them the greatest enjoyment constitutes, they have decided, the happy life. How in this case can everyone love so fervently what not everyone knows? Who can love what he does not know, as I have argued extensively in some of the earlier books of this work?[16] So how is it that happiness is loved by all and yet not known by all? Is it perhaps that everyone knows what it is, but not everyone knows where

it is, and that is what the conflict of opinion is about? As though it were a question of some place in this world where any man who wants to live happily ought to want to live, and the question where happiness is were not the same question as what it is. For of course if it is in bodily pleasure, that man is happy who enjoys bodily pleasure; if in conscious virtue, the man who enjoys this; if in both, the man who enjoys both. So when one man says: "Living happily is enjoying bodily pleasure," and another says: "Living happily is enjoying conscious virtue," is it not the case that either both of them are ignorant of what the happy life is, or that they do not both know what it is? How then can they both love it if no one can love what he does not know? Perhaps then it is untrue, what we have taken for absolutely true and certain, that all men want to live happily. If, for example, to live happily is to live a life of conscious virtue, how can a man who does not want this want to live happily? Would it not be truer to say: "This man does not want to live happily because he does not want to live a life of virtue, which is the only way of living happily"? So all men do not want to live happily, indeed very few want to if the only way of doing so is to live a life of conscious virtue, which many people do not want.

So then, is something false that even Cicero the Academic had no doubt about—and the Academics have doubts about everything? Wishing to begin his dialogue *Hortensius*[17] from an absolutely certain starting point that no one could hesitate about, he said *We all certainly want to be happy*. Far be it from us to say that this is false. So what then? Are we to say that even though living happily is nothing but living a life of conscious virtue, yet a man who does not want this still wants to live happily? This seems to be pure nonsense; it amounts to saying, "Even the man who does not want to live happily wants to live happily." Who can listen to such a contradiction in terms, who can endure it? And yet necessity drives us to it if it is true both that everyone wants to live happily, and that not everyone wants to live in the only way it is possible to live happily.

8. Perhaps we can find a way out of these difficulties like this: we said that people have placed the happy life in whatever they have enjoyed most—thus Epicurus said pleasure, Zeno[18] virtue, someone else something else; so perhaps we can say that living happily is nothing but living according to one's particular form of enjoyment, and so it is not untrue that everyone wants to live happily, because everyone wants to live in a way he enjoys. After all, if this had been proposed to that music hall audience, they would have found it tallied with their wishes. But Cicero too put this argument forward against himself, and refuted it in a way to make its proponents blush. He says, *Here we have, not philosophers but merely people who love an argument, saying that everyone is happy who lives as he likes*—this is the same as what I have just called "in a way he enjoys." Then he immediately went on to add, *But this is false. To want what is not right is itself a very unhappy situation; in fact not to get what you want is not so unhappy a state of affairs as to want to get what you have no business to*. Quite excellently said, and absolutely true. Who could be so mentally blind, so estranged from any light of decency and wrapped in the darkness of infamy as to call happy the man who lives a rotten worthless life, with no one to stop him,

no one to punish him, no one even daring to rebuke him; who with lots of people praising him, since as divine scripture puts it, *The sinner is praised in the desires of his soul, and the man who does iniquity will be called blessed* (Ps 10:3), fulfills all his most criminal and licentious wishes; to call him happy because he lives as he likes, when in fact, though still unhappy, he would at least be less unhappy than this if he could get none of the things he is vicious enough to want? A man is made unhappy just by having a bad will alone, but much more so by the power to fulfill the desires of his bad will.

Therefore, since it is true that all men want to be happy, and yearn for this one thing with the most ardent love they are capable of, and yearn for other things simply for the sake of this one thing; and that no one can love something if he simply does not know what it is or what sort of thing it is, and that he cannot not know what it is that he knows he wants; it follows that all men know what the happy life is. All who are happy have what they want, though not all who have what they want are *ipso facto* happy; but those who do not have what they want, or have what they have no right to want, are *ipso facto* unhappy. Thus no one is happy but the man who has everything he wants, and wants nothing wrongly.

9. Granted then that the happy life consists of these two things, and that it is known to all and dear to all, what are we to suppose is the reason that when men cannot get both of these two things, they choose rather to have everything they want than to want everything rightly even if they have not got it? Perhaps it is just that humankind is so thoroughly warped; it does not escape them that neither the man who has not got what he wants nor the man who has got what he is wrong to want is happy, but only the man who both has the good things he wants and does not want any bad things;[19] yet when it is not given them to have each of these two things which make up the happy life, they in fact choose the one which puts the happy life further out of reach than ever—because the man who gets what he wrongly desires is further away from the happy life than the man who does not get what he desires; when what they should rather choose and prefer is a good will, even without getting the things it wants. For the man who rightly wants whatever he wants is near to being happy, and when he gets them he will be happy. And of course when things do eventually make him happy, it is good things, not bad ones, that do so. He already has one of these good things, one not to be at all underrated, namely a good will, if he does not desire to enjoy any of the good things human nature has a capacity for by committing or acquiring anything bad; and if he pursues such good things as are possible in this unhappy life with a sagacious, moderate, courageous and just mind, and takes possession of them as they come his way. Then even in evil circumstances he will be good, and when all evil circumstances have come to an end and all good ones have been completed he will be happy.

Chapter 3

The author argues that real and total happiness implies and requires immortality; that it is therefore not available in this present life; hence that it is pursued by the philosophers in vain, and that faith alone guarantees the real possibility of a happy immortality through participation in the Word made flesh.

10. It is for this reason that the faith by which we believe in God is particularly necessary in this mortal life, so full of delusion and distress and uncertainty. God is the only source to be found of any good things, but especially of those which make a man good and those which will make him happy; only from him do they come into a man and attach themselves to a man. And only when a man who is faithful and good in these unhappy conditions passes from this life to the happy life, will there really and truly be what now cannot possibly be, namely that a man lives as he would. He will not want to live a bad life in that bliss, nor will he want anything that he lacks, nor will he lack anything that he wants. Whatever he loves will be there, and he will not desire anything that is not there. Everything that is there will be good, and the most high God will be the most high good, and will be available for the enjoyment of his lovers, and thus total happiness will be forever assured.

But now meanwhile the philosophers have all constructed their own happy lives as each has thought best, as though they could manage by their own virtue what they could not manage in their common condition of mortal men, namely to live as they would. They felt indeed that there was no other way for anyone to be happy but by having what he wanted and not enduring anything he did not want. Now who is there who would not want any kind of life that he enjoyed and thus called happy to be so in his own power that he could have it last forever? And yet who is there in such a position? Does anyone want to suffer troubles he would endure bravely, even though he wants to and can endure them if he suffers them? Does anyone want to live in torment, even though he is able to preserve his virtue in it by his patience, and so live laudably?[20] Those who have endured such evils in their desire to have or their fear to lose what they loved, whether their motive was mean or praiseworthy, have thought that the evils would pass away. Many people have bravely fought their way to abiding good things through transitory evils. Such people are *ipso facto* happy in hope even in the midst of the transitory evils through which they come to the good things that shall not pass away.

But a man who is happy in hope is not yet happy. He is waiting in patience for the happiness which he does not yet possess. As for the man who is tortured without any such hope, without any such reward, however much endurance he shows, he is not truly happy but bravely unhappy. You cannot say he is not unhappy just because he would be unhappier still if he underwent his unhappiness without patience. Furthermore, he is not even to be regarded as happy if he does not suffer these things he would rather not suffer in his body, because still he is not living as he wants to. To leave aside other things that without harming the body belong to the trials of the mind which we would rather live without (and they are countless in number), he would of course like if possible to have his body so safe and sound without suffering any trouble from it that he had this possibility really under his control, or had it realized in his body's immunity from all decay. Because he has not got this and is held in suspense, clearly he does not live as he would like. In his courage he may well be prepared to take whatever adversity comes upon him and to bear it with equanimity; but he would prefer it not to come upon him, and if he can he sees to it that it does not. So he is prepared for both eventualities, but in such a way that he hopes for one and avoids the other, and if he runs into the one he would avoid, he willingly bears it because what he wanted could not come about. He endures it therefore in order not to be pushed under completely, but he would rather not be pushed at all. How then can he be said to live as he would like? Because he is willingly brave in bearing unflinchingly what he would rather had not been inflicted on him? But the reason he wills what he can do is that he cannot do what he wills. That is the sum total, whether it makes you laugh or cry, of the happiness of proud mortals who boast that they live as they want because they bear patiently with what they do not want to happen to them. This, they say, is what Terence put so well: "Since what you will can never be, will what you can do."[21] Who would deny that this is very sensibly said? But it is advice given to an unhappy man how not to be unhappier still. To a happy man, however, such as all men want to be, it is neither right nor true to say *what you will can never be*. If he is indeed happy, whatever he wants can indeed be, since he does not want what cannot be. But such a state of things is not for this mortal life; it will only be when there is immortality. If this could in no way be given to man, he would look for happiness in vain, because without immortality it cannot be.

11. All people then want to be happy; if they want something true,[22] this necessarily means they want to be immortal. They cannot otherwise be happy. In any case, if you ask them about immortality as about happiness, they all answer that they want it. But as long as they despair of immortality, without which true happiness is impossible, they will look for, or rather make up, any kind of thing that may be called, rather than really be, happiness in this life. That man lives happily, as we have said above and established firmly enough,[23] who lives as he wants and does not want anything wrongly. But no one is wrong to want immortality if human nature is capable of receiving it as God's gift; if it is not capable of it, then it is not capable of happiness either. For a man to live happily, after all, he must live. How can the happy life remain with him if life itself forsakes him as he dies? When it does forsake him, he is without doubt either unwilling for it to do so, or willing, or neither. If he is unwilling, how is this life happy which is in his will without being in his power? If no one is happy by wanting something and not having it, how much less than happy must he be who is being forsaken against his will not by honor, or possessions, or anything else, but by the happy life itself, when he comes to have no life at all? So even if he has no senses left to be unhappy with (the reason the happy life is leaving

him is that all life is leaving him), still as long as he is conscious he is unhappy because he knows that he is losing against his will what he loves more than anything else, and what he loves anything else for. So life cannot both be happy and forsake a man against his will, because no one is made happy against his will; thus it would make him unhappy if he had it against his will, so how much more will it do so when it forsakes him against his will? If however it is in accordance with his will that it forsakes him, then how can this life have been a happy one that the man who had it wanted to lose?

The only thing left for them to say is that the happy man is conscious of neither attitude; that is, he is neither willing nor unwilling to be forsaken by the happy life when all life forsakes him at death, because he takes up his position between the two attitudes with a steady equanimity. But then his life can scarcely be the happy one if it does not merit the love of the man it is supposed to make happy. How can the life be happy which the happy man does not love? And how can he really love it if he does not care whether it flourishes or perishes? Unless perhaps the very virtues which we only love for the sake of happiness would dare to persuade us not to love happiness itself.[24] If they do this, then we stop loving them too, when we no longer love the happiness for whose sake alone we loved the virtues.

In any case, what will become of the truth of this axiom, so tried, so tested, so clarified, that all men want to be happy, if those who are already happy are neither willing nor unwilling to be so? If they want it, as the truth cries out that they do and as nature compels them to, having this will implanted in it by the supremely good and unchangeably happy creator; if those who are happy do want to be happy, I say, then of course they do not want not to be happy. And if they do not want not to be happy, then without a doubt they do not want their being happy to fade away and cease. They cannot be happy unless they are alive; therefore they do not want their being alive to cease. So anyone who is truly happy or desires to be, wants to be immortal. But a man does not live happily if he has not got what he wants; so it is altogether impossible for a life to be genuinely happy unless it is immortal. Whether human nature is capable of something it confesses to be so desirable is no small question. But if the faith possessed by those to whom Jesus *gave the right to become sons of God* (Jn 1:12) is to hand, then there is no question at all.

12. People have tried to work these things out by human reasoning, but it is the immortality of the soul alone that they have succeeded in getting to some notion of, and then only a few of them, and with difficulty, and only if they have had plenty of brains and plenty of leisure and plenty of education in abstruse learning. Even so, they never discovered a lasting, which is to say a true, life of happiness for this soul. They actually said it returned to the unhappiness of this life after happiness. Some of them, it is true, were ashamed of such an opinion, and thought that the purified soul should be placed in everlasting happiness without the body; yet they have had views about the eternity of the world backward in time that simply contradict this opinion of theirs about the soul. It would take too long to prove this here, but in any case I have sufficiently explained it, I think, in the twelfth book of *The City of God*.[25]

This faith of ours, however, promises on the strength of divine authority, not of human argument, that the whole man, who consists of course of soul and body too, is going to be immortal, and therefore truly happy. That is why in the gospel it did not just stop when it had said that Jesus *gave those who received him the right to become sons of God*, and briefly explained what receiving him meant by saying *to those who believe in his name*, and then had shown how they would become sons of God by adding that[26] they *are born not of blood nor of the will of the flesh nor of the will of the man, but of God* (Jn 1:12). But in case this feebleness that is man, which we see and carry around with us,[27] should despair of attaining such eminence, it went on to say *And the Word became flesh and dwelt amongst us* (Jn 1:14), in order to convince us of what might seem incredible by showing us its opposite. For surely if the Son of God by nature became son of man by mercy for the sake of the sons of men (that is the meaning of *the Word became flesh and dwelt amongst us*[28]), how much easier it is to believe that the sons of men by nature can become sons of God by grace[29] and dwell in God; for it is in him alone and thanks to him alone that they can be happy, by sharing in his immortality; it was to persuade us of this that the Son of God came to share in our mortality.

Chapter 4

The temporal content of faith is examined, namely the incarnation of the Son of God and the life, death and resurrection of the Son incarnate; and the propriety or congruity of this divine economy of salvation is set forth as achieving our deliverance from the evil one by divine justice as well as divine power; whereby a principle is archetypically exemplified, of great consequence for social and political morality, that justice should precede power, and not vice versa.

13. Now there are people who say, "Was there no other way available to God of setting men free from the unhappiness of this mortality, that he should want his only begotten Son, God coeternal with himself, to become man by putting on a human soul and flesh, and, having become mortal, to suffer death?" And it is not enough to rebut them by maintaining that this way God chose of setting us free through *the mediator between God and men the man Christ Jesus* (1 Tm 2:5) is good and befitting the divine dignity; we must also show, not indeed that no other possible way was available to God, since all things are equally within his power, but that there neither was nor should have been a more suitable way of curing our unhappy state. Nothing was more needed for raising our hopes and delivering the minds of mortals, disheartened by the very condition of mortality, from despairing of immortality, than a demonstration of how much value God put on us and how much he loved us.[30] And what could be clearer and more wonderful evidence of this than that the Son of God, unchangeably good, remaining in himself what he was and receiving from us what he was not,

electing to enter into partnership with our nature without detriment to his own, should first of all endure our ills without any ill deserts of his own; and then once we had been brought in this way to believe how much God loved us and to hope at last for what we had despaired of, should confer his gifts on us with a quite uncalled for generosity, without any good deserts of ours, indeed with our ill deserts our only preparation?

14. For even what we call our deserts or merits are gifts of his. In order that faith might work through love,[31] *the charity of God has been poured into our hearts through the Holy Spirit which has been given to us* (Rom 5:5). And he was given to us when Jesus was glorified in his resurrection. It was then that he promised he would send him and that in fact he sent him, because it was then, as had been written and foretold about him, that *he ascended on high, he took captivity captive, he gave gifts to men* (Ps 68:19; Eph 4:8). These gifts are merits by which we arrive at the supreme good of immortal happiness. *But God commends his charity toward us,* says the apostle, *in that while we were still sinners Christ died for us. Much more then, justified now in his blood, shall we be saved from the wrath through him* (Rom 5:8). He drives the point home by adding, *For if while we were enemies we were reconciled to God through the death of his Son, much more being reconciled shall we be saved in his life* (Rom 5:10). The "sinners" of the first sentence he calls "enemies of God" in the last; and those who were "justified in the blood of Jesus Christ" later became those who were "reconciled through the death of the Son of God"; and those who the first time are "saved from the wrath through him" are said later to be "saved in his life." So before receiving this grace we were not just any kind of sinners, but involved in such sins that we were enemies of God. A little earlier we sinners and enemies of God had been called two names in one breath by the same apostle, one the mildest possible and the other brutally harsh, when he said, *For if Christ, while we were still weak, died when the time came for the godless* (Rom 5:6). By "the godless" he meant the same as the ones he had just called "weak." Weakness seems to be a light matter, but sometimes it is such that it gets called godlessness. And yet if it were not weakness it would have no need of a doctor, which in Hebrew is Jesus,[32] in Greek *soter*, and in our language savior. This is a word, *salvator*, that the Latin language used not to have before, but it could have had it, and indeed it was able to coin it when it wanted it. But as I was saying, this earlier sentence of the apostle's, *while we were still weak* he *died when the time came for the godless*, matches these two later ones, in one of which he said "sinners" and in the other "enemies of God," as though applying one each respectively to the first two, referring "sinners" to "weak" and "enemies of God" to "the godless."

15. But what is this *justified in his blood* (Rom 5:9)? What, I want to know, is the potency of this blood, that believers should be justified in it? Is it really the case that when God the Father was angry with us he saw the death of his Son on our behalf, and was reconciled to us? Does this mean then that his Son was already so reconciled to us that he was even prepared to die for us, while the Father was still so angry with us that unless the Son died for us he would

not be reconciled to us? And what about something the same teacher of the Gentiles says elsewhere: *What are we to say to all this? If God is for us, who is against us? He who did not spare his own Son but handed him over for us all, how has he not also made us a gift of all things with him* (Rom 8:13)? Would the Father have not spared his own Son but handed him over for us, if he had not already been reconciled? In fact it seems, doesn't it, as if this text contradicts the former one? There the Son dies for us, and the Father is reconciled to us through his death; but here it is as if the Father were the first to love us, the Father who for our sake did not spare his Son, the Father who for our sake handed him over to death. But if it comes to that, I observe that the Father loved us not merely before the Son died for us, but before he founded the world, as the apostle bears witness: *As he chose us in him before the foundation of the world* (Eph 1:4). Nor does the Father's not sparing him mean that the Son was handed over for us against his will, because of him too it is said, *Who loved me and handed himself over for me* (Gal 2:20). Thus the Father and the Son and the Spirit of them both work all things together and equally and in concord. Yet the fact remains that we have been justified in the blood of Christ and reconciled to God through the death of his Son, and how that was done I shall explain here too[33] as best I can and as fully as seems necessary.

16. By a kind of divine justice the human race was handed over to the power of the devil for the sin of the first man, which passes by origin[34] to all who are born of the intercourse of the two sexes,[35] and involves all the descendants of the first parents in its debt. This handing over was first intimated in Genesis when the serpent was told *You shall eat earth* (Gn 3:14), and the man was told *Earth you are and into earth you shall go* (Gn 3:19). By the words *into earth you shall go* he was given prior notice of the death of the body, because he would not have experienced it if he had remained upright as he was made. As for saying to him while still alive *Earth you are,* he shows thereby that the whole man was changed for the worse. *Earth you are* is the same as *My spirit shall not remain in these men, because they are flesh* (Gn 6:3). So that is when he showed that he had handed him over to the one who had been informed, *You shall eat earth.* The apostle proclaims this fact more openly when he says, *And you when you were dead in your transgressions and sins, in which you once walked according to the course of this world, according to the prince of the power of the air, of that spirit which now works in the sons of unbelief, among whom we too all once conducted ourselves in the desires of our flesh, doing the will of the flesh and of the feelings, and were ourselves by nature sons of wrath just like the rest* (Eph 2:1). The sons of unbelief are the unbelievers, and who is not one of these before he becomes a believer? Thus all men are by origin under *the prince of the power of the air who works in the sons of unbelief* (Eph 2:2). And when I say "by origin" I mean the same as the apostle when he says that he too was "by nature" like the rest, by nature of course as bent by sin, not as created straight in the beginning.

As for the way in which man was handed over into the devil's power, this should not be thought of as though God actually did it or ordered it to be done, but merely that he permitted it, albeit justly. When he withdrew from the sinner, the author of sin marched in. Not of course that God withdrew from his creature in the sense of stopping to present himself to him as the God who creates him and gives him life, and amidst the evils of punishment continues to bestow many good things even on evil men; for he has not *held back his mercies in his anger* (Ps 77:9). Nor did he lose man from the jurisdiction of his own law when he let him be under the devil's jurisdiction, because not even the devil is cut off from the jurisdiction of the Almighty, or from his goodness either for that matter. How would even the wicked angels go on existing with any sort of life at all but for him *who gives life to everything* (1 Tm 6:13)? So if the commission of sins subjected man to the devil through the just wrath of God, then of course the remission of sins has delivered man from the devil through the kindly reconciliation of God.

17. But the devil would have to be overcome not by God's power but by his justice. What, after all, could be more powerful than the all-powerful, or what creature's power could compare with the creator's? The essential flaw of the devil's perversion made him a lover of power and a deserter and assailant of justice, which means that men imitate him all the more thoroughly the more they neglect or even detest justice and studiously devote themselves to power, rejoicing at the possession of it or inflamed with the desire for it. So it pleased God to deliver man from the devil's authority by beating him at the justice game, not the power game, so that men too might imitate Christ by seeking to beat the devil at the justice game, not the power game. Not that power is to be shunned as something bad, but that the right order must be preserved which puts justice first.[36]

How much power in any case can mortals have? Let mortals hold on to justice; power will be given them when they are immortal. Compared with this, the power of those men who are called powerful on earth is shown to be ridiculous weakness, and *a pit is dug for the sinner* (Ps 94:13) in the very place where the wicked seem to be able to do most. The just man sings, *Happy is the man whom you instruct, Lord, and teach from your law, in order to comfort him in evil days, until a pit is dug for the sinner. For the Lord will not reject his people nor forsake his inheritance, until justice turns into judgment, and those who have it are all of upright heart* (Ps 94:12-15). So in this time during which the power of the people of God is being deferred, God will not reject his people nor forsake his inheritance, however bitter and humiliating the trials it suffers in its humility and weakness, until the justice which now belongs to the weakness of the godly turns into judgment, that is until it receives authority to judge, which is being reserved for the just in the end, when power follows in its proper order on the justice that preceded it. Power added to justice, or justice acceding to power makes judicial authority. Justice is a property of good will, which is why the angels at Christ's birth said, *Glory to God in the highest, and on earth peace to men of good will* (Lk 2:14). Power, for its part, should follow justice and not precede it.*

As we were arguing above,[38] two things are required to make you happy: to wish well and to be able to do what you wish. And as we observed in that

---

* *Ideo et in rebus secundis ponitur, id est prosperis; "secundae" autem a "sequendo" sunt dictae.*[37]

discussion, the perversion should be avoided of a man choosing to be able to do what he wants and neglecting to want what he ought, since the first thing he ought to have is a good will, and only after that great power or authority. The good will, of course, has to be cleansed of faults, because if a man is overpowered by these the result is that he wills badly, and then how can his will be good? So it is right to desire power to be given to you now, but against your faults; men hardly ever want to be powerful in order to overpower these, they want it in order to overpower men. What does this mean but that truly speaking they are overpowered, and their overpowering of others is deceptive, and that they are not victors in truth but only in repute? Let a man will to be sagacious, will to be brave, will to be moderate, will to be just, and by all means let him want the power really to manage these things, and let him seek to be powerful in himself and in an odd way against himself for himself. As for the other things that he does well to want and yet is not able to get, like immortality and true and full felicity, let him not cease to desire them and patiently await them.

18. What then is the justice that overpowered the devil? The justice of Jesus Christ—what else? And how was he overpowered? He found nothing in him deserving of death and yet he killed him. It is therefore perfectly just that he should let the debtors he held go free, who believe in the one whom he killed without his being in his debt. This is how we are said to be justified in the blood of Christ.[39] This is how that innocent blood was shed for the forgiveness of our sins. That is why in the psalms he calls himself *free among the dead* (Ps 88:5); he is the only one who ever died free of the debt of death. So too he says in another psalm, *Then I paid what I had not robbed* (Ps 69:4), by robbery meaning sin because it is perpetrated against the law. For the same reason he says through his own mouth in the flesh, as we read in the gospel, *Behold the prince of this world is coming and in me he finds nothing*, that is no sin; *but that all may know*, he goes on, *that I do my Father's will, arise, let us go from here* (Jn 14:30). And he proceeds straight from there to his passion, to pay for us debtors the debt he did not owe himself.

Now would the devil have been overpowered by this most equitable of judgments if Christ had chosen to deal with him by power instead of justice? But he postponed what he had the power to do, in order to do first what he had to do;[40] that is why he needed to be both God and man. Unless he had been man he could not have been killed; unless he had been God no one would have believed he did not want to do what he could do,[41] but they would simply have thought that he could not do what he wanted to; nor would we have imagined that he was preferring justice to power, but simply that he lacked power. As it is, however, he suffered human pains for us because he was man, though if he had not wanted to he would have been able not to suffer so, because he was God. In this way the justice of humility was made more acceptable, seeing that the power of divinity could have avoided the humiliation if it had wanted to; and so by the death of one so powerful we powerless mortals have justice set before us and power promised us. He did one of these two things by dying, the other by rising. What could be more just than to go and face even death on a cross[42] for justice's sake? And what could be a greater show of power than to rise from the dead and ascend into heaven with the very flesh in which he had been killed? So he overcame the devil with justice first and power second, with justice because *he had no sin* (2 Cor 5:21; 1 Pt 2:22) and was most unjustly killed by him; with power because dead he came back to life never to die thereafter.[43] He would have overcome the devil with power even if he could not have been killed by him, though it shows greater power to overcome death by rising than to avoid it by living. But it is by other means that we are *justified in the blood of Christ* (Rom 5:9) when we are delivered from the devil's jurisdiction through the remission of sins; this is a matter of the devil's being overcome by Christ with justice, not with power. Christ was crucified in virtue of the weakness he took to himself in mortal flesh, not in virtue of his immortal power; and yet of this weakness the apostle says, *What is weak of God is stronger than men* (1 Cor 1:25).

Chapter 5

The justice of God manifested in the redeeming death of Christ is further explored, as also the manifold quality of his grace presented to us in the mystery of the incarnation.

19. It is not difficult then to see the devil overcome when the one who was killed by him rose from the dead. It calls for greater and more profound understanding to see the devil overcome when he thought he himself was overcoming, that is when Christ was killed. That is when this blood of his, of one who had no sin at all, was shed for the remission of our sins, and the devil, who once held us deservedly under sentence of death as we were guilty of sin, was deservedly obliged to give us up through him he had most undeservedly condemned to death, though guilty of no sin. This was the justice that overcame *the strong man*, this the rope that *tied him up* so that *his furniture* could be *carried off* (Mt 12:29), and from being *the furniture of wrath* in his house together with him and his angels, could be turned into *the furniture of mercy* (Rom 9:22).

The apostle Paul tells us that the Lord Jesus Christ spoke the following words to him from heaven when he was first called; among the other things that he heard, the following too, he says, was addressed to him: *This is why I appeared to you, to make you a minister and witness of the things you see of me, in which I also go before you delivering you from the people and from the nations, to whom I am sending you to open the eyes of the blind that they may turn from darkness and the power of Satan to God, that they may receive remission of sins and a portion among the saints and faith in me* (Acts 26:16).[44] So the same apostle urges the faithful to give thanks to God the Father by reminding them that *he snatched us from the power of darkness and transported us into the kingdom of the Son of his love, in whom we have redemption for the remission of sins* (Col 1:13). In this act of redemption the blood of Christ was given for us as a kind of price, and when the devil took it he was not enriched by it but caught and bound by it, so that we might be disentangled from his toils. No longer would he drag down with him to the doom of the second and everlasting death,[45] rolled up in the nets of their sins, any of those whom Christ, free of every debt, had redeemed by shedding the blood he did not owe. But those who belong to the grace of Christ, foreknown and predestined and chosen before the foundation of the world,[46] would simply die as Christ himself had died for them, that is to say with the death of the flesh alone and not of the spirit.

20. For although the death of the flesh came itself originally from the sin of the first man, good use of it has made glorious martyrs. That is why not only death but all the ills of this age, the sorrows and hardships of men, have fittingly remained even after sins have been forgiven, although they occur as the deserved consequence of sins and above all of original sin, which is the cause of life itself being constricted by the bonds of death. They provide man with something to struggle against for truth's sake; they train the faithful in virtue, so that the new man may be prepared through the new covenant for the new age amid the evils of this age, wisely enduring the woes which this condemned life has deserved, having the foresight to be thankful that it will all come to an end, faithfully and patiently awaiting the happiness which the emancipated life of the future is going to have without end. For the devil has been turned out of power and out of the hearts of the faithful, in whose condemnation and unfaithfulness he used to be in power though also under condemnation himself. And for the duration of this mortality he is only allowed to lead the opposition to the extent that God knows is good for the faithful. On this point the sacred scriptures ring out loud and clear through the mouth of the apostle: *God is faithful, who does not permit you to be tempted above what you are able for, but with the temptation he will also provide a way out, so that you may be able to endure it* (1 Cor 10:13).

For the faithful who devoutly endure them these evils are very useful, either for correcting sins or for exercising and testing justice or for demonstrating the wretchedness of this life, so that the other one where true and perpetual happiness will be found may be desired the more ardently and sought the more urgently. But all the time what the apostle says holds good for them: *We know that for those who love God all things work together for good, for those who have been called*[47] *according to his purpose. For those whom he foreknew he also predestined to be copies of the image of his Son that he might be the firstborn among many brethren. But those he predestined he also called; and those he called he also justified; and those he justified he also glorified* (Rom 8:28). None of these predestined ones can perish with the devil; none of them will remain until death under the devil's jurisdiction. Then follows what I have referred to above: *What then are we to say to all this? If God is for us, who is against us? He who did not spare his own Son but handed him over for us all, how has he not also made us a gift of all things with him* (Rom 8:31)?

21. And so why after all should Christ's death not have happened? Why indeed should the Almighty not have set aside all the other countless ways which

he could have employed to set us free, and chosen this one specially, in which his divinity suffered no change or diminution, and the humanity he took on conferred such a great benefit on men; in which a temporal death he did not owe was paid by the everlasting Son of God who was at the same time Son of man, in order to deliver them from the everlasting death they did owe? The devil was holding on to our sins, and using them to keep us deservedly fixed in death. He who had none of his own discharged them, and was undeservedly led away by the other to death. Such was the value of that blood, that he who killed Christ even with a momentary death he did not owe would no longer have the right to hold anyone who had put on Christ in an eternal death he did owe. And so *God commends his charity for us in that while we were still sinners Christ died for us. Much more, justified now in his blood shall we be saved from the wrath through him* (Rom 5:8). Justified, he says, in his blood, justified surely in being set free from all our sins, and set free from all our sins because the Son of God, who had none, was slain for us. Therefore shall we be saved from the wrath through him, from the wrath of God that is, which is nothing else but just retribution. God's wrath is not like man's, an emotional disturbance; it is with reference to his wrath that holy scripture says in another place, *But you, Lord of hosts, judge with tranquillity* (Wis 12:18). If then the just divine retribution has received such a name, what can the reconciliation of God mean but the end of wrath in this sense?

Nor for that matter were we really God's enemies except in the sense that sins are the enemies of justice, and when these are forgiven such hostilities come to an end, and those whom he himself justifies are reconciled to the just one. Yet he certainly loved these enemies, seeing that *he did not spare his own Son, but while we were still enemies handed him over for us all* (Rom 8:32). The apostle therefore rightly went on to say,[48] *If while we were enemies we were reconciled to God through the death of his Son*—by which that forgiveness of sins was achieved—*much more, being reconciled, shall we be saved in his life* (Rom 5:10); saved in life after being reconciled by death. Could anyone doubt that he is going to give life to his friends, for whom he gave his death while they were enemies? Not only so, he goes on, *but we also boast in God through our Lord Jesus Christ, through whom we have now received reconciliation* (Rom 5:11). Not only, he is saying, shall we be saved, but we also boast; not in ourselves but in God; not through ourselves but through our Lord Jesus Christ through whom we have now received reconciliation, in the way discussed above.

Then the apostle goes on to add: *For this reason, as through one man sin entered this world and through sin death, and so it passed into all men insofar as*[49] *all have sinned* (Rom 5:12) and so on in the rest of the passage in which he discusses the two men at some length; one, that same first Adam through whose sin and death we his descendants have been tied up in a kind of hereditary evil; the other, the second Adam who is not only man but also God, and who pays for us a debt he did not owe, with the result that we have been set free from debts, both ancestral ones and our own personal ones, which we do owe. So then, just as on that one man's account the devil held in his power all who have been born from that man's vitiated fleshly concupiscence, it is only fair that on account of this one man he should release all of them who have been reborn through this man's untarnished spiritual grace.

22. There are many other things to be advantageously examined and thought about in the incarnation of Christ, which so offends the proud. One of them is the demonstration it affords man of the place he should have in God's foundation, seeing that human nature could so be joined to God that one person would be made out of two substances.[50] That in fact means one person now out of three elements, God, soul, and flesh; and this means that those proud, evilly disposed spirits who offer themselves as mediators, ostensibly to help but really to deceive man, do not now dare to set themselves above him simply because they have no flesh; he[51] particularly chose in fact to die in this flesh to prevent them from inducing men to worship them as gods just because they seem to be immortal.

Another point about the incarnation is that in the man Christ it advertises the grace of God toward us without any previous deserts on our part, as not even he won the privilege of being joined to the true God in such a unity that with him he would be one person, Son of God, by any previous merits of his own; how could he, since from the very moment he began to be man he was also God, which is why it said *The Word became flesh* (Jn 1:14)? Again, there is the point that man's pride, which is the greatest obstacle to his cleaving to God, could be confuted and cured by such humility on the part of God. Man also learns how far he has withdrawn from God, which is useful for him as a remedial pain, when he returns to him through a mediator like this, who comes to aid men as God with his divinity and to share with them as man in their infirmity. And what greater example of obedience could be given to us, us who had been ruined by disobedience, than God the Son obeying God the Father *even to death on the cross* (Phil 2:8)? Where could the reward of obedience be shown to better advantage than in the flesh of such a mediator when it rose to eternal life? It was also a mark of the justice and goodness of God that the devil should be outdone by the same rational creature as he congratulated himself on outdoing, and outdone by one man issuing from that race, which he had held the whole of in his power because its origin had been vitiated by one man.

23. God could of course have taken a man to himself from somewhere else, to be in him *the mediator of God and men* (1 Tm 2:5), not from the race of that Adam who had implicated the human race in his own sin, just as he did not create the one he first created from the race of another. In the same way, or any other way he wished, he could have created another one to conquer the conqueror of the first. But God judged it better to take a man to himself from the very race that had been conquered, in order through him to conquer the enemy of the human race; to take one however whose conception from a virgin was inaugurated by the spirit not the flesh, by faith not lust. There was no desire of the flesh involved, which the rest of men who contract original sin are begotten and conceived by; it was utterly absent when holy virginity conceived by

believing not by embracing, so that what was there born of the stock of the first man would only derive from him a racial not a criminal origin. For what was born was not a nature flawed by the infection of transgression, but the only remedy and cure for all such flaws. What was born, I say, was a man who had not and never would have any sin at all, a man by whom would be reborn those who were to be set free from sin, who could not themselves be born without sin.

For while it is true that the carnal desire dwelling in the genital organs is made good use of by married chastity, still it has its involuntary motions which show that either it could not have been present at all in paradise before sin, or if it did exist there that it was not such as would ever resist the will. But now our experience of it is that it *fights against the law of the mind* (Rom 7:23), and even when it is not required for procreation it goads us on to copulation; if we give in it is sated by sinning, if we do not give in it is curbed by refusal; both situations which no one can doubt were foreign to paradise before sin. After all, the probity of that state would not do anything unbecoming, and the felicity of that state would not suffer anything unsatisfying.[52] It was necessary therefore that there should be none of this carnal desire involved at all when the virgin's offspring was conceived, for the author of death, due to be conquered by the death of *the author of life* (Acts 3:15), was going to find nothing deserving of death in him and yet was going to kill him all the same. Here we have the conqueror of the first Adam, holding the human race in his power, conquered by the second Adam and losing the Christian race, a part of the human race set free from human crime by one who was not involved in the crime though sprung from the race; thus that deceiver could be conquered by the race which he had conquered by his crime. And this was all done in this way in order to prevent man getting conceited, but *he that boasts let him boast in the Lord* (2 Cor 10:17). The one who had been conquered, you see, was only man, and the reason he had been conquered was that he had proudly longed to be God. But the one who eventually conquered was both man and God, and the reason the virgin-born conquered was that God was humbly wearing that man, not governing[53] him as he does the other saints. All these great gifts of God, and any others there may be which it would take too long for us to investigate and discuss now, would have been non-existent if the Word had not become flesh.

Chapter 6

The author places what he has said about the redemption in the last two chapters into his scheme of "wisdom" and "knowledge"; recapitulates the course of the whole book; and concludes by sketching a mental trinity of faith, which belongs to the lower activity of the inner man, and is not yet the mental image of the divine trinity.

24. But all these things that the Word made flesh did and suffered for us in time and space belong, according to the distinction we have undertaken to illustrate, to knowledge and not to wisdom. Insofar as he is Word, he is without

time and without space, coeternal with the Father and wholly present everywhere; and if anyone can utter a true word about this, as far as he is able, it will be a word of wisdom. So it is that the Word made flesh, which is Christ Jesus, has treasures both of wisdom and of knowledge. That is what the apostle says, writing to the Colossians: *I want you to know*, he says, *what a struggle I am having for you and for those at Laodicea and for all who have not seen my face in the flesh, that your hearts may be consoled, bound together in charity and in all the riches of the fullness of understanding, to recognize the mystery of God which is Christ Jesus,*[54] *in whom are hidden all the treasures of wisdom and knowledge* (Col 2:1). Who can ever know how well the apostle knew these treasures, how deeply he had penetrated them and what he had discovered in them? But as far as I am concerned, in terms of his other text, *To each of us is given a manifestation of the Spirit for profit; to one is given through the Spirit a word of wisdom, to another a word of knowledge according to the same Spirit* (1 Cor 12:7), if the difference between these two is that wisdom is attributed to divine things and knowledge to human, I acknowledge each of them in Christ, and so does every believer with me. And when I read *The Word became flesh and dwelt amongst us* (Jn 1:14), in the Word I understand the true Son of God and in the flesh I acknowledge the true Son of man, and each joined together into one person of God and man by an inexpressible abundance of grace. As for what he goes on to say, *And we have seen his glory, glory as of the only-begotten from the Father, full of grace and truth* (Jn 1:14), if we refer grace to knowledge and truth to wisdom, I think we shall not be inconsistent with the distinction between these two things which we have been recommending.

Among things that have arisen in time the supreme grace is that man has been joined to God to form one person; among eternal things the supreme truth is rightly attributed to the Word of God. That the only-begotten from the Father is the one who is full of grace and truth means that it is one and the same person by whom deeds were carried out in time for us and for whom we are purified by faith in order that we may contemplate him unchangingly in eternity.[55] But the most eminent heathen philosophers, who *were able to behold the invisible things of God, being understood through the things that have been made* (Rom 1:20), philosophized nonetheless without the mediator, that is without the man Christ, as they neither believed the prophets that he would come nor the apostles that he had. And so *they held on to the truth*, as it is said of them, *in wickedness* (Rom 1:18). Established as they were at this lowest level of things, they could not but look for some middle level things, by which to reach the topmost things they had understood; and in this way they fell into the hands of fraudulent demons, who brought it about that *they changed the glory of the incorruptible God into the likeness of an image, of corruptible man and birds and quadrupeds and creeping things* (Rom 1:23). Such were the shapes of the idols they set up or worshiped.

Our knowledge therefore is Christ, and our wisdom is the same Christ. It is he who plants faith in us about temporal things, he who presents us with the truth about eternal things. Through him we go straight toward him, through knowledge toward wisdom, without ever turning aside from one and the same Christ, *in whom are hidden all the treasures of wisdom and knowledge* (Col 2:3). But now we are speaking of knowledge; later on we are going to speak about wisdom, as far as he himself enables us to do so. Nor of course should we take these two as if we could never call this one that is concerned with human affairs wisdom, or that one that is concerned with divine things knowledge. In a broader manner of speaking each can be called wisdom and each knowledge. However, the apostle would never have written *To one is given a word of wisdom, to another a word of knowledge* (1 Cor 12:8), were it not that these two things which we are now discussing the distinction of could properly be called by these several names.

25. So now let us see what this long drawn out discussion has achieved, what it has picked up, where it has got to. All men have the will to be happy, but not all have the faith which must purify the heart[56] if happiness is to be reached. So it is that only by way of something that not everybody wants can and should we proceed toward something which there can be nobody who does not want. That they want to be happy is something all men see in their hearts, and such in this case is the unanimity of human nature that a man is not deceived if from his own consciousness he infers this about someone else's; anyway, we just know that everybody wants this. However, many despair of ever being able to be immortal, though without this no one can be what everyone wants to be, that is, happy; they would of course like to be immortal if they could, but by not believing that they could be they fail so to live that they can be. So faith is necessary if we are to obtain happiness with all the potentialities of human nature, that is both of body and soul. But this faith, according to its own belief, has been given actual definite content in Christ, who rose in the flesh from the dead to die no more;[57] and it is only through him that anyone can be set free from the devil's domination by the forgiveness of sins; and in the devil's dominions life can of necessity only be unhappy, and perpetually so, a state that is better called death than life. All this I have discussed for some time in this book as best I could, although I had already said much on the subject in the fourth book of this work. But there it was for a different reason from here: there it was to show why and how Christ was sent in the fullness of time by the Father, because of those people who say that the one who did the sending and the one who was sent cannot be equal in nature; here it has been to distinguish between active knowledge and contemplative wisdom.[58]

26. We had thought it best, you may remember, as we were climbing up, so to say, step by step, to search within the inner man for an appropriate trinity in each of these spheres, just as we had previously searched within the outer man, in order by training the mind at these lower levels to come in our own small measure to a sight of that trinity which God is, at least in a puzzle and in a mirror,[59] if of course we can manage even this much. Suppose then someone commits merely the sounds of the words that express this faith to memory without knowing what they mean—as people who do not know Greek can know Greek words by heart, or Latin ones for that matter, or the words of any other

language they are ignorant of; they[60] have, do they not, a kind of trinity in their consciousness, because the sounds of those words are in his memory even when he is not thinking about them, and from them he forms his attention by recollection when he does think about them; and it is his will to recollect and think that joins the two together. But, when he does this, we said, he is certainly not acting according to a trinity of the inner man but rather one of the outer man, because all that he remembers and looks at when he wishes and as he wishes is something belonging to the sense of the body which we call hearing, nor by such thinking is he dealing with anything but the images of bodily things, namely of sounds.

If, however, he holds in his memory and recollects the meaning of those words, he is now indeed doing something proper to the inner man, but he is not yet to be thought of, or talked of, as living according to the trinity of the inner man, unless he loves what these meanings proclaim, command and promise. He could, after all, remember and think about them because he reckons they are false and wants to try to refute them. So the will which, in this case, joins together what was contained in the memory and what has been imprinted therefrom on the thinking attention does indeed complete a trinity, being itself the third component; but one does not live according to it if one does not approve of what one thinks about as being false. When, however, you believe it to be true, and love in it what should be loved, then you are already living according to the trinity of the inner man; every man lives according to what he loves. How, though, can things be loved that are not known but only believed? This question has already been ventilated in previous books,[61] and we discovered that no one loves what he is totally ignorant of; but that, when unknown things are said to be loved, they are loved in virtue of things that are known.

We must now bring this book to an end with the admonition that *the just man lives on faith* (Rom 1:17),[62] and this *faith works through love* (Gal 5:6); in this way the virtues, too, by which one lives sagaciously, courageously, moderately and justly, are all to be related to the same faith. Otherwise, they could not be true virtues. They are not however of such potency in this life, that it can ever happen here below that no remission of any kind of sins will be necessary; this is only achieved by him who conquered the author of sins with his blood. Whatever notions this faith and such a life produce in the consciousness of the believing man, when they are contained in the memory, and looked at in recollection, and please the will, they yield a trinity of its own kind. But the image of God, which with his help we are going to talk about later on, is not yet to be found in this trinity. Why this is so will appear better when we have shown where in fact the image is. The reader may look forward to this in the next volume.

NOTES

1. It is perhaps worth remembering that it was in the middle of Book XII—probably toward the end of it—that Augustine stopped work on the *De Trinitate* for several years, after tiresome friends had pirated what he had already written. Readers may notice a difference in tone in the last three books, a constant "picking up of threads."

2. *Potestatem*, which does not really mean power, but lawful power, authority, or right.

3. *Viri*, of the male.

4. This text shows admirably how "soul" was no strange mystical concept for Augustine, but a plain reality evidenced by the ordinary experience of individual and social human life.

5. *Conscientia,* in its primary sense of "consciousness."

6. A rather loose expression for sight or possession of the things themselves.

7. *Latinam linguam.*

8. When people read a book in Augustine's day, they almost always read out loud. In the *Confessions* he expresses the astonishment he felt at the sight of Ambrose reading silently (*Confessions* VI, 3).

9. *Species.*

10. See Acts 4:32.

11. This is what he says; but I suppose what he meant to say was that he is as certain about Constantinople as about Rome, even though he had seen Rome and only heard about Constantinople.

12. Reading with M, *qui nequitia majore quam theatrica, propositioni vel pronuniationi theatricae insultent.* CCL reads, . . . *quam theatrica propositione, vel pronuntiationi theatricae insultent;* . . . than the comedian's proposition, who even make nonsense of the actor's utterance.

13. *Largitionis gratia;* literally, for the sake of largesse. But the word often carries the implication of gifts laid out to win popularity.

14. A line from the *Annals* known only from Augustine's quotation of it.

15. *Virtus animi*; my rendering is analogous to "conscious attention" by which I usually translated *acies animi* in Book XI. It is not wholly satisfactory; it sounds more priggish than the original warrants—but then the Stoics, whose view the phrase represents, were such prigs. Perhaps "rational virtue"?

16. Book VIII, 6; IX, 3; and especially X, 1-5.

17. A lost work, fragments of which are known mainly from Augustine's quotations.

18. The founder of the Stoics.

19. Reading with M, *et nulla vult mala;* CCL has *et nulla vult male,* and does not want anything wrongly.

20. The philosophers Augustine is criticizing in this whole section are the Stoics. He is saying that their ideal of *apatheia,* or indifference to passion and suffering, is an illusion, and the cultivation of virtue, especially of patience, without the robust motive of Christian hope, is almost if not quite wholly vain.

21. *Andria* 2, 1, 5-6.

22. *Si verum volunt;* M reads *si vere volunt,* if they want it truly.

23. In the previous chapter, sections 8 and 9.

24. This is the final *reductio ad absurdum* of thoroughgoing Stoicism, or of any moral system that claims to be totally non-self-centered.

25. C.17-20: PL 41, 366-372. The argument here is directed against the transmigrationists. It is a stronger attack on the idea of transmigration of souls than was made at the end of Book XII of this work, where Augustine was criticizing Plato's theory of reminiscence. But then there were platonists—in *The City of God* XII, 20, 3 he mentions Porphyry—who modified the theory, doubtless to meet the kind of objection that is leveled against it here. Or perhaps Augustine is in fact somewhat caricaturing the theory when he represents it as proposing that souls have periodic vacations of bliss in heaven, in the intervals of grim incarnate duty in this visible world; and the genuine theory, stated by Porphyry, merely conceived of transmigration as extending a soul's probationary period from

one life, as Christians would have it, to a variable number of lives. In this form, the theory stands up to Augustine's criticism, since it does not require any vacationary intervals between incarnations.

But then he goes on to object that even in its improved form it is inconsistent with their basic theory of the eternity of the world. As he describes it in *The City of God,* this theory stemmed from a faulty idea of divine knowledge; but anyway it was more or less taken as axiomatic in most philosophical circles. Now what it implied with respect to souls was that they had existed from eternity; that they had originally existed in a state of pure disincarnate bliss, and had been condemned to the body for some fault or negligence committed in that state. So even Porphyry's improved version of transmigration still contained the notion of a fall from bliss, from perfect happiness, as well as a final return to it. And I think Augustine's criticism is that if a soul can fall from perfect happiness once, it can do so again, and therefore in this view (which he would say involves a defective idea of what perfect happiness is) there can be no guarantee that what Porphyry says is a final return to perfect happiness will in fact be so. And if it contains even the fear of a possibility of being forfeited, then of course such happiness is not, according to Augustine's definition of it, true and perfect happiness.

26. *Quia;* M reads *qui* (as part of the quotation), by adding *who are born . . .*

27. He is referring to the body.

28. Reading *nobis* with 4 manuscripts; CCL reads *hominibus,* amongst men; M conflates the two readings into *nobis hominibus,* amongst us men. The sense, in my view, requires *nobis,* since Augustine is explaining in this parenthesis the meaning of his text, and saying in effect that *dwelt amongst us* means "became son of man." I admit that in this case it is hard to explain the reading *hominibus* in the other manuscripts. My hypothesis would be that since the words *hominum* and *hominis* occur frequently in these few lines, one or other just caught the copyist's eye and was written in mechanical error, and that then the corrector, or a further copyist, corrected the resultant solecism to make sense—good grammatical sense, though not such good overall sense, I think, as *nobis.*

29. M adds *Dei,* by God's grace.

30. See Book IV, 1. This whole central section of Book XIII is parallel to the main part of Book IV.

31. See Gal 5:6.

32. Which means "Yahweh saves." The idea of healing or health is contained in the Latin *salus* and the Greek *sōteria.*

33. He is alluding to his already having done so in Book IV.

34. *Originaliter;* hence the term "original sin," meaning not the first sin, but the sin we all contract by our origin.

35. Thus Christ is excluded, being born of a virgin.

36. Explanations of the redemption in terms of justice are not very fashionable nowadays. Indeed they are regarded with a reserve verging on disapproval as being "legalistic" or "feudal" or "juridical"—all of which are very bad names indeed. And even if we can stomach such qualities in a theological explanation, most of us nowadays find it rather peculiar to think of the devil as having legal rights which God has somehow to buy him out of, and we assume that some such idea as this is involved in talking about God overcoming the devil with justice.

The reader must judge for himself whether Augustine's treatment of the theme is open to such criticisms—certainly I should suppose it is rather hard to debit him with feudal concepts. But however that may be, it seems to me that what he has to say has a peculiar significance for us in these late twentieth century times, when we are so acutely aware of the values of social justice and the problems of social revolution, and preoccupied with the question whether and how far a Christian may rightly resort to violence (that is, power) in order to bring about a just society, or alternatively to maintain the stability and order of society.

Current theology, in other words, is involved four square in political thought; it has its political dimension which practically no modern theologian would wish to erase even if he could. And here is Augustine presenting the redemption as an archetypal model of political action, in which justice is uncompromisingly placed before power, just as in the last book he presented the fall as the archetype of all social disarray, in which what is private is disastrously preferred to what is common to the whole human community. It is not for me to discuss the value of what he says to modern currents of theological thought, whether in criticism or in support of them; it is only my responsibility to draw the reader's attention to the relevance of what Augustine has to say.

37. The play on words, which is the whole point of the sentence, is untranslatable. "That is why," he says, "power is counted among the *res secundae,* that is the favorable things or useful things to have; they are called *secundae* from *sequi,* to follow." Perhaps this secondary meaning of *secundus* as "favorable" or equivalent to *prosperus* is derived from nautical language, since a following wind is a favorable wind—or from athletics, in which a second wind is also an advantageous wind!

38. Chapter 2, section 8.

39. See Rom 5:9.

40. What he had to do out of the necessity of justice, not the necessity of nature.

41. That is, avoid being killed.

42. See Phil 2:8.

43. See Rom 6:9.

44. A curious version of an involved text.

45. See Rv 21:8.

46. See Rom 8:29; Eph 1:4.

47. M adds *sancti,* called to be saints, with several manuscripts and the Vulgate. The text of CCL, which is certainly more likely to be Augustine's, is closer to the Greek in another untranslatable little detail; the verb "work together" is in the singular, *cooperatur,* though the subject, *omnia,* is plural; thus the Latin perpetrates a hellenism.

48. Went on from the quotation in the previous paragraph; the text just immediately quoted is a kind of aside.

49. *In quo,* a famous conjunctive phrase, which in his polemic against the Pelagians Augustine interpreted as meaning "in whom," namely in Adam (*Answer to Two Letters of the Pelagians* IV, 4, 7). There he quotes a work of Hilary in support, which the Maurists declare to be from a work by a heretic deacon, also called Hilary. This interpretation is assumed in a famous canon 2 of the Council of Orange, celebrated in the year 529, which was repeated by the Council of Trent in the second canon of its decree on original sin. The interpretation does not in fact make grammatical sense even of the Latin sentence, and is impossible with the original Greek. The translation "insofar as" is what the Latin *in quo* reasonably means in the context, and the wider context of what Augustine is saying here does not require anything else. Therefore I feel it would be unfair to saddle him here with a tortured interpretation that he seems to have adopted, on the strength of a bogus authority, in the heat and pressure of the pelagian controversy. His doctrine of original sin does not in the least depend on this particular *tour de force* interpretation. See Book IV, 15, note 52.

50. He uses the word "substance" in the same sense as Chalcedon was going to talk about "nature"; the two terms are for him in fact practically synonymous, except that "substance" could be said to be "nature" in the concrete.

51. M adds *Filius Dei,* the Son of God particularly . . . .

52. This whole passage contains in a nutshell Augustine's ideas about the connection between sex and original sin. Carnal desire or concupiscence as directed toward sexual intercourse, he thinks, is the bearer of the infection of original sin, and this because it escapes the full control of reason. Thus it is radically symptomatic of that disorder which sin introduced into man's relations with things; he disobeyed God, and found his own body and passions disobeying his reason.

The view derives, in my opinion, not from any manichean horror of the body or of sex, with which Augustine is often credited (the Pelagians were the first to put forward this smear), but from too narrow, too intellectualist an idea of reason, and this was stoic in its derivation.

53. A very neat play on words which I have found no way of bringing out in English: *Deus humiliter non . . . regebat illum hominem, sed gerebat.*

54. Reading *Christus Jesus* with M and one manuscript. CCL omits *Jesus;* in favor of doing so is that it reflects the Vulgate; against it is that the phrase "which is Christ Jesus" a few lines above seems to be an echo of this text.

55. It is bad form for a translator to wring his hands about his material and blame his original for a scarcely intelligible sentence; but this is Augustine at his most intricately dense, and I give the

reader the Latin sentence, in case he can do a better job at it than I have been able to do: *Quod vero idem ipse est unigenitus a Patre plenus gratiae et veritatis, id actum est ut idem ipse sit in rebus pro nobis temporaliter gestis cui per eandem fidem mundamur ut eum stabiliter contemplemur in rebus eternis.* It seems to me that he is trying to make too many points in too short a compass with too clever a rhetoric. He has in fact said it before at greater length, but much more lucidly and in much better style in Book IV, 24; the two paragraphs beginning "But eternal life is promised" and ending "a bridge to eternity."

56. See Acts 15:9.

57. See Rom 6:9.

58. Presumably by illustrating the field of active knowledge in a way needed for restoring the image of God in Everyman redeemed.

59. See 1 Cor 13:12.

60. *Habent:* M reads *habet,* he has, thus tidying up Augustine's syntax.

61. Only in Book VIII, as a matter of fact, in chapter 3, sections 3-8, and in chapter 5, sections 13-14. In Book IX and X he proves that you cannot love what you do not know, without bringing in faith. See Books IX, 3 and X, 1-4.

62. See also Gal 3:11; Heb 10:38 all quoting Hb 2:4.

BOOK XIV

MAN'S CASE HISTORY: THE IMAGE PERFECTED

Chapter 1

The author turns to the discussion of wisdom and its appropriate function of contemplation, in which the true image of God is to be found; but first he picks up a thread from the previous book and examines in more detail why in fact a trinity of faith as the appropriate function of knowledge may not be said to be the image of God.

---

1. Now it is wisdom's turn to be discussed. I do not mean God's wisdom, which is undoubtedly God; it is his only begotten Son that is called God's wisdom. What we are going to talk about is man's wisdom, true wisdom of course which is in accordance with God and is in fact the true and principal worship of him, which in Greek is the single noun *theosebeia*. Our people, as I have already mentioned,[1] translated this by "piety," as they too wanted to find a single noun for it. But piety is more usually called *eusebeia* in Greek; and as *theosebeia* cannot be completely translated by one word, it is better to use two for it and say "God's worship." That this is man's wisdom, as we have already settled in the twelfth volume of this work, is proved on the authority of holy scripture in the book of God's servant Job, where we read that God's wisdom said to man, *Behold piety is wisdom, while to abstain from evils is knowledge* (Jb 28:28).[2] * So God himself is supreme wisdom; but the worship of God is

---

* Some have here translated the Greek word *episteme* by "discipline," which of course derives from *discere*, to learn, and so can mean knowledge, seeing that a thing is only learned in order to be known. But it also has the other meaning, according to which the pains a man suffers for his sins in order to be corrected are commonly called "discipline"; it is used in this sense in the Letter to the Hebrews: *What son is there whose father does not give him discipline?* And even more clearly from the same letter: *All discipline seems at the time to be a matter for sadness, not joy, but afterward it will repay the peaceable fruit of justice to those who have competed through it* (Heb 12:7.11).

man's wisdom, and it is that which we are now talking about. As for *the wisdom of this world, it is folly with God* (1 Cor 3:19). As regards this wisdom, though, which is the worship of God, holy scripture says, *a multitude of wise men is the health of the world* (Wis 6:24).

2. But what are we to do if the discussion of wisdom is the prerogative of the wise?[3] Will we have the nerve to profess wisdom, and if not will our discussion of it not be sheer impertinence? Will the example of Pythagoras not frighten us off? Not daring to profess to be wise, he answered that he was rather a philosopher, that is, a lover of wisdom. From him onward this name found favor among his successors, so that however outstanding a man might seem to be, either in his own or other people's opinion, as a teacher of matters that belong to wisdom, he would never be called anything but a philosopher, a wisdom-lover. Or possibly the reason why none of these men dared to profess to be wise was that they thought a wise man would be entirely without sin. But our scriptures do not say this, because they say, *Rebuke a wise man and he will love you* (Prv 9:8); and presumably they judge a man who is considered to be worthy of rebuke to have sin. Even so, I for one do not dare to profess to be wise. It is enough for me that it is also the business of the philosopher, that is of the wisdom-lover, to discuss wisdom, which even these old philosophers cannot deny. After all, they did not stop doing this, even though they professed to be lovers of wisdom rather than wise men.

3. Now in their discussions of wisdom they defined it as follows: *Wisdom is the knowledge of things human and divine.*[4] That is why in the previous book I expressly said that awareness of each kind of things, namely human and divine, could be called both wisdom and knowledge.[5] But in terms of the distinction made by the apostle, *To one is given a word of wisdom, to another a word of knowledge* (1 Cor 12:8), this definition can be split up, in such a way that knowledge of things divine is properly called wisdom, and of things human is properly given the name of knowledge. I discussed this knowledge in the thirteenth volume, where I did not of course ascribe to it any and every thing a man can know about things human, because this includes a great deal of superfluous frivolity and pernicious curiosity; all I ascribed to it was anything that breeds, feeds, defends, and strengthens the saving faith which leads to true happiness. Very many of the faithful do not excel in such knowledge, though they excel very much in faith itself.[6] It is one thing to know only what a man should believe in order to gain the happy life which is nothing if it is not eternal; quite another to know how the godly are to be assisted in this and how the attacks of the ungodly upon it are to be met, and it is this that the apostle seems to call by the proper name of knowledge. When I was speaking about it above, my chief concern was to commend faith itself, after first briefly distinguishing between eternal and temporal things. While discussing temporal things in that place and deferring eternal ones to this book, I showed that faith in eternal things is also necessary for gaining these eternal things, though faith itself is temporal and finds a temporal dwelling in the hearts of believers. I also argued that faith

in the temporal things, which the eternal one did and suffered in the man he wore in time and bore through to eternity, is equally valuable for gaining these eternal things; and finally that the very virtues by which one lives sagaciously, courageously, moderately, and justly in this time of mortality must be related to this faith which though temporal itself leads to eternity, or they will not be true virtues.

4. Now it is written that *As long as we are in the body we are living abroad from the Lord; for we are walking by faith and not by sight* (1 Cor 5:6). It would seem to follow then that as long as the just man is living on faith[7] he may indeed strive and struggle on by this temporal faith to the eternal truth,[8] and yet in his retaining, contemplating and loving of this temporal faith there is not such a trinity as deserves to be called the image of God, even though he is living according to the inner man; otherwise we would appear to be setting up this image in temporal things, although it should only be set up in things that are eternal. Clearly, when the human mind sees the faith with which it believes what it does not see, it is not seeing something everlasting. It will not always exist, because it will certainly no longer exist when this sojourn abroad comes to an end in which we are living away from the Lord so that we have to walk by faith, and when the sight by which we shall see face to face[9] takes its place. We do not see now, but because we believe, we shall deserve to see, and shall rejoice at having been brought through to sight by faith. Then there will no longer be any faith by which things that are not seen are believed, but sight by which things that were believed are seen. So even though we then remember this mortal life that is over and done with, and recollect from memory that we once believed what we did not yet see, this faith will be reckoned among things that are past and over and done with, not among things that are present and continue for ever. And therefore this trinity too that consists in the memory, observation, and love of faith now present and continuing will be found to be a thing that is past and done with, not still continuing.

From this we conclude that if this trinity is already the image of God, then such an image is not to be located in things that always are but in things that pass away. But it is intolerable to suppose that while the soul is by nature immortal and from the moment of its creation never thereafter ceases to exist, its very best attribute or possession should not last out its immortality. And was anything better created in its nature than its being made to the image of its creator? So whatever it is that must be called the image of God, it must be found in something that will always be, and not in the retention, contemplation, and love of faith, which will not always be.

5. Or should we perhaps spend a little longer on examining more thoroughly and more searchingly whether this is in fact the case? It could, after all, be said that this trinity does not fade out when faith itself passes away. Just as we now retain our faith by remembering, and observe it by thinking, and love it by willing, so too we will retain it then by remembering our having had it, and we

will recollect this fact, and join the two together by willing as the third element, and thus the same trinity will continue in existence.* But if you say this you are failing to distinguish that it is one trinity now when we retain, see, and love faith present in ourselves, and will be another trinity when by recollecting we observe, not faith itself, but so to say its trace image hidden in the memory, and join these two together, that is what was in the retentive memory and what was impressed from there onto the thinking attention, with the will as third element.

To be able to understand this, let us take an example from bodily things, which we spoke about sufficiently in the eleventh book. You will remember that in our ascent from lower things to higher, or our entrance from outer things to inner, we found a first trinity in the body that is seen, and the gaze of the seer which is formed from it when he sees it, and the intention of the will which joins the two together. Now to this trinity let us equate the similar one that arises when the faith that is in us is established in our memory like that body in its place, and from it the thought is formed in recollection just as the gaze was formed from that body in seeing, and to these two to make up a trinity is added the will as the third element which connects and joins together faith established in the memory and a kind of copy of it impressed on the inner gaze in recollection; just as in that other bodily trinity of vision the intention of the will joins together the form of the body that is being seen and the conformation to it which is being produced in the outer gaze by looking. Now let us suppose that that body which was being looked at has fallen to bits and vanished, and nothing of it whatever remains anywhere to which the gaze can turn back in order to see it. The image of course of the bodily thing that is now past, over and done with remains in the memory, and in thought the inner gaze can be formed from it, with the will as the third element joining the two together; but is this to be called the same trinity as the one which existed when the look of the body in its place was being seen? Surely not, it is quite a different one. Apart from the fact that the first one was outside, the second inside, the first was produced by the look of a body present, the second is produced by the image of a body past. So too in the point we are considering now and which we brought up this example to illustrate, faith which is now in our consciousness like that body in its place produces a certain trinity when it is retained, looked at, and loved. But this trinity will not continue to be when faith is no longer in the consciousness like that body no longer in its place. The trinity that will exist then when we recall that faith has been, not is, in us, will be quite a different one. The trinity that exists now is produced by the thing present and affixed to the consciousness of the believer; the trinity that will exist then will be made by the image of the thing past, left behind in the recording

---

* But of course if it leaves no trace of itself in us when it passes away, then indeed we will have nothing of it in our memory to turn back to and recall its having existed in the past, coupling the two together with the intention as third element, namely what was in the memory while we were not thinking about it and what was formed from it by thinking about it.

memory. And as a matter of fact that trinity which does not yet exist will no more be the image of God than this trinity which will not then exist. What we have to find in the soul of man, that is in the rational or intellectual soul, is an image of the creator which is immortally engrained in the soul's immortality.

Chapter 2

The author now begins to look for a trinity in the inner man which will also be the image of God, and recalls what he said in the tenth book about the mind remembering, understanding, and willing itself; it is taken as axiomatic, though an axiom which raises problems, that the mind in some sense always remembers, understands, and loves itself; and yet this trinity is only actualized when the mind thinks about itself; so the place of thought or cogitatio *in the production of the mental trinity is investigated more thoroughly and it is found that without thought there can be no mental word, and therefore no fully actual trinity which will be the actual image of God; thus we again are made to understand that the image of God is only fully realized in certain mental acts, not in mere mental potentialities.*

---

6. We talk about the soul's immortality, of course, with certain qualifications; the soul does have its own kind of death, when it lacks the happy life which ought truly[10] to be regarded as the soul's life; but it is called immortal because it never ceases to live with some sort of life even when it is at its unhappiest. In the same sort of way, though the reason or understanding in it may appear at one moment to be in a coma, at another to be small, at another to be great, the human soul is never anything but rational and intellectual. And therefore if it is with reference to its capacity to use reason and understanding in order to understand and gaze upon God that it was made to the image of God, it follows that from the moment this great and wonderful nature begins to be, this image is always there, whether it is so worn away as to be almost nothing, or faint and distorted, or clear and beautiful. Divine scripture indeed bewails the distortion of its true worth by saying, *Although man walks in the image, yet he is troubled in vain; he treasures up and does not know for whom he gathers them* (Ps 39:6). It would not have ascribed vanity to the image of God unless it had observed that it had been distorted. But it shows clearly enough that this distortion cannot stop its being image by saying, *Although man walks in the image.* So this sentence can be true whichever way round you put it; as well as saying *Although man walks in the image, yet he is troubled in vain,* you could also say "Although man is troubled in vain, yet he walks in the image." Although it is a great nature, it could be spoiled because it is not the greatest; and although it could be spoiled because it is not the greatest, yet because it is capable of the greatest nature and can share in it, it is a great nature still.

Let us search then in this image of God for some special trinity that is *sui generis,* with the help of him who made us to his own image. Without that help we cannot safely investigate these matters or discover anything to do with the wisdom that comes from him. But if the reader has retained in his memory and can recall what we said about the human soul or mind in the previous books, especially the tenth, or if he takes the trouble to look it up in the appropriate places, he will not be requiring here any very lengthy account of the examination of this great question.

7. Among other things, then, we said in the tenth book that man's mind knows itself. The mind knows nothing so well as what is present to it, and nothing is more present to the mind than itself. And we produced other arguments as much as seemed sufficient to prove this with considerable certainty. So what then is to be said about the mind of an infant which is still so small and sunk in such vast ignorance of things that the mind of a man which knows anything shudders at the darkness of that infant mind? Must we perhaps believe that it too knows itself, but that it is wholly preoccupied with the things it is beginning to perceive through the senses of the body with a delight that is all the greater for being new; and so it is not a question of its being able to be ignorant of itself, but of its not being able to think about itself? You can at least gather how intently it is drawn to sensible things from its avidity for drinking in lights. This is such that if anyone is careless enough, or ignorant enough of the consequences, to place a night-light where a baby is lying in such a position that the infant can twist its eyes to the light without being able to turn its neck, it will fix its gaze on it so unremittingly that it will develop a permanent squint, as we know has happened in some cases; the eyes retaining the position which habit fixed them in while still soft and tender. It is the same with the other senses of the body into which the souls of infants compress themselves, so to speak, with all the intensity that that age is capable of, so that they passionately shrink from or grab at whatever offends or attracts the flesh and that alone, but never think of their inner selves. Nor can they be admonished to do this, because they do not know the signs used by the admonisher, among which words have the chief place, and they are as utterly ignorant of these as of anything else.[11] But in any case, that it is one thing not to know oneself and another not to think about oneself we have already shown in the same volume.

8. Let us leave this age of infancy aside, though, as we cannot ask it questions about what is going on in it and we ourselves have thoroughly forgotten it. It is enough to assure ourselves that when a human being is able to think about the nature of his consciousness and find out what is true about it, he will not find it anywhere else but inside himself. And what he will find out is not what he did not know before but what he did not think about before. What after all do we know, if we do not know what is in our own mind, seeing that whatever we know we can only know it with the mind? Such however is the force of thought that the mind cannot even set itself in some fashion in its own view except when it thinks about itself. Nothing is in the mind's view except what is being thought about, and this means that not even the mind itself, which does the thinking about anything that is being thought about, can be in its own view except by thinking about itself.

Though as a matter of fact, how it can not be in its own view when it is not thinking about itself, seeing that it can never be without itself, as though it were one thing and its view another, I cannot really fathom. To be sure, this can be said without absurdity about the eye of the body. The eye is fixed in its place in the body, and its gaze is drawn to things outside, is drawn out indeed as far as the stars. Nor is the eye in its own view, seeing that it has not got a view of itself except when presented with a mirror, which we have already spoken about.[12] But this clearly does not happen when the mind sets itself in its own view by thinking about itself. Does it then see one part of itself with another part of itself when it gets a view of itself by thinking, just as with some parts of our bodies which are the eyes we get a view of the other parts of our bodies which can be in our view? What an absurd idea! Where then is the mind taken from except from itself, and where is it set in its own view except in front of itself? So presumably it will no longer be where it was while it was not in its own view, because it has been set here and taken away from there. But if it has changed places in order to be viewed, where will it stay in order to view? Does it double up, as it were, in order to be both there and here, that is both where it can view and where it can be viewed, so that in itself it is viewing and in front of itself it is viewable? When we consult truth it gives us none of these answers because when we think in this fashion we only think the fabricated images of bodies, and to the few minds which are able to consult truth about this matter it is absolutely certain that mind is not that.

So the only alternative left is that its view is something that belongs to its own nature, and that when the mind thinks about itself its view is drawn back to itself not through an interval of space, but by a kind of non-bodily turning round. But when it is not thinking about itself, it is indeed not in its own view, nor is its gaze being formed from itself, and yet it still knows itself by being somehow its own memory of itself. It is like a man learned in many disciplines; everything he knows is contained in his memory, but nothing is in the view of his mind except what he is actually thinking about. The rest is stacked away in a kind of confidential file of awareness[13] which is called memory. That is why we were constantly presenting a trinity in this way, placing in the memory that from which the gaze of thought is formed, treating the actual conformation as the image that is printed off from it, and finding the thing that joins both together to be love or will. So when the mind views itself by thought, it understands and recognizes itself; thus it begets this understanding and self-recognition. It is a non-bodily thing that is being understood and viewed, and recognized in the understanding. When the mind by thinking views and understands itself, it does not beget this awareness of itself as though it had previously been unknown to itself; it was already known to itself in the way that things are known which are contained in the memory even when they are not being thought about. We say a man knows letters even when he is thinking about other things, not letters. These two, begetter and begotten, are coupled together by love as the third, and this is nothing but the will seeking or holding something to be enjoyed. This is why we thought the trinity of the mind should be put forward under these three names, memory, understanding, and will.

9. We said toward the end of the tenth book, however, that the mind always remembers, always understands and loves itself, even though it does not always think about itself as distinct from things that are not what it is. So we must go on to inquire in what way understanding belongs to thought, while awareness of anything that is in the mind even while it is not being thought about is said to belong only to memory. If this is so, then it did not always have these three in such a way that it remembered, understood, and loved itself, but it only remembered itself, and then came to understand and love itself when it began afterward to think about itself. So let us look a little more closely at the example we employed to show that it is one thing not to know something, another not to think about it, and that it can happen that a man knows something which he does not think about when he is thinking about something else. This man then, learned in two or more disciplines, when he thinks about one of them, he still knows the other or the others even if he is not thinking about them. But can we be correct in saying "This musician certainly knows music, but he does not understand it now because he is not thinking about it; what he understands now is geometry, because that is what he is thinking about"? The absurdity of the sentence is plain to see. What about it if we say "This musician certainly knows music, but he does not love it now because he is not thinking about it; what he loves now is geometry, because that is what he is thinking about now"? Equally absurd, surely. We are however absolutely correct if we say "This man you see now talking about geometry is also an accomplished musician. He remembers the subject, understands it, and loves it; but although he knows and loves it he is not thinking about it now, because he is thinking about the geometry which he is discussing."

This tells us that in the recesses of the mind there are various awarenesses of various things, and that they come out somehow into the open and are set as it were more clearly in the mind's view when they are thought about; it is then that the mind discovers it remembers and understands and loves something too, which it was not thinking about while it was thinking about something else. But if it is something that we have not thought about for a long time and are unable to think about unless we are reminded of it, then in heaven knows what curious way it is something, if you can say this, that we do not know we know. At least it is quite correct for the man who is doing the reminding to say to the man he reminds, "You know this, but you do not know that you know it; I will remind you, and you will discover that you know what you supposed you did not know." Literature performs precisely this function, when it is about things that the reader discovers under the guidance of reason to be true, not simply believing the writer that they are true as when he reads history, but himself discovering with the writer that they are true, and discovering it either in himself or in truth itself guiding[14] the mind. But anyone who is unable to see these things even when he is reminded of them and has his attention drawn to them, is suffering from great blindness of heart and sunk very deep in the darkness of ignorance, and needs very special aid from God to be able to attain true wisdom.

10. The reason why I wanted to introduce some sort of example of thought which could show how the attention is informed in recollection by the things

contained in the memory, and how something is begotten where a man does his thinking that is like what was in him where he was only remembering before thinking, is that the distinction is easier to observe where something crops up in time and where parent precedes offspring by an interval of time. For if we refer to the inner memory of the mind with which it remembers itself and the inner understanding with which it understands itself and the inner will with which it loves itself, where these three are simultaneously together and always have been simultaneously together from the moment they began to be, whether they were being thought about or not, it will indeed seem that the image of that other trinity belongs only to the memory. But because there can be no word in it without thought—we think everything we say, including what we say with that inner word that is not part of any people's language—it is rather in these three that this image is to be recognized, namely memory, understanding, and will. And here I mean the understanding we understand with as we think, that is when things are brought up that were to hand in the memory but were not being thought about, and our thought is formed from them; and the will or love or esteem I mean is the one that joins this offspring to its parent and is in a certain measure common to them both.

It was from this point that I started to lead my slower readers[15] through outward sensible things that are seen with the eyes, in the eleventh book if you remember. And from there I entered with them into that power of the inner man by which he reasons about temporal things, leaving aside for the time being that chief or dominant power by which he contemplates eternal things. I did this in two volumes, distinguishing in the twelfth between these two powers or functions, of which one is the higher the other the lower, which ought to be subordinate to the higher; and in the thirteenth I discussed as truly and as briefly as I could the lower function which includes the salutary knowledge of human affairs, which we need in order to act in this temporal life in a way that will gain us eternal life. At least I succeeded in compressing into one slight volume a vast and many-sided subject which has been debated in many great discussions by many great men,[16] and I showed that here too there is a trinity, but not yet one that can be called the image of God.

Chapter 3

Continuing with his examination of the trinity of the mind's remembering, understanding, and willing itself, and comparing it with the lesser trinities hitherto described, the author finds it to be truly the image of God, because unlike these other trinities it is "coeternal" with the mind itself and is not adventitious to the mind, that is to say, it does not come to it from outside; his presentation of the case involves him in an important explanation or defense of his use of the term "memory" in this context.

---

11. But now we have come to the point of discussing the chief capacity of the human mind, with which it knows God or can know him, and we have

undertaken to consider it in order to discover in it the image of God. For although the human mind is not of the same nature as God, still the image of that nature than which no nature is better is to be sought and found in that part of us than which our nature also has nothing better. But first of all the mind must be considered in itself, and God's image discovered in it before it participates in him. For we have said that even when it has lost its participation in him it still remains the image of God, even though worn out and distorted. It is his image insofar as it is capable of him and can participate in him; indeed it cannot achieve so great a good except by being his image.

Here we are then with the mind remembering itself, understanding itself, loving itself. If we see this we see a trinity, not yet God of course, but already the image of God. It was not from outside that this memory received what it was to retain, nor was it outside that the understanding found what it was to look at, like the eyes of the body, nor was it outside that the will joined these two together like the form of the body and the form derived from it in the gaze of the onlooker. Nor was it the image of a thing that had been seen outside, caught in a certain fashion and stacked away in the memory, which thought discovered when it turned to it, and from which the inner gaze was informed in recollection, with the will as third element joining the two together. This we showed is what happened in those trinities which were discovered in bodily things or drawn inside in a certain way through the senses of the body from bodies, all of which we discussed in the eleventh book.

Nor is it like what happened or appeared when we were discussing that knowledge which is one of the resources[17] of the inner man and had to be distinguished from wisdom. Here the things that are known are adventitious to the consciousness, whether they have been brought in by the acquisition of historical[18] knowledge, like deeds and sayings which occur in time and pass away, or things in nature which occur in their own localities and regions; or whether they are things that have arisen in a man that were not there before, either from the teaching of others or from his own reflections, like faith which we commended extensively in the thirteenth book, or like the virtues which if genuine insure that you live in this mortality in such a way that you will live happily in that immortality which is promised by God.

Now all these and similar cases proceed in a temporal order, one thing after another, which makes it much easier for us to observe the trinity of memory, sight, and love. Thus some of them precede the knowledge that learns about them; they are knowable even before they get known and beget awareness of themselves in the learner. They are there already, either in their own places, or in past time— though of course those in past time are not actually there themselves, but only some sort of signs of their past existence, sight or sound of which produces knowledge that they existed and passed away. Such signs are either put up in places, like tombstones and similar monuments, or to be found in trustworthy writings like any history of sound and approved authority; or even in the minds of those who know them already—they are already known to these people and knowable to others whose knowledge they precede, and who can get to know them if they are taught by those to whom they are already known. All these things produce a kind of trinity when they are learnt, consisting of the look which was knowable even before it was known, and of the learner's awareness joined to this, which begins to be when the thing is learnt, and the will as third element which joins the two together. And after these things are known another trinity is produced inside in the consciousness itself when they are called to mind, one consisting of the images which were impressed on the memory when they were learnt, and of the conformation of thought recalling them with a backward look at them, and of the will as third element which joins these two together.

As for things that arise in the consciousness where they were not to be found before, like faith and similar things, they do indeed seem to be adventitious when they are inserted by teaching, and yet they were never positioned outside, or performed outside like the things that are believed, but quite simply began to be inside in the consciousness itself.[19] Faith is not what one believes but what one believes with; what one believes is believed, what one believes with is seen. And yet because it begins to be in the consciousness which was already a consciousness before faith began to be in it, it seems to be something adventitious, and will be regarded as one of the things in the past when sight succeeds it and it ceases to be; and it produces one trinity now when through being present it is retained, looked at, and loved; it will produce another one then through a kind of trace of itself which it will leave behind in the memory as it passes away, as we have already stated above.[20]

12. The virtues too, by which one lives well in this mortal state, begin to be in the consciousness, which was already there without them and was still consciousness; but whether they too cease to be when they have brought you to eternity is quite a question. Some people think they will come to an end, and when this is said about three of them, sagacity, courage, and moderation, there does seem to be a point there. Justice however is immortal, and will rather then be perfected in us than cease to be. "Tully, the great master of eloquence,"[21] discusses all four of them in his dialogue *Hortensius*. He says:

> If we were allowed when we move on from this life, to spend an immortal age in the isles of the blessed, as the legends declare, what need would there be of eloquence, seeing that there would be no trials or courts? Or for that matter, even of the virtues? We would need no courage where no danger or difficulty faced us; no justice, since there would be no property belonging to others which we could covet; no moderation, to control non-existent lusts; we should not even need any sagacity, not being faced with any choices to be made of good things or bad. So we would be happy with one single awareness of nature, one knowledge, which is the only thing that even the life of the gods is to be praised for. From which we can gather that other things are a matter of necessity, this one thing[22] a matter to be willed for its own sake.

Thus this great orator, reflecting on what he had learnt from the philosophers and explaining it with such grace and distinction, sang the praises of philosophy;[23] and in doing so he stated that the four virtues are necessary only in this life, which we observe to be full of trials and errors; and that none of them is necessary when we move on from this life, if we are allowed to live where one can live happily; but that good souls are happy with awareness and knowledge, that is to say, with the contemplation of nature, in which nothing is better or more to be loved than the nature which created and established all other natures. But if being subject to this nature is what justice means, then justice is quite simply immortal, and will not cease to be in that state of happiness but will be such that it could not be greater or more perfect.

Perhaps then the other three virtues too will continue in that state of bliss, sagacity without any danger now of mistakes, courage without any annoyance of evils to be borne, moderation without any recalcitrant lusts to control. Sagacity will mean not putting any good above or on a level with God, courage will mean cleaving to him with absolute constancy, moderation will mean taking pleasure in no guilty failing. As for what justice does now in succoring the unfortunate, sagacity in taking precautions against pitfalls, courage in enduring trials, moderation in curbing crooked pleasures, there will be none of this where there is quite simply nothing evil. And so these activities of the virtues which are necessary for this mortal life, like faith to which they should all be related, will be reckoned as things of the past. They[24] produce one trinity now when we retain them, look at them, and love them as present; they will produce another one then, when we shall discover them not to be but to have been, by the kind of traces they will leave behind in the memory as they pass away. For then too a trinity will emerge when this kind of trace is both retained in memory and recognized as true and each is joined to the other by will as the third element.

13. In the knowledge of all these temporal things we have mentioned, some knowables precede awareness of them by an interval of time, like those sensible objects that already existed in things before they were perceived, or all the things one comes to know about through history; others begin to be at the same time as the knowledge of them, as though something visible which simply did not exist before were to spring up before our eyes, which would clearly not precede our awareness of it; or as though a noise were to be made in the presence of a listener, in which case both sound and the hearing of it would begin to be simultaneously and cease to be simultaneously. In either case, whether they precede in time or begin to be simultaneously, the knowables beget the knowledge, not the knowledge the knowables. As for the awareness that arises when things that we know and have deposited in memory are looked at again in recollection, anyone can see that retention in the memory is prior in time to sight in recollection and the conjunction of them both by will as the third element.

Now in the case of the mind it is not so. The mind, after all, is not adventitious to itself, as though to the mind which already was came from somewhere else the same mind which was not yet; or as though it did not come from somewhere else, but in the mind which already was should be born the same mind which was not yet, just as in the mind which already was arises faith which was not before; or as though after getting to know itself it should by recollection see itself fixed in its own memory, as if it had not been there before it had got to know itself. The truth of course is that from the moment it began to be it never stopped remembering itself, never stopped understanding itself, never stopped loving itself, as we have already shown. And therefore when it turns to itself in thought, a trinity is formed in which a word too can be perceived. It is formed of course out of the very act of thought, with the will joining the two together. It is here then more than anywhere that we should recognize the image we are looking for.[25]

14. Someone is going to say, "This is not really memory, by which you say that the mind which is always present to itself remembers itself; memory is of things past, not things present." Some writers treating of the virtues, Tully among them, divided sagacity into these three parts: memory, understanding, and foresight; assigning memory to things past, understanding to things present, and foresight to things future.[26] No one has certainty in this last quality except those who have foreknowledge of the future, and this is not a gift enjoyed by men unless they are given it from above, like the prophets. So the book of Wisdom, talking about men, says, *The thoughts of mortals are timid and our foresight unsure* (Wis 9:14). Memory however of past things and understanding of present ones you can be certain about—by present things I mean here non-bodily ones, for it is to the sight of the bodily eyes that bodily things are present.

But if you insist that memory is not of things present, please observe the way secular literature uses words, where there is more concern for the correctness of words than for the truth of things:

No such things did Ulysses endure,
nor did the man of Ithaca
forget himself in that momentous hazard.[27]

When Virgil said that Ulysses did not forget himself, what can he have meant us to understand but that he remembered himself? As he was present to himself, he could not at all have remembered himself unless memory also belonged to things present. As regards things past one means by memory that which makes it possible for them to be recalled and thought over again; so as regards something present, which is what the mind is to itself, one may talk without absurdity of memory as that by which the mind is available to itself, ready to be understood by its thought about itself, and for both to be conjoined by its love of itself.

Chapter 4

The final and perfect image of God is to be found not merely in the mind's remembering, understanding, and loving itself, but in its remembering, understanding, and loving God; it is shown that this trinity is no more adventitious to the mind than that of its self-awareness; and what can be meant by remembering God, understanding him and loving him is discussed.

15. This trinity of the mind is not really the image of God because the mind remembers and understands and loves itself, but because it is also able to remember and understand and love him by whom it was made. And when it does this it becomes wise. If it does not do it, then even though it remembers and understands and loves itself, it is foolish. Let it then remember its God to whose image it was made, and understand and love him. To put it in a word, let it worship the uncreated God, * by whom it was created with a capacity for him and able to share in him. In this way it will be wise not with its own light but by sharing in that supreme light, and it will reign in happiness where it reigns eternal. For this is called man's wisdom in such a way that it is also God's. Only then is it true wisdom; if it is merely human it is hollow. I do not mean it is God's wisdom in the sense of the wisdom by which he is wise; he is not wise by sharing in himself, as the mind is by sharing in God. But I mean it in the same sense as we call God's justice not only that by which he is himself just but also that which he gives to man when he *justifies the godless* (Rom 4:5). This is the justice the apostle sets before us when he says of some people, *Not knowing the justice of God and wishing to establish their own, they did not submit to the justice of God* (Rom 10:3). In the same way it could be said of some people, "Not knowing the wisdom of God and wishing to establish their own, they did not submit to the wisdom of God."

16. So there is an uncreated nature which created all natures great and small, and is without any doubt more excellent than these natures it has created, more excellent therefore than this rational and intellectual nature we are talking about, which is the mind of man made to the image of him who made it. This nature more excellent than others is God, and indeed *He is not set far away from us*, as the apostle says, adding *for in him we live and move and are* (Acts 17:27). If he had meant this in terms of our bodies, it could have been understood of the bodily world also; in it too we live and move and are, as far as our bodies are concerned. So we really ought to take his words in terms of the mind which was made to God's image; this is a more excellent way, being intelligible instead of merely visible. What, after all, is not in God, of whom it is divinely written, *for from him and through him and in him are all things* (Rom 11:36)? So of course if all things are in him, what can things that live live in and things that move move in but in him in whom they are? And yet not all men are with him in the way meant when the psalmist says to him, *I am always with you* (Ps 73:23), nor

---

* It is after all written, *Behold the worship of God is wisdom* (Jb 28:28).

is he with all men in the way meant when we say "The Lord be with you." It is man's great misfortune not to be with him without whom he cannot be. Obviously he is not without him in whom he is; and yet if he fails to remember and understand and love him, he is not with him. But of course if someone has totally forgotten anything, he cannot even be reminded of it.[28]

17. Let us take an example of this from visible things. Somebody you do not recognize says to you "You know me," and to remind you of the fact he tells you where, when, and how you got to know him. If you still do not recognize him when he has produced all the possible pointers that could stir your memory, it means you have forgotten him so completely that all that awareness has been totally rubbed out of your consciousness, and nothing remains but for you to believe him when he tells you that you once knew him; or not even this if the man who is speaking to you does not seem trustworthy. But if you remember, then of course you go back to your own memory and find there what had not been totally erased by forgetfulness. Now let us return to the point we are illustrating by bringing up this example from human intercourse. Among other texts there is Psalm 9: *Let sinners turn back to hell, all the nations that forget God* (Ps 9:17). Then Psalm 21: *All the ends of the earth will be reminded and turn back to the Lord* (Ps 22:27).[29] So these nations had not so forgotten God that they could not even remember when reminded of him. By forgetting God it was as if they had forgotten their own life, and so they turned back to death, that is to hell. Then they are reminded of him and turn back to the Lord, which is like their coming to life again by remembering the life they had forgotten. Likewise we read in Psalm 93: *Understand now, you who are unwise among the people, and learn wisdom for once, you fools. He who planted the ear, will he not hear*, etc. (Ps 94:8)? The psalmist was speaking to people who did not understand God, and so spoke nonsense about him.[30]

18. As for the love of God, many more things are to be found said about this in the divine utterances. The other two can be taken as following on this, because no one loves anything he does not remember and is totally ignorant of. The most important and well known of these texts is the commandment, *You shall love the Lord your God* (Mt 22:37; Dt 6:5). The human mind, then, is so constructed that it never does not remember itself, never does not understand itself, never does not love itself. But if you hate someone you are dead set on doing him harm, and so it is not unreasonable to talk about the mind of man hating itself when it does itself harm. It does not know it is wishing itself ill while it imagines that what it wants is not to its disadvantage, but in fact it is wishing itself ill when it wants something that is to its disadvantage, and that is why it is written, *Whoever loves iniquity hates his own soul* (Ps 11:5). So the man who knows how to love himself loves God; and the man who does not love God, even though he loves himself, which is innate in him by nature, can still be said quite reasonably to hate himself when he does what is against his own interest, and stalks himself as if he were his own enemy. It is indeed a dreadful derangement that while everyone wants to do himself good, many people do nothing but what is absolutely destructive of themselves. The poet describes a disease of this sort that afflicts dumb animals:

Ye gods, for pious men a better lot,
this wild derangement for your foes preserve!
Their own limbs with unsheathed teeth they tore.[31]

Now he was describing a physical disease, so why should he call it a derangement if not because nature prompts every animal to preserve itself as far as it can, and this disease was such that they were tearing to pieces the very limbs of their bodies whose well-being they naturally desired?

But when the mind loves God, and consequently as has been said remembers and understands him, it can rightly be commanded to love its neighbor as itself. For now it loves itself with a straight, not a twisted love, now that it loves God; for sharing in him results not merely in its being that image, but in its being made new and fresh and happy after being old and worn and miserable. It might indeed have loved itself in such a way that if faced with the choice it would have preferred to lose everything beneath itself that it loved rather than be lost itself; and yet by forsaking the one above itself with regard to whom alone it could keep its strength and enjoy him as its light, * it became weak and dark, with the result that it was miserably dragged down from itself to things that are not what it is and are lower than itself by loves that it cannot master and confusions it can see no way out of.[32] From these depths it now cries in repentance in the psalms as God takes pity on it, *My strength has forsaken me and the light of my eyes is no longer with me* (Ps 38:10).

19. And yet in this evil state of weakness and confusion it could not lose its natural memory, understanding, and love of itself. That is why, as I mentioned above,[33] it could properly be said, *Although man walks in the image, yet he is troubled in vain; he treasures up and does not know for whom he gathers them* (Ps 39:8). Why does he treasure up, if not because his strength has forsaken him, by which he would have had God and been in need of nothing else? And why does he not know for whom he gathers them, if not because the light of his eyes is no longer with him? That is why he does not see the truth of what Truth says: *Fool, this night they are claiming your soul back from you. Whose will these things be that you have prepared* (Lk 12:20)? And yet even a man like this still walks in the image, and the mind of the man has memory and understanding and love of self; and so if he were shown that he could not have both, and were allowed to choose one of the two with the loss of the other, either the treasures he has gathered or his mind, is there anyone so mindless that he would rather have the treasures than the mind? Treasures can frequently turn the mind upside down, and the mind that is not turned upside down by treasures can live much more easily and lightly without any treasures at all. But in any case, who can possess any treasures except with the mind? An infant boy may have been born into enormous wealth, and be the master of everything that is his in law, and yet with his mind unawakened he possesses nothing. So I ask you, how on earth

---

* This is of course God, to whom the psalmist sings, *Looking to you I will keep my strength* (Ps 59:9), and in another psalm, *Approach him and be enlightened* (Ps 34:5).

will anyone possess anything if he loses his mind? But why should I speak about treasures and argue that any man if faced with the option would rather lose his treasures than his mind, seeing that nobody would prefer them, nobody would even compare them to the eyes of the body, with which it is not the occasional man that possesses gold but every man that possesses the heavens? Through the eyes in his head everyone possesses whatever he likes to look at. Supposing therefore that a man could not keep both and were obliged to lose one or the other, who would not rather lose his treasures than his eyes? And yet if on similar conditions he were asked whether he would rather lose his eyes or his mind, who can fail to see with his mind that he would rather lose his eyes than his mind? A mind without physical eyes is still human; physical eyes without mind are merely brutish. Who would not rather be a man, even physically blind, than a brute and able to see?

20. I have said all this just very briefly to remind my slower readers into whose hands this work might fall how much the mind loves itself, even when it is weak and confused because it is wrongly loving and pursuing things that are beneath it. And it could not love itself if it did not know itself at all, that is if it did not remember and understand itself. There is such potency in this image of God in it that it is capable of cleaving to him whose image it is. It is so arranged in the order of natures—not an order of place—that there is nothing above it except him. And then when it totally cleaves to him it will be one spirit, as the apostle testifies when he says, *Whoever cleaves to the Lord is one spirit* (1 Cor 6:17). This will come about with the mind attaining to a share of his nature, truth, and happiness, not with him growing in his own nature, truth, and happiness. So when it blissfully cleaves to that nature,[34] it will see as unchangeable in it everything that it sees. Then as divine scripture promises, its desire will be filled with good things,[35] with unchangeable good things, with the trinity its God whose image it is, and to save it from ever again being violated anywhere it will be in the hidden place of his countenance,[36] so filled with his plenty[37] that sinning can never delight it again.

21. For the time being, however, when it sees itself it does not see anything unchangeable. Of this it can have no doubt, since it is unhappy and longs to be happy, and its only hope that this will be possible lies in its being changeable. If it were not changeable it could no more switch from unhappy to happy than from happy to unhappy. And what could have made it unhappy under its omnipotent and good Lord, but its own sin and its Lord's justice? And what will make it happy but its own merit and its Lord's reward? But even its merit is the grace of him whose reward will be its happiness. It cannot give itself the justice which it lost and no longer has. It received it when man was created and it lost it of course by sinning. So it also receives the justice by which it can merit happiness. So the apostle very truly admonishes it, as though it were beginning to get proud of its own goodness, *What have you got that you did not receive? If you received it, why boast about it as though you did not receive it* (1 Cor 4:7)?

But when the mind truly recalls its Lord after receiving his Spirit, it perceives quite simply—for it learns this by a wholly intimate instruction from within—that it cannot rise except by his gracious doing,[38] and that it could not have fallen except by its own willful undoing. Certainly it does not remember its happiness. That was once, and is no more, and the mind has totally forgotten it and therefore cannot even be reminded of it. But it believes the trustworthy documents of its God about it, written by his prophets,[39] when they tell about the bliss of paradise and make known through a historical tradition man's first good and first evil. The mind does however remember its God. He always is; it is not the case that he was and is not, or is and was not, but just as he never will not be, so he never was not. And he is all of him everywhere, and therefore the mind lives and moves and is in him,[40] and for this reason is able to remember him.

Not that it remembers him because it knew him in Adam, or anywhere else before the life of this body, or when it was first made in order to be inserted into this body. It does not remember any of these things at all; whichever of these may be the case, it has been erased by oblivion. Yet it is reminded to turn to the Lord,[41] as though to the light by which it went on being touched in some fashion even when it turned away from him. It is in virtue of this light that even the godless can think about eternity, and rightly praise and blame many elements in the behavior of men. And by what standards, I ask you, do they judge, if not by ones in which they see how a man ought to live, even though they do not live like that themselves? Where do they see these standards? Not in their own nature, since there is no doubt they see them with the mind, and we all agree that their minds are changeable, while anyone who can see this sort of thing can see that these standards are unchangeable. Nor do they see them in the attitude[42] of their own minds, since these are standards of justice, while it is agreed that their minds are unjust. Then where are these standards written down, where can even the unjust man recognize what being just is, where can he see that he ought to have what he does not have himself? Where indeed are they written but in the book of that light which is called truth, from which every just law is copied, and transferred into the heart of the man who does justice, not by locomotion but by a kind of impression, rather like the seal which both passes into the wax and does not leave the signet ring? As for the man who does not do justice and yet sees what should be done, he is the one who turns away from that light, and yet is still touched by it. But the man who does not even see how one ought to live has more excuse for his sin, because not knowing the law he is not a transgressor;[43] yet from time to time even he is touched by the brilliance of truth everywhere present, when he receives a warning reminder and confesses.[44]

Chapter 5

The analysis of the image of God in the mind is concluded with some reflections on the refashioning or refurbishing of the image in a man, which is presented as a lifelong process that will in fact only be completed when God is seen at last face to face.

22. Those who do, on being reminded, turn to the Lord[45] from the deformity which had conformed them by worldly lusts to this world are reformed by him; they listen to the apostle saying, *Do not conform to this world, but be reformed in the newness of your minds* (Rom 12:2). And thus the image begins to be reformed by him who formed it in the first place. It cannot reform itself in the way it was able to deform itself. As he says elsewhere, *Be renewed in the spirit of your minds, and put on the new man who was created according to God in justice and the holiness of truth* (Eph 4:23). "Created according to God" means the same as "to the image of God" in another text. But by sinning man lost justice and the holiness of truth, and thus the image became deformed and discolored; he gets those qualities back again when he is reformed and renovated.

As for his words "in the spirit of your minds,"[46] he does not here mean two things, as though mind were one and the spirit of the mind another. He means that every mind is spirit, though not every spirit is mind. God too is spirit, but he cannot be renewed because he cannot grow old. We also talk about a spirit in man which is not mind, which is the field of our body—like imaginations; he refers to it when he says to the Corinthians, *If I pray in a tongue, my spirit prays but my mind remains without fruit* (1 Cor 14:14). What he means is that what is said is not understood, but it could not even be said unless the images of the physical sounds had preceded the utterances of the mouth in the thought of the spirit. Man's soul is also called spirit, which is the sense of the gospel statement, *Bowing his head he gave up the spirit* (Jn 19:30), which signifies the death of the body on the departure of the soul. One can talk even about an animal's spirit, a usage very clearly employed in Solomon's book Ecclesiastes, where he says, *Who knows if the spirit of the sons of man ascends upward, and if the spirit of an animal descends downward into the earth* (Eccl 3:21)? This meaning also occurs in Genesis where it says that all flesh *that had in it the spirit of life* (Gn 7:22) died in the flood. Wind too is called spirit, a thing that is quite plainly corporeal, and in this sense we have the words of the psalm, *Fire, hail, snow, ice, the spirit of the storm* (Ps 148:8). So because spirit can be used in so many ways, by "the spirit of the mind" he wished to indicate spirit in the sense that mind is called spirit. The same apostle also talks about the stripping off of the body of flesh (Col 2:11). He does not of course mean two things, as though flesh were one and the body of flesh another; but as body is the name of many things, none of which is flesh—apart from flesh there are many heavenly bodies and earthly bodies—he said body of flesh meaning the body which is flesh. In the same way he says spirit of mind, meaning the spirit which is mind.

In another place he mentioned the image more openly, where he gives the same direction in other words: *Stripping yourselves*, he says, *of the old man with his actions, put on the new man who is being renewed in the recognition of God according to the image of him who created him* (Col 3:9). In the other place we read *Put on the new man who was created according to God* (Eph 4:24), and it is the same as what we have here, *Put on the new man who is being renewed according to the image of him who created him.* There he says, "according to God"; here "according to the image of him who created him." For the phrase there "in justice and holiness of truth" he put here "in the recognition of God." So this renewal and reforming of the mind takes place according to God or according to the image of God. It says "according to God" in case we should suppose that it takes place according to some other creature; and "according to the image of God" to help us understand that this renewal takes place in the thing in which the image of God is to be found, that is in the mind; rather as we say that a good man and believer who has departed from the body is dead according to the body, not according to the spirit. Why do we say "dead according to the body" if not to indicate that he is dead in body and not in soul? Or if we say "He is handsome according to the body," or "He is strong according to the body, not according to the character," we mean the same as "He is handsome or strong in body, not in character." We speak like this time without number. So we should not understand "according to the image of him who created him" as though the image according to which it is renewed were something else, and not the very thing that is being renewed.

23. To be sure, this renewal does not happen in one moment of conversion, as the baptismal renewal by the forgiveness of all sins happens in a moment, so that not even one tiny sin remains unforgiven. But it is one thing to throw off a fever, another to recover from the weakness which the fever leaves behind it; it is one thing to remove from the body a missile stuck in it, another to heal the wound it made with a complete cure. The first stage of the cure is to remove the cause of the debility, and this is done by pardoning all sins; the second stage is curing the debility itself, and this is done gradually by making steady progress in the renewal of this image. These two stages are pointed out in the psalm where we read, *He is gracious to all your iniquities*, which happens in baptism, *and heals all your infirmities* (Ps 103:3), which happens by daily advances while the image is being renewed. About this the apostle speaks quite explicitly when he says, *Even if our outer man is decaying, yet our inner man is being renewed day by day* (2 Cor 4:16). It is being renewed, however, *in the recognition of God* (Col 3:10), that is *in justice and holiness of truth* (Eph 4:24), as the apostle puts it in the passages which I have just been quoting.

So then the man who is being renewed in the recognition of God and in justice and holiness of truth by making progress day by day, is transferring his love from temporal things to eternal, from visible to intelligible, from carnal to spiritual things; he is industriously applying himself to checking and lessening his greed for the one sort and binding himself with charity to the other. But his success in this depends on divine assistance; it is after all God who declares, *Without me you can do nothing* (Jn 15:5). When the last day of his life overtakes someone who has kept faith in the mediator, making steady progress of this sort, he will be received by the holy angels to be led into the presence of the God he has worshiped and to be perfected by him and so to get his body back again at the end of the world, not for punishment but for glory. For only when it comes to the perfect vision of God will this image bear God's perfect likeness. Of this the apostle Paul says, *We see now through a puzzling reflection in a mirror, but then it will be face to face* (1 Cor 13:12). Elsewhere he says, *But we with face unveiled looking at the glory of the Lord in a mirror*[47] *are being transformed into the same image from glory to glory as by the Spirit of the Lord* (2 Cor 3:18); this is what is happening from day to day to those who are making good progress. And the apostle John says, *Beloved, we are now sons of God, but that which*[48] *we shall be has not yet appeared. We know*[49] *that when he appears we shall be like him, because we shall see him as he is* (1 Jn 3:2).

24. From this it is clear that the image of God will achieve its full likeness of him when it attains to the full vision of him—though this text from the apostle John might also appear to be referring to the immortality of the body. In this respect too we will be like God, but only like the Son, who alone in the triad took a body in which he died and rose again, carrying it up to the heavenly regions. This too can be called the image of the Son of God in which like him we shall have an immortal body, conformed in this respect not to the image of the Father or the Holy Spirit but only of the Son, because of him alone do we read and receive on wholesome faith that *the Word became flesh* (Jn 1:14). That is why the apostle says, *Those he foreknew beforehand he also predestined to be conformed to the image of his Son, that he might be the firstborn among many brothers* (Rom 8:29). *Firstborn*, of course, *from the dead* (Col 1:18), according to the same apostle; the death by which his flesh was sown in disgrace and rose again in glory (1 Cor 15:48). In terms of this image of the Son to which we are conformed in the body by immortality we also do what the apostle likewise says: *As we have borne the image of the earthen man, we shall also bear the image of the one who is from heaven* (1 Cor 15:49); which means that as we have been mortal after the manner of Adam, so we truly believe and surely and firmly hope that we are going to be immortal after the manner of Christ. For at the moment we can bear the same image, not yet in vision but in faith, not yet in fact but in hope. The apostle was of course speaking about the resurrection of the body when he said this.

25. As for the image, though, of which it was said *Let us make man to our image and likeness* (Gn 1:26), since it does not say "to my" or "to your" image, we believe that man was made to the image of the triad, and as far as we have been able to go with our investigation we have understood what this means. And it is in terms of this image rather that we should also understand what the apostle John says, *We shall be like him because we shall see him as he is* (1 Jn 3:2), for the good reason that he was referring to the one of whom he had just said, *We are sons of God* (1 Jn 3:2). And the immortality of the flesh will be perfected in that moment of which the apostle Paul says, *In the twinkling of an eye, at the last trumpet blast the dead will rise incorruptible and we shall be changed* (1

Cor 15:52). In that twinkling of an eye before the judgment what is now being sown as an animal body in weakness, corruption, disgrace, will rise as a spiritual body in power, in incorruptibility, in glory.[50] But the image which is being renewed in the spirit of the mind in the recognition of God, not outwardly but inwardly from day to day,[51] this image will be perfected in the vision that will then be face to face after the judgment, while now it makes progress through a puzzling reflection in a mirror.[52] It is with reference to this perfection that we should understand the words, *We shall be like him because we shall see him as he is* (1 Jn 3:2). For this gift will be given to us when we are told, *Come, you blessed of my Father, possess the kingdom prepared for you* (Mt 25:34). It is then that the godless man will be taken away so that he shall not see the glory of the Lord,[53] when those on the left hand go to eternal punishment, while those on the right go into eternal life. *But this is eternal life*, as Truth says, *that they may know you*, he says, *the one true God and Jesus Christ whom you have sent* (Jn 17:3).

26. This is the contemplative wisdom which in my view is specifically distinguished in the sacred writings from knowledge and is called precisely man's wisdom, though indeed it only comes to him from the one whom the rational and intellectual mind must share in to become truly wise. Cicero commends it at the end of his dialogue *Hortensius*. He says:

> This is our great hope as we ponder night and day, and sharpen the understanding which is the fine point[54] of the mind and take care it does not get blunt, that is to say as we live in philosophy; either that we will have a cheerful sunset to our days when we have completed our tasks, and an untroublesome and quiet quenching of life, if this capacity of ours to perceive and to be wise is perishable and fleeting; or else, if we have eternal and divine souls,[55] as the ancient philosophers agreed, and they the greatest and far and away the most brilliant, we must suppose that the more these souls keep always to their course, that is to reason and to eager inquiry, and the less they mix themselves up in the tangled vices and errors of men, the easier will be their ascent and return to heaven.

Then he adds this phrase, and ends his discourse by a brief summary:

> Therefore to bring my speech to an end, if we wish either to fade out peacefully when we have finished our lives in these bodies, or to move on from this house to another and infinitely better one without delay, we must devote all our care and energy to these studies.

What astonishes me about a man of such genius is that he should promise men living in philosophy, which makes them happy by contemplation of the truth, a cheerful sunset to their days when they have completed their human tasks, "if this capacity of ours to perceive and to be wise is perishable and fleeting"; as though something here were dying and falling to pieces that we did not love but rather hated savagely, seeing that its sunset makes us cheerful. He certainly did not learn this from the philosophers whose praises he sings so enthusiastically; this opinion smacks of that new Academy in which he was persuaded to doubt even the most evident things.[56] But from the philosophers, as he himself admits, *and they the greatest and far and away the most brilliant,* he had learnt that souls are eternal. It is quite reasonable that eternal minds should be stirred by his exhortation to be found in their course when they come to the end of this life, *that is in reason and in eager inquiry,* and should *mix themselves up less in the tangled vices and errors of men,* to make their return to God all the easier. But this course, which is set in the love of and inquiry into truth, is not enough for unhappy men, that is for all mortals who have this reason alone without any faith in the mediator. This point I have tried to demonstrate as best I could in the previous books, especially in the fourth and thirteenth.

NOTES

1. Book XII, 22.

2. It is interesting he should ascribe these words to divine Wisdom; in the text God is the speaker, but the words are the conclusion of an anomalous poem in the book which is in praise of Wisdom.

3. The same problem arose with "justice" in Book VIII, 9.

4 A commonplace Stoic definition, quoted frequently by Cicero, for example in *De Officiis* 2, 12, 5.

5. Book XIII, 24.

6. That hoary old theological character, the unlettered charwoman of deep and simple faith, who is too often introduced as an excuse for avoiding, or even inhibiting theological thought, was embodied for Augustine in his mother, Monica. But it never occurred to him that his veneration for her should limit the range of his intellectual appetite, and she herself would have been horrified if it had.

7. See Hb 2:4; Rom 1:17; Gal 3:11; Heb 10:38.

8. *Per . . . fidem ad veritatem nitatur et tendat aeternam*; M reads . . . *nitatur et tendat ad eaterna*; strive by this . . . faith to the truth and struggle on to things eternal.

9. See 1 Cor 13:12.

10. *Vere*; M reads *vera*, which ought to be regarded as the soul's true life.

11. For Augustine's infant and child psychology, and his views on rearing children, see *Confessions* I, 6-20. It would be quite unfair to him to conclude that he hated babies and children; he just felt immensely sorry for them in a totally unsentimental way, and regarded childhood as a miserable stage of life to be got through as soon as possible.

12. Book IX, 3.

13. *In arcana quadam notitia.*

14. *In ipsa mentis duce veritate*; M reads . . . *luce veritate*, in truth itself enlightening the mind; this is supported by six manuscripts, and is perhaps the better reading.

15. I do not think that Augustine is really as condescending as he sounds by these occasional reference to the slowness of his readers; after all, a sizeable section of his work, vital to its structure, depends on them! In a sense he sees himself as one of them; it is a slowness of mind common to all fallen humanity, a sluggishness of the intellect consequent on sin.

16. He is probably referring to his discussion of the subject of happiness and man's universal desire for it, a common theme of moralists Christian and pagan, rather than to his survey of faith, to which that discussion was really no more than a preliminary.

17. *Opibus*; M reads *operibus*, activities.

18. This includes what we call natural history.

19. The point of the distinction he is making between faith and the things believed by faith is that awareness of faith is a reflexive awareness, like that of any other psychological event, for example, of knowledge, joy, sorrow, etc.; but yet it is not totally reflexive like the mind's self-awareness.

20. Section 5.

21. Lucan, *Pharsalia* 7.

22. He means wisdom, "the knowledge of things human and divine."

23. Augustine knew Cicero too well to call him a philosopher; he knows—and values—him as recorder of other men's philosophies, and an eclectic whose own dialectical powers are not particularly striking.

24. That is, the *activities* of the virtues, not the virtues themselves.

25. I feel there is a certain uncertainty or haziness about Augustine's thought here. On the one hand he has been arguing that the mind's memory, understanding, and love of itself is the image of God because it is all absolutely contemporaneous with the mind itself, since as he has just said the mind has never stopped remembering, understanding, and loving itself. On the other hand in the last three sentences he makes the very important point that a trinity (and therefore an image) only emerges when the mind actually thinks about itself—which it has often stopped doing—and so a word is begotten and joined by love to the memory it is begotten of.

However, the haziness is, I suggest, more a matter of vocabulary than substance. Augustine seems to lack that very convenient sliding-scale terminology of potency and act which Aristotle bequeathed to the scholastics. But what in fact he is saying is that the mind is always the triune image of God potentially, but that this image is only activated by an act of thought. This is one respect, of course, in which the image falls infinitely short of its examplar, where in Aquinas' language there is no potentiality but pure act, and where therefore in this case the Word is eternally being begotten by an eternal divine act of thought or generation.

It should just be noted, in conclusion, that he is speaking rather loosely in the last sentence but one of this paragraph; the two which the will joins together are not the word and the act of thought, as the sentence might lead one to suppose, but the word generated in the act of thought and the self-memory by which in that act it is begotten.

26. Cicero, *De Inventione*, 2, 53. Augustine summarizes Cicero's division of the virtues in his *Miscellany of Eighty-three Questions*.

27. Virgil, *Aeneid* 3, 628/9.

28. He is a jump ahead of his own thought processes here. He is going on to explain how we can remember (and understand and love) God. And he is going to say that even if we forget him we can be reminded of him, because we are ontologically present—unlike the case here mentioned.

29. Augustine numbers the psalms in the style of the Septuagint.

30. In these last two sentences he has moved from the subject of remembering God to understanding him.

31. Virgil, *Georgics* 3, 513.

32. See Book X, 7; XII, 14.

33. Section 6.

34. M inserts *immutabiliter vivet et*, it will live unchangeably and will see . . . .

35. See Ps 103:5.

36. See Ps 31:20.

37. See Ps 36:8.

38. *Effectu*; M reads *affectu*, affection.

39. M reads *prophetam*, prophet, that is, Moses.

40. See Acts 17:28.

41. See Ps 22:27.

42. *Habitu*; the virtues and vices are called *habitus*; the English "habit" has acquired a rather different connotation.

43. *Non est transgressor legis incognitae*; M rather unimaginatively emends to . . . *cognitae legis*, is not a transgressor of a law he knows.

44. For this concluding paragraph, and its way of proving that, and stating how, the mind can remember God, see Book VIII, 9.

45. See Ps 22:27.

46. This whole paragraph is a long digression on the meaning of "spirit."

47. *Gloriam Domini speculantes*; *speculor* properly means looking from a *specula*, look-out; but here, as he will point out in Book XV, 14, it means looking in a *speculum*, a mirror.

48. *Quod erimus*; M reads *quid*, with Vulgate making it an indirect question.

49. M adds *autem*, But we know . . . .

50. See 1 Cor 15:42.

51. See Eph 4:23; Col 3:10; 2 Cor 4:16.

52. See 1 Cor 13:12.

53. See Is 26:10.

54. *Acies mentis*; when Augustine in Book XI and later used the phrase *acies animi* I regularly translated it "the conscious attention"; but that will scarcely do here.

55. *Animi*.

56. Augustine himself joined the Academics after ceasing to adhere to the Manichees, and before discovering platonism through the *Enneads* of Plotinus, which was the last pre-Christian stage of his intellectual odyssey. See *Confessions* V, 10. The very first work he composed after his conversion, and before he was even baptized, was the *Answer to the Skeptics* (*Contra Academicos*).

Book XV

THE ABSOLUTE INADEQUACY OF THE PERFECTED IMAGE

Prologue

---

1. In pursuance of our plan to train the reader, *in the things that have been made* (Rom 1:20), for getting to know him by whom they were made, we came eventually to his image. This is man insofar as he excels other animals, that is in his reason or understanding and in whatever else can be said about the rational or intellectual soul that may belong to what is called mind or consciousness. Several Latin authors have used this latter word, *animus,* to distinguish what is pre-eminent in man and not found in beasts by a proper name of its own from the soul, *anima,* which is in man and beasts alike. If we then go on to look for something above this nature, and look for something true, there is God, a nature namely that is not created but creator. Whether this nature is a triad we ought to demonstrate, not merely to faith on the authority of divine scripture, but also to understanding, if we can, by some evidence of reason. Why I say "if we can" will appear well enough as our investigation of the subject proceeds.

2. The God himself we are looking for will help us, I confidently hope, to get some fruit from our labors and to understand the meaning of the text in the holy psalm, *Let the heart of those who seek the Lord rejoice; seek the Lord and be strengthened; seek his face always* (Ps 105:3). Now it would seem that what is always being sought is never being found, and in that case how is the heart of the seekers to rejoice and not rather grow sad, if they cannot find what they are looking for? He does not, you see, say "Let the heart of those who find," but "of those who seek the Lord rejoice." And yet the prophet Isaiah testifies that the Lord God can be found provided he is sought, when he says, *Seek the Lord and as soon as you find him call upon him, and when he draws near to you let the godless man forsake his ways and the wicked man his thoughts* (Is 55:6). So if he can be found when he is sought, why does it say *Seek his face always?* Does he perhaps have to be sought even when he has been found? That is indeed how

incomprehensible things have to be searched for, in case the man who has been able to find out how incomprehensible what he is looking for is should reckon that he has found nothing. Why then look for something when you have comprehended the incomprehensibility of what you are looking for, if not because you should not give up the search as long as you are making progress in your inquiry into things incomprehensible, and because you become better and better by looking for so great a good which is both sought in order to be found and found in order to be sought? It is sought in order to be found all the more delightfully, and it is found in order to be sought all the more avidly. This is how we might also take the words of Wisdom in the book of Ecclesiasticus: *Those who eat me will be hungry still and those who drink me will be thirsty still* (Sir 24:29). They eat and drink because they find, and because they are hungry and thirsty they still go on seeking. Faith seeks, understanding finds; which is why the prophet says, *Unless you believe you shall not understand* (Is 7:9, Septuagint). And again, understanding still goes on seeking the one it has found; for, *God gazed down upon the sons of men*, as we chant in the sacred psalm, *to see if there is any who is understanding or looking for God* (Ps 14:2).

3. So then we have spent quite enough time over the things that God has made in order through them to get to know him who made them; *For his invisible things are descried by being understood through the things that have been made from the creation of the world* (Rom 1:20). This is why the book of Wisdom rebukes those who *from the good things that are seen were unable to know him who is, and did not recognize the craftsman by looking at his works, but thought that either fire or wind or whirling air or the circuit of the stars or the violence of the waters or the luminaries of heaven are the gods that rule the world. If they thought them gods because they were ravished by their beauty, let them know how much better is their Lord; it was the begetter of beauty who created them. Or if they were amazed at their might and their activity, they should understand from these how much stronger is he who established them. For from the greatness of the beauty and of the creature the creator of these things can*[1] *knowably be seen* (Wis 13:1-5). I quote this passage form the book of Wisdom in case any of the faithful should reckon I have been wasting time for nothing in first searching creation for signs of that supreme trinity we are looking for when we are looking for God, going step by step through various trinities of different sorts until we eventually arrive at the mind of man.

Chapter 1

The author recapitulates the conclusions he has so far reached, in a brief summary of the previous fourteen books.

---

4. But the requirements of discussion and argument through the course of fourteen books have obliged us to say many things which we are unable to look

at all at once, and so refer them at a glance to the thing we are eager to apprehend. With the Lord's help therefore, I will try as best I can to summarize briefly without argument the points of knowledge which I established by long argument in each book. I will not set before the mind an account of how each proof went but a list of the things proved, so that it may take them in at a single glance, and not find the things that come later so far away from the things which went before, that examination of the former makes it forget the latter. Or at least if this does happen, it will be easy to recall what has slipped the mind by reading it again.

5. In the first book the unity and equality of that supreme trinity is demonstrated from the scriptures. The same point is made in the second, third and fourth books, but a thorough treatment of the question of the mission of the Son and the Holy Spirit produced three books, and it was shown that the one who is sent is not less than the sender just because he was sent and the other did the sending, since the trinity which is equal in every respect likewise also works inseparably, being in its nature unchangeable and invisible and everywhere present.[2]

The fifth book is aimed at those who do not see how the Father and the Son can have the same substance, because they think that everything that is said of God is said substance-wise, and therefore, they argue, since begetting and being begotten, or begotten and unbegotten are contraries, they must be contrary substances. Against them it is demonstrated that not everything said about God is said substance-wise, in the way that he is called good and great substance-wise, and anything else which he is called with reference to self; but that some things are also said of him by way of relationship, that is to say not with reference to self but to another which is not self, as he is called Father with reference to the Son, or Lord with reference to the creation that serves him; it is also pointed out that if he is called anything by a relationship—that is with reference to another which is not himself—that arose in time, as for example, *Lord, you have become a refuge for us* (Ps 90:1), nothing happens to him to change him, but he remains absolutely unchangeable in his nature or being.

In the sixth book we provisionally discuss how the apostle could call Christ *the power of God and the wisdom of God* (1 Cor 1:24), while reserving the question for a more thorough reassessment later on. But we ask whether the one of whom Christ is begotten is not himself wisdom but merely the Father of his own wisdom, or whether it is wisdom that begot wisdom. Whichever of these might be the answer, at least the equality of the triad was made clear in this book, and that God is a triad without being triple, or multiplied by three; and that Father and Son together are not as it were double the single value of the Holy Spirit, since not even all three together are something more than one of them alone. We also discussed the proper way of understanding what bishop Hilary said, *Eternity in the Father, form in the image, use in the gift.*[3]

In the seventh book the question which had been held over is resolved, and it is maintained that God who begot the Son is not only Father of his power and wisdom, but is also himself power and wisdom, as the Holy Spirit is too; and yet there are not altogether three powers or three wisdoms but one power and one wisdom, like one God and one being. Then we talked about how we can talk about one being, three persons, or as some of the Greeks put it, one being, three substances; and we ascertained that it arose from the need for some name which one could use to answer the question what they are three of; since we truly confess that there are three, namely Father and Son and Holy Spirit.

Further reasons were given in the eighth book to make it clear to persons of understanding that in the substance of truth not only is the Father not greater than the Son, but also both of them together do not constitute something greater than any one, nor all three together something greater than any of them singly. Then I urged that an effort should be made to understand the nature, not merely incorporeal but also unchangeable which is God, as far as possible through truth which is beheld by the understanding, and through the highest good from which every good derives, and through justice for which a just soul is loved even by a soul that is not yet just; and finally through charity which in the holy scriptures is called God;[4] and here at last our minds began to perceive some kind of trinity or trio, like lover and what is loved and love.

In the ninth book the discussion reaches the image of God which is man as regards his mind, and a certain trinity is discovered in it, that is mind and the knowledge it knows itself with and the love it loves itself and its knowledge with; and these three are shown to be equal to each other and of one being. In the tenth book the same matter is treated more thoroughly and with more precision, and brought to the point of uncovering in the mind a clearer trinity, consisting in memory and understanding and will. But we also came to realize that the mind could never be in such a case that it did not remember or understand or love itself, although it did not always think about itself; and when it did think about itself it did not always distinguish itself in its thought from bodily things. So we deferred discussion of the trinity which this is the image of, in order also to find a trinity in the sight of bodily things, and to give the reader practice in a more discriminating observation of it.

And therefore in the eleventh book we chose the sense of the eyes, in which we could take whatever we might discover as applying to the other four senses even without our saying it; and thus there came to light first of all a trinity of the outer man in things that are observed outwardly, consisting of the body which is seen and the form which is impressed from it on the attention of the observer and the intention of the will which couples the two together. But it was clear that these three are not equal to each other nor of one substance. Next another trinity was discovered in the consciousness itself, brought in so to speak from the things that had been sensed outside; and here it became clear that the same three are of one substance, namely the image of the body which is in the memory, and the form derived from it when the thinking attention turns to it, and the intention of the will joining the two together. However, this trinity too was found to belong to the outer man, because it has been brought in from bodily things which have been sensed outside.

In the twelfth book we decided a distinction should be made between wisdom and knowledge, and a trinity of its own sort should first be looked for in knowledge properly so called, because it is the lower of the two; a trinity which does indeed belong to the inner man now, but cannot yet be called or reckoned the image of God. This is done in the thirteenth book by a presentation of Christian faith. In the fourteenth book we discuss man's true wisdom, wisdom that is, which is bestowed on him by God's gift in an actual sharing in God himself, something which is distinct from knowledge. And the discussion reaches the point of bringing to light a trinity in the image of God which is man in terms of mind; the mind which *is being renewed in the recognition of God according to the image of him who created* (Col 3:10) man to his own image, and which thus achieves wisdom in the contemplation of things eternal.

Chapter 2

On the strength of Romans 1:20, For his invisible things are descried by being understood through the things that have been made, *the author now tests the possibility of directly descrying the divine trinity by inference from our understanding of creation; and he rules the possibility out, because all the divine perfections which we can infer in the creator from reflection on creation are identical with the divine substance—and thus of course substantively with each other—and therefore common to all three persons of the triad.*

6. Now therefore let us look for the trinity which is God in these eternal things, incorporeal and unchangeable, since the happy life which is nothing if not eternal is promised to us in the contemplation of them. It is not, after all, only the authority of the divine books which asserts that God is; the universal nature of things which surrounds us, to which we too belong, proclaims that it has a most excellent founder, who has given us a mind and natural reason by which to see that living beings are to be preferred to non-living, ones endowed with sense to non-sentient ones, intelligent ones to non-intelligent, immortal ones to mortal, powerful to powerless ones, just to unjust, beautiful to ugly, good to bad, things that cannot decay to things that can, changeless to changeable things, invisible to visible, non-bodily to bodily, happy to unhappy. And so, since we rank the creator without a shadow of doubt above created things, we have to admit that he supremely lives, and senses[5] and understands all things, and cannot die, decay or change; and that he is not a body but the most powerful, just and beautiful, the best and happiest spirit of all.

7. But all this that I have said, and anything else that in a similarly human way of speaking may be regarded as suitable to say about God, fits both the whole trinity which the one God is and each of the persons in this trinity. Will anyone dare to say that either the one God, which is what this triad is, or the Father or the Son or the Holy Spirit does not live, or does not sense or understand anything, or that any of those who are asserted to be equal in that nature is mortal or corruptible or changeable or corporeal? Will anyone deny that any of them

there in the divine sphere is most powerful, just and beautiful, superlatively good and happy? If then all these things can be said both about the trinity itself and each person in it, where or how will trinity be disclosed?

Well, first of all let us reduce these many attributes to a manageably small number. Now what is called life in God is his being and his nature. So the life God lives with is what he himself is for himself. And this life is not such as is found in a tree, where there is no understanding, no sensation; nor such as is found in an animal; the life of an animal has fivefold sensation but understanding it has none. But the life which God is senses and understands all things, and senses with mind not with body, because God is spirit.[6] God does not sense through a body like animals which have bodies, for he does not consist of body and soul. And thus this simple nature senses as it understands, understands as it senses, and its sensing and understanding are identical.

Nor does God live in such a way that he may some time stop being or some time started to be; he is immortal. Nor is it idly said of him that he alone has immortality.[7] His immortality is genuinely immortality, as in his nature there is no change. But that is also genuine eternity by which God is unchangeable, without beginning, without end, and consequently incorruptible. Therefore one and the same thing is being said, whether you say God is eternal or immortal or incorruptible or unchangeable; and again whether you say he is living or understanding, which is the same as wise, the same thing is being said. He has not acquired the wisdom he is wise with, but he is himself wisdom. And this life is the same as the might or power, the same as the beauty, by which he is called powerful or beautiful.[8] What after all could be more powerful or beautiful than wisdom, which *reaches mightily from end to end and arranges all things sweetly* (Wis 8:1)? Again, do goodness and justice differ from each other in God's nature as they do in his works, as though there were two different qualities of God, one goodness, the other justice? Of course not. His justice is the same as his goodness and his goodness the same as his happiness. Finally, God is called incorporeal or non-bodily in order that we should believe or understand him to be spirit, not body.[9]

8. Accordingly, if we say, "Eternal, immortal, incorruptible, unchangeable, living, wise, powerful, beautiful, just, good, happy, spirit," it is only the last of all these that seems to signify substance, while the rest signify qualities of this substance; and yet this is not so in that inexpressible and wholly simple nature. Whatever appears to be predicated of it qualitatively is to be understood as signifying substance or being. It is unthinkable that God should be called spirit by way of substance and good by way of quality; he is called both by way of substance. It is the same with all the other names I mentioned, which we have spoken about at length in the previous books.[10] From the first four names, then, which have just been listed and arranged, that is eternal, immortal, incorruptible, unchangeable, let us choose one, seeing that these four as I have just been arguing signify one thing; otherwise our attention will be over-extended. Let us choose the one mentioned first, that is "eternal." Let us do the same for the second four, which are living, wise, powerful, beautiful. And since some kind

of life is found even in animals in which wisdom is not found; and the next two, wisdom and power, are compared with each other in man in such a way that holy scripture said, *Better a wise man than a strong one* (Wis 6:1, Vulgate); and finally even bodies are commonly called beautiful; let the one of these four which we choose be "wise," even though in God these four are not to be regarded as unequal[11]—they are four names but one thing. As for the third and last group of four, although in God being just is the same as being good, the same as being happy, and being spirit is the same as being just and good and happy, still among men it is possible to be spirit and not happy; it is also possible to be just and good and not yet happy, whereas a man who is happy is automatically just and good and a spirit.[12] So let us choose the one that even among men cannot be found without the other three, that is "happy."

9. So when we say "Eternal, wise, happy," does it mean that these three are the triad which God is called? We reduce those twelve names to this small number of three, but perhaps in the same way we can reduce these three to just one of them. For if wisdom and power or life and wisdom can be one and the same thing in God's nature, why could not eternity and wisdom, or happiness and wisdom, be one and the same thing in God's nature? It made no difference whether we said those twelve names or these three when we reduced the large number to the small one; so it makes no difference either, whether we say these three or that single one of them to which we have shown that the other two can likewise be reduced.

What manner of argument is left then, indeed what force or power of intellect, what liveliness of reason, what needle-sharp thought can show how this one thing "wisdom," not to mention the others which God is called, is also a trinity? God does not get wisdom from someone as we get it from him, but he is his own wisdom; his wisdom is not one thing and his being another, seeing that for him to be is the same as to be wise. In the holy scriptures Christ is indeed called the power of God and the wisdom of God,[13] but we discussed how this was to be understood in the seventh book, in case it should seem to imply that the Son makes the Father wise; and we came to the conclusion that the Son is wisdom from wisdom just as he is light from light, God from God. And we could not conclude anything else about the Holy Spirit, but that he too is wisdom, and together they are all one wisdom, as they are one God, one being. So how then are we going to understand this wisdom, which God is, to be a triad? I did not say "How are we going to believe?" Among the believers this should be no problem. But if there is some way in which we can see intellectually what we believe, what might this way be?

10. If we try to recall where it was in these books that a trinity first began to appear to our understanding, it will occur to us that it was in the eighth book. There we attempted as best we could to raise the attention of the mind by our discussion to understand that supremely eminent and unchangeable nature which our mind is not. We observed it as both not being far away from us and yet being above us, not spacially but in its august and marvelous eminence, and in such a way that it also seemed to be with or in us by the presence of its light.

However, no trinity was yet apparent to us in this, because we could not hold the gaze of our mind fixed on looking for one in that dazzling brilliance; all we were able to perceive was that there is no mass there in which we would have to believe that the size of two or three is something more than that of one. But when we came to charity, which is called God in holy scripture,[14] the glimmerings of a trinity began to appear, namely lover and what is loved and love. However, that inexpressible light beat back our gaze, and somehow convinced us that the weakness of our mind could not yet be attuned to it. So to relax our concentration we turned ourselves back in reflection, between the beginning and the completion of our search, to what could be called the more familiar consideration of our own mind insofar as man has been made to the image of God.[15] And from then on we lingered over the creature which we ourselves are from the ninth to the fourteenth book in order to descry if we could the invisible things of God by understanding them through those that have been made.[16]

So here we are, after exercising our understanding as much as was necessary, and perhaps more than was necessary in these lower things, wishing and not being able to raise ourselves to a sight of that supreme trinity which is God. To be sure, we plainly see some evident trinities, either ones produced outside from bodily things, or ones we see when things that have been sensed outside are thought about; or when things that spring up in the consciousness like faith, like the virtues which are arts of living, are perceived directly by reason and grasped by knowledge; or when the mind itself, by which we know whatever we can say we truly know, is known to itself or thinks about itself; or when it observes something eternal and unchangeable which it itself is not. But just because we see these evident trinities, since they happen in us or are in us when we remember and behold and will these things, does it mean that we also see God as trinity in the same way, since there too we intellectually observe one as uttering, and his Word (that is the Father and the Son) and the charity common to them both proceeding thence, namely the Holy Spirit? Or is it that we see rather than believe these trinities which belong to our senses or our consciousness, while we believe rather than see that God is a trinity? If this is so, it either means that we descry none of his invisible things by understanding them through those that were made,[17] or that if we descry some of them we do not descry trinity among them, and so there is something there which we can descry, and something also which being undescried we must just believe. But the eighth book showed that we do descry the unchanging good which we are not, and so did the fourteenth persuade us of this when we were talking about the wisdom which man has from God.[18] Why then should we not recognize a trinity there? Could it be that this other wisdom which is called God does not understand itself, does not love itself? Who would ever say such a thing? Or does anybody fail to see that where there is no knowledge there cannot possibly be any wisdom? Or is it to be supposed that the wisdom which God is knows other things and does not know itself, or loves other things and does not love itself? It would be folly and impiety to say or believe such a thing. So there we have a trinity, namely wisdom and its knowledge of itself and its love of itself. We found a similar trinity in man, namely the mind, and the knowledge it knows itself with, and the love it loves itself with.

11. However, these three are in man without themselves being man. For man, as the ancients defined him, is a rational, mortal animal.[19] So these three are what is most eminent in man, but not man himself. And one person, that is any single man, has them in his mind, or as his mind.[20] We could also define man like this and say, "Man is a rational substance consisting of soul and body."[21] In this case there is no doubt that man has a soul which is not body and a body which is not soul. Thus here too those three things are not man but something of man's or in man. Leave the body aside and think only about the soul, and mind is something that belongs to it, like its head or its eye or its face—but you must not think of these comparisons in a material way. So it is not the soul but what is pre-eminent in the soul that is called mind. But can we possibly say that a trinity is in God in such a way that it is something of God's, and is not itself just God? And so any single man, who is not called the image of God in terms of everything that belongs to his nature but only in terms of his mind, is one person and is the image of the trinity in his mind. But that trinity he is the image of is nothing but wholly and simply God, nothing but wholly and simply trinity. Nor is there anything belonging to God's nature which does not belong to that trinity; and there are three persons of one being, not, like any single man, just one person.

12. Again there is this enormous difference, that whether we talk about mind in man and its knowledge and love, or whether about memory, understanding, will, we remember nothing of the mind except through memory, and understand nothing except through understanding, and love nothing except through will. But who would presume to say that in that trinity the Father does not understand either himself or the Son or the Holy Spirit except through the Son, or love except through the Holy Spirit, but only remembers either himself or the Son or the Holy Spirit through himself? Or, in the same way, that the Son does not remember either himself or the Father except through the Father, and only loves through the Holy Spirit, while through himself he only understands both the Father and himself and the Holy Spirit? And likewise that the Holy Spirit remembers the Father and the Son and himself through the Father, and understands the Father and the Son and himself through the Son, while through himself he only loves both himself and the Father and the Son? All this, as though the Father were his own memory and the Son's and the Holy Spirit's, while the Son would be his own understanding and the Father's and the Holy Spirit's, and the Holy Spirit his own and the Father's and the Son's charity.

Who would presume to imagine or affirm such a view about that trinity? If the Son alone there does the understanding for himself and the Father and the Holy Spirit, we are back at that absurdity of the Father not being wise with himself but with the Son, and of wisdom not begetting wisdom, but of the Father being called wise with the wisdom he has begotten. For where there is no understanding there cannot be any wisdom, and thus if the Father does not do his understanding for himself, but the Son does it for the Father, it follows that it is the Son who makes the Father wise. And if for God to be is the same as to be wise, it is not the Son who has being from the Father (which is the true position) but rather the Father who has being from the Son, which is the height of absurdity and falsehood. We discussed, showed up, and rejected this absurdity with complete finality in the seventh book.[22]

So therefore, God the Father is wise with the wisdom by which he is his own wisdom, and the Son is wisdom from the wisdom of the Father, which is the Father from whom he is begotten as Son. The consequence is that the Father understands with the understanding by which he is his own understanding—he would not be wise unless he also understood. But the Son is understanding, begotten from the understanding of the Father, which is the Father. The same point could appropriately be made about memory. How can one who does not remember anything, or at least does not remember himself, be wise? It follows then that because the Father is wisdom and the Son is wisdom, the Son does his own remembering[23] just as the Father does; and just as the Father remembers himself and the Son with his own memory not the Son's, so the Son remembers himself and the Father with his own memory not the Father's. Again, who will say that there is any wisdom where there is no love? From this we can infer that the Father is his own love just as he is his own understanding and memory.

So here we are then with these three, that is memory, understanding, love or will in that supreme and unchangeable being which God is, and they are not the Father and the Son and the Holy Spirit but the Father alone. And because the Son too is wisdom, begotten of wisdom, it means the Father does not do his remembering for him or the Holy Spirit his loving any more than the Father or the Holy Spirit do his understanding, but he does it all for himself; he is his own memory, his own understanding, his own love, but his being all this comes to him from the Father of whom he is born. The Holy Spirit too does not have the Father for memory and the Son for understanding and himself for love, because he is wisdom proceeding from wisdom; and he would not be wisdom if another did his remembering and another his understanding for him, and he himself only did his own loving. No, he himself has these three, and he has them in such a way that he is them. But its being so with him comes to him from where he proceeds from.[24]

13. Then how can this wisdom by which God knows all things in such a way that what is called future is not being waited for to happen as though it were not there yet, but things past and future are all present with things present; and things are not thought about one by one, with thought moving from one to another, but all things are grasped in one glance or view; how, I say, can any man comprehend this wisdom, which is simultaneously prudence, simultaneously knowledge,[25] seeing that we cannot even comprehend our own? Things that are present to our understanding or our senses we can at least observe; things that are absent but were present we know by memory, if we have not forgotten them. And we make a guess at future things from past things, not at the past from the future, but without any certainty of knowledge. There are some thoughts of ours which we can see as about to happen in the immediate future with considerable

clarity and certainty; but we do this with the aid of memory when we are able to do it and as far as we are able, and yet memory seems to be concerned with the past and not the future. You can experience what I mean in speeches or songs which we render word for word by memory; clearly, unless we foresaw in thought what was to follow, we would not say it. And yet it is not foresight that instructs us how to foresee, but memory. Until we finish what we are reciting or singing, we have uttered nothing which we have not foreseen. And yet when we do this we are not said to recite or sing from foresight but from memory, and those who are very good at reciting many things of this sort are not usually admired for their foresight but for their memory. We know with complete certainty that these things happen in our consciousness, or proceed from our consciousness. But the more we desire to observe closely how they happen, the more our language begins to stagger, and our attention fails to persevere until our understanding if not our tongue can arrive at some clear result. And shall we suppose that with such feebleness of mental capacity we can comprehend how God's foresight is the same as his memory and his understanding, and how he does not observe things by thinking of them one by one, but embraces everything that he knows in one eternal, unchangeable, and inexpressible vision? It is a relief in this kind of difficulty and frustration to cry out to the living God, "*Your knowledge is too wonderful for me; it is mighty and I cannot attain it* (Ps 139:6) From myself indeed I understand how wonderful and incomprehensible is your knowledge with which you have made me, seeing that I am not even able to comprehend myself whom you have made; and yet *a fire burns up in my meditation* (Ps 39:3), causing me to seek your face always."[26]

Chapter 3

Having shown that a direct intellectual understanding of the trinity in terms of the text of Romans 1:20 is not possible, the author turns to consider the possibility of an indirect vision of the mystery, in terms of 1 Corinthians 13:12: We see now through a mirror in an enigma,[27] *but then it will be face to face. The mirror is interpreted to mean the image of God, which is the human mind, and most of the chapter is devoted to discussing the enigmatic nature of this image, chiefly with respect to the mental word; the chapter closes with a suggested reason why it should have been the Word, not the Father or the Holy Spirit, that became man.*

14. I know that wisdom is a non-bodily substance, and the light in which things are seen that cannot be seen with the eyes of flesh; and yet a great and spiritual man says, *We see now through a mirror in an enigma, but then it will be face to face* (1 Cor 13:12). If we ask what kind of mirror this might be, the thought occurs to us that the only thing ever seen in a mirror is an image. So what we have been trying to do is somehow to see him by whom we were made by means of this image which we ourselves are, as through a mirror. The same

thing is referred to in another text of the same apostle's, *But we with face unveiled, looking at the glory of the Lord in a mirror, are being transformed into the same image from glory to glory as by the Spirit of the Lord* (2 Cor 3:18).

By *speculantes*[28] he means seeing in a *speculum* (a mirror), not looking out from a *specula* (a look-out point). In the Greek from which the apostle's letter was translated into Latin there is no ambiguity. In that language the *speculum* in which the images of things appear differs completely in the sound of the word from the *specula* from whose height we gaze out into the distance. And it is quite clear that the apostle here said *speculantes the glory of the Lord* (2 Cor 3:18) from *speculum* a mirror, not from *specula* a look-out point. As for what he said, *we are being transformed into the same image,* he clearly wants us to understand it as the image of God, and he calls it the same, meaning this one we are looking at in the mirror. For the same thing is both image and glory of God, as he says elsewhere: *The man ought not to cover his head, as he is the image and glory of God* (1 Cor 11:7). We discussed this text in the twelfth book.[29] So, *we are being transformed,* he said; we are being changed from form to form, and are passing from a blurred form to a clear one. But even the blurred one is the image of God, and if image then of course glory, in which men were created surpassing the other animals. It is of the whole nature of man that it is said, *The man ought not to cover his head, as he is the image and glory of God.* And when this nature, the most excellent of created things, is justified by its creator from its godlessness, it is transformed[30] from an ugly form into a beautiful one. The more damnable a fault its godlessness is, the more surely admirable is its nature.[31] And that is why he added *from glory to glory* (2 Cor 3:18), meaning from the glory of creation to the glory of justification. Though it is true that *from glory to glory* here could be understood in other ways: from the glory of faith to the glory of sight;[32] from the glory by which we are sons of God to the glory by which we shall be like him, because we shall see him as he is.[33] As for his concluding words, *as by the Spirit of the Lord* (2 Cor 3:18), they indicate that the good of such a desirable transformation is conferred on us by God's grace.

15. I have said all this in explanation of the apostle's saying that we now see *through a mirror* (1 Cor 13:12). But he added, *in an enigma,* and many people do not know what this means, since they are not acquainted with those textbooks that teach us about the figures of speech which the Greeks call "tropes." We too use this Greek word in Latin, Indeed, just as we more commonly say "schemata" than "figures," so we more commonly say "tropes" than "modes" in this connection. As a matter of fact, it is extremely difficult and most unusual to put into Latin the names of all the modes or tropes, and give each one its own particular name. Some of our translators, unwilling to use a Greek word for the apostle's phrase, *these things are put in an allegory* (Gal 4:24), have translated with a circumlocution and said, "these things are signifying one thing from another."

Of this trope, that is allegory, there are various species, and among them the one called enigma. Now the definition of the general term must necessarily embrace all its species. And thus in the same way as every horse is an animal while not every animal is a horse, so every enigma is an allegory while not every allegory is an enigma. An allegory is nothing but a trope in which one thing is understood from another, as for example this to the Thessalonians: *So let us not sleep like the others, but let us keep awake and be sober. For those who sleep sleep at night, and those who are drunk are drunk at night; but we who are of the day should be sober* (1 Thes 5:6). But this allegory is not an enigma, as its meaning is obvious except to the unusually slow-witted. An enigma, to put it briefly, is an obscure allegory, like *The blood-sucker had three daughters* (Prv 30:15), and other sayings like that. But when the apostle talked of allegory, he did not find it in words but in a fact, arguing that the two testaments are to be understood from the two sons of Abraham, one born of the slave woman, the other of the free; this was not just said—it happened. And before he explained it its meaning was obscure. So an allegory of this sort, called such by the general name, could specifically be called an enigma.

16. However, it is not only people unacquainted with the textbooks in which you can learn about tropes who want to know why the apostle said that we see now in an enigma; people who know about enigmas are anxious to know in particular what this enigma is in which we now see. We have to find a solution that covers both parts of the sentence, both his saying *We see now through a mirror* and his adding *in an enigma* (1 Cor 3:12). After all, it makes one whole sentence, running *We see now through a mirror in an enigma.* As far as I can see then, by the word "mirror" he wanted us to understand an image, and by the word "enigma" he was indicating that although it is a likeness, it is an obscure one and difficult to penetrate. Now we can indeed take it that by the use of the words "mirror" and "enigma" the apostle meant any likenesses that are useful for understanding God with, as far as this is possible; but of such likenesses none is more suitable than the one which is not called God's image for nothing.

No one therefore should be surprised that in this fashion of seeing which is allowed us in this life, namely through a mirror in an enigma, we have a struggle to see at all. If it was easy to see, the word "enigma" would not be mentioned in this connection. And what makes the enigma all the more puzzling is that we should be unable to see what we cannot not see. Who fails to see his own thoughts? And on the other hand who does see his own thoughts—and I do not mean with the eyes of flesh but with the inner gaze? Who fails to see them and who does see them? After all, thought is a kind of sight of the consciousness, whether things are present that are seen with the bodily eyes or sensed with the other senses, or whether they are not present and their likenesses are observed in thought; or whether none of these are being thought about, but only things that are neither bodily nor the likenesses of bodies, such as virtues and vices, such indeed as thought itself; whether they are things that are taught by the disciplines of a liberal education,[34] or whether the higher causes and ideas of all these things are being thought about in their unchanging nature; whether we are thinking of bad and idle and false things either without the consent of sense or with an erring consent.

17. But now let us talk about things which we think of when we are aware of them, and have in our awareness even if we are not thinking about them, whether they belong to that contemplative knowledge which I have maintained

is properly to be called wisdom or to that active knowledge which is properly called knowledge. Both together they belong to one mind and make one image of God. But when it is a question specifically and separately of the lower function, then it should not be called the image of God, although even then a certain likeness can be found of that trinity, as we showed in the thirteenth volume.[35] Now however we are speaking of men's knowledge in general and all together, in which everything is known to us that *is* known to us, and it must all be true, otherwise it would not be known. No one knows false things except when he knows them to be false. If he knows this he knows something true, since it is true that they are false. So now we are discussing things which we think of when we are aware of them, and which we are aware of even when we are not thinking of them. But to be sure, if we wished to utter them we could not do it unless we thought about them. Even if no words are spoken, the man who is thinking is of course uttering in his heart.

Thus we have the text in the book of Wisdom: *They said to themselves, thinking unsoundly* (Wis 2:1); he explained what "they said to themselves" means when he added "thinking." We have a similar thing in the gospel about some scribes who heard the Lord say to the paralytic, *Courage, son; your sins are forgiven you. They said to themselves, This man is blaspheming.* How did they say to themselves, except by thinking? Anyhow, it goes on, *And when Jesus saw their thoughts he said, Why are you thinking evil things in your hearts* (Mt 9:2)? So Matthew. Luke, however, tells the same story as follows: *The scribes and Pharisees began to think, saying, Who is this that speaks blasphemies? Who can forgive sins but God alone? But as Jesus knew their thoughts he answered and said to them, What are you thinking in your hearts* (Lk 5:21)? What the book of Wisdom expresses as "they said thinking" is here put as "they thought saying." In both places it is shown that this saying to oneself and in one's heart is[36] a saying by thinking. "They said to themselves," and they were asked "What are you thinking?" And of that rich man whose fields produced a fat harvest the Lord himself says, *And he thought to himself, saying* (Lk 12:17).

18. So thoughts are a kind of utterance of the heart, which also has its mouth, as the Lord showed when he said, *It is not what goes into the mouth that defiles a man, but what comes out of the mouth, that is what defiles a man* (Mt 15:11). One sentence includes the two sorts of mouth a man has, one of the body, the other of the heart. Clearly, what they thought a man is defiled by goes into the mouth of the body; but what the Lord said a man is defiled by issues from the mouth of the heart. That is how he himself explained what he said; a little later he spoke to his disciples about this matter: *Are you too still without under-standing? Do you not understand that everything that goes into the mouth passes into the belly and is got rid of in the privy* (Mt 15:16)? Here, certainly, he was obviously alluding to the mouth of the body. But in what follows he points to the mouth of the heart: *But things,* he says, *that issue from the mouth come out from the heart, and they defile a man. For from the heart come out evil thoughts,* etc. (Mt 15:18). What could be clearer than this explanation?

However, just because we say that thoughts are utterances of the heart, it does not mean that they are not also seeings, arising when they are true from the seeing of awareness. When these things happen outwardly through the body, speech is one thing, sight another; but when we think inwardly they are both one and the same; just as hearing and seeing are two things that differ from each other among the senses of the body, while in the consciousness it is not one thing to see and another to hear. And thus while, outwardly speaking, utterance is not seen but rather heard, the holy gospel says that inward utterances, that is thoughts, were seen by the Lord, not heard. *They said to themselves*, it went, *This man is blaspheming*; and then it added, *And when Jesus saw their thoughts* (Mt 9:3). So he saw what they said. With his thought he saw their thoughts which they imagined that they alone could see.

19. If anyone then can understand how a word can be, not only before it is spoken aloud but even before the images of its sounds are turned over in thought—this is the word that belongs to no language, that is to none of what are called the languages of the nations, of which ours is Latin; if anyone, I say, can understand this, he can already see through this mirror and in this enigma some likeness of that Word of which it is said, *In the beginning was the Word, and the Word was with God, and the Word was God* (Jn 1:1). For when we utter something true, that is when we utter what we know, a word is necessarily born from the knowledge which we hold in the memory, a word which is absolutely the same kind of thing as the knowledge it is born from. It is the thought formed from the thing we know that is the word which we utter in the heart, a word that is neither Greek nor Latin nor any other language; but when it is necessary to convey the knowledge in the language of those we are speaking to, some sign is adopted to signify this word. And usually a sound, sometimes also a gesture is presented, the one to their ears the other to their eyes, in order that bodily signs may make the word we carry in our minds known to their bodily senses. What after all is gesticulating but a way of speaking visibly? The holy scriptures support this view with their evidence; we read in the gospel according to John: *Amen, amen I tell you, that one of you will betray me. So the disciples looked at each other, uncertain whom he was speaking of. So one of the disciples whom Jesus loved was*[37] *in the bosom of Jesus. So Simon Peter gesticulated to this one and said to him, "Who is it he is talking of"* (Jn 13:21)? There you have him uttering with a gesture what he did not dare to utter aloud. Such at any rate are the bodily signs which we present to the ears or eyes of those we are speaking to, if they are present. Letters too[38] were invented so that we might also be able to converse with those who are absent; but these are signs of vocal sounds, while the vocal sounds of our speech are signs of the things we are thinking of.

20. Thus the word which makes a sound outside is the sign of the word which lights up inside, and it is this latter that primarily deserves the name of "word."[39] For the one that is uttered by the mouth of flesh is really the sound of a "word," and it is called "word" too because of the one which assumes it in order to be manifested outwardly. Thus in a certain fashion our word becomes a bodily sound by assuming that in which it is manifested to the senses of men, just as the Word of God became flesh by assuming that in which it too could be

manifested to the senses of men. And just as our word becomes sound without being changed into sound, so the Word of God became flesh, but it is unthinkable that it should have been changed into flesh. It is by assuming it, not by being consumed into it, that both our word becomes sound and that Word became flesh.

Therefore if you wish to arrive at some kind of likeness of the Word of God, however unlike it may be in many ways, do not look at that word of ours which sounds in the ears, neither when it is uttered vocally nor when it is thought of silently. The words of all spoken languages are thought of silently, and people run over songs in their minds while their mouths remain silent; and it is not only the number of syllables either, but the notes of the melodies as well, all of them bodily realities pertaining to the bodily sense called hearing, that the thoughts of those who are thinking them over, and silently pondering them all, find ready to hand in their own kind of non-bodily images. But we must go beyond all these and come to that word of man through whose likeness of a sort the Word of God may somehow or other be seen in an enigma. I do not mean the word of God which came to this or that prophet, and of which it is said, *The word of God was increasing and multiplying* (Acts 6:7);[40] and of which it is also said, *Therefore faith comes through hearing, hearing however through the word of Christ* (Rom 10:17); and again, *When you received from us the word of hearing about God, you did not receive it as the word of men, but as the word of God which it really is* (1 Thes 2:13). And countless other such things are said in the scriptures about the word of God which is spread abroad through the hearts and mouths of men in the accents of many different languages. The reason it is called the word of God is that it conveys divine not human teaching. But the Word of God we are now seeking to see, however imperfectly, through this likeness, is the one of which it was said, *The Word was God* (Jn 1:1); of which it was said, *All things were made through him* (Jn 1:3); of which it was said, *The Word became flesh* (Jn 1:14); of which it was said, *A fountain of wisdom is the Word of God on high* (Sir 1:5).

And so we must come to that word of man, the word of a rational animal, the word of the image of God which is not born of God but made by God, the word which is neither uttered in sound nor thought of in the likeness of sound which necessarily belongs to some language, but which precedes all the signs that signify it and is begotten of the knowledge abiding in the consciousness, when this knowledge is uttered inwardly just exactly as it is. When it is uttered vocally or by some bodily sign, it is not uttered just exactly as it is, but as it can be seen or heard through the body. So when that which is in the awareness is also in a word, then is it a true word, and truth such as a man looks for so that what is in awareness should also be in word and what is not in awareness should not either be in word. It is here that one acknowledges the *Yes, yes; no, no* (Mt 5:37; 2 Cor 1:17; Jas 5:12). In this way this likeness of the made image approaches as far as it can to the likeness of the born image, in which God the Son is declared to be substantially like the Father in all respects.

There is another likeness to the Word of God that can be observed in this enigma; just as it is said of that Word, *All things were made through him* (Jn 1:3), stating that God made all things through his only-begotten Word, so too there are no works of man which are not first uttered in the heart. That is why it is written, *The beginning of every work is a word* (Sir 37:16).[41] Here too, if it is a true word, it is the beginning of a good work. And a word is true when it is begotten of the knowledge of how to work well, so that here too one may apply the *Yes, yes; no, no*; so that if it is yes in the knowledge by which one ought to live, it should be yes in the word through which one has to work, and if no, no. Otherwise such a word will be a lie and not the truth, and from it will come a sin, not a right work. There is also this other likeness to the Word of God in this likeness which is our word, that we can have a word which is not followed by a work, but we cannot have a work which is not preceded by a word, just as the Word of God could be, even without any creation coming into existence, but there could not be any creation except through that Word through which all things were made. And the reason why it was not God the Father, not the Holy Spirit, not the trinity itself, but only the Son who is the Word of God that became flesh (although it was the trinity that accomplished this), is that we might live rightly by our word following and imitating his example; that is, by our having no falsehood either in the contemplation or in the operation of our word. However, this is a perfection of the image that lies some time in the future. To achieve it we are instructed by the good master[42] in Christian faith and godly doctrine, in order that *with face unveiled* from the veil of the law *which is the shadow of things to come* (Heb 10:1; Col 2:17), *looking at the glory of the Lord through a mirror, we might be transformed into the same image from glory to glory, as by the Spirit of the Lord* (2 Cor 3:13)[43] according to our earlier discussion of these words.[44]

Chapter 4

The image seen enigmatically in the mirror is now examined to bring out its inadequacy, or unlikeness to the original; and first of all, in this chapter, with reference to the first eternal procession in God, that of the Son from the Father.

21. So then, when this image is renewed to perfection by this transformation, we will be like God *because we shall see him*, not through a mirror but *as he is* (1 Jn 3:2); what the apostle Paul calls *face to face* (1 Cor 13:12). But now, in this mirror, in this puzzle, in this likeness of whatever sort, who can adequately explain how great the unlikeness is? However, I will touch upon a few things as best I can, which will serve to bring this point home to us.

Take first of all the knowledge from which our thought is truly formed when we utter what we know; how much and what sort of knowledge can really accrue even to the most learned and knowledgeable of men? Apart from things that come into the consciousness from the senses of the body, so many of which are other than they appear that an insane person excessively crammed with convincing delusions about them thinks he is sane—which is why the philosophy of the Academics developed to the point of doubting everything and so landed itself in a much more wretched kind of insanity;[45] apart then from these things that come into the consciousness from the senses of the body, what is there left that we know as surely as we know that we are alive? In this matter at least we are never afraid of being deceived by some delusion, because it is quite certain that even a man who is being deceived is alive. And this is not one of those visible things that are externally presented in such a way that the eye is deceived, as it is deceived for example when an oar seems to be broken in the water, and when the lighthouse seems to those sailing past it to be moving, and a thousand and one[46] other things that are not what they seem; but this is not something that is seen by the eyes of flesh.

The knowledge by which we know that we are alive is most intimately inward, and cannot be touched by an Academic saying, "Perhaps you are dreaming, and do not know it, and all you are seeing is dreams." Who is unaware that what dreamers see is often extremely like what waking people see? But the man who is certain of his knowledge that he is alive is not saying on the strength of it "I know I am awake," but "I know I am alive." It is impossible in this particular point of knowledge to be deceived by dreams, because even sleeping and seeing things in dreams is proper to someone who is alive. Nor again can the Academic say against this knowledge, "Perhaps you are crazy, and you do not know that what crazy people see is very like what sane people see." But if a man is crazy, he is alive; and against the Academics he is not saying "I know that I am not crazy," but "I know that I am alive." So someone who says he knows he is alive can never be lying or be deceived. Let a thousand kinds of illusion be objected against the man who says "I know I am alive"; none of them will worry him, since even the man who suffers from an illusion is alive.

But if this is the only kind of thing that really pertains to human knowledge, then there are extremely few instances of it—except that any point of knowledge can be so multiplied that its instances, far from being few, turn out to extend to infinity. Thus the man who says "I know I am alive" says he knows one thing; but if he says "I know that I know I am alive," there are two things. The fact that he knows these two things makes a third knowing; and in this way he can add a fourth and a fifth and a countless number more, if he has the time. But because he cannot either comprehend an innumerable number by adding up single ones or give it innumerable expression, what he certainly does comprehend is both that this is true, and that it is so innumerable that he cannot comprehend or express the infinite number of its word.[47]

The same thing can be observed with the certitude of the will. If somebody says "I want to be happy," would it not be sheer impudence to answer him, "Perhaps you are deceived"? And if he says "I know that I want this, and I know that I know it," to these two things can be added the third, that he knows these two; and a fourth, that he knows he knows these two things, and so he can go on to infinity. Again, if someone says "I do not want to be mistaken," then whether he is mistaken or not, it will surely be true that he does not want to be mistaken. Would it not again be sheer impudence to say to him, "Perhaps you are deceived," since it is obvious that in whatever case he is deceived, he is not deceived about not wanting to be deceived? And if he says he knows this he can add as big a number as he likes of things known, and observe that the possible number is infinite. The man who says "I do not want to be deceived, and I know that I do not want this, and I know that I know this," can go on from here to show an infinite number, even if he cannot find a suitable expression for it. And there are other instances one could bring up in order to confute the Academics who contend that nothing can be known by man.

But we must set a limit to this discussion, especially as this is not the task we have undertaken in this work. There are however the three books of mine on the subject[48] written at the time of my conversion, and anyone who wishes and is able to read them, and understands them when he has read them, will certainly find that none of the many arguments the Academics have brought up against the perception of truth will be able to move him. There are, after all, two sorts of things that can be known, one the sort that the consciousness perceives through bodily sensation, the other the sort it perceives through itself. Now these philosophers were constantly prating against bodily sensation,[49] but as regards certain absolutely solid perceptions of the consciousness about true things through itself, such as the one I mentioned, "I know that I am alive," they were not able in the least to call them in question. But in any case, far be it from us to doubt the truth of things we have learnt through the senses of the body. It is through them that we have learnt about heaven and earth and all that is known to us in them, as far as their creator and ours has willed them to be known to us. Far be it from us either to deny that we know what we have learnt on the testimony of others; otherwise we would not know the Ocean[50] exists; we would not know that there are countries and cities commended to us by their celebrity and renown; we would not know that the men and their works which we have learnt about from our historical reading really existed; we would not know the things that are reported to us every day from all sides, which are confirmed by constant[51] and consistent indications; finally we would not know where we were born or of what parents, because these are all things that we have believed on the testimony of others. If it is absurd to say such things, then it has to be admitted that a very great deal has been added to our knowledge by the senses of other people's bodies as well as of our own.[52]

22. All these things then that the human consciousness knows by perceiving them through itself or through the senses of its body or through the testimony of others, it holds onto where they are stacked away in the treasury of memory. From them is begotten a true word when we utter what we know, but a word before any sound, before any thought of sound. For it is then that the word is most like the thing known, and most its image, because the seeing which is thought springs direct from the seeing which is knowledge, and it is a word of no language, a true word from a true thing, having nothing from itself, but everything from that knowledge from which it is born. And it makes no dif-

ference when the man who utters what he knows learnt it—sometimes he utters it as soon as he learns it—provided it is a true word, that is one that has arisen from things known.

But did God the Father, from whom is born the Word as God from God, did God the Father then, in that wisdom which he is for himself, learn some things through the senses of his body, others through himself? Would anyone dream of saying this who is able to think of God not as a rational animal but as above the rational soul, as far of course as he can be thought about by those who rate him above all animals and all souls, even though they see him only by inference through a mirror and in a puzzle, and not yet face to face as he is?[53] As regards those things which he knows, not through a body which he has not got but through himself, did God the Father learn them from anyone, or need messengers or witnesses in order to know them? Of course not. That perfection is sufficient to itself for knowing all the things it knows. He does indeed have messengers, that is angels, but not for telling him what he does not know—there is nothing he does not know. Their privilege is to consult his truth about their works, and this is what it means to say they tell him things; not that he learns from them, but they from him through his Word without any physical sound. They are also sent by him to tell what he wants to whom he wants, and they hear it all from him through that Word of his; that is they find in his truth what they have to do, and what is to be told to whom and when.

We too pray to him, and yet we do not teach him about our needs. *For your Father knows*, says his Word, *what you need before you ask him* (Mt 6:8). To know this he did not get to know it at a certain time, but without beginning he foreknew beforehand all future temporal things, and among them what we were going to ask him for and when, and whom he was going to listen to or not listen to, and about what things. It is true of all his creatures, both spiritual and corporeal, that he does not know them because they are, but that they are because he knows them. He was not ignorant of what he was going to create. So he created because he knew, he did not know because he had created. Nor did he know them as created otherwise than as to be created; nothing accrued to his wisdom from them, but when they came into existence as required and when required, it remained just as it had been. So it is written in the book of Sirach: *Before they were created all things were known to him, so too after they were completed* (Sir 23:20). "So," he says, not otherwise; "both before they were created and after they were completed, so they were known to him."

Our knowledge therefore is vastly dissimilar to this knowledge. What is God's knowledge is also his wisdom, and what is his wisdom is also his being or substance, because in the wonderful simplicity of that nature it is not one thing to be wise, another to be, but being wise is the same as being, as we have already said often enough in previous books.[54] But *our* knowledge, as regards most of its objects, can be both lost and acquired for the very reason that for us to be is not the same thing as to know or to be wise, since we can be, even if we do not know and are not wise to things we have learnt from elsewhere. That is why, just as our knowledge is so dissimilar to that knowledge of God's, so our word is dissimilar to that Word of God which is born of the Father's being. (It would amount to the same thing, of course, if I said "of the Father's knowledge, of the Father's wisdom"; or even more precisely, "of the Father who is knowledge, of the Father who is wisdom.")

23. So the Word of God, the only-begotten Son of the Father, like the Father and equal to him in all things, God from God, light from light, wisdom from wisdom, being from being, is exactly and absolutely what the Father is, and yet is not the Father because this one is Son, that one Father. And thus he knows everything that the Father knows, but his knowing comes to him from the Father just as his being does. For here knowing and being are one and the same. And thus just as the Father's being is not from the Son, so neither is his knowing. Hence it is as though uttering himself that the Father begot the Word equal to himself in all things. He would not have uttered himself completely and perfectly if anything less or more were in his Word than in himself. There supremely can we recognize *Yes, yes; no, no* (Mt 5:37; see 2 Cor 1:19-20; Jas 5:12). And the reason this Word is truly truth is that whatever is in the knowledge of which it was begotten is also in it; and anything that is not in that knowledge is not in it. And this Word can never have anything false in it because it unchangeably finds itself exactly as he from whom it is finds himself. For, *The Son cannot do anything of himself except what he sees the Father doing* (Jn 5:19). He is powerfully unable to do this, nor is this weakness, but the strength by which[55] truth cannot be false. So the Father knows all things in himself, knows them in the Son; but in himself as knowing himself, in the Son as knowing his Word which is about all these things that are in himself. Likewise the Son too knows all things in himself, that is to say as things that are born from the things that the Father knows in himself, and he knows them in the Father as the things from which are born all the things that he as Son knows in himself. Therefore the Father and the Son know each other, the one by begetting, the other by being born. And all the things that are in their knowledge, in their wisdom, in their being, each of them sees all at once, not bit by bit and one by one, nor by turning his gaze from here to there and there to here, and again from there or there to this and that, as though he could not see some things unless he stopped seeing others. But as I said, each sees all things together, and there is nothing that he does not see always.

24. But our word, the one that has neither sound nor thought of sound, the one that belongs to the thing we utter inside as we see it and thus not to any language, and hence the one that in this puzzle[56] is at least something like that Word of God which is also God, since this one is born of our knowledge as that one was born of the Father's; such a word of ours then we have found to be somehow or other like that one. But now we should not be reluctant to observe also how unlike it is, as far as we are able to state it.

Is our word only born of our knowledge? Do we not also utter many things which we are ignorant of? We say them of course without hesitation, supposing them to be true. And if they do happen to be true, they are true in the things themselves we are talking about and not in our word, because a word is not true unless it is born of a thing that is known. In this way then our word is false, not when we are lying but when we are mistaken.[57] When however we are in doubt, there is as yet no word about the thing we are doubtful of, but there is a word about the doubt itself. We do not know whether the thing we are doubtful about is true, but we do know that we are doubtful, and thus when we say so our word is true, because we are saying what we know. What about our also being able to lie? When we do this we willfully and knowingly have a false word, where the true word is that we are lying; this after all is what we know. And when we admit that we have been lying we are saying something true, because we are saying what we know; we know that we have been lying. But that Word which is God and is more powerful than us cannot do this. For he *cannot do anything except what he sees the Father doing* (Jn 5:19). And he does not speak of himself, but everything he speaks comes to him from the Father,[58] because the Father speaks to him alone. And it shows the great power of that Word that he cannot lie, because there cannot be there any *Yes and no*, but only *Yes, yes; no, no* (2 Cor 1:18).

"But if it is not true, it should not even be called a word." So be it; I entirely agree. But even when our word is true and therefore rightly called a word, it can to be sure be called sight from sight or knowledge from knowledge, but can it also be called being from being, as that Word of God is supremely called and supremely should be called? Hardly. And why not? Because for us it is not the same thing to be as to know. We know many things which live after a fashion by being remembered and which thus die after a fashion by being forgotten;[59] and thus while they are no longer in our awareness, we still are, and while our knowledge has perished from us by slipping from the consciousness, we still live.

25. There are, certainly, things which are so known that they can never escape us, because they are present and belong to the very nature of the consciousness, like our knowing that we are still alive. This remains as long as the consciousness or mind remains, and as the mind always remains, so does this always remain. This and similar cases that could be found, in which the image of God is for preference to be observed, may indeed always be known, but they are not always being thought about, and so it is difficult to see how one can talk of an everlasting word about these things, since our word is only uttered by our thought. To be alive is everlasting for the mind and to know that it is alive is everlasting. But to think about its life or about its knowledge of its life is not everlasting, since when it begins to think about something else it stops thinking about this, although it does not stop knowing it. It follows then that if there can be some everlasting knowledge in the mind, while there cannot be everlasting thought about this knowledge, and if our true and innermost word is only uttered by our thinking, only God can be understood to have an everlasting Word co-eternal with himself. Unless perhaps you could say that the very possibility of thought, given that what is known can be truly thought about even when it is not being thought about, is a word as continuous as the knowledge itself is continuous. But how can that be a word which has not yet been formed in the sight which is actual thought? How will it be like

the knowledge it is born from if it does not have its form? Is it already to be called a word because it can have this form? That amounts to saying that it should already be called a word because it can be a word.

But in that case, what is it that can be a word and therefore already deserves the name of word? What, I ask, is this formable not-yet-formed thing, but something of our mind which we cast about hither and thither with a kind of chopping and changing motion as we think about now this and now that just as it occurs to us or comes our way? And the time you get a true word is when this thing that I have said we cast around with a chopping and changing motion falls onto something we know and is formed from it and takes on its exact likeness, so that the thing is thought about exactly as it is known, that is to say is uttered in the heart without either voice or thought of voice which would *ipso facto* belong to some language. And thus even if we concede, to avoid thrashing around in an argument about words, that something of our mind which can be formed from our knowledge should already be called a word even before it has been formed, because it is already, so to say, formable; still, who could fail to see what a vast dissimilarity there is here to that Word of God which is in the form of God[60] without first being formable and afterward formed, and which could never ever be formless, but is simple form and simply equal to him from whom it is and with whom it is wonderfully co-eternal?

For this reason it is called God's Word without also being called God's thought, to avoid the assumption that there might be in God anything like a chopping and changing element, which will now receive, now regain a form in order to be a word, and which can lose it too and so somehow roll formlessly around. It was an outstanding master of words, one who knew them well and had looked closely into the bias of thought, who said in his poem:

> and to himself he rolls
> his mind around the varied course of war,[61]

that is to say, he thinks about it. So the Son of God is not called the thought of God but the Word of God. But as for our thought, when it comes upon something we know and is formed from it, it is our true word. And therefore, without any idea of God thinking, the Word of God should be understood as a simple form, which does not have something formable in it that could also be formless. The holy scriptures admittedly talk about the thoughts of God,[62] but with the same figure of speech as they talk about God's forgetfulness,[63] which of course is not properly speaking to be found in God at all.

26. And so since there is now such a great unlikeness to God and the Word of God in this puzzle,[64] though at the same time a genuine likeness has also been discovered there, we must admit further that even when we are like him, when we shall see him as he is[65]—that not even then shall we be equal to him in nature. The nature that has been made is always less than the one that made it. Then, to be sure, our word will never be false because we shall neither lie nor be deceived. Perhaps too our thoughts will no longer chop and change, going and coming

from some things to others, but we shall see all our knowledge in one simultaneous glance. And yet even when this happens, if it does happen, it will be a creature that was once formable which is formed, so that it now lacks nothing of the form to which it was intended it should come; but even so it will not be right or possible to put it on the same level as that simplicity in which there is not something formable that has been formed or reformed, but just form. Neither formless nor formed is that eternal and unchangeable substance.

Chapter 5

The author goes on to point out the dissimilarity of the mental image with reference to the second eternal procession, that of the Holy Spirit from the Father and the Son; though in fact he seems rather to forget his precise intention, only reverting to it at the very end of this chapter; and with scarcely any reference to the image, or its third element of will or love, he discusses at length the propriety of the names we give to the Holy Spirit.

---

27. We have talked enough about the Father and the Son insofar as we have been able to see them through this mirror and in this puzzle.[66] Now we must discuss the Holy Spirit as far as it is granted us with God's help to see him. According to the holy scriptures this Holy Spirit is not just the Father's alone nor the Son's alone, but the Spirit of them both, and thus he suggests to us the common charity by which the Father and the Son love each other. However, to put us through our paces, the divine word has made us search with greater diligence into things that are not set out in open display, but have to be explored in obscurity and dragged out of obscurity. So scripture did not say "The Holy Spirit is charity"; if it had, it would have eliminated the major part of this problem. What it said was, *God is charity* (1 Jn 4:8.16), thus leaving it uncertain, and something to be investigated, whether God the Father is charity or God the Son or God the Holy Spirit, or simply God the triad. Nor are we going to say that God is not called charity because charity is a substance that is worthy of the name of God, but simply because it is God's gift, rather as it is said to God, *you are my patience* (Ps 71:5). This of course is not said because our patience is God's substance, but because it comes to us from him; as in fact it says elsewhere, *For from him comes my patience* (Ps 62:5). Scripture's way of talking, indeed, easily refutes such an interpretation.[67] *You are my patience* is the same sort of statement as *Lord my hope* (Ps 71:5), and *My God my mercy* (Ps 59:17), and many others like that. But in this case it does not say "Lord my charity," or "You are my charity," or "God my charity," but it says *God is charity* (1 Jn 4:8.16) just as it says *God is spirit* (Jn 4:24). Anyone who does not see this should ask the Lord for understanding, not me for an explanation; I could not put it any more plainly.

28. So *God is charity*. But the question is whether it is the Father or the Son

or the Holy Spirit or the triad, because this triad is not three Gods but one God. But now I have already argued earlier on in this book[68] that the trinity which is God cannot just be read off from those three things which we have pointed out in the trinity of our minds, in such a way that the Father is taken as the memory of all three, and the Son as the understanding of all three, and the Holy Spirit as the charity of all three; as though the Father did not do his own understanding or loving, but the Son did his understanding for him and the Holy Spirit his loving, while he only did the remembering for himself and for them; and the Son neither remembered nor loved for himself, but the Father did the remembering and the Holy Spirit the loving for him, while he only understood for himself and for them; and again the Holy Spirit neither remembered nor understood for himself, but the Father did the remembering and the Son the understanding for him, while he himself only did the loving for himself and for them. It is rather that all and each of them has all three things each in his own nature.[69] Nor do these three differ in them, as in us memory is one thing, understanding another and love or charity yet another; but it is all one thing which has all these values, like wisdom; and it is so possessed in the nature of each that each one who possesses it is what he possesses, an unchangeable and simple substance. If all this then has been understood, and has been shown to be true as far as it is granted us to see or infer in such deep matters, then I do not know why Father and Son and Holy Spirit should not all be called charity and all together be one charity, just as Father and Son and Holy Spirit are all called wisdom and are all together not three wisdoms but one wisdom. In the same way the Father is God and the Son is God and the Holy Spirit is God, and they are all together one God.

29. And yet it is not without point that in this triad only the Son is called the Word of God, and only the Holy Spirit is called the gift of God, and only the Father is called the one from whom the Word is born and from whom the Holy Spirit principally proceeds. I added "principally," because we have found that the Holy Spirit also proceeds from the Son. But this too was given the Son by the Father—not given to him when he already existed and did not yet have it; but whatever the Father gave to his only-begotten Word he gave by begetting him. He so begot him then that their common gift would proceed from him too, and the Holy Spirit would be the Spirit of them both. This distinction then within the inseparable trinity must be diligently looked into and not casually taken for granted. It is this that allows the Word of God also to be called distinctively the wisdom of God,[70] even though both Father and Holy Spirit are also wisdom. If therefore any of these three can be distinctively named charity, which could it more suitably be than the Holy Spirit? What is meant is that while in that supremely simple nature substance is not one thing and charity another, but substance is charity and charity is substance, whether in the Father or in the Son or in the Holy Spirit, yet all the same the Holy Spirit is distinctively named charity.

30. In the same sort of way all the books of the Old Testament of the holy scriptures are sometimes signified by the name of the law. When the apostle quotes the testimony of the prophet Isaiah, where he says, *In other tongues and*

in other accents shall I speak to this people (Is 28:11), he prefaces it by saying, *It is written in the law* (1 Cor 14:21). And the Lord himself says, *In their law it is written that they hate me for nothing* (Jn 15:25), though we find this in a psalm.[71] But sometimes it is what was given through Moses that is distinctively called the law, and accordingly it is said, *The law and the prophets until John* (Mt 11:13), and, *On these two commandments hangs the whole law and the prophets* (Mt 22:40). Here clearly it is the law from Mount Sinai that is being distinctively so called, while the psalms are also included here under the name of the prophets; and yet in another place the Savior himself says, *It was necessary for all the things to be fulfilled that are written about me in the law and in the prophets and in the psalms* (Lk 24:44). Here on the contrary he meant the name of the prophets to exclude the psalms. So "the law" is used generally to include the psalms and the prophets, and it is also used distinctively to mean what was given through Moses. And "the prophets" can be used as a common name to include the psalms, and it can be used distinctively to exclude the psalms. And many other examples could be given to show that many names of things are both used generally and applied distinctively to particular things—but in such an obvious matter one must avoid being too long-winded. I have only said all this in case anyone should consider that it is unsuitable for us to call the Holy Spirit charity, on the grounds that God the Father and God the Son can also be called charity.

31. Just then as we distinctively call the only Word of God by the name of wisdom, although the Holy Spirit and the Father are also wisdom in a general sense, so the Spirit[72] is distinctively called by the term charity, although both Father and Son are charity in a general sense. But the Word of God, that is the only-begotten Son of God, is openly called wisdom by the mouth of the apostle where he says, *Christ the power of God and the wisdom of God* (1 Cor 1:24). We can however find where the Holy Spirit is called charity if we carefully examine the words of the apostle John. After saying, *Beloved, let us love each other because love is from God*, he went on to add, *and everyone who loves is born of God. Whoever does not love does not know God, because love is God* (Jn 4:7). Here he made it clear that he called that love God which he had just said was from God; love therefore is God from God.[73] But besides the Son being born of God the Father, the Holy Spirit proceeds from God the Father, and so the natural question is about which of them we should here take it as said, that love is God. The Father alone is God in such a way that he is not from God, and thus the love which is God in such a way that it is from God must either be the Son or the Holy Spirit. But in the next few lines, after mentioning the love of God, not the one we love him with, but the one with which *he himself loved us and sent his Son as an atoner for our sins* (1 Jn 4:10), and going on from there to urge us to love one another and so have God abide in us, because of course he had already called love God, he now wished to say something a little more plainly about this matter, and so he said, *In this we know that we abide in him and he in us, because he has given us of his Spirit* (1 Jn 4:13). So it is the Holy Spirit of which he has given us that makes us abide in God and him in us. But

this is precisely what love does. He then is the gift of God who is love. Finally, after repeating this a little later and saying, *Love is God*, he immediately added, *and whoever abides in love abides in God, and God abides in him* (1 Jn 4:16), about which he had said above, *In this we know that we abide in him and he in us, because he has given us of his Spirit* (1 Jn 4:13). He then is the one meant when we read, *Love is God* (1 Jn 4:8.16). So it is God the Holy Spirit proceeding from God who fires man to the love of God and neighbor when he has been given to him, and he himself is love. Man has no capacity to love God except from God. That is why he says a little later, *Let us love because he first loved us* (1 Jn 4:19). The apostle Paul also says, *The love of God has been poured out in our hearts through the Holy Spirit which has been given to us* (Rom 5:5).

32. Nothing is more excellent than this gift of God. This alone is what distinguishes between the sons of the eternal kingdom and the sons of eternal perdition. Other endowments too are given through the Spirit,[74] but without charity they are of no use. Unless therefore the Holy Spirit is imparted to someone to make him a lover of God and neighbor, he cannot transfer from the left hand to the right.[75] Why is the Spirit distinctively called gift? Only because of the love without which the man who has not got it, though he speak with the tongues of men and of angels, is booming bronze and a clashing cymbal; and if he has prophecy and knows all mysteries[76] and all knowledge and has all faith so as to move mountains, it is nothing; and if he distributes all his substance, and if he gives over his body to burn, it does him no good.[77] What a great good must it be then, without which such great goods cannot bring anyone to eternal life! But if a man has this love or charity (they are two names for one thing), and does not speak with tongues or have prophecy or know all mysteries and all knowledge or distribute all his property to the poor, either because he has not got any to distribute or because he is prevented by some family obligation, it brings him home to the kingdom; yes, even faith is only rendered of any use for this purpose by charity. Faith there can indeed be without charity, but it cannot be of any use. That is why even the apostle Paul[78] says, *In Christ Jesus neither circumcision nor foreskin is of any value, but faith which works through love* (Gal 5:6); in this way he distinguishes it from the faith with which even the demons believe and tremble.[79] So the love which is from God and is God is distinctively the Holy Spirit; through him the charity of God is poured out in our hearts,[80] and through it the whole triad dwells in us. This is the reason why it is most apposite that the Holy Spirit, while being God, should also be called the gift of God. And this gift, surely, is distinctively to be understood as being the charity which brings us through to God, without which no other gift of God at all can bring us through to God.

33. But must we also prove this, that the Holy Spirit is called the gift of God in the sacred writings? If this is expected of us, we have in the gospel according to John the words of the Lord[81] Christ saying, *If anyone is thirsty, let him come to me and drink. Whoever believes in me, as scripture says, rivers of living water shall flow from his belly.* Then the evangelist goes on to add: *This he said of the Spirit which those who believed in him were going to receive* (Jn 7:37). That is

why the apostle Paul as well says, *And we were all given one Spirit to drink* (1 Cor 12:13). But what we are asking is whether this water which is the Holy Spirit is called the gift of God. Now just as we find here that this water is the Holy Spirit, so do we find elsewhere in the same gospel that this water is called the gift of God. When the same Lord was talking to the Samaritan woman at the well, and had said to her, *Give me a drink,* and she had answered that Jews did not mix with Samaritans, *Jesus answered and said to her, If you knew the gift of God and who it is that says to you, Give me a drink, you would perhaps have asked him and he would have given you living water. The woman said to him, Sir, you have nothing to draw with, and the well is deep. So where can you get living water from?* etc. *Jesus answered and said to her, Everyone who drinks of this water will be thirsty again; but whoever drinks of the water which I shall give him will not be thirsty ever, but the water which I shall give him shall become in him a fountain of water leaping up into eternal life* (Jn 4:7-14). Thus because this living water is the Holy Spirit, as the evangelist explained it, there can be no doubt that the Holy Spirit is the gift of God of which the Lord says here, *If you knew the gift of God and who it is that says to you, Give me a drink, you would perhaps have asked him and he would have given you living water.* In the other place he says, *Rivers of living water shall flow from his belly* (Jn 7:38); and it is the same as what he says here, *It shall become in him a fountain of living water leaping up into eternal life.*

34. Then there is the apostle Paul: *To each one of us,* he says, *is given grace according to the measure of the donation of Christ;* and to show that the donation of Christ is the Holy Spirit he went on to add, *That is why it says, he ascended on high, he took captivity captive, he gave gifts to men* (Eph 4:7). But it is public knowledge that when the Lord Jesus had ascended to heaven after his resurrection from the dead he gave the Holy Spirit; and being filled with it those who believed began to speak with the tongues of all peoples.[82] And do not let it worry you that he says "gifts," not "gift." He was quoting the text from a psalm, and what we read in the psalm is, *you have ascended on high, you have taken captivity captive, you have received gifts among men* (Ps 68:18). This is the reading of most codices, especially the Greek ones, and we have it translated like this from the Hebrew. So the apostle said "gifts" just as the prophet did, not "gift"; but while the prophet said "You have received them among men," the apostle preferred to say "he has given them to men," in order that we might get the fullest meaning[83] from both statements, the one prophetic the other apostolic, since each has the authority of the divine utterance behind it. Each after all is true, both that he has given to men and that he has received among men. He has given to men as the head to its members; he in turn of course received among men his members,[84] the members on whose account he cried out from heaven, *Saul, Saul, why are you persecuting me* (Acts 9:4)?; the members of whom he said, *When you did it to one of the least of mine, you did it to me* (Mt 25:40). So this Christ both gave from heaven and received on earth. But now both of them said "gifts," both the prophet and the apostle, because through the gift which the Holy Spirit is in common for all the members of Christ, many gifts which

are proper to them severally are divided among them. They do not each have all the gifts, but these have some and those have others, although all have the gift by which their special gifts are distributed to each, that is the Holy Spirit. Elsewhere he mentions many gifts, and then says, *All these does one and the same Spirit achieve, distributing them severally to each as he wills* (1 Cor 12:2). The same word is found in the Letter to the Hebrews, where it is written, *God bearing witness with signs and portents and various mighty deeds and distribution of the Holy Spirit* (Heb 2:4). In this place too, after saying *he ascended on high, he took captivity captive, he gave gifts to men,* he goes on, *But that he ascended, what is it but that he also descended into the lower parts of the earth? He who descended is the one who ascended above all the heavens that he might fill all things; and he gave some to be apostles, some evangelists, some shepherds and teachers* (Eph 4:8-11). So there you have the reason why he talked about gifts. Just as he says elsewhere, *Are all of us apostles, are all prophets?* etc. (1 Cor 12:9), so here he added *for the perfection of the saints toward the work of the ministry, for the building up of the body of Christ* (Eph 4:2). This is the house which as the psalm declaims[85] is being built after the captivity, because it is from those who have been delivered from the devil by whom they were held captive that the body[86] of Christ is built; and this house is called the Church. And he took this captivity captive by conquering the devil. To stop him from dragging down to eternal punishment with himself those who were going to be members of the holy head, he first bound him with the bonds of justice and then with those of power.[87] So it is the devil who is called the captivity which was taken captive by him who ascended on high and gave gifts to men or received them among men.[88]

35. What the apostle Peter said we can read in that canonical book in which the Acts of the Apostles are recorded; speaking about Christ to the Jews who were moved in their hearts and saying, *What shall we do, brothers? Show us,* he said to them, *Repent, and let each one of you be baptized in the name of*[89] *Jesus Christ for the forgiveness of sins, and you shall receive the gift of the Holy Spirit* (Acts 2:37). Again, we read in the same book that Simon the magician wanted to give the apostles money in order to receive power from them by which the Holy Spirit might be given through the imposition of his hands. Peter again answered him, *Your money go with you to perdition, because you have reckoned on acquiring the gift of God for money* (Acts 8:18). There is another place in the same book where Peter was speaking to Cornelius and his people, telling them the good news and proclaiming Christ to them, and scripture says, *While Peter was still speaking these words the Holy Spirit fell upon all who were listening to the word, and the faithful of the circumcision who had come with Peter were astounded, because the gift of the Holy Spirit was poured out among the nations also. They could hear them speaking with tongues and magnifying God* (Acts 10:44). Then afterward Peter was giving the brethren at Jerusalem, who were worried about the matter, an explanation of his action in baptizing the uncircumcised, and saying that it was because the Holy Spirit had cut the knot of this particular question by coming upon them before they were baptized, and

he said, *When I had begun to talk to them the Holy Spirit fell on them as he did on us at the beginning, and I remembered the word of the Lord, how he had said that John indeed baptized with water, but you shall be baptized with the Holy Spirit. If therefore he has given the same gift to them as to us who believed in the Lord Jesus Christ, who was I to be able to forbid God to give them the Holy Spirit* (Acts 11:15)? And there is a lot more scriptural evidence which all conspires to prove that the Holy Spirit is the gift of God, in that he is given to those who love God through him. But it would take far too long to collect it all. And what could satisfy people anyway, if they are not satisfied by the evidence I have quoted?

36. Insofar as people do now see that the Holy Spirit is called the gift of God, they must realize of course that when they hear the phrase "the gift of the Holy Spirit" they are to recognize the same figure of speech as in the phrase "in the stripping of the body of flesh."[90] Just as the body of flesh is nothing but flesh, so the gift of the Holy Spirit is nothing but the Holy Spirit. So he is the gift of God insofar as he is given to those he is given to. But in himself he is God even if he is not given to anyone, because he was God, co-eternal with the Father and the Son, even before he was given to anyone. Nor is he less than they because they give and he is given. He is given as God's gift in such a way that as God he also gives himself. You can scarcely say he is not his own master,[91] the one of whom it is said, *The Spirit breathes where he will* (Jn 3:8), and in the text of the apostle's we have quoted above, *All these things does one and the same Spirit achieve, distributing them severally to each as he wills* (1 Cor 12:11). In this case there is no question of the subject condition of the one given and the ownership rights of the givers, but simply of the unanimity of the one given and the givers.

37. As[92] then holy scripture proclaims that charity is God,[93] and as it is from God and causes us to abide in God and him in us,[94] and as we know this because he has given us of his Spirit, this Spirit of his is God charity. Again, if there is nothing greater than charity among God's gifts, and if there is no greater gift of God's than the Holy Spirit, what must we conclude but that he is this charity which is called both God and from God? And if the charity by which the Father loves the Son and the Son loves the Father inexpressibly shows forth the communion of them both, what more suitable than he who is the common Spirit of them both should be distinctively called charity? This, surely, is the most sensible way for us to believe or understand the matter, that the Holy Spirit is not alone in that triad in being charity, but that there is a good reason for distinctively calling him charity, as shown above. In the same way he is not alone in that triad in being either holy or spirit, because the Father too is holy and the Son too is holy, and the Father too is spirit and the Son too is spirit, a truth about which piety can have no hesitations; and yet he is distinctively called the Holy Spirit, and with good reason. Because he is common to them both, he is called distinctively what they are called in common.

Otherwise, if the Holy Spirit alone in that triad is charity, it will immediately follow that the Son is found to be the Son, not of the Father alone but of the

Holy Spirit as well. It is said of him in countless places that he is the only-begotten Son of the Father, but without prejudice to the truth of what the apostle says about God the Father: *Who snatched us from the power of darkness and transported us into the kingdom of the Son of his charity* (Col 1:13). He did not say "of his Son," though it would have been absolutely true if he had said it, because it was absolutely true on the many occasions when he did say it; but he said "the Son of his charity." So he is also the Son of the Holy Spirit, if the Holy Spirit alone in that triad is the charity of God. If on the other hand this is an absurd conclusion, it can only mean that it is not the Holy Spirit alone who is charity there, but that for reasons I have sufficiently discussed he is distinctively so called. As for the expression "Son of his charity," it means no more than "His beloved Son," no more in the last resort than "Son of his substance." For the charity of the Father in his inexpressibly simple nature is nothing but his very nature and substance, as we have often said already and are not tired of often repeating. And thus "the Son of his charity" signifies none other than the one who is born of his substance.

38. All this goes to show how ridiculous the logic of Eunomius is, the father of the Eunomian heretics.[95] He was unable to understand and unwilling to believe that the only-begotten Word of God through whom all things were made[96] is the Son of God by nature, that is, he is begotten of the substance of the Father; and so he said that he is not the Son of the nature or substance or being of God but the Son of his will. He wished of course to assert that the will by which God begot the Son is something accidental to him, on the grounds apparently that we sometimes will something that we were not willing before—as though this were not proof of the changeableness of our nature, a thing we could not possibly believe to be the case in God. The only reason it is written *Many are the thoughts in the heart of a man, but the counsel of the Lord abides for ever* (Prv 19:21) is to make us understand (or at least believe) that just as God is eternal so is his counsel eternal, and therefore unchangeable just as he himself is. What can be said of thoughts can be said with equal truth about wishes: "Many are the wishes in the heart of man, but the will of the Lord abides for ever." To avoid saying that the only-begotten Word is the Son of the Father's counsel or will,[97] some have said that this Word simply is the counsel or will of the Father. But I consider it better to call him counsel from counsel and will from will, just as he is substance from substance, wisdom from wisdom; or we shall find ourselves in the absurdity we have often refuted of saying that the Son makes the Father wise or willing, if the Father does not have counsel or will in his own substance.

But now this heretic once cunningly asked whether God begot his Son willingly or unwillingly. If you answer "Unwillingly," then the point he intended to make follows this unbeatable argument, namely that he is not Son by nature but by will. But someone gave him a very shrewd answer; he was wide awake enough to ask him in turn whether God the Father is willingly or unwillingly God. If he answered "Unwillingly" the consequence would be an even more total divine unhappiness, which it would be the height of lunacy to believe about God; and if he said "Willingly" he could be answered, "Therefore he is God by will and not by nature." What remained for him then but to shut up, and see that his own question had tied him in an insoluble knot? But if any person in the trinity is to be distinctively called the will of God, this name like charity fits the Holy Spirit more than the others. What else after all is charity but the will?

39. I see that in this book I have been arguing about the Holy Spirit according to the scriptures;[98] and it should be enough for the faithful who already believe that the Holy Spirit is God and not of a different substance nor less than the Father and the Son, which we established as true according to the same scriptures in earlier books.[99] As far as we could, we have also used the creation which God made to remind those who ask for reasons in such matters[100] that as far as they can they should descry his invisible things by understanding them through the things that are made,[101] and especially through the rational or intellectual creature which is made to the image of God; so that through this, as a kind of mirror, as far as they can and if they can, they might perceive in our memory, understanding and will that God is a trinity. Anyone who has a lively intuition of these three (as divinely established in the nature of his mind) and of how great a thing it is that his mind has that by which even the eternal and unchanging nature can be recalled, beheld and desired—it is recalled by memory, beheld by intelligence, embraced by love—has thereby found the image of that supreme trinity. To the memory, sight, and love of this supreme trinity, in order to recollect it, see it, and enjoy it, he should refer every ounce and particle of his life. But I have sufficiently warned him, so it seems to me, that this image, made by the trinity and altered for the worse by its own fault, is not so to be compared to that trinity that it is reckoned similar to it in every respect. Rather, he should note how great the dissimilarity is in whatever similarity there may be.

Chapter 6

The author concludes his examination of the dissimilarity of the image trinity to the divine Trinity with some general observations, not peculiar to either of the divine processions or any of the divine persons; then commends the image trinity, for all its inadequacy, as a means of access to communion with the divine; and finally reverts as a kind of afterthought to the problem of why the Holy Spirit is not said to be born, though he proceeds from the Father; and the only reason he can find for this is that the Holy Spirit also proceeds from the Son as well as from the Father.

40. Certainly I have been trying as best I could to delineate God the Father and God the Son—that is God the begetter, who in his Word co-eternal with himself somehow or other uttered all that he has substantially, and God this Word of his, who also substantially has neither more nor less than what is in him who begot him as a true and not a false Word—I have been trying to

delineate all this, not as it might already be seen *face to face* (1 Cor 13:12), but as it might be seen by whatever kind of limited inference from this likeness *in a puzzle* (1 Cor 13:12), which we find in the memory and understanding of our mind. In this likeness I have been attributing to memory all that we know even though we are not thinking about it, and to intelligence in the proper sense a kind of formation of thought. It is when we think about something we have found to be true that we are primarily said to understand it; and then we deposit it again in the memory. But there are more hidden depths in our memory, where we found this thing even when we thought about it for the first time,[102] and where the innermost word is born that does not belong to any language—born as knowledge from knowledge and sight from sight, and as understanding which is manifested in thought from understanding which was already lurking, but hidden, in memory; although if even thought did not have some kind of memory of its own, it would never return to things it had deposited in the memory when it started to think about something else.

41. As far as the Holy Spirit is concerned, the only thing I pointed to in this puzzle as seeming to be like him is our will, or love or esteem,[103] which is will at its most effective—because of course our will, which is implanted in us by nature, has various moods according as it is involved with, or comes up against, things that either attract or repel us. What is the position then? Are we to say that when our will is right it does not know what to go for and what to avoid? But if it knows, then it thereby has its own kind of knowledge, and this cannot exist without memory and understanding. Should we really even listen to some-one who says that charity, which *does not act mistakenly* (1 Cor 13:4),[104] does not know what it is doing? So, just as there is understanding and just as there is love in that primordial function of memory[105] in which we find everything we can come at by thinking filed and ready (because we found these two there when we found by thinking that we both understood something and loved it, and they were there even when we were not thinking about it); and just as there is memory and there is love in this understanding which takes form with thought and which we utter as a true word independent of any nation's language when we utter what we know (because the gaze of our thought only goes back to something by remembering, and only bothers to go back to it by loving); so too the love which joins together the sight settled in memory and the sight of thought that is formed from it, as parent and offspring, would not know what to love rightly unless it had some knowledge of desiring things, which it could not have without memory or understanding.

42. But when these three things are found in one person, such as man is, someone could well say to us: "These three, memory, understanding and love, are mine, not their own; and whatever they do, they do it for me and not for themselves—or rather, I do it through them. It is I who remember with memory, understand with understanding, love with love. And when I turn the focus of my thought onto memory, and thus utter in my heart what I know, and a true word is begotten of my knowledge, each is mine—both the knowledge, that is to say, and the word. For it is I who know, I who utter what I know in my heart.

And when by thinking I find that I already understand, already love something in my memory, and that this understanding and love were there even before I thought about it, I find my understanding and my love in my memory, where it is I who understand, I who love, not they. Again, when my thought remembers and wishes to go back to what it had deposited in the memory, and on understanding it to observe it and utter it inwardly, it remembers with my memory and wishes with my will, not its own. My love too, when it remembers and understands what it ought to go for and what to avoid, remembers with my memory, not its own; and with my understanding, not its own, it understands whatever it understandingly loves."

To put it in a nutshell we can say: "It is I who remember, I who understand, I who love with all three of these things—I who am not either memory or understanding or love, but have them." This can indeed be said by one person who has these things and is not himself these three things. But in the simplicity of that supreme nature which is God, although God is one the persons are three, Father and Son and Holy Spirit. So the trinity as a thing in itself is quite different from the image of the trinity in another thing. It is on account of this image that the thing in which these three are found is also simultaneously called image;[106] just as a canvas and what is painted on it are both called an image, but the canvas is only called an image simultaneously on account of the picture which is on it.

43. But such is the inseparability that reigns in that supreme trinity which incomparably surpasses all things, that while a triad of men cannot be called a man, that triad is called, and is, one God. Nor is it a triad in one God—it *is* one God. Nor is that triad like this image, man, which is one person *having* those three things; on the contrary, it *is* three persons, the Father of the Son and the Son of the Father and the Spirit of the Father and the Son. It is true that man's memory (and particularly the kind of memory which animals do not have, in which intelligible things are contained that have not come into it through the senses of the body) has in its own little way some sort of likeness in this image trinity to the Father, however immeasurably inadequate the likeness may be. Again it is true that man's understanding, which is formed from memory by directing thought onto it when what is known is uttered, and which is an inner word of no particular language, has in its enormous inequality some kind of likeness to the Son; and that man's love, proceeding from knowledge and joining memory and understanding together, as being itself common to parent and offspring (which is why it cannot be itself regarded as either parent or offspring) has in this image some likeness, though a vastly unequal one, to the Holy Spirit. And yet, while in this image of the trinity these three *are* not one man but *belong to* one man, it is not likewise the case in that supreme trinity of which this is the image that those three belong to one God: they *are* one God and they *are* three persons, not one.

It is certainly a marvelously inexpressible and an inexpressibly marvelous thing that while this image of the trinity is one person and that supreme trinity is three persons, that trinity of three persons should still be more inseparable than this trinity of one. In the nature of divinity, or of the deity if you prefer it,[107] that triad is what this nature is, and is unchangeable and always equal within itself; nor was it some time not or some time different. But these three in the unequal image may not indeed be separated from each other by space, since they are not bodies, yet now in this life they are separated among themselves by their respective "sizes." Just because there is no physical mass involved, it does not mean that we do not see that memory is bigger in one man than under-standing, in another the other way round; that in a third both these are surpassed in size by love, whether the two of them are equal to each other or not.[108] And thus the lesser are outweighed by the greater, whether it is two by one or one by two or one by another. And even when the time comes that they are equal to each other, cured of all weakness, even then it will not be possible to equate with a thing unchangeable by nature a thing that is freed from change by grace, because creature is not to be equated with creator; and in any case, when it is cured of all weakness it will change.

44. But when the sight comes that is promised us *face to face* (1 Cor 13:12), we shall see this trinity that is not only incorporeal but also supremely in-separable and truly unchangeable much more clearly and definitely than we now see its image which we ourselves are. However, those who do see through this mirror and in this puzzle,[109] as much as it is granted to see in this life, are not those who merely observe in their own minds what we have discussed and suggested, but those who see it precisely as an image, so that they can in some fashion refer what they see to that of which it is an image, and also see that other by inference through its image which they see by observation, since they cannot see it *face to face*. For the apostle did not say "We see now in a mirror," but *We see*[110] *by a mirror* (1 Cor 13:12).

So those who see their mind insofar as it can be seen, and in it this trinity which I have discussed from many angles as best I could, but do not believe or understand it to be the image of God, see indeed a mirror, but are so far from seeing by the mirror the one who now can only be seen by a mirror, that they do not even know the mirror they see *is* a mirror, that is to say an image. If they did know this, they would doubtless perceive that the one whose mirror it is should be looked for in it, and seen in it for the time being, at least to some extent. Faith unfeigned[111] would be purifying their hearts[112] in order that the one who is now being seen in a mirror might one day be seen face to face. But by despising this faith that purifies hearts, what are they doing in understanding the nature of the human mind, with their subtle discussions about it, but condemning themselves on the very evidence of their own understanding? For in their exercise of it they would certainly not meet the difficulties they do, only reaching any certitude with the greatest labor, unless they were wrapped in a penal darkness and burdened with a corruptible body that weighs down the soul.[113] And what can have deserved the infliction of such an evil, when all is said and done, but sin? So, warned by the magnitude of such an evil they ought to follow the Lamb *who takes away the sin of the world* (Rv 14:4; Jn 1:29).

As for those who belong to him, though they may be far less intelligent and talented than these people, the jealous powers who slew the Lamb though he owed no debt of sin, and whom he overcame by the justice of his blood before doing so by the might of his power,[114] have no rights over them to hold them in bondage, once they are released from the body at the end of this life. Thus freed from the power of the devil, they are taken up by the holy angels, delivered by *the mediator between God and men, the man Christ Jesus* (1 Tm 2:5). For as the divine scriptures agree in declaring, both the old which foretell Christ and the new which tell of him, *There is no other name under heaven by which men may be saved* (Acts 4:12). Cleansed from all infection of corruption, they are established in tranquil abodes until they get their bodies back—but incorruptible bodies now, which will be their guerdon, not their burden.[115] For it is the decree of the most wise and excellent creator that the spirit of the man who is devoutly subject to God would have his own body blissfully subject to himself, and that this bliss should continue without end.

45. There we shall see the truth without any difficulty, and enjoy it in all its clarity and certitude. There, there will be nothing for us to seek with the reasonings of the mind, but we will perceive by direct contemplation why the Holy Spirit is not a son, though he proceeds from the Father. In that light the question will not arise. But here I have been acutely conscious of the enormous difficulty of the effort to perceive this, and I have no doubt that my careful and intelligent readers will be equally conscious of it. So great has this difficulty been, that every time I wanted to bring out some comparative illustration of this point in that created reality which we are, having promised in the second book of this work that I would talk about the matter later on,[116] I found that no adequate expression followed whatever understanding I came to; and I was only too well aware that my attempt even to understand involved more effort than result. In the one person which a man is I did indeed find an image of that supreme trinity; and it was my purpose, above all in the ninth book, to point out those three[117] in a changeable object, to enable us the more easily to comprehend them as deployed through intervals of time. And yet the three things of one person were quite unable to match those three persons in the way our human plan requires, as we have been demonstrating in this fifteenth book.

In any case, in that supreme trinity which God is there are no intervals of time by which it could be shown, or even asked, whether the Son was first born from the Father, and afterward the Holy Spirit proceeded from them both, seeing that the holy scripture calls him the Spirit of them both. It is he, after all, of whom the apostle says, *But because you are sons, God sent the Spirit of his Son into our*[118] *hearts* (Gal 4:6); and it is he of whom the Son says, *For it is not you who speak, but the Spirit of your Father who speaks in you* (Mt 10:20). And many other texts of the divine utterances can be brought in evidence to prove that the one who is properly called in the trinity the Holy Spirit is the Spirit of the Father and the Son; the Son himself says of him, *whom I shall send you from the Father* (Jn 15:26), and in another place, *whom the Father will send in my name* (Jn 14:26). He is proved to proceed from each of them, because the Son himself says, *he proceeds from the Father* (Jn 15:26); and then after rising from the dead and appearing to the disciples, *he breathed on them and said, Receive the Holy Spirit* (Jn 20:22) in order to show that the Spirit too is the virtue which went out of him, as we read in the gospel, and healed them all.[119]

46. As for the reason why he first gave the Holy Spirit on earth after his resurrection and then sent him from heaven, I think it is because charity is poured out in our hearts through this gift, charity by which we are to love God and neighbor according to those two commandments on which the whole law depends and the prophets.[120] It was to signify this that the Lord Jesus gave the Holy Spirit twice, once on earth for love of neighbor, and again from heaven for love of God. Some other reason could doubtless be found for the double giving of the Holy Spirit; but that it was the same Spirit[121] given when Jesus breathed on them as he mentioned shortly afterward when he said, *Go and baptize*[122] *the nations in the name of the Father and of the Son and of the Holy Spirit* (Mt 28:19), the text which presents this trinity to us the most plainly, that is something we should not have the slightest hesitation about. So he it is who was also given from heaven on the day of Pentecost, that is ten days after the Lord had ascended into heaven.

How then can he who gives the Holy Spirit not be God? Indeed, how much must he who gives God be God! None of his disciples ever gave the Holy Spirit; they prayed that he might come upon those on whom they laid hands, they did not give him themselves. The Church in its bishops still observes this custom. Finally, when Simon the magician offered the apostles money, he did not say, *Give me this power that* "I might give the Holy Spirit," but that *whomever I lay hands on might receive the Holy Spirit* (Acts 8:19). for scripture had just said, not "Simon seeing that the apostles were giving the Holy Spirit," but *Simon seeing that the Holy Spirit was given through the laying on of hands by the apostles* (Acts 8:18).

That is why the Lord Jesus himself not only gave the Holy Spirit as God but also received him as man, and for that reason he was called *full of grace* (Jn 1:14). It is written of him more openly in the Acts of the Apostles, *that God anointed him with the Holy Spirit* (Acts 10:38), not of course with a visible oil but with the gift of grace which is signified by the chrism the Church anoints the baptized with. Nor, to be sure, was Christ only anointed with the Holy Spirit when the dove came down upon him at his baptism;[123] what he was doing then was graciously prefiguring his body, that is his Church, in which it is particularly those who have just been baptized that receive the Holy Spirit. But we must realize that he was anointed with this mystical and invisible anointing when the Word of God became flesh, that is when a human nature without any antecedent merits of good works was coupled to the Word of God in the virgin's womb so as to become one person with him. This is why we confess that he was born of the Holy Spirit and the virgin Mary.[124] It would be the height of absurdity to believe that he only received the Holy Spirit when he was already thirty years old—that was the age at which he was baptized by John;[125] no, we must believe that just as he came to that[126] baptism without any sin, so he came to it not without the Holy Spirit. If it is written of his servant and forerunner John, *he shall be filled with the Holy Spirit even from his mother's womb* (Lk 1:15), because although he was engendered by his father he received the Holy Spirit once he was formed in the womb, what are we to understand or believe about the human being Christ, the actual conception of whose flesh was not fleshly but spiritual? In another text, where it is written of him that he received the promised Holy Spirit from the Father and poured it out,[127] both his natures are indicated, that is to say the human and the divine. He received it as man, he poured it out as God. As for us, we can receive this gift in our own small way, but we certainly cannot pour it out upon others. That this might happen, though, we invoke over them the God by whom it is done.

47. So then, can we even ask whether the Holy Spirit had proceeded already from the Father when the Son was born, or whether he had not yet done so, and only once the Son had been born did he proceed from them both, seeing that there is no such thing as time in that sphere? We were able to ask this kind of question where we found that will proceeds first in time[128] from the human mind to look for something which when found might be called offspring; and when this[129] was already brought forth or begotten, that earlier will was perfected by resting in it as in its end, and so what had begun as a questioning appetite ended as an enjoying love which now proceeded from both, that is from the begetting mind and the begotten notion, as from parent and offspring. Such a question cannot possibly be asked where nothing begins in time, so as to be completed in the time that follows. Therefore anyone who can understand the generation of the Son from the Father as timeless should also understand the procession of the Holy Spirit from them both as timeless. And anyone who can understand that when the Son said, *As the Father has life in himself, so he has given the Son to have life in himself* (Jn 5:26), he did not mean that the Father gave life to the Son already existing without life, but that he begot him timelessly in such a way that the life which the Father gave the Son by begetting him is co-eternal with the life of the Father who gave it, should also understand that just as the Father has it in himself that the Holy Spirit should proceed from him, so he gave to the Son that the Holy Spirit should proceed from him too, and in both cases timelessly; and thus that to say that the Holy Spirit proceeding from the Son is something which the Son has from the Father. If the Son has everything that he has from the Father, he clearly has from the Father that the Holy Spirit should proceed from him. But one must not think of any time in this matter, which would include before and after, because there is absolutely no such thing as time there at all.

Clearly then it would be the height of absurdity to call the Holy Spirit the son of them both, since just as generation from the Father bestows being on the Son without any beginning in time, without any changeableness of nature, so does procession from them both bestow being on the Holy Spirit without any beginning in time, without any changeableness in nature.[130] For the reason why we do not dare to call the Holy Spirit unbegotten, even though we do not say that he was begotten, is to avoid the suggestion this term might convey of there being two Fathers in that trinity, or two who are not from another. The Father alone is not from another, and therefore he alone is called unbegotten, not indeed in the scriptures but in the conventional usage of those who discuss the matter and employ such language as they are able to in so deep a mystery. But the Son is born of the Father and the Holy Spirit proceeds from the Father principally,[131] and by the Father's wholly timeless gift from both of them jointly. He would be called son of the Father and of the Son if both of them begot him, which is repugnant to the feelings of all sane people. So he is not begotten by either of them, but he proceeds from each of them as the Spirit of them both.

48. It still remains of course extremely difficult to distinguish generation from procession in that co-eternal and equal and incorporeal and inexpressibly unchangeable trinity. So I hope it will suffice those who cannot stretch their minds any further over the matter to read what I said about it in a sermon preached to the Christian people, which I later had written down. Among other things, I had been teaching from the evidence of the holy scriptures that the Holy Spirit proceeds from them both. I then went on to say:

So if the Holy Spirit proceeds from both the Father and the Son, why did the Son say *he proceeds from the Father* (Jn 15:26)? Why indeed, do you suppose, unless it was the way he was accustomed to refer even what was his very own to him from whom he had his very self?—for example, that other thing he said, *My teaching is not mine but his who sent me* (Jn 7:16). If in this case we can accept that it is his teaching, which he says however is not his but the Father's, how much more should we accept in our other case that the Holy Spirit also proceeds from him, seeing that he said, *he proceeds from the Father*, without also saying "he does not proceed from me"? He from whom the Son has it that he is God—for he is God from God—is of course also the one from whom he has it that the Holy Spirit proceeds from him as well; and thus the Holy Spirit too has it from the Father that he should also proceed from the Son as he proceeds from the Father. Here we begin to see some sort of reason, as far as people like us can understand it, why the Holy Spirit is not said to be born but rather to proceed. For if he too were called Son he would be called the Son of them both, which is the height of absurdity. The only two that anyone is the son of are father and mother. It is unthinkable we should imagine any such thing between God the Father and God the Son; for in any case a son of human beings does not proceed from his father and mother simultaneously, but when he proceeds from his father into his mother he does not then proceed from his mother, and when he proceeds from his mother into the light of day he does not then proceed from his father. But the Holy Spirit does not proceed from the Father into the Son and then proceed from the Son to sanctify the creature. He proceeds simultaneously from them both, even though the Father gave the Son that the Spirit should proceed from him as he does from himself. Nor can we say that the Holy Spirit is not life, while the Father is life and the Son is life. And thus just as the Father, while having life in himself, also gave the Son to have life in himself, so he gave him that life should proceed from him as it proceeds from himself.[132]

I have transcribed this from that sermon into this book but of course I am not addressing unbelievers in this passage but believers.[133]

49. But if these people are not quite capable of observing this image and of seeing in what way these three things in their mind are true, which are not three like three persons but belong all three to man who is one person; why in that case do they not rather believe what is to be found in the sacred writings about that supreme trinity which God is, instead of demanding the most stringent proof to be given them, which in any case the human mind in its slowness and weakness could not grasp? And when they have placed their unshakable trust in the holy scriptures as the truest of witnesses, let them pray and seek and live rightly, and in this way take steps to understand, that is to be able to see with the mind, as far as it can be seen, what they hold on faith. Who is to stop them doing this? Indeed who would not encourage them to do this? But if they suppose that these truths are to be denied because they cannot observe them with their blind minds, then people who are blind from birth should deny that there is such a thing as the sun. So the light shines in the darkness,[134] and if as darkness they do not comprehend it, let them first be enlightened by God's gift and become believers, and begin to be light in comparison with unbelievers; and after laying this foundation, let them build themselves up to see the things, which they now believe in order that one day they may be able to see them. Some things which we believe are such that they simply cannot now be seen at all. Christ is never going to be seen on the cross again; but unless we believe that he was once so to be seen, in a manner in which there would be no expectation of seeing him again, we shall not come to see Christ as he is to be seen forever. But as far as concerns that supreme, inexpressible, incorporeal and unchangeable nature and the perception of it in some measure or other by the understanding, there is nothing on which the human mind could better practice its gaze (provided of course that it is governed by the rule of faith) than on that which man has in his nature that is better than other animals, better even than the other parts of his own soul; and this is the mind to which has been allotted a kind of power to see invisible things, and to which the senses of the body also bring all things for judgment as it presides, so to say, in the innermost and uppermost place of honor, and which has nothing above it to whose government it is subject except God.

Epilogue

The author first addresses his soul in a soliloquy, and then concludes the work with a prayer to God.

50. But you, O my soul, among all these things that I have said about that supreme trinity—and I dare not claim that any of them is worthy of this unimaginable mystery, but must rather confess that his knowledge is too wonderful for me and has been too mighty and I have not been capable of

it[135]—where do you perceive that you are among all these things, where do you lie or where do you stand until all your sicknesses are healed by him who has shown himself gracious to all your iniquities?[136] You certainly realize that you are in that tavern to which that Samaritan brought the man he found half-dead from the many wounds inflicted on him by robbers.[137] And yet you have seen many true things, and I do not mean with these eyes which see colored bodies, but the ones the man was praying about who said, *Let my eyes see justice* (Ps 17:11). So then, you have seen many true things, and distinguished between them and the light by which you have seen them. Lift up your eyes to that light and fix them on that if you can. Thus you will see how the birth of the Word of God differs from the procession of the gift of God; which is the reason why the only-begotten Son said that the Holy Spirit proceeds from the Father,[138] not that he is begotten of him; otherwise he would be his own brother. And hence while the Spirit of them both is a kind of consubstantial communion of Father and Son, he is not (it is just unthinkable) called the Son of them both. But you are unable to fix your gaze there in order to observe this clearly and distinctly. You cannot do it, I know. I am telling the truth, I am telling it to myself, I know what I cannot do. However, this same light has shown you those three things in yourself, in which you can recognize yourself[139] as the image of that supreme trinity on which you are not yet capable of fixing your eyes in contemplation. It has shown you that there is a true word in you when it is begotten of your knowledge, that is when we utter what we know, even if we do not think or speak a meaningful sound in the language of any people; provided our thought is formed from what we know, and the image in thinking attention is completely like the awareness[140] which was already contained in memory, with will or love as the third element joining these two together as parent and offspring. That this will proceeds from awareness—for no one wants anything if he is totally unaware of what it is, or what sort of thing it is—and yet that it is not itself an image of awareness, and that thus in this intelligible case there is suggested a certain difference between birth and procession, because to observe by thought is not the same thing as to desire or even to enjoy by will; that all this is so, let him note and discern who can. You yourself have been able to do this, although you could not and cannot explain in adequate language what you have only seen with difficulty in the thick clouds of body likenesses which never cease to loom up in front of human thoughts.

But that light which is not what you are, also shows you that these bodiless likenesses of bodies are one thing and the truth which we observe with the intelligence when we turn them down is another. These things and others equally certain has that light shown to your inner eyes. What is the reason then that you cannot fix your gaze on it to see it, but weakness obviously; and what brought this weakness on you but wickedness obviously? Who then is to heal all your infirmities but he who is gracious to all your iniquities?[141] So now let us bring this book to a close at last with a prayer in preference to an argument.

Prayer

51. O Lord our God, we believe in you, Father and Son and Holy Spirit. Truth would not have said, *Go and baptize*[142] *the nations in the name of the Father and of the Son and of the Holy Spirit* (Mt 28:19), unless you were a triad. Nor would you have commanded us to be baptized, Lord God, in the name of any who is not Lord God.[143] Nor would it have been said with divine authority, *Hear O Israel, the Lord your God is one God* (Dt 6:4),[144] unless while being a triad you were still one Lord God. And if you, God and Father, were yourself also the Son your Word Jesus Christ, were yourself also your gift the Holy Spirit,[145] we would not read in the documents of truth *God sent his Son* (Gal 4:4), nor would you, only-begotten one, have said of the Holy Spirit, *whom the Father will send in my name* (Jn 14:26), and, *whom I will send you from the Father* (Jn 15:26). Directing my attention toward this rule of faith as best I could, as far as you enabled me to, I have sought you and desired to see intellectually what I have believed, and I have argued much and toiled much. O Lord my God, my one hope,[146] listen to me lest out of weariness I should stop wanting to seek you, but let me seek your face always,[147] and with ardor. Do you yourself give me the strength to seek, having caused yourself to be found and having given me the hope of finding you more and more. Before you lies my strength and my weakness; preserve the one, heal the other. Before you lies my knowledge and my ignorance; where you have opened to me, receive me as I come in; where you have shut to me, open to me as I knock.[148] Let me remember you, let me understand you, let me love you. Increase these things in me until you refashion me entirely.

I know that it is written, *In much speaking you will not avoid sin* (Prv 10:19). If only I only spoke when preaching your word and praising you! Not only would I avoid sin, I would acquire good merit, however much I spoke like that. Nor would a man blessed by you have enjoined a sin upon his own son in the faith, to whom he wrote to say, *Preach the word, be urgent in season, out of season* (2 Tm 4:2). Can it be said that this man did not speak much, who did not keep quiet about your word out of season, let alone in season? But perhaps it was not really much, because it was so necessary. Deliver me, my God, from the much speaking which I suffer from inwardly in my soul, which is so wretched in your sight and flies to your mercy for refuge. My thoughts are not silent even when my voice is. And of course, if I thought nothing but what is pleasing to you, I would not ask you to deliver me from this much speaking. But many of my thoughts are of the kind of which *you know the thoughts of men that they are vain* (Ps 94:11). Grant me not to consent to them, and if ever they delight me grant that I may reject them and not linger over them in a kind of doze. Let them not so prevail over me that any action of mine proceeds from them, but let my judgment at least be preserved from them, and my conscience, with you to preserve me. A wise man was speaking of you in his book which is now called Sirach as its proper name, and he said, *We say many things and do not attain, and the sum of our words is, he is all things* (Sir 43:27).[149] So when we do attain to you, there will be an end to these many things which we say and do not attain, and you will remain one, yet all in all, and we shall say one thing praising you in unison, even ourselves being also made one in you.

O Lord the one God, God the Trinity, whatsoever I have said in these books is of you, may those that are yours acknowledge; whatsoever of myself alone, do you and yours forgive.[150]

Amen.

NOTES

1. *Poterit*; M *poterat*, could.

2. The line of reasoning seems to be: as the three operate inseparably, the Father sending the Son cannot mean his sending him to do a job for him which he was not personally performing himself; and that is the kind of sending that implies the subordination of the one sent.

3. *De Trinitate*, II, 1, 1 (PL 10, 51).

4. See below, section 10, note 14.

5. He will say in the paragraph after next just what he means by God sensing things.

6. See Jn 4:24.

7. See 1 Tm 6:16.

8. Reading *speciosus* with M; CCL has *speciosius* with most manuscripts, but it seems an obvious scribal slip, caused by the word occurring in the next sentence.

9. Against those like Tertullian who thought that "non-bodily" meant the same as "non-substantial," hence non-real, a mere abstraction.

10. Chiefly in Book V.

11. Reading *inaequalia* with M and three manuscripts; CCL has *aequalia*; sense of a sort could be made of this—in God these four are not equal, they are identical. But he has been arguing from their inequality in creatures in favor of choosing "wise"; and having done so he puts in a proviso to remind us that we must not transfer their creaturely connotations to God. The substitution of *non aequalia* for *non inaequalia* could be a pure slip of the pen.

12. Provided, of course, you take "happy" (*beatus*) in the sense he is using it in, which he discussed at great length in Book XIII, 7-9. In this sense no man can be called truly happy this side of heaven.

13. See 1 Cor 1:24.

14. 1 Jn 4:8.16; there is no doubt, as the reader will later perceive, that Augustine took *Deus caritas est* to mean "love is God" just as much as "God is love."

15. See Gn 1:27.

16. See Rom 1:20.

17. See Rom 1:20.

18. Book VIII, 4-5; Book XIV, 26; but the justice of this latter reference seems to me doubtful.

19. For example, Cicero, *Academica Priora* 2, 7, 21.

20. *Habet illa . . . in mente, vel mentem*; M omits *vel mentem*.

21. For example, Cicero, *De Finibus Bonorum et Malorum*, 5, 12, 34.

22. Section 1.

23. *Sibi meminit*; M reads *sui meminit*, remembers himself.

24. It may perhaps help if we summarize the argument of this chapter, which has been a little obscured by the wealth of embellishment Augustine has given it. In essentials he is giving two reasons why in fact we are unable to see the divine trinity intellectually, or descry it through rational inference from creation, or prove it without recourse to the authority of scripture; and the second follows from the first, so that we may indeed say he gives one reason, and that is the absolute simplicity of the divine nature.

Thus we can make a list of divine attributes, inferred from reflection on creation; he gives a list of twelve. But they are reducible to three, and then to one, because they are all identical with the divine being or substance, and hence with each other. Having reduced the twelve to a representative three, he has to admit that of course these three are not the divine trinity we are looking for.

Having further reduced the three to one, which he characteristically makes "wisdom," he goes on to suggest that perhaps we do have a lead into the trinity here, because this divine wisdom must know itself and love itself, as we have seen that the human mind does in its function as image of God. But then comes the second part of his argument; we cannot make wisdom remembering itself into the Father, wisdom understanding itself into the Son, wisdom loving itself into the Holy Spirit; for the three divine persons are not in fact functions of the godhead, as the elements of our mental trinity are functions of our mind. They are the godhead all together, and each of them severally is the godhead. Given the simplicity of the divine substance, this must be so. For the same reason each of the divine persons is wisdom remembering, wisdom understanding, and wisdom loving.

Thus on the authority of revelation, or on the basis of faith, we keep on having to make affirmations about the trinity which cut the ground from under any probative force we may at first feel that our created analogies could be expected to have. It remains true that we cannot *directly* descry all the invisible things of God by understanding them through the things that are made. In the next three chapters he will be asking if we may not perhaps be able to do it *indirectly*, as through a mirror in a puzzling reflection.

25. God's wisdom is simultaneously prudence, by which he knows the future (*prudentia* in the rare sense of *providentia*), and knowledge, by which he knows the past. The whole of this and the next paragraph form a rather odd disgression, which seems little to the point.

26. See Ps 105:4.

27. Throughout this chapter I will translate *per speculum in aenigmate* in this over literal fashion, for a reason that will be obvious to the reader. Elsewhere I have translated "through a puzzling reflection in a mirror."

28. Translated above as "looking . . . in a mirror;" see Book XIV, 23, note 47.

29. Sections 9 and 10; there, in fact, he interprets the text, not "of the whole nature of man," but of the higher, wisdom function of the mind. But here, by "the whole nature of man," he is probably intending to indicate the inclusion of both sexes.

30. *Transformatur*; M reads *transfertur*, with 2 manuscripts, and probably rightly; the relevant phrase runs, in M, *a deformi forma formosam trnsfertur in formam*. The word-play is just tolerable as it stands. I think Augustine is far more likely to have written *transfertur*, which makes a better cursus, and does not overdo that "form"; and it is easy to explain how a copyist could have inadvertently changed it.

31. On the principle of *corruptio optimi pessima*.

32. See 2 Cor 5:7.

33. See 1 Jn 3:2.

34. A liberal education means one in which the liberal arts are taught—that is, skills appropriate to free people. They are opposed to the mechanical arts. They are: grammar, logic, mathematics, music, rhetoric, medicine and astronomy.

35. Section 26; see also Book XII, section 4.

36. Reading *esse*; M with most manuscripts reads *est*, giving the sense; "Both places show this saying to oneself and in one's heart, that is saying by thinking."

37. M adds *recumbens*, reclining.

38. *Etiam*; M reads *autem*, however.

39. This is not etymologically, or even semantically true of the Latin *verbum*, or its English cognate "word," which primarily signify the vocalized utterance; but it is true of the Greek *logos*.

40. A very careless quotation, since the subject of "multiplying" is in fact "the number of disciples."

41. Augustine's version is here true to the Greek, which the Vulgate very freely paraphrases. But the paraphrase, oddly enough, seems to be reflected in Augustine's next sentence; it runs, *Before all works let a true word precede you.*

42. See Mk 10:17.

43. After *gloriam Domini speculantes* Augustine adds the explanatory phrase, *per speculum scilicet intuentes.* I had to leave it out, otherwise my text would have run, "looking at the glory of the Lord through a mirror, that is looking through a mirror . . . "

44. Section 14. His closing argument is rather elliptical. The line of thought, I suggest, is something like this: all things were created through the Word, that is through the wisdom, the intelligence, the reason of God—the created universe is a rational and intelligible creation. Now we, in harmony with it, are meant to live rational, intelligent, that is good lives. To restore to us the possibility of doing this, it was the wisdom, the intelligence, the reasonableness of God (the Word, precisely) that became flesh, to *enlighten* us.

45. See the end of Book XIV, 26, note 56.

46. The equivalent Latin number appears to be 600, *sexcenta.*

47. *Verbi*; M reads *vere*, a reasonable emendation of the *veri* of some six manuscripts: so innumerable that he truly cannot comprehend . . . its infinite number. I myself find it hard to comprehend or express this whole desperate sentence. I presume all he wants to do is add yet another point of certain knowledge, namely the impossibility of expressing infinity.

48. *Answer to the Skeptics* (3 books) (*Contra Academicos Libri III*), the earliest of his surviving writings.

49. That is, against its reliability as a source of true knowledge.

50. A proper name for the ancients, signifying the Atlantic.

51. *Constantibus*; M reads *contestantibus*, testificatory.

52. He has evidently forgotten that what he started to do at the beginning of this section was to show how little even the most learned man can really know.

53. See 1 Cor 13:12; 1 Jn 3:2.

54. Books V-VIII, *passim.*

55. Reading *qua* with M and two manuscripts; CCL reads *quia*, nor is this weakness but strength, because truth cannot be false.

56. See 1 Cor 13:12.

57. But in the rather odd case he has just been envisaging we are not even mistaken, because what we have said happens to be true. Where then is the mistake, and where the falsity of our word? In the fact that we thought we knew it was true, while in reality we did not know it; in this case its happening to be true was just a lucky fluke. I suppose the sort of thing he has in mind is most usually verified in claims we make to know what is going to happen. We say we know such-and-such is going to happen; we say it because we "know" that in all probability it will happen. But in fact all the probabilities in this case are against its happening, so our "knowledge" and hence our word is false. And yet after all the thing does happen—against all the probabilities. So in its content our statement that the thing would happen was true—it was true in the thing itself we were talking about; but as a statement of our knowledge of the thing it was false.

58. See Jn 12:49.

59. There seems to be an oblique allusion here to Jn 1:4, *What has come to be in him (the Word) was life.* I am inclined to think that it was not meant to be an oblique allusion, and that he intended to quote the verse to make the contrast, but inadvertently left the sentence out.

60. See Phil 2:6.

61. Virgil, *Aeneid* 10, 159-60; the word in question is *volutat.*

62. For example Is 55:8.

63. Not a very good comparison, as it is hard to find a genuine instance. The best I could find is the psalmist asking God how long he will forget him, Ps 13:1.

64. See 1 Cor 13:12.

65. See 1 Jn 3:2.

66. 1 Cor 13:12.

67. As that God is called charity in the same way as he is called my patience, because it is his gift.

68. Section 12.

69. *In sua quisque natura.* This is a very loose expression, because in the strictest theological use of "nature" in this context the divine persons do not have distinct natures, but have and are the one divine nature. What he is stressing is that each is a complete person, unlike their analogues in the human image person; one might perhaps have translated *natura* here by "personality."

70. See 1 Cor 1:24.

71. See Ps 35:19; 69:4

72. M adds *sanctus*, the Holy Spirit.

73. This comment seems to me to prove conclusively that Augustine sometimes took *Deus caritas est* to mean "Love is God;" see section 10, note 14.

74. M adds *sanctus*, the Holy Spirit.

75. See Mt 25:33.

76. *Sacramenta.*

77. See 1 Cor 13:1-3.

78. "Even Paul," because he is the protagonist of justification by faith alone—so at least he appears to be in Romans, interpreted in isolation.

79. See Jas 2:19.

80. See Rom 5:5.

81. M adds *Jesu.*

82. See Acts 2:2.

83. *Sensus plenissimus*: the idea of what they call the *sensus plenior* has in recent years been taken up by a number of Catholic biblical theologians as a hermeneutical instrument or principle. As I understand it, this has really been an attempt to transcend the traditional distinction between the literal and the spiritual senses of scripture, which really goes back to Origen, was neatly tidied up, on the surface at least, by Aquinas, and seems to have meant almost diametrically opposite things at different periods of the Church's history. One might perhaps describe the *sensus plenior* concept as the idea that a text of scripture, precisely as the vehicle of divine revelation, may often mean more than what its author, in the context in which he wrote, actually intended it to mean; but that this "more" is not simply other than the literal meaning of the text, to be set side by side as a distinct and separate meaning; rather it underlies, or grows out of the literal meaning, whichever way you prefer to look at it; the literal sense is itself pregnant with the *sensus plenior*. Authors differ in the rules they lay down for detecting such possible pregnancies, and for bringing the *sensus plenior* to birth.

On the whole subject see two articles by Raymond E. Brown, "The History and Development of the Theory of a Sensus Plenior," *Catholic Biblical Quarterly* 15 (1953) 141-162; and "The Sensus Plenior in the Last Ten Years," *ibid*, 25 (1963) 262-285.

84. Reading *accepit in hominibus idem ipse utique membra sua*. I have reluctantly felt obliged to emend the text here, as neither CCL nor M gives a reading that really makes any sense at all. The whole sentence runs in CCL:*Dedit hominibus tanquam caput membris suis; accepit in hominibus idem ipse utique in membris suis . . .* M only differs in omitting the *in* before the second *membris*. One manuscript, and Bede in a collection of Augustinian texts, put the disputed clause in the margin; a corrector of the same manuscript and a second manuscript omit it altogether.

The problem of course is that as it stands in the editions the clause gives no object to *accepit*, and in the context, where the author is telling us what gifts Christ received among men, an object for this verb is absolutely mandatory; also within the context it seems clear that what Christ did receive among men was his members. Hence my emendation. It is slightly supported by M's reading;

I take it that the first vitiation of what I am supposing to be the original occurred when a copyist wrote *membris suis* for *membris sua*, his eye caught by the *membris suis* of the preceding clause. Then another wrote in the *in*, to put this second *membris suis* into apposition with *in hominibus*. Finally a few copyists left the whole clause out, either by an extended haplography, or because they could not make sense of it.

85. Ps 96: title, LXX.

86. *Corpus*; M reads *domus*, the house.

87. See Book XIII, 17.

88. See Eph 4:8; Ps 68:19.

89. M adds *domini*, the Lord.

90. See Col 2:11.

91. *Non esse suae potestatis.* That is like a slave, who could be given away without also giving himself.

92. *Sicut*: M reads *si*, if.

93. See 1 Jn 4:8.16.

94. See 1 Jn 4:7.13.

95. Otherwise known as Anomoeans, extreme Arians, who denied that the Son is even like the Father.

96. See Jn 1:3.

97. Behind this *consilium seu voluntas*, I suspect, lies the Greek word *boule*, which means a mixture of both.

98. He seems to be half admitting that he has not in fact done what he set out to do at the beginning of this chapter.

99. Books I-IV.

100. See Book I, 1 and 4.

101. See Rom 1:20.

102. Provided it is a non-adventitious thing, like self or God.

103. *Amorem seu dilectionem*; I usually translate *dilectio* by "love," except when forced to vary the word, as here.

104. The *non agit perperam* of the Latin is a neat transliteration but a faulty translation of the Greek *ou perpereuetai*, which means "is not boastful."

105. *Illi memoriae principali*; memory is the mental *principium* or source from which the other two functions of understanding and willing proceed or evolve, just as the Father is the divine *principium* or source from which the other two divine persons proceed, or in a manner of speaking evolve—no more inadequate a manner of speaking, really, than to say they proceed.

106. That is, man is called image because the triadic image properly so called is found in him.

107. See Book I, 15, note 38.

108. He seems to contradict here what he said in earlier books about the essential equality of these three mental acts (IX, 4-8; X, 18). But there he was talking about perfect mental acts, here it seems about imperfect mental capacities.

109. See 1 Cor 13:12.

110. M adds *nunc*, now.

111. See 1 Tm 1:5.

112. See Acts 15:9.

113. See Wis 9:15.

114. See Book XIII, 17; also XV, 34, note 87.

115. *Quae ornent non onerent.*

116. Book II, 5, note 11.

117. Which three? The divine persons or the mental acts? It is not clear.

118. *Nostra*; M reads *vestra*, your.

119. See Lk 6:19.

120. See Mt 22:40.

121. M adds *sanctum*, the same Holy Spirit.

122. M adds *omnes*, all nations.

123. See Lk 3:22.

124. In the African baptismal creed. See J.N.D. Kelly, *Early Christian Creeds* (London, 1960, 2nd ed.), especially chapter 6.

125. See Lk 3:23. The supposition that Augustine rejects as the height of absurdity was in fact made by the Adoptionist heresy, which declared that Jesus (a mere human being) was *adopted* as Son of God at his baptism, when the Holy Spirit came upon him.

This particular heretical belief had more or less faded away by Augustine's time, and so he does not refer to it explicitly here. As a heresy, we can probably say, it only represented a hardening or freezing of an archaic understanding of the person of Jesus Christ which found expression in the story of his baptism.

What seems to have happened, according to modern New Testament scholars, is that the primitive christology underlying the New Testament texts developed backward. The earliest strand saw Jesus as made or appointed Christ, Lord, Son of God by being raised from the dead (Acts 2:36; 13:33; Rom 1:4; see also Mt 28:18).

But as accounts of his ministry, his miracles, teaching and passion were collected and pondered, it was felt that his status as Christ, Lord, Son of God must have already been his in order to give authority and meaning to his life and ministry. So the baptismal legend was developed, and he was proclaimed Son of God and anointed with the Holy Spirit at his baptism, which thus inaugurated his ministry. This theological development was also of use in explaining what must have been the exceedingly awkward fact for the first Christian generation of Jesus having been baptized by John with the *baptism of repentance for the forgiveness of sins.*

But this "baptismal christology" could hardly remain definitive. If Jesus Christ is more than just the greatest of the prophets, if he is (as Christians from the beginning have been convinced that he is) a *unique* human being—Son of God in a manner no other human being can share—then he must always have been like this. And so we have the christology of the infancy narratives, according to which he is "*born* king of the Jews" (Mt 2:2), and *conceived* by the Holy Spirit (Mt 1:18.20; Lk 1:35).

Finally, he is apprehended as Son of God in an even more primordial sense, and we have the fully developed christology of John, and the doctrine of the incarnation of the eternal Word.

For a careful statement of this development, see Raymond E. Brown, *The Birth of the Messiah* (London, 1977), especially the Introduction, page 29.

126. *Ad illud*; M reads *illum ad*, he came to baptism.

127. See Acts 2:33.

128. Reading *tempore* with one manuscript; both CCL and M read *tempora*; see next note.

129. Reading *qua* with M and most of the manuscripts; CCL reads *quia*.

It is impossible really to make sense of the text as it is given in CCL; I think the editor has carried the principle of "the more difficult reading is to be preferred" to an unworkable extreme here. We have a control to what Augustine is saying here, because he has said it all at somewhat greater length already, at the very end of Book IX, 18. And he says it here too, if we take the readings I follow in this and the preceding note. The whole sentence in CCL runs (from the beginning of the paragraph— it is one sentence in the Latin), *Numquid ergo possumus quaerere utrum jam processerat de patre spiritus sanctus quando natus est filius . . . ubi nulla sunt tempora, sicut potuimus quaerere ubi invenimus* tempora *voluntatem prius de humana mente procedere ut quaeratur quod inventum proles vocetur, quia jam parta seu genita voluntas illa perficitur eo fine requiescens, ut qui fuerat appetitus quaerentis sit amor fruentis . . .* The two disputed words are left in roman type.

As regards the first word: if we leave *tempora*, as in both CCL and M, it can only be construed as the object of *invenimus*; this leaves the accusative and infinitive clause *voluntatem . . . procedere* hanging in the air without a verb to govern it. The problem is solved if we read *tempore* instead of *tempora*. This could have been altered to *tempora* by a very easy slip, given the occurrence of *tempora* in the preceding line.

As regards the second word: if we leave *quia*, then *parta seu genita* can really only be construed as nominative qualifying *voluntas illa*. But Augustine never speaks of *voluntas* as brought forth or begotten; the whole gist of his argument, here and in book IX, is against it. But if instead, with great support from the manuscripts, we read *qua* with M, then we have a neat relative clause in the ablative absolute, in which *parta seu genita* refers to the *proles* of the previous clause. How *qua* could have been changed to *quia* is slightly more problematic; it could have been just a slip of the pen, or it could have been a copyist who did not really understand the sentence trying to be clever. But to my mind there can be very little doubt as to which is the correct reading.

130. This is more an assertion than an argument. Its character as such appears clearly in the last sentence but one of this paragraph. Some kind of argument may emerge in the next paragraph.

131. See Section 29 above.

132. *Homilies on the Gospel of John* 99, 8-9.

133. Does this imply that the *De Trinitate* is addressed to unbelievers? In part, yes—at least to those whom he immediately goes on to talk about, who demand reasons before believing. See Book I, 1.

134. See Jn 1:5.

135. See Ps 139:6.

136. See Ps 103:3.

137. See Lk 10:30. By an almost universal consensus of the Fathers, the Good Samaritan was interpreted as Christ, the victim of the robbers as mankind wounded by sin, the inn or tavern as the Church.

138. See Jn 16:26.

139. *Te*; M reads *tu*, in which you can recognize the image.

140. *Cognitionis/cognitione* in all three places; M reads *cogitationis/cogitatione*, thought.

141. See Ps 103:3.

142. M adds *omnes*, all.

143. This remark is aimed at the Arians, who denied the true divinity of the Son and the Holy Spirit.

144. M omits *Deus*, God; perhaps in this context the preferable reading, though Augustine is not consistent in the way he quotes this text.

145. The Sabellian view.

146. See Ps 91:9.

147. See Ps 105:4.

148. See Rv 3:7; Mt 7:7.

149. *Universa est ipse*. This evidently sounded pantheistic to someone, and the Vulgate reads *ipse est in omnibus*, he is in all things. Augustine had a less queasy theological stomach.

150. He ends with a typical piece of word play, untranslatable and not outstandingly elegant: *quaecunque dixi in his libris de tuo agnoscant et tui; si qua de meo, et tu ignosce et tui. Amen.*

INDEX OF SCRIPTURE

(The numbers after the scriptural reference refer to the particular book and its section)

Old Testament

Genesis

1:1	I, 24
1:3	II, 17
1:3.6	II, 14
1:26	I, 14; VII, 12; XII, 6; XIV, 25
1:27	XII, 6, 7, 8, 10
2:20	XII, 20
2:24	XII, 3, 8
3:5	XI, 8
3:8	II, 18
3:9	II, 17, 18
3:11	XII, 20
3:14	XIII, 16
3:19	XIII, 16
4:14	II, 18
6:3	XIII, 16
6:7	I, 2
7:22	XIV, 22
9:6	IX, 17
12:1	II, 19; III, 25
12:7	II, 19; III, 25
18:1	II, 19, 34; III, 25
18:2	III, 25
18:33	II, 21
19:1	II, 21
19:17	II, 22
22:1	III, 25
22:10	III, 25
22:12	I, 23; III, 25
22:13	III, 25
22:15	III, 25

Exodus

3:1	II, 23
3:6, 2	III, 20
3:14	I, 2, 17; V, 3; VII, 10
8:15	III, 12, 18
13:21	II, 24
16:10	II, 24
19:18	II, 25, 26
20:5	I, 2
20:18	II, 25
20:21	II, 25
24:10	II, 25
24:17	II, 26
33:11	II, 27
33:13	II, 27, 28
33:18	II, 27
33:20	II, 28
33:21	II, 30
33:22	II, 31

Numbers

11:17	V, 15
21:9	III, 20

Deuteronomy

6:4	V, 12; VII, 8; XV, 51
6:5	X, 9; XIV, 18
6:13	I, 13; II, 19

Job

7:1	IV, 5
28:28	XIV, 1, 15

Psalms

1:2	I, 5
2:7	II, 19, 33
3:8	XII, 7

5:5	I, 17
5:13	II, 1
7:14	IX, 14
8:6	IV, 17
8:8	II, 33
9:2	X, 9
9:17	XIV, 17
10:3	XIII, 8
11:5	VIII, 9, 18; XIV, 18
14:1	XIII, 2
14:2	XV, 2
15:2.1	IV, 6
16:11	I, 17
17:8	I, 2
17:11	XV, 50
18:28	IX, 2
18:29	XII, 7
19:1.5	IV, 15
19:3	IV, 29
19:6	I, 24
22:1	IV, 6
22:27	XIV, 16
24:7	I, 24
27:4	I, 20, 31
31:20	I, 31
31:23	IV, 1
32:1	II, 31
32:4	II, 31
32:8	III, 19
34:5	XIV, 18
36:10	VII, 4
38:10	XIV, 18
39:3	XV, 13
39:6	II, 28; XIV, 6, 19
45:5	XII, 7
45:8	II, 11; III, 20
49:12	XII, 16
50:7	III, 20
57:7	IV, 7
59:9	XIV, 18
59:17	XV, 27
62:5	XV, 27
63:8	VI, 7
68:9	IV, 2
68:18	IV, 17; XIII, 14; XV, 34
69:4	XIII, 18
71:5	XV, 27
72:18	I, 11
73:1	I, 31
73:23	XIV, 16
73:26	IV, 1
73:27, 28	VI, 7
77:9	XIII, 16
80:2	V, 9
82:6	I, 13

85:12	IV, 24
86:10	V, 9
88:5	XIII, 18
90:1	V, 17; XV, 5
91:16	I, 17
94:8	XIV, 17
94:11	XV, 51
94:12-15	XIII, 17
94:13	XIII, 17
102:26	III, 8
102:27	I, 2
102:28	V, 9
103:3	XIV, 23
104:4	III, 9
104:6	V, 9
105:3	XV, 2
105:4	I, 5; IX, 1
110:1	II, 19
110:3	I, 24
112:7	I, 31
112:8	I, 16
122:3	III, 8
139:6	XV, 13
139:7	II, 7
139:8	II, 7; V, 9
143:2	II, 28; IV, 5
146:6	IV, 25
148:8	III, 19; XIV, 22

Proverbs

8:22	I, 24
8:25	I, 24
9:8	XIV, 2
10:19	XV, 51
19:21	XV, 38
30:15	XV, 15

Ecclesiastes

1:18	IV, 1
3:21	XIV, 22

Song of Songs

1:10	I, 16
1:11	I, 17

Wisdom

1:7	III, 3
1:13	IV, 15
2:1	XV, 17
3:9	VIII, 11
6:7	XV, 8

6:24	XIV, 1
6:25	I, 8
7:7	II, 27
7:24	IV, 18
7:25	IV, 27
7:26	IV, 27, 28
7:27	II, 14; IV, 27
8:1	II, 7, 25, 30; III, 6; IV, 18
9:10	IV, 27, 28
9:14-16	III, 21
9:15	II, 28; III, 10; IV, 5; VIII, 3
9:17	III, 21
11:20	III, 16; XI, 18
12:18	XIII, 21
13:1-5	XV, 3
16:24	II, 11; III, 6

Sirach

1:5	XV, 20
18:7	IX, 1
19:1	XII, 15
23:20	XV, 22
24:5	I, 10; IV, 28
24:21	XV, 2
37:16	XV, 20
43:37	XV, 51

Isaiah

5:18	XI, 10
6:10	II, 31
7:9	VII, 12; XV, 2
9:6	II, 23; III, 23
11:2	II, 27
28:11	XV, 30
35:10	I, 21
40:5	II, 11
48:16	II, 8
55:6	XV, 2
61:1	I, 22
66:1	II, 30

Jeremiah

23:24	II, 7

Daniel

7:9-14	II, 33
7:10	VIII, 3
9:21	III, 25

Habakkuk

2:4	I, 16, 17
2:8	II, 33

Zechariah

12:12	I, 31

New Testament

Matthew

1:18	II, 8, 9
2:12	IV, 15
3:16	II, 10
3:17	II, 18
5:6	IV, 1
5:8	I, 17, 28, 30, 31; VIII, 6
5:37	XV, 20, 22
6:8	XV, 22
6:11	V, 15
6:12	XII, 18
7:12	VIII, 10
7:21	IX, 15
8:12	XI, 10
8:22	IV, 5
9:2	XV, 17
9:3	XV, 18
10:20	XV, 45
10:28	II, 15; IV, 6
11:13	XV, 30
11:27	I, 16; VII, 4
11:28	VIII, 11; IX, 14
11:29	VIII, 11
12:29	XIII, 19
12:32	I, 22
12:35	I, 31
12:37	IX, 14
12:40	IV, 6, 10
13:15	II, 31
14:31	XIII, 5
15:11	XV, 18
15:16	XV, 18
15:18	XV, 18
15:28	XIII, 5
16:18	II, 28
17:5	I, 7; II, 18
19:7	I, 31
19:17	I, 31
20:23	I, 24, 27
22:37	II, 28; XIV, 18
22:39	II, 28

22:40	VI, 7; VIII, 10; XV, 30
24:19	IX, 14
25:21	I, 31
25:31	I, 28
25:32	I, 29
25:34	XIV, 25
25:37	I, 31
25:40	XV, 34
25:41.34	I, 31
26:38	I, 22
28:19	XV, 46, 51

Mark

1:11	I, 7
10:17	I, 31
10:18	V, 9
12:33	VIII, 9
13:32	I, 23
15:34	IV, 6
15:39	IV, 16
15:42	IV, 10

Luke

1:15	IV, 5; XV, 6
1:17	V, 15
1:34	II, 8
2:14	XIII, 17
3:6	II, 11
4:18	I, 22
5:21	XV, 17
9:60	IV, 5
10:38	I, 20
10:42	I, 31
11:3	V, 15
11:20	I, 22
12:17	XV, 17
12:20	XIV, 19
15:13	IV, 1
18:19	V, 9
20:36	IV, 5
21:18	IV, 6
24:26	II, 31
24:39	IV, 6
24:44	XV, 30

John

1:1	I, 9; II, 9, 27; VI, 3, 4; VII, 4; XV, 19, 20
1:1, 3	VII, 1
1:1-3	IV, 3
1:1-6	IV, 3
1:1-14	XIII, 2

1:2	I, 9
1:3	I, 12, 14, 22, 26, 31; II, 14, 15, 25, 28; IV, 3, 25, 26; VII, 4; XII, 5, 6; XV, 20
1:3-4	IV, 3
1:4	IV, 3, 4
1:5	IV, 3, 28
1:9	VII, 4
1:10	II, 7; III, 3; VII, 5
1:11	II, 7
1:12	V, 17; XIII, 11, 12
1:14	I, 9; II, 9; IV, 4, 28; VII, 4; XIII, 12, 22, 24; XIV, 24; XV, 20, 46
1:29	II, 11; XV, 44
2:19-21	IV, 9
2:21	IV, 9
3:14	III, 20
3:17	IV, 30
4:7	XV, 31
4:7-14	XV, 33
4:10	V, 10, 12
4:13	IX, 14
4:24	V, 12; XV, 27
5:19	I, 11; II, 3, 5; XV, 24
5:21	I, 11
5:22	I, 29, 30; II, 3
5:24	I, 30
5:25	I, 30
5:26	I, 22, 26, 29, 30; II, 3, 4; VII, 4; XV, 47
5:27	I, 30; II, 3
5:28	I, 30
5:36; 14:31	I, 26
5:46	III, 26
6:38	I, 22
7:16	I, 22,26; II, 4, 5; XV, 48
7:37	XV, 33
7:39	IV, 29
7:38	XV, 33
8:15	II, 9
8:25	I, 24; V, 14
8:31	IV, 24
8:42	II, 9
8:50	I, 29
10:30	I, 17, 22, 25; II, 3; V, 4, 10; VI, 3; VII, 12
10:36	II, 9
11:51	IV, 22
12:28	I, 7; II, 18
12:44	I, 27
12:47	I, 26, 27, 29
12:48	I, 26
12:49-50	I, 26
12:50	I, 26

13:1	II, 29
13:21	XV, 19
14:1	I, 27
14:8	I, 17
14:9-11	I, 17
14:9	IV, 26
14:15-17	I, 18
14:16	I, 19
14:17	I, 19
14:21	I, 18, 28, 30, 31
14:22	I, 18
14:23	VII, 12
14:25	I, 25
14:26	II, 7; IV, 26, 29; XV, 45, 51
14:28	I, 15, 18; VI, 10
14:30	XIII, 18
15:5	XIV, 23
15:13	IV, 17
15:15	I, 23
15:25	XV, 30
15:26	II, 5; IV, 29; V, 12, 15; XV, 45; 48, 51; XII, 5
16:6	I, 18
16:7	I, 24; II, 7
16:12	I, 23
16:13	I, 18; II, 5, 23
16:14	II, 5
16:15	I, 22
16:19	I, 25
16:22	I, 20, 31
16:25	I, 21
16:26	I, 21
16:27	I, 21
16:28	II, 7; IV, 28, 30
17:1.5	II, 6
17:3	I, 17, 30, 31; IV, 24; VI, 10; XIV, 25
17:4	II, 1, 6
17:5	I, 31
17:10	I, 22
17:19	II, 9
17:20	IV, 12
17:22	IV, 12; VI, 4
17:23	IV, 12
17:24	V, 17
19:11	III, 12
19:30	IV, 16; XIV, 22
20:17	I, 18; IV, 6
20:22	IV, 29; XV, 45
20:28	IV, 6

Acts of the Apostles

2:1	II, 26
2:2	II, 10
2:3	II, 11
2:11	III, 11
2:37	II, 31; XV, 35
4:12	XV, 44
6:7	XV, 20
7:2	III, 24
7:29	III, 24
7:51	III, 26
8:18	XV, 35, 46
8:19	XV, 46
8:20	V, 9, 12
9:4	XV, 34
10:38	XV, 46
10:44	XV, 35
11:15	XV, 35
15:9	I, 17
17:27	IV, 3; VII, 5; XIV, 16
17:28	IV, 23
26:16	XIII, 19

Romans

1:4	XII, 7
1:17	IV, 5, 20; XIII, 26
1:18	XIII, 24
1:20	II, 25; IV, 21; VI, 12; XIII, 24; XV, 1, 3
1:21	VI, 12
1:23	XIII, 24
1:25	I, 13
3:26	I, 24
4:5	I, 24; IV, 5; XIV, 15
4:13	I, 4; IV, 5
4:25	II, 29
5:5	VII, 5; VIII, 10; XIII, 14; XV, 31
5:6	XIII, 14
5:8	IV, 2; XIII, 14, 21
5:9	XIII, 15, 18
5:10	XIII, 14, 21
5:11	XIII, 21
5:12	IV, 15; XIII, 21
6:6	III, 20; IV, 6
6:13	IV, 6; XII, 17
7:23	XIII, 23
7:24	XII, 16
8:9	V, 12
8:10	IV, 5
8:11	IV, 5
8:13	XIII, 15, 20
8:18	IV, 5
8:23	II, 29; III, 10
8:24	I, 17
8:26	I, 20
8:28	XIII, 10, 20

8:29	XIV, 24
8:30	I, 24
8:31	IV, 2; XIII, 20
8:32	I, 21; II, 9; XIII, 21
8:34	I, 21
9:5	II, 23
9:22	XIII, 19
10:3	XIV, 15
10:9	II, 29
10:17	XIII, 5; XV, 20
11:33-36	I, 12
11:36	I, 12; II, 25; III, 9; V, 9; VI, 7, 12; XIV, 16
12:2	VII, 12; XI, 8; XII, 21; XIV, 22
12:3	III, 22
13:8	VIII, 9

1 Corinthians

1:21	IV, 28
1:24	I, 10; VI, 1, 2; VII, 1, 2, 4; XV, 5, 31
1:25	XIII, 18
1:30	VII, 4
2:2	I, 3, 23
2:6	I, 23
2:8	I, 24, 28
2:11	I, 18; V, 15
2:14	VII, 11
2:15	I, 18
3:1	I, 23
3:1-2	I, 3
3:6	III, 14
3:7	III, 11
3:8	VI, 4
3:12	XV, 16
3:16	VII, 6
3:19	XIV, 1
3:22	VI, 10
4:5	I, 17
4:7	V, 15; XIV, 21
5:6	XIV, 4
6:15	I, 13
6:16	VI, 4
6:17	VI, 4, 6, 7, 9; XIV, 20
6:18	XII, 15
6:19	I, 13, 23; VII, 6
6:20	I, 13; II, 23
8:1	IV, 1
8:2	IX, 1
8:3	VIII, 10
8:5	II, 19
8:6	I, 12
10:4	II, 11
10:11	III, 24

10:13	XIII, 15, 20
11:3	I, 12
11:3	VI, 10
11:7	VII, 12; XII, 9, 10, 12; XV, 14
11:10	XII, 10
12:2	XV, 34
12:3	IX, 15
12:6	IV, 29; V, 14
12:7	XIII, 24
12:7-11	V, 14
12:8	XII, 22, 25; XIII, 24; XIV, 3
12:9	XV, 34
12:10	III, 18
12:11	XV, 36
12:13	XV, 33
13:4	VIII, 11; XV, 41
13:12	I, 3, 4, 16, 28, 31; II, 6, 28; III, 1, 9, 10; V, 1; VI, 2, 12; VII, 6; VIII, 3; IX, 1; XII, 22; XIV, 5, 23; XV, 3, 4, 6, 15, 21, 40, 44
14:14	XIV, 22
14:21	XV, 30
15:21	IV, 15
15:23	IV, 6
15:24	I, 15, 16, 17, 18, 20, 21, 28, 31
15:25	I, 16
15:26	II, 33
15:27	I, 15
15:28	I, 15, 20, 28
15:48	XIV, 24
15:49	XIV, 24
15:52	XIV, 25

2 Corinthians

1:17	XV, 20
1:18	XV, 24
1:19-20	XV, 23
2:10	VII, 8
3:13	XV, 20
3:17	II, 19
3:18	XIV, 23; XV, 14
4:6	IV, 10
4:13	III, 22
4:16	IV, 5, 6; XI, 1; XIV, 23
5:6	I, 17; II, 28
5:7	VIII, 6
5:21	XIII, 18
6:2-10	VIII, 13
10:17	XIII, 23
11:14	IV, 13
12:9	IV, 2

Galatians

2:20	II, 9; XIII, 15
3:19	III, 26
3:26	XII, 12
4:4	I, 14, 22; II, 8, 9, 12; III, 3; IV, 10, 26, 28, 30; XV, 51
4:6	XV, 45
4:9	IX, 1
4:24	XV, 14
4:26	III, 8
5:6	XIII, 5, 26; XV, 31
5:14	VIII, 10
6:2	VIII, 10
6:14	II, 28

Ephesians

1:4	V, 7; XIII, 15
2:1	XIII, 16
2:2	XIII, 16
4:2	XV, 34
4:3	VI, 7
4:5	XIII, 5
4:7	XV, 34
4:8	IV, 17; XIII, 14
4:8-11	XV, 34
4:22	IV, 6
4:23	XII, 12; XIV, 22
4:24	XIV, 23
5:1	VII, 12
5:8	IV, 10
5:14	IV, 5

Philippians

1:18	III, 14
1:23	III, 10
2:6	I, 12, 14, 31; II, 3, 20, 28; V, 4; VI, 5; VII, 5
2:7	I, 14, 18, 20, 21, 22; II, 5, 20
2:8	I, 22; III, 20 XIII, 22
2:8-11	I, 29
2:9	I, 29
3:3	I, 13
3:12	I, 8
3:13	IX, 1
3:15	I, 5
3:20	I, 15
3:21	IV, 6

Colossians

1:13	XIII, 19; XV, 37
1:15,17	I, 24
1:18	I, 24; VII, 5; XIV, 24

1:24	IV, 6
2:1	XIII, 24
2:3	I, 3; XIII, 24
2:11	XIV, 22
2:14	IV, 17
2:15	IV, 17
2:17	XV, 20
2:20	II, 28
3:1	IV, 6
3:3	I, 16
3:9	XII, 12; XIV, 22
3:10	VII, 12; XI, 1; XII, 12; XIV, 23; XV, 5

1 Thessalonians

2:13	XV, 20
5:6	XV, 15

2 Thessalonians

2:9	IV, 13

1 Timothy

1:5	VIII, 6
1:7	II, 32
1:15	VII, 5
1:17	II, 14, 20
2:5	I, 14, 16, 20; III, 26; XIII, 13, 23; XV, 44
2:14	XII, 11
3:16	IV, 27
5:5	XII, 11
5:6	IV, 5
6:13	XIII, 16
6:14	I, 10
6:15	II, 14
6:16	I, 2, 10; II, 1, 15, 32, 33, 34

2 Timothy

4:1	I, 27
4:2	XV, 51

Hebrews

1:13a	III, 22
2:1	III, 22
2:3	III, 22
2:4	XV, 34
2:8	II, 33
5:14	XII, 20
10:1	XV, 20
11:1	XIII, 3

12:7.11	XIV, 3
12:22	III, 8

James

1:15	IX, 14
1:17	I, 2
5:12	XV, 20, 23

1 Peter

2:22	XIII, 18
3:18	IV, 17

1 John

1:5	VII, 4, 6; VIII, 3, 12
2:10	VIII, 12
3:2	I, 17; II, 28; IV, 5; XII, 22; XIV, 23, 25; XV, 21

4:7	VIII, 12
4:8	VIII, 11, 12
4:8. 16	VI, 7; VII, 6; IX, 1, XV, 27, 31
4:10	XV, 31
4:13	XV, 31
4:16	VIII, 10, 12; XV, 31
4:19	XV, 31
4:20	VIII, 12
5:7	IV, 29
5:8	IX, 18
5:20	I, 9, 22, 26

Revelation

1:5	I, 21, 24
1:7	I, 28, 29, 31
5:11	VIII, 3
14:4	XV, 44

INDEX

(prepared by Joseph Sprug)

(the numbers refer to the particular book and its section)

A

Abraham:
  "Now I know that you fear God," I:23
  voice of the Lord; appearance, II:19
  three men at the oak of Mambre, II:19-21, 34; III:25
  the Lord (i.e. angel) appeared to, III:24-25
Academics, on knowledge, XV:21
acrobatic feats, IV:14
action/activity:
  foreshadowing joy, by Mary and Martha, I:20
  temporal things; knowledge, XII:22
Adam and Eve:
  Genesis: God walks/talks with Adam, II:17, 18
  seeing God with physical eyes, II:18
  hiding from God's face, II:18
  punishment of, XII:13
  forbidden fruit, XII:17
  sin; reconciliation through second Adam, XIII:21, 23
agriculture, agents in, III:14
Alexandria, VIII:9
allegory (enigma), XV:15
angel(s):
  sovereignties no longer needed, I:16
  theophanies and utterances (O.T.), II:21-22; III:6; III:22-27; IV:30, 31
  announcer or messenger, II:23
  burning bush; angel of the Lord, II:23
  representing God in manifestations, III:4
  the making of physical manifestations, III:5
  knowledge of our bodily changes, III:5
  rebel angels, and wizards, III:13
  good, do as God commands; bad, as God permits, III:13
  divine limitations on good and bad, III:18
  divine prohibition (bad angels), III:18
  person of God represented by, III:19
  marvelous acts, III:20
  speaking in person of God; example, III:20
  pillars of cloud and fire, III:21
  God works through, even bad, angels, III:21
  the "Lord" appeared to Abraham, III:25
  sometimes called "men," III:25
  law proclaimed by (Stephen), III:26
  mortal men made equal to, IV:12
  past and future equally present to, IV:22
  wisdom, IV:27
  Christ as model for, VII:5
  all together do not make one God, VIII:3
  time and, XII:10
  said to tell God all things, XV:22
  see also theophanies
animals:
  outer/inner man and, XII:1
  sensing outside bodies, XII:2
Anna, IV:29
annunciation, date of, IV:9
apparitions, demonic, IV:14
appetite, in pursuit of knowledge, IX:18; XII:17
Arians:
  substance-wise statements about God, V:4, 7
  Christ: power and wisdom of God, VI:1
  the Son as not true God, VI:10
ascension: equality with the Father, I:18
attention:
  act of recall, XI:6
  memory, inner sight, and will, XI:11-12
  will, sensation, and memory, XI:14-15
  recollection of things in memory, XIV:10
Augustine, Saint:
  covenant with the reader, I:5, 8
  tongue and pen driven by Charity, III:1
  would rather read than write, III:1
  a word to critics, III:2
authority:
  holding fast to, IX:1
  justice combined with power, XIII:17
awareness, see mind

B

baptism:
  made sons of God by, XII:12
  the uncircumcised; the Holy Spirit, XV:35
  sent in name of the trinity, XV:51

beauty:
  perception of, IX:11
  spirit roused by talk of, X:1
  knowledge through senses, XIII:4
being:
  change and, V:3
  as genus or species word, VII:11
birth: beginnings from hidden seed, III:13
blasphemy: against the Son; against the Holy
    Spirit, I:22
blind, XI:2
bliss, *see* happiness
body (-ies):
  temples of the Holy Spirit, I:13
  perishibility, IV:5
  death: being forsaken by spirit, IV:16
  size, color, shape, VI:8
  substance both simple and multiple, VI:8
  division; part and whole in, IX:7
  its image in our consciousness, IX:16
  parts of soul we share even with animals,
    X:7
  part(s) of highest value, X:9
  visible: sense of sight, XI:2
  limits of sensing set by, XI:14
  consciousness, XII:1
  traces of spiritual things in, XII:5
  sinning against one's own, XII:15
  represented by serpent, not woman, XII:20
  live, move, are — in him, XIV:16
  see also senses
body and soul:
  interaction of, III:15
  need of healing and resurrection, IV:5
  outer/inner parts of man, XIII:2
books: value of several authors, I:5
buying and selling, XIII:6

                    C

Cain, II:18
Carthage, VIII:9
Catholic Church:
  judgment day: protection by right faith, I:31
  faith: beholding Christ's back (hu- manity),
    II:28
  standing on the rock, II:30
cause:
  primary and ultimate; example, III:8
  visible and changing events, III:8
  physical species and motions, III:9
  generation of animals, III:15, 17
  secondary causes; natural order, III:16-17
  angels, and the proximate causes of things,
    III:17
  no changeable goods, without the un-
    changeable good, VIII:5
censure: not feared by lover of truth, II:1
certainty:
  things minds know about themselves, X:14
  see also knowledge
chance:
  made by God, without change in God, I:3

changeableness, and mortality, II:15
  natural causes; will of God, III:19
  the changeable and eternity, IV:24
  being and, V:3
  modifications, V:5
  nothing simple; everything created, VI:8
  "changeable" must not be thought of God,
    VIII:3
  hope in soul being changeable, XIV:21
character:
  praiseworthy: memory, under- standing,
    and will, X:17
charity, *see* love
children: memory, understanding, and will,
    X:17
Christ, *see* Jesus Christ
christian life:
  hidden with Christ in God, I:16
  God inwardly effecting, III:14
  partakers in his divinity, IV:4
  Paul on how one should live, VIII:13
Christmas: date of [note 31], IV:9
church:
  body of Christ, IV:12
  house built after the captivity (devil),
    XV:34
  prefigured: Christ anointed with Holy
    Spirit, XV:46
Cicero:
  on the happy life, XIII:8
  on four basic virtues, XIV:12
  on living in philosophy, XIV:26
circus prodigies, IV:14
City of God, The:
  on the soul, XIII:12
cogitation, *see* thought
commandment(s):
  reward for keeping, I:18
  eternal life, I:26
common good: self-enjoyment and, XII:17
consciousness:
  sense knowledge, IX:16
  intention: sense of seeing, XI:2
  power of fabricating, XI:8
  the outer man, XII:1
  raised to highest in spiritual things, XII:1
  not common to man and beast, XII:2, 3
  found only inside self, XIV:8
  faith and, XIV:11
  virtues begin in, XIV:12
  focus of book XI, XV:5
  perceptions through, XV:21, 22
  see also mind; thought
contemplation:
  mediator will bring us to face to face vision,
    I:16
  promise: eternal perfection, I:17
  rejoicing in hope, I:17
  reward of faith, I:17
  the clean of heart, I:17
  inseparability of persons, I:17
  I will show myself to him, I:18

believers brought to, I:20
God will be all in all, I:20
of God; eternal life, I:31
eternal things; wisdom, XII:22
wisdom: the light shines in darkness, XIII:2
courage: Cicero on four basic virtues, XIV:12
covetousness:
    true love opposed to, VIII:10
    creature loved on its own account, IX:13
    forsaking better things, XI:8
creation:
    scripture's words, when referring to God, I:2
    of things in time, I:3
    all things made through the Son/Word, I:9; XV:20
    "all things were made through him" (Jn I:3), I:12; IV:3
    Genesis: person(s) involved in, II:17
    obedience to its maker; theophanies, III:6
    God as inmost cause of, III:16
    creator: the one who fashions things in their principles, III:18
    one creation, one life, IV:3
    interlock of, IV:4
    the sixth day, IV:7
    all should bear witness to creator, IV:25
    both Father & Son are called origin, V:14
    everlastingly lord, V:17
    lower creatures; remote likeness to creator, XII:5
    knowing the God who made them, XV:3
creator:
    his nature more excellent than created natures, XIV:16
    ranks above created things, XV:6
creature(s):
    every substance that is not God, I:9
    enjoyment of created things, IX:13
    all are known by God, XV:22
critics: a word to his readers, III:2
cross: prefigured by Moses' arms outstretched, IV:20
crucifixion:
    the Lord of glory, in form of a servant, I:28
    "why have you forsaken me," IV:6
    see also death; Jesus Christ; redemption
curiosity:
    distinguished from the studious person, X:3, 4

D

Daniel:
    the Son: appearance in physical form, II:33
darkness:
    foolish minds of men, IV:3
    heart: the light shines in darkness, XIII:2
days: calculation, dark to light, IV:10
death:
    serpent stands for, III:20
    decay of the outer man, IV:5
    body and soul; difference, IV:5

the Lord's death: model for death of outer man, IV:6
God as cause, IV:15
little fear of, IV:15
man's inclination: flesh or spirit, IV:15
companionship of Son of God, IV:17
way chosen by God to free us from mortality, XIII:13
devil using our sins to keep us fixed in, XIII:21
defect: finding fault with, IX:16
demons:
    unlike proud people, they cannot die, IV:18
    offer selves as mediators, XIII:22
desire:
    for temporal goods, IX:14
    directed to sensible things, XI:7
    see also covetousness
devil:
    airy body, IV:14
    died in spirit by godlessness, IV:15
    false mediator, IV:15, 18
    deceiver: mediator to death, IV:17
    temptation of Christ, IV:17
    death of the Lord and, IV:17
    in everlasting fire, IV:18
    desire to be worshipped, IV:19
    proudest of all spirits, IV:20
    handed over to, by original sin, XIII:16
    subject to the Almighty, XIII:16
    overcome by God's justice, XIII:17, 18
    overcome (and man freed from) by Christ's death, XIII:19, 22
    turned out of hearts; power limited, XIII:20
    outdone by a rational creature: the God-man, XIII:22
    conquered by second Adam, XIII:23
    called "captivity which was taken captive," XV:34
    overcome by blood of the Lamb, XV:44
discernment of spirits, III:18
discipline: meanings, XIV:1
divine persons, *see* persons; Trinity
divinity: not seen by human sight, I:11
doctrine: "my doctrine is not mine," I:27
doubt:
    Augustine's goal: overcoming, I:4
    things the mind knows with certainty, X:14
    use of mind's faculties, X:14
    true/false words, XV:24
dove: Pentecostal, II:11
dreams: deluded by images, XI:7

E

earth:
    love for the good things of this earth, VIII:4
Elijah: prayer; drought, III:11
enigma (allegory), XV:15
enjoyment:
    use of created things, IX:13
    will: things can be enjoyed or used, X:13
    using, with actual joy, X:17

equality:
    proven from scripture, I:7-13
    "did not think it robbery . . . ," I:12; V:4;
        VI:5
    ascension to the Father, I:18
    Son hearkens to us with the Father, I:21
    the Son in form of God, I:22
    belief in Jesus, as we believe in the Father,
        I:27
    the Son's substance, no lesser good than the
        Father's, I:31
    scripture: substance of Father and Son, II:3
    work of Father and Son is indivisible, II:3
    the form-of-God rule, II:4
    greater: one who sends; one is sent, II:7
    three men at the oak of Mambre, II:20
    the one sent (Son) and sender (Father),
        IV:26
    Christ: power and wisdom of God, VI:1
    in virtues, VI:6
    Father and Son: same substance, VI:6
    wisdom and charity in God, VI:7
    one is as much as three together, VI:11
    no single person is less than the trinity itself,
        VIII:1
    when complete: mind, knowledge, love,
        IX:4
    focus of book I, XV:5
    man: in nature never equal to God, XV:26
error:
    three types, thinking about God, I:1
    remembering sensed thing falsely, XI:17
eternal life:
    the Father's word and commandment, I:26
    the Son: begotten to unchangeable life, I:26
    "he who listens to my word . . . ," I:30
    sight not granted to the wicked, I:30
    answer to young man asking about
        achieving, I:31
    contemplation of God; everlasting joy, I:31
    to know the one true God, I:31
    the changeable and faith, IV:24
    truth abides: immortal, imperishable,
        unchanging, IV:24
    truth and faith, IV:24
eucharist:
    unique sign, III:10
    infants' knowledge of the celebration,
        III:21
Eunomius (heretic), XV:38
Eve, see Adam and Eve
existence: no thing brings itself into, I:1
Exodus, The:
    theophanies, II:23-27, 32
eyes, see seeing; sight

                            F

faith:
    vigor of mind, I:4
    love: through faith, to sight, I:21
    beholding Christ's back (humanity), II:28
    resurrection of Christ gives value to, II:29

    temporal/eternal things and, IV:24
    things done in time for our sakes, IV:24
    becomes truth by seeing, IV:24
    following Christ; four stages, IV:24
    "unless you believe . . . ," VII:12
    firm assent, even if understanding is
        unclear, VIII:1
    believing (hoping, loving) what it cannot
        yet see, VIII:6
    fabrications of imagination, VIII:7
    physical appearance irrelevant to, VIII:7
    fabrication; false beliefs, VIII:8
    help in knowing and loving God, VIII:13
    certitude of, initiates knowledge, IX:1
    acceptance of historical events, XIII:2
    in things that are false, XIII:3
    seen, with certitude, in the heart, XIII:3, 5
    meaning not perceived by bodily sense,
        XIII:4
    a thing of heart, not of bodily sense, XIII:5
    comes by hearing, XIII:5
    each has his own consciousness of, XIII:5
    necessary in this mortal life, XIII:10
    promise of immortality, XIII:12
    necessary for happiness of body and soul,
        XIII:25
    works through love, XIII:26
    leads to true happiness, XIV:3
    a temporal thing, XIV:3
    to be replaced by sight, XIV:4
    retaining, observing, loving, XIV:5
    in our (temporal only) consciousness,
        XIV:5
    recollection: image hidden in memory,
        XIV:5
    consciousness and, XIV:11
    seeking God, XV:2
    can have, without love, XV:32
    purifies hearts, XV:44
fall of man: happiness not remembered, XIV:21
family, as a trinity, XII:5, 8
fancies:
    desiring covetously, XI:8
    memory and thought in, XI:17
Father:
    distinct person, I:7
    he alone, addressing his Son, I:7, 8
    as greater than the Son, I:14
    greater than Son (in form of servant), I:15
    Philip, "whoever has seen me . . . ," I:17
    Son shall tell you openly about Father, I:21
    the Father's doctrine is his Word, I:27
    all judgment given to the Son, I:29, 30
    the getting of being, II:2
    "He gave the Son life," II:4
    nowhere said to have been sent, II:8
    not sent; physical manifestations, II:12
    delusions re texts on the Father "alone,"
        II:14-15
    appearing visibly to human eyes, II:18
    voice at baptism & transfiguration of Jesus,
        II:18

the invisible and only God, II:20
scriptures: never found as "being sent,"
    II:22
never appeared to the patriarchs, II:32
never presented in bodily guise, II:34
said to have sent, not to have been sent, III:3
as known by someone in time, IV:28
source of all godhead, IV:29
voice heard, after the incarnation, IV:31
begetter of his own attributes, VI:2-3
wisdom begotten by, VI:2, 3
begetter of greatness, VI:3
as "greater," VI:5
Arians: only true God, VI:10
Hilary on eternity in, VI:11
called so, with reference to Son, VII:1
question: powerful or wise, taken singly,
    VII:1
Christ: power of God, wisdom of God
    (text), VII:1-2, 4
as not wise with himself, but with the Son,
    XV:12
senses of Word of God and, XV:22
alone is called unbegotten, XV:47
see also God; persons; Trinity
fear:
    senses shrinking from sensible things, XI:7
fire:
    Pentecostal, II:11
    Mount Sinai manifestation; Pentecost, II:26
flesh (a term for "man"), II:11
form:
    observed by eye of the mind, IX:12
    true knowledge of things, IX:12
    observing and loving, X:2
    begotten by visible object, XI:3
    luminous body, changing colors, XI:4
    likeness remains in memory, XI:6
    things stored in memory, XI:13
friends:
    analogy: knowledge and knower, IX:6
future:
    philosophers, prophets, and historians,
        IV:21-22
    foretelling: angels and the airy powers,
        IV:22
    philosophers are not to be consulted, IV:23
    guess at, from past things, XV:13

G

gesture: a way of speaking, XV:19
gift, contrasted with donation, V:16
giving: from the Father to the Son, I:29
glorification:
    Jesus, in form of a servant, I:24
    Holy Spirit, the Father also, glorifies Son,
        II:6
glory: from faith to sight, XV:14
God:
    conceived of, in bodily terms, I:1
    error: God begets himself, I:1
    false ideas about, I:1

scripture's use of corporeal words, I:2
true immortality, I:2, 10
knowledge of God's substance, I:3
being God, and being true God, I:10
the Father himself loves us, I:21
face to face seeing, by the clean of heart,
    I:28
his goodness manifested to the pure of
    heart, I:31
that one who alone is good, I:31
"no one is good except the one God," I:31
"who alone has immortality," II:15
has shown himself only through a created
    bodily substance, II:16
Moses demands a true spiritual vision of,
    II:27
substance cannot be physically seen, II:35
power to produce sensible effects through
    spiritual agents, III:6
his will as ultimate cause, III:8
invisibly produces visible and sensible
    effects, III:10
the one creator, III:18
physical objects sometimes represent
    God's person, III:19
unchangeable substance, therefore
    invisible, III:21
hearts purified, to see substance of, III:26
longing for God, IV:1
unchangeable: eternity, truth, will, IV:1
extent of his love for us, IV:2
cannot be measured by changeable things,
    V:1
think about always, V:1
accidental predications [Aristotle's], V:2
substance or being, V:3
no modifications in, V:3, 5
unchangeable, V:5
nothing said of him modification-wise, V:6
substance-wise references to himself, V:7,
    9
"you alone are the great God," V:9
metaphors of time, place, etc., V:9
the one God is a trinity, V:9
predications about, V:11
his loving "temporally" is unthinkable,
    V:17
lord of time, V:17
past and future in, V:17
relationship modifications, V:17
said to be "angry," V:17
Father of power and wisdom, VI:1, 2
virtues: simple multiplicity, VI:6
called great in multiple ways, VI:8
the trinity as only true God, VI:10
greatness of, not separate from being God,
    VII:1
cause of his being, VII:2
to be, the same as to be wise, VII:2
truth in thinking/talking about, VII:7
being: I am who I am, VII:10
improperly called substance, VII:10

to be is to subsist, VII:10
able to know what he is not, VIII:3
the good of every created good, VIII:4
the good in which we live, move, are, VIII:5
beholding permitted only to the pure in
    heart, VIII:6
loving related to knowing, VIII:6
inward presence, VIII:11
God is love, VIII:11
cause of not seeing God: not loving brother,
    VIII:12
ourselves made better by knowing God,
    IX:16
the wish to claim God's inner beauties for
    self, X:7
source of goods making men happy,
    XIII:10
his "wrath" is not emotional, XIII:21
supreme wisdom, XIV:1
body and soul: we live in him, XIV:16
memory erased by forgetfulness, XIV:17
seeking the Lord always, XV:2
incomprehensibility, XV:2
when found, seek more avidly, XV:2
a triad without being triple (book VI), XV:5
anything said about, also fits the trinity,
    XV:7
genuinely immortal, eternal, unchangeable,
    XV:7
goodness and justice identical, XV:7
life in, XV:7
sensing and understanding identical in,
    XV:7
wisdom, XV:7-9
qualities signifying substance, XV:8
eternal, wise, happy, XV:8-9
enigma: we see now through a mirror . . . ,
    XV:16, 44
his knowledge is also his wisdom, XV:22
simplicity, XV:22
unchangeable, XV:38
see also creation; Father; Holy Spirit; Jesus
    Christ; persons; trinity
godlessness:
    getting further away from him who alone
        can satisfy, X:7
    forgetting God, as forgetting one's own life,
        XIV:17
    result: weakness, darkness, XIV:18
    light in the heart of man, XIV:21
    transformed from, XV:14
good and evil:
    divine causality, III:14
    love for the good things of this earth, VIII:4
    no changeable goods, without the
        unchangeable good, VIII:5
    failing to love the good that makes things
        good, VIII:5
    using/enjoying things badly, X:13
    likeness to the highest good, XI:8
    abstaining from evil, in time, XII:22
    wisdom and knowledge, XII:22

God: source of goods making men happy,
    XIII:10
devil imitated: devoted to power, not
    justice, XIII:17
evils remain, after forgiveness of [original]
    sin, XIII:20
making good use of evil, XIII:20
all works together for, for those who love
    God, XIII:20
see also happiness; sin
good example:
    building up one's neighbor, II:28
good person:
    good things from good treasure of his heart,
        I:31
    love for, even if never seen, X:1
good will: perversion of, XIII:17
good works:
    rest, the eternal reward for, I:20
    words from the heart, IX:14
    services of mercy, XII:11
government:
    chain of beings; hierarchy, III:9
    human affairs in hands of wise men, III:9
grace:
    gratis: voluntary rain, IV:2
    sons of God by, XIII:12
    knowledge and, XIII:24
greatness:
    predication, V:11
    the equally true must be equally great,
        VIII:2
greed: root of all evils, XII:14
Greek works, III:1
guilt: purged by Christ's death, IV:17

H

happiness:
    fullness of, I:18
    following God-made-man, VII:5
    final end, XI:10
    sequence of wills as ladder to, XI:10
    loved, but not known, by all, XIII:7
    variety of wishes re, XIII:7
    in bodily pleasures, XIII:7
    unhappiness from bad will, XIII:8
    definition of the happy man, XIII:8-9
    philosophers on the happy life, XIII:8, 10
    having the good things wanted; not wanting
        anything bad, XIII:9, 10, 11
    eternal, XIII:10
    waiting in hope of, XIII:10
    adversity, XIII:10
    immortality and, XIII:11
    unhappy: not loving one's life, XIII:11
    all have desire for, XIII:11, 25
    everlasting, XIII:12
    wishing well and being able to do what you
        wish, XIII:17
    eternal and temporal things, XIV:3
    Cicero on four basic virtues, XIV:12
    sin, and God's justice, XIV:21

before the fall of man, XIV:21
men living in philosophy (Cicero), XIV:26
harmonia (the word), IV:4
hate: loving evil, is hating self, XIV:18
head: analogy with mind, IX:6
health, IV:24
hearing: love commonly results from, X:1
heart:
　blessed are the clean of heart, I:17, 31
　the blessed clean of heart, will see God,
　　I:28, 30, 31
　good things from good treasure of his heart,
　　I:31
　fancies of, IV:1
　words from the heart, IV:6; IX:14
　justice: light in the heart of man, XIV:21
　seeking the Lord always, XV:2
　what comes from the "mouth" of, XV:18
heaven:
　will of God presiding in, III:9
　direct contemplation of divine persons,
　　XV:45
　see also contemplation; eternal life
heretics:
　use of the scriptures, I:6
　only the Father is God, II:23
　unbelievers in the Church, II:30
Hilary, on the trinity, VI:11
historians:
　philosophers and the future, IV:21
history:
　knowledge in awareness of, XIII:2
Holy Spirit:
　distinct person, I:7
　form of a dove, I:8
　problem of begetting of, I:8
　bodies as temples of, I:13
　consubstantial and co-eternal, I:13
　God, not creature, I:13
　Spirit of truth, I:18
　will teach you all truth, I:18
　abode, along with Father and Son, I:19
　advocate to be with you, I:19
　"I shall send him to you," I:25
　"the Father will send in my name," I:25
　he will not speak from himself, II:5
　neither a son, nor begotten, II:5
　proceeds from the Father, II:5
　glorifying the Father, II:6
　the virgin birth, II:9
　form of a dove, II:10, 11
　created form not assumed by, II:11
　sent; physical manifestations, II:12; III:3;
　　IV:30
　as angel, II:23
　Mount Sinai manifestation; Pentecost, II:26
　sent to the world (where he already was),
　　III:3
　gift of knowledge (note 3), IV:1
　not the Father's and the Son's, IV:29
　not yet given (Jn VII:39), IV:29
　procession of, IV:29

only person called gift of God, IV:29;
　XV:29, 33-36
manifestations, after the incarnation, IV:31
called the gift of God, V:12
Spirit of both Father and Son, V:12, 13;
　VI:7; XV:27, 37
right to be called origin, V:14
to each is given a manifestation of, V:14
Father and Son as origin, V:15
Spirit of Elijah, V:15
why not a Son also, V:15
being-gift by being given, V:16
proceeds from eternity, V:16
as gift, and as donation, V:17
unity and equality of substance, VI:7
as wisdom, VII:6
re being called Son, IX:17
as mother of the Son, XII:5
charity of God poured into our hearts,
　XIII:14
mission: focus of books II-IV, XV:5
distinctively named charity, XV:29, 31
abiding in God, XV:31
love which is from God and is God, XV:32
nothing more excellent than this gift of
　God, XV:32
gifts/endowments given through, XV:32,
　34
living water, XV:33
distribution of, XV:34
speaking with tongues, XV:35
co-eternal with the Father, XV:36
not alone in being God-charity, XV:37
best fits name: will of God, XV:38
like him: will, love or esteem, XV:41
given by the Son, XV:45
given through laying on of hands, XV:46
sent from heaven by the Son, XV:46
proceeds from Father and Son, XV:47-48
proceeds from the Father, XV:50
see also Pentecost; persons; Trinity
hope: eternal contemplation of God, I:17
human body, *see* body
human condition:
　weakness; longing for God, IV:1
　seeking eternity, truth, happiness, IV:2
　men by nature; not just by sin, IV:4
　see also death; sin
human mind, *see* mind
humility:
　look at self in God's light, IV:1
　love brought to perfection in, IV:2
　made weak by being humbled, IV:2
　Christ vs devil, IV:13
　example of the Magi, IV:15
　borne on the wood of the cross, IV:20
　of the incarnation, VIII:7
　Jesus: learn of me . . . , VIII:11

I

image of God:
　made by the Father through the Son, VII:5

refashioning, VII:5
let us [plural] make man, VII:12
similarity, not equality, VII:12
seeing the image in ourselves, IX:2
man as image of the trinity, IX:2; XII:6-8
the outer man (senses), XI:1
realized in father-mother-child, XII:8-9
man or woman as, XII:9-10
woman with her husband, XII:10
no bodily sex in, XII:12
rational mind as, XII:12
preserved only when facing him, XII:16
attributed to the man only, XII:19
to be found in human soul, XIV:5, 6
reform: turning to the Lord, XIV:22
full knowledge, with full vision, XIV:24
from blurred form to clear one, XV:14
being transformed into, XV:14, 21
word of man; Word of God, XV:20
memory, understanding, will, XV:39
see also trinities
images (perceptions):
mind hooked on bodily images, X:11
knowledge through senses, XIII:4
retained in memory, XIV:5
imagination:
fabricating physical features, VIII:7
desiring covetously, XI:8
immoderation, IX:15
immortality:
unchangingness, I:2, 10
partakers in life everlasting, I:10
"who alone has immortality," I:11
controversy: Jesus pre-incarnation, II:15
invisible and unchangeable divine
substance, II:16
happiness and, XIII:11
human reasoning, XIII:12
cease to desire; patiently wait, XIII:17
image of the Son, XIV:24
perfected on the last day, XIV:25
incarnation:
the Son alone, I:7, 8
the Son, same substance as the Father, I:9
everlasting substance prior to, I:14
form of God not lost in, I:14
belief in, as Son of God, I:30
the annunciation, II:8
working of Father and Son, II:9
the invisible three produce the visible Son,
II:18
participation in the Word, IV:4
the just man to intercede for sinful man, IV:4
how accomplished, IV:31
Son of God: remained God, became man,
XIII:13
advertises grace of God, XIII:22
three elements in one person, XIII:22
conception by believing, XIII:23
the supreme grace, XIII:24
individual:
memory, understanding, love, XV:42, 43

infants: soul; senses, XIV:7
inner man, *see* mind; soul
inquisitiveness, IX:18
intellect: best thing in our nature, V:2
inventio (the word), X:10
irreligion, *see* godlessness
Isaiah: seek/find God, XV:2

J

Jacob:
colors of his flocks, III:15; XI:5
anointed stone stands for Christ, III:20
Jesus Christ:
human weakness: crucified, I:3
question of divinity of, I:9
divinity not seen by the Jews, I:11
will transfigure body of our lowliness, I:15
handing over kingdom to the Father, I:15,
16, 17, 18, 20, 21
rejoice at my going to the Father, I:18
as priest, I:20
acts, in form of a servant, I:22
text: future time as though it were past, I:23
human power: "it is not mine to grant," I:25
"it is not I that will judge," I:26, 27
he who believes in me . . . , I:27
belief in, as we believe in the Father, I:27
"name above every name," I:29
form of God, form of servant, II:2
"my teaching is not mine," II:4, 5
all that the Father has is mine, II:5
"I did not come from myself," II:9
held to be mortal pre-incarnation, II:15
angel of great counsel, II:23
prefigured: "you shall see my back," II:28
death and resurrection prefigured, III:20
Moses' rod; Jacob's stone, III:20
proclamation of the law (Moses), III:26
true mediator, III:26; IV:12-19
his death as model, IV:6
his death as sacrifice [note 18], IV:6
materialistic thoughts about, IV:6
not to touch, until he has ascended, IV:6
burial; the new tomb, IV:9
death: 3 days in tomb, IV:9-10
consubstantial equality, IV:12
death: amazement of those present, IV:16
true mediator of life, IV:17
effects of his death on mankind, IV:17
devil: scoffing at death of, IV:18
Word made to receive our faith, IV:26
sacrament: Word become flesh, IV:27
God and man, IV:31
whole man: body and soul, IV:31
as wisdom, VII:4
as model, VII:5
emptied himself, VII:5
use of power, VIII:11
chose not to use power to avoid humiliation,
XIII:18
death: doing the Father's will, XIII:18
the devil overpowered by his death, XIII:18

crucified as man, rose as God, XIII:18
death for justice's sake, XIII:18
power: rising from the dead, XIII:18
sin; reconciliation through second Adam,
   XIII:21
why should his death not have happened?
   XIII:21
no sin ever, XIII:23
treasures of wisdom and knowledge,
   XIII:24
power and wisdom: focus of book VI,
   XV:5, 9
thought of as blaspheming, XV:17
as man, received the Holy Spirit, XV:46
born of the Holy Spirit, XV:46
see also crucifixion; incarnation; persons;
   redemption; resurrection; Son of God;
   Word of God
Job: tested, III:12
John, apostle, evangelist:
   on brotherly charity, VIII:12
   beginning of his gospel (I:1-14), XIII:2
John the Baptist:
   filled with Holy Spirit, IV:29; XV:46
   historicity, XIII:2
   witness to the light, XIII:4
joy:
   foreshadowing by Mary and Martha, I:20
   contemplation of God; eternal life, I:31
   see also enjoyment
judgment day:
   "it is not I that will judge," I:26, 27
   the Lord of glory, crucified, I:28
   "I in turn will love him," I:28
   handing over the kingdom, I:28
   the wicked will see him in form of man,
      I:28, 30
   the Son of man will/will not judge, I:29
   the Son in form of man, I:29, 30
   the Son: visible to good and bad alike, I:30
   the judge will not seem good to the wicked, I:31
   "come, blessed of my Father," I:31
   "go into everlasting fire," I:31
   faith in the Catholic Church, I:31
   our supreme good: sight of God, I:31
   image of God perfected on, XIV:25
justice:
   beauty of mind, VIII:9
   knowing what "just" is, VIII:9
   defination of a just mind, VIII:9
   love men (neighbor) because of justice,
      VIII:9
   form we judge by found in God, VIII:13
   one loving perfectly is already just, IX:14
   a property of good will, XIII:17
   devil imitated: devoted to power, not
      justice, XIII:17
   immortal, XIV:12
   divine, XIV:15
   meriting happiness, XIV:21
   turning from light in the heart of man,
      XIV:21

justification:
   justified in his blood, XIII:15, 18, 21
   see also redemption

K

kingdom of God:
   handing over, to the Father, I:15, 16, 17, 18,
      20, 21
   Daniel: the Father giving, the Son
      receiving, II:33
know thyself, X:12
knowing oneself: beauty of, X:5
knowledge:
   value, IV:1
   certitude completed after this life, IX:1
   equal with mind, when complete, IX:4
   greater than the body known, IX:4
   specific or generic, IX:9
   a word, or only loved knowledge, IX:15
   likeness to the thing known, IX:16
   of quality, IX:16
   ourselves made better by knowing God,
      IX:16
   knowable, but not yet known, IX:18
   preceded by inquisitiveness, IX:18
   thing known co-generates knowledge of
      itself, IX:18
   appetite for learning, IX:18
   what mind knows, the whole of it knows,
      X:6
   hankering after temporal things, XII:16
   of changeable things, XII:17, 25
   good within its proper limits, XII:21
   necessary for virtue, XII:21
   action; temporal things, XII:22
   distinguished from wisdom, XII:23, 24;
      XIII:2; XIV:11
   conscious reasoning; sense images, XIII:4
   grace and, XIII:24
   of things human, XIV:3
   only possible in the mind, XIV:8
   needed, in temporal life, XIV:10, 13
   knowables beget knowledge, XIV:13
   man's wisdom (Cicero), XIV:26
   knowing something as true, XV:17
   a word is born from, XV:19
   certainty of being alive, XV:21
   innumerable numbers, XV:21
   two kinds of perceptions, XV:21
   human: can be both lost and acquired,
      XV:22
   for man: not the same to be as to know,
      XV:24
   called word even before being formed,
      XV:25
   everlasting, in the mind, XV:25
   see also trinities

L

language(s):
   scriptures speak in common human usage,
      I:23

negative adjectives, V:8
beauty; usefulness, X:2
studious about learning your own, X:2
to hear nobody as a foreigner, X:2
law: term for Old Testament books, XV:30
learning:
  pursuit and acquisition of, IX:18
  arousal of interest in studying, X:1, 2
  partial knowledge needed for pursuit of, X:3
  memory, understanding, and will, X:17
life:
  God animates all things as they are born,
    III:11
  forms; seed, III:13
life everlasting, *see* immortality
light:
  Wisdom: brightness of eternal light, IV:27
  God is (spiritual) light, VII:4
  image of God, VII:5
  not in God, not in light, VIII:12
literature, and truth, XIV:9
logic:
  genus/species names, VII:7-8, 11
  inadequacy of human speech, VII:9
look of the body:
  four "looks" brought to light, XI:16
Lot, two angels came to, II:21-22
love:
  keeping the commandments, I:18
  for us, by the three persons, I:21
  through faith, to sight, I:21
  building up one's neighbor, II:28
  yearning to behold God, II:28
  brought to perfection in humility, IV:2
  persuaded of God's love for us, IV:2
  substance of God, VI:7
  for God, as being good itself, VIII:4
  for good things of this earth, VIII:4
  failing to love the good that makes things
    good, VIII:5
  clinging to this good (God) in love, VIII:6
  loving God before one knows him, VIII:6
  believing the trinity which we do not know,
    VIII:8
  what one believes but does not see, VIII:9
  form and truth which the one loving sees in
    self, VIII:9
  love men (neighbor) because of justice,
    VIII:9
  loving oneself unjustly, VIII:9
  true love vs covetousness, VIII:10
  abiding in God, VIII:10
  definition of true love, VIII:10
  scripture sometimes refers to only one love
    command, VIII:10
  of God and neighbor (commands), VIII:10;
    XIV:18
  cause of not seeing God: not loving brother,
    VIII:12
  charity herself loved, VIII:12
  God understood in brotherly charity,
    VIII:12

  trinity seen in, VIII:12
  our brother as ourselves, VIII:12
  the two commandments cannot exist alone,
    VIII:12
  unites good angels and men in bond of
    holiness, VIII:12
  three: the lover, being loved, love, VIII:14;
    IX:2
  what does loving itself mean? IX:2
  with mind, one spirit, IX:2
  in the knowledge of the lover, IX:8
  kindled when hearing of great acts, IX:11
  for creatures, related to creator, IX:13
  as image or word, IX:17
  mind does not beget love of itself, IX:18
  for something quite unknown, X:1, 2, 3, 4
  mind loves the very knowing of "know
    thyself," X:5
  involved with senses of the flesh, X:7
  deserving, X:17
  of body-seen; alienation, XI:9
  of something not known, but only believed,
    XIII:26
  command to love neighbor as self, XIV:18
  straight, when God is loved, XIV:18
  for things beneath mind, XIV:20
  transferring: temporal to eternal, XIV:23
  God is charity; love is God, XV:27, 28, 31,
    37
  nothing, if without love, XV:32
  primordial function of memory, XV:41
  human: likeness to the Holy Spirit, XV:43
  see also covetousness; trinities

M

Magi, IV:15
man(-kind):
  cannot see God's face and live, II:28
  light of men: rational minds, IV:3
  mortal men made equal to angels, IV:12
  definition, XV:11
  a triad cannot be called one man, XV:43
  see also body; human condition; image of
    God; senses; soul
Martha and Mary, I:20
Mary, Blessed Virgin:
  filled with Holy Spirit, IV:29
  physical appearance, VIII:7
materialism:
  notions re God's Word and Wisdom, II:14
mediator:
  true: Jesus; false: devil, IV:13-19
  see also Jesus Christ; Son of God
memory:
  images stored in, IX:10, 11
  self-awareness of remembering, X:13
  image of divine trinity in the mind, X:17-19
  thought; recollection, XI:6
  memory, inner sight, and will, XI:11-12
  gives light on things looked at in thoughts,
    XI:14
  will, sensation, and attention, XI:14-15

remembering sensed thing falsely, XI:17
measure, XI:18
thoughts committed to, XII:23
false memories; dreams, XII:24
knowledge through senses, XIII:4
a confidential file of awareness, XIV:8
as limited to things past, XIV:14
forseeing by (not by foresight), XV:13
knowledge and, XV:40
a likeness to the Father, XV:43
see also trinities
mercy: good works, XII:11
metheglin (the word), X:2
mind:
    purification necessary, to see God, I:3
    vigor through faith, I:4
    darkness: foolish minds of men, IV:3
    chief part of man, VI:10
    its beauty cannot be seen, VIII:9
    we know others from knowing our own,
        VIII:9
    we know what (our) mind is, VIII:9
    a just mind: seeing the inner truth, VIII:9
    loving itself, IX:2
    with love, one spirit, IX:2
    must know itself in order to love, IX:3
    knowledge, when it knows itself, IX:4, 6
    love, when it loves itself, IX:4, 6
    love and knowledge in, substantially, IX:5,
        6
    wholeness; knowing/loving itself
        completely, IX:7
    change, with new knowledge, IX:11
    word joined to mind with love, IX:15
    as cause of its love of itself, IX:17
    begets knowledge of itself, IX:18; XIV:7
    can know itself as in a mirror, X:5
    love, when seeking to know itself, X:5
    knows itself to be mind, X:6
    commanded to know itself, X:7, 13, 16
    thinking of itself as if it were a body, X:8
    conceived of as mortal, X:9
    looks for things looked for by senses, X:10
    used to being with bodily images, X:11
    looking for itself as if it were absent, X:11
    looking for/finding itself, X:11
    things known with certainty, X:14
    as substance; as subject, X:15
    knows itself, even when looking for itself,
        X:16
    rational performance of bodily/temporal
        actions, XII:3
    looking for a trinity in, XII:4
    image of God, XII:4, 12, 15, 20; XV:5
    reaching for the eternal, XII:10
    common nature of man, woman, XII:12
    awareness: in temporal/eternal matters,
        XIII:1
    awarenesses in, XIV:9; XV:18
    inner-memory, -understanding, -will,
        XIV:10
    chief capacity: knowing God, XIV:11

live, move, are — in him, XIV:16, 21
always remembers, understands, loves
    itself, XIV:18, 19
possessions, treasures, XIV:19
changeable, XV:10
image of the trinity, XV:11
pre-eminent in the soul, XV:11
power to see invisible things, XV:49
see also attention; consciousness; thought;
    trinities
ministry:
    Paul on how God's ministers should live,
        VIII:13
miracles:
    signs of divine power, III:11
    staff of Moses into serpent, III:11
    water into wine, III:11
    wonderful works of God, III:11
    witchcraft, III:12
    tell us something about God, III:19
mirror:
    enigma: we see now through a mirror . . . ,
        XV:14, 16, 21, 44
missions:
    Old Testament theophanies, II:1-35
    going forth from the Father, into the world,
        II:7
    greater: one who sends; one is sent, II:7
    sendings of Son and Holy Spirit, II:7-11
    Son/Holy Spirit sent to where they already
        are, II:8
    sent by the Father; yet, he sent himself, II:9
    form of servant; form of God, II:9
    sent: the one who appeared in the flesh, II:9
    Son sent by Father and his Word, II:9
    outward sights, II:10
    symbolic actions (O.T.), II:11
    questions re Holy Spirit's physical
        manifestations, II:12
    O.T., the Son and Holy Spirit, II:13
    from world of spirit into public gaze, III:3
    persons: O.T. manifestations, III:3
    Son and Spirit in Old Testament, III:4
    use of physical creatures for bodily guise,
        III:4
    the one sent (Son) equal to the sender
        (Father), IV:26, 32
    Son not sent because Father is greater,
        IV:27
moderation:
    Cicero on four basic virtues, XIV:12
modification (the term), V:5
modifications:
    separable/inseparable, V:5
    whatever can be lost or diminished, V:6
    relationship terms in God, V:17
Moses:
    mission: lead people out of Egypt, II:23
    Mount Sinai; the ten commandments,
        II:25-26
    the Lord spoke to Moses face to face, II:27
    favor in God's sight, II:28

rod into serpent; meaning, III:20
appearance called both angel and Lord, III:24
belief in (Christ), III:26
law given to, by angels, III:26
cross prefigured by arms outstretched, IV:20
Spirit given to, V:15
Mount Sinai: the ten commandments, II:25-26
mouth:
    word from the heart, IX:14
    man defiled by what comes out of, XV:18
    of the body; of the heart, XV:18
music: fix in memory, XII:23

N

natural history:
    study, by philosophers, IV:21
natural phenomena:
    none is independent of God's will, III:7
nature:
    serves the divine command, III:7
    phenomena as work of God, III:11
    primary and secondary causes in, III:16-17
    normal course of, III:19
    sameness of nature and being in, VI:4
    contemplation of (Cicero), XIV:12
needs: ministering; good works, I:20
neighbor: scripture on command to love, II:28; VIII:9, 10, 12; XIV:18
numbers, innumerable, XI:12; XV:21
numerical harmony:
    number 3, IV:10
    number 4 & 40, IV:7-8, 10
    number 6, IV:7-8, 10

O

obedience:
    reward of Christ's obedience unto death, XIII:22
Old Testament:
    books included in "the law," XV:30
    see also prophets; theophanies
omnipotence:
    humility of the incarnation, VIII:7
omnipresence of God, II:7
original justice:
    carnal desires in paradise, XIII:23
original sin:
    handed over to devil's power, XIII:16
    evils remain, after forgiveness of sin, XIII:20
outer man: recollection, XII:1
    see also body

P

paradise: as physical locality, II:18
passover: lamb slain at, III:26
patience: comes to us from God, XV:27
Paul, Saint, apostle:
    his knowledge of the people he taught, I:23
    proclaiming Jesus Christ, III:10

why we love him, VIII:8, 9, 13
a just mind, VIII:9
mission given to, by Christ, XIII:19
Pentecost:
    the Holy Spirit alone, I:7, 8
    a violent wind; tongues as of fire, II:10, 11
    speaking in languages, IV:29
    given from heaven, XV:46
perfection: pressing on intently for, IX:1
persons:
    distinction of, in one God, I:7
    inseparable; work inseparably, I:7-8, 12, 15
    God and human bodies, I:13
    abode with those who love, and keep commandments, I:18
    each suffices by himself, I:18
    scripture shows one is from, not less, than other, II:3
    Holy Spirit, the Father also, glorifies Son, II:6
    presence everywhere (O.T. texts), II:7
    controversy re immortality, II:15
    invisible and unchangeable substance, II:16
    voices heard by Adam, II:18
    the name "Lord," II:19
    burning bush; angel of the Lord, II:23
    Mount Sinai: which person is not clear, II:26
    seeing, with the physical eye, II:27
    having been sent does not affect equality, III:3; IV:32
    acting through angels, III:26
    sender and sent are one, IV:29
    the Spirit of God is one, IV:29
    separate names; cannot be said as one, IV:30
    relationship-wise differences, V:6, 9, 11
    begetter, begotten and unbegotten (terms), V:7, 8
    trinitarian logic, V:8
    adding up in all three, to a singular, V:9
    "I and the Father are one," V:10
    called both holy and spirit, V:12
    relationship-wise predication, V:14
    "in the beginning was the Word," VI:3
    always in each other; never alone, VI:9
    supreme equality of, VI:10
    bounded or determined by each other, VI:11
    each in all, and all are one, VI:11
    Father, image, gift, VI:11
    called "Father," "Son" with reference to each other, VII:2
    one being, one God, VII:6
    terminology of Greeks and Latins, VII:7
    genus/species names, VII:7-8
    inadequacy of human terminology, VII:9
    why we say "three persons," VII:11
    no one excels in greatness, VIII:2
    partaking in the redemption, XIII:15
    on being "greater," (book VIII), XV:5
    memory, understanding, will, XV:12

wisdom, understanding, memory, XV:12
each sees all things together, XV:23
all together: one charity, XV:28
wisdom of God, XV:29
intervals of time in processions of, XV:45
distinguishing generation from procession, XV:48
see also equality; missions; predication; processions; Trinity
Peter, apostle: boldly preaching Christ, II:30
Philip, apostle: "whoever has seen me" . . . , IV:26
philosophers:
ridiculing Christ, IV:20-21
historians and the future, IV:21
not to be consulted re the future, IV:23
calling themselves wise . . . , IV:23
on the happy life, XIII:8, 10
disbelief; without the mediator, XIII:24
the term, since Pythagoras, XIV:2
without faith, insufficient for happiness, XIV:26
piety, XIV:1
pillars of cloud and fire, III:21
plagues of Egypt, III:12
Plato: on the soul, XII:24
pledge (the word), V:13
power:
taking pleasure in, VIII:11
devil imitated: devoted to power, not justice, XIII:17
limited in this life, XIII:17
desire power over your faults, XIII:17
a triad without being triple (book VII), XV:5
praise:
flattery, II:1
wanted by all people, XIII:6
prayer to the trinity, XV:51
preaching:
both good men and bad men can preach, III:14
predication:
affirmations and denials, V:8
substantive and relative, V:8, 11
of each person by himself, VII:1
of relationship, VII:2
presumption:
holders of false presumptions, II:1
pride:
devil: death, IV:13
value the devil more than Christ, IV:18
ashamed of the cross, IV:20
greatness of this vice, IV:20
obstacle to cleaving to God, XIII:22
priest: sacrifice for sin, IV:19
private property: greedy for more, XII:14
processions:
love is God, XV:31
intervals of time in, XV:45
timeless, XV:47
with no change in nature, XV:47

prophets:
sometimes represent God's person, III:19
expression "says the Lord" used by, III:25
foretelling the future, IV:22
true piety of, IV:23
O.T.: can include the psalms, XV:30
psalms: included with the prophets, XV:30
punishment: cause: deserts of the crime, IV:15
pure in heart:
blessed: they shall see God, VIII:6
purification:
of mind, to see God, I:3
by one's own power, IV:20
adaptation to eternal things by temporal means, IV:24
Pythagoras, XIV:2

Q

quality: positive knowledge of, IX:16

R

reader(s): covenant with, I:5
reason:
role in temporal affairs, XII:13
knowledge of changeable things, XII:17
recollection:
conscious attention to memory, XI:6
will acting on attention, XI:8
memory, inner sight, and will, XI:12
redemption:
Christ died for us, still sinners, IV:2
blood of the just man, IV:4
the many saved by the One, IV:11
chains of many sins broken by Christ's death, IV:17
God chose to suffer death, XIII:13
reconciliation through death of the Son, XIII:14, 21
the Father did not spare the Son, XIII:15
primacy of justice over power, XIII:17, 18
devil overcome (and man freed from) by Christ's death, XIII:19
incarnation: way chosen by God, XIII:23
relationship:
each being is something besides the relationship, VII:2
being and subsisting, VII:9
use of the plural, VII:12; VIII:1
remembering:
memory, inner sight, and will, XI:11-12
previous incarnations, XII:24
renewal:
put on the new man, XIV:22
reform: turning to the Lord, XIV:22
stages; day by day progress, XIV:23, 25
see also spiritual life
repentance:
soul resuscitated by, IV:5
crucifixion of the inner man, IV:6
cry for pity, XIV:18
resurrection (of Christ):
Christ wants us to believe, II:29

faith in, saves and justifies, II:29
afterwards, many believed, II:31
Christ bestowed two resurrections on us,
IV:6
model for our bodies' resurrection, IV:6
sacrament of our inner resurrection, IV:6
called to new life, justified, IV:17
resurrection of the body:
through his Spirit, IV:5
pre-enacted by Christ, IV:6, 11
end of the world, XIV:23
image of the Son, XIV:24
resurrection of the dead:
Jesus, mediator of life, IV:15
faulted by philosophers, IV:21

S

Sabellius, VII:9
sacrament: Word become flesh, IV:27
sacrifice:
evil spirits and true sacrifice, IV:19
four elements in each, IV:19
offered for purification of human faults,
IV:19
one true mediator, IV:19
sagacity: Cicero on four basic virtues, XIV:12,
14
saints:
sharing in the selfsame, III:8
demons and, IV:14
loved, and predestined, by God, V:17
salvation: giver and receiver, V:15
salvator (the word), XIII:14
scripture:
use of words taken from corporeal things,
I:2
heretics' use of, I:6
language: common human usage, I:23
see also theophanies
security: loss of sense of, X:7
seed: forms of life, III:13
seeing:
most excellent of the senses, XI:1
a trinity in the act of, XI:2
thing seen, the sight, conscious intention,
XI:2
will to see has sight as its end, XI:10
see also sight
seeking God:
error: forsaking God's inward presence,
VIII:11
faith seeks, understanding finds, XV:2
self:
not knowing, not thinking, of self, X:7
loving, hating, XIV:18
self-enjoyment: a private good, XII:17
selfsame (the term), III:8
sending, *see* missions
senses/sensation:
images absorbed by, IX:10, 11
mind looks for things looked for by senses,
X:10

sensation divided in five parts, XI:1
analogies of the trinity in, XI:1-17
conscious soul and body senses, XI:2
necessary for memory of anything bodily,
XI:14
material things, XII:17
power, in men and in animals, XII:20
knowledge through, XIII:4
the outer man (book XI), XV:5
perceptions through, XV:21
serpent:
stands for death, III:20
sensation represented by serpent, not
woman, XII:20
sex: when not required for procreation, XIII:23
sex differences:
head-covering: man, woman, XII:12
man represents mind; woman, sensation,
XII:20
sight:
visible form impressed on eyes, XI:2
visible object; seeing subject, XI:3
seeing double flame of candle, XI:4
role of will in sight, XI:5
form of body from which it is produced,
XI:9
partly spiritual, XI:9
resting place of the will, XI:10
will, sensation, and attention, XI:14-15
sensation of, from external body, XI:16
remembering sensed thing falsely, XI:17
number, XI:18
brutish, without mind, XIV:19
sign: hearing an unknown sign, X:2
Simeon, IV:29
sin:
few care about not sinning, IV:15
our death; Christ's death, IV:15
road to death, IV:15
sacrifice for sin, IV:19
weight of love of temporal things, IV:24
words from the heart, IX:14
list of objectives, XII:14
seeks to obtain things sensed through body,
XII:15
in thought or in deed, XII:17-18
commission; remission, XIII:16
enemies of justice, XIII:21
singing: harmony, IV:4
Son of God:
distinct person, I:7
life everlasting, I:10
as servant: the Father's inferior, I:14
equality: the form of God, I:14-21
"emptied himself; form of a servant," I:14,
18, 20, 21, 22, 31; II:20
the "Father is greater than I," I:15, 18
the "Son himself shall be made subject . . . ,"
I:15, 20
Holy Spirit will teach you all truth, I:18
sufficing us, by himself, I:18
differing in substance, I:20

Jesus, in form of God, I:22
the Spirit of the Lord is upon me, I:22
form of God; form of a servant, I:22, 24
glorifies his saints, I:24
whom he justified, them he also glorified,
    I:24
as judge on the last day, I:26
"I speak just the Father told me," I:26
begotten to unchangeable life, I:26
life in himself, I:26
the word the Son has spoken judges, I:26
"have not spoken as from myself," I:26
texts: the Father has "given" to the Son, I:29
all judgment given to, I:29, 30
life in himself, I:30
the getting of being, II:2
God from God, II:2
lesser as to changeable human substance,
    II:3
birth in eternity (from the Father), II:3
doing only what he saw the Father doing,
    II:3, 5
the form-of-God rule: equal to, yet from,
    the Father, II:4
in form of servant: can do nothing of
    himself, II:5
He was in the world (Jn I:10-11), II:7
mission: made of a woman, II:8
called a rock, II:11
God and man, II:11
lamb of God, II:11
held to be mortal before incarnation, II:15
said to be visible before incarnation, II:15
as having appeared to Abraham, II:20
back visible; face invisible, II:31
visible, in form of servant, II:31
appearance to Daniel in physical form,
    II:33
sent to the world (where he already was),
    III:3
purpose: by faith to lead us to his truth,
    IV:24
purpose of his mission, IV:25
mission in this world, IV:30
"begotten" means the same as "son," V:8
coeternal with the Father, VI:1, 3
"God from God, light from light," VI:3
only the Son is Christ, VI:10
as Word, as Wisdom, VII:3
mercy: became man for us, XIII:12
Word made flesh, XIII:24
mission: focus of books II-IV, XV:5
called the Word, not thought, of God,
    XV:25
only person called Word of God, XV:29
"Son of his charity," XV:37
begotten by will of God, XV:38
see also Jesus Christ; Wisdom; Word of
    God
Son of man:
    will judge by his authority as Son of God,
        I:28, 30

power to do judgment, II:3
assumed by Word of God, II:11
soothsayers, IV:22, 23
sorrow: longing for God, IV:1
soul:
    differing in substance, I:20
    spiritual substance; invisible, II:14, 16
    divine will uses the just and the bad for his
        purposes, III:8
    sharing in changeless wisdom, III:8
    body's life; changeable, IV:3
    ungodliness as death of, IV:5
    godless; returned to life, IV:5
    death: why have you forsaken me, IV:6
    lives more when it is wise, V:5
    spirit received so as to be man, V:15
    time of creation of, V:17
    nature not simple but multiple, VI:8
    simple; no mass spread, VI:8
    whole in any part of body, VI:8
    becoming wise, VII:2
    expression: a good soul, VIII:4
    turning away from highest good, VIII:5
    some parts we share even with animals, X:7
    conceived of as fifth elementary substance,
        X:9
    pursuing likeness to God, XI:8
    the inner man, where reason begins, XII:13
    goal: higher things, not possessed privately,
        XII:15
    image of God, XIV:6
    life immortal, XIV:6
    rational and intellectual, XIV:6
    of infants, XIV:7
    reasoning about temporal things, XIV:10
    called spirit, XIV:22
    eternal, XIV:26
    image of God, XV:1
    mind belongs to, XV:11
    Augustine's soliloquy to, XV:50
    see also body and soul; immortality; mind;
        spirit
speech: vocal sound as sign, XV:19, 20
spirit:
    life; faith, IV:5
    death: forsaken by God, IV:16
    of more value than body, IV:16
    by cleaving, made one with God's Spirit,
        VI:4
    virtues, VI:6
    better, by cleaving to creator, VI:9
    human: called true/great, VIII:3
    each mind is spirit, XIV:22
    the term, used in many ways, XIV:22
    see also soul
spirits:
    angel-messengers, III:9
    airy bodies (demonic), IV:14
    difficult concept: without bodies, VIII:3
spiritual life:
    cannot see God's face and live, II:28
    dying to fleshly attachments, II:28

renewal; growth, IV:5
put falsehood aside, IV:6
renewal; repentance, IV:6
progress in time; not in this world, IV:28
the Word is sent to souls knowing him,
    IV:28
Word perceived according to one's
    progress toward God, IV:28
when the lesser cleaves to the greater, VI:9
imitation (paradoxes), VII:5
mind intent on invisible things, XII:21
failing to live . . . in him, XIV:16
one spirit: cleaving to the Lord, XIV:20
see also renewal
Stephen, the martyr, III:24, 26
study: love as motivation for, X:2
substance:
    argument: Father & Son differ in substance,
        V:4
    hypostasis (Greek term), V:10
    in predication, all are called together, VI:3
    unity of Father and Son, VI:4
    both simple and multiple, VI:8
    Father and Son: each is one substance,
        VII:2
    relationships, VII:2
    terminology of Greeks and Latins, VII:7
    predication as relationship, VII:9
    changeable things, VII:10
    subsisting, VII:10
    mind, love, knowledge (in one being), IX:8
    memory, understanding, and will, X:18
    Father and Son: focus of book V, XV:5
    qualitative predications, XV:8
suicide, IV:16
summary of books I-XIV, XV:4-5
symbols: Old Testament phenomena, II:11

T

teletai (the word), IV:13
temporal (the word):
    that which has originated, IV:24
temporal goods:
    adaptation to eternal things, IV:24
    diminishing or increasing, VIII:5
    failing to love the good that makes things
        good, VIII:5
    love of; conception of a word, IX:14
    not satisfying, even when gotten, IX:14
    dangerous advances into, XII:10
    reason's role in, XII:13
    reasonable use of, XII:21
    rational cognizance of, XII:25
    needed: knowledge of human affairs,
        XIV:10
    no need to tell God our needs, XV:22
temptation: able to endure, XIII:20
ten commandments: Mount Sinai, II:25-26
theophanies (Old Testament), II:1-35
    fire in the bush; speaking by the Father, II:12
    ascertaining which person(s) appeared,
        II:13

creatures formed for; angels, II:13
Genesis: God walks/talks with Adam,
    II:17, 18
Abraham: come away from your country . . . ,
    II:19
the name "Lord," II:19
three men at the oak of Mambre, II:19-21
burning bush; angel of the Lord, II:23;
    III:23
from the book of Exodus, II:23-27, 32
Exodus: pillar of cloud/fire, II:24
which person is not clear, II:24, 26
creature control; visible, perceptible, II:25
Mount Sinai; the ten commandments,
    II:25-26
Mount Sinai: which person is not clear,
    II:26
creation serving God's purposes, II:27
Moses demands: show me your majesty,
    II:27
the Lord spoke to Moses face to face, II:27
"you shall see my back," II:28
to Moses: you cannot see my face and live,
    II:28
soul ravished with desire for, II:28
God manifested in symbolic manner, II:32
Daniel of the Ancient of Days, II:33
seeing God (persons) with bodily eyes,
    II:34
senses of mortal man, II:35
identifying the one who appeared, III:3
persons in bodily manifestations, III:3
achieved through created objects, III:22
angels: testimony of New Testament, III:22
angels as secondary agents of, III:22-27
Son of God, called "angel," III:23
the Lord (i.e. angel) said to Moses, III:23
Stephen: angel appeared to Moses, III:24
the Lord spoke through angels, III:26
manifestations (O.T./N.T.) differ, III:26
pre-incarnation, work of angels, III:26
likenesses of Christ, IV:11
seen by the fathers before he was sent,
    IV:26
produced by trinity together, IV:30
produced before the incarnation, IV:31
theosebeia (the word), XIV:1
thought:
    memory, innar sight, will, XI:6, 12
    as sights seen in, XI:13
    brought out from things stored in memory,
        XI:13
    sense experience basic to, XI:14
    sight of, formed from internal memory,
        XI:16
    sinful pleasures, XII:18
    formed on image retained in memory,
        XIV:5
    understanding belongs to, XIV:9
    inner-words, XIV:10
    word formed in act of thought, XIV:13
    as sight of consciousness, XV:16

seeing one's own thoughts, XV:16
"they said to themselves . . . ", XV:17
awareness, XV:17
utterances of the heart, XV:18
our true word, XV:25
see also form; knowledge
time:
    Jesus: future time as though it were past,
        I:23
    the day and the hour, I:23
    the Son, begotten before creation, I:24
    timelessly contained in eternal Wisdom,
        II:9
    the sixth age, IV:7
    tripartite division of, IV:7
    cycles of the year, IV:8
    did not begin in time, V:17
    God does not see in, XII:10
transformations: by angels, III:5
treasures: possessions, and the mind,
        XIV:19
trinities (analogues of the divine trinity):
    memory, understanding, will, IV:30;
        X:17-19; XIV:8, 10
    the lover, being loved, love, VIII:14; IX:2
    the mind, its love and knowledge, IX:4, 6,
        7, 8, 15, 18
    analogy: three rings from the same gold,
        IX:7
    image, likeness, equality, IX:16
    disposition, learning, practice, X:17
    analogies from the outer man (senses),
        XI:1-17
    thing seen, the sight, conscious intention,
        XI:2
    memory, inner sight, and will, XI:6, 11-12;
        XIV:12, 13
    senses, memory, attention, XI:14
    looking for, in the mind, XII:4
    family: male, female, offspring, XII:5, 8, 9
    memory, thought, will, XII:25; XIII:26;
        XIV:8
    memory, observation, love, XIV:4
    none deservedly called image of God,
        XIV:4
    memory, recollection: will, XIV:5
    image, attention, will, XIV:11
    the look, awareness, will, XIV:11
    mind: remembering, understanding, loving
        itself, XIV:11, 13, 14
    memory, sight, love, XIV:11; XV:39
    virtues: retaining, looking, loving, XIV:12
    memory, understanding, love, XIV:13;
        XV:42, 43
    lover, what is loved, and love, XV:10
    wisdom, knowledge, and love, XV:10
    respective sizes, XV:43
Trinity:
    goal: give people reasons for this teaching,
        I:4
    inseparable substance, I:7
    "all things were made through him," I:12

awareness of, when persons are referred to
    singly, I:19
indivisible operation of one substance, I:25
work of Father and Son is indivisible, II:3
voices heard by Adam, II:18
thoughts inadequate to object, V:1
things-said-about are in singular, not plural,
    V:9, 11
"the Lord your God is one Lord," V:12
relationships within, V:15
fitting traces appear in creation, VI:11
whoever understands, even in part, thank
    God, VI:11
the question: Three What? VII:7
"three persons," why not "three Gods?",
    VII:8
belief in, VII:12
comparison of things known to, VIII:8
seen in charity, VIII:12
remain firm in faith while searching for, IX:1
seeking to understand, IX:1
man made in image of, IX:17; XII:6-8;
    XIV:25
believe rather than see (unlike trinities),
    XV:10
quite different from image(s) of, XV:42
three persons, one God, XV:43
seeing, face to face, XV:44
believe scriptures, rather than demand
    proof, XV:49
see also Father; Holy Spirit; persons; Son
    of God; trinities
tropes (figures of speech), XV:15
trust:
    no trust in our weakened selves, IV:2
truth:
    praise/condemnation of the author, I:6
    Holy Spirit will teach you all truth, I:18
    censure not feared by lover of, II:1
    wise man submits to eternal truth, III:8
    divine: unchangeable, IV:1; IX:9
    abides: immortal, imperishable,
        unchanging, IV:24
    eternal life, IV:24
    nothing is greater, unless more truly, VIII:2
    God is truth: do not ask what truth is, VIII:3
    searching re what is to be understood, IX:1
    form; judgment of, IX:10, 11
    wisdom and, XIII:24
    light in the heart of man, XIV:21
    knowing something as true, XV:17
    learnt from testimony of others, XV:21

U

understanding:
    anger: people told they are unfit for, I:3
    serious study, I:5
    difficulties presented by scriptures, II:1
    faint glimpse of truth re trinity, VII:9
    firm faith, even if unclear, VIII:1
    search truth about what is to be understood,
        IX:1

image of divine trinity in the mind, X:17-19
belongs to thought, XIV:9
as referring to things present, XIV:14
finding God, XV:2
likenesses useful for, XV:16
memory and love in, XV:41
a likeness to the Son, XV:43
see also trinities
unity:
  proven from scripture, I:7-13
  scripture: substance of Father and Son, II:3
  one in Christ, the mediator, IV:12
  "that we and they may be one," VI:4
  imitate this mutuality by grace, VI:7
  memory, understanding, and will, X:18
  image in memory, sight, conscious attention, XI:7
  focus of book I, XV:5
use: putting something at will's disposal, X:17

V

Virgil, XIV:14, 18
  virgin birth: working of Father and Son, II:9
virtues:
  cannot be separated from each other, VI:6
  knowledge necessary for, XII:21
  loving, for sake of happiness, XIII:11
  temporal life; related to faith, XIV:3
  begin in consciousness, XIV:12
  Cicero on four basic virtues, XIV:12

W

weakness: knowledge of one's own, IV:1
widow: the "true" widow (Paul), XII:11
will:
  perfecting the soul in good, VIII:5
  no voluntary act without previously uttered word, IX:12
  calling on, to direct mind, X:11
  resting, delighted, in things for their own sakes, X:13
  self-awareness of willing, X:13
  image of divine trinity in the mind, X:17-19
  desire directed to sensible things, XI:7
  role in recalling, XI:7, 8
  fixed on either inner or outer man, XI:8
  role in sight and body-seen, XI:9, 10
  its resting place, XI:10
  memory, inner sight, and will, XI:11-12
  memory, sensation, and attention, XI:14-15
  as parent or offspring, XI:18
  image in memory, joined to thought, XIV:5
  name "will" best fits the Holy Spirit, XV:38
  likeness to Holy Spirit, XV:41
  see also trinities
wisdom (both divine and human):
  the Son speaks with voice of, I:10
  divine; unchangeable, II:14
  seeing (Christ) with the physical eye, II:25
  achieves what she wills, III:6
  soul sharing in the selfsame, III:8
  wise man: sharing in eternal truth, III:8

interaction of body and soul, III:15
soul is wisdomless when God leaves, IV:5
angels, IV:27
brightness of eternal light, IV:27
outflow of glory of God, IV:27
lost by the unwise, V:5
equal to the Father, VI:7
Christ: power of God, wisdom of God (text), VII:1-2, 4
called wise with reference to itself, VII:2
Father and Son: one Wisdom, VII:3, 4
as begotten or made (in scripture, VII:4
enlightening us, VII:4
the Father utters, to be his Word, VII:4
follow the Son by living wisely, VII:5
the Holy Spirit as, VII:6
feminine gender, XII:5
holding, dear in charity, XII:16
unchangeable, spiritual things, XII:17, 25
contemplation, XII:22
distinguished from knowledge, XII:23; XIII:2, 24
truth and, XIII:24
as worship of God, XIV:1
defined, by philosophy, XIV:3
knowledge and, XIV:11
worship: becoming wise, XIV:15
a triad without being triple (book VII), XV:5
focus of books XII & XIV, XV:5
divine, XV:7
comprehending God's wisdom, XV:13
we see now through a mirror . . . , XV:14
  see also trinities
wish: unknown: the wishes of others, XIII:6, 7
witchcraft:
  miracles, III:12
  power from above, III:12
wizards:
  and rebel angels, III:13
  as creators, III:18
  their serpents stand for the dead, III:20
women:
  touch Christ only after he has ascended, IV:6
  image of the trinity, XII:9-10
  head-covering: man, woman, XII:12
  sensation represented by serpent, not woman, XII:20
Word of God:
  same substance as the Father, I:9
  after judgment day, I:15
  begotten by the Father, I:26
  the Father's doctrine is his Word, I:27
  without a beginning in time, II:9
  in flesh; being flesh, II:11
  son of man assumed by, II:11
  materialistic ideas re, II:14
  participation in, IV:4
  contemplation in eternity, IV:26
  "and the Word was with God," VI:3
  Christ: power of God, wisdom of God (text), VII:1

Father and Son are not together one Word, VII:3
word of man as likeness of, XV:20
likeness in works of man, XV:20
spoken by the prophets, XV:20
absolutely same as Father is, XV:23
begotten: the Father uttering himself, XV:23
truth cannot be false/lie, XV:23, 24
co-eternal with God himself, XV:25
form of God, XV:25
distinctively called wisdom of God, XV:29, 31
counsel or will of the Father, XV:38
word(s):
temporal and passing, VII:4
no voluntary act without previously uttered word, IX:12
conceived by wanting, born by getting, IX:14
definition [Augustine's usage], IX:15
love with knowledge, IX:15
rightly disliking things, IX:15
study of unknown words, X:2
meanings, sounds, XIII:4
without thought: no words, XIV:10
formed in act of thought, XIV:13
begotten from knowledge, XV:19, 20
sign, XV:19, 20

as likeness of the Word of God, XV:20
knowledge; awareness; truth, XV:20
true word: beginning of a good work, XV:20
true word begotten from consciousness, XV:22
human: dissimilar to Word of God, XV:22
human: false when mistaken, XV:24
human: somewhat like the Word of God, XV:24
birth; innermost mind, XV:40
work:
works of man: first uttered in the heart, XV:20
world:
cannot know God by [human] wisdom, IV:28
see also creation; temporal goods
worship:
wisdom as, XIV:1
becoming wise, XIV:15
writing:
reaction on first-time hearing about, X:1

Z

Zachary, IV:29